MONEY/SPACE

Bringing together in one volume the most important writings of Andrew Leyshon and Nigel Thrift on money and finance, including the unpublished classic, 'Sexy Greedy', this collection examines the economic, social and cultural manifestations that go to make up a multiple vision of money.

Since the mid-1980s, attention to the role played by money and finance in the processes of social and economic change has become pervasive across the social sciences. The documentation of monetary and financial matters reflects growing concern with the 'power of money' and the ways in which this power has the force to influence the conduct of social and economic life across a range of geographical scales. *Money/Space* describes the economy of international money, linking it with the distribution of social power. It looks at some of the ways in which this world of money, exemplified by finance capital and financial markets, is discursively constituted through particular social-cultural practices and shows how the world of money is constructed at a number of spatial scales.

Andrew Leyshon is Reader in Geography and **Nigel Thrift** is Professor of Geography, both at the University of Bristol.

MONEY/SPACE

Geographies of Monetary Transformation

ANDREW LEYSHON
and
NIGEL THRIFT

LONDON AND NEW YORK

First published 1997
by Routledge
11 New Fetter Lane, London EC4P 4EE

Simultaneously published in the USA and Canada
by Routledge
29 West 35th Street, New York, NY 10001

© 1997 Andrew Leyshon and Nigel Thrift

Typeset in Baskerville and Helvetica by
Keystroke, Jacaranda Lodge, Wolverhampton

Printed and bound in Great Britain by
TJ Press (Padstow) Ltd, Padstow, Cornwall

British Library Cataloguing in Publication Data
A catalogue record for this book is available from the British Library

Library of Congress Cataloging in Publication Data
Leyshon, Andrew.
Money/space : geographies of monetary transformation / Andrew
Leyshon and Nigel Thrift.
p. cm. — (International library of sociology)
Includes bibliographical references and index.
ISBN 0–415–13981–3 (hb). — ISBN 0–415–03835–9 (pb)
1. Money. 2. International economic relations. 3. Power (Social
sciences). I. Thrift, N. J. II. Title. III. Series.
HG220.A2L49 1996
332.4—dc20 96–18262

... money is like love, she thought at once. Once you have some, it can go on multiplying, each part dividing itself, doubling and doubling like the cells of an embryo.

H. Mantel (1989: 181)

That money talks
I'll not deny
I heard it once:
It said 'Goodbye'.

Richard Armour (cited in Dunkling and Room (1990: 130))

Suppose someone is too poor to visit her sister in Bristol . . . as far as her freedom is concerned, that is equivalent to 'trip to Bristol' not being written on someone's ticket in . . . [an] . . . imagined non-monetary economy. The woman has the capacity to go to Bristol. She can board the underground and approach the barrier she must cross to reach the train. But she will be physically prevented from passing through it ... the only way you won't be prevented from getting and using things is to offer money for them.

G.A. Cohen (cited in M. Roberts (1995: 21))

CONTENTS

FIGURES

TABLES

PREFACE

Towards the end of *Loyalties*, one of Raymond Williams's last novels, a besieged South Wales mining community awaits its nemesis in the miners' strike of 1984. One of the miners, Dic, with his blood up, shouts defiance, 'let the buggers come, we'll see in the end of it'. But Gwyn, a more cosmopolitan character, offers a warning in response: 'they don't have to come, Dic. They can do it from where they are. This is a world of paper and money. It's taken priority over coal, people, anything else that's real and alive' (Williams 1985: 341).

This is a book about this world of paper and money. Williams was surely right to stress the importance of this world, and its ubiquity. But he was wrong to characterise it as an impersonal force. If there is one message that we want to impart more than any other in this book, it is that money is a social process.

In exploring the conundrum of money, this book's chief aims are therefore fourfold. The first aim is simply *to describe the economy of international money*. In carrying out this aim, we intend to make a contribution to a number of literatures but most especially the literature on the new international political economy with its emphasis on the interconnectedness of international economics, international politics, national economics and national politics. A second aim is *to link the economy of international money with the distribution of social power*. Here we see our chief contribution being to the burgeoning area of economic sociology and most especially to the work on the social and cultural embeddedness of finance capital and financial markets. Our third aim is *to show some of the ways in which this world of money is discursively constituted* through particular social–cultural practices. Here we conceive of money as information circulating in specific, separate but overlapping actor–networks, made up of actors, texts and machines, which think and practise money in separate but overlapping ways. Then, finally, our fourth aim is *to show how the world of money is constructed out of and through geography*, and at a number of different spatial frames. In particular, this book operates within four such frames: the global monetary economy, the national space of Britain, the regional space of the south of England, and the concentrated urban space of the City of London. Our intention here is to contribute, in particular, to the debates on the global and the local.

This book has been a long time in the writing. It represents the fruits of a collaborative writing project on the geographies of money and finance that now spans a decade. We first began writing together in 1986, brought together by an Economic and Social Research Council (ESRC) funded research project which was based in the Department of Geography, Saint David's University College, Lampeter. Andrew Leyshon was employed as the project's researcher while Nigel Thrift was one of the principal investigators (along with Peter Daniels, then in the Department of Geography, University of Liverpool). In the years that followed, we have continued to work together, off and on, and have explored a wide range of issues surrounding money and finance, both individually and collectively.

Although our collaborations date from the mid-1980s, a concern with matters monetary and financial predates our joint writings. Thus, Nigel Thrift's interest in these issues dates from the early 1980s, and was the result of three stimuli. This first of these was some early direct empirical work on money and financial institutions carried out mainly in Australia and the Pacific Basin (see especially Taylor and Thrift 1982; Hirst *et al.* 1982; Thrift 1986a). Not only did this work show many silences in our knowledge of the geography of money, but it also showed up yawning gaps in how to study this geography. The second stimulus was the issue of social equity. It seemed obvious that the operation of money and the monetary system was bound up with problems of poverty but the connections were sometimes opaque (Thrift 1979). The third stimulus was theoretical. In particular, it was the magnificent Marxian account of money offered by David Harvey in Chapters 9 and 10 of *The Limits to Capital* which proved to be both an inspiration and, at the same time, something of a puzzle (Harvey 1982). Harvey both outlined and expanded on a number of Marxian concepts of money (like fictitious capital) but he also left too little room for the myriad of everyday practices which propelled the whole system forward and which, in his scheme of things, were too often treated like incidentals to the real business of theory (Thrift 1983).

Andrew Leyshon arrived in Lampeter in early 1986 to work on a research project on the geography of 'professional' producer service firms. The project, undertaken with Peter Daniels, was intended in part to respond to the first research stimulus outlined above, to deliver theoretically informed empirical research on the geography of money and finance. The project generated a range of publications on industries associated with the financial system (Daniels *et al.* 1988a, b; Daniels *et al.* 1989; Leyshon *et al.* 1990), and was the catalyst for a series of studies undertaken at a range of geographical scales, from the local to the global. We began to investigate the rise of particular local financial spaces, such as provincial financial centres. We also began to consider the rise and fall of 'financial regions' through an analysis of the south east of England. At a still higher level of spatial aggregation we turned our attention to different national financial systems, such as those of Britain and Japan, and have considered the possibilities of creating a distinctive European financial space within the EC. Finally, we have looked at more general processes of financial restructuring, from the less developed countries' debt crisis and the rise of a 'new international financial system', to more fundamental transformations in the regulation of the global financial system.

The reply to the second research stimulus mentioned above has been to undertake research on the impacts of financial crisis and subsequent restructuring upon poorer communities and especially to focus upon the withdrawal of formal monetary systems from these communities. Initially we pursued this work through a study of the international debt crisis. More recently, our attention has been focused, again with the aid of an ESRC grant, on the impacts of financial infastructure withdrawal on poorer communities in Britain and the United States (Leyshon and Thrift 1994a).

In all this work, we have been concerned to respond to the third research stimulus, that of theory. We have sought to maintain a balance between theoretical elaboration and empirical detail, and as we have done so, our theoretical account of money, which started out as Marxian, with a dash of Simmel, has changed. It first mutated as we attempted to bring in social and cultural factors to leaven the economic determinisms of the Marxian account. Latterly, we have thrown away many of the Marxian traces and our theoretical account of money is now much more concerned with what we call at various points in this book a discursive approach, which emphasises the role of culture in both defining what does and does not count as money, and in elevating specific monetary practices to the forefront of study. In other words, we have come to be suspicious of accounts that try to make a clear distinction between the economic sphere (to which money is often confined) and other spheres (onto which the economic sphere is too often unproblematically mapped), on the grounds that such a distinction itself presumes cultural norms which may indeed be constitutive but by no means need to be regarded as inevitable. Most particularly, we see money as based in particular, overlapping social networks which provide the ground through which money obtains meaning and is practised as specific monetary forms. This kind of anthropological approach questions the apparent ascendancy of commodity relationships which are so central to the Marxian account and gives equal weight to the actual or perceived bond of trust central to many monetary transactions. Such an approach is able to bring understanding to even the least propitious of situations (see e.g. Mars 1982; Zelizer 1994; Carrier 1995) because

> commodity logic is not some residual propensity to truck and barter that finds expression when it is liberated from social constraint. Rather it is a social value that binds and obligates potential transactors to each other. It is a way that people maintain personal identities that reflect as much adherence to a set of moral values . . . as they do the desire to maintain personal repute or secure the economic means of survival.
>
> (Carrier 1995: 91)

In all of the work we have done, one space has been pre-eminent. That space has been the City of London (Chapters 4,5,9 and 10). When we first became interested in this space, there was remarkably little contemporary academic writing to draw on, apart from the work of Dunning and Morgan (1971), Coakley and Harris (1983) and Ingham (1984). In geography, the situation was even worse, with only the pioneering work of Goddard on offices and communications in the City to act as a signpost (Goddard 1968a, b). Over the years since our initial explorations (e.g. Thrift 1985a, b) we have explored this subtle, understated and yet extraordinarily powerful location in more detail, and have found that the City exerts power in ways that are quite different from those which are imagined by those who are still weighed down by a heavy baggage of old cultural prejudices (e.g. see Hutton 1995). Moreover, we like to think that we have had a hand in stimulating the growing body of work in geography on the City of London now being published (for reviews, see Leyshon (1995, 1996a)).

This book, then, is the record of a journey which has certainly not ended yet. Along the way, we have encountered a number of fellow travellers to whom we want to extend our thanks. There is, first of all, the small but growing band of geographers and sociologists who are interested in matters monetary and financial: these include Gordon Clark, Stuart Corbridge, Nigel Dodd, Geoffrey Ingham, Mike Pryke, Mike Taylor and Adam Tickell. We are particularly grateful to Adam for allowing us to use the material included in Chapter 8, which he co-wrote. We would also like to acknowledge the contribution of Peter Daniels, who worked with us in the early days of this project. We are also grateful for the contributions made by John Allen, Alan Cochrane, Chris Hamnett, Nick Henry, Doreen Massey, Linda McDowell and Phil Sarre, who, under the auspices of an Open University research project on the south east of England, involved us in many useful discussions and provided provocative and useful criticisms of our work as it developed.

Finally, we want to thank John Urry who, as series editor of the *International Library of Sociology*, has continued to encourage us, even when the nearly completed manuscript of a book called *Making Money* fell at the final hurdle.

A book of this kind relies on the labour of others. In particular, we want to thank Sarah Howell, Kit Kelly, Liz Humphries, Anna Pazkowicz and Hanne Page, who produced a clean manuscript, and Simon Godden, Paul McSherry and Keith Scurr, who drew all the maps and diagrams.

Thornbury and Bath
September 1995

ACKNOWLEDGEMENTS

The authors gratefully acknowledge permission to reproduce the following copyright material:

Chapter 2 is a revised version of 'The transformation of regulatory order: regulation in the global economy and environment', by Andrew Leyshon, first published in *Geoforum*, Vol. 23, pp. 249–67, 1992, and is published here with permission from Elsevier Science Ltd, Pergamon Imprint, The Boulevard, Langford Lane, Kidlington, OX5 1GB, UK; Chapter 3 is reprinted from 'Liberalization and consolidation: the Single European Market and the re-making of European financial capital', by Andrew Leyshon and Nigel Thrift, first published in *Environment and Planning A*, Vol. 24, pp. 49–81, 1992, and is published here with permission of Pion Ltd; Chapter 4 first appeared in 1987 as a Producer Service Working Paper in a series produced by the University of Liverpool and Saint David's University College, Lampeter; Chapter 5 is reprinted from 'In the wake of money: the City of London and the accumulation of value', by Nigel Thrift and Andrew Leyshon, in L. Budd and S. Whimster (eds) *Global Finance and Urban Living: A Study of Metropolitan Change*, Routledge, London, pp. 282–311, 1992; Chapter 6 is reprinted from 'The restructuring of the UK financial services industry in the 1990s: a reversal of fortune?', by Andrew Leyshon and Nigel Thrift, first published in *The Journal of Rural Studies*, Vol. 9, pp. 223–41, 1993, and is published here with permission from Elsevier Science Ltd, Pergamon Imprint, The Boulevard, Langford Lane, Kidlington, OX5 1GB, UK; Chapter 7 is reprinted from 'Geographies of financial exclusion: financial abandonment in Britain and the United States', by Andrew Leyshon and Nigel Thrift, first published in *Transactions of the Institute of British Geographers*, New Series, Vol. 20, pp. 312–41, 1995, and is published here with permission from the Royal Geographical Society–Institute of British Geographers; Chapter 8 is reprinted from 'Money order?: The discursive construction of Bretton Woods and the making and breaking of regulatory space', by Andrew Leyshon and Adam Tickell, first published in *Environment and Planning A*, Vol. 13, pp. 299–327, 1994, and is published here with permission from Pion Ltd; Chapter 9, 'A phantom state? the de-traditionalisation of money, the international financial system and international financial centres', by Nigel Thrift and

Andrew Leyshon, first published in *Political Geography*, 13, pp. 299–327, 1994, is published here with permission from Butterworth–Heinemann, The Boulevard, Langford Lane, Kidlington, OX5 1GB, UK; Chapter 10, 'New urban eras and old technological fears: reconfiguring the goodwill of electronic things', by Nigel Thrift, first published in *Urban Studies*, vol. 33, 1996, is pubished here with permission from Carfax Publishing Company.

CHAPTER 1

INTRODUCTION

Money, it seems, is the great god of our age, so it is entirely appropriate to write about it. But money is not so easy to write about, because it is a multiple vision. Money is an economy. It is often described as the 'central nervous system' of capital but like the central nervous system it is easier to see than to understand. Money is a sociology. In capitalism, according to some, it provides the 'real community' (Marx 1973: 225), a community in which rational calculation is mixed with a quasi-religious faith in the power of its bonds. Money is an anthropology. Its meanings are multiple. They deeply affect and are deeply affected by culture (Parry and Bloch 1989; Zelizer 1989, 1994). Finally, money is a geography, and a curious geography too. It is, apparently, 'everywhere but nowhere in particular' (Harvey 1989a: 167). How, then, to grasp the conundrum of money? This book represents our attempt to do precisely that, and to do it in a way which attempts to give equal weight to money's economic, social and cultural manifestations.

This task can no doubt be completed in a number of ways. For example, one might experiment with an idiom that might be called 'postmodern'. Money could be depicted as a kind of supernatural deity which, through the power of commodification, is gradually fracturing subjects into fragments of symbolic delirium, commodities into aesthetics, and consumption into a spectacle of simulated desire. One could then stir into this heady brew the shock of a new round of time–space compression, being sure to remember to scatter references to Baudelaire and Benjamin liberally through the text. We would not advise travelling down this path. Writing in this idiom seems to us to be a kind of flummery, a way for academics to take on a 'prophetic role' (Bourdieu 1988), a way for them to 'spectacularise' themselves (Friedman 1987). We have taken another path, one that leads away from the undoubted attractions of *homo academicus gallicus* and also from his or her American gothic cousin. The path that we have chosen in our writings on money is different in four ways. First, we have tried to take the particularities of histories seriously. We do not believe that histories can be reduced to theory: we believe that histories provide the grounds in which theory must operate. It is symptomatic of a number of current intellectual tendencies in social science that we feel we have to restate such a basic premise. Second, we have attempted to take the particularities of geography seriously. Again, we do not believe that geography can be reduced to theory: geographies provide the grounds in which theory must operate. The implication of both these preceding strictures is that theory always has to be tied to particular local contexts in ways which have important *theoretical* connotations (Birmingham 1989; Probyn 1991). But this is not, we should hasten to add, just that old cry to respect difference which is heard so often nowadays. We believe that too often this call is being used simply to avoid theorising the very things that need to be theorised. As Eagleton (1989: 406) puts it, 'one might agree that it is some post-modernists who are the true levellers and homogenisers in this respect, for all their cult of the heterogeneous'. Third, we believe that theories of epochal transition from one form of economy, society, culture or geography to another one are unhelpful unless they are extremely carefully phrased. For example, what is striking about the case of Britain, which we examine at some length in the chapters that follow, is that economic, social, cultural and geographical continuity is as important as novelty. Theories of transition also need to be carefully phrased because otherwise they become overly normative (Thrift 1989a). Histories and geographies are judged against a theoretical role model which only reveals the modern world's self-image of its own distinctiveness and, inevitably, in the face of this hubris, an 'aesthetic of disappointment' (Pfeil 1990) sets in which is both seductive and debilitating. Fourth, and finally, there is a question of style which is also a question of content. We reject the stylistic overtones of too much writing which claims to be in a postmodern vein in which

> teachers . . . are generating increasingly parasitical forms of metaphors and are themselves subject to a tyrannical pressure not only to have absorbed all the latest products of the theory industry but if possible to have got the better of them: to be in a position to have the cleverest last say on them, or even better the most pointedly ironical last laugh.
>
> (Soper 1990: 19)

The position that Soper describes seems to us to be untenable when studying money and money making. The world of money may sometimes seem to have only a tenuous connection to people's everyday lives but its effects on these lives are often devastating and cannot be skated over. There are general moral principles at stake here concerning justice, power and equity and there are also more specific issues of culpability which must be exposed.

This is not, of course, to say that we have not tried to come to terms with some of the issues raised by postmodernism or poststructuralism. For example, we take discourse seriously and below we argue that discourses about money form a vital element of their constitution as money. To quote Soper (1990: 11) once more:

> It is a question, in short, of preserving a certain dialectic between the material and the linguistic, the verbal and the non-verbal: a complex

dialectic which it is difficult to specify since it is true, as the poststructuralist critique has rendered clearer to us, that the relationship here is not simply one of representation between word and thing. . . . I can share with discourse theory the insight that the role of discourse in the construction of existence does not operate as a semiotic level of which another 'truer' and more 'material' level finds expression, but what I cannot accept is that discourse is exhaustive of reality, or that there are no relations of necessary dependence between what is sayable at any time and the ways the world happens to be materially organised.

Indeed, we would want to resist actively any attempt to understand money, as Parsons, and post-Parsonians (like Habermas and Luhmann) and, interestingly, a number of postmodernist authors (in so far as they say anything about money at all) have, as just a medium of communication, through an analogy with language. Ganßmann (1988: 312) explains why:

> I find it more plausible to follow Marx in the opinion that, to a decisive extent, money has turned into or is available as a substitute for power, influence, commitment, etc. '(I)n place of brightly coloured cohesive means of humanity' (Marx, 1954: 874), we now find the 'silent force of economic relations'. It is expressed with money. Ask those who don't have any.

By way of an introduction to the geographies of money, this chapter recounts some of the ways in which the world has become saturated with the practices and symbols of money. Its first section is concerned with the transformation of monetary forms. This history of the instruments and institutions of finance points to five different forms of money, namely: 'primitive' or premodern money; commodity money; money of account; state money; and virtual money. The second section considers the way in which space has made a difference to this history of money. Money does not just have a geography; *money is itself a geography*. The third section considers the symbolic dimension of money through an analysis of some of the dominant leitmotifs in discourses about money. In each case, we have restricted ourselves to primarily western examples (and especially the case of England) to illustrate our arguments, but it is important to acknowledge here the diversity of monetary experiences around the world which do not, and never can, add up to one single story (see Angell 1930).

MONEY

Five chief forms of monetary practice can be distinguished in the historical record. None of these forms of monetary practice are destroyed by the succeeding form. Rather, they join with the preceding forms to produce new hybrid combinations. Each form can be thought of as consisting of a particular set of formal *instruments* of money, a particular set of financial *institutions and practices*, and a broadly conceived set of *interpretations* of what money is and what it does. It is true to say that theoretical understanding of these different forms of money has usually run behind their actual use. As Cencini (1988: 3) puts it, 'Apart from the rare moments of high theory, when analysis was playing a leading role, economists have mostly tried to catch up with the practical historical development of money.' That said, these rare moments of high theory do crystallise out some of the chief features of each form of money, and the accounts of Marx, Keynes and Cencini loom large in what follows, although it is also important to bear in mind Dodd's (1994: xv) observation that, 'most definitions of money tend to reveal as much about the interests of the theorists who formulate theory as they do about money itself'.

Before we embark upon this evaluation of different monetary forms and practices, we need to answer a rather important question: what exactly is money? While this may seem to be an apparently straightforward question, coming up with a satisfactory answer to it proves more difficult. Most conventional interpretations see money as evolving in parallel to and then supplanting barter systems of exchange. But it is important to note that the process by which money supplemented barter has not led to its complete eradication; it survives in certain contexts to this day. Rather, the emergence of money provided an additional means of engaging in exchange, just as subsequent developments in monetary forms and practices have complemented those that already existed, without ever completely overwhelming them.

Nevertheless, each development has occurred because new monetary forms and practices contain distinctive advantages over prevailing systems. Thus, the advantages of money over barter are legion:

> Monetary exchange is more convenient than barter. It saves on the time and effort needed to search for potential co-transactors and to compromise or extend the relationship when the requirements of each transactor do not match. In barter, the key requirement of transactors is for information. This mostly concerns the location and trustworthiness of potential co-transactors. Money paid or received can be handed on elsewhere at a later date. Once money is received as payment for something, the relationship between transactors can be concluded rather than extended into the future by promises or other obligations. The process of search and compromise necessary in barter is effectively performed by money rather than by transactors themselves. Crucially, money does not carry or transmit the information required in barter but replaces it with information of its own: that it can be re-used in the future, that it will be accepted by other members of a society or social group, and that it truly represents its face-value and will continue to do so over time.
>
> (Dodd 1994: xxii–xxiii)

So far, so good, but we still have not answered our initial question: what *is* money? In theory and in practice money can be, and has been, a wide range of physical objects, from shells to porpoise teeth, from precious metal to stones (Angell 1930; Davies 1994; Einzig 1966; Galbraith 1975). But it is not the materiality of money that matters so much as the ability of money to perform two key roles in the process of economic exchange, namely to act as both a medium of exchange and as a store of value. In performing these roles, money necessarily takes on two additional roles, as a unit of account and as a means of payment. The utility of money is that it therefore acts both as a lubricant of exchange and as an independent expression of value. But this duality of money, while advantageous in many ways, has also served to introduce an important dynamic into monetary forms and practices. Thus, as Dodd has pointed out, the ability of different types of money to perform the functions of a medium of exchange *and* of a store of value tends to be 'inversely proportional' (1994: xviii), so that money forms which perform admirably in the capacity of the former, tend to perform less well in the capacity of the latter:

> For example, legal-tender notes tend to lose value over time as a result of inflation, and so are best used chiefly for exchange and payment purposes. Assets which store value stably over time or even appreciate in value, on the other hand, are linked to securities or other investments which make them difficult to convert into a form suitable for payment or exchange, perhaps losing value on conversion or carrying a time constraint delaying conversion.
> (Dodd 1994: xviii)

It is the differential performance of each and every type of monetary form in this regard which has introduced a dynamic element within the evolution of money, so that the monetary system is characterised by a range of alternative and complementary forms of money, examples of which will be considered below.

This is not the only implication of money's dual role as both a medium of exchange and a store of value. In certain circumstances these roles may be seen as contradictory, for if the value of money begins to fall while acting as a lubricant of exchange, money may be withdrawn from circulation owing to its ability to exist independently as a store of value. It is precisely this contradiction that led commentators such as Marx, Keynes and others to link crises in the monetary system to more general economic crises (Altvater 1993). We will explore the connections between monetary uncertainty and economic crisis at more length later in this book. But now we wish to return to the embodiment of money itself, and outline five key monetary forms.

Premodern money

Before money, exchange revolved around barter. The advantages of money over barter have already been laid out, but there is a general consensus amongst historians and anthropologists that money did not arise in the first instance in order to circumvent the 'cumbersome awkwardness' of barter (Davies 1994: 9). Rather, the origins of money are cultural, inasmuch as the use of money arose in processes of exchange that were firmly non-economic in their orientation. According to Davies, the economic use of money occurred almost as an accidental oversight, as a social discovery that followed on from well-established cultural practices:

> The most common non-economic forces which gave rise to primitive money
> may be grouped together thus: bride-money and blood-money; ornamental
> and ceremonial; religious and political. Objects originally accepted for one
> purpose were often found to be useful for other non-economic purposes, just
> as they later, because of their growing acceptability, began to be used for
> general trading also.
>
> (Davies 1994: 23–4)

In other words, money evolved from relatively narrow, culturally
specific uses, to take on later a much broader range of social and economic
functions commonly associated with money.

This evolutionary interpretation of money is closely associated with the
work of Karl Polanyi who distinguished between 'primitive' and 'modern'
money on the basis of the range of functions each type of money performs
(Polanyi 1968). For Polanyi, modern money is 'all-purpose money', so
called because it performs equally well all the key functions ascribed to
money: that is, means of exchange; store of value; unit of account; and
means of payment. Premodern money, meanwhile, tends to perform some,
but not all, of the functions associated with modern money. Premodern
moneys, therefore, are described as 'special-' or 'limited-purpose' moneys:

> In primitive economies – i.e. small-scale economies not integrated by market
> exchange – different uses of money can be instituted separately in different
> monetary objects to carry out reciprocal and redistributive functions . . . the
> items which perform non-commercial money uses need not be full-time
> money, so to speak; they have uses and characteristics apart from their ability
> to serve as a special kind of money.
>
> (Dalton 1965: 48)

This distinction between general-purpose and special-purpose money is
analytically useful, inasmuch as it draws attention to the ways in which
money objects have their origins in quite specific cultural practices that
are distinctive from the process of market-based exchange. These non-
commercial monetary exchanges may be relatively infrequent, and may
involve the use of different types of 'money' for each type of exchange
(Dalton 1965).

However, there are also problems with drawing a distinction between
premodern and modern moneys on the basis of the range of functions that
each perform. This is not so much because primitive moneys are seen as
'special-' or 'limited-purpose' moneys; rather, the difficulty arises because
of the premise that modern money is somehow 'all-' or 'general-purpose',
'which as a single currency, unburdened by ritual or social controls, can
function effectively as a universal medium of exchange' (Zelizer 1994: 22).
For example, according to Dodd (1994: xviii):

> The idea that modern money is general-purpose, fulfilling all the possible
> monetary tasks, is simply incorrect. There exists no form of money which
> serves all such tasks simultaneously. Legal tender notes are rarely used to

store value in practice. Notes and coins represent standard units of value without literally embodying them; indeed, if they did so they would be worth considerably more than their legal-tender equivalent. Cheques, credit cards and bank drafts serve only as means of payment. It is absurd to regard these monetary forms as general purpose.

Zelizer (1989, 1994) has also argued that the links between premodern and modern moneys are more tangible than most people suspect. Thus, while 'multiple moneys in the modern world may not be as visibly identifiable as the shells, coins, brass rods, or stones of primitive communities . . . their invisible boundaries work just as well' (Zelizer 1994: 24). 'How else', Zelizer argues, 'do we distinguish a bribe from a tribute or an allowance, a wage from an honorarium, or an allowance from a salary? How do we identify ransoms, bonuses, tips, damages, or premiums?' (ibid.).

Given the weight of such criticisms, the notion that single-purpose primitive moneys surrendered in the face of incursions by an all-purpose modern money form needs to be treated with care. Davies (1994: 24) treads an advisably cautious line in his description of the decline of single-purpose premodern moneys, arguing that 'primitive moneys originating from one source or from one use came to be used for similar kinds of payments elsewhere spreading gradually without necessarily becoming generalised'. In other words, it is possible to trace a line from a multiplicity of premodern moneys to a more limited number of modern monetary forms, but without surrendering to the view commonly held by classical social theorists who, 'impressed by the fungible, impersonal characteristics of money . . . [have] emphasised its instrumental rationality and apparently unlimited capacity to transform products, relationships, and sometimes even emotions into an abstract and objective numerical equivalent' (Zelizer 1989: 347).

Indeed, there is growing archaeological evidence to refute the view that the march of modern money brought with it an irrevocable transformation of social practices. Rather it seems that modern monetary systems could be subverted and money put to use in non-economic social practices. For example, in a review of the archaeological literature on coin hoards in Roman Britain, Aitchison (1988) dismisses the widely held view that all such hoards were deposited in response to economic motives. According to this view such hoards, of which around 1,500 have been discovered, were either laid down in order to safeguard monetary wealth during times of uncertainty, or merely dumped and discarded when the coins, for some reason or another (e.g. inflation), lost their economic value. However, while such economic motives may be the cause of some of the deposits, they cannot explain all of them. Many hoards seem to have been laid down as votive offerings to gods and deities. Aitchison argues that, despite the introduction to Britain of a monetary system based on the circulation of Roman coins, these coins were also used for other purposes reminiscent of the uses of premodern moneys. In other words, coins which were produced to circulate within a modern monetary system sometimes moved beyond this system into 'an "alternative economy" within which coins circulated which cannot be distinguished from social and ritual practices of the Iron Age or of those lands beyond the Imperial frontiers' (Aitchison 1988: 279).

The range of objects and materials that have been used as premodern money is extremely large (e.g. see Einzig 1966). The movement towards a more generalised money form which, literally, gained a wider currency beyond the very specific social and cultural conditions that gave it birth is generally argued to be linked to the use of metallic-based premodern moneys. These were often made of a precious metal, such as silver, which had a culturally determined economic value, which made them particularly suited to serving as a medium of exchange. These premodern moneys existed initially merely as lumps of silver, uneven in size and form, which readily served as the raw material for the manufacture of a whole series of metal artefacts. Thus, these metallic moneys had a use value as well as an exchange value. The first tentative steps towards the creation of modern money came with efforts to standardise the appearance of premodern moneys (Dalton 1965). This process of standardisation led to the eventual creation of coinage:

> The most obvious and direct route to coinage was . . . through the improvements in quality and authority of the kind of large silver blobs or 'dumps' such as those in use in Knossos in the Second millennium. These Minoan pre-coins were ... not very uniform and required either a state seal or a punched impression to help their still hesitant circulation. However such metal quasi-coins gradually became more plentiful in Greece, including the Greek islands and the eastern Mediterranean, during the first half of the first millennium BC, during which the final stages in the inventive process took place quite rapidly. In retrospect we can see that this invention meant that a new monetary era had definitely begun.
>
> (Davies 1994: 61)

The significance of this development cannot be overestimated for, as Davies (1994: 64) observes, ever since, 'the financial history of the world has undergone a series of revolutionary changes around the central, relatively unchanging core of coinage, which has meant that for most people, most of the time, money has simply meant coins'.

Commodity money

The development of coins led to the development of a set of monetary practices that revolved around the notion of *commodity money*. In a system of commodity money, money functions as a medium of exchange and as a store of wealth and the value of coins therefore emanates from their embodiment of the value of the precious metals that they are made from. The key institution of the commodity money system, then, is the mint that transforms the precious metals into coins.

Not surprisingly, the direct link between money and precious metals brought about a search for reserves, followed in short order by large-scale mining wherever they were found. For example, by the middle of the first millennium BC, thousands of slaves were at work extracting silver from the mines that fed the Mediterranean city states of Athens, Aegina and Corinth (Davies 1994: 70), each of which had their own coinage systems.

As the coins from these rival systems came into contact with one another through trade, trade which was in part made possible through the economic wealth commodity money systems engendered, so there emerged a need for a whole new set of skills and competencies associated with the exchange of one type of coin into another, 'creating a persistently powerful and widespread demand for "bankers" who could find their way through the money maze' (Davies 1994: 72). However, despite the use of accounting *systems* at this time, there was no real development of money beyond its commodity form, which left commodity money-based economies and societies highly exposed if they were cut off from the mines which fed their systems of coin production.[1]

Despite such attendant threats and the dangers of debasement, the coin became the world's dominant monetary form, due in large part to the later expansion of the Roman Empire and its propagation of commodity money. According to Davies (1994: 110)

> in the thousand years between 600 BC and AD 400 the whole of the [western] world had become accustomed to coinage as the basis of its monetary systems. At one time or another, between 1,500 and 2,000 mints were busy turning out the coins required in the non-Chinese and non-Indian areas of the . . . world.
>
> (Davies 1994: 110)

But as the Roman Empire collapsed in the middle of the second millennium AD, so did the dominance of the commodity money form, which disappeared altogether for hundreds of years in some of parts of Europe, including Britain (Spufford 1988).

However, by the second millennium, the situation had recovered somewhat, so that by the eleventh century even the lowliest members of a number of communities in Europe might have expected to use coin, however periodically. By the thirteenth century cash rents were common in the countryside and by the beginning of the fourteenth century, peasants in some communities had begun to amass savings in coin. The switch to money rents and the evidence of saving are symptomatic of new interpretations of money, and of a 'whole revolution in attitudes to money' (Spufford 1988: 245). For example, cultivable land came to be regarded as a source of money and not just a use value. Other resources were regarded in a similar manner. The new outlook soon spread. Richer peasants bought tenancies and parts of tenancies from their neighbours, so changing patterns of landownership.

The revival of the commodity money form was due in large part to the rise of the European monarchical state, the rulers of which promoted the use of a standardised monetary unit in order to further their military and economic ambitions. Rulers of such states began to exert a growing influence over money, which in turn led to the production of increasingly distinctive financial territories, characterised by monetary systems based on different types of commodity money.

The development of a consistent system of coinage had distinct economic advantages for the rulers of these territories. For the most part, these advantages stemmed from assurances over the value and worth of tributes and taxation extracted from the populations they ruled over (Davies 1994; Dodd 1994; Giddens 1985). To guarantee the value of the returns realised through what was effectively an emerging fiscal policy, it paid rulers to attempt to 'regulate' the quality of the money in circulation in the territories they controlled. For example, from the tenth century onwards English monarchs expressed a close interest in the quality of money through their efforts to oversee the production of coins in circulation. Control was achieved by establishing a network of official mints, by watching over the issue of dies and by strictly regulating the money-makers. The result was that it was possible to produce 'a coinage of uniform type and standard' (Davies 1994: 130). The reasons for such surveillance and control were fairly straightforward, to do with the way in which commodity money was seen to 'embody' economic value. Regulating the production of commodity money was a way of ensuring the value of the revenue received by the monarch in the form of tribute and taxation.

The forging of a bond between fiscal objectives and the development of authoritative control over money accelerated in eleventh-century England in the wake of the Norman invasion. The Doomsday survey was a central component of a strategy designed to create a national system of taxation. In order to be sure of the value of the taxes and tributes it was clearly necessary for the monarch to be assured of the quality of the money flowing into the state's coffers, particularly when extracting large sums to fund extraordinary expenses. The dilemmas are outlined by Davies (1994: 136–7):

> The King's finances were derived mainly from five sources: first, directly from the proceeds of his own estates, the 'Crown lands'; secondly, from regular customary and therefore normally fixed payments made by the shires and boroughs; thirdly, from the fines and other fluctuating profits resulting from the maintenance of justice; fourthly, the mostly arbitrary profits from issuing the King's dies and minting the King's coins; and fifthly, in order to meet exceptional expenditures, a general tax on the land, the 'geld'. . . . It follows that the greater the yield of the first four sources, the fewer and the less heavy would be the exceptional gelds. Despite his improved administration, William found it necessary to levy five gelds during his 21-year reign. Because the gelds were usually very heavy and were paid in cash, they had a close relationship with the demand for coinage. Furthermore, it becomes clear that only an efficient tax-gathering system could guarantee that the quality of English coinage would be maintained.

Exercising no control over the commodity money in circulation left the system of taxation and tribute open to abuse and exploitation by the monarch's subjects. Maintaining absolute control over the production and distribution of coinage meant that rulers were able to gather to themselves the ability to extract value through the exploitation of coinage and the arbitrary profits derived from minting referred to above. These profits could be realised by means of regular and almost imperceptible rounds of debasement. Episodes of 'recoinage' would involve the recall of all existing coins which, if taken to the network of official mints scattered across the territory,[2] could be exchanged for coins of an identical face value but which might be slightly smaller in size and/or made up of a reduced volume of precious metal (Davies 1994: 131). In this way, monarchical rulers could extract economic profits from altering the physical make-up of money, while prohibiting their subjects from doing the same.[3]

The economic benefits derived from control over the monetary system were closely linked to military imperatives of the monarchical state, because the economic gains helped fund the cost of military campaigns. Yet, despite this imperative, the military ambitions of such states would often come up against the limits of a monetary system that relied upon a direct link between precious metal and coinage. Despite the periodic episodes of recoinage, there was only so much money to go around. This constraint was instrumental in bringing into being a new monetary form which, unlike commodity money, was more an expression than an embodiment of value.

Money of account

Beginning in the eleventh century and increasing in importance in the twelfth and thirteenth centuries, money began to take on a new form: *money of account*. This new monetary practice derived its name from its function. It is a measure of value used almost exclusively for accounting purposes.

The origins of this new form of money lay in the problems that monarchical rulers were facing in raising funds in a medieval monetary system based on commodity money. Under such a system the supply of money was ultimately constrained by the European supply of silver and gold. Money of account emerged as a way of boosting the supply of money 'beyond the limits of minting' (Davies 1994: 149). The emergence of money of account is linked to the growth of *credit money*, and its roots can be traced back to the focus on fiscal and monetary policies within the medieval monarchical state, as discussed earlier.

For example, in the case of medieval England the interrelated nature of these two functions was expressed in the fact that the institutions responsible for their administration, the Royal Treasury and the Royal Mint, were located in close proximity to each other in the royal household. However, the growing complexity of money flows caused by the imposition of taxation required a more specialised range of accounting skills. Thus, the Treasury became 'the first section of the Royal household to be organised as a separate department of state clearly distinguishable from, although inevitably still very closely associated with, the management of the royal household' (Davies 1994: 147). The move towards increased specialisation was critically important in the history of money for it led to the eventual creation of a new financial instrument that was in a credit-based monetary system:

> As early as the Middle of the twelfth century [the Royal Treasury's] increasing workload caused it to become divided into two sections, one specialising in the receipt, storage and expenditure of cash and other payments, and the other into recording, registering and auditing the accounts. The first section, the Exchequer of Receipt, was also known as the Lower Exchequer, while the second section, the Exchequer of Account, was called the Upper Exchequer. For ease in reckoning and 'checking' the cash payments, the Exchequer tables ten feet by five, were covered with a chequered cloth, either black-lined with white, or green with red-lined squares, which custom gave its name not only to the institution but also subsequently to the cheque or, as still in America, the 'check'. The Exchequer of Receipt made increasing use of an ancient form of providing evidence of payment by issuing 'tallies', and developed this system so much that the history of the Treasury is inseparably connected with that of the tally.
>
> (Davies 1994: 147)

The tally was nothing more than a wooden stick upon which grooves, cuts and notches could be scored to record payment of differing amounts and which served as durable receipts. However, in time the tally began to be used by the Treasury as a way round the limit set on the supply of money imposed by a commodity-based monetary system. The tally was transformed into money of account:

> The first stage in this process was the 'assignment', by which a debt owed by the king, shown physically by the tally stock held in the exchequer, could be used by the king to pay someone else, by transferring to this third person the tally stock. Thus, the king's creditor could then collect payment from the king's original debtor. Alternatively this new creditor might decide to hold the tally to pay his share of taxes required in a subsequent tax season . . . what soon became clear from as early as the twelfth century onward, was that 'the exchequer of receipt was tending to become more and more of a clearing house for writs and tallies of assignment and less and less the scene of cash transactions'. The resulting economy in the use of coinage and the relief of pressures on minting were again of obvious importance. . . . A considerable increase in the flow of tallies, and therefore a corresponding increase in credit, occurred when royalty began habitually to issue tallies in anticipation of tax receipts.
>
> (Davies 1994: 150)

The circulation of tallies signalled the rise of a form of credit money. The value of the tally was its embodiment of a claim to a specified volume of commodity money held elsewhere, which was realisable on the physical presentation of the tally to the counterparty. However, the circulation of these tallies led to severe problems of time–space co-ordination. Those who were issued tallies by the Exchequer might find that in order to take delivery of commodity money they had to travel the length and breadth of the country to find the counterparty to the tally they were holding. It was in order to overcome such problems of time–space co-ordination that an embryonic private finance market developed where it was possible to sell the tallies at a discounted price. The centre of the market was in London, for it was there that the tallies were issued. Merchants offered the holders of tallies the opportunity effectively to move forward in time by taking immediate delivery of commodity money, thus avoiding the delay and expenses that would be incurred in tracking down the counterparties to each individual tally. In return, the owners would forgo part of the full value of the tally, which the merchant took as payment for the service offered (Davies 1994: 150).

The initial development of a private capital market in medieval England and elsewhere in Europe was of immense importance because it signalled that a major social economic transformation was under way, a transformation which involved a major shift in power and which, in part, helped bring the medieval period to a close. As Davies (1994: 168) puts it, 'Medieval money was above all monarchical money', but the development of private capital markets saw the control of money shift away from the absolute control of the rulers of feudal states, so that the development of credit money 'helps distinguish modern from medieval times' (ibid.).

The major force driving the later development of money of account was the increasing complexity of commercial trade. The 'commercial revolution' brought with it a considerable increase in the volume of international trade. But international trade was no easy matter. Partly this was because of the large number of extant currencies; a monetary map of late medieval Europe (Figure 1.1) resembles a monetary map of the world today in its scope and complexity. More particularly, the physical transport of coin or ingot was both difficult and dangerous. In order to surmount these difficulties, new monetary instruments came into existence, fostered by new monetary institutions. In international trade, the most important instrument was the *bill of exchange* and the most important institution was *merchant banking* (focused on Tuscany) (Figure 1.2). By the first half of the fourteenth century, the Italian innovation of the bill of exchange had become a normal way of making commercial payments, enormously expanding the supply of money available for international transactions between the main cities of Europe. Initially, bills of exchange were used only by merchants but the convenience that they offered, cancelling the need to barter, clear books face to face, or make payments in coin or ingot, meant that they soon spread to other members of the population. Merchant banking evolved out of the invention of the permanent partnership (rather than one lasting a single voyage) and the effects of the bill of

Figure 1.1 Principal currencies of late medieval Europe
Source: Spufford (1988)

exchange on trade in goods. 'As the bill of exchange developed it became possible for the merchant to sell or buy in one direction only, against bills of exchange. Before long, trade in goods became less interesting for some, and a number of merchants developed into dealers in bills of exchange or into bankers' (Kindleberger 1984: 35). This prototypical international monetary system had a strong geographical structure, based to begin with on the financial centres of Italy, and on firms which over the course of time became cemented in place (Centre for Medieval and Renaissance Studies 1979). Changes in local banking and practices were also important. Most particularly, there was the development of transfer of accounts within the same bank, and then the transfer of accounts between different banks. By the fourteenth century, written instruments or *cheques* had become common, as had current accounts and overdrafts. International and local banking amalgamated when bills of exchange were able to be debited from bank accounts.

Once certain levels of monetary activity were reached, quantitative changes in the money supply led on to qualitative changes in the nature of bank money. In particular, there were radical changes in the practices and interpretations of credit as the discovery was made 'that for many purposes the acknowledgements of debt are themselves a serviceable substitute for money proper in the settlement of transactions' (Keynes 1930: 5).

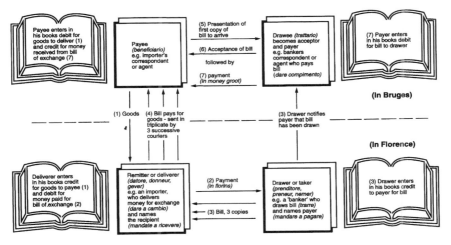

Figure 1.2 The parties to a normal bill of exchange (e.g. one to enable an importer in Florence to pay his or her correspondent in Bruges)
Source: Spufford (1988)

The credit economy grew rapidly in size with the advent of the bill of exchange. Credit was effectively given even when the request was ostensibly for payment at sight simply because the mails of the day took time to reach correspondents. Bills of exchange were soon joined by simple finance bills, effectively bills drawn by an individual without any underlying trade transactions (Kindleberger 1984). Thus bills of exchange began to have less and less correspondence with particular consignments of commodities, or indeed with commodities at all. In time, then, 'bank money' developed to the point at which acknowledgements of debt could be substituted for commodities as such in the settlement of transactions. Thus separate acknowledgement of debt could be issued by any bank and represented through bank money.

As the move to a new bank money, increasingly independent of trade in commodities and with its own rules and rhythms, developed, so four further dramatic changes occurred. Most important of these changes was the formation of an *international capital market*. This market formed in the seventeenth and eighteenth centuries as a result of three chief determinants (Neal 1990): the advent of highly profitable long-distance voyages which created incentives to mobilise large sums, for long periods, amongst principals separated by greater distances than before; the scattering of influential but persecuted religious minorities, especially Huguenots and Jews, whose movements and kin networks created a web of reliable business contacts in major cities like London, Amsterdam and Hamburg; and the increasingly voracious fiscal requests of states with increasingly voracious imperial ambitions. By the eighteenth century, large and established capital markets existed in London, Amsterdam and Hamburg.

A second, important change consisted of the creation of new financial instruments and organisations that would support the burgeoning credit economy. Thus, the bill of exchange became more sophisticated. The transferable perpetual share was invented (in the sixteenth century). Markets for these bills and shares developed although the discounting of bills was at first hampered by usury laws. As an example of this process, by the end of the seventeenth century London was already offering the first regular price quotations for actively traded securities and a wide range of financial intermediaries had grown up as Tudor money scriveners were replaced by bill brokers while specialist dealers in stock were replaced by brokers and jobbers (Morgan and Thomas 1962; King 1972). In turn, these new or improved financial instruments and markets relied on organisational developments, most especially joint stock companies (which originated in the sixteenth century), and a range of different kinds of banks (in Britain, private banks, country banks and merchant banks, for example) which in turn were to lead on to the formation of joint stock banks in the early nineteenth century.

A third major change was the increasing frequency of financially led crises, usually the result of excessive speculation around all manner of objects, based in the expanded ability to obtain credit, coupled with the increasing dematerialisation of money. Increasingly, money was being transformed into *fictitious capital*, most especially through the development of new ways of buying ahead, sometimes to lay off risks, which themselves became tradable instruments. Thus, by the late seventeenth century, the London capital market was using time bargains and dealing in options.

But London was put into the shade by the Amsterdam capital market which earlier in the century had already developed many sophisticated techniques for trading, including short selling, puts and calls (options to buy or sell stocks at a stipulated price over a stipulated period of time), and futures trading in commodities. The status of some of these techniques is well described by the Dutch description of options trading – *windhandel* – or trading in air. Certainly it is no surprise that insurance began to be used as a way of reducing risk: for example, the first insurance company in England started in 1680 with a considerable expansion taking place in 1720 (Kindleberger 1984) but, again, the Dutch were effectively first in the field. However, overshadowing each of these three changes was a fourth and that was the increased involvement of the nation state in the financial system. This was to bring into being a new set of monetary forms, institutions and practices.

The rise of money of account also brought with it changing attitudes to and interpretations of money as the 'old incumber'd villainy' of the monarchical state and landed aristocrats was challenged by new centres of power, including especially the merchant classes. These changing attitudes to and interpretations of money are clearly complex but the example of England shows some of the kind of changes that occurred in many of the countries of the west. In England, these changes were fourfold. First, 'credit' becomes a key figure in the imaginary, a figure of anxiety which is all the more pronounced because of money's increasingly paper form, and which changed decisively the ways in which people thought and wrote about themselves and the world:

> The power of the imaginary [of credit] was becoming a moving force in secular material transformations of human relationships and circumstance. If biblical faith could move mountains then business confidence, through systems of credit, would sail ships and drive an economy. As faith is increasingly placed in paper forms pledging invisible futures for the sale of returns which may or may not materialise, the medium of change, money itself (but now not even metal specie, but paper notes of credit), and not the goods that money supposedly exists to circulate, increasingly signified the substance of wealth. . . . Defoe brings into the light of Day the issues being raised. 'Is it a true story', he asks, 'that nations should grow rich by War? . . . Why do *East India* Company's Stock rise when Ships are taken? Mine adventures raise Annuities when Stocks fall; lose their Vein of Oar in the Mine, and yet find it in the Shares; let no man wonder at the Paradoxes, since such strange things are practised every Day among us? If any Man requires an answer to such things as these, they may find it in this Ejaculation. Great is the Power of Imagination.'
>
> (Nicholson 1994: 46)

'Inconstant' credit was seen to bring into existence new forms of personality, was seen to refashion natural desire as fevered acquisition, and was seen to challenge traditional hierarchies. Most commonly, when writers cast around for a figure with which to embody credit, it was presented as a self-willed but persuadable woman.[4] In other words, 'the rhetoric of Eve as fateful temptress survives in altered usage' (Nicholson 1994: xi).

Second, and coincident with the importance of credit, there is the spectre of debt which also vexed writers of the time.[5] The possibility of imprisonment for debt in debtors prisons like the Fleet sketched in books like *The Cry of the Oppressed*, the later plates of *The Rake's Progress* and plays like Goldsmith's *The Good-Natured Man*, shows the concern with which debt was handled, a concern buttressed by Christian injunctions against getting into debt at all (Barty-King 1991). Third, the subject of money opened up a space for public discourse, a space which was strengthened by the Lockean idea of a 'contract'[6] as being as or more important than ancient custom, and the growing realisation by writers that they were themselves a part of the sphere of commerce, reliant on agents, publishers, painters, and the like. Finally, there was an increasing development of the notion of risk as something that could be set apart from mere gambling. Gambling was a 'passion' which eroded self-control, erased past commitments and threatened future duties (Hirschman 1977). In seeking out risk, gamblers lost all sight of their social obligation. But now types of financial instruments (like insurance) were able to break the link between gambling and risk and refigure risk as a quantifiable estate of uncertainty which was morally tenable (Knights and Vurdubakis 1993).

State credit money

The rise of money of account and the growth of bank credit money had led to a falling away of the influence of the state over money. The state still remained important, of course, particularly in the creation and validation of commodity money which, despite the growth of money of account, was still widely perceived as the ultimate source of value within the monetary system. However, beyond this, responsibility for regulating the financial system fell to the growing band of private merchants and bankers who effectively oversaw and supervised the circulation of money and credit, often through informal but closely knit networks for the exchange of business and information.

For example, Quinn (1995) has shown how in the seventeenth century a network of goldsmith–bankers in the City of London used their reserves of gold to develop markets in short-term debt. The possession of a receipt or note from a goldsmith 'was evidence of ability to pay; of money in the bank' (Davies 1994: 251). In this way, these early banking institutions facilitated the growth of credit money instruments such as bank notes and cheques, helping them become established as readily acceptable means of payment.

But these privatised financial instruments and the institutions that issued them were never entirely free of the influence of the state. For example, many of London's goldsmith–bankers came to grief in the 1670s when, in the face of their refusal to increase their loans to the Crown in order to fund a further round of naval expansion, Charles II prohibited the payment of royal debt.[7] And, during the eighteenth century, the state's influence over the finance system began to reassert itself. There were three main reasons for this. The first of these was the creation of national debts (chiefly, it should be noted, through the need to finance wars). State means of financing debts had often been haphazard so that 'the total picture prior to 1700 was best described as chaotic' (Kindelberger 1984: 76). However, after 1700, markets for debt both broadened and deepened and, as a result, government debt was consolidated and extended. States became borrowers on a large scale. For example, as late as 1824 the paid-up capital of all the domestic companies trading on the London Stock Exchange was £34 million. This compared with a public debt of over £800 million (Neal 1990). The second reason for increasing state involvement was the creation of limited monarchies. Once absolutist states were overthrown, the risk of arbitrary seizure of assets was much reduced and lending to states became a more sober and reliable business. Finally, there was the creation of national banks which in time took on a range of regulatory functions. Public banks had been founded in Europe from an early date. The first state deposit bank had been established in Geneva in 1407 and further such banks followed in Spain and Sicily. Increasing sophistication came with the founding of the Bank of Amsterdam in 1608 and the first true state central bank, the Swedish Riksbank, established in

1656 and taken over by the Swedish state in 1668. However, it is still generally reckoned that it is the founding of the Bank of England in 1694 that signalled the most important innovation in state finance (Fay 1988). The Bank was founded to market the national debt but ended up managing it and regulating the British financial system to boot. Yet the history of the Bank of England is a history of only grudging acceptance of a role as the focus of the British financial system, a role forced on it by various financial crises. Most importantly of all, under the Bank Act of 1844, the Bank became a lender of last resort. By 1890 the Bank was acting as a full lender of last resort, arranging to guarantee the liabilities of Barings in a way that it would not have done in previous years (Roberts and Kynaston 1995).

The idea of a central state bank acting as lender of last resort then spread to the rest of the world. In doing so, it produced a new kind of money, what Keynes called *state credit money*, in which the state becomes the guarantor of public debts, using its ability to issue money. What distinguishes bank credit money from state credit money 'is the fact that the former defines a private debt whereas the latter does not. Thus the determining factor is not the private or public character of the institution which is getting spontaneously indebted but the nature of its debt' (Cencini 1988: 46). State credit money reached its apotheosis in the years after the Second World War. At that time, an international system of state money seemed to be coming into existence, as a result of the Bretton Woods agreement of 1944 and the subsequent postwar settlement. The function of lender of last resort between nations was a role discharged by the World Bank and the International Monetary Fund (IMF), as well as by the central bank swaps which grew up outside the IMF.

However, the ascendancy of state credit money was always contested. Even at its height, the state was never unambiguously in charge of money. The internationalisation of money, the growth of the power of banks and the increase in private commercial lending, as opposed to state lending, provided countervailing forces. Even in 1906, one London commentator, with a degree of prescience if not accuracy, could write that 'Lombard Street has been more under the control of the Japanese banks than of the Bank of England' (cited in King 1972: 283). State banks were able to fend off countervailing forces through more active banking strategies and the Bretton Woods agreement seemed to signal the final success of state credit money. But in the late 1960s and early 1970s, the strength of countervailing forces was significantly boosted. Most especially, much of the international capital market moved outside of state control through the growth of the Eurocurrency and other markets. Other woes piled up thick and fast: the opportunities to create and distribute fictitious capital became much greater because of the invention of new financial instruments (some of which were precisely designed to avoid state regulation); state regulation of national financial systems tended to become less rigid if not less extensive (Helleiner 1994, 1995); as a result of successive bouts of reregulation financial service companies began to move across established regulatory boundaries; systems of monetary transmission and clearing went electronic, becoming harder to track. The result was that it was no longer possible, as it had still been in the early 1970s, to use the weight of government in the gross national product to control or even direct the private sector (Minsky 1982).

The interpretations that were current in the period when state credit money reigned are again complex in their genealogy and contradictory in their effects. As the case of England shows, to an extent the concerns of the previous period were still prevalent. For example, credit and debt remained critical sites of the imagination, especially for the many women for whom, at least at the beginning of the period, 'the world of credit with its ever-present threat of prison for unpaid bills was directly in . . . experience' (Copeland 1995: 4). Again, the public sphere expanded, and one of its chief concerns became money and how to get and manage it. For example, Copeland (1995: 7) notes that money, like the weather, 'is one topic on which every novel has an opinion'.

But there were also some important changes and each of these can be traced to the growth in influence of the state. The first was the growth of state action upon the monetary front which significantly affected the lives of many ordinary people. Most particularly, in 1869 imprisonment for debt was abolished. Then there was the growth of insurance which, although not state controlled, was certainly sponsored by the state.[8] And, finally, and most importantly, there was the growth of the welfare state. Second, there was the growth of a 'domestic attitude' to money. Management of money was to be modelled on a domestic budget (Copeland 1995), which arose from the new discourse of family responsibility being promoted by Hannah Moore, Samuel Smiles and the like and from a direct comparison between the accounts of states and households.[9] 'Prudence requires that we pitch our scale of living a degree below our means rather than up to them, but this can only be done by carrying out faithfully a plan of living by which both ends may be made to meet' (Smiles 1859). As a result, after 1800,

> money finds a far less anxious place in the women's novel. Women's fiction abandons bit by bit, its narrative of economic victimisation to embrace a narrative of economic empowerment, a fictional world in which women assertively participate in the economy as managers of the domestic budget.
>
> (Copeland 1995: 61)

Virtual money

It is now possible to talk about a new kind of money coming into existence: *virtual money* (or book entry money) (Cencini 1988). This is money reduced to a numeraire – Walras in action. Money becomes an activated double book entry, a spontaneous acknowledgement of debt that is no longer a commodity. This new system of fleeting *instants* is based on quasi-private institutions and on the full range of instruments of fictitious capital (Hart 1986). 'Money is accepted on the belief that whoever offered it will make it good *in the future*. Money is to that extent partly a fiction, the stuff that dreams are made of' (Desai 1988: xiii).

It is possible to make virtual money seem as though it is insubstantial, what Poster (1990) calls a 'messagerie' constantly circulating intentions in an electronic space. In some accounts, often following Baudrillard, virtual money achieves lift-off from the real world:

> only signs, representations and simulations of the real circulate. In fact this is the reality of 'Wall Street'. Go back to the floor of the Stock Exchange, and re-examine the green computer screens of the young bankers. . . . Numbers flashing across screens, numbers which can be erased with a touch of the finger, or a loud voice. Numbers which point to imaginary properties of imaginary things. Companies with made-up names whose productivity is measured by imaginary accounts. Money attached to nothing by imaginary numbers attached to made up accounts, built on who can best manipulate this imaginary political economy of signs.
>
> (Denzin 1991: 40)

But it has to be understood that virtual money cannot be reduced to this romance of the unrepresentable. *It consists of a set of social practices just like any other.* It is not just a ghost in the machine.

Further, this new set of practices will continue in combination with other older forms of monetary practice in new combinations. For example, although the use of cash payments has declined in Britain, cash seems likely to remain important for many years yet, and not just because of the underground economy. In 1994, for example, according to Bank of England figures, 16 million out of 26 million recorded monetary transactions in Britain were in cash (Coyle 1995). And in 1995 the use of cash-intensive services, a boom in tourism, and even a heat wave in July and August (which increased spending on cash items like drinking and ices) boosted the use of cash. Further, electronic developments often *seem* more extraordinary than they are. Certainly it is possible to point to the remarkable spread of automated transactions machines (ATMs), often functioning on an intercontinental scale (Thrift 1995). The use of these machines has grown rapidly, in Britain up from 8,625 in 1986 to 14,096 in 1994, as has the number of transactions involving them (496 million in 1986, 1.3 billion in 1994). Similarly, there is the increasing use of debit cards, launched in Britain in 1988. And yet, what are these innovations mostly used for? In the case of the ATM, to withdraw *cash*. And in the case of the debit card, one of the reasons for its success in Britain has been the offering of 'cash-back' facilities.[10]

Virtual money also has its characteristic interpretations. In some senses, these interpretations might be regarded as a 'return' to those of the era of money of account. In England, for example, the increasingly rapid circulation of increasingly virtual money seems to have produced the same degree of suspicion of money's chimerical qualities, allied to a suspicion of the City of London as the centre of this virtual world, which is to be found in Addison or Pope or Gay or Swift, a point made clear by Churchill's (1987) play *Serious Money* which is prefaced by a scene from Thomas Shadwell's 1692 play, *The Volunteers, or the Stockjobbers* (1692).

But there have also been many changes. Of these, the most important is clearly the growth of a more accommodating attitude to the existence of credit and debt over the whole population which is, roughly speaking, based on the principle that 'everyone should be free to obtain as much credit as he (sic) could get, on the terms available to the market. But that was not to say that people had a right to it, that they were entitled to it' (Barty-King 1991: 171). But, even here, there are traces of older attitudes, attitudes that certainly go back to the era of money of account, and earlier.

> There is a very clear dichotomy in the British attitude to credit/debt. At its most basic assumption, credit is when you can afford the loan and debt is when you cannot, but I suspect that a lot of the ambivalence goes back to the medieval Christian theory of the Just Price and the medieval Christian view that usury was a sin. Certainly approximately 70 per cent of the population disapprove of debt, and 70 per cent of the British population are in debt. There is disapproval in principle and approval in practice, or is it hating the sin and loving the sinner?
>
> (Cunningham, cited in Barty-King 1991: vi)

Certain things immediately become clear from this short history of the transformation of money. The first of these is that this is a history of what Marx and others called the *dematerialisation* of money. Money is no longer a commodity which is transported hither and thither. It no longer even consists of paper, in the main. Increasingly, money is a set of double entries briefly etched in computer memories. The second thing that emerges is the crucially important role of *space*. Space is wrapped up with the history of the transformation of money because money is a means of linking what are often widely scattered interchanges, connecting credit and liability. As Giddens (1990: 24) puts it:

> Money is a means of bracketing time and so of lifting transactions out of particular milieu of exchange. More accurately put . . . money is a means of time–space distanciation. Money provides for the enactment of transactions between agents widely separated in time and space.

MONEY AND SPACE

The importance of space is worth expanding on, because the history of money and credit has been a geography too, and that geography has been and is constitutive of what money and credit now are. However, the importance of geography in the evolution of money has not always been recognised. In particular, there has been a failure to be suitably sensitive to the interplay between money, space and place, to see that monetary forms, practices and institutions are contingent in both space and time, and that money has often evolved in order to solve more general problems of time–space co-ordination; that is, money allows social relationships to be extended across space and time. To understand money, then, we must consider its historical geography. Each monetary form has its own geography, and the transformation from one monetary form to another has important geographical implications. It is, therefore, possible to identify different geographies of money.

Mapping the geography of '*premodern money*' would reveal a patchwork of discrete monetary systems scattered widely over space and through time, each system reflective of specific social and cultural conditions. If the incidence of such systems were mapped over time, then one would find that the systems that survived longest, in many cases well into the modern period, were a part of societies and cultures which maintained some degree of isolation from economies which used modern money forms. It is in this sense highly appropriate that the second chapter of Einzig's (1966) influential book on premodern money is entitled, 'Is primitive money still Terra Incognita?'. Einzig was making reference to the level of knowledge amassed by western academics on the subject, but the term has a deeper meaning than Einzig intended. For the survival of premodern money is inversely related to the degree of contact between the societies in which it circulates and western culture. It is no coincidence then that it was in Oceania and parts of Africa that premodern money systems appear to have survived longest (Einzig 1966), or long enough at least to have them documented by western anthropologists (although such acts of documentation often also sounded the death-knell for many premodern money systems, signalling as they did a greater degree of contact between such societies and a more powerful cultural form which used modern money (Gewertz and Errington 1995)).

Dodd (1994) appears to suggest that these initial acts of documentation and revelation have ensured that the possibilities of writing a systematic historical geography of premodern moneys are not propitious. Most of our knowledge of premodern money systems has been amassed by anthropologists but, according to Dodd at least, this knowledge is flawed, tainted by the idiographic biases of anthropological enquiry:

> The empirical study of pre-modern money has been misled by a preoccupation with the physical and symbolic properties of monetary objects. This precludes examination of the social and cultural conditions which enable monetary transaction, using any object whatsoever, to take place. To focus on the features of monetary objects can obviously be informative. But it is also too specific, providing no exhaustive guide to understanding the preconditions for establishing money as a social institution within a particular society or social group, however limited its use and functions might be.
>
> (Dodd 1994: xxi)

Such limitations would indeed make the writing of a convincing geography based on such anthropological accounts rather difficult. But the more interesting issue, from a geographical perspective at least, is not the empirical mapping of a constellation of premodern money forms, but the documentation of episodes of monetary incursion of exogenous monetary forms, practices and institutions and interpretations. As Dalton (1965: 66) has astutely observed, 'cases of monetary incursion deserve examination for reasons that are of interest to students of community economic development as well as economic anthropology'. Dalton is specifically concerned with the effects of 'western' money on 'traditional social organisations and cultural practices' in less developed countries, among the most important of which is the fusion of non-commercial obligations and commercial payments. However, the lessons of historical episodes of monetary incursion may also be of value to those interested in the possibilities of creating 'alternative' financial institutions in the 'west', such as local exchange and trading systems (LETS) (Lee 1995; Williams 1995), which, at a pinch, may be interpreted as the reassertion of premodern moneys in the midst of modern monetary systems.

The history of these monetary incursions really begins with the development of *commodity money*. The early history of commodity money is in large part one of incursion and invasion, for the development of coinage made it far easier to mobilise military action at a distance. As Davies (1994: 108) describes it, 'Coins followed – indeed accompanied – the sword', so that 'payment for troops and for their large armies of camp-followers was generally the cause of minting'. The Greek and Roman armies were paid in coin and well paid too in order to maintain their loyalty. It has been estimated that it would require 1,500,000 silver denarii per annum to support a single Roman legion, so that the majority of the silver flowing into Rome from the mines scattered throughout the empire was transformed into coins to support the Roman army (Davies 1994: 88).

At the same time, as the armies went on their military campaigns they became vehicles of monetary expansion and incursion, for they took their coins with them, which subsequently became used as money in the territories they appropriated. The effect of these actions was to bring about a degree of financial homogenisation over space. One way in which this came about, of course, was through direct force, as more powerful states imposed their money on weak states, thereby easing economic integration and eliminating the uncertainties associated with monetary exchange. Just such an episode occurred in Greece in the middle of the first millennium BC:

> In 456 BC Athens forced Aegina to take Athenian 'owls' and to cease minting their own 'turtle' coinage. In 449 BC Athens in furtherance of greater uniformity issued an edict ordering all 'foreign' coins to be handed in to the Athenian mint and compelling all her allies to use the Attic standard of weight, measures and money.
>
> (Davies 1994: 76)

Here is an example of financial homogenisation occurring across spaces already dominated by commodity money. But of more importance to the argument being pursued here was the extension of commodity money networks into spaces previously dominated by exchange based on premodern moneys. However, while such incursions were undoubtedly important in extending the geographical influence of modern money, to recall the instance of Roman Britain discussed earlier, the degree to which early monetary networks extended beyond the key cities of the empire into the vast territories that surrounded then is still the subject of much debate (Aitchison 1988: 277–8).

In many cases, the 'infilling' of commodity money into the spaces that surrounded these nodal centres did not occur until much later with the rise of the fiscal policies of the early monarchical states, a process that was facilitated by the construction of an extensive network of official mints. At the same time, there occurred a marked increase in the level of trade, often across large geographical distances, despite the inherent inconveniences of conducting exchange at long distance using heavy coinage, with the result that until about the fifteenth century the history of money includes often heroic efforts to transport commodity money over long distances. However, during the fifteenth century a new monetary era hove into view, due in large part to a series of social innovations which caused a radical shift in the time–space co-ordinates of the financial system:

> The modern monetary age . . . began with the geographic discoveries, with the full fruition of the Renaissance, with Columbus and El Dorado, with Leonardo da Vinci, Luther and Caxton; in short with improvements in communications, minting and printing. A vast increase in money, minted and printed, occurred in parallel with an unprecedented expansion in physical and mental resources. The invention of new machines for minting and printing were in fact closely linked in a manner highly significant for the future of finance. At first the increase in coinage was to exceed, and then just to keep pace with the increase in paper money; but eventually and inexorably paper was to displace silver and gold, and thereby to release money from its metallic chains and anchors.
>
> (Davies, 1994: 174)

The advent of credit money served to reshape the geography of the financial system. The clearest sign of the birth of this new monetary era was the increasing use of the bill of exchange. When the first bills of exchange appeared, presenting the first means of distanciating credit, distance was, not surprisingly, the crucial factor in calculating the maturity of a bill. Thus the 'usuance' or 'usance' of a bill, the period between its creation and maturity, was simply an acknowledgement of distance:

> Mails . . . took time. Bills were payable at sight, at 'usuance', or sometimes half-usuance or double-usuance. Usuance was the standard credit period for a given trade. From Geneva at the beginning of the sixteenth century it ran five days for Pisa, six for Milan, fifteen for Ancona, twenty for Barcelona, thirty for Valencia and Montpellier, two months for Bruges and three for London. From London, usuance was one month to Antwerp, two to Hamburg and three to the northern Italian cities. It was seldom changed: the

one month between London and Antwerp lasted from the fourteenth
century to 1789.

(Kindleberger 1984: 39)

As money and capital markets became more extensive, so geography
was again crucial. There are numerous examples of the constitutive role of
space in the development of money. As noted above, the need to finance
highly profitable but also risky long-distance voyages led to the invention of
perpetual transferable shares. More important even than the invention of such new financial instruments was the way in which the constraints
of space were overcome, so as to make these instruments tradable over
greater and greater distances, through the marrying of improvements
in transport and communications to specific market nodes, usually large
urban centres, so as to produce an increasingly compressed financial
space (Castells 1989; Harvey 1989b). It is worth dwelling on this point by
considering the example of the circulation of financial documents.
Financial practices have always generated large amounts of records and
communications. For example, when one sixteenth-century merchant
of Prato died he left 150,000 letters, 500 account books and ledgers, 500
deeds of partnership and several thousand bills and checks. Again, at the
end of the eighteenth century, the clerk of one Hamburg banker wrote
200 letters a day and when the ice broke up in 1795 and thirteen English
posts came in at once, it took the banker concerned three days to read
them all (Kindleberger 1984).

The way in which systems of financial communication and transmission
came about as specific articulations of space is perhaps best illustrated
through the historical geography of the development of bank clearing in
England and Wales (Kindleberger 1984). By the seventeenth century
London had already become the major clearing centre for national
payments. The London banks issued a few bank notes of their own. They
settled balances with each other, on their own accounts and the accounts
of their correspondents, in Bank of England notes. The banks kept
running accounts with one another which enabled them to cancel out offsetting claims. This activity was soon transferred to a public house and then
in 1773 to a rented building in Lombard Street which was dubbed as the
clearing house. Not all of the City of London banks joined this institution
and, as if to demonstrate the importance of even small distances, none
of the banks in the West End of London became members. Private banks
continued to dominate London clearing even after joint stock banks were
formed after the Bank Acts of 1826 and 1833. The new joint stock banks
were only finally admitted to the London clearing in 1854.

Clearing was clearly slow to form in London but in time it became an
institution, based on a tightly regulated micro-space of specific distances
(only offices within one-half a mile of the clearing house were allowed
in the system) and specific times (the afternoon settlement deadline),
integrated by the 'walks' of messengers and couriers around the offices
picking up drafts and cheques to take to the clearing house for settlement.

However, if clearing was slow to form in London – and spatially specific even there – it was slower still in the provinces. There, the system was regional in emphasis. A system of exchanging bank notes on a friendly basis was developed by Scottish banks as early as 1752. In England, before that date, there were, in any case, few banks, perhaps a dozen in all. But after that date the number of 'country banks' grew almost exponentially and the need for some system of clearing became pressing (Presnell 1956). For example, by the 1780s eight country banks in Newcastle were exchanging notes at regular intervals. By the early nineteenth century banks in the north were coming together at weekly or even biweekly intervals using Bank of England notes, then cheques, to settle any outstanding balances. After the Bank Act of 1826, Bank of England branches spread out over the country (Black 1989). These branches became the natural foci for settlement, and by the later nineteenth century all principal cities had their own clearing houses.

However, if *intra-regional* settlement was now proceeding on national lines, *inter-regional* settlement was still something of a problem. Indeed, bills of exchange were still being used well into the nineteenth century. The domestic bill of exchange only finally declined for a number of reasons, chief amongst which were the rise of the telegraphic transfer, wide circulation of Bank of England notes, the rapid growth of bank depositors and bank deposits and, most important of all, the rise of joint stock banks with extensive branch networks which meant that inter-regional clearing moved from the inter to the intra-organisational domain (King 1972). As a result, clearing through London gradually became the norm. For example,

> in 1858 the National Provincial Bank thought it preposterous for a bank in Manchester to collect a cheque on Newcastle-upon-Tyne by way of London. . . . By 1866, however, it was ready to give up the note issue privilege, start a London banking office, and settle for its system through the regular London clearing.
>
> (Kindleberger 1984: 79)

This brief example shows a financial system progressively coalescing at different spatial scales from the inter-regional to the national. It also illustrates the ways in which more or less uniform national financial spaces are formed based upon state money, brought into being through the regulation of money by the state:

> The creation of what can be described as 'national financial space' was part and parcel of the evolution of the state system between the sixteenth and eighteenth century, upon which the capitalist system was grounded. Along with the development of a centralised legal order and taxation system, the emergence of national monetary systems organised and policed by state authorities was central to the emergence of what later became the nation-state (Giddens, 1985). National financial spaces were predicated upon the circulation of 'state' or 'fiduciary money'; that is, money that has no inherent value of itself, such as commodity money, but is guaranteed

through the state's supervision and surveillance of the national financial system (Giddens, 1985, page 155). In seeking to maintain the worth of fiduciary money, the state is forced to sanction those economic institutions that, through 'improper' financial practice, are seen to be undermining faith in fiduciary money as the medium of exchange and the measure of value in exchange. Through the social practice of regulation (Marden, 1992), the state seeks to control the institutions within a financial system, ushering in 'safe and sound' financial practice, while at the same time crowding out alternatives to fiduciary money within the national financial space.

(Leyshon 1996a: 76)

The above example also begins to show the increasing importance of electronically mediated indirect communication. Indirect communication has, of course, been a vital part of monetary systems for a very considerable length of time, as the examples of the heavy use of the mails by the merchant of Prato and the banker of Hamburg, laid out above, showed. This indirect communication was never simply technical. Along with the gold, bills, notes, drafts and contracts flowed a ceaseless stream of intelligence and comment, about money market conditions, news of business failures and the fate of expeditions, as well as all manner of political and religious interpretation: money has never been able to be separated from the discourse about money. But such communication, even with the advent of the railways, still took up time and space. Electronically mediated indirect communication altered the terms of this equation (Thrift 1990b). Time and space were so compressed by the time Simmel was writing in the first decade of the twentieth century that it was quite clear to him that money was a bridge over distances:

the role of money is associated with the spatial distance between the individual and his possession ... only if the profit of an enterprise takes a form that can be easily transferred to any other place does it guarantee to property and the owner, through their spatial separation, a high degree of independence or in other words, self-mobility. ... The power of money to bridge distances enables the owner and his possessions to exist so far apart that each of them may follow their own precepts to a greater extent than in the period when the owner and his possession still stood in direct mutual relationship, when every economic engagement was also a personal one.

(Simmel 1978: 332–3)

This compression of time and space was already laying the foundations for *virtual money*, as the example of the coalescence of an international money and capital market around the telegraph in the nineteenth century shows. The formation of such a market was hampered by distance and the currency of bills was accordingly longer. Thus, the usuances for bills drawn on domestic inter-regional trades were usually three months; for the export trade four months' drafts were common, drawn on the merchant houses of London and Liverpool. But for imports, drafts were often six months and could be twelve months or even more (Chapman 1984), especially when trade was with India, the East Indies and China (King

1972). The international bill market became increasingly important through the 1840s and 1850s, especially as a result of the increasing use of the system of acceptance credits, a system that 'was practised on a much larger scale than ever before, and was extended to trades and areas in which it had previously been only exceptionally used' (King 1972: 177), especially to the Americas, Scandinavia, China and the East. As the domestic bill market waned, the international bill market waxed. Bills were 'cleared' in London through a troika of banks, accepting houses, and bill brokers. Through the nineteenth century the market became increasingly international with the acceptances of the large London houses being employed as a kind of international currency. But as the market internationalised so the problem of international interest rates became a pressing one. Already by 1819 it was recognised that a differential between London and continental rates might have an important effect on London credit conditions. Still rates did not equalise rapidly. This was hardly surprising in days when mail from London to New York, for example, took at least two weeks: rapid adjustments in rates were simply impossible.

The advent of the telegraph was therefore extraordinarily important: it was fundamental to the creation of an integrated international money market. The telegraph was first used by banks between London and Hamburg.

> The earliest reference in surviving records to the use of the telegraph by merchant banks occurs in 1845, when Rothschilds and Behrens of Hamburg opened a telegraphic correspondence to swap information on prices on the international stock and currency exchanges. Behrens wrote 'As far as we know, no Hamburg bankers have yet taken advantage of this means of communication. It is, so far, used only by the grain trade and other merchants.' But Behrens proposed to use it only once a week and, twenty years later, the weekly routine at Barings still revolved around the foreign post days.
> (Chapman 1984: 108)

But if Barings used the telegraph in a limited way, others did not. By the early 1870s, the telegraph had considerably accelerated the tempo of financial business worldwide. Nowhere was this clearer than in the case of business between London and New York. The first Atlantic telegraph opened for traffic in August 1858. About eight years later New York foreign exchange rates were being regularly advised by cable (King 1972). By 1872, when Isaac Seligman was sent to represent his brother's New York house in London, he recalled the nervous strain of 'sending and receiving telegrams every few minutes' (Chapman 1984: 108). In particular, the telegraph meant new opportunities for arbitrage. But even more importantly, the use of the telegraph suggested new ways of doing international financial business so that by 1877, 'The *Economist* was remarking that telegraphic transfers, together with international coupons, were superseding the bill (of exchange) as a means of remittance' (King 1972: 269).[11]

Virtual money would spring out of these and other developments in electronically mediated telecommunications, as communication in monetary systems became increasingly indirect, and instantaneous. This increase in indirectness and instantaneity can be measured in all kinds of ways, from a simple increase in the use of computers and telecommunications, allowing double-entry book-keeping to glue the world economy together, to the invention and increasing sophistication of the credit card, which may well in time mean a farewell to cash.[12] As a matter of record, the first credit card was invented by Diners Club for use in the United States in the 1950s. American Express followed suit in 1958. Bank Americard was issued by the Bank of America in California in 1959 and licensed in other states in 1966. The American Express Card was introduced to Britain in 1963. Barclaycard was introduced by Barclays in 1966. Its main rival, Access, did not appear until 1972 (Dunkling and Room 1990; Zelizer 1994; Ritzer 1995).

What must be noted about this new system, with its compressed electronic geography, is that it accentuates a need for *trust* but at the same time, precisely because so much communication is distanciated, indirect and impersonal, it undermines the basis on which trust is usually extended. What then replaces face-to-face contact as a way of extending trust? The answer, as Giddens (1990) has pointed out, is *expert systems*. These systems are intended to construct and guarantee trust in money through the deployment and display of particular *knowledge structures* (Strange 1988). Such systems, in turn, are monitored in all kinds of ways for their trustworthiness, through state surveillance and regulation, through branding, through the critiques offered by the media, and so on. Thus, as Giddens (1990: 28) points out:

> Export systems are disembedding mechanisms because, in common with symbolic tokens (like coins), they remove social relations from the immediacies of context. Both types of disembedding mechanism preserve, yet also foster, the separation of time and space as the condition of the time–space distanciation which they promote. An expert system disembeds in the same way as symbolic tokens, by providing 'guarantees' of expectations across distanciated time–space. This 'stretching' of social systems is achieved via the impersonal nature of tests applied to evaluate technical knowledge and by public critique (upon which the production of technical knowledge is based), used to control its form.

The problem of course is that the extension of trust must be, in large part nowadays, based on *belief* since it is impossible to validate most knowledge. This is a double-edged sword, and leads directly to a major theme of this book, the prevalence of fictitious capital in systems of virtual money:

> Money is accepted on the belief that whoever offered it will make it good in the future. Money is to that extent partly a fiction, the stuff that dreams are made of. Normally institutional regulations, traditional habits of caution on the part of bankers and sheer luck make the outcome not too different from the fiction: the money accepted yesterday can be 'cashed' in goods today. But

a lot of it is fictitious. Indeed many of the trillions of dollars that were wiped out on 19th October, 1987 were fictitious capital to which nothing 'real' corresponded. It is this habit of money to be tolerably unreal in normal times, but wildly fictitious in times of speculation, that has yet to be accommodated in monetary theory.

(Desai 1988: xiii–iv)

MONEY AND ITS INTERPRETATIONS

Money and its practices saturate our language. In the most general sense, it provides many of the metaphors through which we constitute reality (Lakoff and Johnson 1980). More specifically, money is the begetter of a rich fabric of words, phrases and sayings, and general slang. There is hot money, funny money, pin money, slush money and old money. There is having money to burn, and launder. There is money for jam, or old rope. There is cash on the barrel. There is a quid and a pony. There is a lolly, dosh (originally a West Indian term), brass, dough . . . the list goes on (Dunkling and Room 1990).

Within the general flow of everyday language about money, there exists a more specialised language used by the community that is professionally involved in making money. In the financial press, for example, 'a luxuriant language runs riot. . . . An engineering company sees a "hint of silver on the horizon"; the champagne trade is "not bubbling over with joy"; "Colorol shares take a pasting"; "Marmite spread over the UK"; and so on and so on' (Enzensberger 1990: 85). It is a rhetoric of those who belong to the financial world and it simultaneously defines those who are members and those who are not. No wonder that Enzensberger (1990: 86–7) writes:

> I can't get rid of the feeling that as a reader (of the financial press) I'm out of place. The commentator is pleased because the New Zealand loan has been taken up so well. On the other hand, Paris was listless at the close of trading; goldmines lost some ground and liquidations were noted amongst professional traders. Hapag-Lloyd, we have learned, wants to raise earnings and Mannesman's profits have increased again. It all goes on, day in, day out, behind my back as it were. I must admit that I don't belong to this 'economy'. If at least I were an ordinary saver, or a small shareholder! Because these characters are welcomed with open arms, and the editors' concern for them is moving, as if they were dealing with the walking wounded, even if an undertone of condescension is also unmistakeable. These people belong but only as onlookers. I by contrast, only participate in economic life, if at all, in a quite subordinate way, as an employee for example, or as a 'consumer'; in a word, as an object of the 'economy'; i.e. as its fool.

Finally, there is the language used by the various occupational communities in finance and banking. This is a language of extreme specialisation. Whole glossaries exist that name all different kinds of financial instruments now in use, and the various ways of buying and selling them. Then there are all the different languages of the traders and the setters-up of deals. For example, slang names have always been given to shares. Even in 1895, A.J. Wilson found eighty 'slang, or corrupted names from the London Exchange. *Marbles* stood for Marbella Iron Ore Shares and *Imps* for Imperial Tobacco Company Shares. Aerated Bread Shares were *Breads*, while fractions of these shares were Bread Crumbs' (Odeat 1990: 226). The language can become forcefully representative. In the 1980s mergers and acquisitions provided a plethora of terms: white knights, corporate raiders, poison pills, greenmail, sleeping beauties, and so on. So did trading.

Interestingly, many of these different specialised vocabularies are suffused with images of sexuality and violence. For example, in particular trading rooms these languages can become a kind of parody of masculinity and masculine violence (Odeat 1990; McDowell and Court 1994). The classic example here is found in Lewis's account of his initiation into the Salomon Brothers trading culture in New York in the 1980s. Here was a world in which the successful traders were 'big swinging dicks', the trading floor was a 'jungle', and one of the chief business aims was to 'rip the opposition's face off'. Sometimes the scatological intensity of these languages reached parodic level:

> The piranha didn't talk like a person. He said things like 'if you fuckin' buy this bond in a fuckin' trade, you're fuckin' fucked. And if you don't pay attention to the fuckin' two year, you get your fuckin' face ripped off'. Noun, verb, adjective: fucker, fuck, fucking. No part of speech was spared. His world was filled with copulating inanimate objects, and people getting their faces ripped off.
>
> (Lewis 1989: 65)

But are there any traditions of judgement that unite all these different languages of money? In the broadest sense, at least, the answer is yes. Two discourses can be identified. One is a discourse of suspicion. The other is a discourse of liberation.

In the first discourse, money – and those who are associated with money – are treated with the deepest of suspicion. Three judgements seem to recur constantly. First, money itself is often seen as a system that is *out of control*. Second, those who deal in money, and especially credit, are *placed beyond the pale*. They are even *parasitic*. Third, money acts as a *corrosive force* in human societies, especially as part of the rise of *individualism*.

Such judgements as these can be found as early as the work of Aristotle, according to whom

> Profit-oriented exchange is . . . unnatural, and is destructive of the bonds between households. Prices should therefore be fixed and goods and services remunerated in accordance with the status of those who provided them. Money as a tool intended only to facilitate exchange is naturally barren and, of all ways of getting wealth, lending at interest – where money is made to yield a 'crop' or 'litter' – 'is the most contrary to nature'.
>
> (Parry and Bloch 1989: 2)

Aristotle's views about money were taken up by Thomas Aquinas and through him they achieved considerable currency in the economic thought of the Middle Ages: 'One of the major problems was that the merchant apparently created nothing; while the usurer earned money even as he slept. "The labourer is worthy of his hire", but it was not at all clear that the merchant and the money lender laboured' (Parry and Bloch 1989: 3). The persistence of this medieval unease about money is most forcefully illustrated by the history of the usury laws that have had such a purchase on European economic history. These laws were the province of the church and only died out very slowly in Europe (they are, of course, still current in many Moslem countries). The history of these laws of usury in Britain is exemplary (Angell 1930). There, lending at interest became acceptable when Henry VIII broke away from the Church of Rome. The usury laws of 1487 and 1495 were relaxed in 1545 when a 10 per cent limit was set to the interest that could be charged.

> Edward VI restored the prohibition against changing interest but in 1571 Elizabeth I removed it again. Thereafter the limit to interest that was not usurious was gradually lowered to 8 per cent under James I in 1624, 6 per cent under Charles II in 1660 and 5 per cent under Queen Anne in 1713.
>   (Kindleberger 1984: 41)

The laws against usury were finally dropped in Britain, Holland, Belgium and north Germany between 1854 and 1867 (Hobsbawm 1975). Long before this, such laws had become something of a fiction honoured only in the breach. But their continued existence still demonstrated a powerful suspicion of lending with interest – and of those who lent at interest. This point is further demonstrated by the way in which money lenders have often been from different ethnic groups or religions. In Europe these 'pariah capitalists', to use a Weberian term, were often Jews – but it is dangerous to make too much of this; at least in part the Jewish concentration in money lending was because Jews were forbidden to own land.

The discourse of suspicion about money is perhaps most visible in the history of economic thought. There we often find money depicted as out of control. Such a depiction is especially found in the work of Keynes. For Keynes the whole monetary system was, in the last resort, a species of illusion, 'a contrived system of pretty, polite techniques, made for a well-panelled board room and a nicely regulated market' (Keynes 1936: 214). It was an exercise in making uncertainty respectable. Most worrying of all, to Keynes, was speculation. 'Keynes had an almost obsessive fear that speculation or gambling would predominate over investment based on the best genuine long-term expectations' (Frankel 1977: 78). No wonder that Keynes saw money as a force that had to be reined in by the state. Again, those who deal in money are constantly berated as unproductive labour, especially in the corpus of classical economics. For example, in Marx, both the most comprehensive and the narrowest of the classical economists, finance and banking fell as activities within the realm of circulation, as necessary but unproductive. Money is a 'mere circulation machine' (Marx 1885: 139). Finally, money is often depicted as a corrosive force. Many economists who have made an excursion into sociology have seen money as a kind of acid, making the personal into the impersonal and the different into the indifferent. For Marx, for example, money is clearly a corrosive force;

> if money is the bond which ties me to human life and society to me, which links me to nature and to man, is money not the bond of all bonds? Can it not bind and loose all bonds? It is therefore not the universal means of separation? It is the true agent of separation and the true cementing agent, it is the chemical power of society.
>
> (Marx 1973: 377)

Money is also the great leveller, it 'does away with all distinctions' because it reduces everything to the same yardstick, collapsing differences of quality into mere quantity. And money is a perfect example of commodity fetishism with the power to reproduce itself; money breeds money just as 'it is an attribute of pear trees to bear pears . . . ' (Marx 1961). Then again, money conceals the origin of the commodity. The value of the commodity is expressed in money terms and the labour which went into its production is veiled. Worse still, money comes back to haunt humankind, as a disembodied force that takes on a life of its own:

> Money abuses all the gods of mankind and changes them into commodities. It has, therefore, deprived the whole world, both the human world and nature, of their proper value. Money is the alienated essence of man's work and existence, this essence dominates him and he worships it.
>
> (Marx 1963: 37)[13]

But there is another discourse, one in which money is not the great Satan and those who deal in money are not necessarily counted as, to use a phrase of Burke's (1978: 268), 'sophisters, oeconomists, and calculators'. This discourse of money as an enlightened force also has deep roots in history although they are probably not as deep as those of the discourse of suspicion (Reddy 1987). In France, for example, Montesquieu traces out a history of money and commerce as an enlightened and anti-autocratic force. For example, in part four of *Esprit des Lois*, Montesquieu describes how commerce was hampered by accusations of usury from the church, and consequently was taken up by the Jews. But the Jews suffered violence and constant extortion at the hands of the monarchy and industry, to which they reacted by inventing the bill of exchange. Montesquieu's conclusions are striking, especially from the modern perspective:

> through (the bill of exchange) commerce could elude violence and maintain itself everywhere: for the richest trader had only invisible wealth which could be sent everywhere without leaving any trace. . . . In this manner we owe . . . to the avarice of rulers the establishment of a contrivance which

somehow lifts commerce right out of their grip. Since that time, the rulers have been compelled to govern with greater wisdom than they themselves might have intended.

(cited in Hirschman 1977: 72)

Similar arguments were made by Spinoza, Steuart and Adam Smith.

Such documents may now appear extravagant, yet they provide a useful counterbalance to the discourse of suspicion, and are not without some merit. Thus, in many modern critiques, money and capitalism are still depicted as alienated forces. But from the perspective of the discourse of liberation,

> this accusation seems a bit unfair, for capitalism was precisely expected and supposed to repress certain human desires and productivities and to fashion a less multifaceted, more predictable and more 'one-dimensional' human personality. This position . . . arose . . . from concern over the destructive forces unleashed by the human passions with the only exception . . . of 'innocuous' avarice. In sum, capitalism was supposed to accomplish exactly what was soon to be denounced as its worst feature. For as soon as capitalism was triumphant and 'passion' seemed indeed to be restrained and perhaps even extinguished . . . the world suddenly appeared empty, petty and boring and the stage was set for the romantic critique of the bourgeois order as incredibly impoverished in relation to earlier ages . . . considerable traces of this nostalgic critique can be found in subsequent social thought from Fourier's advocacy of passionate attraction to Marx's theory of alienation, and from Freud's thesis of libidinal repression to Weber's concept of Entzauberung (progressive disintegration of the magical vision of the world).
>
> (Hirschman 1977: 132–3)

Of course, most accounts of money mix these two discourses together. For example, Keynes' almost obsessive fear of monetary speculation[14] was matched by an attention to the advantages of modest accumulation that could have come from Montesquieu or Dr Johnson:

> Dangerous human proclivities can be canalised into comparatively harmless channels by the existence of opportunity for money-making and private wealth which, if they cannot be satisfied in this way, may find their outlet in cruelty, the reckless pursuit of power and authority, and other forms of self aggrandisement. It is better that a man should tyrannise over his bank balance than over his fellow-citizens; and whilst the former is sometimes denounced as being but a means to the latter, sometimes at least it is an alternative.
>
> (Keynes 1936: 374)

But there is one writer who is usually thought of, more than any other, as writing on money in ways which unite and transcend these discourses. That is Simmel (see Simmel 1978, 1990; Frisby 1992; Poggi 1993; Grenier *et al.* 1993). At first glance, Simmel's views may seem very close to those of Marx. After all, Simmel wanted to construct a 'new storey beneath historical materialism' by considering the 'psychological or even metaphysical pre-conditions' of the modern form of economic life (Simmel

1978: 56). But Simmel, although he was willing to recognise historical materialism as a legitimate method of analysis and as a heuristic model of social change, wanted to lay much more weight on the symbolic dimension of human societies as well as extraneous economic or material causes.

For Simmel, then, money is 'the symbol of the completely dynamic character of the new world'. It is the most ephemeral thing in the external practical world which is both concentrated by the modern *money metropolis*, with its requirements for exactitude and calculability, and diffused by the modern *economy*. The frenzied activity of the modern money metropolis 'carries the person as if in a stream, and he hardly needs to swim for himself' (Wolff 1964: 410). The increase in nervous life that results leads to indifference, dissociation, cynicism and blasé attitudes, all necessary forms of self-preservation which in some senses are liberating: the progressive emancipation of the individual from various kinds of social tie is, for Simmel, the most important and beneficent aspect of monetary order (Frankel 1977).

Thus, money becomes the community holding everything together but at the price of inventing new distinctions between people. It is an instrument of freedom, and a condition of the extension of the individual personality. But at the same time money constitutes a threat to the moral order: 'while money enlarges the field of our desire by making all things for a price, it also absorbs our desire by becoming an end in itself' (Frisby 1992: 305). Money sets us free to buy everything but it cannot guide us in deciding what to do with that freedom (Simmel 1978). For Simmel, then, the negative aspect of money is that:

> it places us at widening distance from the objects of our own concern. Thus immediacy of impression of things and of our interests becomes weakened. Our contact with them becomes interrupted: we sense them only through the mediation of money which however can never fully express their unique and genuine character.
>
> (Frankel 1977: 14)

It is difficult not to conclude that Simmel's philosophy of money is in fact a schizophrenic one. There is a sense through all his work on money of a romantic critique of a psychically impoverished 'modern' order which is the result of the mapping of money's 'complete heartlessness' onto society. This involves:

- The imposition of an 'unconditionally interchangeable' system of numbers (p. 444), whose 'uncompromising objectives' (p. 373) threaten all qualitative distinctions.
- The interpretation of all non-economic restrictions on money as atavistic 'sentimentalities that lose their significance completely with the growing indifference of money' (p. 441).
- The reduction of space to a plaything because 'owing to the abstractness of its form, money has no definite relationship to space; it can exercise its effects upon the most remote areas' (p. 504).

- The condemnation of money dealing. The sites of this activity are 'the nurseries of cynicism . . . those places with huge turnovers, exemplified in stock exchange dealings, where money is available in huge quantities and changes owners easily' (p. 256).

To summarise, 'the more money becomes the sole centre of interest, the more one discovers that honour and conviction, talent and virtue, beauty and salvation of the soul are exchanged against money' (p. 256).

But, at the same time, Simmel is quite willing to recognise that the practice of money can only be sustained by social relationships of some depth. Thus Frisby (1992: 93–4), quoting Simmel, notes how although

> money is the reified function of being exchanged; it is 'the reification of the pure relationship between things expressed in their economic motion', it 'stands in a realm organised according to its own norms', it is 'an absolute intermediary' [still] this mediation is . . . only possible on the basis of other social functions such as trust, embodied in guarantors, the largest of which is 'the central political power'.

Indeed, Simmel notes how

> money transactions would collapse without trust . . . [but] . . . there are nuances of this trust. The assertion that money is always credit because its value rests upon the recipient's confidence that he will be able to acquire a certain quality of goods in exchange for it is not entirely adequate . . . in the case of credit, of trust in someone, there is an additional element which is hard to describe: it is most clearly embodied in religious faith (p. 179).

Simmel's schizophrenic condition suggests that there are severe problems with a definition of money which views it solely as an objectifying force (Dodd 1994; Zelizer 1994) which cannot be solved by simply acknowledging that money has a symbolic dimension (Harvey 1989a). The search is therefore on for a model of money which can satisfy at least five criteria (Zelizer 1994). First, money is clearly a key tool within the modern market economy, but it cannot be cloistered within it. It is therefore bound to be strongly influenced by the social and cultural spheres (Lamont 1992). Second, no single, uniform and generalised money exists. Rather

> People earmark different currencies for many or perhaps all types of social interactions, much as they create distinctive languages for different social contexts. And people will in fact respond with anger, shock, or ridicule to the 'misuse' of moneys for the wrong circumstances or social relations, such as offering a thousand dollar bill to pay for a newspaper or tipping a restaurant's owner. Money used for rational instrumental exchanges is not 'free' from social constraints but is another type of socially created currency, subject to particular networks of social relations and its own set of values and norms.
>
> (Zelizer 1994: 19)

Third, the classic functions model of money, which we referred to in the first part of this chapter, is too narrow because it assumes that all money is 'market' money. A broader model is needed. Fourth, the protean and unchecked power of money which is so often a feature of writing on money is seen to be an exaggeration. Social and cultural structures set limits on what is thought of as money, how it is controlled, and on flow and liquidity. Fifth, geography is not an incidental to money, it is constitutive of it: 'despite its transferability, people make every effort to embed money in particular times, places, and social relations' (Zelizer 1994: 18).

What Zelizer's criteria suggest is the need for a more differentiated model of money which stresses the importance of social networks, prevalent discursive regimes, and the circulation of information. In the second part of this book we have tried to edge towards such a model.

Part I

HIGH SUMMER

High Summer

PART I

INTRODUCTION

The chapters in this part of the book share two main characteristics. First, they were all written during the mid- to late 1980s and very early 1990s, an era dominated by the triumphalism of Thatcherism and Reaganomics. In the financial sphere, re-regulatory programmes associated with these neo-liberal projects brought about what Magdoff and Sweezy (1987) have aptly described as a 'financial explosion'. Despite an unpropitious start to the decade, which was overshadowed by the emergence of the less developed countries' debt crisis, the 1980s was therefore a kind of financial high summer, during which the financial services industry enjoyed the fruits of an unprecedented period of growth. The chapters which follow represent our attempts to document this period of growth and to figure out the urban and regional consequences of the 1980s' financial boom.

The second characteristic that these chapters have in common is that they were written from a broadly political economy perspective. Our early work on the geography of money and finance was strongly influenced by Marxist theory. In this, like many others, we were influenced by David Harvey (1982, 1985, 1989a, b), whose work in this area has tended to ensure that geographers undertaking analyses of money and finance have produced studies of geographical political economy (see Leyshon 1995). Our initial attempts to discern the dynamics and mechanisms of the financial system were greatly enhanced through an understanding of the Marxist model of money. One of the reasons for this is that money is afforded a special place in Marxist economic theory, performing a key role in the circuit of capital. In the guise of what Marx describes as banking capital, it is also one of the three main forms of capital that structure he body of capitalism. For reasons which we shall elaborate upon later, we are now far less enamoured with this model than we once were. Nevertheless, below we offer our interpretation of the Marxist model of money. We do this both by way of an introduction to this part of the book and to give a clearer indication of the type of theoretical thinking that strongly influenced us when we wrote many of the chapters which follow.

THE MARXIST MODEL OF MONEY

Money is afforded a special place in Marxist theory. Money is regarded as a key component in the engine of the capitalist system and its central role is illustrated in Marx's schematic representation of the circuit of productive capital:

$$M - C \overset{MP}{\underset{LP}{\diagup\diagdown}} \dots P \dots C' - M'$$

Here, M represents money advanced for the purchase of commodities (C) in the form of the means of production (MP) and labour power (LP), which through production (P) are transformed into new commodities (C'). When sold, these new commodities realise a sum of money (M') which exceeds the value of that originally advanced. Capital is said to have been *valorised* when it increases in value through production, generating *surplus value* through the difference between the value of the money capital originally advanced and the value contained within the transformed commodities. If surplus value generated from the circuit of production is then advanced for the purchase of more commodity inputs, then the cycle can be repeated and so the realisation of surplus capital continues. Therefore, money is presented prior to production, and through production is transformed into an increased volume of money.

Marx distinguished between three forms of capital, which are defined in relation to the role they play within the circuit of productive capital. Thus, *productive capital* is the form of capital which exists when it is articulated within the productive circuit itself, that is when capital is translated into commodity inputs, which are in turn transformed into new commodities within the production process. According to Marx, this is capital existing as capital in its true form (Marx 1959: 343). However, forms of capital exist outside the productive circuit, but are nevertheless essential for the continued reproduction of productive capital.

Banking capital, or what we shall from now on call *financial capital*, is the form of capital which is advanced in the form of money prior to production.[1] This is interest-bearing capital, and is advanced by money-owners in return for an eventual share of the surplus value produced within production. The share of surplus value is repaid by the productive capitalist to the money-owner in the form of interest on the original capital advanced. The interest rate, therefore, represents the 'price' paid by the productive capitalist for the use value of money as capital, which is exchanged for commodities which are introduced into the production process to generate surplus value. The productive capitalist therefore buys the value-producing potential of money (Thompson 1977: 237–8).

The determination of the price of money – the interest rate – is unusual in Marxist analysis in that it is the only phenomenon that is not held to be determined by a fundamental underlying law. It is seen as being largely arbitrary, in that it is determined by the relationship between supply and demand as well as by tradition and custom (Harvey 1982: 259). The interest rate, therefore, can be seen as a representation of the relative balance of power which exists between financial capital and productive capital, in that the interest rate determines the division of surplus value between the interest paid to financial capitalists and the profit of enterprise retained by productive capitalists. Financial capital is always advanced for a share of surplus value (Harvey 1982: 257), whether interest payments are funded directly, as in the case of advances made to productive capitalists, or indirectly, as for example in the case of advances made to property companies, where the repayment of interest is funded out of rents gathered from productive capitalists who in turn pay their rents out of the surplus value they derive from production.

The third form of capital defined by Marx is *commercial capital*. This form of capital exists only in exchange relations, and is extended through the purchase and resale of commodities at a higher price. It does not enter production, nor is it advanced for production to take place. It is purely a market-based form of capital: 'Commercial capital requires nothing more for its development than the circulation of commodities (however produced) mediated by monetary relations in a market' (Ingham 1984: 86). Therefore, commercial capital does not contribute directly towards the creation of surplus value. As Marx put it, 'If equivalents are exchanged no surplus value results, and if non-equivalents are exchanged we still have no surplus value. Circulation or the exchange of commodities creates no value' (cited in Ingham (1984: 86)).

Commercial capital is considered to be extended at the expense of productive capital by securing a share of surplus value. This it does either via arbitrage – buying cheaper and selling dearer – and/or via the charging of a fee for facilitating the circulation of commodities. A subform of commercial capital that is of particular importance here is that of *money-dealing capital*. Money-dealing capital engages in those activities 'associated with the function of money in circulation' (Thompson 1977: 243). Money-dealing capital is extended through the fees charged for facilitating the circulation of money (as in money broking and dealing and the validation of both money accounts and the legality of money exchange) and through arbitrage within money markets (the buying and selling of financial instruments for profit).

Both financial and commercial capital can exist outside the circuit of productive capital. Indeed, in the forms of usurer's capital and merchant's capital respectively, financial capital and commercial capital were constituent parts of pre-capitalist social formations. However, since Marxist theory denies that these types of capital can actually produce value in their own right, the creation of value within the capitalist mode of production is essential for the expansion and extension of both financial and commercial capital. In turn, financial and commercial capital exist in a symbiotic relationship with one another, for they provide the means by which the circulation of capital is speeded up, thereby increasing the rate at which money is borrowed and lent out (so extending financial capital) and the rate at which commodities are bought and sold (so extending commercial capital).[2]

The role of money

In common with conventional economic thinking, Marxist theory sees money as performing two very important functions within the process of capital accumulation: as a medium of exchange and as a measure of value. Money operates as a medium of exchange at two critical points in the circuit of productive capital, facilitating first the exchange between M–C, and then the exchange between C'–M'. Therefore, money lubricates the circuit of productive capital, providing both free exchange between a wide range of commodities and a universally recognisable medium. However, money is much more than just a signatory to an exchange of commodities. To be a medium of exchange money must also be a measure of value, otherwise the process of exchange would not be possible. Money acts as a universal equivalent against which the values of commodities can be judged. In Marxist analyses, money adopts the mantle of the universal equivalent by way of its representation as the socially recognised incarnation of human labour expanded in the production process. Human labour is conceived as the sole generator of surplus value, representing the difference between the money advanced and the money realised through the sale of commodities transformed within the production process (Harvey 1982: 241). Money, therefore, possesses all the hallmarks of a true commodity. It has an intrinsic value, which is the amount of human labour expended in production. It has an exchange value, in relation to the value of other commodities, and it has a use value, as a medium of circulation in the process of exchange. However, its role as the universal equivalent and as a measure of value confers upon money a status above all other commodities. As such it is the ultimate expression of social power: commodities are not exchanged in pursuit of other commodities, as believed by classical economists (e.g. Adam Smith); commodities are exchanged in the pursuit of money (Clarke 1988).

For Marxists, this tail-chasing characteristic endows money with a dominant role within the circuit of productive capital and within the cycle of capitalist accumulation as a whole. But this dominant role is also responsible for a systemic weakness within the capitalist system of production, the cause of which is buried within the nature of money. The dual roles of money, as both a lubricant of circulation and exchange and as an independent expression of value, are ultimately contradictory, for if money begins to fail while acting as a lubricant of exchange it will be withdrawn from circulation. To illustrate how this contradiction manifests itself, let us return to the circuit of productive capital. For the circuit to operate effectively, money must constantly be made available to allow the initial purchase of commodities which are thrown into production. Money must also be available to allow the exchange of transformed commodities back into money. Money will only be invested in production for as long as M is successfully transformed into M', through the generation of surplus value and ensuring an increase in the store of money. If, for any reason, the circuit of productive capital begins to fail, leading to a decline in the production of surplus value, then money may be withdrawn from circulation altogether and hoarded for its utility as an independent expression of value. This withdrawal will, of course, preclude its use as a medium of circulation. The diversion of money away from the circuit of productive capital will therefore precipitate a crash in the capitalist system as a whole, which becomes unable to reproduce itself. Such crises in capitalism are systemic, and can be traced back to the contradictory nature of the dual role of the money commodity, to its dominance as the denominator of social power and to its ability to exist as a valuable commodity outside of and external to the production cycle (Harvey 1982: 284).

The ability of financial capital to assert its dominance over productive capital is linked to a more fundamental contradiction within the structure of the capitalist system. This contradiction manifests itself in a tension between, on the one hand, the central dynamic within the system towards the production of output for the realisation of surplus value, and, on the other, the ability of this output to be consumed by society as a whole, that is, the limit of the market. This tension and contradiction have been described by Clarke (1988: 101–2):

> The historical tendency of the capitalist mode of production, its law of motion, is determined by the insatiable thirst of capital for surplus value, and the incessant accumulation of capital. This tendency drives the capitalist to intensify labour and constantly to revolutionise the methods of production. The result of this tendency is a constant increase in the mass of commodities produced. However, these commodities have not been produced as use values in accordance with the consumption needs of society. . . . The capitalist throws them in to circulation not to convert them into use values, but to convert them back into the money form of capital. Nevertheless, if this capital is to be realised in the form of money, the commodities have to prove themselves as use-values by finding a consumer. Consumption appears to the capitalist . . . not as the sole end of production, but as a barrier to the realisation of his capital.

The tendency to revolutionise the methods of production leads to an 'overaccumulation of capital'. Production proceeds until the supply of commodities exceeds the demands and capacities of the market, causing a fall in prices. For those capitalists that have introduced new methods of production, this may not be a problem, since new production processes may reduce the costs of production sufficiently that a fall in the sale price of commodities can be accommodated without lowering profit levels. However,

> less efficient capitalists and petty producers will come under more intense pressure (while) the fall in prices will still not lead to the immediate

contraction of production to the limits of the market. Petty producers will respond to the decline in their incomes by working harder, mobilising the entire labour at the disposal of the household, and so will increase production, until the fall in price is such that . . . domestic manufacturers can no longer renew their means of production. . . . The less efficient capitalists will continue to produce so long as they can cover their current costs, and will try to reduce costs by cutting wages, extending the working day and intensifying labour . . . until they have exhausted their capital and are driven into liquidation. Better placed capitalists may seek to reduce their costs by introducing the new methods of production in their turn, further contributing to the escalating over-production of commodities. The most advanced capitalists . . . may increase their investment, intensify labour and extend the working day in the hope of capitalising on their good fortune before events take an unfavourable turn. However, the very success of capitalists in improving the conditions for the production of surplus value by forcing down wages, intensifying labour, and introducing new methods of production merely intensifies the tendency to the over-production of commodities and so the pressure of competition.

(Clarke 1988: 103)

Therefore, the extension of productive capacity beyond the limit of the market first causes prices, then profits, to fall. Bankruptcies escalate and the overall productive system begins to collapse as the owners of money refuse to introduce it into the circuit of productive capital. Money-owners, in the realisation that the chances of them obtaining a return on money invested is increasingly unlikely, choose instead to hoard their money for its self-contained value. It is this ability of money to possess a value that is autonomous from the circuit of productive capital that lends financial capital its supremacy over productive capital within the capitalist accumulation cycle.

For Marxists, crises of the sort described above are cyclical and systemic within capitalism. However, the period of time between crises has tended to increase, and this can be attributed in part to the growth of *credit money*. The development of credit money has been important in postponing financial crashes, because credit money extends the limits of the market by granting purchasing power to those who do not possess money but expect to gain possession some time in the future.[3] At the same time credit money reduces the cost of and speeds up the circulation of commodities. The next section describes the processes by which credit money superseded commodity money as the most important money form within the capitalist system.

The State and the development of credit money

Over much of the history of the capitalist system precious metal – commodity money – existed as the representation of value in its ultimate irreducible form (Mandel 1984). Silver or gold was the final arbiter of value; all other commodities had prices that reflected their values in relation to commodity money. The utility of commodity money is that it has a material form which renders it 'as precise and unambiguous as possible' as a 'measuring rod' of value (Harvey 1982: 293). However, while commodity money functions well as a measure of value, it functions less well as a medium of exchange. If commodities are to circulate efficiently, there must be a supply of gold equivalent in principle to all the value contained within all the commodities in circulation. But gold is itself a commodity, and one that is produced through a particularly difficult production process, as is the case with all precious metals. As such, the supply of gold as commodity money cannot be immediately expanded in response to an increase in the demand for the medium of circulation, and this effectively constrains the circulation of commodities. This is not the only problem, for the 'weighing and calibration of gold is both risky and a nuisance' and it is 'inflexible, costly and inconvenient when used as a pure money commodity' (Harvey 1982: 243).

These latter problems have been overcome by developing substitutes for commodity money in the form of coins or notes. Of course, coins need not be separate in any way from commodity money. If they are made from gold, their direct link to commodity money is not broken. However, if coins are not made from gold then, like notes, they become merely symbols or tokens of the money commodity (Lipietz 1985). For these symbols to be universally accepted it must be acknowledged that in the last resort they are redeemable for their face value in 'real' or commodity money. The movement away from the use of commodity money requires faith. Users of credit money must believe that there is no gap between the nominal and the real values of non-commodity money.

Of course, this faith in the validity of non-commodity money must be fostered. It is at this point that the state's role is crucial. It intervenes to validate non-commodity money by taking responsibility for the minting of coins and for the issuing of notes. However, belief in non-commodity money can also be fostered through market-based exchange relations, merely by experiencing a series of successful redemptions of token money into commodity money as and when required. For example, in Britain and in Europe more generally the bill of exchange became an accepted and important form of debt settlement (Collins 1988). In the first instance, the bill of exchange was effectively a trade credit and represented little more than an IOU. A merchant wishing to purchase manufactured commodities for resale to consumers would present the manufacturer with a bill of exchange equivalent to the value contained within the commodities. The bill would be redeemable at a point in the future, when the merchant had hopefully made sufficient profit on the resale of the commodities to cover at least the cost of purchasing the commodities in the first place.

Over time these bills began to operate as symbols of commodity money, for they could be exchanged for other commodities as it became widely recognised that they could successfully be converted into commodity money on the date the bill was due for redemption. Thus, they became a form of credit money. 'Faith' in the bill of exchange as a convertible symbol of commodity money was helped by the emergence of financial institutions that adopted the role of guarantor in the last resort, promising to redeem the bills of exchange issued by merchants for commodity money should the issuer default. These institutions profited by exchanging the bills of exchange presented to them prior to their due redemption date for a volume of commodity money lower than that indicated on the face of the bill. This discount represented the fee charged for facilitating the circulation of commodities. When the institutions themselves presented the bill to the original issue on the due date they received the full amount. However, to protect themselves from insolvency, the institutions that discounted bills of exchange took it upon themselves to regulate efficiently the issue of such bills, by agreeing to endorse only those issued by merchants with a very low risk of default.

The bill of exchange can therefore be seen to be a relatively early form of credit money, a form of money which 'represents a value in the course of realisation' (Lipietz 1985: 86). Credit money is the symbolic representation of 'real' money and represents a claim upon a quantity of commodity money. However, the ability to transform this claim into actual commodity money is dependent not only upon the validity of the claim being universally accepted, but also upon the transformation being backed up by a regulatory authority that will validate this claim. In the case of bills of exchange, they became a form of credit money and a medium of circulation when merchants and manufacturers realised that in the last resort the bills endorsed by financial institutions could be transformed into the money commodity, even if the issuer refused to honour the bill.

The next logical stage for the institutions endorsing bills of exchange was to become banks, and issue their own bank notes. A bank note is 'nothing but a draft drawn upon a banker, payable at any time to the bearer, and given by the banker in place of private drafts' (Marx 1959: 403), so financial institutions found it more cost-effective to substitute their own bills of exchange (i.e. bank notes) for those of a large number of individual producers. The reason for this transition lay in the fact that the general acceptability of the bill of exchange as a form of credit money resided in the authority lent them by the endorsement of banks. Consequently, the name of the financial institution on the bill became more important than the name of the original issuer. To obtain endorsement from the financial institution, the merchant or manufacturer had to demonstrate financial soundness. Similarly, merchants and manufacturers could draw drafts on the bank in the form of bank notes only if they demonstrated they were financially 'sound'. Therefore, for merchants and manufacturers, bills of exchange, and then bank notes, were validated as credit money only because the banks promised in the last resort to convert the bills and notes they endorsed into commodity money.

Banks, therefore, adopted the role of *de facto* regulators, supervising the soundness of money and acting to maintain the link between the nominal value of credit money and the real value of commodity money. However, as Harvey (1982: 247) makes clear, the primary function of a bank is not to act as an objective regulator of monetary relations. A bank is a private enterprise engaged in competition with other banks in the pursuit of profit. The competitive search for new business can cause banks to relax the stringency of their assessments of 'good and sound' financial risks when they endorse bills or issue notes. In the long run, this behaviour can threaten the banks' ability always to convert the form of credit money they endorse into commodity money as defaults escalate and creditor claims grow. The failure of one bank to act on its promise to transform credit money into commodity money casts doubt upon the ability of all banks to do so. Doubt and uncertainty are only compounded in a situation where there is a fragmentary credit money system with many banks all issuing their own notes and where knowledge of the financial soundness of each and every bank cannot be gathered easily. In such a state of affairs, the validity of credit money is brought into question, prompting economic agents to return to 'real' money by reclaiming commodity money.

The solution that prevents a dissolution of the credit money system is the development of a further tier of regulatory authority to regulate the behaviour of banks. This level of regulation is usually (but not always) the preserve of the nation state and is performed by a central bank. The bank is granted special powers by the state, in return for which it attempts to preserve the viability of national monetary relations:

> Most central banks are . . . set apart from other banks by the granting of certain monopoly privileges. Absolved from the necessity to compete, the central bank can dedicate itself to its sole task: to perform this function, the central bank becomes the guardian of the country's gold reserves. This gives it the power to drive out 'bad' bank money by refusing convertibility into central bank money, which is the only kind of money which is freely convertible into gold.
>
> (Harvey 1982: 248)

In this way the central bank becomes the lender of last resort within a nation state. The validity of credit money is backed up by the promise of the central bank to convert it back into commodity money. But the central bank is only able to do this so long as it can exercise financial discipline over the banks, who as part of this disciplinary exercise are in turn forced to exercise financial discipline over their customers. The result is a hierarchical form of regulatory control, with the central bank at the apex of the hierarchy, ensuring the continued link between the nominal value of credit money and the real value of commodity money. In addition, by securing the nation's store of gold reserves as commodity money the central bank increases the efficiency of monetary exchange by permitting it to take place purely in the form of credit money, obviating the need for transfers between institutions of a bulky and inconvenient material.

The need for this hierarchical structure of regulation is a direct result of the problems of attempting to reconcile the inherently contradictory roles of money as both a measure of value and a medium of circulation. While credit money operates supremely well as a medium of circulation, it is inevitably distanced from 'real' money. Hence a need develops for a regulatory authority that will constantly validate credit money as truly representative of the value inherent within commodity money. A further example of how this contradiction manifests itself can be seen when the central bank, directed by the state, acts to develop the medium of circulation *par excellence* – the non-convertible currency. When a currency is declared to be no longer convertible into the commodity form of gold then its claim to be an objective measure of absolute value is removed. Although the non-convertible currency is the most flexible form of credit money there is, since its supply can be increased or decreased extremely rapidly by the state in response to circulatory demands, it becomes beholden upon the state to provide 'political and legal backing (to) replace the backing provided by the money commodity if users of pure paper moneys are to have confidence in their stability and worth' (Harvey 1982: 244). This function is the essence of financial regulation.

However, the problem of exchange between economic units at the same level of the regulatory hierarchy then reappears. When banks acted as regulators of merchants and manufacturers issuing bills of exchange, the nature of the relations between banks necessitated the development of the higher regulatory authority. Similarly, when nation states enter into exchange relations between one another, problems of validation re-emerge:

> As guardian of the national stock of gold, the central bank can guarantee the quality of money only within the territory of the nation state. The central bank then takes on the task of balancing payments between nations. All the time that central bank money is convertible into gold, the latter functions as the universal equivalent in world exchange. But once countries abandon convertibility within their own borders, then it becomes progressively more difficult to keep the gold standard intact on an international scale (particularly when capital becomes multinational). If the only way to balance the accounts between nations is by means of the different national currencies, then those have to be freely convertible into each other at some determinate rate of exchange. The problem then arises of guaranteeing the quality of national moneys on the world market'.
>
> (Harvey 1982: 248)

Thus the problem of validating credit money is solved at each level of the regulatory hierarchy only to be exposed at its pinnacle. At this level, national currencies (and through them central banks and states) are effectively in competition with one another, maintaining the link between currency and value through the controlling actions of central banks and states.

Although the contradictory nature of money is eventually exposed at the highest level of supervisory regulation, the other levels of the regulatory hierarchy serve to subjugate productive capital to the dominance of financial capital in the bid to maintain the link between credit and commodity money. According to Thompson (1977: 270–1), in the most general terms the practices of productive capital can be described as accumulationist; rationalisation and technocracy are combined with a propensity for risk taking in the overall pursuit of surplus value. However, the practices of financial capital are better described as consolidationist. These practices, like money itself, are revealed to be contradictory. Financial capital is concerned above all else with preserving the value of money. But at the same time financial capital also requires its own extension through the appropriation of surplus value, which of course can only be achieved by advancing money for a future share of value produced in production, so incurring risk. The contradictory nature of these practices makes financial capital 'the most "cautious" form of capital, requiring firm "collateral" before any credit can be given' (Thompson 1977: 270). Or, indeed, before credit will be given at all, for, as we have noted, financial capital is concerned with capital extension through risk minimisation. Through its possession of the embodiment of the ultimate form of social power – money – financial capital has ensured the development of a plethora of financial and legal controls to which all other forms of capital have to submit before they can gain access to the credit advanced by financial capital. Therefore, all other capitalists are 'called to account' before they can hope to be 'worthy' of the credit of financial capitalists. Financial capital is aided and abetted in this domination of all other forms of capital by the subform of commercial capital, money-dealing capital. It is this latter form of capital that performs the accounting and legal functions devised to monitor individual capitals to ensure their activities conform to financial orthodoxy, obliging such capitals to act in such a way as not to undermine the value of money.[4]

However, it should be re-emphasised that although financial capital may be dominant over all other forms of capital, it is not independent of them. For example, although financial capital is extended by appropriating part of the surplus value created in production by productive capital, financial capital, and the credit system it supports, are necessary to the successful operation of the circuit of productive capital. The relationship between financial, commercial and productive capital is revealed to be ultimately symbiotic.

The credit system, the circulation of capital and the creation of fictitious capital

The existence of the credit system is essential for the reproduction of the capitalist mode of production. Some of the more important functions performed by the credit system are: the mobilisation of money as capital; the reduction of the time and cost of circulation; the easing of long-term investment and consumption; and the creation of markets for fictitious capital (Harvey 1982: 262–70).[5] Each of these functions will briefly be discussed in turn.

For productive capital to reproduce itself, money needs to be made available as capital ready to be thrown into production. The credit system, through the intermediation of financial institutions, helps mobilise money as capital through the centralisation of previously individualised stores of money, which on their own would be insufficient to kick the circuit of productive capital to life. The actions of financial institutions which receive money as savings and then redistribute these as loans (or, as money capital), permit

> capitalists who are saving [to] lend at interest to capitalists who are reinvesting [which] cuts down on levels of hoarding because capitalists can amass credits while keeping their monetary reserves active as interest-bearing capital.
>
> (Harvey 1982: 262)

However, it is not only capitalists who have savings. Workers too introduce money to the credit system through savings and these may also be pooled and converted into money capital by financial institutions (Hannah 1986). The credit system also serves to cut down on the transaction costs associated with exchange. Credit money itself is physically easier to exchange than commodity money while the centralisation of credit functions within financial institutions further diminishes costs by 'netting' exchanges and transactions.

The credit system further smooths the functioning of the capitalist mode of production by allowing large-scale investments to be paid in periodic instalments rather than in one payment (i.e. by allowing the pooled money capital to pay by the initial purchase, with the productive capitalist paying back in periodic instalments to the financial capitalist). This characteristic of the credit system encourages investment in fixed capital, accelerating the rate at which commodities are produced. At the same time, repayment through periodic instalments can also be used to encourage the purchase of these finished commodities, thereby lubricating the process of circulation and consumption.

Perhaps the most important function the credit system performs in assisting the smooth operation of the circuit of productive capital is through the creation of markets for *fictitious capital*. Fictitious capital represents a form of 'speculative value', and is a logical extension of the speculative quality of credit money. Credit money represents a future claim upon a specified volume of commodity money. However, until the transformation from credit to commodity money is completed, credit money remains a form of speculative holding, for it can never be known with absolute certainty whether the link between the nominal value of the credit money is reconcilable with the real value of the credit money. Until that transformation is made the value is 'fictitious', waiting to be realised. Similarly, the advancement of credit money as money capital represents the creation of fictitious capital; the value of the money capital is merely 'value in process', which has to be proved at the resolution of the productive cycle (Lipietz 1985). Fictitious capital can therefore be viewed as

> financial assets created by the capitalisation of an income stream where the asset does not have a counterpart in an equivalent sum of productive capital. The representative example of fictitious capital examined by Marx was shares in joint-stock companies traded on the Stock Exchange where the price, being the capitalised value of the entitlement to future dividends that they represented, exceeded the value of the funds invested in the company through the initial share subscription.
>
> (L. Harris 1988: 21)

In the final analysis, despite financial capital's many attempts to remove risk from the process, the advancement of money capital will always involve an element of speculation since it is advanced for a share of value that has yet to be created. The money capital that is advanced is therefore in constant danger of being devalued. When money capital is advanced it is viewed by the financial capitalist as an asset, since it represents a claim upon an appropriated share of surplus value. But until this value is realised there is always the danger of a divide opening up between the fictitious value of the asset and the actual value realised through production.

Given this uncertainty, there is a danger that no money will be advanced at all. Money-owners might prefer to hoard their money rather than risk devaluation through its conversion from money capital into fictitious capital. Such a tendency would of course threaten the circuit of productive capital and the overall reproduction of the capitalist mode of production. The institution of markets for fictitious capital helps to facilitate the continued advance of money capital (Harvey 1982). The formation of fictitious capital markets has the effect of offering financial capitalists the prospect of diversifying their risk by offering their advances across a range of borrowers. In the first instance, the formation of fictitious capital markets requires borrowers to sell titles to a share of future surplus value in return for an advance of money capital. Financial capitalists are attracted to those titles because they have secondary resale value, which permits lenders to realise their money capital and liquidate their investments by selling the right to the income stream on to a third party. The existence of secondary markets is an important adjunct to the creation of fictitious capital, for it allows individual lenders to redeem their credit without diminishing the total volume of credit advanced (Thompson 1977: 258). Therefore, the creation of markets for fictitious capital helps to preserve the existence of credit, and allows economic units such as productive capitals to draw periodically upon money capital needed for entering into production. Simultaneously, markets for fictitious capital ensure that financial capitalists have the opportunity to extend continually their capital via the appropriation of surplus value, but also to realise the capital they have advanced through the liquidation of their fictitious capital assets within secondary markets. This prevents money capital from existing as merely 'capital in the process of being realised' for the temporal duration of the circuit of productive capital.

Fictitious capital markets are administered by economic agents that may be classified as part of money-dealing capital. But these markets are driven by institutions which belong to the fraction of financial capital. These institutions act as intermediaries in the circulation and recirculation of surplus value by offering interest payments in exchange for the individualised holdings of money capital that are deposited with them as savings (or investments). These are pooled, and then lent to borrowers in return for a share of future surplus value. This share may be derived directly, as when money capital is borrowed by productive capitalists, or indirectly, as when borrowed by individual employees, who repay out of earnings, earnings which are themselves paid out of surplus value. Financial institutions minimise the risk of fictitious capital being devalued by diversifying the money capital across a range of borrowers. These institutions are able to profit by striking different bargains with borrowers and lenders of money, with the rate of interest offered to borrowers being higher than that offered to lenders.

The volume of fictitious capital claims circulating within the economy varies in relation to the unfolding of the capitalist accumulation cycle. Demand begins to grow in a period of initial expansion following a recovery from an economic crash, as the capacity of productive capitalists to finance investment from their own or rival's cash reserves is exhausted (Harvey 1982: 303). It is at this point that productive capitalists turn to the credit system and secure money capital advanced to them by money-owners, thereby facilitating the creation of fictitious capital. As firms come up against the inevitable limit of the market so the credit system and the volume of fictitious capital in the system are extended still further as they seek out yet more money capital to assist their competitive position via the technological reorganisation of production. Markets for fictitious capital expand exponentially, as the creation of an initial fictitious capital instrument is matched by another designed to counter its price movement in a hedging or risk-management exercise. These instruments may in turn be hedged by the creation of yet more parallel instruments. However, instruments that are used for risk management can also be used for speculation. It is this contradictory quality inherent within fictitious capital instruments that can lead to the ultimate undoing of the credit system, especially when demand for credit is so great that it becomes increasingly profitable for business organisations to divert money away from the circuit of productive capital and transform it into fictitious capital (Bond 1990). The disproportionalities that result from this diversion then undermine the validity of fictitious capital itself, for the productive sector cannot keep up with the rate of surplus value production necessary to satisfy the outstanding claims made upon it. Fictitious capital therefore runs the risk of being devalued, and the resultant rapid liquidation of fictitious capital holdings into money can cause a threat to the whole credit system and therefore to the capitalist system as a whole. Since the credit system and the capitalist system now operate at the global scale, this raises the spectre of regular global financial crashes such as the one witnessed in 1987 (Bose 1988).

BEYOND THE MARXIST MODEL OF MONEY

As we indicated earlier, the Marxist model of money was extremely influential and instructive in fashioning our thinking on the dynamics of the global financial system. However, the adoption of such a model clearly has important drawbacks, some of which have already become clear, and these have to be faced. Nearly all of these drawbacks come from the historically specific nature of Marx's account of money. The classical economists, of which Marx was one, effectively and unsurprisingly assumed that they were dealing with a system of commodity money (Foley 1989). The only exception to this rule was the analysis of inconvertible paper money issued by the state. But, since the time of the classical economists history has, of course, rewritten their texts. The rise of the state and state money, the growth of credit, the decline of gold and the greater role of the financial system in the world economy, the explosion in fictitious capital through a system of virtual money – all these, and many other events, have changed the landscape of money. Therefore, the Marxian model has to be, at the very least, supplemented while some may feel that the extent of these historical changes is sufficient that the model can no longer exist in the same way as before.

In particular, four changes need to be made. The first of these revolves around the affinity of the Marxian model with production. As Foley (1989: 255) points out:

> The characteristic theme of classical analysis was the subsidiary importance of money in relation to production. Money was seen as adapting to economic activity, either by automatic adjustments in the quantity of money, or in real quantities of money through changes in the prices of commodities.

Money was considered to be a part of the sphere of circulation and, effectively, functioned as a drain on the economy of producers of things. Workers in the money and finance sectors were deemed to be 'unproductive', despite the fact that 'a capitalist in the circulation sphere hires and exploits labor like the industrial capitalist, and earns the going rate of profit on the investment' (Boss 1990: 97–8). This is clearly an unsustainable position. It has become increasingly difficult to countenance the financial system as *necessarily* linked to productive capital at all. Even Harvey (1989b: 194) has written of the ways in which 'the financial system has achieved a degree of autonomy from real production unprecedented in capitalism's history, carrying capitalism into an era of equally unprecedented financial dangers'. But how to interpret this rupture? There are two alternatives. One is to argue that the coupling between productive and financial capital is historically specific, based on a mode of factory production that is no longer as relevant as it was. A more radical argument is to suggest that the dichotomy between production and circulation implicit in the Marxian model is simply without foundation:

> What would Marxian economics lose were it to drop the production circulation dichotomy? Possibly the hardest pill to swallow would be the implied inclusion within the productive domain of financial services capital-istically organised, which [Marx] regarded as a straightforward drain on the economy of real producers of things. ... In so far as the growing importance of the financial sector was one of Marx's major predictions about the evolution of the capitalist mode, and had an important role in realisation crises, it is difficult to justify relegating banks and finance to the analytic sidelines.
>
> (Boss 1990: 103)

The second change required is connected with the role of the state. Apart from the role played through the co-ordination of the central bank, the Marxian model of money does not envisage the state as a major actor in the financial system. And yet, state intervention in the contemporary financial system is now constant and constitutive (Helleiner 1994, 1995; Moran 1991).

The third change required is a product of the proliferation of credit. The Marxian model does not give sufficient role to credit in its numerous forms. As national and then international markets for credit have grown and coalesced, as the value of speculation has increased, and as large-scale movements of money have taken place, so the Marxian model is increasingly revealed as inadequate.

Fourth and finally, although one of the most important aspects of the Marxian model is its recognition that money is a form of social interaction between people, involving classes for example, it pays little or no attention to a number of other social and cultural dimensions of money. Money essentially is seen in terms of abstract exchange (indeed, that is its chief characteristic in capitalist societies), the accumulation of wealth and alienation. But hardly any attention is paid to the way in which the financial system manages to sustain itself, despite the apocalyptic claims of impending crisis and disaster that are so common in Marxian analyses of money. Although the financial system is an increasingly complex and probably riskier place to do business, that it survives at all seems to be due in no small part to the role of *trust*, which is cultivated through social networks and backed up by abstract expert systems:

> Abstract systems depend on trust, yet they provide none of the moral rewards which can be obtained from personalised trust. . . . Moreover, the wholesale penetration of abstract systems into daily life creates risks which the individual is not well placed to confront: high consequence risks fall into this category. Greater interdependence, up to and including globally inter-dependent systems, means greater vulnerability when untoward events occur that affect these systems as a whole. . . . The money a person possesses,

however little it may be, is subject to the vagaries of the global economy which even the most powerful of nations may be able to do very little about. A local monetary system may collapse completely, as happened in Germany in the 1920s; in some circumstances which we might not envisage at all, this might perhaps happen to the global monetary order, with disastrous consequences for billions of people.

(Giddens 1991: 136)

That monetary systems do not constantly fall into disastrous crises is due, at least in part, to numerous, cross-cutting regulatory systems based upon networks of trust as well as of coercion and censure. For these reasons the history of financial regulation in all its guises is crucial to our understanding of the financial system.

THE CHAPTERS

Make the money-spinner spin! For you only stand to win,
And you'll never with dishonesty be twitted,
For nobody can know, to a million or so,
To what extent your Capital's committed.
Gilbert and Sullivan, *Utopia Limited*

The role of financial regulation is a recurring theme in this part of the book and in Chapters 2 and 3 the regulation of money and finance is addressed directly. In Chapter 2, we consider the changing bases of financial regulation within the world economy since the nineteenth century. Over time there has been a shift away from abstract concepts of regulation towards more concrete and contextual regulatory mechanisms. In the nineteenth century, regulation revolved around the rule of money through the international gold standard. Between 1945 and the early 1970s an attempt was made to regulate the world economy through a set of institutions which sought to create an international regulatory space, within which the power of money was subordinated to politically and economical sovereign states. The breakdown of this system in the early 1970s resulted in a more explicit form of geo-economic competition between states, and a widespread restructuring of regulatory frameworks. International regulatory mechanisms are being reconstructed as part of negotiated competition between nation states. We argue that the tendency towards geo-economic competition within the global economy might well preclude the construction of international regulatory mechanisms capable of controlling the tendency towards overaccumulation on a world scale.

In Chapter 3 we turn our attention to the European Community's efforts to restructure the European financial services industry, as part of the Single European programme. These efforts embodied impulses towards both the liberalisation and the consolidation of the industry, impulses which were often at odds with one another. The chapter examines the state regulation of money and financial institutions, considers the tendencies towards liberalisation and the opposing tendencies towards consolidation, and considers the implications of the outcome of the programme, particularly the struggle between finance and financial capital models of state regulation of money and finance.

The remaining chapters in this part of the book focus more upon the urban and regional consequences of the growth of financial markets, with a particular focus upon the City of London, which in so many ways was symbolic of a series of economic, social and cultural changes in 1980s Britain. Chapter 4, originally written in 1987, considers the implications for London and the South East of the rise of the City of London to a position of pre-eminence within the international financial system of the 1980s. The chapter attempts to forge a link between the restructuring of financial capital on an international scale and social and economic change at the national and subnational level via an analysis of labour market restructuring in the City of London. As the City's labour market became more international it also became more remunerative. The sharp rise in City incomes consequent upon the greater international role played by the City of London in the international financial system during the 1980s saw a significant number of individuals generate wealth which had direct impacts on class formation. The combination of labour market change in the City of London, wealth generation and class formation played a central role in the pre-eminence of the South East region within the British economy during the 1980s.

Chapter 5 develops the analysis initiated in the previous chapter. This chapter takes account of the economic, social and cultural aspects of the City's influence on Britain in the 1980s. The first part of the chapter considers the growth of the City labour market in the 1980s, paying particular attention to the escalation of incomes that accompanied the growth in jobs. The large salaries and bonuses paid to many of those working in the City during the 1980s were converted into personal wealth, which in turn was used for the purchase of 'positional' goods. The second part of the chapter therefore considers the choices that were made by the newly wealthy of the City, concerning which goods and services were particularly appropriate to buy, such as country houses. Assets such as country houses were purchased not only to serve as stores of economic value but also as expressions of social and cultural value. The purchase of these assets became one of the ways in which the City's newly wealthy defined themselves socially and culturally. Over time, this definition spread to other parts of the business community, becoming more general in the process, both socially and geographically.

CHAPTER 2

THE REGULATION OF GLOBAL MONEY

INTRODUCTION

This chapter sketches a cursory outline of the changing regulatory basis of capitalism from the nineteenth century to the present day. Throughout this period there has existed a search for mechanisms capable of ordering the dynamics of capitalist accumulation. However, over time there has occurred a progressive move away from abstract, ahistorical concepts of regulation towards more concrete, contextual regulatory mechanisms. The second section examines the role of regulation and outlines the main responses to the recent round of regulatory dislocation within the global economy. The third section looks at regulation in the nineteenth century, which revolved around the rule of money and a belief in the self-regulating capabilities of capitalist markets. The fourth section looks at regulation in the period after 1945, the form of which was conditioned by the operation on an international scale of a set of regulatory institutions created to facilitate order within the international monetary and trade systems. The last section concludes this chapter by considering the implications for regulation of the rise of an intensified geo-economic competition within the global economy.

THE ROLE OF REGULATION

During the 1980s and early 1990s the issue of regulation rose to the top of academic and political agendas as a wave of regulatory reform swept through the world economy. Researchers and politicians alike struggled to make sense of and respond to the unfolding of an unprecedented round of international regulatory restructuring. Despite the weight of recent attention it would be wrong to suggest that a concern with the phenomenon of regulation is altogether novel. The inherently volatile and crisis-ridden nature of capitalist accumulation has long engendered an academic and political interest in the concept of regulation. Yet, despite a long and rich history and the recent analytical turn towards the subject, the concept of regulation remains stubbornly elusive of an all-encompassing definition, and is used as a metaphor to encapsulate a wide range of social practices.

Two uses of the term regulation predominate over all others (Hancher and Moran 1989: 130). First, regulation is used to describe the maintenance of a *systemic equilibrium*, analogous to 'processes of regulation found in many physical systems which are maintained at, or tend towards, some state of equilibrium' (ibid.). In this sense regulation describes an independent dynamic, such as an economic or social system, which is controlled by a 'governing mechanism' which seeks to ensure the system reproduces itself. Hancher and Moran (1989: 132) give as an example the first twenty-five years or so of the post-1945 economic order which was 'regulated' by the economic and political hegemony of the United States, the authority of which acted as the 'governor' of the capitalist world economy. Second, regulation can be used to describe a framework of legal and administrative rules. These two interpretations of regulation are frequently constituent of one another; the form of systemic equilibrium in operation at any time will influence the drafting and administration of a system of legal rules and guidelines, which are used to define the range of permissible practices open to economic agents. Thus, to refer back to the earlier example of regulation as a form of systemic equilibrium, the existence of an international economic order 'governed' by the United States had implications for policy making not only within the United States but also within other rule-making institutions of the international economic system.[1]

Given the intermittent but regular occurrence of capitalist crises, most regulatory impulses have historically tended towards the imposition of order upon what is interpreted to be an otherwise anarchic and ultimately self-destructive process of capitalist accumulation. As Moran (1991) has noted in the context of financial regulation, new forms of regulation are most frequently drafted and administered in response to incidents of crisis. Yet, despite the regular imposition of the restraining influence of regulation, crises remain a persistent feature within capitalist economies. The reason for the perpetual occurrence of crises is the inherently fragile and temporal nature of all systems of regulation within a highly dynamic and spatially variegated capitalist system. For example, merely determining the most appropriate level of regulation is highly problematic, given that a fundamental paradox exists within all forms of capitalist regulation. According to Giddens (1990: 165):

> to claim that capitalist markets must be 'regulated' in order to remove their erratic qualities leads us to a dilemma. Subjecting markets to the centralised control of an all-encompassing agency is not economically efficient and leads to political authoritarianism. Leaving markets free to operate more or less without any restriction, on the other hand, produces major disparities between different groups and regions.

Giddens could additionally have drawn attention to the systemic risk which also emerges from the unfettered progress of capitalist markets. Clearly, this paradox defines the polarities of the regulatory impulse; the imposition of high levels of surveillance and restriction on the one hand, against a permissive freedom on the other. Nevertheless, these contradictory impulses reveal the dialectic at the heart of capitalist regulation, which ensures that the durability of all regulatory forms, however restrictive or permissive, is strictly limited.

Two reasons in particular help explain why every regulatory 'fix' is necessarily temporary. First, regulatory systems can be undermined by what can be described as a process of *systemic dislocation*; the nature of activities being regulated may change in such a way as to make existing governing mechanisms redundant, as the former equilibrium of the system becomes disturbed by some unforeseen development. In such an instance the accepted order of the regulatory system is undermined and a search begins for a new governing mechanism or mechanisms. Systemic dislocation is a product of the inherently competitive structure of capitalist accumulation, and of the perennial search by economic agents for ways to surmount barriers to the generation of profits and value (Clarke 1988: 101). Regulatory boundaries are frequently constituted as barriers to accumulation, and their successful circumnavigation by pioneering economic agents can confer significant competitive advantages. It is for this reason that so much store is set by the successful development of new markets through innovation (Best 1990). Not only do innovative agents enjoy a period of monopoly or near monopoly profits in newly developed markets, but agents also have the opportunity to operate in markets of such novelty that for a time at least they operate relatively free from regulatory surveillance. As Hancher and Moran (1989) indicate, the recent history of financial markets bears testament to the profit-seeking impulses which underlie the development of new markets relatively unconstrained by regulatory supervision (see also Thrift and Leyshon 1988).

Second, the spatially bounded nature of regulation further facilitates the process of regulatory dislocation. Most regulatory systems are tied to particular geographical–political formations, most typically in the form of the nation state. It is possible, therefore, for economic agents to move between different 'regulatory spaces' in order to obviate any perceived constraints associated with particular regulatory regimes (Dicken, 1992a). The instances of such 'regulatory arbitrage' have increased markedly in the postwar era as improvements in communications and technology have enabled economic institutions to co-ordinate successfully their activities over large expanses of international space (Ohmae 1990). This form of regulatory dislocation has also loomed large in the recent history of the financial services industry, which is replete with examples of institutions organised to take advantage of geographical differences in regulation (Naylor 1987), the most infamous recent example being that of the Bank of International Credit and Commerce, which for many years engaged in a wide variety of unorthodox and illegal banking practices before eventually being closed down by the Bank of England in 1991 (Lascelles *et al.* 1991).[2]

Regulatory dislocation has become increasingly prevalent within recent years, as the competitive and spatial bases of regulatory systems have been undermined. The international economic order has been disturbed by shifts in the balance of geo-economic power, and in particular by the waning inclination of the United States to propagate international economic growth through the management of international regulatory mechanisms in favour of a narrower focus on the pursuit of national economic competitive advantage. At the same time, the globalisation of markets and firms has served to undermine the coercive power of regulatory systems which are embedded within particular geographical–political jurisdictions.

There have been several regulatory responses to these developments, of which two have been of particular significance. First, there has occurred an atomisation of regulation as international regulatory co-operation has increasingly been replaced by national regulatory competition. This movement is captured by Phillip Cerny's notion of the *competition state* and what Robert Cox has described as a *state–capitalist* model of development (Cerny 1990, 1991; Cox 1987). Both authors compare these new state forms with that of the 'welfare state', the regulatory form of which was a national expression of a prevailing international, welfarist-oriented, co-operative regulatory order held together under the hegemony of the United States:

> The state–capitalist approach is grounded in an acceptance of the world market as the ultimate determinant of development. No single national economy – not even the largest – can control the world market or determine its orientation. Furthermore . . . the state-capitalist approach does not posit any consensual regulation of the world market as regards multilateral trade and financial practices. States are assumed to intervene not only to enhance the competitiveness of their nation's industries but also to negotiate or dictate advantages for their nation's supporters. The world market is the state of nature from which state-capitalist theory deduces specific policy.
>
> (Cox 1987: 290)

Whereas the welfare state was predicated upon a series of different 'interventions' which sought to promote full employment, socio-spatial redistributive transfer payments and social service provision on a *national* scale, the collapse of the international regulatory order and the intensification of international competition demand new interventions which revolve around the promotion of enterprise, innovation and profitability within an *international* context (Cerny 1991: 179). Despite the retreat from a consensual international regulatory order there has occurred a tendency towards regulatory harmonisation around norms better fitted towards the imperatives of international competition. This development is captured by McMichael and Myhre (1991: 84) in their identification of the *transnational* state, 'in which domestic social and political relations are increasingly shaped by global capital circuits'. They argue that a system of national and international regulation has been undermined and replaced by a tentative form of global regulation, more attuned to the accumulative imperatives of capitalism, effectively reworking a thesis previously developed around the same theme by Andreff (1984).

A second regulatory response has seen the tentative development of a form of transnational regulation. Through policy co-ordination between different geographical political jurisdictions, transnational regulation has sought to prevent more coercive forms of regulation being undermined by economic agents through regulatory arbitrage. These developments have been taken furthest within the financial sector, in an attempt to offset the threat of systemic disorder caused by an international financial crisis. The harmonisation of capital adequacy requirements for international banks by the Bank of International Settlements (BIS) is the leading exemplar of such developments (Hall 1990). However, it is difficult to disentangle such transnational regulatory motives from wider geo-economic struggles now being played out between the competition states of the world economy. As Underhill (1991) makes clear, geo-economic considerations were deeply implicated within the final form of the BIS regulations, as the capital adequacy ratios finally agreed upon bore a great similarity to those originally put forward by United States and British financial regulators. These ensured that the regulations were set at a level low enough not to confer any undue competitive advantage upon German banks, which traditionally have capital bases much higher than American and British banks, but at the same time the regulations were high enough to ensure that Japanese banks, which during the 1980s had succeeded in carving out large shares of the global banking market on capital to asset ratios which were low by international standards, would be forced to restructure their balance sheets by disposing of assets in order to meet the new regulatory conditions (Leyshon 1994).

This ever more explicit instrumentality of the new geo-economic struggle has important implications for efforts to impose a measure of co-ordinated regulatory control over those economic and social practices which threaten to further destabilise the global economy and environment. The globalisation of capital may be bringing about the imposition of some sort of capitalist regulation on a global scale; but this same process of globalisation, based as it is upon a form of capitalism still wedded to an exploitative form of industrialism (Giddens 1990), is simultaneously causing a dislocation of physical systems of equilibrium, the long-term effects of which are still unclear. Nevertheless, the situation is likely to get worse without some form of concerted, co-operative intervention at an international level. But as the 1992 United Nations Earth Summit clearly demonstrated, the current climate of geo-economic competition acts as an effective deterrent against the imposition of any form of international regulation, which might help slow the degradation of the global environ-ment but which might also serve to restrict the regulatory flexibility of the competition states of the northern hemisphere. In the sections that follow. an attempt will be made to place the recent round of regulatory restructuring and dislocation within an historical context by examining the making and breaking of earlier systems of international regulation in the nineteenth and twentieth centuries.

MONEY, THE INTERNATIONAL GOLD STANDARD AND THE SELF-REGULATING ECONOMY

During the nineteenth century international economic regulation was based upon the rule of money in its most abstract form. In this sense, the international order was an extension of the regulatory order operating in Britian, the leading economic power of the age. The nature of the regulation was strongly influenced by the seminal British select committee and parliamentary debates of the early nineteenth century which represented the first systematic appraisal by any state of the relationship between economic growth and the regulation of money.[3] These debates generated a consensus of opinion that the uncoupling of Bank of England notes from a fixed metallic standard at the end of the eighteenth century had directly caused the inflationary conditions which destabilised the economy, and that it was consequentially a task of the utmost importance to reimpose order on the economy by *ordering* money, by linking currency to an intrinsic source of value in the form of commodity money and by more effective regulation of the banking system. The restoration of currency convertibility occurred in 1821, while the *Bank Act* of 1844 enshrined the regulatory authority of the Bank of England over the financial system (Walter 1991).

The return to gold ensured that economic adjustment processes would be dictated by the anti-inflationary imperatives of financial capital, and represented the first of many victories for monied interests over the more developmentalist and inflationary tendencies of industrial capital in a series of wider struggles over regulation. The regulatory structure of the nineteenth century was designed to prevent generalised crises occurring as a result of overaccumulation and the overextension of credit, and the subsequent 'debasement' of the circulation medium at the heart of the exchange process. The link between credit and a physical money form limited the extension of credit beyond certain limits, since an extension beyond the ability of borrowers to cover their debts by increasing their revenues would lead first to a series of defaults on credit and then to a monetary crisis in which there was a retreat to the commodity money form. Thus, the primary form of economic adjustment was dictated by a *fractioning logic*, which imposed the discipline of money directly upon those economic agents involved in the overextension of production and credit: that is, upon 'those producers with the greatest excesses of anticipated receipts (and corresponding repayment commitments) over actual ex-post receipts, and [upon] those banks with greatest concentrations of failed bills of exchange'. Through the abstract rule of money the economic system was locked into a form of systemic equilibrium, in which errant fractions of industrial and financial capital would be disciplined by the ultimate sanction of bankruptcy and liquidation, as assets were recovered to make good their profligate debts. An alternative form of economic adjustment, what Burkett calls *a centralising logic*, was rejected due to the ascendant social and political power of Britain's financial capitalists. Under a centralising logic, the costs of adjustment are not directly borne by the producers and financial institutions most deeply implicated in a crisis of overproduction and the overextension of credit. Rather, the adjustment process is spread through the economy as a whole, as the shortfall between anticipated receipts and *ex-post* receipts is covered by the provision of new credit. In this way, overproducing industrial capitals and overlending financial capitals are not exposed to the discipline of money. Under a centralising logic, the costs of adjustment are generalised throughout the economy as a whole and 'the losses which would [otherwise] be incurred by particular private agents under fractioning logic are socialized as decreases in the purchasing power of the medium of exchange' (Burkett 1989: 45).

For most economic agents this second form of adjustment is less painful in the short term, even if it represents merely the postponement rather than the reconciliation of a crisis, although over the longer-term period inflationary conditions arise due to the injection of new purchasing power into the economy. It was this latter consequence that made this form of economic adjustment so unacceptable in nineteenth-century Britain, for it devalued the financial assets of the ruling classes. David Ricardo, a keen advocate of the need to link money to an intrinsic form of value in the form of a metallic base, was well aware of this connection, commenting that the

depreciation of the circulating medium has been more injurious to monied men . . . It may be laid down as a principle of universal application, that every man is injured or benefited by the variation of the value of the circulating medium in proportion as his property consists of money, or as the fixed demands on him in money exceed those fixed demands which he may have on others.

(quoted in Galbraith 1975: 53)

In other words, inflation tends to reduce the wealth of creditors and investors, but is beneficial to debtors since it acts to devalue debt in real terms.

During the last quarter of the nineteenth century, this form of economic adjustment was extended to the international arena and used as the model for international economic regulation. The construction of an international gold standard represented an attempt to create an abstract form of economic regulation at an international level, above and beyond the irrationalities of national political formations:

the classical advocates of the GS [gold standard] usually made two major arguments in its favour. They asserted that the international adjustment mechanism under the GS [was] essentially automatic in that international payments imbalances [would] tend to be eliminated fairly rapidly by gold flows which are their counterpart. A second and connected claim is that the existence of a fixed gold price for domestic currency [ensured] that the central banks which abuse[d] their privileged position by indulging in or permitting inflationary financing [would] suffer a loss of reserves. The system therefore ensure[d] that the rates of credit creation in the various countries [could not] differ significantly over time, and that in the long run world prices [would] be determined by the quantity of gold in the reserves of central banks.

(Walter 1991: 54)

In this way, states and economies were ordered and constrained by the disciplining power of money, which imposed an economic rationality which was considered to be above politics (Clarke 1988: 204). However, the international power of money was in fact highly reflective of British economic and political power, and forced other countries to adhere to the same form of financial rationality and economic liberalism which governed development within Britain (Polanyi 1957: 24). The adherence to the principle of international 'free trade' militated against the development of coherent national economies. Instead, there emerged a distinctive set of regional economies, which were often more highly integrated with international than with national markets. The relative growth or decline of these regions was determined not only by the changing geography of Ricardian comparative advantage, with competitive success in international markets being determined by relative levels of productivity, but also by the changing geography of Smithian absolute advantage, as industries competed on the basis of low-cost production (cf. Porter 1990: 11). For example, the South Wales coal industry embodied the classical forms of economic regulation of the age, as the large combines of the region competed in world markets for coal on the basis of a search for extreme absolute advantage, which was facilitated by directly linking wages to the price of coal on world markets (Cooke 1985: 235), ensuring that labour rather than capital would bear the costs of adjustment.

However, this form of regulatory order was soon to be undermined by two highly significant and interrelated developments. The first was the development of a nation state system, in which states acted as reflexive, competitive economic entities in their own right (Giddens 1985). The existing international regulatory order was of British making and firmly in British interests, as the rule of money consolidated the power of the City of London, while the adherence to free trade and open economies enabled its producers to compete on the basis of absolute and comparative advantage. Combined with the deflationary tenets of the gold standard, however, this system also served to consolidate the existing pattern of international uneven development. The growth of local industries in countries outside Britain to a scale of operations sufficient to compete successfully in the world market was continually under threat, not only as a result of the periodic fractioning logic of the international financial system, but also because of the constant exposure of local markets to foreign competition. The move by political authorities beyond Britain to resist the restrictive and disciplining authority of international capital not only sounded the death-knell of this particular regulatory order, but also constituted the rise of the modern nation state system which resulted from a conscious and deliberate attempt to draw a regulative boundary between an internal, domestic market enclosed within the borders of the state, and an external, international market which existed beyond these territorial boundaries (Agnew 1991; Mann 1984). Thus, it is at the end of the nineteenth century rather than in the contemporary period that we see the first emergence of the competition state, as a new form of nationally regulated capitalism began to emerge, most notably in the form of rising industrial powers such as the United States and Germany (Dunford and Perrons 1983; Born 1983; Picciotto, 1991), but also in the guise of formerly feudal states such as Japan (Leyshon 1994). The developmentalist orientation of these new state forms involved some degree of closure from the international economy, normally achieved through the erection of protectionist barriers to trade and capital. This development not only afforded domestic capital a degree of refuge from international competition and encouraged a greater integration of industrial and financial capital than had ever developed in Britain, but also enabled firms in the competition states of Germany and the United States 'to prepare for [an] assault on the world market' (Clarke 1988: 186). In this way, the classic liberal tenets of the nineteenth century were replaced by a more instrumental, neomercantilist and developmentalist brand of economic regulation.

A second and closely related development was a disjuncture in the basis of economic competition. The spatially equilibrating assumptions of the prevailing regulatory order were increasingly brought into question as industries in the United States and Germany, highly aware of the need to penetrate markets controlled by British producers, sought to capture market share through processes of capital deepening rather than through processes of capital widening, as was more prevalent within Britain (Overbeek 1990). In this way, American and German industries competed much more on grounds of comparative rather than absolute advantage. The strains upon the equilibrating assumptions were taken to breaking point following the path-breaking advances made in industrial productivity and organisation in the United States during the first two decades of the twentieth century. The reorganisation of the labour process in accordance with the principles of Taylor and Ford, and the reorganisation of the administrative basis of firms in accordance with the principles of Sloan, conferred significant competitive advantages upon US producers (Best 1990). These developments overrode the prevailing regulatory mechanisms of the international order, which was wholly unable to cope with the structural imbalances which followed the shifting of political and economic competition onto entirely new grounds.

The retreat from the gold standard which followed the outbreak of the First World War accelerated the movement towards a more autarchic, nationally focused and instrumental form of economic development. In the immediate postwar years the fact that currencies were no longer tied to gold speeded the recovery of Europe's war-damaged economies, as governments were able to implement expansionary monetary policies in order to revive accumulation free from the threat of sanction by the co-ordinating discipline of gold. However, as time went on, economic expansion began to tend towards overaccumulation, as producers once more began to come up against the limits of their national markets. Overcoming such barriers through the internationalisation of accumulation was now much more difficult, given that currencies were now unstable and extensive tariff barriers had been drawn around national economies. In response to such problems, several attempts were made to reconstruct an international regulatory order on the lines of the nineteenth-century model. However, the reassertion of an abstract and aspatial form of adjustment upon an international economy that was becoming ever more spatially variegated and traversed by ever more internationally mobile capital was doomed not only to end in failure but also in an unprecedented economic crisis. According to Polanyi (1957), the monetary and financial crisis of 1929 and the economic depression of the 1930s which followed, can be traced directly to efforts by the United States and Britain (which had returned to the gold standard in 1925) to bolster the old international regulatory order through a pioneering form of monetary policy co-ordination:

> when Great Britain and France reverted to gold, the burden on their stabilized exchanges began to tell. Eventually, a silent concern for the safety of the pound entered into the position of the leading gold country, the United States. This preoccupation which spanned the Atlantic brought America unexpectedly into the danger zone . . . American support of the pound sterling in 1927 implied low rates of interest in New York in order to avert big movements of capital from London to New York. The Federal Reserve Board accordingly promised the Bank of England to keep its rate low; but presently America herself was in need of high rates as her own price system began to be perilously inflated.
>
> (Polanyi 1957: 26)

Thus developed a supreme irony. To ensure the imposition of the rule of money at an international level it was necessary first for the discipline of money to be relaxed within the United States, which possessed by far the most powerful economy within the international system, and which was the automatic refuge for the growing pools of internationally mobile funds of financial capital. But the cost of preventing the mass transfer of specie from Europe to the United States, which would otherwise have inexorably led to the demise of the gold standard, was a rapid expansion of credit and the development of an incipient speculative crisis within the United States (Kindleberger 1986). Credit conditions were already tight in Europe, where interest rates were kept high in order to offset capital flight to the United States; following the stock market crash and the subsequent liquidity crisis of the US financial system, these conditions became generalised right across the international economy.

The attempt to restore the international gold standard in its nineteenth-century guise was finally abandoned when in 1933 the United States severed the link between the dollar and gold. While the ending of the gold standard enabled national economies some respite from specie discipline, the external financial threats to their currencies still existed; indeed, the removal of the link between currencies and gold made the foreign exchange markets even more volatile (Brown 1987). As the old international regulatory order faded away, the new anarchy of international competition resulted in a growing spiral of barriers to trade and the movement of capital as nation states took refuge in a mode of development which was based ever more firmly upon a conceptual divide drawn between the internal and the external, between the national and the international economy:

> Import quotas, moratoria and stand-still agreements, clearing systems and bilateral trade treaties, barter arrangements, embargoes on capital export, foreign trade control and exchange equalization funds developed in most countries to meet the same set of circumstances. . . . The frantic efforts to protect the external value of the currency as a medium of foreign trade drove the peoples, against their will, into an autarchized economy. The whole arsenal of restrictive measures ... formed a radical departure from traditional economics.
>
> (Polanyi 1957: 27)

These developments furthered the emergence of the *welfare–nationalist* state model, which was a 'compound of nationalism, social security, planning, and corporatism' (Cox 1987: 161) in which 'the state supplemented the market-sustaining functions of the liberal state with new functions intended to compensate for the negative effects of the market on significant numbers of citizens' (ibid.: 165). Such tendencies had first begun to develop from the late nineteenth century onwards, consonant with the rise of the nation state as a reflexive economic actor in its own right, but reached their apotheosis in the mid- to late 1930s as states sought to deal with the grave social and economic problems caused by the collapse of the old regulatory order (Dunford and Perrons 1983) by turning their face away from the international economy and towards the ordering of national economy and society:

> Step by step with the building of the welfare-nationalist-state institutions went an increasingly profound knowledge of economic and social processes and a search for ways in which the state could influence or control these processes. The observation that there were regular recurrent cycles in economic activity, phases of investment and labor absorption followed by phases of stagnation and unemployment, led to speculation about the causes of these cycles and thus to the identification of remedies through which the state

could act to moderate or counter these cycles. *Concern to correct the market's social defects thus moved toward a project for regulating the market itself, for making the state into the market's tutor* while at the same time preserving the market's preeminence in the economy.

(Cox 1987: 166) (emphasis added)

However, while the bid to temper some of the more damaging effects of market discipline upon the working classes through regulation succeeded in bringing a measure of social advance, the overtly nationalist orientation of this state form, particularly in its fascist variation, led to growing interstate tensions and eventually to the conflagration of the Second World War.

BRETTON WOODS: A MANAGED INTERNATIONAL REGULATORY ORDER

The immediate postwar era witnessed the construction of a new regulatory order within the international capitalist economy. It was a hybrid regulatory order, which incorporated aspects of the internationalist, abstract model of the nineteenth century and elements of the welfarist–nationalist state order. From the nineteenth-century regulatory order was inherited a link between currencies and gold, in an attempt to anchor money to a residual form of value, and a commitment to a more or less open economy for the progress of international trade. However, at the same time the political and economic sovereignty of the nation state was recognised, and legislated for within the new regulatory order. The regulation of the postwar economy was conditioned by the Bretton Woods system which represented an attempt to build an international economic order in which separate national accumulation strategies could be pursued, but which would not permit states to retreat into the defensive, autarchic blocs that developed in the 1930s (Ikenberry 1992). As in the nineteenth century, states were called to order through the regulatory power of money, although in a more tempered and less draconian fashion than ever occurred under the international gold standard. Under the Bretton Woods system, only the dollar was linked directly to gold, with all other currencies being linked indirectly through their fixed exchange values against the dollar. The creation of a system of fixed exchange rates sought to introduce a degree of stability and predictability into the currency markets which would facilitate the development of international trade. In effect, the disciplining effects for all states other than the United States proved to be very similar to those which had existed under the gold standard, only now states had to balance their trade and current accounts to prevent a depletion of dollars rather than gold. States with deficit problems were, however, assisted in the process of adjustment by an international stabilization fund, in the form of the International Monetary Fund (IMF), which provided short-term loans. Nevertheless, the deflationary adjustment processes necessary to overcome balance-of-payments problems were still enforced (Brett 1985), resulting in the unleashing of periodic rounds of fractioning logic within deficit countries. In other words, 'the pain that gold inflicted immediately, the IMF mission inflicted a little later' (Galbraith 1975: 273). Meanwhile, the General Agreement on Tariffs and Trade (GATT) was established to ensure the progressive liberalisation of trade between nations, to ensure that states could trade their way out of any balance-of-payments difficulties.

Therefore, the postwar years saw the construction of an *international regulated space*, comprised of a constellation of nation states linked one to another through reciprocal flows of money, goods and services, complemented by a set of international institutions which existed to manage processes of adjustment within the international economy. According to Ikenberry (1992: 289),

> the new system was different than anything the capitalist world had seen before. The Anglo-American agreements established rules for a relatively open and multilateral system of trade and payments, but they did so in a way that would reconcile openness with trade expansion with the commitments of national governments to full employment and economic stabilization.

However, the new international regulatory order contained within it a number of destabilizing contradictions.

First, a critical contradiction existed between the disciplining role attributed to money at an international level and the pursuit of welfarist-orientated accumulation strategies on a national scale. At a national level political and financial authorities became more permissive of a centralising form of capital adjustment, as the quest for growth and a commitment to full employment overcame traditional reservations over the inflationary conditions which resulted from a looser form of monetary policy (Burkett 1989: 52–3). However, states were nevertheless faced with the pressures for a fractioning logic at an international level, first under the aegis of the IMF, and then from 1958 onwards in the form of the increasingly powerful foreign exchange markets, which began to place considerable strains upon the fixed exchange rate system as money moved between national economies on the basis of the real rate of return on financial investments. Therefore, detachment from the old international gold standard gave nation states more flexibility over the regulation of national accumulation strategies, although these strategies were ultimately constrained by the disciplining power of money enshrined within the international regulatory order.

Second, there was a critical contradiction between the role of the United States as both the governor and guarantor of this regulatory order on the one hand, and its position as a competitive geographical–political jurisdiction in its own right on the other. The United States was able to use its considerable structural power during the construction of the Bretton Woods system to insist upon a central role for the dollar in the new monetary order, instead of the new international currency proposed by Keynes, who led the British negotiating team. The dual role of the dollar, as both a national and *the* international currency, meant that the United States, unlike other members of the new regulatory order, was liberated from the disciplining power of money because balance-of-payments difficulties could be countered simply through an expansion of domestic credit (Strange 1988). It was the ability of the United States to pursue a policy of expansionary growth over a long period that served to increase significantly the volume of credit circulating within the international financial system, which was to prove the ultimate undoing of the international regulatory order.

The contradiction between the US roles as both guarantor of and competitor within the postwar regulatory order came into even sharper focus within the field of international trade. Although the United States had pressed hardest for a multilateral, open-trade postwar order during the Anglo-American negotiations over the shape of the postwar order (Ikenberry 1992), it was the United States which first breached the regulatory order. Worries over the impact the growing volumes of cheap textile imports from Japan were having upon domestic producers led to the United States breaking with the spirit, if not the rules, of GATT by using its geo-economic power to effect the imposition of voluntary export quotas on Japanese producers (Tussie 1991). This move, which was to herald the development of a progressively more negotiated international trade system in the postwar era, was in large part the product of the dialectic character of an international regulatory order which sought to reconcile domestic accumulation strategies with a competitive international economy. However, the United States' role as the pilot of the postwar economy meant that tensions between nationally and internationally orientated capital spilled over into the management of the regulatory mechanisms of the international order. According to Tussie (1991: 86), '[h]istory shows a policy of having to take one step backward to placate the protectionist lobby for every step forward required by sectors interested in foreign markets' which meant that the 'dualism of U.S. trade interests was reproduced in GATT as a natural development of U.S. economic prominence'.

A third and related contradiction lay in the geographical configuration of the postwar regulatory order, which was based upon a system of nation states, each of which was deemed to be both politically and economically sovereign. This reification of the state and the presumption of national economic closure ignored the clear tendencies towards the internationalisation of accumulation which had both prefigured and been encouraged by the development of welfarist–nationalist state forms – as producers resorted to production within foreign markets to avoid the effects of spiralling tariff barriers – and which would gain further momentum in the more open economy of the postwar era (Taylor and Thrift 1982). The reasons these tendencies were overlooked and ignored reflected the conceptions of space which prevailed within the *interpretative community* of politicians and economists involved in the construction of the post-war regulatory order (Agnew 1991). Although the attempt to build a new international order was clearly infused with elements of idealism, the prevailing philosophy of international relations was firmly *realist* in its orientation. The realist school of international relations asserts that sovereign states are the dominant actors within the international system, and that the course of international events is determined by the relationships between states in their pursuit of power (Agnew 1991; Liefferink and Moi 1991). The ascendancy of realist thought, particularly within the US political community, served to ensure the primacy of national spaces within the new regulative order. Meanwhile, the incorporation within the regulatory order of the 'new economics' of Keynesianism also tended towards the reification of national space, which was deemed to be the most appropriate container of economic activity. As Radice (1984: 12) has cogently argued, Keynesian economic theory presupposes the existence of a national economic space:

> The constituent elements of the General Theory are economic aggregates – output, employment, investment, consumption, etc. – or synthetic averages – rate of interest, real wage, money wage level, price level: in either case, these are defined and measured over a given *geographical–political* space, that of the national economy. Further, distinct aggregates – imports, exports, capital flows – and averages – exchange rates, terms of trade – are defined and measured to capture all economic transactions *between* national economies. The existence of a unique yardstick of measurement, the national currency, is also taken for granted . . . . The point is that Keynes developed *an economic theory of the national economy*, in which abstract propositions are formulated in terms of a coherent set of economic aggregates.
>
> (*original emphasis*)

However, this was a fairly novel proposition at the time. Before the Keynesian economic revolution 'doubts about the feasibility and utility of aggregate measures of product and income were strong . . . the German economist Amonn, for instance, held that, since the nation as a whole was not an economic *agent*, its income was a statistical fiction of no special purpose' (Boss 1990: 228). Nevertheless, the ideological appeal of Keynesianism and the possibilities it offered for the political management of economic processes prompted an extensive and self-justifying search for appropriate measures of national income and expenditure to assist national macro-economic management.

The dominance of these political and economic interpretations of space ensured that the territorial borders of the nation state became ever more firmly synonymous with the boundaries of *the economy*. In consequence, international economic relations became viewed as precisely that; economic transfers between national economic spaces. The vision was of a system of sovereign political and economic states engaged in reciprocal trade relations, supported by a stable and complementary international monetary regime. But when economic activity began to be internationalised much of the spatial logic to the regulatory order began to be undermined, as the geographical integrity of national economies was eroded, while the ease with which multinational corporations could engage in regulatory arbitrage did much to circumscribe the regulatory autonomy of individual nation states (McMichael and Myhre 1991; Dicken 1992a).

The combined effect of these various contradictions was to lead to the unravelling of the postwar regulatory order by the early 1970s. The regulatory 'fix' of Bretton Woods was immediately put under pressure as postwar economic recovery in the core capitalist countries ensured that within each state accumulation soon came up against the limits of the national market. As an increasing number of corporations began to extend their operations beyond the borders of their home state, the process of regulatory dislocation began to unfold. By far the most important aspect of this development was the destabilising of the Anglo-American system of international monetary regulation, which was the central plank to the entire postwar regulatory order. Monetary regulation was the issue upon which the American and British architects of the Bretton Woods system were in full agreement as being the most important requirement for the reconstruction of the world economy after 1945, and served as the basis of Anglo-American compromise upon a series of other regulatory issues (Ikenberry 1992). The importance attached to international monetary regulation was a consequence of the widely held desire to prevent a recurrence of the monetary perturbations which had served to disrupt and inhibit economic development during the nineteenth century and during the era of 'welfare-nationalist' capitalism during the 1930s. The New Deal reforms in the United States had already done much to constrain the activities and influence of the financial sector within the US economy (Van der Pijl 1984; Frieden 1987). Similar anti-financial capital sentiments had been expressed on the other side of the Atlantic. In common with the New Deal reformers, Keynes wished to restrict the mobility and freedom of financial capital to permit the construction of a more productivist, industrial form of capitalist development. However, whereas in the United States the New Deal regulators were concerned with drawing structural barriers between different domestic financial markets and around state banking markets to prevent the spatial and systemic contagion of financial crises within the national economy, Keynes' clarion call for the 'euthanasia of the rentier' was predicated upon a clear understanding of the power of financial capital at an international level. Thus, Keynes was concerned not only to eliminate what he clearly saw as a class of parasitical bankers and financiers but to limit the recurrence of international financial capital flows, which could be used to compromise the autonomy of national accumulation strategies:

> the transformation of society, which I preferably envisage, may require a reduction in the rate of interest towards a vanishing point within the next thirty years. But under a system by which the rate of interest finds a

uniform level, after allowing for risk and the like, throughout the world under the operation of normal financial forces, this is mostly unlikely to occur. Thus, for a complexity of reasons, which I cannot elaborate in this place, economic internationalism embracing the free movement of capital and of loanable funds as well as of traded goods may condemn my own country for generations to come to a much lower degree of material prosperity than could ever be attained under a different system.

(Keynes, quoted in Radice (1984: 123–4))

Therefore, on both sides of the Atlantic there existed a strong urge to regulate and control money and finance, in order to move away from the harsh regulatory order of the nineteenth century and to prevent a return to the economic chaos and depression of the 1930s.

The international mobility of financial capital was to be muted both by the existence of limitations on the movement of capital across national borders, exercised through exchange controls, and the 'crowding out' of financial capital by the IMF and the World Bank, which ensured that managed international capital flows significantly outweighed profit-seeking, private capital flows.

However, the contradictions inherent within the regulatory order soon led to a growth in the volume of private financial capital circulating on an international scale, to the empowerment of international financial capital, and to the decay of the authority and logic of the international regulatory order. Two processes were of particular importance in this development. The first was the rapid expansion in the volume of extant world money which followed from the pursuit by the United States of a national accumulation strategy based upon a centralising logic, as its financial system was given over to the creation of large amounts of cheap credit. The second was the internationalisation of these supplies of world money, both as a result of state action and of the behaviour of private economic agents and institutions. On the one hand, significant volumes of dollars were pumped into the world economy in the immediate postwar years as the United States attempted to revive capitalism in Western Europe through the Marshall Plan, and to suppress the rise of communism in Asia through military spending, first in Korea and then on a much larger scale in Vietnam. On the other hand, the internationalisation of production facilities by US manufacturing corporations introduced even more dollars in to the world economy, as firms sought to exploit the competitive advantages they held over foreign rivals in production technology and in organisational capabilities by setting up facilities directly in foreign markets. The internationalisation of financial institutions followed in strict order, as the United States began to establish branches overseas so that they could continue to service their clients in foreign markets.

By the early 1960s American banks no longer needed the excuse of a client with international operations to justify opening an overseas branch. The reluctance of many states and multinational firms to repatriate dollars to the United States, where their financial assets would come under the regulatory jurisdiction of that country, led to the institutionalisation of a set of money and credit markets which existed beyond the effective jurisdiction of *any* national or international regulatory authority. The growth of the *euromarkets*, in which states and multinational corporations issued debt denominated primarily in offshore dollars, marked an important disjuncture in the postwar world economy, as there emerged for the first time an essentially *de-territorialised* economic phenomenon, which possessed a logic and a dynamic completely at odds with the national–centric order of the international regulatory system. Despite the fact that the euromarkets were based for the most part in the City of London, they remained outside the remit of British financial regulation; indeed, their development was encouraged and welcomed by the Bank of England, whose concerns over issues of systemic risk were more than outweighed by its desire to use the development of these large but unregulated markets to propel the City of London to its former position as the world's premier international financial centre (see Chapter 3). The lack of regulation enabled those banks active in the euromarkets to invent 'new' financial instruments free of central bank censure. The novelty of these instruments revolved around the fact that for the most part that they ran counter to the central tenet of national banking regulation that banks should not lend to one another. As the euromarkets expanded, so did the interbank lending markets, until these markets soon became by far the largest form of euromarket.

Once established the euromarkets took on a momentum of their own, although the burgeoning size of the euromarkets was also due in large part to the continuing prosecution of a centralising logic of economic adjustment by the United States, which ensured a constant supply of new money and credit, much of which was later internationalised. But as the euromarkets grew, and as the volumes of unregulated financial capital circulating within the international economy increased, so the strains upon the international regulatory order began to tell. First, while the existence of plentiful supplies of international credit served to facilitate economic recovery and growth outside the United States, it also served to increase the level of economic competition within the world economy as the euromarkets facilitated the internationalisation of European and Japanese firms who began to erode the long-held dominance of US producers. Second, while the macroeconomic autonomy of states other than the United States had long been constrained by the need to run balanced budgets, freedom of movement became ever more restricted as an empowered international financial capital began to censure inflationary economies through the foreign exchange markets, forcing states to deflate their economies, leading to ever more volatile cycles of stop–start growth. Third, the institutions of international monetary adjustment became increasingly ineffective, as the volumes of capital available to the IMF and the World Bank were surpassed by the volumes of private international financial capital (Evans 1988). Fourth, and finally, by the late 1960s the power of international financial capital even began to have a constraining effect upon the US economy. Although the foreign exchange markets were not yet able to force a *reorientation* of US domestic economic policy, the total stock of dollars in existence was sufficient to threaten US gold supplies, a state of affairs which began to cast doubt upon the long-term viability of an expansionary monetary policy.

The strains on the Bretton Woods system finally caused it to collapse in 1971 when the United States unilaterally terminated the right of dollar holders to convert notes into specie. The severing of the link between currencies and gold, which served as an anchor of the international monetary system, led directly to the breakdown of the fixed exchange system in 1973. The collapse of the system of international monetary management signalled the end of an era of political regulation and the installation of market forms of regulation within the world economy (Hübner 1991). The United States abruptly abandoned any pretence to be an impartial 'governor' of the economic regulatory order and moved ever more strongly onto a competition state footing, signalling the dawn of an era in which the United States would range a series of geo-economic offensives against Europe and Japan. Indeed, severing the link between the dollar and gold represented the first round of this new geo-economic struggle, as the dollar was immediately devalued against both the deutschmark and the yen, by 12 and 17 per cent, respectively (Galbraith 1975: 310). As the threat to its gold supplies was removed, the United States was now free to continue to push ahead with its expansionary monetary policy which had the dual effect of stimulating domestic accumulation and reducing the value of the dollar to support US exports within the world economy.

As the old regulatory order collapsed, the costs of economic adjustment, which had formerly been subject to a process of collective international economic management, were directly imposed upon individual states. Although as indicated earlier the fixed exchange rate system allowed only a limited degree of autonomy in the configuration of national accumulation strategies, the new regime of flexible exchange rates enabled the deflationist, fractioning logic of financial capital to gain further ascendancy over the centralising, productivist logic which had prevailed in most core capitalist countries during the postwar order. Inflationary states could now be quickly and effectively disciplined through the foreign exchange markets as selling pressure upon the currencies of recalcitrant states would necessitate a defence of the currency through interest rate rises (Gill and Law 1989). The postwar model of an international order comprised of a set of interrelated but economically sovereign nation states was finally exploded by an invigorated and, by virtue of significant advances within the field of communications and information technology (Langdale 1985, 1987), an increasingly mobile international financial capitalism. The dismantling of the regulatory order at an international level led to a struggle over the structure of national regulatory forms, as a 'new, aggressively orthodox liberalism pitted the propertied classes against the Keynesian welfare states and the mode of accumulation of which they were the complement' (Van der Pijl 1984).

A number of European states sought to insulate themselves from the disciplining and destabilising effect of the new international monetary disorder through experiments with exchange rate co-ordination, leading to the eventual formation of the European Monetary System (EMS) in 1979 (Thompson 1990b). However, while the linking together of currencies served to stabilise exchange rates amongst EMS members, it proved impossible to insulate macroeconomic policies from the international financial system as a whole, and EMS states fell in line behind a deflationist strategy led by the West German economy whose currency anchored the entire exchange rate mechanism (Leyshon and Thrift 1994b).

The collapse of international monetary regulation and the fixed exchange rate system also saw the demise of the principal means of international trade regulation, as exchange rates were decoupled from trade flows (Tussie 1991) and the emphasis was turned towards the 'financing rather than [the] balancing of deficits' (Van der Pijl 1984: 263). These changes in the international regulatory order and the accompanying resurgence of the power of financial capital caused a radical reorientation of economic policy within the core capitalist countries. In particular, there was a move away from attempts to promote growth within the national economy through macroeconomic measures, for fear of the inflationary and financial disciplining consequences which would follow, and towards a focus upon micro-economic policy which would have an effect upon the competitive standing of economic actors within the national economy, with the intention that this would improve competitive advantage within the wider international economy (Cerny 1991).

The facilitation of national competitive advantage became imperative from the late 1970s onwards, when even the United States was forced by the international financial markets to rescind its long-term policy of monetary expansion and revert to more deflationary monetary policies. In 1978, the value of the dollar plunged in the foreign exchange markets as international investors began to unload their holdings of a currency which it seemed was destined only to be devalued (Leyshon 1990). From this moment on the United States accelerated the rate at which it launched geo-economic offensives against its economic rivals in Europe and Asia. At least four offensives have been ranged, with varying degrees of effectiveness. The first offensive was the 'Reaganomics' experiment itself, which combined a deflationary monetary policy with an expansionary fiscal policy, which used high interest rates to draw in financial capital from the rest of the world which were then recycled in the form of defence spending and tax breaks. The pursuit of what has been described as 'Keynesianism in one country' (Streeck and Schmitter 1991: 145) was designed to achieve a form of entrepreneurial, high-technology growth which would confer upon US producers competitive advantages within the international marketplace. However, the offensive backfired somewhat when the rise in interest rates caused the less developed countries' debt crisis, thereby effectively closing a number of important US export markets, and turning the United States into the world's largest debtor nation (Corbridge and Agnew 1991). Subsequent offensives were less unilateral and represented a move to a position of *negotiated competition*, in which the United States took the lead in an attempt to remake the regulatory basis of competition between states (Thompson 1990b). Thus, the second major geo-economic offensive saw the United States open up a trade front, using the threat of exclusion from the US market to force through a series of price-fixing or quota agreements amongst importers to the United States to restrict the volume of imports (Tussie 1991), while at the same time intervening strongly within the Uruguay Round of GATT negotiations to ensure the inclusion of service industries, in which it was perceived the United States had a competitive advantage (McCulloch 1988). The third offensive saw the United States attempt to use the meetings between the leading industrial nations (Group of Ten, Groups of Seven, and Group of Five) to engineer a reorganisation of international macroeconomic conditions favourable to US interests (Thompson 1990b; Leyshon 1994). The fourth major offensive was launched against Japan, the country which posed the greatest threat to US geo-economic supremacy (Ó Tuathail 1992b). The yen–dollar talks, which began in 1984, were the main vehicle through which the United States sought to rectify the structural distortions within the Japanese economy which, it was claimed, conferred upon Japanese corporations an 'unfair' competitive advantage within the global economy (Leyshon 1994).

REGULATION IN AN ERA OF GEO-ECONOMIC COMPETITION

The growth of geo-economic competition within the world economy can be seen to be the result of a breakdown of the Anglo-American system of regulation which governed both international monetary and trade relations until the early 1970s. The increasingly volatile and erratic trajectory of the international economy in the past twenty years or so (Thrift 1989b) has in large part been caused by the unravelling of this regulatory order. In its wake, there has been a reawakening of historical debates over both the most appropriate forms of, and the spatial frames for, regulation.

On the one hand, there have been moves towards the construction of an *inclusionary* regulatory order, which would establish regulative norms at a transnational level, and, as was indicated earlier, have been taken furthest within the arena of financial regulation (OECD 1992a). But even here, attempts to develop an internationally co-ordinated system of regulation represent a very different form of regulation from that of the grand plan drawn up and implemented in the immediate postwar period. According to Picciotto (1991: 56), transnational financial regulation in the era of geo-economic competition revolves around 'a motley collection of semi-formal, informal and often secret organisations and meetings of officials, advisers and consultants'. The regulatory authority ceded to such institutions is symbolic of a shift in the spatial and regulatory logic of the nation state: attempts to intervene within accumulation processes to reach an accommodation between capital and labour at a national level have been abandoned in favour of 'a tendency for the state to act more as a facilitator of the requirements of global capital' as 'states attempt to manage their finances by yielding to the logic of the global wage relation' (McMichael and Myhre 1991: 99–100). But such developments are also symbolic of a reluctance on the part of governments to agree upon truly transnational regulatory structures for fear that the subsequent loss of regulatory flexibility would restrict the range of policy options available to them as competition states within the new geo-economic struggle.

On the other hand, there have been moves which have revealed tendencies towards the construction of more *exclusionary* regulatory norms. Associated with the construction of regional economic blocs within the global economy (Taylor 1989: 51), these impulses seek to establish regulatory norms within clearly defined spatial areas, creating new spatial frames for systems of regulation. The most developed example of this tendency is the process of European integration driven by the European Community, which seeks to break down national regulatory structures and to replace them with a syncretised regulatory structure applicable across an integrated economic space, thereby combining processes of integration with reregu-lation (Streeck and Schmitter 1991). However, the fact that such processes of regulation require an initial impulse towards liberalisation means that it becomes doubly difficult subsequently to install a more coercive regulatory authority through reregulation (Leyshon and Thrift 1994b).

Therefore, the main effects of both regulatory impulses have tended to be in the same direction: the stripping down of the regulatory mechanisms of the period of postwar reconstruction and their replacement with mechanisms which are seen to fit better the economic globalization and geo-economic competition of the late twentieth century (Cerny 1991). Although these regulatory norms do not preclude the possibility of economic growth, they do condemn the world economy to a more erratic and perhaps even self-destructive forms of economic growth. The ascendancy of the power of financial capital since the 1970s has seen first the developing countries and then the core capitalist countries become enmeshed in a web of debt crisis and broken credit agreements (Cleaver 1989: Bond 1990), as entire economies have become subordinated to the inherent tendency towards overaccumulation and the overextension of credit which earlier forms of regulation were introduced to placate. At the same time, the tendency towards geo-economic competition tends to preclude the construction of international regulatory forms which would seek to prevent the environmental degradation caused by an exploitative industrialised capitalism. Binding international agreements are resisted by states which fear the competitive implications of environmental regulation. Similar competitive concerns discourage the unilateral development of regulatory safeguards for the environment.

CHAPTER 3

LIBERALISATION AND CONSOLIDATION

The Single European Market and the remaking of European financial capital

INTRODUCTION

The European Commission's programme for the completion of an internal market by 1992 was without doubt an extraordinary exercise in multi-national regulatory restructuring. The key aims of the 1992 programme, as set out in the 1985 European Commission White Paper and enshrined in the Single European Act of 1987, were, as far as possible, to establish 'four freedoms' within the European Community by the end of 1992. The four freedoms were: the freedom of individuals, the freedom of goods, the freedom of services, and the freedom of capital. The free movement of labour, commodities, services, and capital within the Community was to be achieved via the dismantling of a series of physical, technical and fiscal barriers previously organised on a national basis within the EC. The removal of these barriers was designed to facilitate the development of community-wide markets in each of these phenomena, based as far as possible upon the law of one price. The 1992 project was promoted as a vehicle that would deliver substantial economic benefits to the EC as a whole.

However, it is important to recognise that, although the EC's advocacy of market integration was consistently voiced in the language of economics, the 1992 project was always driven by political forces. As Cutler *et al.* (1990: 4) have argued, 'the transcendent objective [of the 1992 programme] is the unification of Europe . . . this programme is ultimately desirable because it promotes European unity and will strengthen Europe in global political competition against Japan and the United States'. Underlying the explicit aims of the programme, therefore, was a scarcely concealed agenda for the creation of a single, and probably federal, European state, which would assume a position of considerable geopolitical power within the world economy.

The restructuring of financial services assumed a position of vital importance within this programme. There were several reasons for this, of which three were particularly significant. First, the financial services sector was effectively doublecounted in the setting out of the 'four freedoms', for it is extremely difficult to draw a conceptual distinction between the liberalisation of capital movements and the liberalisation of financial services, because the two phenomena are intimately related. Second, the liberalisation of capital and financial services was recognised by the European Commission to be a necessary precondition for the establishment of a single market in labour, commodities, and services, based upon the law of one price (Servais 1988). In the influential Cecchini Report, for example, it is argued that the economic benefits accruing from the community-wide integration of financial services would be 'substantial', with benefits accruing from the

> unique, pivotal rule played by financial services in catalyzing the economy as a whole. Removal of barriers here, and of the costs linked to them would lead to three interlocking effects: a surge in the competitiveness of the sector itself; a knock-on boost to all businesses using its increasingly efficient services; and more generally, a new and positive influence on the conduct of macro-economic policy in the EC.
>
> (Cecchini 1988: 37)

Thus in the Cecchini Report it is estimated that the liberalisation of financial services would produce direct economic benefits of 22 billion ECU (1985 prices), equivalent to 27.5–33.8 per cent of the total economic gain anticipated from the completion of the Single European Market.[1] Third, the liberalisation of capital and financial services is important to the 1992 project because the liberalisation of financial capital flows across Europe helps reveal the considerable economic and political tensions which are inherent within the integration process. The most important of these tensions is the formal surrendering by individual European states of pretensions to national economic sovereignty to a supranational political organisation. This tension is apparent across the whole of the 1992 programme. But the EC directives which affect the organisation of the financial services sector strike at the 'holiest of holies' of all the forms of economic regulation conducted by nation states. The ability of a nation state to control money and its agents is seen as an essential prerequisite of national economic sovereignty (Harris 1988), for traditionally it has only been via the control of key monetary levers that the pace and direction of growth within an economy can be influenced (Lipietz 1987). For many European states, the EC directives on capital and financial services will act to alter the level of control they have over their domestic financial system, with important implications for notions of national economic and political sovereignty.

For all these reasons, the liberalisation of capital and financial services within the European Community occupies a special place within the 1992 programme. However, the impact of the 1992 programme upon the organisation of flows of money and finance in Europe should not be overemphasised. The 1980s was a decade of substantial change within the international financial system, during which money and finance achieved a remarkable liberalisation from the control of the state, effectively preempting many of the liberalising measures advocated by the EC. Indeed, the restructuring of the international financial system was so extensive during the 1980s that by the early 1990s the EC's prescription for the reform of the financial services sector had already begun to appear outdated in several respects. Much of the preparatory research for the 1992 programme was conducted in the early to mid-1980s. But the anatomy of the financial sector changed so much in the late 1980s and early 1990s that many of the objectives of the 1992 project relating to financial services, such as the liberalisation of finance and capital from the direct control of the nation state, were to a large extent achieved ahead of the 1992 deadline. Long-run tendencies towards financial innovation, rapid advances in the capabilities of communication and information technologies, and the growing internationalisation of accumulation processes combined to engineer a significant liberalisation of money from the control of individual nation states. These developments were associated with a tendency for money to become more spatially mobile, as money-owners became more discerning and international in their investment choices. The allocation of money on an international scale increasingly came to be based on appraisals of the likely effects of national macroeconomic policies upon the value of money. Money-owners, typically in the form of international financial institutions, began to display their readiness to switch money rapidly between national economies, practising policies of spatial arbitrage. The spatial switching of investments was often driven by the diversion of money out of economies undergoing relatively high levels of inflation, to avoid a devaluation of money capital. External evaluations of national macroeconomic policies by money-owners were usually signalled through currency exchange rates as investors bought and sold currencies.

To avoid destabilising episodes of exchange rate volatility, national economic policies became increasingly sensitive to the power of international money and orientated to the pursuit of conditions of low inflation and of relative price stability. By the late 1980s, external financial pressures had forced several industrialised nation states (e.g. the United Kingdom) to acknowledge just how little economic sovereignty they still possessed, as economic and monetary policies were ultimately framed within the context of seeking to satisfy the anti-inflationary imperatives of international financial capital. It was the ability to attract and retain the 'hot money' controlled by international investment institutions which came to signify the 'successful' prosecution of national macroeconomic policy (Jessop *et al.* 1990).

This growing power of financial capital *vis-à-vis* the state at an international level was paralleled by an inability of nation states to control the creation and circulation of money within the national economy. Advances in information systems within the financial labour process accelerated the rate of product and process innovation within the financial sector, which enabled financial institutions to circumvent the forms of structural regulation which had traditionally served to partition the financial system and so control the production and circulation of money and credit within the economy. Formerly single-function financial institutions began to move into new areas of credit creation and circulation, a tendency that accelerated during the 1980s, following the election to power of neo-liberal governments in many industrialised states, governments which were committed to the rolling back of the state and the free play of market forces (Overbeek 1990). In many states, the advocacy of market liberalisation was extended to the financial sector, and competition and risk taking were encouraged among financial institutions. Consequently, the breakdown of forms of structural regulation within the financial sector proceeded still further, and ensured that the 1980s was a period of widespread regulatory reform (Dale 1989; Gardener and Molyneux 1990; Llewelyn 1989; Moran 1991).

These changes have to be recounted in order to emphasise the fact that the 1992 programme is not the only force working towards the liberalisation of financial capital and financial services from the control of the state in Europe. Indeed, despite the EC's vociferous advocacy of market liberalisation, it may be that in the case of financial services the establishment of a Single European Market will actually work in the opposite direction, and provide the framework for the imposition of a *higher* level of state control over money and finance within Europe than hitherto.

The remainder of this chapter is therefore divided into four parts. In the second part we consider in more detail the tensions which exist between the political and economic authority of nation states and the innovative tendency of financial capital by means of an analysis of the recent evolution of the international financial system. In the third part we focus upon the EC's attempt to restructure European financial capital through the 1992 initiative, and examine the main types of response to these changes in the form of institutional and spatial restructuring by financial institutions. The 1992 project is generally portrayed as a programme of liberalisation. However, the fourth part reveals the countertendencies towards a reassertion of state power over financial capital contained both within the 1992 programme and within the parallel programme of European Monetary Union. The conclusions are presented in the final part of the chapter.

STATES AND MONEY: REGULATION, FINANCIAL CAPITAL AND THE RESTRUCTURING OF THE INTERNATIONAL FINANCIAL SYSTEM

The regulation and supervision of money have traditionally been seen as tasks of considerable importance for any nation state (Harris, L. 1988). The monopoly the state holds over money is seen to be an essential condition of national sovereignty, and provides the state with a degree of economic autonomy that would not otherwise be possible. To this end, the state attempts to take legal control of the stock of money in circulation, which includes the cash and bank deposits created by the banking system. The state must also endeavour to validate a system of monetary regulation in order to facilitate the smooth circulation of commodities within the economy. The state, through its central bank, seeks to ensure that the liabilities created by the system are readily accepted as means of exchange, and does this by intervening in the process of monetary exchange. However, the task of regulating money is highly problematic, as is revealed when one attempts to identify the *object* of financial regulation:

> The state . . . cannot operate directly either on the stock of money or on its circulation. It is not as if the state controls a printing press which is the sole source of money (as it appears to do in simple macro-economic models); or enforce strict ratios between gold reserves and the stock of money in circulation (as simple theories of the gold standard would have it); or can control the total money stock by strictly controlling the monetary base of high-powered money created by the state and allowing banks to reach an equilibrium position (as modern advocates of the monetary control base would have it). The money stock consists primarily of financial instruments which appear on the balance sheets of financial institutions, traditionally defined as bank deposits of various types. Their quality, character and role depended on the financial institution's own behaviour in relation to other agents.
>
> (Harris 1988: 15–16)

Therefore, being unable to regulate money *per se*, the state attempts to enforce financial prudence and responsibility by constraining the behaviour of financial institutions. In many nation states the regulation of money has, therefore, traditionally revolved around the balkanisation and segmentation of financial markets and financial institutions. Such structural regulation demarcates the financial system and is designed to restrict financial institutions to prescribed areas of financial activity (Gardener and Molyneux 1990). Different branches of the financial system are compartmentalised to ensure as far as possible that the development of a financial crisis within one branch of the financial system cannot easily spill over into other branches, thereby undermining not only the rest of the financial system but also exchange processes within the economy as a whole. However, whereas the partitioning of the financial system by the state is designed to constrain the activities of financial institutions, and thereby offset the development of a systemic crisis, the framework of structural regulation tends to be undermined by the inherent tendency for financial institutions to engage in the process of 'financial innovation' (de Cecco 1987). Financial innovation is the process by which financial institutions develop new financial instruments, thereby enabling them to move outside existing regulatory frameworks and into new areas of financial activity as yet unconstrained by regulatory control. Financial institutions engage in financial innovation because, for the most part, they are profit-seeking organisations, whereas the existence of forms of structural regulation ultimately serves to constrain profit-seeking behaviour by prohibiting certain types of financial institutions from engaging in certain types of financial activity. However, should the level of competition within financial markets intensify, then financial institutions will often seek to break free of the constraints placed upon them by structural regulation (Llewellyn 1989). Ironically, increased levels of competition between financial institutions are often initiated by the state, as it seeks to accelerate or cheapen the process of credit creation by lowering certain structural barriers between financial markets, usually allowing new participants into credit markets.[2] But the intensification of competition between financial institutions within financial markets eats into profits and so drives a process of financial innovation, as financial institutions engage in a search for new profit-making opportunities outside existing regulatory structures. The tendencies towards financial innovation also ensure that the regulatory and supervisory authorities of the state are faced with the constant task of reappraising and restructuring the regulatory framework.

The ability of individual nation states to maintain control over their financial systems via regulatory control has greatly deteriorated in recent years because of the growing tide of financial innovation. Individual nation states have increasingly found themselves powerless to resist successive rounds of innovation which have often assumed international and even global proportions. Nation states can only really exert control over the financial system when the process of credit creation, and the financial institutions responsible for such credit creation, are nationally bounded. Here the state can ensure that the process of credit creation is conducted according to the guidelines of financial regulation laid down by its financial authorities, subject of course to the constant process of revision and redrafting which is necessary to take account of the historical tendency towards financial innovation within any financial system. However, when the process of credit creation assumes an international dimension, the ability of the state to intervene in this process becomes heavily circumscribed. In recent years, as the process of credit creation has become more tenuously connected to individual nation states (Strange 1988), the intervention of nationally based regulatory authorities in the circuit of financial capital has become less proactive and more reactive, and increasingly symbolic of a willingness on the part of individual nation states to reach an accommodation with the interests of international financial capital.

The tendency for the power of international financial capital to wax, and for the economic power of individual nation states to wane, may be seen as an outcome of the ways in which the process of credit creation has been internationalised. Although it is not possible here to undertake a detailed analysis of the deterritorialisation of the credit creation process,[3] it is nevertheless important to outline the process by which credit provision has tended to become decoupled from national space economies, because it has considerable implications for the level of control that nation states are able to exercise over money and credit.

Money and credit in the international financial system

The nature of credit provision within the postwar international financial system has undergone a continual process of evolution, in response both to the growing pursuit of capital accumulation on an international and even a global scale (Clarke 1988), and to changes in the framework of financial regulation constructed by nation states and supranational regulatory authorities. The deterritorialisation of credit provision during this era should be viewed as an historical process, representative of the unravelling of the structure of international financial regulation developed by the United States and its Allies during the Second World War. The unfolding of this historical process can be partitioned into successive periods, in which the principal mode of credit provision was characterised by particular functional and spatial characteristics. Each of these periods revolves around particularly important disjunctures in national and international financial structures.

The first period: late 1940s to late 1950s

In this period, credit was for the most part advanced in the form of credit money, denominated in domestic currency, and was created by the expansion of the balance sheets of banks. In spatial terms, credit provision was largely nationally bounded, which served to consolidate the functional dominance of the advance of credit money as the primary mode of credit provision. The free circulation of financial capital was discouraged, for fear that this would disrupt the reconstruction of West European economies, which was being undertaken via the generalised application of nationally centric Keynesian policies of demand management, fuelled by the Marshall Aid programme (Clarke 1988). It was only in 1958 that reconstruction was deemed to have progressed sufficiently to allow the partial relaxation of currency exchange controls in Europe (Strange 1988). The reopening of a market in foreign exchange facilitated the growth of international portfolio investment, the absence of which in the earlier postwar period had seen capital markets depend solely upon the circulation of domestic investment funds. The limited supply of funds entering capital markets made this form of credit provision relatively expensive, ensuring that securitised forms of credit provision played only a minor role during this period.

The second period: late 1950s to late 1970s

In this period, credit was still predominantly advanced in the form of credit money, although the volume of securitised credit increased strongly over the period, a product of the growing volume of international portfolio investment which found its way into capital markets, and the growing importance of institutional investment organisations such as pension funds and insurance companies in systematically organising this investment.[4]

However, from the late 1950s there was a marked transformation in the spatial dimensions of the process of credit creation. Anomalies between the structures of financial regulation in the United States and in Europe encouraged the export of financial capital from the United States to financial centres in Europe (Strange 1988; Urry 1990). The growth of the 'euromarkets', which developed for the most part in the City of London (Clarke 1965; Sampson 1965), saw the emergence of offshore credit money markets denominated largely in expatriate US dollars, which were then pooled into loans by the international banks which flocked to the City to participate in this new debt market. The volume of funds in the euro-markets increased rapidly from the late 1960s and early 1970s onwards as money continued to flow overseas from the United States. The export of money from the United States was further accelerated by domestic policy measures introduced to speed up the rate of capital accumulation within the US economy and through the cheapening of credit, and pumping demand into the economy.[5] The cheapening of credit led to a marked increase in the volume of money circulating within the US economy, and then through capital export, also within the rest of the international financial system, leading to a marked increase in the volume of extant global monetary reserves (Parboni 1981). The euromarkets, into which these funds predominantly flowed, expanded still further after 1974 as OPEC nations deposited the superprofits they derived following the steep rise in oil prices.

The mid- to late 1970s marked the high point of this phase of credit creation within the international financial system, and revealed the growing divide between processes of credit creation and structures of regulatory control; the first were largely conducted on an international scale, whereas the second operated at the level of the nation state. The ability of financial institutions to advance credit largely unconstrained by the dictates of good banking practice led first to a series of financial crises, as banks began to extend credit beyond the capacity of borrowers to pay it back, and then in response to these crises, to the tentative organisation of forms of supra-national financial regulation, designed to overcome the spatial mismatch between the processes of credit creation and the framework of regulatory control over the credit system.[6] However, attempts to reassert regulatory control over the international financial institutions participating in the offshore credit markets at this time were both too little and too late, as an overextension of credit and an important disjuncture in the trajectory of global macroeconomic development ushered in a new era of credit provision within the international financial system.

The third period: late 1970s to late 1980s

A third phase of credit creation within the postwar international financial system began to emerge in the late 1970s, but was only really fully installed in the early 1980s. This phase saw a deepening of the deterritorialisation of the credit system combined with a switch to more securitised forms of credit provision. The move to more disintermediated means of debt organisation initially began as a response to the success of national regulatory authorities in reasserting some semblance of control over the process of international credit provision through the construction of multinational regulatory structures. These structures consisted largely of the setting of multinational measures of financial prudence, typically requiring banks to hold 'prudent' levels of capital as reserves against money lent out to borrowers. However, the moves to standardise capital-to-asset ratios among international banks had the effect of constraining profit growth for many such institutions, for asset-base expansion was ultimately limited by the market value of the bank. These moves undermined the popularity of traditional means of bank intermediation within the international financial system, as lending was penalised by financial regulation which gradually began to be extended into the international arena of the credit system.

As the world economy entered the 1980s, the international credit system was still based on the creation of 'intermediated credit', with the large international banks booking loans on their balance sheets. However, during the 1980s, both the principal process of credit creation and the spatial dimensions of this process were transformed. The functional trans-figuration of the credit creation process was propelled by a sea change in US monetary policy from the late 1970s onwards. Problems of rising infla-tion and growing selling pressure on the dollar in the foreign exchange markets in the late 1970s encouraged the United States to check its policy of monetary laxity which it had used to drive domestic accumulation. Interest rates began to rise, making credit more expensive, and so cooling demand within the domestic economy. The 'high interest rate, strong dollar' policy was extended still further after 1980 as the Reagan adminis-tration pursued a defence-led expansion of the economy through the use of imported money; high interest rates attracted in the globally mobile international financial capital needed to fund the project (Leyshon 1990; Lipietz 1989; Thrift and Leyshon 1988).

However, the rise in US interest rates was transmitted through the rest of the international financial system, and pushed debt repayments on intermediated credit to crippling levels. Developing countries, which had borrowed heavily in the euromarkets during the 1970s, found they were unable to pay the interest, let alone the principal, on the debt they had accumulated. The breaking of the developing country debt crisis set off a series of reactive developments within the international financial system which helped install a new regime of credit creation. On the one hand, investors chose not to invest their money with banks, for fear that the banks were too heavily implicated in the developing debt crisis for their money to be absolutely safe. Instead, investors increasingly began to lend their money directly to borrowers, through the purchase of securities and various forms of commercial paper. On the other hand, the shift to off-balance-sheet financing was consolidated by renewed postcrisis attempts by financial authorities to impose multinational regulatory safeguards upon bank lending, by insisting upon higher capital-to-asset ratios, further curtailing the ability of banks to engage in asset-based expansion. In the search for profits, banks began to engage in fee-earning and income-earning activities, which did not expand their balance sheets. These activities, which included the issue of securities for borrowers, created new problems for regulatory authorities, for not only was the creation of credit via securitisation more difficult to constrain by conventional means of financial regulation, but the process of disintermediation also set in train a wave of financial innovation, which greatly multiplied the ways in which borrowers could gain access to credit. Many of the new financial instruments were highly esoteric and often extended not only beyond the control of the regulatory authorities but also sometimes beyond their comprehension.

The transformation of the process of credit creation was paralleled by a reorientation of the spatial movement of credit flows. During the 1970s credit flows moved primarily between the industrialised, OPEC and developing nations, in a process of 'financial recycling' which was organised in the euromarkets and mediated by international banks. Following the debt crisis, the developing countries were subjected to a process of exclusion from international credit markets, cut off from the supply of new funds by their financial position. This saw the international financial system experience a process of spatial concentration, as the circulation of credit was increasingly restricted to a cohort of core industrial nations. In particular, financial flows began to move in response to a new process of recycling, which was necessitated by the widening budget imbalances emerging between industrialised nations (Figure 3.1). The largest imbalance opened up between the United States and Japan, which resulted in large volumes of funds being diverted from Japan to the United States, with the bulk of this money being placed in securitised investments.[7] Consequently, financial, economic and geopolitical relations between the two most dominant national economies began to exercise an increasingly pervasive influence upon the trajectory of world economic development. In the new international financial system of the 1980s, New York performed a role akin to global financial sink, as money was sucked in to fund the growing deficit, while Tokyo acted as a financial fountainhead, providing the liquidity which helped lubricate processes of accumulation. The flows of financial capital moving between Japan and the United States became the dominant feature of the international financial system of the 1980s, and saw both New York and Tokyo assume the position of the world's premier financial centre at different times during the decade.

Europe in the global financial system

For the most part, European financial centres have occupied subordinate positions within these new international financial markets. The securitised

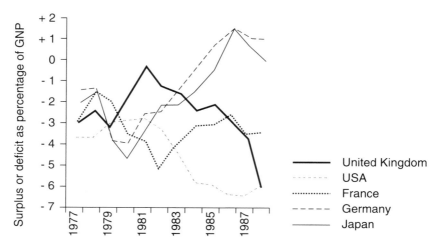

Figure 3.1 Budget surplus or deficit of Group of Five industrial nations
Source: Financial Times (1989)

credit markets of Japan and the United States dwarfed those of Europe, and the low liquidity of the European markets had a deterrent effect on many international financial institutions with large volumes of financial capital to invest. These investors were further deterred from active involvement within the European financial markets by the divisive structures of financial regulation operated within several states, which although they were increasingly ineffective at controlling flows of financial capital, nevertheless had the effect of making the cost of buying and selling investments relatively expensive on a global scale (Pagano and Roell 1990).

The existing regulatory framework within Europe was, therefore, proving to be doubly ineffective in a new regime of international credit provision. On the one hand, regulatory fragmentation within Europe served to provide windows of opportunity for international financial capital to engage in pan-European speculative investment. Yet, on the other hand, the fragmentation of the European capital market on a nation state basis meant that the European states looked set to continue to play a subordinate role to the credit markets of the United States and Japan. The role of European centres in the new international financial system was to act as 'spatial maklers' (Lash and Urry 1987) for the flows of global financial capital moving east to west, as funds were diverted from Tokyo to New York. European financial centres provided international investors with opportunities for engaging in a process of 'spatial arbitrage' between financial markets. There evolved what became known as the 'European trading day', which followed the Tokyo trading day and preceded the New York trading day.

The European financial centre which more than any other succeeded in carving out a functionally important position within this new international financial system was London. The City of London had been the world's leading financial centre in the 1960s and 1970s, as the focus of the euro-markets. However, the rise of a more disintermediated form of financial system, and the growing importance of Tokyo–New York capital flows saw London's position as a premier international financial system come under threat. The enforced restructuring of the City in 1986 ('Big Bang') was the British government's attempt to preserve the City's status as a pre-eminent financial centre, as arcane and restrictive practices were thrown out, and foreign financial institutions and new ways of making money let in. This process of competitive reregulation (Moran 1991) consolidated the City's position as Europe's premier financial centre, and enabled it to capture a large proportion of financial business flowing into Europe as well as sig-nificant volumes of financial business generated within Europe. The City's renewed financial pre-eminence was accomplished through a willingness of the UK state to bend the structure of financial regulation towards the new imperatives of the international financial system.

Regulatory regimes in other European financial centres and financial systems remained orientated first and foremost to controlling the circula-tion of intermediated credit within the domestic economy. Many European states retained restrictions on the movement of financial capital through exchange controls, thereby hanging on to the traditional levers of monetary and economic growth. Moreover, capital markets were relatively undevel-oped in several important European states, especially when compared with similar markets in the United Kingdom (or the United States) (Franks and Mayer 1990). In countries such as Germany and France securitised forms of credit provision remained a relatively unimportant source of new fund-ing compared with the advance of credit money in the form of loans. For example, the persistence of intermediated credit as the principal form of debt provision in Germany was partly a product of financial history, and partly a product of regulation. It was a product of history in that German banks began as early as the nineteenth century to cultivate long-term lending relationships with domestic industrial borrowers because the inter-national capital markets were tightly controlled by the financial institutions based in the City of London (Born 1983). In these lending relationships, the banks often established themselves as the largest shareholders of the companies they lent to, thereby short-circuiting the development of a credit market based on the exchange of corporate ownership. Similar bank-orientated financial systems also existed in several other EC states (e.g. France). The stagnant nature of the market for corporate ownership, and the relative illiquidity of the German capital markets, effectively acted as a deterrent to those funds circulating within the global economy which might otherwise have entered the country in the form of securitised investments. Other forms of national regulation exacerbated the illiquidity of capital markets in several important European countries. For example, taking the example of Germany again, the legal entitlement for managers, employees and their representatives to obtain positions on the supervisory boards of companies meant that interests other than those of shareholders had to be taken into account when attempts to purchase large tranches of shares affected the ownership of the firm (Franks and Mayer 1990). Therefore, whereas German banks participated successfully in the circuit of disintermediated credit circulating on a global scale, at home a series of barriers to the penetration of securitised form of credit provision meant that the German economy remained a bastion of credit provision through the release of intermediated credit from banks to their long-term industrial borrowers.

The securitised forms of debt provision which increasingly dominated the international credit system failed to penetrate other European economies because of the maintenance of structural forms of financial regulation, which not only prevented domestic financial institutions from engaging in certain types of financial activity, but also curtailed the activities of the foreign financial institutions established in these countries. The maintenance of strong forms of structural regulation within states such as France, Italy and Spain meant that the institutional structure of credit markets in these countries was highly stable, with financial profits being generated without recourse to the highly aggressive business strategies practised by banks participating in the competitive global circuit of capital (United Nations Centre on Transnational Corporations 1988, 1990). The restraint of processes of competition within such domestic financial markets saw the balance of power within the credit markets tipped firmly in favour of the banks, whereas the intensification of competition within financial markets operating at an international level empowered investors, as margins were shaved and the cost of credit lowered.

To summarise, the maintenance of restrictive forms of financial regulation within several European states had the effect of undermining the international competitiveness of European financial centres, in that regulation discouraged the import of flows of highly mobile financial capital, while at the same time the cost of credit within domestic financial systems began to appear increasingly expensive compared with the cost of credit available in deterritorialised credit markets.[8] These regulatory anomalies allowed one financial centre – the City of London – to capture a significant volume of financial business through a process of competitive reregulation.[9] Regulatory fragmentation also ensured that the institutional structure of European financial markets had become highly variable, with some financial systems producing large, highly capitalised and efficient financial institutions capable of taking on the best of the US and Japanese banks, whereas others had produced numerous small, domestically orientated institutions that would find it difficult to survive in competition with international financial institutions should they ever be exposed to the full force of open competition. However, at the same time structural regulation was patently failing to ensure financial prudence for, through internationalisation, banks and other financial institutions were able to escape the spatial frame of such regulation by setting up operations in foreign financial centres such as the City of London, so entering into the unregulated and risk-laden circuit of disintermediated credit.

The persistence of regulatory fragmentation in the European credit system severely threatened the EC's plan to harmonise the conditions of exchange across national boundaries as part of its progression towards the creation of a unified European state. The EC's bid to remould the structure of European finance consisted of a parallel programme of liberalisation and consolidation.

Below we analyse these related strategies of liberalisation and consolidation. We do this in two stages. First, we analyse the 1992 programme as it affects the organisation of the European financial sector. We then go on to look at the programme which seeks to forge monetary integration within Europe, examining the bid to establish European Monetary Union.

THE REMAKING OF EUROPEAN FINANCIAL CAPITAL: FINANCIAL SERVICES AND THE SINGLE MARKET

The 1992 programme and financial services

The broad aims of the 1992 project were fairly straightforward: they were to boost the effectiveness and efficiency of European economic activity through the easing of barriers to market processes. A wave of direct economic benefits would ensue from the removal of an array of non-tariff barriers which had hampered the flow of capital and commodities between EC member states. It was further anticipated that the locomotive effect of the removal of barriers would generate a series of even more substantial indirect economic benefits. One of the primary indirect benefits sought by the EC was an increase in the general level of 'economic efficiency', derived from the specialisation and rationalisation of economic activity in Europe as firms pursued economies of scale, and processes of capital centralisation and concentration unfolded within the unified market. The harmonisation of markets would have the effect of opening up formerly protected markets to foreign competition, ensuring that less efficient domestic firms would no longer be defended by protective governmental regulation. The EC hoped that the prising open of markets in this way would allow more efficient firms to command more of the European market, either by driving less successful firms out of business or by absorbing such firms through processes of capital centralisation. Thus, it is important to note that the 1992 programme was steeped in an ideology of economic orthodoxy. The plans for the Single Market were grounded in notions of perfect competition, of comparative advantage and in a belief in the supreme allocative efficiency of markets. The neo-liberal dimensions of this strategy conveniently overlooked the worries expressed by commentators more sensitive to the relationships between processes of capital centralisation, capital concentration and market power, who argued that the emergence of a relatively small number of giant pan-European companies was more likely to denude levels of competition than increase it (Cutler *et al.* 1990).

Nevertheless, it might be argued that, if a blueprint for economic change based upon economic orthodoxy has any relevance, it probably has most relevance for change within the financial sector. For example, 'wholesale' financial markets, in which international investment institutions, transnational corporations and nation states borrow and lend money and buy and sell financial products to one another, are probably among the most transparent and 'market efficient' of all branches of economic activity. However, it is important to recognise that this is only one branch of financial activity. Wholesale financial markets, which have been subject to extensive processes of deterritorialisation, are in consequence only lightly regulated. These markets are driven by institutional money-owners and are highly price-sensitive. Market conditions are very different on the retail side of the financial services sector, where the balance of power between economic agents in the market is much less equal (Grilli 1989). Moreover, there is little evidence to suggest that the pursuit of economies of scale in financial services will necessarily produce the efficiency gains anticipated by the EC, in either wholesale or retail financial markets:

> Financial economists have long questioned the view that larger banks are more efficient.... The many empirical studies have found...that scale economies in banking are limited to smaller institutions, and the average cost curve for producing the main products of banking (loans and deposits) seem to be U-shaped.
>
> (Gardener and Molyneux 1990: 216)

What a strategy of capital centralisation *does* deliver to a financial institution is greater market power within the areas in which it operates, for such a strategy helps extend processes of capital concentration and increase levels of market capitalisation. But an increase in the market power of those financial institutions who prosecute strategies of merger and acquisition does not necessarily square with the EC's mission to deliver measurable increases in market efficiency across the Community.

The financial services directives

The EC's attempt to restructure the financial services sector revolves around the reorganisation of three key areas of financial activity: banking, the securities industry and insurance (Kay 1991). The attempt to restructure the EC *banking industry* revolved around the implementation of the Second Banking Directive, which sought to harmonise rules on levels of capital, control, solvency ratios, deposit ratios, deposit guarantees and the qualifications of managers, and represented an important extension of the process of multinational regulatory harmonisation initiated by the EEC in the 1970s. Under the Second Banking Directive 'home countries' assumed responsibility for the issue of operating licences to banks, and for ensuring that basic operating standards were adhered to, while 'host countries' were free to enforce their own operating rules. The purpose of the directive was to liberalise the European banking market, and to open up domestic banking systems to market forces by ensuring that incoming banks were not faced with the bureaucratic obstacles of being forced to obtain separate operating licences in every EC country in which they wish to operate (Davis and Smales 1989). However, it is important to note that banks were not granted total freedom of operation, because individual countries could still proscribe certain types of financial activity through the imposition of national operating rules associated with structural forms of financial regulation, although all non-host-country EC banks were at least assured of equal treatment with host-country banks. Therefore, although the rationale underlying the Second Banking Directive has commonly been described as a 'passport principle' in EC banking, Davis and Smales (1989) have more accurately identified the directive as introducing a 'driving licence principle' into European banking, where banks registered in the EC are free to operate across the Community so long as they conform to local rules and guidelines.

The restructuring of the European *securities industry* was similarly governed by a 'passport' or 'driving licence principle'. The key elements of EC legislation affecting the securities industry were the UCITS (Undertakings for Collective Investments in Securities) Directive and the Investment Services Directive. The UCITS Directive established the principle that a unit trust which met the basic standards laid out in the directive could be approved in one EC country and sold anywhere in the EC. The Investment Services Directive was to the securities industry what the Second Banking Directive was to the banking industry. The directive proposed a pan-European Community licence, where investment services established in one country could be marketed throughout the Community. However, the Investment Services Directive contained a grey area similar in kind to that included within the Second Banking Directive; that is, between rules of establishment and rules of operation (Davis and Smales 1989).

The legislative changes to the *insurance industry* revolved around the Second Non-Life Directive. The directive drew an important distinction between large risks (underwritten risks) and mass risks (insurance services, such as motor car insurance). Only the first type of insurance market was subject to regulatory change, with insurance companies being able for the first time to transact large-risk business transactions across national boundaries within the Community. However, mass-risk business remained subject to local regulations, which varied considerably. Therefore, it was only the large-risk insurance business that was to be transformed via regulatory change, providing price reductions only to those corporate bodies large enough to generate large individual-risk liabilities.

The explicit objective of the various financial service directives was to harmonise the cost of financial services in Europe around a lower average. Research commissioned by the EC during the mid-1980s discovered that marked differences existed in the cost of financial services across Europe (Table 3.1). The EC attributed these price differences to the fragmented regulatory and institutional structures of the Community. A process of regulatory and market harmonisation, the EC argued, would serve to bring costs down around a lower average (Cecchini 1988). However, this was a strictly non-contextual and non-spatial interpretation of price variation, and was an interpretation which stemmed from the ideology of economic orthodoxy which pervaded EC thinking on market integration. The fact that the cost of credit and of insurance is closely tied to notions of risk, and that the riskiness of economic activity is socially constructed and varies spatially, because of geographical variations in the nature of such social constructions, does not seem to have been entertained by the EC in its deliberations on price variability.[10]

A recognition of spatial variations in the riskiness of extending both credit and insurance would by itself have dispelled any anticipation of a sudden Community-wide harmonisation of the prices of EC financial services on 1 January 1993, because such variations would not be immediately removed. There were other reasons why the 1992 deadline itself could not be taken as a clear watershed date, neatly marking the end of an old European financial order and heralding the birth of another. On the one hand, some of the measures to be implemented under the Single European Market Act were staggered, so that, whereas some measures were scheduled to come into force on or before the end of 1992, some countries were able to defer the implementation of certain directives until well into the mid-1990s. In addition, a series of *derogations* was attached to certain of the directives in some EC countries, which enabled the pace of reform to be slowed if the reregulatory measures were deemed to have induced destabilising effects upon the domestic economy, particularly if flows of money and finance were dangerously disturbed. On the other hand, the 1992 deadline could not mark a clear watershed because certain processes associated with the Single Market programme began to unfold several years prior to the deadline.

Perhaps the most visible example of such proactive processes was the wave of corporate restructuring which began to preoccupy European financial institutions from the mid-1980s onwards. In anticipation of a unified market in financial services in the EC after 1992, financial service firms began to engage in extensive rounds of capital centralisation, thereby pre-empting one of the main indirect benefits anticipated by the EC from the creation of the Single Market. However, the proactive character of the capital centralisation behaviour in the European financial sector was one of the reasons why the links forged between institutions before 1992 were often characterised by caution and hesitancy, with organisational tie-ups falling far short of complete takeover. Such behaviour illustrated that many financial institutions were effectively covering their options, allowing themselves maximum operational flexibility in their eventual choice of organisational strategy within the unified regulatory

Table 3.1 Percentage differences in prices of standard financial products compared with average of the four lowest national prices

Name of standard service	Description of standard service	Bel	Ger	Spa	Fra	Ita	Lux	Net	UK
Banking services									
1 Consumer credit	Annual cost of consumer loan of 500 ECU. Excess interest rate over money market rates	−41	136	39	na	121	−26	31	121
2 Credit cards	Annual cost, assuming 500 ECU debit. Excess interest rate over money market rates	79	60	26	−30	89	−12	43	16
3 Mortgages	Annual cost of home loan of 25,000 ECU. Excess interest rate over money market rates	31	57	118	78	−4	na	−6	20
4 Letters of credit	Cost of letter of credit of 50,000 ECU for three months	22	−10	59	−7	9	27	17	8
5 Foreign exchange drafts	Cost for a large commercial client of purchasing a commercial draft for 30,000 ECU	6	31	196	56	23	33	−46	16
6 Travellers' cheques	Cost for a private consumer of purchasing 100 ECU worth of travellers' cheques	35	−7	30	39	22	−7	33	−7
7 Commercial loans	Annual cost (including commissions and charges) to a medium-sized firm of a commercial loan of 250,000 ECU	−5	6	19	−7	9	6	43	46
Insurance services									
1 Life insurance	Average annual cost of term (life) insurance	78	5	37	33	83	66	−9	−30
2 Home insurance	Annual cost of fire and theft cover for house valued at 70,000 ECU with 28,000 ECU contents	−16	3	−4	39	81	57	17	90
3 Motor insurance	Annual cost of comprehensive insurance, 1.6 litre car, driver with ten years' experience, no-claims bonus	30	15	100	9	148	77	−7	−17
4 Commercial fire and theft	Annual cover for premises valued at 387,240 ECU and stock at 232,344 ECU	−9	43	24	153	245	−15	−1	27
5 Public liability cover	Annual premium for engineering company with twenty employees and annual turnover of 1.29 million ECU	13	47	60	117	77	99	−16	−7
Brokerage services									
1 Private equity transactions	Commission costs of cash bargain of 1,440 ECU	36	7	65	−13	−3	−7	114	123
2 Private gilts transaction	Commission costs of cash bargain of 14,000 ECU	14	90	217	21	−63	27	161	36
3 Institutional equity transactions	Commission costs of cash bargain of 288,000 ECU	26	69	153	−5	47	68	26	−47
4 Institutional gilt transactions	Commission costs of cash bargain of 7.2 million ECU	284	−4	60	57	92	−36	21	na

(*Source*: Cecchini 1988: table 6, pp. 38–9).

structure. But this was not the only reason why financial institutions did not seek the full-blooded mergers implicitly favoured by the EC in the search for absolute economies of scale. The organisation of much of the European financial sector was contingent upon spatial variations in social and cultural constructions. Even if the EC did not recognise this in their blueprint for a single market in financial services, many financial service firms did, placing themselves among a growing cohort of capitalist organisations which became increasingly sensitive to the geography of consumption and exchange.

The institutional restructuring of financial capital in the EC

Corporate restructuring was driven both by offensive and by defensive market strategies, as financial institutions jockeyed for position prior to the harmonisation of regulatory conditions. Amidst the maelstrom of mergers, takeovers and alliances, all of which took place within a relatively short period of time, it was possible to identify a set of distinctive processes through which the institutional structure of the European financial sector was reshaped. For example, Gardener and Molyneux (1990) have put forward a fivefold typology of restructuring processes consisting of (1) the forging of alliances, with firms taking non-predatory minority interests in other firms; (2) blocking strategies, through the acquisition of strategic minority interests in other firms; (3) cross-border acquisitions; (4) national mergers and acquisitions; (5) cross-border mergers (Gardener and Moly-neux 1990: 213). This basic typology can be developed to take greater account of the spatial dimensions of the restructuring processes. Therefore, we would wish to distinguish between national and cross-border alliances, and between national and cross-border mergers and acquisitions. We do not find it especially useful to distinguish between cross-border mergers and cross-border acquisitions. Thus, our revised typology might consist of (1) cross-border alliances, (2) national alliances, (3) cross-border mergers and acquisitions, (4) national mergers and acquisitions, and (5) strategic minority share holdings (Table 3.2). The last category is the least important, and was associated with minority, but nevertheless substantial, share purchases in firms which were either being considered as likely full-bid targets or effectively 'taken out of play' in order to prevent a bid from a rival organisation. In the analysis which follows we will concentrate upon the two main forms of restructuring activity which took place ahead of the Single Market: merger and acquisition activity and the forging of alliances between financial institutions.

As Table 3.2 reveals, processes of institutional restructuring within the European banking industry were dominated by straightforward merger and acquisition activity. The number of merger and acquisition deals greatly outweighed the number of agreements forged between institutions seeking more co-operative ways of preparing for the Single Market. At a purely

Table 3.2 The restructuring of the European banking sector ahead of the Single Market – some examples of merger and acquisition behaviour, up to the end of 1990

Institution	Location of investment	Date	Nature of deal
(a) *Cross-border alliances*			
Commerzbank (Germany)	Spain	1984	Acquired 10% of Banco Hispano-American, BHA, in exchange for 5% of Commerzbank
San Paolo Bank (Italy)	UK	1986	Acquired 6% of Hambros Bank
Skandinaviska Enksilda Bank (Sweden)	Denmark	1986	Acquired 5% of Privatbanken
	Norway	1986	Acquired 6% of Bergen Bank
	Finland	1986	Acquired 3% of Union Bank of Finland
Deutsche Bank (Germany)	UK	1987	Acquired 5% of Morgan Grenfell
San Paolo Bank (Italy)	France	1987	Acquired 1.1% of Compagnie Financière de Suez
Generale Bank (Belgium)	France	1987	Acquired 1.5% of Compagnie Financière de Suez
Banco Bilbao (Spain)	UK	1987	Acquired 5% of Hambros Bank
Cariplo (Italy)	Spain	1988	Acquired 1% of Banco Santander
Banco Santander (Spain)	UK	1988	Acquired 10% of Royal Bank of Scotland, in exchange for 2.5% of Banco Santander
Generale Bank/Amro	Belgium/ Netherlands	1988	Exchange of 10% equity holdings. Holdings later reduced to 5%
Paribas (France)	Denmark	1989	Link with Hafnia (insurance company)
DG Bank (Germany)	Spain	1989	Joint venture, Banco Co-operativo Español, formed with Spanish rural savings banks
San Paolo Bank (Italy)	USA	1989	Acquired 5% of Salomon Brothers, but represented move of Salomon Brothers into Italian retail banking
Nomura (Japan)	Spain	1989	Acquired 1.5% of Banco Santander, and 10% of Banco Santander subsidiary, Banco Santander des Negocios
Banesta (Spain)	Portugal	1989	Acquired 3.3% of Banco Tottae Acores
Baltic (Denmark)	UK	1989	Acquired 9% of Hambros Bank
Taiyo Kobe Bank (Japan)	Italy	1989	Cooperative agreement with Monte dei Paschi, and 5% stake in Monte dei Paschi subsidiary, Credito Commercial
Mitsui Bank (Japan)	UK	1990	Acquired 5% of Hambros Bank
Monte dei Paschi (Italy)	Germany	1990	Exchanged 5% of equity in its Credito Commercial subsidiary for Bayerische Landesbank's 10% stake in Bankhaus Aufhauser
(b) *National alliances*			
Banque Nationale de Paris	France	1989	Share-link and cross-marketing deal with state-owned Union des Assurances de Paris (insurance company)

Table 3.2 (continued)

Verenigde Spaarbank	Netherlands	1989	Alliance with Amex (insurance company)
Dresdner Bank	Germany	1989	Agreement with Allianz (insurance company) to distribute products
San Paolo Bank	Italy	1989	Agreement with Guardian Royal Exchange (UK insurer) to buy three Italian insurance companies in joint venture

(c) *Blocking or strategic minority interests*

Hongkong Bank (HK)	UK	1987	Acquired 15% of Midland Bank
Cartera Central (Kuwait, Spain)	Spain	1988	Acquired 12% of Banco Central
Cariplo (Italy)	Spain	1988	Acquired 30% of Banco Jover
Banco Santander (Spain)	Italy	1988	Acquired 30% of IBI
Crédit Agricole (France)	Italy	1989	Acquired 13.3% of Nuovo Banco Ambrosiano

(d) *Cross-border mergers and acquisitions*

Barclays (UK)	Spain	1981	Acquired Banco de Valladolid from Regulatory Authorities
Citicorp (USA)	Spain	1983	Acquired Banco Levante
Citicorp (USA)	Italy	1984	Acquired Banco Centrosud from Banco di Roma
Lloyds Bank (UK)	Germany	1984	Acquired Schröder, Münchmeyer Hengst Bank
National Australian Bank (Australia)	UK/Ireland	1987	Acquired Clydesdale Bank
Bank of Ireland (Ireland)	UK	1987	Acquired Bank of America's UK mortgage loan subsidiary
Banco Santander (Spain)	Germany	1987	Acquired CC bank from Bank of America
Crédit Lyonnais (France)	Netherlands	1987	Acquired Nederlandse Credietbank from Chase Manhattan
San Paolo Bank (Italy)	France	1987	Acquired control of Banque Vernes from Suez Group
Populare di Novaro (Italy)	France	1988	Acquired 80% of Banque de l'Union Maritime
Banque Nationale de Paris (France)	UK	1988	Acquired Chemical Bank's UK mortgage loan subsidiary
Dresdner Bank (Germany)	UK	1988	Acquired 70% of Thornton Fund Management
Banco Santander (Spain)	Belgium	1988	Acquired Belgium subsidiary of Crédit du Nord
Midland Bank (UK)	Italy	1989	Controlling stake in Euromobiliare bank
Westdeutsche Landesbank (Germany)	Various	1989	Purchase of Standard Chartered's European branches (except in Frankfurt and Switzerland)
Société Générale (France)	UK	1989	Acquired Thornton, Touche Remnant (fund management)
Hypo Bank (Germany)	UK	1989	Acquired 50% of fund managers Foreign and Colonial
Deutsche Bank (Germany)	UK	1989	Acquired Morgan Grenfell for £950 million

Table 3.2 (continued)

Banque Nationale de Paris (France)	Spain	1989	Acquired eighty-five branches of Banco Bilbao Vizcaya
Banco Bilbao Vizcaya (Spain)	France	1989	Acquired eighty-five branches of Banque Nationale de Paris' Crédit Universel consumer finance chain
Crédit Lyonnais (France)	Italy	1989	Purchased 30% of Credito Bergamasco
Société Générale (France)	Germany	1989	Acquired SG Alsassische Bank
Société Générale (France)	Netherlands	1989	Acquired Inguersen (brokers)
Deutsche Bank (Germany)	Netherlands	1989	Acquired Albert de Bary (merchant bank)
NMB (Netherlands)	Belgium	1989	Acquired Royal Bank of Canada's Belgian banking operations
Banco Bilbao Vizcaya (Spain)	Belgium	1989	Acquired Banque Crédit Commercial
Banco Hispano (Spain) and BACOB (Belgium)	Belgium	1989	Joint acquisition of Continental Bank
Banque Bruxelles Lambert (Belgium)	France	1989	Acquired Dreyfus (investment bank)
Deutsche Bank (Germany)	Spain	1989	Acquired Banco Commercial Transatlantico
	Portugal	1989	Acquired MDM (merchant bank)
Dresdner Bank (Germany)	France	1989	Acquired Banque Internationale de Placement
Bank in Lichtenstein (Lichtenstein)	UK	1989	Acquired GT Management (fund management)
Bank in Yokohama (Japan)	UK	1989	Acquired Guinness Mahon for £94.5 million
National Australian Bank (Australia)	UK	1990	Acquired Yorkshire Bank for £976.5 million

(e) *National mergers and acquisitions*

Banco de Bilbao/Banco de Vizcaya	Spain	1988	Merger
ABC Bank	Norway	1985	Savings bank merged with central savings bank
NMB	Netherlands	1989	Merger with Postbank
Risparmio di Roma	Italy	1989	Acquired 51% of Banco Spirito Santo
Credito Italiano	Italy	1989	Acquired large stake in Banca Nazionale dell'Agricoltura
Nuova Banco Ambrosiano	Italy	1989	Acquired Banca Cattolica de Veneto
San Paolo Bank	Italy	1989	Acquired large stake in Crediop
Den Norske Creditbank	Norway	1989	Merger with Bergen Bank
Sparekassen SDS	Sweden	1989	Merger with Privatbanken
Den Danske Bank	Denmark	1989	Merger with Copenhagen Handelsbank
PK Banken	Sweden	1990	Merger with Nordbanken
Svenska Handelsbanken	Sweden	1990	Planned merger with Skanska Banken
Amro	Netherlands	1990	Planned merger with ABN

(*Sources*: Gardener and Molyneux (1990) and authors' own observations)

national level, such behaviour was clearly driven by defensive motivations. Intranational merger and acquisition activity was undertaken mainly by financial institutions which tended previously to operate for the most part within the confines of their domestic economy. These firms reacted with alarm to the prospect of larger, more heavily capitalised financial institutions encroaching into their home markets, and to the possibility of being caught up in a price war which foreign and more strongly capitalised firms would be better placed to win. Such reactive behaviour was particularly rife in Italy from the mid-1980s onwards, where a history of strong structural regulation and constraints on bank branching had created a compartmentalised and geographically differentiated banking system. The low levels of competition which the regulatory structure had engendered saw Italian banks fall behind on a number of critical measures of cost-effectiveness. According to Friedman,

> The level of customer service is horribly poor. The payments system is so ineffective it can take up to a month for cheques to clear. . . . A senior foreign banker . . . poses the problems in even starker terms: 'If Italian banks don't put their houses in order, and quickly, they're going to get killed by international competition in the future.'
>
> (Friedman 1989: 8)

In response to such fears, Italian banks embarked upon a state-sponsored round of internal merger and acquisition activity in an attempt to build institutions capable of standing up to more competitive foreign financial service organisations. Similar nationally based rounds of capital centralisation unfolded elsewhere within the EC, particularly in Denmark and the Netherlands, and were even witnessed in non-EC countries such as Norway and Sweden, where domestic financial institutions began to merge in response to the regulatory reform of their domestic financial systems intended to regularise the flow of money and capital between their countries and their primary trade partners within the EC (Taylor 1990). Similar processes of capital centralisation also unfolded within the European insurance sector, as national insurance companies engaged in intranational rounds of merger and acquisition. However, it was on an international scale that merger and acquisition among European financial institutions was most prevalent. But, although numerous deals were struck, closer examination reveals that this form of institutional restructuring was characterised almost entirely by large financial institutions buying much smaller organisations (Gardener and Molyneux 1990). Therefore, although this form of activity was numerically important, it was not as functionally important as the numbers of deals alone would suggest. For example, no 'European superbanks' were created through such processes. Indeed, the one deal struck which explicitly sought to form such a supranational institution – the share swap between Belgium's Generale Bank and the Netherlands Amro Bank – broke down in 1989. Rather, the merger and acquisition activity which did take place saw small, essentially nationally orientated financial institutions absorbed into larger foreign groups seeking to extend their operations into new national markets.

Links forged between *large* financial institutions ahead of the Single Market were in fact characterised by the striking of alliances and co-operative agreements, often involving the reciprocal exchange of capital and equity. Such behaviour took place at both a national and an international level, but it was the forging of alliances across borders which were most numerous. The large number of alliances struck between financial service firms in Europe ahead of the 1992 deadline may have in part reflected the unwillingness of some large institutions to commit themselves. Indeed, when financial service firms were canvassed for their views on the future shape of the market the results normally revealed a gradualist approach to corporate restructuring. For example, a Bank of England survey of British financial institutions revealed that

> few firms perceived the single market as an entirely new phenomenon; most expected it rather to give added impetus to current trends in European and [global] markets. It was generally accepted that any major effects would occur only gradually over a period of years, not as sudden or dramatic changes in the demand for financial services, or in the nature and organization of the firms supplying them.
>
> (Bank of England 1989: 407)

In any case, by the late 1980s and early 1990s many large banks had very little option but to adopt a cautious attitude in their pursuit of strategies of capital centralisation. Earlier rounds of merger and acquisition, in particular those associated with the restructuring of London's capital markets in 1986, had blown large holes in their balance sheets, and growing levels of international competition and the slowdown in the growth of financial markets following the crash of October 1987 had cut deeply into profit margins. The optimism that had encouraged banks to enter into extravagant corporate shopping sprees in the early to mid-1980s (Reid 1988) had all but disappeared after the trauma of 1987, as banks were forced to recognise that the value of corporate investments could go down as well as up. The lures of buying into a new, more competitive market were easier to resist second time round.

However, this line of reasoning may perhaps overstate the degree to which restraint had penetrated the boardrooms of the large international banks which operated, or hoped to operate, on the European stage. Even those banks which felt financially sound enough to embark upon a round of substantial merger and acquisition behaviour were faced with some fairly difficult hurdles to overcome. First, the number of banking institutions available for outright purchase remained relatively small (Molyneux 1989), given that national governments are inherently nervous of domestic banks falling into the hands of foreign owners. (The tendency to see foreign purchases of major national banks as unacceptable extends even

to the United Kingdom, which in most other respects has been the
European state which has demonstrated most enthusiasm for the exposure
of economic agents to international market forces.) The nervousness
associated with foreign takeovers of domestic banks would seem to be
a product of the role banks play within the credit system, giving rise to
chauvinistic fears that elements of control over national money will slip
into foreign hands.[11] In addition to such national regulatory barriers, the
multinational capital adequacy ratios recently introduced by the Bank
for International Settlements (BIS) have also served to make large capital
outlays more difficult (Hall 1990). Under these new rules, by the end
of December 1990 every bank which operated in international markets
and was based in a country whose regulatory authorities participated in the
formation of the BIS conditions (apart from the Japanese banks, who had
until March 1991) was required to have a minimum capital to assets ratio
of 7.25 per cent, rising to a ratio of 8 per cent by 1993 (Lewis and Marsh
1990). Although compared with US and Japanese banks, most European
banks appeared relatively cash rich with ratios well in excess of the minimum standards (*The Economist* 1991), the need to cast a more prudent
eye over the use of valuable capital militated against extensive rounds of
capital centralisation. These various constraints combined to make merger
and acquisition a less important phenomenon than it would have been
in an earlier era. As Gardener and Molyneux have argued, the new
BIS regulations represent 'probably the most severe restriction on major
banking acquisitions across Europe. . . . The deductibility from Tier 1
capital of any premium (or goodwill) above the asset value acquired in an
acquisition is likely to precipitate a need for fresh capital' (1990: 213).

In this context, the striking of alliances with financial institutions in other
countries provides a viable alternative to extending operations into new
EC markets through the pursuit of strategies of organic growth. The construction of new branch networks with EC banking markets would be an
extremely expensive undertaking, and unlikely to pay off in anything
but the very long term.[12] The striking of co-operative agreements between
financial service firms from different countries facilitates the introduction
of their financial products into national financial service markets through
established domestic financial service providers, avoiding the heavy costs
involved in the outright acquisition of distribution networks or in the
construction of distribution networks through the pursuit of organic growth
strategies. This was certainly one of the reasons which underlay the alliances
struck between insurance companies and banks at both an intranational and
an international level, as insurance companies aligned themselves to banks
who could provide them with a ready-made distribution network through
which they could sell complementary but not competing financial products
(Cockburn 1989).

Examples of such linkups were many and varied. The number of alliances
struck between financial service firms led in some cases to a quite complex
intermeshing of links and interests among European financial institutions

(Figure 3.2). From the late 1980s onwards, the threads of agreement and co-operation began to be cast much further afield as non-EC financial institutions began to position themselves within the European market through similar processes of alliance building with European financial service firms.

The growing number of links between non-EC and EC financial institutions was also driven by fears of reciprocity clauses included in the main EC Financial Service Directives, which enabled the EC to impose reciprocal levels of discrimination against financial service firms from

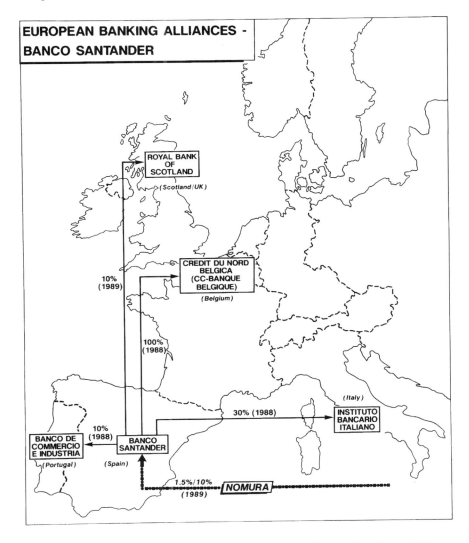

Figure 3.2 European banking alliances: (a) Banco Santander (Spain); (b) Hambros (UK)

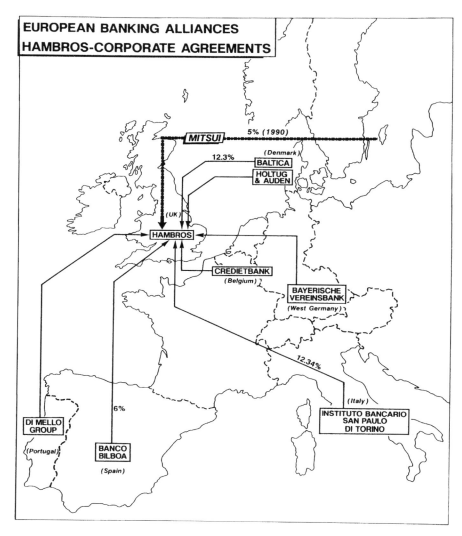

Figure 3.2 (continued)

those non-EC countries judged to have discriminated against EC financial institutions within their financial markets. However, these reciprocity clauses were not to be retrospective, so institutions established in the community prior to the creation of the Single Market cannot be discriminated against even if reciprocity is not achieved after 1992. Hence, non-EC financial institutions eagerly sought entry into Europe in order to guard against their possible exclusion from the new market, adopting the same process of alliance building and share exchange described earlier, for much the same reasons of caution and cost.

A new spatial order? 1992 and the geography of European money

The advent of the Single European Market in financial services was clearly responsible for ushering in a protracted round of corporate restructuring among financial institutions. However, the spatial implications of this round of restructuring were often fairly limited. This is because not all international financial service firms organise their operations according to the same spatial rationale (Diacon 1990). In general terms, it can be argued that those financial institutions which operate primarily within the wholesale, corporate-orientated financial markets tend to run a 'global strategy', within which operations in different countries are co-ordinated in relation to one another. These operations tend to be highly geographically concentrated within the key financial centres of individual countries, and serve to channel flows of capital and information from one centre to another. This form of organisation is typical of large investment banks and securities firms. However, those international financial service firms which operate primarily within retail financial markets tend to operate what can be described as 'multi-domestic strategies', where 'competition in one country is essentially independent of competition in other countries' (Diacon 1990: 209). In other words, retail-orientated financial service firms build up distribution networks for the sale of financial products tailored to particular national and regional markets. This form of organisation is typical of the insurance and retail banking industries.

These organisationally specific spatial rationales help us to understand why the geography of European finance will not be subject to a process of radical spatial reorientation in the 1990s. First let us consider the spatial organisation of wholesale financial markets in Europe. The geography of these markets has long been dominated by the City of London, the importance of which in the co-ordination of the global credit system has seen it overshadow its nearest European competitors. The extent of the City's financial supremacy within Europe is graphically revealed in Table 3.3. However, it was anticipated by some commentators that the process of regulatory restructuring unleashed by the 1992 programme would lead to a progressive deconcentration of certain types of wholesale financial market (Dale 1990). In particular, it was expected that the harmonisation of regulatory structures would have the effect of eroding many of the operational advantages traditionally enjoyed by European financial service firms conducting business in the City of London. Dale estimated that because of tax variations between Germany and the United Kingdom around '30 per cent of the turnover of German government bonds, 50 per cent of the turnover in international DM straight issues, 80–90 per cent of the turnover of DM floating rate notes and 15–20 per cent of turnover in . . . German equities takes place in London' (1990: 8). Financial activity generated in other European countries also migrated to the City for similar reasons. Therefore, the harmonisation of regulation was widely

Table 3.3 Financial centres and financial markets in Europe: market
capitalisation of listed domestic equities, 1986-9

Country	Exchange[a]	Market capitalisation at year end				Percentage share 1989 [b]
		1986	1987	1988	1989	
Belgium	Brussels	25,146	23,013	32,487	48,815	0.7
Denmark	Copenhagen	11,744	10,840	29,353	23,730	0.4
France	Paris	116,667	92,117	123,729	226,671	3.5
Germany	FoE	178,791	116,710	139,307	227,939	3.5
Greece	Athens	763	2,393	2,380	na	na
Ireland	Dublin	3,389	3,267	5,298	7,476	0.1
Italy	Milan	95,859	64,425	75,245	105,622	1.6
Luxembourg	Luxembourg	na	3,828	4,662	6,353	0.1
Netherlands	Amsterdam	56,721	46,106	63,036	95,886	1.5
Portugal	Lisbon	na	3,320	4,662	6,411	0.1
Spain	Madrid	31,544	38,399	50,300	76,267	1.2
Sweden	Stockholm	46,365	41,156	55,617	74,000	1.1
Switzerland	Zurich	87,664	68,301	77,768	na	na
United Kingdom	ISE	304,865	349,239	377,162	507,159	7.7
Total		956,518	863,114	1,041,007	1,511,052	23.1

Source: International Stock Exchange (1990: table 4.1)

[a] FoE Federation of Exchanges; ISE International Stock Exchange
[b] Percentage share of global market capitalization 1989
na not available

expected to encourage the repatriation of certain types of financial
business activity away from the City of London and back to European
financial centres such as Frankfurt, Amsterdam and Paris, because the
conduct of business in London would no longer present the same obvious
cost advantages. However, the 1992 programme also acted as the catalyst
for a series of processes which served to reinforce and even to deepen the
concentration of wholesale financial markets within the City of London.

As one example, the City of London has long been Europe's leading
centre for corporate finance activity, a position which the City acquired
through the active role in developing this market played by the City's
merchant banks, the disproportionate size of the City's capital markets,
and the fact that corporate control is seen to reside entirely with shareholders, all making for a deep, liquid and transparent market in equities,
in stark contrast to other core European economies (Franks and Mayer
1990). As we have seen in our analysis of the financial sector, the advent
of the Single Market programme encouraged extensive rounds of capital
centralisation, processes which were replicated across a wide range of
industrial sectors in Europe. Much of the deal making which accompanied
these processes of capital centralisation was conducted in the City, for
two main reasons. First, the openness and transparency of the UK capital
markets meant that British firms were easier to buy than other EC firms.

For example, the proportion of money expended on the purchase of UK companies in 1989 represented 48 per cent of the total volume of money invested in the purchase of companies in nine leading EC countries (Table 3.4). The 20,832 million ECU expended on the purchase of UK companies made the City an extremely lucrative location for the merger and acquisition departments of international financial institutions. Second, the relatively long history and prominence of the City's market in corporate finance meant that firms active in this market proved highly successful in capturing the increased volume of business in this field generated across the breadth of Europe. The City's financial institutions were not only active in the sale and acquisition of UK companies, but also successfully penetrated the corporate finance markets of other EC markets, often by drumming up business on their own initiative:

> Schroeders, for example, came up with the idea for and advised on Credit Lyonnais's $390m (£201m) purchase of a stake in Credito Bergamasco last year. Warburg advised on the merger of NMB and Postbank in the Netherlands, the acquisition of the Spanish Plus Ultra by the Norwich Union, and the share exchange between Guinness and Louis Vuitton Moet Hennessey. Warburg is also the third biggest player in the domestic French M&A market.
>
> (Waller 1990: 21)

Table 3.4 Cross-border acquisitions in Europe, 1989

Target nation	ECU (million)	Total number of deals [a]	Acquiring nation	ECU (million)	Total number of deals [a]
United Kingdom	29,831.8	237.8	USA	13,802.2	185.1
Germany	5,710.3	215.9	France	9,674.4	167.5
France	5,366.0	191.4	Germany	6,647.0	128.5
Italy	4,121.9	104.1	United Kingdom	5,512.0	281.6
Spain	2,689.4	128.4	Italy	1,681.4	52.0
Netherlands	1,883.3	98.5	Japan	1,481.6	54.6
Belgium	1,285.6	61.5	Sweden	1,381.6	120.7
Sweden	762.1	34.9	Belgium	1,016.3	27.9
Denmark	543.8	34.5	Switzerland	926.4	82.9

[a] Fractions of deals arise from deals being split between more than one nation
Source: de Jonquieres (1990)

Therefore, the high level of corporate finance expertise accumulated within the City of London, and the large number of mergers and acquisitions involving a UK partner, had the effect of generating a lucrative stream of new business for financial institutions based in the City of London. This helped counterbalance the future effects of any tendency towards the repatriation of other types of financial business which had migrated to the City to take advantage of spatial anomalies in regulation.[13] Moreover, the process of regulatory harmonisation contained within the

1992 programme looks set to maintain the existing pattern of spatial concentration over the medium term at least, because the syncretism of regulatory structures makes it more difficult for EC financial centres to attempt to divert new business away from rival centres through a strategy of competitive unilateral reregulation.

Changes in the geography of the retail-orientated financial service industry are likely to be similarly gradual and long term, not least because entry into new national markets has been pursued through strategic alliances and merger and acquisition, rather than through processes of direct entry involving the construction of new distribution networks for the sale of financial products. Such strategies were pursued for reasons of cost and caution, as outlined earlier. But these were not the only reasons. The selling of financial services to individuals is a very different process than is the selling of services to professional investors or corporate treasurers. The selling of personal financial services still relies heavily upon the collection and utilisation of local knowledge, in which the tailoring of services to local tastes and habits is paramount (Davis and Smales 1989). The failure of the Prudential insurance company to break into the UK estate agency business serves as an instructive example of the difficulties that large financial institutions face in breaking into retail-orientated markets (Beaverstock *et al.* 1990). Prior to invasion by large corporations, the organisation of the UK estate agency industry tended to vary spatially, with modes of operation tailored to suit the dynamics of different types of housing market. Moreover, most firms traded heavily upon acquired local reputations. The movement of the Prudential insurance company into the estate agency business, through an extensive round of mergers and takeover activity in which the company absorbed many regional and local estate agency firms, saw the imposition of both a national brand image and a set of standard operating rules through the setting of national rates of commission on sales upon all the firms they bought. The eradication of highly valued local estate agency names with their own operating structures was deemed to be one of the primary reasons why the Prudential suffered disproportionately badly from the downturn in the UK housing market from 1988 onwards, prompting the company to put its entire estate agency chain up for sale towards the end of 1990. This cautionary tale illustrates the difficulty of propounding a thesis that rounds of capital centralisation within the retail financial sector will necessarily generate a radical overhaul of the functional or spatial organisation of such service provision. Even where national retail-orientated financial service firms have been taken over ahead of the creation of the Single Market, it can be anticipated that these firms will continue to enjoy a relatively high level of operational autonomy. Otherwise, the purchase of financial service firms would also risk the loss of local market intelligence through the imposition of inflexible operating procedures from above.

FINANCIAL CONSOLIDATION IN EUROPE: MULTINATIONAL FINANCIAL REGULATION AND EUROPEAN MONETARY UNION

The processes of restructuring described above were corporate responses to the 1992 programme of market liberalisation. However, this programme, and the institutional response it generated, represented only part of the EC's wider bid to remake the order of European financial capital. To some it might appear that the 1992 programme was designed merely to allow financial capital to run untrammelled across the EC. But the liberalisation programme was not a one-way street. The 1992 programme, having served to undermine the traditional national spatial frame of financial regulation, also laid the grounds for the creation of an enlarged spatial frame extending across the then twelve member nations, in which a new structure of monetary regulation could be constituted. By forcing individual European states to surrender control of money and finance at a national level, the 1992 programme may eventually serve to redress the growing empowerment of international financial capital, within the European sphere at least. A single European state would enjoy much greater immunity from the power of financial capital than do the individual European states at present. It is important, therefore, to recognise that the restructuring of financial services in Europe ahead of the 1992 deadline was driven by complex, and often apparently contradictory, processes. On the one hand, there was the explicit drive to harmonise regulation and to free the flow of financial capital across the Community. But on the other hand, there would seem to be an implicit attempt to reassert control over money, because the harmonisation process could undermine the tendency for financial capital to engage in spatial arbitrage within the Community. The harmonisation of regulation would promote the homogeneity of Europe as an investment arena and act as a deterrent to the rapid switching of hot money between European states. Moves towards political and economic union in Europe would further undermine the power of money as the centralisation of political and economic power within a European state would provide another bulwark against the growing power of financial capital and its ability to erode economic sovereignty. Seen in this light, the 1992 programme can be seen as an example of international regulatory co-ordination through which the growing power of financial capital can be countered.[14] There are precedents. It was the European Community which pioneered moves to counter the tendency for financial institutions to free themselves from the shackles of financial regulation through internationalisation when in 1972 it established the 'Groupe de Contact', a forum in which EEC bank regulators could attempt to forge some harmonisation of banking supervision across the Community (Llewellyn 1989). Seen in this context, the liberalisation of money and finance demanded by the 1992 programme can be seen as a means to an end. Individual European nation states are being encouraged to surrender control of national levers of financial regulation.

But in return, they are being offered the implicit bargain of a more rigorous and more effective control of finance exercised by the EC within the European sphere as a whole.

Such processes of consolidation were taken still further in a strategy which ran almost parallel to the 1992 programme; the attempt to further the centralisation of financial and political power in the hands of the EC through European Monetary Union (EMU). On the surface, the EC's advocacy of monetary union was couched in conventional economic language. Without some form of currency union, the argument ran, the full range of economic benefits of the 1992 programme would not be delivered, for regulatory and bureaucratic processes connected with the management of national currencies would serve to distort the operation of an otherwise unified economic system (Eichengreen 1990; Servais 1988). But it was clear that beneath these apparently 'economically rational' arguments, there lay barely concealed hopes that EMU would also deliver to the EC a level of economic and monetary control which had long been lost by all but the most powerful of its member states.

The vehicle which provided the blueprint for union was the European Monetary System (EMS). The EMS was originally set up in 1978 to counter the exchange rate volatility and currency weakness experienced by several EC countries. However the EMS also brought with it prolonged price stability, a consequence of the dominant role in the EMS's exchange rate mechanism played by the Deutschmark, against which all currencies were pegged; the Bundesbank's overriding commitment to price stability was channelled through the EMS. Although the cost of stability was often high in economic and social terms, as countries became locked into a process of 'competitive disinflation' (Wolf 1990), by the end of the 1980s its effects were clearly reflected in the convergence of national rates of inflation in EMS countries around a lower average (Table 3.5). The EMS was seen as being economically successful, in that it helped defend EC currencies from the power of international financial capital in the foreign exchange markets and helped deliver price stability. But in addition, the EMS

Table 3.5 The convergence of annual rates of inflation in EMS member countries, 1980–8

Country	Annual rate of inflation	
	1980	1988
Belgium	6.6	1.2
Denmark	12.3	4.6
France	13.6	2.7
Germany	5.5	1.2
Italy	21.2	5.0
Ireland	18.2	2.1
Netherlands	6.5	0.7

Source : Wolf (1990)

engendered a harmonisation of national monetary policy around the anti-inflationary strategy pursued by the Bundesbank.[15] However, there were fears in some quarters that the demands of the 1992 programme might put unbearable strains upon the EMS, as the drive for liberalisation undermined the ability of the member states to exert the necessary level of control over their financial systems to retain the anti-inflationary discipline necessary to maintain exchange rate parities:

> despite the success of the EMS, many of its supporters feared for its future unless the system were strengthened by institutional steps towards economic and monetary union. The Bank of Italy in particular, feared that the planned abolition of exchange controls in most EC countries in 1990 would confront the EMS members with an impossible task of reconciling free trade, full capital mobility, fixed exchange rates and national monetary autonomy.
>
> (Holberton 1989: 3)

Thus the EMS gradually came to be seen not as an end in itself, but just as a stage along a process of economic harmonisation, involving a more explicit linking of monetary policies at a supranational scale, culminating in a process of European Monetary Union. If the EC could achieve monetary union, the elevation of economic and political power beyond the control of individual European states would be complete, and the orchestration of monetary policy would be vested largely in the hands of the EC. In this way, the EC's bid to forge a new economic superpower could be realised, as any single European currency would be backed by a large proportion of world GDP. The report produced by the Delors Committee in April 1989, which presented a three-stage plan towards monetary union, represented the clear statement by the EC that it was determined to pursue a path towards full economic and monetary union, which could be completed before the end of the 1990s. Whether such a programme is eventually triumphant, the chief motive behind it is clear:

> the real spur to currency union ... comes not from contemplations of marginal extra gains in efficiency but from the fear that the current EMS will not long survive complete freedom of international capital and other flows, that *de facto* fixing of exchange rates is not a viable alternative to currency union.
>
> (Franklin 1991: 20)

CONCLUSIONS

In this chapter we have attempted to illustrate that the EC's attempt to restructure European financial capital was characterised by parallel strategies of liberalisation and consolidation. The 1992 programme embodied the strategy of liberalisation, forcing through regulatory harmonisation to liberate previously tightly policed national financial markets. The move towards EMU embodied the strategy of consolidation, although elements of the 1992 programme also pushed in this direction.

At first blush, it may appear that these parallel strategies were complementary. The 1992 programme could be used as a weapon to break the nationally based structure of financial and monetary control in Europe, and the forging of EMU would help remake the European regulatory structure, but on a pan-European scale. The disempowering of financial capital which this would engender would then allow interventionist economic policies to be placed once more on the European agenda. However, in another light, these parallel strategies can be seen to be contradictory. For it is not clear what model of financial organisation the EC wishes to see installed in the European arena.

There are, of course, various forms of financial organisation which encompass different levels of state and financial involvement in the credit creation process (Cox 1986; Zysman 1983). But the liberalisation and consolidation strands seem to be identified with two particularly distinctive forms of financial organisation. The push towards the liberalisation of economic exchange across Europe embodied within the Cecchini Report would seem to be closely identified with the UK model of financial organisation, where activities have traditionally been only lightly regulated and where competition between financial institutions has pushed down the cost of financial transactions. However, within this mode of financial organisation, financial capital is given free rein to assert its dominance over other interests, and in particular over those of productive capital, as witnessed in the periodic but regular accusations from the manufacturing sector and its representatives that the financial sector (usually identified as 'the City') is given to adopting short-term investment policies (National Association of Pension Funds 1990; Plender 1990a, b). The detachment between finance and industry in the United Kingdom is not only an historical phenomenon, a product of the early ascendancy of British financial capital within the world economy which saw international and commercial investments given priority over national and industrial investments (Anderson 1987; Ingham 1984), but it is also a product of its orientation towards disintermediated credit in highly competitive financial markets. Competition between financial institutions undermines their capacity to engage in relatively long-term investments, for in the end, financial institutions are competing with one another on the basis of returns on investment.

This willingness rapidly to restructure investment portfolios is very different from the attitude displayed by financial institutions within the German banking system, which is most closely aligned to the strategy of consolidation. Here, as described earlier, financial institutions have traditionally taken a much longer perspective on return on capital investment, often because financial institutions are the single largest shareholder in companies. The alignment of interests between financial and productive capital has underpinned the remarkable growth of Germany in the postwar era, as financial institutions have facilitated a steady stream of relatively cheap intermediated credit for long-term investment in productive capacity.

It is perhaps no coincidence that financial and productive capital enjoys a similar intimacy in Japan, where the *Keiretsu* groups have facilitated the forming of close relationships between banks and their industrial clients (Goldsmith 1983; Hayes and Hubbard 1990; Scott 1986), underpinning the remarkable transformation in the productive capacity of that country.

Indeed, on a global scale, this form of financial organisation might seem to be best suited to a new fourth period of credit creation which appeared to be forming in the late 1980s and early 1990s. The inflationary pressures generated by the credit surge of the 1980s resulted in the raising of interest rates within the largest industrialised economies. This, combined with the more stringent capital to asset ratios imposed by the Bank for International Settlements, served to make credit not only more expensive but also more difficult to raise. In an era of relative credit shortage, one would anticipate industrial borrowers seeking to establish longer-term relationships with banks from which they could gain access to relatively long-term and relatively cheap credit.

However, it is unlikely that this model of financial organisation will be generalised across Europe during the 1990s and beyond. The German banking system is able to produce relatively cheap credit for its industrial borrowers through a process of cross-subsidisation, by channelling retail deposits into industrial loans. This is only profitable because of the existence of strong forms of structural regulation within the German banking system which serve to limit the returns on investment enjoyed by retail investors. However, the 1992 programme will prise open these markets letting in financial institutions offering more competitive returns on investment, which will eventually force German banks to do the same. Thus, cross-subsidisation is likely to prove increasingly untenable, cutting off the flow of cheap and long-term funds to the industrial sector.

In such an event, the struggle between the forces of liberalisation and consolidation would result in a decisive victory for the liberalisation camp. The transformation of the German financial system from one based on a *finance* capital model to one which more clearly resembled the *financial* capital model of the United Kingdom (which the liberalisation programme seems sure to bring about) will make the task of bringing money back under control within the EC all the more difficult. The EC will certainly succeed in its bid to remake financial capital in Europe. But in what form? The generalisation of the UK model of financial organisation across the rest of the EC is not a particularly edifying prospect.

CHAPTER 4

'SEXY GREEDY'

The new international financial system, the City of London and the south east of England

INTRODUCTION

There's ugly greedy and sexy greedy, you dope.
At the moment you're ugly which is no hope.
If you stay ugly, god knows what your fate is.
But sexy greedy *is* the late eighties.[1]

This chapter is concerned with the urban and regional impacts of an international financial centre upon its immediate hinterland. More particularly, it considers some of the economic and social effects of the City of London upon the south east of England in the 1980s. In a short chapter like this one it is not possible to catalogue all of the effects of the City on the South East (see Leyshon *et al.* 1987). Instead we have chosen to examine the effects flowing from the concentration of the City's labour market on wealth generation and class formation.

In order to get to the point where it is possible to examine these effects it is first necessary to outline briefly the genesis and functioning of the 'new international financial system' (NIFS) in the 1980s (chapter 2, this volume), how and why this system has led to changes in the City of London (the so-called 'Big Bang' or 'City Revolution') and what these changes have consisted of. This outline makes up the first major section of the chapter.

The second major section of the chapter considers how the changes in the City have affected its labour market, especially by making it more international and more remunerative. In particular, it will be argued that the boost to City incomes has led to considerable generation of wealth which has had direct impacts upon class formation.

This argument leads to the third major section of the chapter which considers how the City triptych of labour market change, wealth generation and class formation can be translated into the arena of the south east of England. In particular, a direct connection will be made between this triptych and the pre-eminence of the South East within the British space economy via the demand for goods and services.

To summarise, this chapter attempts to forge a set of links between the restructuring of banking and commercial capital on the international scale

(Ingham 1984; Thrift 1987c) and social and economic change on the national and subnational scales. The argument is set out in schematic form in Figure 4.1.

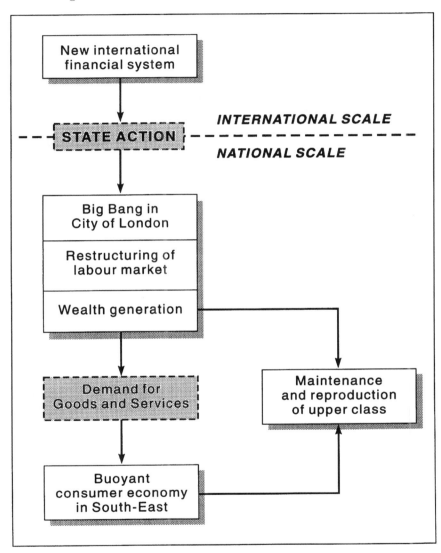

Figure 4.1 The argument in this chapter

NIFS, STATE ACTION, BIG BANG

Since Big Bang the floor is bare,
They deal in offices on the screens.
But if the chap's not really there
You can't be certain what he means.

Crisis and change

Since the early 1980s the world's financial markets have undergone a process of restructuring which has resulted in the emergence of a new international financial system (NIFS). This new phase in the development of the international financial system has been characterised by a radical change in the nature and direction of international capital flows. The new era is also characterised by a further erosion of Pax Americana and the continued economic advance of Japan (Nomura Research Institute, 1986).

The emergence of the NIFS marks a second major phase in the restructuring of the world's financial markets since the Second World War. The restructuring process has served to break down the closely regulated international financial regime which was dominated by the United States for the bulk of the postwar period. This first phase of this process hinged upon the decline of the value of the dollar in the late 1960s and the emergence of differential national rates of inflation. This led directly to the abandonment of the dollar's convertibility into gold in 1971 and also to the subsequent dismantling of the Bretton Woods regime, which ushered in a period of floating exchange rates and volatility in the world's financial markets. The catalyst for the second phase of restructuring and the formation of the NIFS was the developing country debt crisis of the late 1970s and early 1980s which dramatically altered the provision of international debt, and had far-reaching consequences for borrowers and financial institutions alike.

From debt crisis to closed financial system

At the heart of the developing country debt crisis was the recycling of the 'petrodollars' of the oil-producing states into loans for Third World sovereign borrowers. Following the 1973 price rise by the OPEC nations the international banks performed intermediary roles in the redistribution of the funds that flowed from the oil-producing states to the euromarkets based in London. The international banks banded together in lending syndicates to redistribute the capital to Third World sovereign borrowers. By 1979 the volume of syndicated loans arranged in the euromarkets reached $80 billion (Plender and Wallace 1985).

However, the organisation of debt in this way fell apart in the early 1980s, hitting both borrowers and intermediaries. Developing debtor countries were severely affected by the worldwide deflationary trends that followed the oil price fall from 1981 onwards, which brought in its wake high real interest rates and damaging new repayment obligations. Furthermore, the monetarist policy of the Reagan administration and its expansion of the US budget deficit simultaneously pushed interest rates higher and strengthened the dollar, which further increased the real repayment cost of dollar-denominated debt. Consequently, borrowers started to suspend repayments in 1982. In doing so they immediately revealed the vulnerability of the leading lending banks who had become dangerously exposed to repayment default as a result both of their imprudence in lending and their involvement in oversyndication. By 1984 some thirty-five sovereign borrowers were unable to service their debt (Plender and Wallace 1985).

The debt crisis abruptly ended the recycling of capital from the First to the Third World and created a closed financial system where funds are transferred predominantly between western industrialised nations. The restriction of capital flows resulted from the behaviour of the three principal groups involved in the organisation of debt – banks, borrowers and investors. First, to prevent any further entanglement within the crisis, banks stopped lending money to Third World sovereign borrowers by effectively drawing up a blacklist of states (Lim 1986). Second, in the wake of the crisis, many banks suffered a decline in their credit-worthiness ratings, so that western sovereign borrowers and multinational corporations discovered it was they that were the better investment risk and that debt could be obtained on better and more flexible terms by approaching investors directly rather than by going through the intermediation of a bank. The growth of disintermediation has seen the issuing of interest-bearing bonds become the principal form in which international debt is now organised. For example, between 1983 and 1985 the volume of international lending rose from $76.7 to $167.7 billion, with the proportion of debt obtained in the form of bonds rising from 65 per cent to 81 per cent of the total (OECD 1986). Third, the securitisation of debt has been bolstered by investors who have preferred not to deposit capital within the commercial and money centre banks directly embroiled in the debt crisis but instead to lend directly to borrowers via the purchase of bonds and securities, representing a 'flight to quality' (Plender and Wallace 1985). In this way the euroloan was replaced by the eurobond as the principal instrument of international debt provison. The retention of capital within the First World system has been such that the developing nations are now net exporters of capital. For example, since 1982 international banks have received $100 billion net from South America in the form of interest and amortisation payments (Lawless 1987).

Investor power

Of the three groups mentioned above – banks, borrowers and investors – it is the investors that are the driving force behind the NIFS. Pension funds and insurance companies have amassed large capital funds that need to be invested to cover future disembursements, and have developed into highly professional institutional investment vehicles. They are responsible for over two-thirds of the funding on most stock exchanges and exercise considerable customer power. The search for high-quality investments has seen the institutions become increasingly international in their investment

outlook. Although all the western industrial nations have their own institutional investors, by far the most important in the NIFS are the Japanese.
In 1985 Japan became the world's leading creditor nation, and its investments in foreign securities totalled some $128 billion (Nomura Research
Institute 1986). The outflow of money from Japan has been further
stimulated by the success of Japanese multinational corporations who have
sought investment outlets for their cash surpluses at home. The inability
of the Japanese economy to absorb all this money has seen corporate
profits and the funds of investment institutions increasingly forced overseas. The securities investments of these organisations are immense (Table
4.1). The flow will inevitably increase still further in future as the progressive deregulation of the Japanese financial system results in the lifting
of the present ruling that allows life insurance companies to invest only
25 per cent of their assets abroad (Marsh 1986). Consequently, Japan's
gross balance of overseas assets was expected to surpass $1 trillion by 1995
(Nomura Research Institute 1986).

Table 4.1 Security assets held by leading Japanese institutional investors,
March 1986

	$bn
Trust banks	
Sumitomo Trust and Banking	50.56
Mitsubishi Trust and Banking	48.209
Mitsui Trust and Banking	38.542
Yasuda Trust and Banking	33.170
Toyo Trust and Banking	28.399
Chuo Trust and Banking	20.490
Nippon Trust and Banking	6.614
Life insurance companies	
Nippon Life Insurance	29.314
Dai-Ichi Life Insurance	17.144
Sumitomo Life Insurance	16.170
Meiji Mutual Life Insurance	10.876
Asahi Mutual Life Insurance	9.490
Yasuda Life Insurance	6.046
Taiyu Life	4.876
Non-life insurance	
Tokio Marine and Fire Insurance	6.268
Yasuda Fire and Marine Insurance	3.654
Others	
Daiwa Bank	47.281
Norinchukin Bank	67.739
Kampo	95.719

Source: Adapted from *Euromoney* (1987a: 123)

The global centralisation of financial services

In the past decade, the emergence of the NIFS has brought about a considerable realignment in the rankings of leading international banks (Table 4.2). There have been two main changes. First, there has been a marked decline in the status of US money centre and commercial banks such as Citicorp and BankAmerica whose balance sheets grew fat during the 1970s on the loans they arranged for Third World sovereign borrowers, especially in South America. The leading banks of the NIFS are now Japanese. Their assets are buoyed by the massive foreign earnings of Japanese multinational corporations. Second, the move towards the securitisation of debt has acted in favour of investment banks and securities houses. Prior to the advent of the NIFS, such institutions acted primarily as underwriters and traders of securitised financial instruments such as government securities and equity stock. The securitisation of cross-border international debt has meant that the investment banks and securities houses were well placed to perform a similar role in the eurobond market. The prerequisites for banking success in the NIFS are sufficient capital adequacy to be able to underwrite whatever size bond issue is required by a borrower plus an efficient distribution and sales network able to unload the bonds to investors. These are characteristics more typical of securities houses and investment banks than the euroloan giants of the 1970s.

The transformation of international debt has also meant an upheaval in the relationship between borrower and client banks.[2] Long-term relationship banking has largely been replaced by service-driven links, a process which has ultimately resulted in the centralisation of financial provision among the world's leading banking institutions. The ability to provide an effective securities distribution system and a comprehensive set of financial instruments is an option open only to the largest and most powerful banks.

Technological change

Technological change has played an important part in facilitating the development of the NIFS. Advances in information technology are constantly improving the external and internal efficiency of financial markets (Ayling 1986). The external efficiency of markets is improved by the increasing speed and capacity of financial information systems which enable market participants to make better informed and quicker decisions. Data production and distribution are increasingly subject to computer application and is now supplied 'on-line' to market practitioners by financial information companies.

The internal efficiency of markets is enhanced by improved links between markets, institutions and individuals. Dealing and settlement systems are increasingly being automated while electronic links enable traders to participate in 'remote' trading. In the NIFS, technological

Table 4.2 The world's largest banking institutions by market capitalisation, 1976–86

1976		1981		1986	
1 BankAmerica Corp (US)	4,404.79	1 Dai-Ichi Kangyo Bank (Jap)	5,020.46	1 Sumitomo Bank (Jap)	35,366.53
2 Citicorp (US)	4,085.92	2 Fuji Bank (Jap)	4,963.50	2 Nomura Securities (Jap)	33,909.82
3 Union Bank of Switzerland (Swi)	2,455.60	Sumitomo Bank (Jap)	4,963.50	3 Industrial Bank of Japan (Jap)	33,909.82
4 Deutsche Bank (WG)	2,158.47	4 Mitsubishi Bank (Jap)	4,933.11	4 Dai-Ichi Kangyo Bank (Jap)	29,639.09
5 Credit Suisse (Swi)	1,914.10	5 Sanwa Bank (Jap)	4,933.11	5 Fuji Bank (Jap)	27,200.68
6 Nomura Securities (Jap)	1,755.88	6 Union Bank of Switzerland (Swi)	4,663.01	6 Mitsubishi Bank (Jap)	27,059.13
7 Sumitomo Bank (Jap)	1,746.70	7 Nomura Securities (Jap)	4,130.58	7 Sanwa Bank (Jap)	21,948.05
8 Mitsubishi Bank (Jap)	1,734.53	8 Industrial Bank of Japan (Jap)	3,677.60	8 Sumitomo Trust Banking Co. (Jap)	16,875.50
9 Sanawa Bank (Jap)	1,734.53	9 Credit Suisse (Swi)	3,281.30	9 Mitsubishi Trust Banking Co. (Jap)	16,750
10 Dai-Ichi Kangyo Bank (Jap)	1,731.55	10 Swiss Bank Corp Int. (Swi)	3,240.57	10 Union Bank of Switzerland (Swi)	15,040
11 Fuji Bank (Jap)	1,722.36	11 Deutsche Bank (WG)	2,871	11 Deutsche Bank (WG)	13,816.63
12 Dresdner Bank (WG)	1,502.09	12 Long Term Credit Bank (Jap)	2,637.56	12 Long Term Credit Bank (Jap)	13,655.43
13 Swiss Bank Corp Int. (Swi)	1,134.35	13 Tokai Bank (Jap)	2,626.19	13 Mitsui Bank (Jap)	13,377.96
14 Industrial Bank of Japan (Jap)	1,224.04	14 Mitsui Bank (Jap)	2,605.91	14 Daiwa Securities (Jap)	13,144.33
15 Long Term Credit Bank (Jap)	1,075.68	15 Barclays Bank (UK)	2,443.70	15 Nikko Securities (Jap)	13,060.41

Source: Euromoney (1987b: 85–95)

change is transforming securities trading from a primarily exchange-based activity into an electronic marketplace conducted within the dealing rooms of financial institutions.

The increasing automation of financial transactions has dramatically increased turnover in financial markets. The number of transactions is increasing for three main reasons. First, the development of automatic execution systems for the trading of small lots of securities speeds up dealing as it eliminates the need for counterparties to contact one another. Second, turnover is being increased by the progressive introduction of 'expert systems' in financial trading that will automatically alert dealers to profit-making opportunities as they arise in the market. Third, the reduction in execution time and in costs facilitated by technological application encourages institutional investors to become more 'active' in their management of investment portfolios, a tendency which is further encouraged by banks who are bidding for the right to restructure the entire portfolio of investment fund managers.

New markets and capital substitution in the NIFS

The interaction of technological change and securitisation has spawned a series of new financial markets as financial instruments are increasingly transformed into tradable commodities. Relatively recent innovations such as financial futures and options are now commonplace in the NIFS. There is even a secondary market in Third World sovereign debt where developing country borrowing repayments can be purchased at a discount of the original loan (French 1987). However, perhaps the most important new market in the NIFS has been the emergent 'swap' market which is bringing about an increasingly integrated world financial system. The burgeoning swap market is a largely unregulated market that emerged during the early 1980s. A swap is a financial transaction in which two parties agree to exchange a predetermined series of payments over time (Hammond 1987) which serves to circumnavigate market imperfections and inefficiencies:

> Since their inception, swaps have been used to arbitrage different perceptions of credit risk; different perceptions of interest rate risk and exchange rate risk; imperfections arising from systems of taxation, regulation or accountancy; differential access to information; market illiquidity; and transaction costs.
>
> (Hammond 1987: 66)

The earliest swaps were currency based and were used to arbitrage between different financial regulatory environments. However, currency swaps have been surpassed in volume by interest rate swaps which pivot upon the different credit perceptions of borrowers between segmented markets. For example, while the volume of outstanding currency swaps rose from $2-3 billion to $80-100 billion between 1982 and 1986, the volume of outstanding interest rate swaps rose from $2–3 billion to $350 billion over the same period (Hammond 1987). The rise to dominance of interest rate swaps has been paralleled by a tendency for intermediary banks to build up portfolios of swaps, rather than, as previously, enter into a series of matched deals (*Euromoney* 1987c). The portfolio or 'warehousing' approach means that banks will arrange interest rate swaps for clients without possessing immediate offsetting agreements. This development has encouraged the rise of a secondary swap market and the transformation of the interest rate swap into a tradable instrument (Hammond 1987). The swaps market is dominated by a handful of predominantly US financial institutions (*Euromoney* 1987c) and the ten leading banks accounted for some 70 per cent of all activity in the market during 1986 (Hammond 1987).

The success of the swap is based upon its capacity to overcome market imperfections. Swaps allow borrowers to engage in transnational capital substitution by removing imposed market variations. By allowing such substitution swaps can be seen as an important driving force in creating a more integrated global market.

Spatial centralisation of financial activity

Despite the fact that technological advance is increasing the locational capacity of financial activity as never before, there is in fact a process of spatial concentration under way. In particular, activity is concentrating in three major centres – New York, Tokyo and London. This process is a reversal of the trend of the 1970s when there was a multiplication of financial centres and a general lessening of the disparity between centres (Browning 1986). The three major centres accounted for almost 50 per cent of all international banking activity in 1985 (Table 4.3), and are the largest capitalised stock markets in the world (Figure 4.2). This concentration of activity arises first because of the role each centre performs as a regional financial centre – New York for North America, Tokyo for Asia and the Pacific, and London for Europe (and the euromarkets) – and second, because of their strategic locations within different time zones. Their respective positions allow for a continuous global market to develop where transactions can be pursued twenty-four hours a day by passing on deals from market to market. For example, in a working day lasting from 6.00 a.m. to 6.00 p.m. communications and dealing technology enable a dealer based in London to catch the end of trading on the Tokyo exchange, trade through the entire working hours of the London market and work for over half the hours of the New York exchange. Although only foreign exchange dealing is a truly developed, twenty-four-hour global market at present, other markets such as secondary trading in eurobonds, international equities and futures are increasingly becoming so (Figure 4.3).

Table 4.3 The three premier world financial centres

	London	New York	Tokyo
Foreign banks	399	254	76
Foreign Stock Exchange members	22	33	6
Share of international banking (1985, %)	24.9	15	9.1
Share of foreign exchange turnover (1984, %)	32.6	22.3	5.3
Stock market turnover (1985, £bn)	52.8	671.3	271.5
Stock market capitalisation (1985, £bn)	244.7	1,302.2	648.7

Source: Price (1986: 16)

Evidence for this spatial concentration is displayed in Figure 4.4 which shows the office locations of seventeen leading investment banks and securities houses in 1985–6. The dominance of the three centres as locational bases is clear. The consequences of this process of spatial concentration are that the three premier cities are increasingly becoming the 'transactional centres' of the NIFS, while other financial centres are increasingly becoming important for their business generation capacity and as sales outlets.

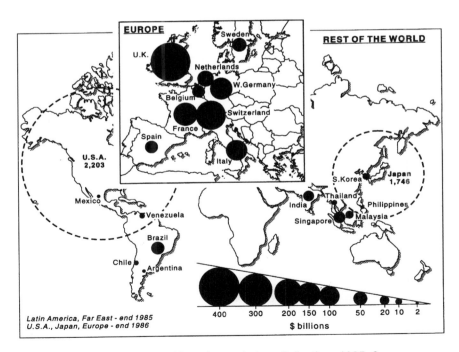

Figure 4.2 World equity market capitalisation, 1985–6

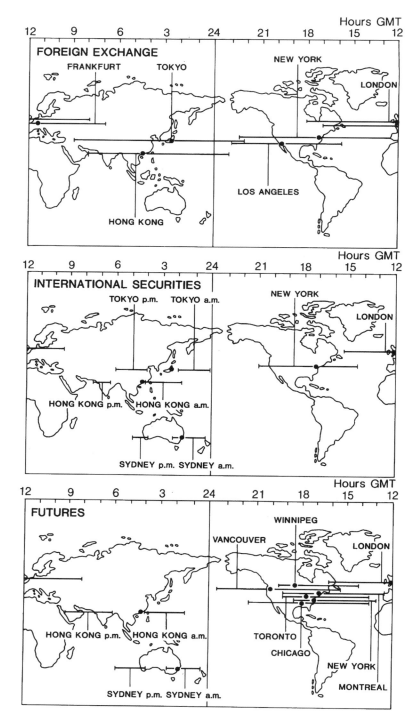

Figure 4.3 Global trading in three financial markets
Source: Clarke (1986a: 119–21)

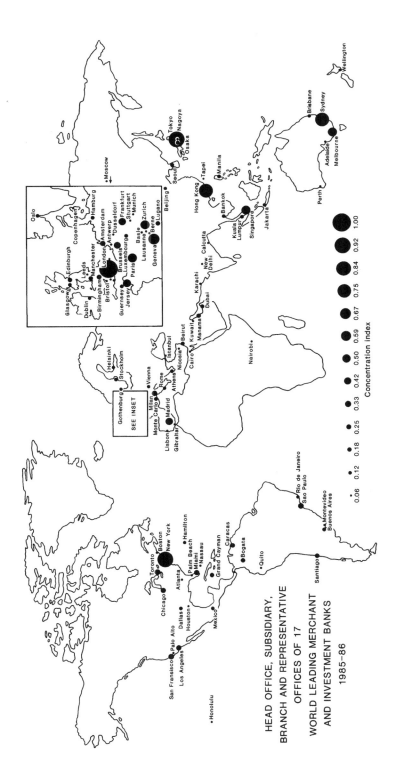

Figure 4.4 Office locations of seventeen leading investment banks

To summarise, the rise of the NIFS has seen a move towards the greater integration of the world's financial markets. Facilitated by technological advances and the behaviour of international financial institutions, banking and commercial capital is becoming ever more transnational. The ability of individual governments to control capital flows has been seriously undermined in this new environment. Indeed, even the setting of strictly internal financial measures such as interest rates can be overcome in the NIFS by the ability of financial institutions to create 'synthetic' government securities through the utilisation of the swap market and capital substitution. The interest rates on these securities will therefore be linked much more closely to sentiment in the global market than that of any local domestic economy (see Goodhart 1987). This externalisation of financial control effectively means that the controlling functions formerly performed by central bankers have been subjugated to the market. In effect, regulatory authority has been privatised (Plender 1987).

The impact of the NIFS on financial centres

For most of the postwar period regulatory controls in financial centres have been nationally based, instigated by governments who have wanted to establish orderly domestic markets (Price 1986). The most common forms of regulation are controls of external capital flows (exchange controls), limits on interest rates and the separation of markets and practitioners into clearly divided functions. The latter form of regulation purposely segments and partitions financial markets. For example, until October 1986, entirely separate roles were performed in the UK by commercial banks, merchant banks, stockbrokers, stockjobbers and building societies.

However, changes in international markets associated with the emergence of the NIFS have made the operation of closely regulated domestic markets increasingly untenable. First, the broadening horizons of the investment institutions have led to capital flows becoming increasingly mobile and international as funds have sought investment outlets based on a risk/return allocational criterion rather than on an administrative rationale. Consequently, funds have began to move towards less highly regulated financial markets. Second, the advent of securitisation and disintermediation has effectively fused the activities of debt provision with that of securities trading. However, the rigorous division of these activities insisted upon in many domestic financial markets meant that many institutions were hamstrung in their ability to adapt to the changes unfolding around them, since they were usually allowed to engage in banking or in securities trading but not in both. Third, and finally, the ability of regulatory authorities to control the activities within financial markets has been progressively undermined by the increasing application of new technology. Technological advances and volatility within financial markets have given birth to a plethora of new financial instruments (see Table 4.4) beyond the control (and frequently beyond the comprehension) of the regulators.

Table 4.4 US financial innovations, 1970–82

Types	Exogenous causes*							
	(a)	(b)[1]	(c)	2	3	4	5	6
A Cash management								
1 Money market mutual funds	*							
2 Cash management/sweep accounts	*							
3 Money market certificates	*				*			
4 Debit card	*					*		
5 NOW accounts	*				*			
6 ATS accounts	*				*			
7 Point of sale terminals					*			
8 Automated clearing houses					*			
9 CHIPS (same-day settlement)					*			
10 Automated teller machines					*			
B Investment contracts								
(i) Primary market								
1 Floating rate notes				*				
2 Deep discount (zero coupon) bonds	*	*		*				
3 Stripped bonds	*	*		*				
4 Bonds with put options or warrants	*			*				
5 Floating prime rate loans				*				
6 Variable rate mortgages				*				
7 Commodity linked (silver) bonds				*				
8 Eurocurrency bonds	*						*	
9 Interest rate futures				*				
10 Foreign currency futures						*		
11 Cash settlement (stock index) futures				*				
12 Options on futures			*	*				
13 Pass-through securities				*				
(ii) Consumer type								
1 Universal life insurance				*				
2 Variable life policies		*						
3 IRA/Keogh accounts			*	*				
4 Municipal bonds funds			*	*				
5 All-saver certificates	*			*				
6 Equity access account	*			*				
C Market structures								
1 Exchange-traded options								*
2 Direct public sale of securities								
Green Mountain Power Co.				*				
Shelf registration				*		*		
3 Electronic trading								
NASDAQ					*			
GARBAN					*			
4 Discount brokerage						*		
5 Interstate depository institutions					*	*		
D Institutional organization								
1 Investment bankers/ Commodity dealers Salomon/								

cont . . .

Table 4.4 US financial innovations, 1970–82 (continued)

Phibro, Goldman Sachs/ J. Aron, DLJ/ACLI	*		*		
2 Brokers/general finance Shearson/Amex, Bache/Prudential Schwab/ Bank of America					*
3 Thrifts with commercial banks	*		*	*	
4 Financial centres (Sears Roebuck)					*

*Column headings: 1 = inflation; (a) = level of interest rates; (b) = general price level; (c) = tax effects; 2 = volatility of interest rates; 3 = technology; 4 = legislative initiative; 5 = internationalization; 6= other

Source: Kaufman (1986: 22–3)

At the same time transactions have increasingly become electronically based, removing the need for fixed central marketplaces, the traditional powerbase of the regulatory authorities.

Therefore, faced with the combination of the internationalisation of capital, securitisation and new technology, many financial centres realised that survival in the NIFS meant attracting both capital and international financial institutions: attempts to impose stringent controls were becoming less and less effective, and to the degree that they were ultimately self-defeating in that they tended to drive capital away. As a result, the 1980s have seen the worldwide dismantling of domestic financial restrictions. Australia, Canada, Finland, France, Norway, New Zealand, Portugal, Singapore, Sweden, Switzerland, South Korea and West Germany are among those countries that have recently embarked upon the progressive deregulation of their financial systems (A. Hamilton 1986; Ayling 1986). All of these moves have been designed to help capture a share of the burgeoning cross-border financing business in the NIFS. Similar moves have also been made in the three premier world financial centres. There was New York's early abolition of fixed commissions in securities trading in 1975, and the establishment of 'offshore' international banking facilities in 1981 (A. Hamilton 1986). Tokyo too is in the grip of a (slow) process of deregulation that will allow Japanese capital greater access to world financial markets and foreign financial institutions greater access to the Japanese financial market (Marsh 1986). However, it has been within the City of London that adaptation to the conditions of the NIFS has been the most radical, as state-imposed change has forced the complete overhaul of practices within its domestic securities markets.

Deregulation in the City of London

The transformation of the world's financial markets in the wake of the NIFS meant that during the late 1970s and 1980s the City was increasingly placed at a considerable competitive disadvantage. This was for two main reasons. First, the wide-scale application of technology in financial markets served to make the process of capital formation in the UK look both expensive and inefficient because of its exchange-floor-based, single-capacity, fixed-commission system. Given the increased mobility of capital, this threatened the long-term attractiveness of London as an investment outlet. Second, in a period when financial centres worldwide had been loosening regulatory controls, the domestic UK financial system remained sharply balkanised. London's rise to prominence in the 1960s and 1970s was based on the regulation-free environment it offered to international banks operating in the euromarkets. However, when the emphasis in international debt shifted from loans to securities, UK institutions were stymied by their historical compartmentalisation of function and had difficulty in competing with the more diversified European 'universal banks' and the investment banks and securities houses of the United States and Japan which were better suited to the sales-driven orientation of the new securitised environment. However, the UK equivalent to the Japanese and American securities houses, the member firms of the Stock Exchange, remained comfortably cosseted by the large earnings that could be earned in the restricted, fixed-commission domestic securities market, and did not venture too far into the more competitive international arena. At the same time, the weakening pound and the size of the UK domestic market meant that the capitalisation of the internationally orientated British-owned institutions was significantly lower than that of their foreign competitors. As competitive pressure in the international securities market has increased, so *profit margins* have tended to decrease. However, *profit levels* can be maintained by participation in larger deals. However, this option is open only to those organisations that are sufficiently well capitalised to be able to absorb large securities issues without reducing liquidity.

The restructuring of the City of London was a process initiated by state action in 1976 and finally agreed to by the Stock Exchange in 1983.[3] It was designed to overcome the two problems outlined above. The 'Big Bang', as it became known, essentially revolved around a state-enforced transformation of one financial market, the market for domestic securities. However, the restructuring of the equities and gilts market was used as a catalyst for a wider reorganisation of UK financial institutions with the underlying hope that the synergy achieved from the fusion of formerly separate financial institutions would propel UK institutions to the forefront of the NIFS.

The 'new City' was unveiled on 27 October 1986. The totem of change was the scrapping of fixed commissions on all domestic securities trans-actions, a move strongly welcomed by the investment institutions in the equities market and by the state itself in the gilts market. However, this move in turn necessitated other changes. First, under a regime of competitive commissions, the single-capacity system of market-making jobbers and agency brokers was considered to be unworkable. Previously, jobbers had earned income from the difference between the buying and selling prices of stock, while brokers had earned theirs from charges to clients for transactions executed in the market. However, it was felt that brokers would not be able to survive on reduced commission fees alone. Hence, a dual-capacity trading system was introduced where individual firms would be able to perform both market-making and agency roles. This change, in turn, led to a second necessary change: the opening up of the exclusively domestic membership of the Stock Exchange to outside financial institutions. The restrictive nature of the fixed-commission, single-capacity system allowed firms to operate at remarkably low capitalisation levels. Indeed, all member firms had operated as partnerships.

However, in a competitive, dual-capacity regime greater levels of capital would be necessary to allow participation in more frequent and larger deals so as to protect profit levels as margins declined. The necessary injections of capital came from UK and overseas financial institutions who on the announcement of the opening up of the Exchange embarked on a frenzied shopping spree as they anxiously purchased domestic securities expertise within the UK market.

The reformulation of the market was completed by the instigation of a screen-based dealing system. SEAQ (Stock Exchange Automated Quotations), closely modelled on the US over-the-counter electronic dealing system NASDAQ (National Association of Securities Dealing Automatic Quotations), soon removed dealers from the floor of the Exchange into the dealing rooms of the new financial conglomerates.

Impacts of deregulatory change in the City

The restructuring of the market has had two major impacts upon the functioning of the City. First, the centralisation of capital that has already occurred as a result of the balkanisation of the market is likely to increase still further. The overcapacity in the new market is already leading to a shakeout of participants. Before Big Bang the equities market contained five main jobbers and three smaller ones; the new market contained thirty-five market-makers. Similarly, in the gilts market, the two largest jobbers had accounted for over 75 per cent of turnover; the new market contained twenty-seven primary dealers (Farmborough 1987). The scale of over-capacity in the gilts market can be gauged by the fact that although the US government securities market is ten times the size of the UK market it supports only thirty-seven primary dealers (Hewlett and Toporowski 1985). As a result of the increased competition, profits have been slashed as equity transactions have fallen by as much as 50 per cent (Ingram 1987; Barrett 1987). Moreover, a small group of firms has quickly risen to dominance, so that in the equities market the leading ten firms account for 80 per cent of all trading (*The Economist* 1987g). The competition is already beginning to tell. Midland Montagu withdrew from equity market making in March 1987, while Lloyds Bank pulled out of gilts three months later.

Second, although the British banks have entered securities trading for the first time, transforming them into entities that resemble the European universal banks, British purchases were more than matched by foreign buyouts of Stock Exchange firms thus resulting in a sharp increase in the foreign presence in the City. For example, at the time of Big Bang over half of the twenty-seven firms making a market in gilts were overseas institutions. Moreover, in the new highly competitive regime it is the foreign institutions that are expected to be the beneficiaries of the British casualties in the market. It is the British merchant banks suffering from inadequate levels of market capitalisation that are the prime target for takeover, as predators position themselves for bids:

> Hill Samuel is still for sale – two Australians hold almost 27% of it . . . Equiticorp, a New Zealand financial services company, offered £218m ($350m) for the two-thirds of Guiness Peat it does not own . . . Hanson Trust, which specialises in buying companies wholesale and selling them themselves retail, revealed it has a small stake in Morgan Grenfell.
>
> (*The Economist* 1987h: 16)

To summarise, faced with an increasingly internationalised financial system, largely dominated by foreign institutions, there were two options open to the City. It could either have remained firmly behind a barrier of restrictive controls as business steadily migrated elsewhere, or it could attempt to introduce international 'financial best practice' (Goodhart 1987) into its operations. Forced by state pressure into the latter course, the viability of the City as a financial centre has been considerably enhanced.[4] However, it has been at the cost of diminished national involvement in domestic financial transactions.

LABOUR MARKET, WEALTH, CLASS

I told him for what he's getting for my team, why be a meanie,
He got rid of the BMWs and got us each a Lamborghini.

The changes induced by the forced adjustment of the City of London to the NIFS have had numerous urban and regional effects. Many of these have been summarised by us elsewhere,[5] including: the office building boom in the City of London and elsewhere; the effects on the rental and freehold housing markets in London; changes in the level and pattern of commuting in and out of London; multipliers from the expenditure on new technology in the shape of jobs in computing and telecommunications firms; and so on (Leyshon *et al.* 1987). In this chapter we will limit our horizons to three interrelated effects, namely the City's labour market, the generations of wealth and changes in social class.

The City of London labour market

There has always been an international professional and managerial labour market but for numerous reasons it has of late been increasing dramatically in scope. These reasons include: the increasing internationalisation of already multinational corporations (especially as Japanese and European corporations have moved into the United States); the increased propensity to regard an international posting as a vital part of a career in a corporate bureaucracy; and the increase in the number of international financial centres and of jobs in these centres. The case of Britain is distinctive in this regard. Using International Passenger Survey data, Findlay (1987) has shown that there has been a steady increase in the number of professional and managerial workers leaving and re-entering the UK in the 1980s, signifying in the main an increase in short-term job transfers (41 per cent of professional and managerial workers re-entering Britain between 1980 and 1985 had been abroad for less than two years).[6]

A special subset of this professional and managerial labour market is the international labour market for those working in financial services. Of late, this part of the international labour market has been growing particularly rapidly, in line with growth in financial services worldwide (Key 1981). It is particularly orientated to the so-called world cities like London (see Thrift 1986a, 1987c). But until the period leading up to the Big Bang, from 1984 on, the City of London had been able to insulate itself from the international labour market to an extent (see Cobbett 1986). In the early 1960s when one bank managing director went there, all was tradition still:

> 'I started on a stool by a mahogany sloping desk in the postage department, writing every address into a leather-bound book . . . . In those days there were no graduate recruitment schemes. Whether one started from University, school or army, advancement was always from the bottom. Snails would have appreciated the pace of progress, with six months spent in every department over as many years.' Then, Porter recalls, everyone wore his old school tie on Fridays. The reason was never clear.
>
> (Bowen 1986: 39)

The growth in foreign banks coincident with the rise of the eurodollar market in the late 1960s was the first real crack in the clannish, clubbish wall of privilege and tradition surrounding the City's labour practices. Aggressive New Yorkers were suddenly to be found in the confines of the City. The growth of foreign exchange trading following the floating of exchange rates in the early 1970s meant another crack in the wall (the City had to meet the threat by allowing working-class clerical labour with sharp wits to move on to the dealing floors). The growth of the eurobond market in the late 1970s again brought more foreign banks and foreigners into the City. Each of these events meant an increase in the presence of foreign firms in the City (Table 4.5), bringing labour practices foreign to the City with them, and more Britons working abroad and being introduced to foreign labour practices whilst there. However, the events from 1984

Table 4.5 Foreign banks and securities houses in London, 1968–86 (directly represented through a rep. office, branch or subsidiary)

Nationality	1968*		1977		1986	
	No.	Employees	No.	Employees	No.	Employees
USA	24	2,673	103	10,345	101	23,559
Japan	12	487	32	1,177	72	4,500
Others	89	5,936	165	12,772	227	25,774
Total	125	9,096	300	24,294	400	53,833

*Excluded securities houses
Sources: *The Banker*, 1968, 118: 915–23; 1977, 127: 129–77; 1986, 136: 69–132

onwards changed the City labour market irrevocably, fully articulating it into the international labour market and bringing other changes as well. Table 4.6 shows the client characteristics of the City labour market in 1981. Since 1984 this labour market has undergone at least five significant changes. First, there has been a growth of the labour market in simple absolute terms coincident with a general increase in financial services employment and a bull market. Exact numbers are not available but the 25.9 per cent increase in foreign bank employees in 1986, from 42,767 to 53,833, is a particularly dramatic example of this growth.[7] Second, and as already inferred, the labour market has become more international. There are more Americans, Japanese, Europeans, expatriate Britons returning to their homeland. The numbers are quite dramatic. One estimate is that there are 40,000 to 50,000 Japanese in London (Holberton 1987).

Third, the City labour market has become more 'skilled'. Graduate employment in the City has become something of a norm whereas before it was relatively unusual. The City now takes larger and larger numbers of graduates. In 1985 just over 18 per cent of British graduates went into finance, many into the City (see Pagano 1986; O'Leary 1986). Fourth, and related to the third change, the City labour market has become more specialised. There are few generalists now. As financial markets have become more numerous and complex, and as methods of analysing their twists and turns have become more sophisticated, so the demand for specialists has increased, especially those with appropriate qualifications. Maths and natural science graduates are now quite common where before they were almost unheard of:

> Peter, aged 27, is a classic example. He finished his PhD in nuclear physics about two years ago. He is now writing computer programmes for the options trading desk and working on new products for one of the US's biggest investment banks based in London.
>
> (Pagano 1986: 22)

Fifth, the labour market has become much less rigid in terms of mobility. People are more willing to switch jobs. They are not looking for

Table 4.6 The City of London labour market, 1981: employment by SIC (80) division and class

Division	Male		Female		Total	
	No.	%	No.	%	No.	%
Energy and water supply industries	3,275	1.3	1,606	1.1	4,881	1.3
Extraction and manufacture of minerals and metals	695	0.3	410	0.3	1,105	0.3
Metal goods and motor vehicles etc.	3,674	1.5	1,129	0.8	4,803	1.2
Other manufacturing industries	28,034	11.3	6,273	4.4	34,307	8.8
Construction	3,311	1.3	203	0.1	3,514	0.9
Distribution, hotels and catering; repairs	20,026	8.1	12,912	9.0	32,938	8.4
Transport and communications	48,098	19.4	11,892	8.3	59,990	15.4
Banking, finance, insurance, leasing, etc.	114,570	46.3	81,491	57.0	196,061	50.2
(of which)						
Banking and finance	47,861	19.3	37,772	26.4	85,633	21.9
Insurance, not compulsory social security	16,205	6.5	9,711	6.8	25,916	6.6
Business services	49,404	20.0	33,361	23.3	82,765	21.2
Retailing of movables	224	0.1	56	0.1	280	0.1
Owning and dealing in real estate	876	0.4	591	0.4	1,467	0.4
Other services	25,676	10.4	26,902	18.8	52,578	13.5
Unclassifed by industry	138	0.1	91	0.1	229	0.1
Total	247,497	100.0	142,909	100.0	390,406	100.0

Source: Census of Employment (1981)

a sinecure but for early responsibility and 'serious money'. The issue of 'serious money' leads to the next subsection.

The generation of wealth

Initially, wage rates in the City labour market had been cheap by international standards. However, during the 1980s this situation began to change. Salaries began to catch up with those in other international financial centres (Table 4.7). There were four main reasons for this narrowing of the wages gap. First, with the increase in the permeability of the City labour market to the international financial labour market,

Table 4.7 Rates of pay in international financial centres in 1986

City	National head of department ($pa)
1 Geneva	100,767
2 New York	93,860
3 Brussels	80,410
4 Frankfurt	80,197
5 Vienna	79,617
6 Paris	79,167
7 The Hague	74,918
8 Stockholm	68,302
9 Copenhagen	67,383
10 Rome	65,659
11 Oslo	60,458
12 Luxembourg	61,736
13 Helsinki	57,146
14 *London*	*52,194*
15 Madrid	47,675
16 Dublin	43,228
17 Athens	28,505
18 Lisbon	22,542

Source: Taylor (1987)

there was bound to be some levelling up of salaries, as too many people were re-entering Britain with raised financial expectations:

> London has been lagging behind its rivals, New York and Tokyo, for several years in the level of renumeration being paid. Finance is one of the most international of all trading commodities and it was clear that employers would eventually have to pay the guy dealing in equities in London, earning perhaps £20,000 five years ago, the quadrupled salary level his equal in New York would be earning.
>
> (Pagano 1986: 22)

Second, substantial skill shortages became apparent as the new markets of the NIFS (e.g. swaps, caps, or swap options) flickered into existence,[8] as existing markets (e.g. dealers in eurobonds) expanded, and as the rate of technological change hotted up (e.g. software writers). This phenomenon was only helped by increased specialisation. Third, firms, especially large foreign firms, began to bid for this labour, often quite frantically. In doing so, they forced the level of salaries up. Fourth, information on the labour market became easier to find. As salaries become an important issue, so several specialist firms have started up supplying information on the going rates for different kinds of employee (Table 4.8). Fifth and finally, people working in the City themselves became more aware of their worth:

> banks, brokers and dealers (scrambled) over each other in the mad dash to double salaries overnight by offering themselves – or teams – to rival firms.

Table 4.9 Full-time adult rates of pay, in the City of London, the South East and Britain 1986

	City of London			South East (excl. Central London)			Britain		
	10% earned less than	Average	10% earned more than	10% earned less than	Average	10% earned more than	10% earned less than	Average	10% earned more than
All males	152.8	340.0	579.5	113.2	212.8	332.7	111.4	207.5	320.8
Non-manual males	157.9	365.2	629.0	124.9	247.2	384.5	124.6	244.9	383.2
Manual males	133.4	248.7	395.4	107.2	175.8	254.6	105.5	174.4	253.9
All females	122.9	201.8	301.0	81.9	138.3	207.6	80.3	137.2	209.8
Non-manual females	126.7	204.6	303.7	86.3	145.0	216.5	85.0	145.7	219.7
Manual females	na	na	na	71.2	109.2	156.1	69.9	107.5	151.3

Source: Department of Employment (1986)

Salaries over £100,000 are now fairly common in the following jobs: corporate finance senior executive, corporate finance specialist, project finance manager, bonds origination manager, bonds marketing executive, euronotes marketing executive, bonds sales/traders, equity funds manager, leasing senior manager (Remuneration Economics 1987). One estimate is that in August, 1986, about 2,000 people were earning £100,000 plus salaries, most of them drawn from the marzipan layer (Pagano 1986).

It is important to note here that many of the people in the marzipan layer had their salaries boosted by various 'golden hellos' and 'golden handcuffs', often of up to £200,000 (*Guardian*, 12 August 1986), intended to tempt employees to new firms, or to keep them satisfied with the firms they were in. (One bank actually *did* switch its fleet of BMWs to a fleet of Lamborghinis to keep a dealing team happy!)

Third, there is the large number of people, especially but not exclusively young or youngish graduates, who are not, or not yet, in the high-flying positions. They have all seen their salaries increase substantially from starting salaries for graduates, now averaging £16,000,[9] right through to those higher up the career ladder but not yet at the top. Differentials are now quite often to do with skill shortages. The example of computing experts is instructive in this regard. There is a general computing skill shortage in the City and as a result computing jobs command, on average, a 10 per cent premium over other specialists (May 1987). Thus compared with nationally, salaries are generally higher in the City for the same job, at a younger age (Table 4.10).

In each of the above three categories the figures mentioned are only *salaries*. They do *not* include other important monetary incentives. In particular, bonuses are vital. They can bring some people's annual earnings overall to well over £100,000 (Table 4.11) and they generally upgrade the earnings of very many people. In addition, there are various perquisites, most notably a carefully graded company car, health insurance, life insurance and mortgage subsidy, which again add to the overall earnings take, even if indirectly.

One last category is missing: the final set of workers in the City, the lower paid, constituting probably about half the workforce concentrated in clerical jobs, personal services like chauffeuring and so on (*Labour Research* 1986). Many of these jobs are held by women. A secretary in the City can expect to earn £10,000 to £12,000, plus receiving a mortgage subsidy, cheap loans, health insurance, a pension scheme and incentive payments, all of which could add another £2,000 to £3,000 in value (*Sunday Times*, 24 May 1987: 49). This is quite high in comparison with national figures (but note the higher London cost of living). But it is not high comparatively within the City, especially since secretarial work is becoming deskilled and repetitive (especially through the introduction of word processing systems) (Table 4.12). Further, salary figures like this do not apply to the many temporary clerical workers in the City, who are often paid considerably less (see Townsend 1987).

Table 4.10 Rates of pay for computer managers in the City and Britain, 1987

Managers of	National average salary	Av. age	City average salary	Av. age	% salary difference
Data processing	31,384	43	39,906	42	27
Systems development	26,437	40	34,592	39	31
Computer services	25,739	41	35,012	39	36
Systems	22,838	40	27,952	40	22
Programming	21,378	38	25,237	37	18
Systems and Programming	23,466	39	30,057	40	28
Operations	20,323	39	25,474	40	25
Technical support	22,319	39	28,799	37	29
Communications	22,044	40	28,895	39	31
Information centres	20,771	38	25,757	37	24

Source: The Times, 21 July 1987

Table 4.11 Average rates of pay for selected high-earning jobs in the City (with bonuses added), early 1987

Job	Basic* £	Bonus £	Total £
Investment dealer	65,984	36,629	102,613
Chief eurobond dealer	66,660	17,473	84,133
Manager, eurobond trading	52,820	26,822	79,642
Manager, equity trading	58,833	19,383	78,216
Manager, new business dev.	50,121	25,289	75,410
Director, corporate finance	54,719	7,683	62,402
Forex and money manager	49,921	10,402	60,323
Head of swaps	48,432	10,859	59,291
Inst. salesperson, capital markets	40,097	15,471	55,568
Head of credits	45,127	6,928	52,055
Director, portfolio management	40,793	9,644	50,437
Chief dealer	40,144	7,992	48,136
Corporate finance executive	34,754	7,965	42,719
Manager, Forex dealing	34,500	7,615	42,115
Senior FRN dealer	36,296	5,685	41,981
Project finance manager	35,964	4,749	40,713
Senior futures trader	32,933	5,985	38,918
Chief sterling dealer	33,088	4,420	37,508
Manager, capital mkt docum.	32,539	4,861	37,400
Head of trade finance	33,203	2,567	35,770
Head of personnel	30,417	2,823	33,240
Manager, Eurosettlements	28,248	3,199	31,447
Syndications manager	27,888	3,053	30,941

*Combined weighted average

Source: The Sunday Times, 24 May 1987: 73

Table 4.12 Lower rates of pay in the City, 1987

Job	Lowest salary (£)	Highest salary (£)
Executive secretary	9,250	14,000
Secretary	7,650	12,000
Shorthand typist	6,000	9,000
Chauffeur	7,500	9,250
Filing clerk	5,000	8,950
Receptionist/telephonist	6,000	10,750
Messenger	6,000	10,000
Telex operator	7,000	12,000
Word processor operator	7,250	11,500

Source: Remuneration Economics (1987: 39).

This said, what the earnings explosion of the last few years has meant for people in the City has been a vast increase in personal wealth for a considerable number of people:

> This week Smith New Court financial services group published figures showing that the average basic salary of its directors (excluding the boss) is between £90,000 and £95,000 this year. On top of this they will get at least £40,000 in bonus or commission. The highest paid directors will take home £194,000 this year. The favoured few get much more than this in other firms.
>
> (*Guardian*, 6 June 1986, quoted in Townsend (1987: 68))

This City wealth can be quantified at least to an extent, in three different categories: earnings, total income and wealth.

Probably at least one-half of the City workforce (some 190,000 people) were earning more than the top 10 per cent (pretax) national wage of £16,681 in 1986. Of those our estimate[10] is that *with bonuses* about 4,000 people were earning £100,000 or more in 1986, including directors and partners. Some of course were earning substantially more than £100,000. With bonuses, a further 10–15,000 people were earning between £50,000 and £100,000 and another 80–100,000 were earning between £20,000 and £50,000. Using the most recent data on income distribution (Board of Inland Revenue 1987), we might estimate that those in the City had 11.5 to 14 per cent of all incomes in Britain between £20,000 and £50,000, 23 to 34 per cent of all incomes in Britain between £50,000 and £100,000 and 50 per cent of all salaries over £100,000 (see Thrift 1987b).

In terms of total income (including income from rents, stocks and shares, dividends, bank and building society interest, etc.) we would estimate that these percentages might even increase. City people would naturally invest much of their money, but they would be able to get a better return, through extra expertise and information. The same stricture applies in terms of property speculation etc.

Finally, in terms of wealth, our estimate would be that City people would have amassed considerable wealth. It is important to remember that a number of those working in the City emanate from upper-class and upper middle-class backgrounds and are already likely to be more wealthy than the population as a whole. Thus to those that have will be given more. Taking this factor into account, our estimate is that of the 20,000 millionaires to be found in Britain in 1986 (Shorrocks, cited in Rentoul 1987) probably at least 3,000 (or 15 per cent) were in the City.[11] For those who are moderately wealthy (according to *New Society* (1986) the top 0.1 per cent of the population with assets of over £740,000) the figure is probably nearer 30 per cent.[12] After all, there are many who are in the position of the 43-year-old commodity market company director:

> He said he now receives about £1000 per week or £50,000 per annum, plus £1500 for meals expenses, £2000 pension payments, £2,500 life insurance and £450 medical insurance. He had a 'windfall' in the previous twelve months through his associations with the Company of £175,000. His wife earns £10,000 per annum in a fashion business. They own assets of well over half a million pounds: two homes, one in a fashionable part of central London, worth a total of £275,000, company shares worth over £300,000 and nearly £100,000 more in jewellery, antiques, cars, a computer, wine, savings and the encashable value of life assurance. They had taken out a new loan of £100,000 on the rising value of their London home because of the tax relief obtained on the payments.
>
> (Townsend 1987: 66)

Class

The changes in the City labour market, manifested in growth in salaries, are important in understanding class restructuring in the City. Traditionally, the City has been a preserve of the British upper class, 'men who walk in lockstep from Eton to the grave, lingering in the City en route' (*The Economist* 1985: 40). Even now the City is surprisingly homogeneous in class terms, at least in its upper reaches. *Becket's City Directory* reveals that one-quarter of UK merchant bankers and stockbrokers went to Eton (Bowen 1986) and a public school background is the rule rather than the exception for those at the top of the occupational hierarchy. On average, some 74 per cent of top executives in merchant banks, stockbrokers, clearing banks, accountancy firms, insurance companies and insurance brokers went to public school. A staggering 96 per cent of top stockbrokers have a public school background (Table 4.13). This narrowness of educational background amongst those presently at the top of the executive hierarchy is reproduced at university level (Table 4.14). On average 68 per cent of the top City executives with degrees went to Oxford or Cambridge. This is no surprise. Until quite recently, many City institutions had a tradition of automatically interviewing all candidates from Oxbridge, while candidates from other universities were screened in advance of interview. These indices of upper-class supremacy at the top of the City ignore the presence of the aristocracy, which is extensive. For example, the merchant bank

Table 4.13 Top executives in City institutions by school, 1986

City institution	School		
	Public	Grammar	Other
Merchant banks	83	8	9
Stockbrokers	96	4	0
Clearing banks	56	21	23
Accountants	72	18	10
Insurance companies	58	15	27
Insurance brokers	77	13	10
Mean	74	13	13

Source: Bowen (1986: 39)

Table 4.14 Top executives and new entrants in City institutions by university, 1986 (per cent)

City institution	University					
	Top executives			New entrants		
	Cambridge	Oxford	Others	Cambridge	Oxford	Others
Merchant banks	37	35	28	37	27	36
Stockbrokers	37	43	20	26	15	59
Clearing banks	36	18	46	16	13	71
Accountants	23	29	48	1	1	98
Insurance companies	23	36	41	12	1	87
Foreign banks	Mostly foreign educated			28	23	49
Mean	31	32	27	20	13	67

Source: Bowen (1986: 39)

Kleinwort Benson has six lords amongst its employees, including some hereditary peers (*Business,* June 1987: 18).

However, beginning in the late 1960s the upper-class ascendancy in the City did begin to break down. The first shock to the City was the influx of American banks in the 1960s in the euromarket boom which were more likely to recruit meritocratically and trained people for early advancement. The floating of exchange rates in the early 1970s was another shock to the system. This ushered in 'the lads from Newham', or working-class foreign exchange dealers. Finally, the Big Bang has also opened up the City, for at least three reasons. First, recruitment procedures have become more systematic and promotion procedures more meritocratic. Second, the restructured firms have become larger, making it more difficult for them to recruit exclusively upper-class candidates or keep an exclusively upper-class atmosphere. Third, and in a related vein, because of the wider competition for Oxbridge graduates many firms have been forced to take graduates from other sources (Table 4.14). As a result of the Big Bang there has, therefore, been a general dilution of the upper-class presence in the City, *but* it is by no means certain that there has been lessening in absolute numbers. Indeed, given the *greater* flow of Oxbridge graduates into the City representation, this may have actually *increased*. For example, 26 per cent of Oxford's graduates went into commerce or chartered accountancy in 1986, many of them into the City. The figures were somewhat less for Cambridge but in both cases they have been growing rapidly in recent years.

It is certainly too early to tell whether the influx of graduates from universities other than Oxford and Cambridge means that the social class profile of the City will be indelibly changed as these students work their way up the City career ladders turning the City into a service-class preserve. There are certainly forces working against that possibility. First, the expansion of foreign banks and securities houses in the lead up to the Big Bang has not necessarily meant a bias against the old class ways. Indeed, foreign banks and securities houses have taken the second largest proportion of Oxbridge students (Table 4.14). The major Japanese securities house, Nomura, took up 28 graduate students in 1986, all from Oxford or Cambridge. Second, the social linkages of the 'old boys' network', although weakened by the influx of new players, do still influence employment opportunities. Even in 1986, an eminent stockbroker could still suggest that the best way to obtain a job interview was through 'the personal recommendation from some family friend' since it is 'much more difficult to refuse an interview if it is at the request of a mutual acquaintance' (J.D. Hamilton 1986: 177). Third, much of the influx of graduates seems to be a replacement for formerly 'unskilled' labour. For example, in the foreign exchange market:

> the original barrow boys are being squeezed out both by the growing complexity of instruments such as swaps and options and by the vastly increased reservoir of graduates willing, desperate even, to join the red Ferrari brigade. 'The barrow boy type is a pretty rare animal these days,' says Dudley Edmunds, director of specialist headhunter Roger Parker. 'Now there is a move towards graduates and people with higher degrees: five to ten years ago, it didn't matter if you had an O-level to your name.'
>
> (Bowen 1986: 41)

Fourth, it is difficult to know whether a filtering of graduates will not take place in which only Oxbridge graduates become the top executives. Alternatively those middle-class graduates that succeed may simply be incorporated into the upper class.

What does seem to be happening is that it has become very difficult for upper-class idiots to survive in the restructured City of London. In Lloyds, for example, 'there are a number of (upper class) brokers swanning around with not necessarily a lot between the ears' but if 'the families are still there . . . only the bright members survive in terms of becoming a big noise' (Bowen 1986: 41). But it is a big step from observing the winnowing of the less mentally agile upper class to saying that the City will no longer be an upper-class preserve. If anything, it might be argued that the injection of wealth into the City before and after the Big Bang has enabled the many upper-class people already in the City to consolidate their wealth and induced many more brighter, young upper-class people to move onto the first rung of the earnings ladder than would have been the case previously.

THE CITY IN THE SOUTH EAST

Now as a place to live, England's swell
Tokyo treats me like a slave, New York tries to kill me, Hong Kong
I have to turn a blind eye to the suffering and I feel wrong.
London, I go to the theatre, I don't get mugged, I have classy friends,
And I go to see them in the country at weekends.

The south east of England has had a long history of regional dominance in Britain which a cynic might think was based on the maxim, 'where there was commerce, finance or trade, money was made more readily than where there was manufacturing or industry'. Recently work in economics and social history has helped to confirm this maxim, demonstrating that much of the dominance of the South East in the nineteenth century was the result of a combination of 'international trade and particularly investment, the consumer demand sustained by many centuries' accumulation of landed wealth and the self-sustaining capacity of affluence' (Lee 1984: 154). In other words, wealth, pure and simple, and the buoyant demand for goods and services that this wealth generated accounted for a good part of the relative dominance of the South East; 'an affluent, service-owned economy can to some considerable degree sustain its own well being' (Lee 1984: 153).

In turn, much of the South East's fund of wealth was accumulated (and then reinvested) in the City of London. Rubinstein (1977) has pointed out that between 1858 and 1914 out of 151 millionaires who died in Britain, seventy-seven came from London and forty-nine of these hailed from the City. Similarly, out of 403 half millionaires, 167 came from London, and 117 of these came from the City (see also Rubinstein 1980).

In this final section, we want to hazard the argument that much the same situation now pertains in the South East[13] as during much of the nineteenth century and for reasons that are not dissimilar: that is, wealth and the demand for goods and services that this wealth still generates forms its own momentum in the South East, and amongst the chief beneficiairies are those working in the City of London.

Wealth is disproportionately gathered in the South East, whether in the form of earnings (Table 4.9), total income (Figure 4.5), investment income (Figure 4.6) or accumulated assets. Thus, according to *New Society* (1986) 58 per cent of those earning over £50,000 in Britain lived in the South East where the average earnings are generally much higher than in the rest of the country (Table 4.5). Some 51 per cent of those with a total

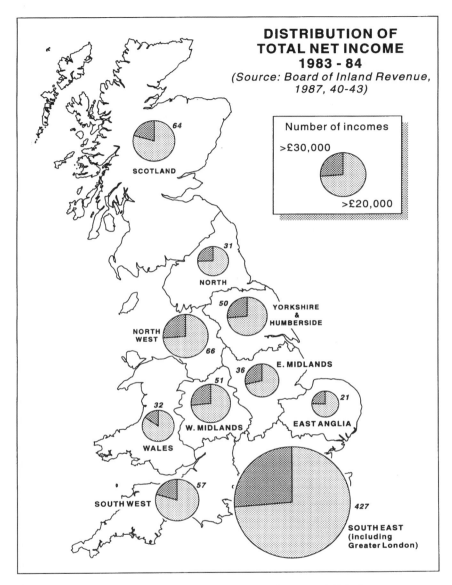

Figure 4.5 Distribution of total net income, 1983–4
Source: Board of Inland Revenue (1987: 40–3).

income of over £20,000 in 1983–4 in Britain lived in the South East (Board of Inland Revenue 1987) (Figure 4.5); 42 per cent of millionaires also lived in the South East (*New Society* 1986).

Since 1979 wealth has increasingly been redistributed to the wealthy (see Rentoul 1987) and the number of moderately and very wealthy has accordingly increased quite rapidly (see Thrift 1987b). For example,

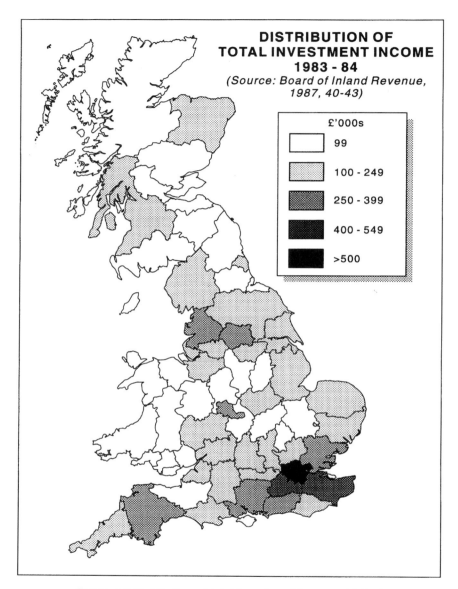

Figure 4.6 Distribution of total investment income, 1983–4
Source: Board of Inland Revenue (1987: 40–3).

Shorrocks (cited in Rentoul (1987)) calculates that the number of millionaires increased from 13,000 in 1983 to 20,000 in 1986. A number of reasons have been proffered for the increase in the ranks of the wealthy including factors such as: rapidly increasing executive incomes; a favourable taxation environment; very favourable rates of return on capital; a bullish stock market (most people who are wealthy own a greater proportion of their assets in stocks and shares than the average for the population and so have benefited from the rising stock market disproportionately); low rates of inflation; and high house price inflation.

It would make a pleasingly symmetrical arrangement to argue that a spatial concentration of wealth in the South East has also occurred since 1979, over and above its already high levels of wealth. But there is only very limited data to confirm this argument. Certainly earnings have increased faster in the South East than elsewhere, especially for top earnings bands (Department of Employment 1986). The limited data on incomes (Board of Inland Revenue 1987) also suggest a degree of concentration. However, data on wealth are almost entirely lacking although one might assume that those with substantial assets have increased faster in the South East than in other parts of the country for various reasons including: the greater preponderance of unlisted stock market firms in the South East than elsewhere;[14] the presence of the City of London with its spiralling incomes (see above); and, of course, above-average house price inflation. Over the past twelve years, house prices in London and the South East have out-stripped the national average by at least 25 per cent. Set against this fact has to be the increased amount of income required to meet the generally higher level of mortgage repayments in the South East. Even so, members of households are accumulating tangible assets, backed by ready availability of mortgage loans.

The concentration of wealth in the South East has generated a buoyant economy (Table 4.15), compared with the rest of the country. It is an economy buoyed up by the consumption of goods and services. The South East's average level of consumer spending is much higher than in other regions. Even allowing for a higher cost of living, its inhabitants spend more on almost every category of household expenditure, absolutely (Table 4.16). Proportionately more of their household expenditure goes on 'housing', 'durable household goods', 'other goods' and 'transport, vehicles, services and miscellaneous', than in most other regions. Similarly, much of the South East's prosperity seems to come from services gener-ated by income. In a crude replication of the exercise by Lee (1984) we found the same causal relationship between income and service provision ratio (i.e. the amount of service employees per capita per region).

The City as a wealth generator

What has been the role of the City in bolstering the South East's dominance within the British space economy, especially in the lead up to, and after, the Big Bang? Our estimate is that, as in the nineteenth century, the City[15] has produced a disproportionate amount of wealth which has then spread out through London and the South Eastern economy, in the shape of demand for goods and services, producing more jobs and more wealth in a 'virtuous' circle (Figure 4.7). This is not an easy argument to confirm without analysing considerable amounts of data and undertaking

Table 4.15 The South East economy within Great Britain

| Region | Usually resident population 1984 | | Service provision ratios 1984 (employment per 10,000 pop) | | | Average unemployment rate, 1985 |
	No.	%	All services	Distribution, hotels and catering; repairs	Banking, finance insurance, business services and leasing	
South East	17,112,400	31.2	3058.95	865.5	575.96	9.9
North	3,093,100	5.6	2104.36	651.1	223.08	18.9
Yorkshire and Humberside	4,904,300	8.9	2175.03	740.2	235.92	15.1
East Midlands	3,874,300	7.1	2043.21	689.4	221.72	12.7
East Anglia	1,939,600	3.5	2279.88	334.4	282.02	10.7
South West	4,461,200	8.1	2311.04	790.4	313.59	12.0
West Midlands	5,176,000	9.4	2132.92	704.8	292.50	15.3
North West	6,395,500	11.6	2248.99	737.7	287.39	16.3
Wales	2,807,250	5.1	1973.14	587.1	198.77	16.9
Scotland	5,145,700	9.4	2389.18	737.9	284.12	15.6
Great Britain	54,909,300	100.0	2466.21	764.1	362.05	13.5*

*UK

Source: Calculated from Regional Trends (1986) and Employment Gazette (1987)

Table 4.16 Household expenditure on commodities and services by region 1983–4

	Average Total expenditure per person	Housing	%	Fuel light and power	%	Food	%	Alcoholic drink	%	Tobacco	%	Clothing and footwear	%	Durable household goods	%	Other goods	%	Transport vehicles, services and misc.	%
								Average weekly household expenditure (£ per week)											
United Kingdom	55.5	146.5	23.2	16	9.3	6	30.5	21	7.1	5	4.3	3	10.6	7	10.9	7	11.4	8	39.2	27
North	47.8	124.2	17.1	14	8.6	7	28.0	22	7.6	6	5.0	4	9.8	8	9.8	8	9.0	7	29.4	24
Yorkshire and Humberside	50.2	132.9	19.4	15	8.7	6	28.6	22	7.2	5	4.4	3	9.5	7	10.1	8	10.2	8	34.8	26
East Midlands	55.4	146.3	25.4	17	8.9	6	30.3	21	6.8	5	4.2	3	10.0	7	11.1	7	11.8	8	37.8	26
East Anglia	53.4	134.1	21.7	16	9.8	7	28.7	21	5.2	4	3.2	2	8.4	6	10.1	8	10.7	8	36.3	27
South East	65.4	169.6	30.0	18	9.3	5	32.9	19	7.5	4	3.8	2	12.0	7	13.0	8	13.8	8	47.3	29
South West	56.0	142.6	22.8	16	9.6	7	28.8	20	6.0	4	3.5	2	9.6	7	10.1	7	11.2	8	40.9	29
West Midlands	51.9	143.1	23.7	17	9.1	6	30.3	21	7.0	5	4.0	3	10.1	7	9.9	7	10.1	7	38.8	27
North West	51.9	137.4	21.2	15	9.2	7	29.3	21	7.7	6	4.7	3	9.6	7	9.9	7	9.9	7	35.8	26
England	56.7	148.8	24.6	17	9.2	6	30.5	20	7.1	5	4.1	3	10.5	7	11.1	7	11.6	8	40.1	27
Wales	48.4	134.2	17.0	13	10.0	7	30.6	22	7.0	5	4.9	4	10.5	8	10.3	8	10.3	8	33.4	25
Scotland	51.8	136.6	16.4	12	9.5	7	30.1	22	7.2	5	5.6	4	11.4	8	10.2	8	10.4	8	35.9	26
Northern Ireland	44.0	129.5	15.9	12	13.4	10	32.3	25	4.2	4	4.5	4	10.8	8	7.1	6	9.5	7	31.7	24

a series of local studies. Therefore what follows is a preliminary, impressionistic analysis concentrating on personal wealth only. However, it is important to note the other impacts of the Big Bang on the South East emanating from the corporate sector (Figure 4.7).

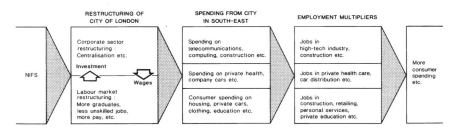

Figure 4.7 Impacts of the City of London on the South East

In 1986, the City's 390,444 workers had, because of their relatively high salaries, a gross income of about £5,423,980,000. Allowing for tax and other deductions, they were left with probably some £3,254,388,000 in actual income.[16] It should be noted that this figure is very conservative since it does not include indirect spending by firms in the City on items like company cars, private health schemes, and the like, or boosts to housing spending in the form of mortgage subsidy.

This money was spent all over the South East. Allowing for items like reinvestment of income (often flowing back into the City), foreign travel (but booked through South Eastern travel agents!), commuter travel, expenditure in central London (on items like consumer goods, the theatre, restaurants, clubs, etc.) and so on, we can make the assumption that the residue was spent at or near the home locations of City workers. Most disposable income would be spent at or near the home locations of professional and managerial workers, rather than clerical and other workers, and at the home locations of men rather than women, there still being an obvious and unfortunate correlation between professional managerial workers and men and clerical workers and women. We can obtain a very crude idea of the spatial pattern of spending by assigning average salaries of men and women in accordance with the spatial distribution of male and female workers in the City gleaned from 1981 census data as in Figure 4.8. Not surprisingly, this brings the result that most disposable income is being spent in the better-off areas of London and the classical commuter belt settlements, generating jobs, and more affluence. (This finding is confirmed by the information we have been able to obtain on the home locations of professional and managerial City workers, in aggregate and by individual firms (Figures 4.9, 4.10, 4.11).) In turn, we might expect that the affluence of these localities is partially connected with the spending power of City workers (the exact relation will obviously vary according to the proportion and type of City worker to be found).

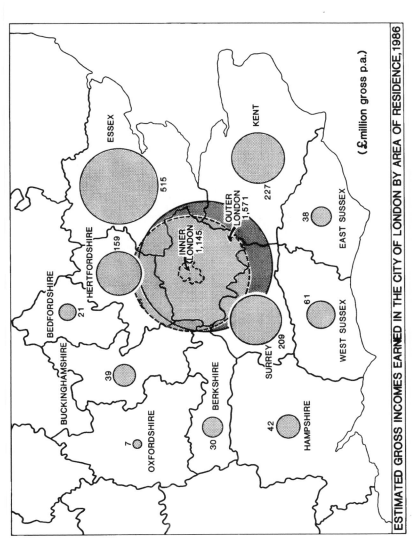

ESTIMATED GROSS INCOMES EARNED IN THE CITY OF LONDON BY AREA OF RESIDENCE, 1986

(£million gross p.a.)

Figure 4.8 Spatial distribution of City earnings

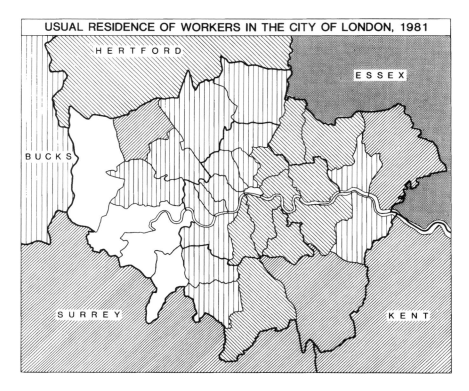

USUAL RESIDENCE OF WORKERS IN THE CITY OF LONDON, 1981

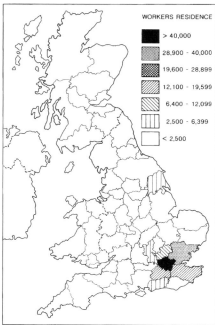

WORKERS RESIDENCE

> 40,000

28,900 - 40,000

19,600 - 28,899

12,100 - 19,599

6,400 - 12,099

2,500 - 6,399

< 2,500

Figure 4.9 Geographical distribution of the residences of City of London workers, 1981
Source: Census

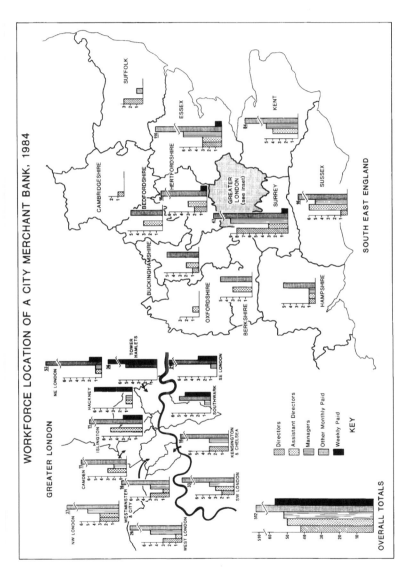

Figure 4.10 Geographical distribution of the residences of workers in a City merchant bank, 1984

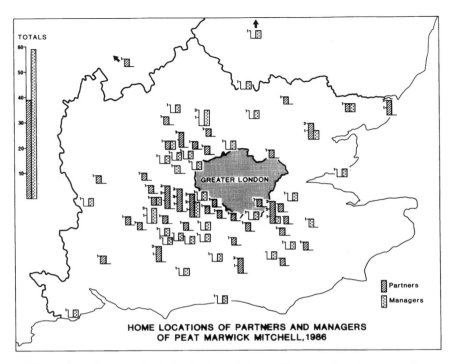

Figure 4.11 Geographical distribution of the residences of workers in a City accountancy firm, 1986

What is the income being spent on? Obviously much of the income will be spent on essentials. But the more wealthy City workers would have considerable amounts of discretionary income to spend on goods and services. From our limited research, this discretionary income is being spent primarily demonstrating 'taste' (Bourdieu 1984; Thrift 1987b).

Spending on goods

In the case of goods, discretionary income tends to be spent either on status goods like cars, or on a subset of status goods, 'positional' goods (Hirsch 1977) which are scarce by reason of short supply, and which gain their value from being scarce, items like antiques or fine art. Commodities like these demonstrate the 'nobility' of their buyers.

The case of country houses, a classical positional good, is particularly instructive, demonstrating as it does the particular demand for such goods in the South East stimulated by City workers with boosted spending power in the wake of the Big Bang. The market in country houses has boomed since the Big Bang and without doubt much of the activity in this market can be traced to the new City rich, especially when the houses are in commuting distance of London:

More than anything else, the 'Big Bang' in the City of London has altered people's attitudes to country houses. For one thing it has produced overnight a generation of young people who can afford to buy the houses that their elders have been struggling to keep up for years. For another, it has magnified the importance of accessibility to London, resulting in the present distortion of property prices in the South-East. The stockbrocker who has now to be in front of his SEAQ computer at 7 am does not want to live too far away from London.

(Country Life 1987: 10)

Figure 4.12 shows the current (1987) values of country houses, while Figure 4.13 shows the rise in country house prices since 1981. As would be expected, the rise was mainly concentrated in the South East, but it has also spread along the M4 corridor.

The profile of typical country house owners confirms expectations (Savills 1987a). Most come from the City. They are relatively young, with most men in their forties and most women in their thirties. They are well off, with 74 per cent earning more than £50,000 per annum and 41 per cent earning more than £100,000. Most were looking for houses in the £250,000 to £350,000 price range. Over half would purchase with cash. Those who had loans were often paying more than £2,000 per month for a mortgage.

Consumption on tasteful goods like country houses demonstrates the cultural nobility of the moderately and very wealthy. That taste is upper class or middle class imitating upper class. Consumption is aimed at reproducing upper-class lifestyles through a constellation of goods, each of which reciprocally confirms the taste and background of their owner (Thrift 1987b). Thus the country house is a shell for consumption of other goods – the Range Rover, the tweedy country clothes, the stable and so on.

Spending on services

Not all discretionary income is spent on goods, of course. Much of it is also spent on services (Gershuny and Miles 1983). Of course, the consumption of tasteful goods can often imply the use of services. There are often substantial multipliers even here. The purchase of a status car supports a network of distributors and repair shops. The purchase of a country house might require an estate agent, an accountant, a construction company to do the renovations, plus cook, nanny, gardener,[17] and so on. But other services are also important. From our limited research, much of the discretionary spending on services by more affluent City workers seems to be bent towards maintaining and reproducing upper class, and middle class imitating upper class, 'lifestyles' (see Ascherson 1986a, b, c).[18] That might just mean appropriate restaurants but it can also mean education of children.

In fact, the case of private education is particularly instructive. Most affluent City workers send their children to a private school and, given the

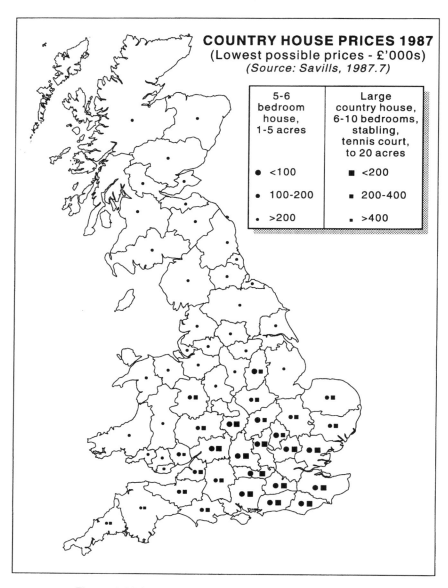

Figure 4.12 Lowest country house prices (£000s), 1987
Source: Savills (1987a: 7)

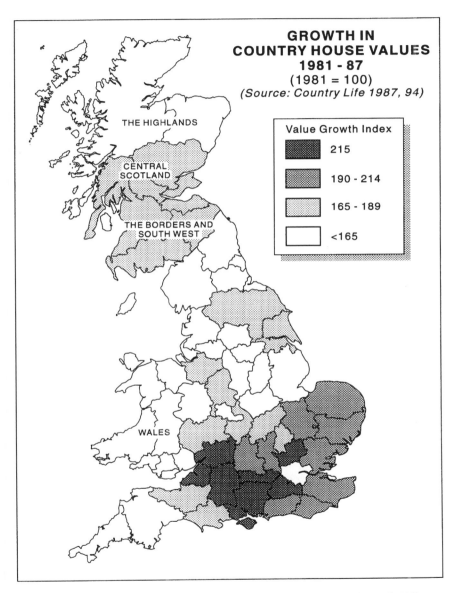

Figure 4.13 Growth in country house values, 1981–7 (1981 [equal] 100)
Source: *Country Life* (1987: 94)

number of workers involved, children with City parents must account for a considerable number of the 440,864 pupils being educated in private schools in the UK in 1986–7 (about 7 per cent of the total UK school population). Some 34 per cent of these private school pupils were being educated in schools in Greater London and the South East (Figure 4.14). In turn, spending on private education then keeps others employed. For example, in the UK as a whole, 33,248 teaching staff were employed in 1986–7 (Independent Schools Information Services 1987). (It is interesting to note that pupil numbers have been increasing in private schools at between 1 and 2 per cent per year since 1984 and the growth has been most apparent in the South East, where most public schools are concentrated.)

Consumption of services like private education demonstrates how such services can be bent towards the reproduction of particular classes, in this case most prominently the upper and upper middle class. The case of private schools is indeed exemplary. Routinely, private school pupils win about 50 per cent of Oxbridge places (in 1987, 46 per cent of Oxford places went to private school candidates, and 49 per cent of Cambridge places (*Times Higher Education Supplement* 28 August 1987: 1)). Whilst at Oxbridge they are likely to be snapped up by City firms, a likelihood strengthened by their private school background. They are consequently paid high salaries, and so the round continues.

CONCLUSIONS: AN UPPER-CLASS REVIVAL?

> The British Empire was a cartel
> England could buy whatever it wanted cheap
> And make a profit on what it made to sell.
> The empire's gone but the City of London keeps
> On running like a cartoon cat off a cliff – bang.

In this chapter we have tried to link together, albeit in an exploratory fashion, the restructuring of the international financial system in the 1980s, the 'Big Bang' in the City of London, and the south east of England. What we have seen has been a flow of great wealth from the City into the South East similar to that found by Rubinstein and Lee in the later nineteenth century, and with many quite similar effects including especially a strong demand for goods and services which has helped to keep the South East relatively prosperous.

Perhaps the least expected effect has been the consolidation and even expansion of the British upper class. The extant British upper class has received an injection of wealth from jobs in the City which has enabled it to reaffirm its position and its culture (through the consumption of the appropriate goods and services). In addition, a number of the middle classes have accumulated sufficient wealth from the City to enable them to join the ranks of the upper class,[19] or if not them then at least their suitably educated and probably independently wealthy children. These economic and social changes have a spatial expression in the tenacity

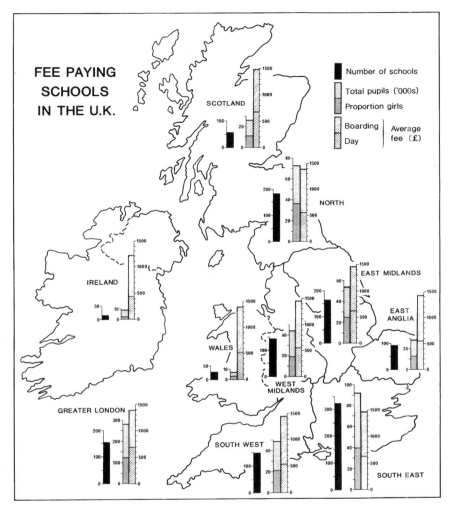

Figure 4.14 Fee-paying schools in the UK
Source: ISIS

of the South East as the dominant region of Britain and the main site for the reproduction of the upper class.[20] Much has changed in the modern international world but some changes, it seems, can act to block change.

CHAPTER 5

IN THE WAKE OF MONEY

The City of London and the accumulation of value

> What does it do, in detail, to people; this pride of class and wealth; this indifference of trade; this reduction of human connections to their convenience for business?
>
> (Williams, Introduction to Dickens, *Dombey and Son* 1970:25)

> As individuals succeed in wealth creation there can be no doubt that the majority will strive to exhibit that success by moving to the country.
>
> (Lilwall and Allcock 1988: x)

Over the last 150 years the City of London has often been described as a separate world from that inhabited by the vast majority of the British population, as a complex of wealth, prestige, authority and power dependent upon the rest of the world for its survival as much as upon Britain, and 'all the more formidable because of its geographical concentration, and the mutual sympathies of the men who ultimately control it' (Sandelson 1959: 141). Of course, it is possible to argue about the degree to which, over the course of history, the wealth and power generated by the City has cohered, and the degree to which it has influenced the British economy, state, society and culture. But it is clear that in the 1980s the City became more visible to the public gaze as a result of the interaction between changes in British society and changes in the City. In the case of the economy, the visibility of the City was made more acute by a general worldwide boom in the financial services industry and by specific increases in financial services employment in many parts of Britain, drawing new workers into the financial services labour force (Leyshon *et al.* 1989b). In the case of the state, the City's visibility grew with the increasing scale and influence of large financial services conglomerates which periodically were able to outflank the various state controls based upon the Bank of England and assorted regulatory mechanisms. In the case of British society, the more dynamic sections of the City became part of a new 'disestablishment' (Lloyd 1988a, b, c, d; Perkin 1989), a highly visible coalition of private business interests that was 'meritocratic rather than egalitarian, efficient rather than generous, individualistic rather than corporate' (Lloyd 1988d:

155). Finally, the City became imprinted on the national culture as an exemplar of a new Britain which was more conscious of wealth and more careless of egalitarian concerns. The rapidly growing cultural industries were able to serve up the City to audiences as a set of stereotypes. For example, young men and women working in the City were interpreted as Thatcher's stormtroopers in large numbers of plays, television series and films, and books, all the way from *Serious Money*, through *Capital City*, to *Nice Work*. It is thus that *Dombey and Son* takes on a new life.

This chapter will take the measure of some of the economic, social and cultural aspects (the three are inseparable) of the City's influence on Britain in the 1980s. The argument is a straightforward one that starts with the payment of large salaries and bonuses to many of those working in the City in the 1980s. In turn, these salaries and bonuses were converted into personal wealth. One of the ways in which this conversion was accomplished was via the purchase of scarce assets which therefore had a 'positional' value (Hirsch 1977). Such positional assets have appreciated particularly rapidly in the 1980s. But these assets are not just a store of economic value. They also have a social and cultural value (indeed, this is one of the ways in which their positionality is defined). The purchase of these assets, therefore, became one of the ways by which the City's newly wealthy defined themselves socially and culturally and, over time, this definition (or set of definitions) spread to other parts of the business community, becoming more general in the process, both socially and geographically.

Accordingly, this chapter is in three parts. The first part considers the growth of the City's labour market in the 1980s, paying particular attention to the escalation in incomes that accompanied this expansion. The second part considers the choices that were made by the newly wealthy of the City, concerning which goods and services were particularly appropriate to buy. Particular attention is paid to the market in country houses. Finally, some brief conclusions are drawn.

MAKING MONEY: THE GROWTH OF THE CITY OF LONDON THROUGH THE 1980S

It is not our concern in this chapter to provide a full account of the economic growth of the City of London in the 1980s. That has already been done elsewhere (Chapter 4, this volume). Instead, our intention is to select aspects of that growth which are most closely related to the chief theme of this chapter: the way that money earned in the city has contributed to the social and cultural transformation of Britain by the business community. In particular, this means focusing on the expansion of the City's labour market and the parallel increase in incomes.

Through the 1980s the City of London's labour market grew rapidly. There are, of course, considerable problems in defining what is meant by the City's labour market. Thus, the pattern of demand for labour has changed as the City's institutions have spilled out of the traditional area of City activity, the Square Mile, into the rest of inner London and even further afield. The pattern of supply of labour has also changed. Although the bulk of the City's labour force still comes from London, through the 1980s the long-established tendency to draw labour from the South East and farther out was strengthened by an increase in long-distance commuting by rail (Leyshon *et al.* 1989a). Given the constantly shifting boundaries of the City's labour market, in both demand and supply terms, it is clearly difficult to provide exact quantitative estimates of the numbers employed in the City or their places of residence. So far as the administrative area of the Square Mile is concerned, numbers in employment have increased from 390,215 in 1981, to 413,711 in 1984, to 415,435 in 1987. Of these employees, 341,567 were engaged in service activities in 1981 (a definition nearer to indicating City types of activities), 357,939 in 1984 and 380,370 in 1987. Within financial and producer services, 186,235 were employed within the City administrative area in 1981, 206,452 in 1984 and 250,150 in 1987 (Census of Employment). A better estimate of total City employment would be provided by including those working in City types of activities in inner London. No official data series provides such information. However, a survey by Rajan and Fryatt (1988) found that in 1987 the City administrative area accounted for only 71 per cent of employment in six key City activities (banks and discount houses, other credit-granting institutions, securities, insurance, accountancy and management consultancy, software services) and, given more recent moves out of the City by financial institutions, the percentage can only decrease in the future.

So far as supply of labour is concerned, similar difficulties are presented. Figures 5.1 and 5.2 show the place of residence of those working in the City in 1981 (the last date for which census figures are available). Not surprisingly, there was a clear pattern of decay with distance from the City and from the major road and rail links. Since 1981, this pattern has been 'stretched' with the development of Docklands, at least parts of which are enclaves for City workers, and by the continuing tendency for the City to draw its workers from farther and farther out from London (Evans and Crampton 1989).

In summary, the City's labour market expanded rapidly throughout the 1980s. The rate of expansion is in some dispute, but Rajan and Fryatt (1988) calculate that in the particularly frantic 'Big Bang' to 'Big Crash' period from 1984 to 1987, the average annual growth rate of employment was as much as 7.5 per cent. In the period from 1987 to 1992, Rajan and Fryatt calculated that the growth rate would still be in the order of 3 per cent per annum with the most sustained growth, over both periods, being found in banking, accountancy and management consultancy, and software services. This expansion in the numbers employed in the City was accompanied by an expansion of the City's labour market over space, in both demand and supply terms.

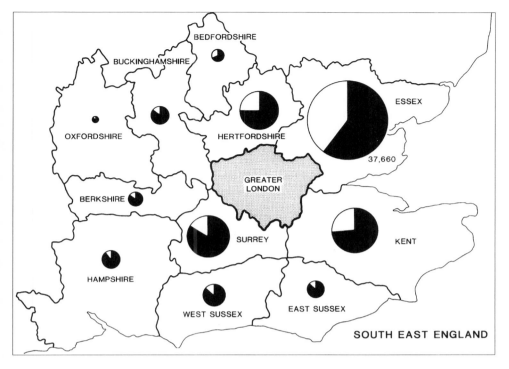

Figure 5.1 City workforce by area of residence, 1981
Source: Census of Population

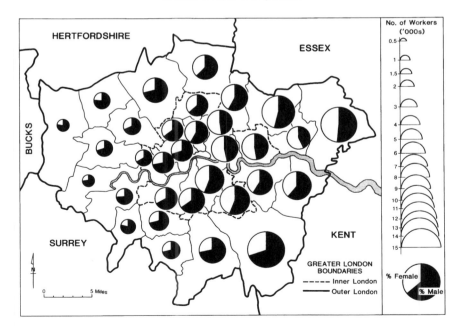

Figure 5.2 Number of City workers within Greater London boundaries, 1981
Source: Census of Population

Of course, the City's labour market is not an undifferentiated mass. Over time, its composition has been changing as a result of changes in employer demand. Most importantly, the 1980s saw a general upgrading of the City's skills base which meant hiring more school leavers with 'A' levels, more diploma holders, more graduates and more of those with postgraduate qualifications. Thus, in Great Britain as a whole, banking, finance and insurance raised its share of graduate employment from 13.8 per cent in 1983 to 17.7 per cent in 1987. This increase coincided with the deregulation of financial services associated with Big Bang. This rise was particularly marked for males whose share rose from 14.8 to 19.7 per cent, but also concerned females, up from 11.2 to 13.2 per cent (Creigh and Rees 1989: 21).

In turn, this upgrading of the City's skills base has meant that the proportion of employment in managerial and professional occupations increased, whilst the share of employment held by clerical staff decreased relatively (Rajan and Fryatt 1988). The shortages of skilled labour induced by the City's need to upgrade its skills base also meant that through the 1980s more women and those from ethnic minorities have been hired. However, these groups remained under-represented and tended to be concentrated in the poorer-paying clerical jobs which still account for nearly one-half of the City's jobs.

The spatial extent of the labour markets of each of these different groups clearly varied. Thus, at one extreme, the City acted as a kind of 'vacuum cleaner', sucking up highly skilled labour. For example, graduates were pulled into the City from all parts of Britain to live in London and the south east of England. At the other extreme, women and ethnic minorities (seen as undifferentiated groups) tended to be drawn from nearer to London, and to be more or less coincident with the pattern of supply of the City's clerical labour force (Figures 5.1 and 5.2).

PAY IN THE CITY IN THE 1980S

According to New Earnings Survey data, earnings in the City underwent a dramatic increase in the course of the 1980s. Average earnings were not just above average earnings in Britain, but also above average earnings in the rest of London, and in the south east of England. More spectacularly, the disparities have increased over time (Figure 5.3).

The reasons for such a rapid increase in earnings were many but amongst them the most important was a skills shortage induced by the general trend towards more skilled jobs in the City, coupled with the willingness of some firms to pay inflated salaries to buy in these skills. In the context of the City, 'skills' does not just mean proficiency in using particular management techniques or a particular technology, it also means the social proficiency associated with access to a web of contacts which provide new customers and other important information on markets and business more generally. One important manifestation of the

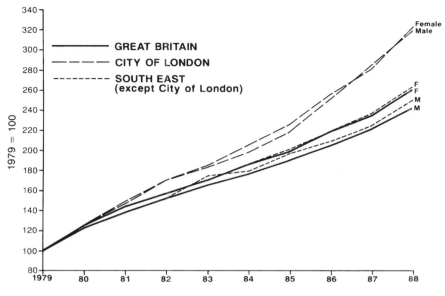

Figure 5.3 Full-time adult gross average earnings, 1979–88
Source: New Earnings Survey

skills shortage (which was obviously greater in certain kinds of jobs than others) was the constant poaching by firms of people or teams of people with particular skills/contacts from other firms, even in the less favourable market conditions of the late 1980s. This behaviour leads to particularly strong salary inflation because the value of such people or teams of people often comes to be associated with the salaries that they earn. Other factors also come into play in explaining the City's above-average earnings. First, through the 1980s the City increasingly became part of an international labour market for upper-echelon financial services workers based in the financial centres of the world. At the beginning of the 1980s salaries in the City were comparatively low by the standards of many of those centres. Through the 1980s the City was in the process of catching up, spurred on by an influx of foreign (especially US) firms used to paying higher salaries. In addition, more and more foreign nationals began to work in the City and in many cases they were used to higher salaries. Second, the institutional structure of the City's labour market became more complex: headhunting firms were commonly used to find particular kinds of workers (Byrne 1987; Jones 1989); labour market information (especially on salaries) became more freely available to both firms and workers; and so on. Third, and finally, career and salary expectations undoubtedly changed. Workers, in the upper echelons at least, became more likely to expect higher salaries and to expect to switch jobs in order to get them.

It is important to note here that earnings in the City do not consist only of salaries. In many City jobs, additions to basic salary are of crucial importance in boosting income (Reid 1988). Amongst these, the most important is the use of bonuses. These can be linked to the performance of the firm, or to individual performances (by, for example, traders) and can consist of straight cash bonuses or various share options schemes. In a number of cases these bonuses can form a very substantial proportion of final income. Another important addition to salary will consist of various perquisites, including mortgage subsidy, a company car or allowance for use of own car, help with costs of rail travel, life insurance, free medical assurance, low-interest loans, subsidised meals and subsidised private telephone. These additions to basic salary are clearly unequally distributed according to seniority and type of job, but it would be surprising to find that in the 1980s those occupying managerial positions were not earning at least another 15 per cent of their salary through them.

In summary, it is clear that the number of well-off people in the City increased quite rapidly in the 1980s as a result of generally improved levels of income, combined with a gradual increase in the number of professional and managerial workers who were the chief beneficiaries of these increases in income, both relatively and absolutely.

But the story cannot stop with income. It is important to point out that the high incomes of the kinds which could be found in the City can be rapidly converted into a stock of assets, into personal wealth. The use of stock options as bonuses is just the most direct conversion of income into assets that is offered to those with substantial incomes. More usually, they make the conversion themselves by buying stocks, and shares, or opening deposit accounts, which provide them with another stream of income. Alternatively, they can buy appreciating assets like houses, or antiques and other collectables.

The process by which income was converted into personal wealth by the better-off workers in the City was aided by four important processes. First, especially in the period leading up to Big Bang, many people gained instant wealth via golden 'handshakes', 'hellos' or 'handcuffs', large payments aimed at: buying partners or directors out of small firms which were to be integrated into larger ones; tempting people or teams of people with particular skills to join another firm; and persuading people or teams of people with particular skills to stay put. Second, many of those who work in the City do not have to accumulate wealth from scratch using only their salary and bonuses as a stake. In the City's upper echelons before Big Bang many of its leading firms had had a clear preference for recruiting into managerial or prospective managerial positions from a small pool of people (Thrift *et al.* 1987). These new entrants to the City labour market were more likely to have upper- or upper middle-class backgrounds associated with the major public schools and universities. They were therefore more likely to be wealthy, or to have wealth thrust upon them via inheritance (see Tables 4.13 and 4.14). With the increase in the number of foreign firms in the City, whose recruitment practices are more meritocratic, and the general increase in the size of the City labour force, the degree of selection from a narrow set of class backgrounds has clearly diminished but not, perhaps, as much as might be thought. Thus, many foreign institutions have shown the same bias towards products of Oxford, Cambridge and other top-rank universities like Bristol as their British counterparts. Again, it remains to be seen whether the leaders of City institutions in the late 1990s and 2000s will not prove to have the same narrow backgrounds as at present (Greenshields 1989) as the process of selection for higher office works through the system of promotion. In other words, in the case of the City the old adage 'to him who hath will be given more' may still have some force; the link between wealth and access to high incomes with which to generate more wealth has not necessarily been broken.

Third, the process of conversion of income into wealth has been helped by the active intervention of the British state. Various rules on capital transfer and capital gains have helped to make wealth accumulation more feasible but undoubtedly the chief instruments of aggrandisement came in the successive budgets of the 1980s and most especially the 1988/9 budget which abolished all but one higher-rate tax band. Many studies (Stark 1989) have documented the galvanising effect of these budgets on the potential for wealth accumulation amongst those with high incomes. For example, a 35-year-old City investment analyst with a modest income of £72,000 (made up of £70,000 salary and £2,000 investment income) would have paid out £32,881 in income tax in 1987/8 but only £23,945 in 1989/90 (Knight, Frank and Rutley 1989). Fourth and finally, wealth accumulation has been made easier by soaring asset price inflation running far above the rate of product price inflation (Reading 1989a, b). Thus until 1987, at least, the market in stocks and shares boomed (and well-off people are more likely to keep their money in shares). Then, after 1987, a period of high real interest rates meant that those who had switched their assets into bank or building society deposits still gained. Even more strikingly, throughout the 1980s, markets in housing, antiques, fine art and other such assets all ran enthusiastically onwards and upwards (*The Economist* 1989).

It is, of course, exceedingly difficult to put exact figures on the total amount of income earned by City workers, but even the crudest calculations suggest that the gross annual earnings of City workers were £3.4 billion in 1981, £4.9 billion in 1984 and £6.9 billion in 1987. Taking into account the effect of tax, this left £2.2 billion to spend in 1981, £3.2 billion in 1984 and £4.5 billion in 1987. (This is a most conservative estimate since it does not include bonuses or the effects of various perquisites.) More mysterious is the amount of personal wealth that has been created out of the figures for income, but amongst the top 10 per cent of City workers (who earned £535 million in 1981, £763 million in 1984 and £1.4 billion in 1987) it can be safely assumed that personal wealth was being laid down at a very considerable rate.

SPENDING MONEY

The effects of the spending power provided by the boosted incomes and enhanced personal wealth formation of the City on the economy and society of London, the south east of England and Britain as a whole remain a matter of fierce debate. Lee (1984, 1986) has argued that, in the mid- and late nineteenth century, the high levels of consumer spending in London and the South East (including those of workers in the City of London) were a powerful stimulant to the economy of the region, both qualitatively and quantitatively. Similarly, Rubinstein (1977, 1980, 1986, 1987) argues that the disproportionate concentration of high incomes and personal wealth in London and the South East was an important determinant of the region's economic and social success relative to the north of England, and that this concentration flowed from finance and 'from London's other role as the centre of wealth, display, retailing, the professions, the press, and service industries' (Rubinstein 1987: 102). Clearly, such arguments are controversial, especially in the degree to which they underestimate incomes and wealth drawn from sources other than finance and commerce, and the degree to which they confuse pattern with process (Daunton 1989). However, even so, it seems clear that by the end of the nineteenth century, and probably before, definite and extensive impacts were being felt on the economy and society of London and the south east of England as a whole, as a result of making money from finance and then spending it.

In the twentieth century, there seems little reason to suppose that these impacts have not continued, although on what scale they now affect the structure of demand is clearly extremely difficult to measure.

What seems certain is that spending generated by the incomes and personal wealth connected to the City of London has had identifiable effects on particular high-value markets. Of these markets, the most visible are those which have not only economic but also social and cultural resonance: that is, in which demand for goods and services is socially and culturally defined. These are markets in which money is deployed to buy goods and services which, when combined with other goods and services in particular practices, produce social and cultural advantage, what Bourdieu (1979, 1980, 1984, 1987) identifies as the accruing of 'social' and 'cultural' capital. Social capital refers to each person's insertion into, and accumulation of, a network of 'relationships of acquaintance and mutual recognition', that is a network of family, friends and business contacts. Cultural or symbolic capital refers to each person's accumulation of a stock of socially accepted competences all the way from a family name through ownership of 'appropriate' goods to formal educational qualifications. Roughly, the distinction Bourdieu draws is between knowing the right people and knowing the right things, although clearly the two are heavily interrelated, not least through their geography. Being in the right place is a crucial element of each type of capital. For example, to be seen at the right places, the right ski resorts in winter and the right watering places in summer, is important both for the symbolic capital involved and for the social and quasi-professional contacts that can be made or confirmed by simultaneous presence.

(Marceau 1989: 146)

For those in the City who, in the 1980s, found themselves in possession of substantial incomes and, in some cases, considerable personal wealth, the challenge was to spend their money in tasteful ways, that is in ways which would accrue social and cultural capital for themselves and their children. The new City wealthy were not alone in this objective. It was one shared by the rising 'disestablishment' which needed to stamp its authority on Britain, not just in the economic realm, but in the social and cultural realms too. In other words, Marx's abstract community of money had to be transformed into a concrete community of the moneyed. That required seeking out goods and services that could become a part of practices that would allow this to happen. Examples of markets for such goods and services were legion in Britain in the 1980s, extending all the way from the boom in simple status goods that demonstrate what Bourdieu calls 'honourability' (like expensive automobiles or antiques), through the expansion of arenas for aiding the formation of social capital (such as the interrelated rise of the Season and the corporate hospitality business, or the rise of certain field sports), to the rise of private day school education (which allows a child to accrue both social and cultural capital). In the rest of this chapter we will concentrate on just one of these markets in social and cultural transformation, the country house.

THE COUNTRY HOUSE MARKET

At the outset, it is important to define as precisely as possible what the commodity, 'a country house', consists of. Conventionally, the country house market is divided into three segments. The first and cheapest of these segments is the 'cottage'. Usually set in a rural village, it will have three bedrooms, two reception rooms, a bathroom and a kitchen and will also have about half an acre of garden (although this will vary quite dramatically). The second segment of the country house market is the five- or six-bedroom 'period house'. It will have three bathrooms, three reception rooms, a kitchen and a utility room, plus garaging for two cars and a considerable amount of land (up to five acres). It will often have been formerly a farmhouse. The third and final segment is the full-scale 'large country house' or 'manor'. This will have six to ten bedrooms, four bathrooms, three reception rooms, a study, a kitchen and most probably domestic accommodation (perhaps in a cottage set off from the main house). It will have extensive land (at least fifteen acres) and garaging for three cars. It will almost certainly have outbuildings (especially stables) and most likely will include a tennis court and a swimming pool amongst its particulars.

The country house market has a number of common features which define it above and beyond the formal architectural parameters. Three of these stand out. First, the country house is 'historic'. Although there are examples of country houses built after the Second World War (Robinson 1984), they are rare and, significantly, they are likely to command a premium only if they are in a period style. In most places, more than 90 per cent of applicants to agents specialising in country house sales specifically want a period property, preferably Grade II listed (Paice 1989). Second, the country house should be vernacular in the broad sense; that is, it is built in materials and style typical of its local area and therefore blends harmoniously into the landscape. Third, and related, country houses should, as the term implies, be in rural locations. A quiet and attractive country setting is an integral part of the attraction of a country house. Thus 'Surrey has gone out of fashion . . . it is regarded as insufficiently rural and as one agent observed: "Today everybody thinks he's a squire"' (*Country Life* 1989: 20).

The pages of *Country Life* attest to the fact that a country house market existed before the 1980s but, except for some areas in and around London and the Home Counties, it was not a particularly active market. This was partly because the wealth and capital gains were not there to support it, partly because a national market did not exist, but rather a set of localised and often quite distinct submarkets, and partly because tastes ran counter to many of the values represented by the country house. In the 1980s all this changed: the market exploded into life. First of all, the wealth became available. In the first instance, this was undoubtedly the result of an injection of wealth from the City of London.

> More than anything else, the Big Bang in the City of London has altered people's attitudes to country houses. For one thing, it has produced overnight a generation of young people who can afford to buy the houses that their elders were struggling to keep up for years.
>
> (*Country Life* 1987: 10)

But if it was people from the City who set the market running, they were soon followed by other members of the newly wealthy private sector business class who had found a market which combined capital gains with social and cultural gains. An examination of typical country house owners carried out in 1986 confirms expectations (Savills 1987b). In 1986, most new owners still came from the City. They were relatively young, with most men in their forties and most women in their thirties. They were well off with 74 per cent earning more than £50,000 per annum and 41 per cent earning more than £100,000. Over half were purchasing their houses with cash. Those who had loans were willing to pay more than £2,000 a month for a mortgage. As money from the newly wealthy started to pour into the country house market so substantial capital gains became possible, adding further to the market's attractions. Country houses are, after all, an important part of the British positional economy (Hirsch 1977), made up of goods which are inherently scarce. Seen in this sense, country house value comes from their absolute scarcity (since there can only ever be a limited stock) and their positioning in settings which are similarly in short supply. As one agent put it more succinctly, 'substantial demand plus fixed supply equals rising price. A period cottage away from neighbours and in pretty countryside will always perform well because it cannot be recreated' (*Country Life* 1989: 20).

Second, the 1980s saw a truly national market for country houses gradually come into existence. Before the 1980s, there were few chains of estate agents large enough to provide a national market in these houses. But in the 1980s, as the market grew, so those agents expanded apace, partly keeping up with it and partly creating it. Specialist agents like Savills, Knight, Frank and Rutley, Chestertons, Cluttons and Lane Fox all expanded and integrated their office networks; they began to do serious research on the market and to target potential buyers. By the year ending April 1988, one of the largest specialist agents, Savills, had a country house division turnover of £183 million. It sold 809 country house properties around Britain at an average price of £225,000 (Savills 1988). The expansion by specialist agents was paralleled by increasing interest being shown in the market by the large agency chains that were being set up by banks, insurance companies and building societies in the latter part of the 1980s. For example, Prudential Property Services set up a Prestige and Country Homes division in 1987.

Third, the 1980s saw tastes changing. The country house has been a potent symbol in Britain for a considerable period of time, whether at its most blatant as the patrician grand home, 'the abstraction of success, power and money . . . founded elsewhere' (Williams 1973: 299), or in its more domestic manifestations as the solid patrician period farmhouse, complete with squire, or as the Helen-Allingham-like period cottage. In the 1970s these symbols were tarnished by a combination of recession and the prevailing structure of feeling, which was still based in the public sector and its associated modernist imagery (Wright 1988). In the 1980s these symbols were dusted off. The fog of the 1970s was blown away. Most particularly, country houses have become both a part of and a way of reflecting back a set of larger cultural discourses in a way that advantages the person who owns them. Their value as cultural capital has been inflated. These discourses are many but chief amongst them we can count the revival of historical feeling in the 1980s, helped along by the growth of conservation movements and the use of the past as a resource by the retailing and heritage industries (Wright 1985; Hewison 1987; Samuel 1989; Thrift 1989c), and the increased interest in nature and the countryside, aided by the new devotion to pastoral versions of Englishness and the growth of the environmental movements (Samuel 1989; Howkins 1986; Thrift 1989c). The country house has, in its different forms, amplified and extended these discourses, buoyed up by a wave of publications which have all helped to focus and fuel the fires of desire for ownership, ranging from stalwarts like *Country Life*, through the agents' advertising and advertising-related magazines like *Savills Magazine* (first published in 1980) or Prudential's *Prestige and Country Homes* (first produced in 1988), to the vast flood of country house books which shows no signs of ebbing.

It is no surprise to find that, in these circumstances, those who buy country houses, as many surveys have shown, seem intent on buying a ticket to the past. Ideally, a house should be listed (in late 1987 there were 6000 Grade I listed buildings in England, a further 20,000 listed Grade II and 420,000 listed Grade III) and it should be recognisably 'historic'. In the 1980s, current cultural mores dictated that this meant chiefly houses in the Georgian or Queen Anne style. 'Working out what does constitute most prospective buyers' ideal of a classic country house is no problem at all for Jeremy Blanchard, of Humberts: " . . . Georgian," he declared' (Brennan 1989). This anecdote is borne out by a survey carried out by Savills (1987b) which showed that 17 per cent of country house owners sought Georgian homes as their ideal, a further 15 per cent Queen Anne and 10 per cent Regency. Again, a country house needs to be in an un-ambiguously rural position to take maximum cultural advantage:

> [H]ouse-buyers are now seeking what one agent describes as 'a very comfortable form of the good life' where they can bring up their children in an attractive country environment within a rural community to which they can contribute. Through that they achieve a sense of belonging which enhances their quality of life.
>
> (*Country Life* 1989: 19)

The importance of a rural backdrop is not just about cultural mores. It also implies a quite specific set of social relations: cultural capital and social capital are interrelated. The 1980s have seen tastes change to the undoubted advantage of the country house. Buyers strive for monetary rewards, but the cultural and social rewards of ownership are not far behind. Certainly, the ultimate goal is clear.

Twenty estate agents were asked what their buyers would regard as an ideal country house. On this there was astonishing unanimity of view. It can be summed up in the description of one agent:

> [I]t is in a very underpopulated part of the country, which never sees tourists, but from which it is easy to get to London when wanted. There is a happy rural community where people know and like each other. The house itself is set in a park surrounded by a wall and entered by lodges. The drive sweeps up past beautiful trees. Then the house comes into view – slightly raised, overlooking a lake. It is not too big: seven or eight bedrooms and one good drawing room. The scale is fine but not grand. The style is Queen Anne or Georgian, and it must have 100 acres of land.
>
> (*Country Life* 1989: 22)

The origins of the revival of the country house market and its subsequent pattern of expansion can be traced through the market's geography. Undoubtedly, in the early years of the revival, proximity to

London was a critical factor. Country houses had to be within commuting distance of London: 'the stockbroker who now has to be in front of his SEAQ computer at 7 am does not want to live too far away from London' (*Country Life* 1987: 10). But the country house buying habit soon began to spread outwards from the immediate environs of London, for at least five reasons. First, there was the sheer expense of country houses nearer the capital. For example, by the year ending 30 April 1988, the average price of houses sold by Savills' Henley office was £380,000 in contrast to the average for the Norwich office of £134,000. This expense pushed buyers without the requisite capital out of areas nearer to London. The effect was cumulative over time – as the frontier of high prices moved further and further out so those coming into the market were less likely to have the requisite capital and had to move further out again to find a house. Second, improved communications helped to open up certain areas to interested London buyers, especially the completion of the M25, and faster train times on some intercity rail lines. The most famous example of this effect was the town of Grantham in Lincolnshire. With the introduction of high-speed trains, journey times to London were reduced to seventy-five minutes, and electrification subsequently reduced them to an hour. The result was an influx of more than 200 London commuters and a country house price increase of 45 per cent in 1987 (Van Cutsem 1988).

Third, the stock of country houses near London is finite. Thus the search had to be extended outwards. Certain counties, like Oxfordshire, have a very limited stock of country houses relative to demand so that prices in these counties spiralled rapidly upwards. Other counties with a greater stock saw more moderate rises (it is important to note that there are no extant stock figures for counties, a situation which clearly makes it extremely difficult to estimate exact supply/demand relations).

Fourth, there was the increasing spread of agents' offices out from London and of information about houses in the rest of the country back into London. Finally, there was the large rise in London house prices in the 1980s. This resulted in a considerable pool of people, who already had large salaries and were in a position to trade up, using their capital gains. For example, by mid-1987, an average four-bedroom family house in Fulham cost between £300,000 and £350,000 with a journey time to the City, door to door, of about forty-five minutes. At the same time, a six-bedroom period house set in two acres of ground near Ipswich would have cost £275,000 to £300,000, with a journey time to the City, door to door, of 75–90 minutes (Van Cutsem 1988).

Thus the London buyer spread outwards (Figures 5.4 and 5.5). In the period from 1984 to 1986, 15.3 per cent of country house buyers at Savills' Norwich office came from London. By 1987 the proportion had increased to 21 per cent. The Cambridge office saw an increase between the two periods from 14.1 to 17.5 per cent, Banbury from 11.7 to 22.2 per cent, Salisbury from 15.8 to 26.8 per cent, Hereford from 6.5 to 8.2 per cent and

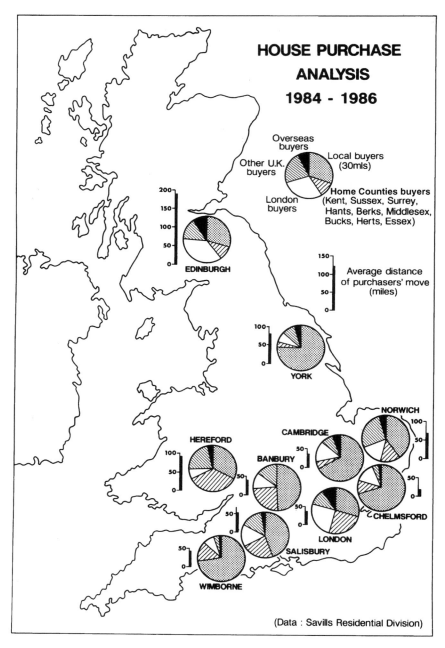

Figure 5.4 House purchase analysis, 1984–6
Source: Savills Residential Division

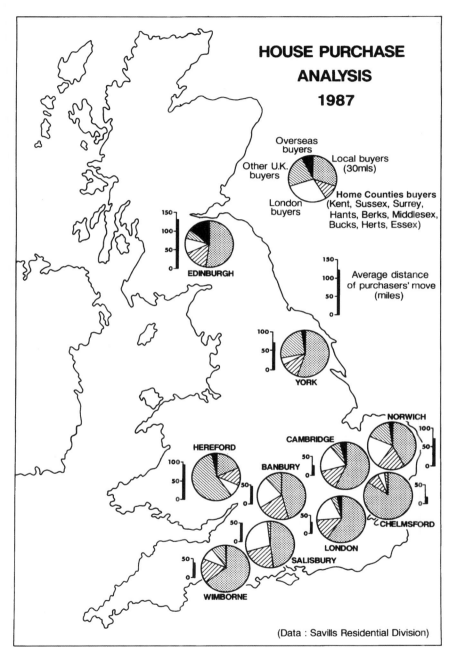

Figure 5.5 House purchase analysis, 1987
Source: Savills Residential Division

Wimborne from 3.8 to 7.6 per cent. (Meanwhile, offices nearer to London came to rely increasingly on buyers from London and the Home Counties as the only purchasers able to afford the prices.)

But, even in the mid-1980s, the country house market was clearly not restricted only to London (and especially City) buyers. The increasing wealth of the wealthier parts of the population in other parts of the country meant that the country house market was to some extent becoming independent of London. This was partly the result of the increasing economic prosperity of a number of different parts of the country, which was producing large concentrations of higher incomes (Leyshon *et al.* 1989b), and partly because these wealthier parts of the country outside London experienced their own house price booms, which allowed people in these areas to trade up to country houses in areas further out again. Thus by 1987 a number of major cities were forcing up country house prices within their own spheres of influence.

> Birmingham now affects Staffordshire almost as much as Warwickshire, while Hereford and Worcester are not far behind . . . Shropshire lags and continues to show plenty of scope for price improvement to match the other counties barely further in miles from Birmingham. Manchester's influence on Cheshire has produced in excess of a two-fold increase but Derbyshire and Lancashire have been less responsive. Bristol's interest in Gloucestershire, Avon and Somerset now collides cheerfully with that of London to bring about pronounced price increases.
>
> (Lilwall and Allcock 1988: x)

Throughout the 1980s the highest country house prices were found in the Home Counties but over time the price differential between London, the Home Counties and the rest of Britain tended to decrease as country house prices in other parts of Britain rose: 'London is no longer in the position of rich relation to impoverished country cousins. Gone are the days when one could buy a Herefordshire manor house for the price of a terrace-house in Fulham' (*Country Life* 1989: 13). But undoubtedly a wedge of relatively high country house prices in the Home Counties persisted through the 1980s and was gradually joined in the course of the decade by the counties of Hampshire, Oxfordshire and Gloucestershire, all counties with a limited stock of country houses and a 'smart' image. Outside this privileged wedge, there was an intermediate zone of high country house prices created more recently that reaches west (to Wiltshire, Avon, Dorset, Somerset and Devon), north (to Essex, Cambridgeshire and Leicestershire) and east (into Norfolk and Suffolk).

By the end of the 1980s, the country house market had taken on all the characteristics of a mature market. It was liquid, it was national, it was split into identifiable market segments, based on different kinds of purchasers. Most important of all, it had the capacity to become self-generating as the wealth of the 1980s made in the City and elsewhere flowed through it in separate but related circuits of money, social and cultural capital. Thus one survey by Crowley Financial Services (Stewart 1988) identified three different kinds of purchaser based on the degree of their income or capital. The first of these consisted of younger purchasers looking for properties valued at under £250,000. They were taking the first step into the country house market via a mortgage financed by an income which would certainly be under £100,000. Usually these buyers required a 95 per cent mortgage but they might also have access to some capital in the form of gains on a house in London or an inheritance. The second type of purchaser consisted of older executives with substantial incomes, often already established in the country house market but wanting to trade up. The majority of purchasers in this group were in the 35–45 age bracket with young or grown-up children and were seeking a better quality of life in the country – with riding, shooting, fishing, tennis, sailing and swimming nearby. They were also the highest-paid group and were confident of borrowing £300,000 to £500,000, when perhaps they would have been reluctant to borrow even £50,000 half a decade earlier. These people required properties in the £250,000 to £1 million price range and already owned property which itself had increased in value so that their borrowings were usually no more than 70 per cent of the purchase price (Stewart 1988: 10).

Finally, there was a group of the very rich with sufficient capital to ensure that income was no longer a consideration. These purchasers made their money in company flotations and sell-outs. They rarely needed to borrow and were generally not concerned about the price of the house they bought. However, they were often prepared to pay a premium of anything up to 30 per cent for a property that was really outstanding. Importantly, within these gradations of purchaser, there emerged a clearly defined country-house-buying life cycle that made the country house market self-sustaining (Table 5.1). Knight, Frank and Rutley (1989) looked at three 'typical' households in this life cycle. The first consisted of a young couple (aged 35 and 32) with two children buying their first country house. The husband was an investment analyst in the City. They lived in London in Clapham or Battersea. They made considerable capital gains in the London housing market and may also have had access to a gift from parents or to an inheritance. They were in the market for a period farmhouse or perhaps a period cottage for weekend use. The household cycle is next picked up when the husband is a 45-year-old company director trading up from a period farmhouse to a manor house. Finally, the household life cycle is completed when both heads of household are in their sixties. They have decided to trade down to a period village house and to distribute the excess proceeds to their children. The whole process then starts again.

CONCLUSIONS

This chapter has attempted to trace some of the effects of the proliferation of high incomes in the City of London and consequent changes in patterns

Table 5.1 The country house-buying life cycle

	Household 1	Household 2	Household 3
Size of household	Husband 35 Wife 32 Two children	Husband 45 Wife 42 Three children	Husband 68 Wife 65 Three children
Current house	London, five bedrooms three reception rooms, valued at £325,000	Period farmhouse, six bedrooms, three reception rooms, valued at £450,000	Period manor, eight bedrooms three reception rooms valued at £1 million[plus]
Aspirations	Period farmhouse	Period manor house	Period village house
Job of husband	City investment analyst	City company director	Retired City company director
Salary	£70,000 pa plus profit share	£130,000 pa plus profit share	£80,000 (pension)
Other income	£2,000 pa investments	£20,000 pa from investments	£26,000 pa from investments
Capital	£80,000 invested in stocks, shares, deposits	£350,000 invested in stocks, shares, deposits	£650,000 invested in stocks, shares, deposits
Total income after tax	£48,055	£75,655	£68,455
Existing borrowings	£40,000 mortgage	£50,000 mortgage (reduced from when present house bought)	£30,000 mortgage (reduced from when present house bought)
Borrowing power	£175,000	£400,000 (on income only)	–
Inheritance money from family	–	£220,000	–
Total funds	£450,000	£1,000,000	£1,000,000 (£600,000 for village house, £400,000 to be distributed to children)

Source: Knight, Frank and Rutley (1989)

of demand and consumption on the economy, society and culture of Britain. This has been done by reference to one commodity market only, the market for country houses. In the process it has demonstrated the importance of positional goods in asset appreciation. Positionality is the result of a complex interaction between not only economic but also social and cultural processes of the definition of scarcity. The country house market thrived in the 1980s because the commodities that it had on offer held out not only the possibility of economic gain, but also social and cultural gains. Indeed, it was precisely the ability of the country house to act simultaneously as a store of economic, social and cultural value which was its attraction. The scarcity of the commodity on offer was clearly an essential part of that ability. In particular, country houses were seized on by the new private sector 'disestablishment' as a way of accumulating assets, and as a way of providing themselves with social and cultural credibility.

The argument in the chapter could be extended much further if space did not preclude it. However, two points need to be made in conclusion. First, the chapter has only begun to explore the effects of the proliferation of higher incomes in the City, and more generally, on the pattern of expenditure in Britain. A laborious audit of a whole series of other commodity markets would be needed before the full measure of these effects could be understood. What is certain is that expenditure by those with higher incomes has hardly been restricted to the country house market. A whole constellation of goods and services is involved. Paradoxically, perhaps, this point can be well illustrated by turning back to the example of the country house. Expenditure on country houses hardly stops with the purchase of the house. It involves a whole series of other commodities, all of them with their effects on the structure of demand for particular goods and services. As Table 5.2 shows, buying a country house is likely to mean calls on the time of the chartered surveying and legal

Table 5.2 Expenditure on a country house

Initial outlay (purchase price plus agents' fee, stamp duty, etc.)	£537,500
Immediate expenses (conservatory etc.)	£54,000
Annual running costs (oil central heating, electricity, poll tax, etc.)	£5,150
Staff (gardener, domestic, nanny)	£16,840 pa
Garden and land (swimming pool, tennis court, etc.)	£62,350

Source: Stewart (1989: 57)

industries immediately, followed in short order by the removals and construction industries and the furniture industry (no doubt including antiques and restorations) and the gardening industry. It may add to the growth of employment in domestic service. It will almost certainly help the fashion industry as the new owners 'tog up for the country' (Glancy 1988).

Second, it is important not to lose sight of the fact that commodities are part of the process of social relation. They are not something separate. The country house provides the example again. Country houses are simply one of the most visible parts of a wider process of social interaction and class formation. The dinner parties, the weekend visits by friends or acquaintances, the reciprocal visits to kin, all these social activities centred around the country house will help to build up the 'invisible resources' (Marceau 1989) that will sustain the new disestablishment over future generations. The wake of money is long and sinuous.

Part II

FALL

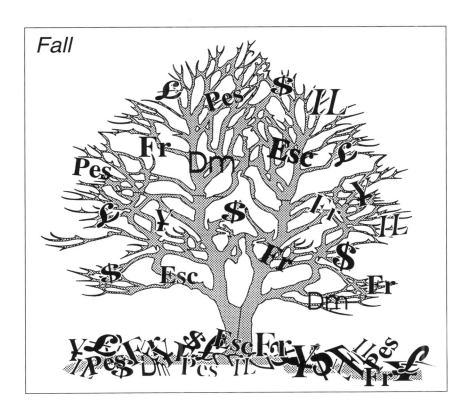

Fall

PART II

INTRODUCTION

There is a long history of writing on money and finance in the literature of Britain (e.g. Jackson 1995).[1] It is a history which is usually recorded as a struggle between the eternal values of art and the insubstantial and diabolical quantities of money. A typical history begins with a quotation from the Bible, is usually followed by Paul's plaintive question 'Papa' what's money?' in Dickens' *Dombey and Son*, moves on to Trollope and then T.S. Eliot (working at his desk at Lloyds Bank in the City of London)[2] and ends up in the Thatcherite 1980s with that demon of the chattering classes, the yuppie, a staple of numerous books of that time. One writer is usually exempted from this literary odyssey and that is R.H. Mottram. Mottram is, of course, famous for the First World War epic, the *Spanish Farm Trilogy* (1924).[3] But shortly thereafter Mottram also wrote *A History of Financial Speculation* (1929). Like Eliot, Mottram had worked as a bank clerk (but in Norwich, not London) and all his life he kept up the links with matters financial as well as literary.

Mottram, then, provides a kind of model for these five chapters in that he never made an attempt to separate out meaning from money. He tried to listen to the song of money in each and every register – the 'social', the 'culture' and the 'political', as well as the 'economic' – for, in a globalizing world, no other choice is possible.

> On all sides, politically as well as economically, national barriers are being broken down and overridden. Individual states, sunk beneath debt, or clamouring for capital they cannot themselves mobilise, must take wide views and show themselves capable of new qualities, if they are to maintain their financial integrity. Speculative habit, rightly used and necessarily controlled, may do much but only on condition that there can be created for its direction a body of intelligence and initiative that can put it adequately at the service of those humble laborious classes upon whose consent and co-operation it and the very daily existence of civilized states depend.
>
> (Mottram 1929: 314)

In this introduction, we want to provide a background to these chapters. We therefore begin in the 'economic' register, move on to the 'social' and 'cultural' registers and end up in the 'political' register.

ACCOUNTING FOR MONEY

There is a dominant model of the social and cultural effects of money. In it, money 'objectifies' human life. In particular, this process of objectification involves a direct mapping of money as a quality-less exchange relationship onto human life, so that human relationships are gradually stripped of all their older, customary aspects. So, apparently like money, human life becomes abstract, impersonal, instrumental, calculative and disembedded. Such a model of money as, to use Marx's term, a 'radical leveller', is found most clearly in the work of nineteenth-century social theorists – Marx, Weber and Simmel – but it has echoes in more contemporary writers like Parsons, Giddens and Harvey. It is best summed up by Simmel (1990: 346): 'the complete heartlessness of money is reflected in our social culture, which is itself determined by money'. Zelizer (1994) has suggested that this dominant model of money is based on five main assumptions.

First, the cultures and characteristics of money are defined strictly as 'economic'. Where the symbolic dimension of money is recognised it simply reinforces such a definition, by suggesting that all social life is becoming more 'economic'. Second, all money is regarded as the same. Differences in quantity replace differences in quality. Third, money is regarded as profane and utilitarian. Fourth, monetary concerns are seen to erode, corrode and corrupt all areas of life because money is interpreted as the vanguard of the overall commodification of society. Fifth, money is seen to have the power to transform non-pecuniary values but the reciprocal power of non-pecuniary values to transform money is rarely or never entertained.

However, as the later chapters in the second part of this book make clear, there is another way of proceeding which argues that money has never been as it is portrayed in the dominant model of money; this model is, to a large extent, an historically specific fantasy that was generated in the era of state money. Then, since this dominant model does not hold, there is no need to keep faith with its apparent effects on society.

Thus Zelizer (1994) shows how the dominant model of money – which she calls market money – was born out of the specific historical conjuncture of state credit money, and especially the convergent impulses of the growth of specific state monetary practices (of which the forging of a uniform national currency to replace the numerous monies that existed beforehand, which were gradually made illegal, is the most obvious) and the growth of discourses of the market. Yet, she also shows how, even at the high watermark of state credit money, there was clear resistance to the notion of monetary uniformity:

> even congress resisted when the government's efforts to homogenise currency went too far. Consider, for instance, the intense debate provoked in 1908 by the proposal to restore the inscription. 'In God We Trust', which had been removed by presidential order, on United States gold coins.

Although a few Congressmen applauded President Roosevelt's sensible decision to remove the motto insisting that 'our coin . . . is a medium of secular,
and not sacred, transactions', their more successful opponents argued elo-
quently in favour of the ritual marker, insisting that while 'the removal of
(the motto) did not depreciate (money's) monetary value . . . it depreciated
its sentimental value'. The United States, said the representative of Georgia,
should not coin an 'infidel money'.

(Zelizer 1994: 17)

How, then, might models of money be forged that offer some degree of
historical and geographical generality without spilling over their time and
place? The answer to this question can be found in the work of sociologists
like Zelizer and Dodd, and anthropologists like Bloch, Carrier and Parry,
whose orientation to money is as a determinedly partial and necessarily
anthropological phenomenon; that is, money is constituted in a number
of different networks of human practices, and used and thought of in different ways in these networks. Such an answer belies the idea of a single,
centred model of money in favour of series of differentiated, but overlapping models of monetary custom. In practice, this means conceiving
of money as a series of transactional networks, bound together by the
communication of information, which allow certain forms of uncertainty
to be at least controlled if not eliminated, and which depend for their
upkeep on often distinctive concepts, texts and instruments (Serres 1982;
Latour 1993; Law 1994). Seen in these terms, even the most minimally
extensive of monetary networks seems to rely on five properties (Dodd
1994, 1995). These five properties are:

1   *Calculative practices.* Each monetary network requires some kinds of
    calculative practices to sustain it, practices that, like what we now call
    'accountancy', organise monetary activities through particular notions
    of what money and monetary activity is (Hopwood and Miller 1994;
    Knights and Vurdubakis 1993; Power 1993).
2   *Regulative practices.* Each monetary network requires some degree of
    legal or other forms of sanction to back up merely consensual
    relationships, rules which will usually be administered by a wide
    variety of overlapping, non-contiguous institutions that fight for
    dominance and territory.
3   *Spatial practices.* Each monetary network takes up space and space is
    constitutive of each network. Space has to be understood as not just
    the delimitation of territory but also as a necessary part of how
    monetary networks operate: space has to be both overcome and used
    in order to create these networks.
4   *Reflexive practices.* Each monetary network is constructed from
    information within which is included expectations about the future
    which are incorporated into the process of monetary transaction
    itself. Thus reflexivity is a necessary condition of monetary networks,
    as a form of reasoning, as a means of constructing the future, and as
    a condition of monetary institution.

5   *Practices of sociability.* Each monetary network depends upon the striking up of particular social relationships which are *both* calculating *and* aimed at promoting sociability for its own sake. Thus:

> it is far from clear that the kinds of myths, superstitions, beliefs, fears and hopes which tend to be bound up with the use and operation of money should be confined to the margins of monetary analysis, treated as inconsequential failures to understand what money really is and how it really works.
>
> (Dodd 1995: 28)

To summarise, money *in use* can never be identified as one money, but only as a set of overlapping monetary networks which have profound effects on flow and liquidity. These 'special' or, more accurately, 'multiple' monies can never be reduced to one money (Zelizer 1994). A process of social earmarking of money is always at work which is based on the location of particular monetary forms within defined monetary networks:

> A fully sociological model of money must show how, how much, and why, even in the heartland of capitalism, different networks of social relations and systems of meaning mark modern money, introducing controls, restrictions and distractions that are as influential as the rationing of primitive money. Multiple monies in the modern world may not be as visibly identifiable as the shells, coins, brass rods or stones of primitive communities, but their invisible bodies work just as well. How else, for instance, do we distinguish a bribe from a tribute or a donation, a wage from an honorarium, or an allowance from a salary? How do we identify ransom, bonuses, tips, damages, or premiums? True, there are quantitative differences between these various payments. But surely the special vocabulary conveys much more than different amounts. Detached from its qualitative distinctions, the world of money becomes indecipherable.
>
> (Zelizer 1994: 24–5)

THREE LITERATURES

This kind of move towards an emphasis on the cultural construction of money and finance can be seen at work in each of the three bodies of literature that inform the succeeding chapters. The first of these is so-called international political economy. International political economy is, of course, a very broad church, a heterodox collection of approaches as diverse as regime theory and regulation theory. But in practically every corner of international political economy, the same phenomenon can be recognised: an increased emphasis on the discursive constitution of economic life, including financial systems. For example, Jessop's work on 'third-wave' regulation theory argues that social regulation can only be understood by activating the discursive dimension:

> In short, let us recognise that 'society' is simply a fluid interdiscursive space . . . a terrain in which different social forces compete to stabilize orientations and expectations around rival societal projects.
>
> (Jessop 1990: 335)

In more conventional work in international political economy, this discursive dimension is also crucial. For example, Sinclair (1994) has pointed to the crucial importance of credit-rating agencies as discursive prime movers in the international financial system.

In the body of literature known as economic sociology, similarly, an emphasis is on culture is becoming apparent:

> it is . . . argued that the cultural dimension – meaning historically constructed sets of group meaning and social 'scripts' – is present in all varieties of economic activity. Programmatic statements . . . stress the danger of narrowness of investigation if culture – in addition to social structure – is not included in the study of market, consumption, and workplace interaction.
>
> (Smelser and Swedberg 1994: 19)

For example, the work of Giddens on money as a disembedding mechanism has recently been challenged by the work of Dodd and Zelizer who conceive of money in more intimate terms, as a set of constantly practised monetary networks (but see Leyshon (1996b)).

Then, finally, there is a body of literature which is either poststructuralist or heavily influenced by poststructuralist motifs. Again, this is a broad church, spanning approaches as different as critical geopolitics and actor-network theory but held together by some common assumptions. In particular:

> by focussing on language and stressing the instability of meaning in language, poststructuralist theory undermines the effort to dissolve communication into a 'real' of action or into a universal definition of the human. At the same time, it calls into question versions of the relation of theory and history/context which present the latter as a closed or totalised field that seem to turn theory into ideology, into a discourse whose assumptions are disavowed or made invisible.
>
> (Poster 1995: 75)

Because poststructuralism emphasises communication and abhors fixity, it is a particularly good means for theorising the fluid and fast-moving international financial system. Of course, like any theoretical approach poststructuralism can become its own caricature, but international political economy and economic sociology can exert a calming influence by constantly reminding the reader that one rule is paramount in social science: 'always come back to the practice'. Why? Because

> practice identifies the self as it identifies the world. It is not the application of a code to the organisation of the world by a methodological individual or actor. It is a highly motivated practice rooted in the way immediate experience is structured in definite social contexts.
>
> (Friedman 1995: 86)

The move towards an emphasis on the cultural construction of money and finance that we have attended to has been accompanied by a linked move towards a greater appreciation of the role of space. Why has this linkage occurred? For three interrelated reasons. First, because the increasing hybridity of culture is also a postcolonial map of comings and goings which shows that the world is globally interconnected (Bhabha 1994; King 1995). Second, because the now-persistent questioning of the notion of 'modernity' is, in part, a questioning of why certain parts of the world should be privileged over others. Third, because the definition of culture (and identity) as a discrete and enclosed space has been revealed as suspect but the spatial metaphors that might replace such a definition are still in formation, so we are left with rather unsatisfactory metaphors of mixing and hybridity which, in part, still retain elements of the old definition (but see Gilroy 1993; Friedman 1995). Our more recent work on money and finance is part of this simultaneous move towards culture and space. In particular it questions simple binary notions like the global and local, the embedded and the disembedded, and the spatial and the temporal.

THE STATE WE'RE NOT IN

It follows from what has already been written that our analysis of a number of aspects of political economy is rather different from that currently found in the literature on the role of money and finance. In this final section we want to take issue with one current interpretation of the financial system, most particularly because it has become almost hegemonic in the imaginary of the British Left, especially as a result of the popularisation of the work of latter-day Hobsonites like Cain and Hopkins (1993a, b), Hutton (1995) and Kynaston (1995).

The Hobsonite account (Brewer 1990) starts with the identification of a tightly knit body of finance capital, an identification which serves three main purposes. First, it points to the articulation between finance and industry. Second, it domesticates finance by tying it to industry as a phenomenon which should rightly service the needs of production. But then, third, such a move also enables finance to be blamed for nearly all of the predicaments of industry.

In Britain, these assumptions are given a local spin by being tied to and motivated by a cultural formation known as 'gentlemanly capitalism' (Cain and Hopkins 1993a, b)[4] which, simply stated, assumes that British capitalists were either gentlemen or aspired to gentlemanly qualities arising out of a landed capitalism heavily influenced by pre-capitalist notions of order, authority and status and reliant upon values like 'honour, dignity, integrity, considerateness, and chivalry' (Thompson 1963: 16), all values which sprang from the nature of life on a country estate and from the practices of paternalism this engendered. This loosely knit club of capitalists has had a decisive and generally negative effect on the British economy because of its disdain of the world of industry and work (Wiener 1981).

The gentlemanly capitalist had a clear understanding of the market and economy and how to benefit from it; at the same time, he kept his distance from the everyday and demanding world of work. In an order dominated by gentlemanly norms, production was held in low repute. Working for money, as opposed to making it, was associated with dependence and cultural inferiority.

(Cain and Hopkins 1986: 505)

In particular, the City of London is usually identified in this account as the root of the British economic boil, which must now be lanced. Thus, so the account goes, through the nineteenth century entrepreneurs who had made fortunes in the City gradually moved into the lower and then the upper regions of the aristocracy, as a result of intermarriage, the purchase of large estates, the reliance of many landed aristocrats on City wealth and expertise, and

the fact that some forms of 'entrepreneurial' wealth were closer to the gentlemanly ideal than others. A line has to be drawn not just between rentiers and entrepreneurs but between those whose relationship with the production process was direct and those whose involvement was only indirect. Manufacturing was less eligible than the service sector: even at the highest levels, captains of industry could not command as much prestige as bankers in the City.

(Cain and Hopkins 1986: 506)

The combination of this process of assimilation and the unique features of the City's economic structure based on high profits (since only small amounts of capital were needed), on numerous small firms, and on the highly personalised nature of transactions, in which a knowledge of other people's standing was crucial to the operation of trust, meant that the City rapidly became an important branch of gentlemanly capitalism.

High finance, like high farming, called for leadership from 'opinion makers', and trust from associates and dependants. A gentleman possessed the qualities needed to inspire confidence; and because his word was his bond transactions were both informal and efficient. Shared values, nurtured by a common education and religion, provided a blueprint for social and business behaviour. The country house led to the accounting house. The public school led to the service sector; the London club supported the City. Gentlemanly enterprise was strongly personal and was sustained by a social network which, in turn, was held together by the leisure needed to cultivate it. The predominance of inter-group marriage . . . was not a gesture to traditionalism, but a strategy to reinforce group solidarity, to create economic efficiency and political stability, and to take out an option on the future by ensuring dynastic continuity. Social proximity was aided by geographical concentration: both came together in London, the focal point of the gentleman and his activities. In this world conspicuous consumption was not merely wasteful: it was a public manifestation of substance, a refined advertisement which used hospitality to sustain goodwill, to generate new connexions, and to exclude those of low income or low repute.

(Cain and Hopkins 1986: 508–9)

As we hope is already clear, we believe that this kind of gentlemanly capitalist explanation is both overstated, and too slippery. As an explanation of Britain's economic problems, 'the concept is simply not up to the task' (Ingham 1995: 11) and for four main reasons.

First of all, it is much too easy to use it as a means of characterising the City of London as a unified and homogeneous bloc acting to conspire against the rest of British industry, in a way that harks back to Hobson's anti-semitic characterisation of financiers as a Jewish cabal (Hobson 1902)[5] but now with the British gentleman in the driving seat. In turn, by positioning the City as a unified and homogeneous bloc, it is possible to overstate the City's influence on government policy by positing a City–Bank–Treasury nexus which was nearly always more diffuse than commentators like Anderson (1987) or Leys (1988) have made out. In fact, the City has never been a dynastic social bloc. The City has split over numerous economic issues. It has nearly always included a very large foreign component (e.g. in 1914 twelve of the leading twenty merchant banks were of foreign origin and Chapman (1992) is able to devote a whole chapter of his authoritive work on merchant enterprise in Britain to the international houses). And the history of the City has been regularly marked by the bankruptcies of gentlemanly family firms – hardly a testament to cohesion. In other words, 'the most essential feature of mercantile activity in Britain from the eighteenth to the twentieth centuries has been its ethnic, cultural and organisational diversity' (Chapman 1992: 312).

Second, there is the difficulty of straightforwardly ascribing cultural motives to economic strategies. For example, when City financiers bought land it was by no means always a slavish strategy to curry social influence: just as often it was a way of finding an alternative source of income to minimise the risk of failure from other business interests (Harris and Thane 1984). And, even when a gentlemanly capitalist lifestyle was being aspired to, research shows that it was rarely achieved.[6] Most so-called gentlemanly capitalists worked hard and long.

> For the many, it must have been a lifestyle that was a seldom achieved reward. In particular, it might spur on those without the discipline of religious sanctions or ethnic restraints, and it ensured that mediocre heirs could be diverted from the trading successes. Like the contemporary legend of self-help, it contains sufficient truth to be plausible and have wide appeal, but its relevance to economic reality is evidently limited, even for the most successful families, who had to work hard to maintain their fortunes.
>
> (Chapman 1992: 312)

Even more caution must be expressed in ascribing cultural motives to middle-class aspirants in finance. As Gunn (1988), Perkin (1989) and others have shown for the nineteenth century these aspirations were nowhere near as conformist as they are often portrayed, and there is no reason to believe that this is any more the case now.

Third, too often the idea of gentlemanly capitalists conflates what is a structural necessity of the business of international money – the need to forge social relationships – with its City variant, thus making the case of the City seem more extreme than it usually is. Fourth and finally, the gentlemanly capitalist thesis is too often used to exaggerate the importance of the City of London in the British economy. Thus, Ingham (1984) calculates, following Imlah, that in the 1820s the City's income including earnings (excluding investment income to rentiers) amounted to about 30 per cent of the value of exported products. By the 1880s, this proportion had grown to nearly 50 per cent. But this was probably the high point. Again, the personal fortunes made in the City were probably not as large as has sometimes been made out by commentators like Rubinstein (1980), and their effect on the structure of demand in the South East was correspondingly less marked. The fortunes made in industry outside the South East may also have been rather larger than has sometimes been stated (Daunton 1989).

Let us be clear: we do not believe that 'gentlemanly capitalism' ever existed as a coherent social formation in Britain or the City of London. That does not mean that a gentlemanly discourse has not existed and has not been powerful at certain points in the City's history (see Chapter 5). But, whatever the case, by the 1960s, whatever effects such a gentlemanly discourse might have had were fast dying and, as examples like the death of Barings and the takeover of Warburgs, Smith New Court and others in the mid-1990s show, that shrinking segment of the City which did still cleave to some gentlemanly values, which the Left, since the growth of work on the 'Establishment' in the 1950s (e.g. Thomas 1959) has so often fixed on and taken to be pivotal, has now all but died out.

Of course, we do not want to absolve international finance, as practised by the City, of blame for all the British economy's problems. It is undoubtedly the case that the short-termism of the capital markets is a problem for certain parts of British industry, although the problem is by no means universal. But, it is also the case that what Kay (1993, 1995) calls the 'architecture' of many British firms was and is deficient, let alone the other assets these firms might have. And it is also the case that British industry suffered and still suffers from a serious management deficit. We believe, then, that the 'republicanisation' of finance which Hutton (1995) calls for, and about which we have some reservations (mainly to do with the state-centred nature of the project), must be balanced by other policy actions. No doubt, such actions will lack the glamour which attacks on the City have for the British Left, which for a long time has constructed the City as an economic and, as importantly, a cultural enemy. But they may well turn out to be rather more important. Whatever the case, a first step towards understanding the City is to dispel the aura of matters both sexy and arcane that still surrounds it and a number of the chapters that follow are intended as contributions towards that aim.

THE CHAPTERS

I tell thee, Rica (the commerce of stock jobbers) is Lying, Political Lying: and tho' each Man knows the other to deal in this Commodity, yet no one Day passes, in which some of these fellows do not grow rich, and others are outdone as they *out-lye* one another, or as the lye of one gains more credit than that of *another*. They call the chief nominal Commodity which they deal in SOUTH SEA STOCKS. This is worth more or less in Idea only, as the *Lye of the Day* takes or does not take. Thou wilt think that I rave, that I talk idly, when I tell thee here are many People, whom I have convers'd with, and who appear, in other particulars, to be Men of *Reason*, and yet, on the first of these Syllables *South Sea Stock*, lose at once all reflection and comparison. They told me that, in the year 1720, they carry'd this Ideal-Value of their Stocks so high, that what, in the beginning of the Year, was not valued at 1000 *Piastres*, mounted to more than 10,000 in less than the space of seven moons: that is every Man had agreed to call himself exceedingly rich. . . . But at last . . . the People awoke from their Golden Dreams.

(*The Craftsman*, 27 May 1727, cited in Nicholson (1994: 1))

If the 1980s was high summer for the world of money and finance, then the 1990s was the fall. Golden Dreams were exchanged for dreams of silver or bronze. The chapters that follow provide, then, a kind of financial evensong. And yet, at the same time, they also show the invention of new monetary forms and financial practices which have allowed the international financial system to stutter on.

Even under substantial pressures, there has been no breakdown of the sort that threatened the world through the 1920s when the international financial system of R.H. Mottram's day served up some awful warnings. Most specifically, then, of course there was the case of Germany and Austria, which suffered hyperinflation on a scale rarely known before or since in world history. The scale of inflation was such that by August 1923 the whole German and Austrian monetary system had all but collapsed.

> When cheques are presented for payment at a bank, the bank now charges 2 per cent a day on the face of the cheque until it is now cleared. As it takes about four days this reduces the value of the cheque by 8 per cent. When cheques are presented on provincial banks – which take about ten days to clear, owing to the general breakdown – it has been found cheaper to send a messenger to the provincial bank to get the cash. For example, on a cheque for £5 on a Hamburg bank (about 100,000,000 marks) a Berlin bank would deduct 20,000,000 marks for collection, whereas a messenger could be sent, at third class fare, to Hamburg and back for only 3,000,000 marks.
>
> (Newspaper correspondent cited in Angell (1930: 334))

In the 1990s, the financial systems of the United States, Britain and many other countries have been through the mill. Chapter 6 charts the British experience, showing how a combination of bad loans, technological change and cost pressures forced the British financial system to retrench, with drastic effects on employment in financial services, effects which are still rolling on.

Some of the adverse effects of financial system decline are hinted at in this chapter by alighting on the example of the United States, most particularly the damage done to poorer people who are forced out of the system by a so-called 'flight to quality' either by price or by simple administrative fiat. These kinds of adverse effects are described more fully in Chapter 7 which documents the process of withdrawal of financial services from poorer communities in the United States and Britain. The chapter is concerned both with the changes that might be made to extant financial structures so that they are more open to the needs of poorer people and with the possibilities of building alternative financial institutions, all the way from community banks, through women's banks, credit unions, rotating credit associations, and even those ancestors of Robert Owen's 1832 Equitable Labour Exchange, the growing number of LETS (local exchange and trading systems) (Angell 1930; Ardener and Burman 1995; Reifner and Ford 1992).

These chapters take a broadly political economy perspective but, increasingly throughout the 1990s, we have begun to develop another approach, one that we might call 'discursive'.[7] This approach sees international financial systems as essentially a communicative entity, made up of networks of interdependent texts, technological devices, and people which shuttle information back and forth (Dodd 1994; Law 1994) passing on the 'lye of the day', and so both making money and reconstituting money for another first time. This approach sees each network as being the heir to quite specific practices including particular forms of social affiliation, particular monetary forms and particular notions of what 'money' actually is. The last three chapters provide explanations and amplifications of this approach. Thus Chapter 8 both provides a critique of political economic approaches and outlines the importance of a discursive approach. The chapter analyses the 'ordering' of the international financial system through a consideration of the Bretton Woods system. It points to the way in which the world of money is increasingly one of interpretive power struggles where competing sets of scripts and discourses conjure up alternative plausible interpretations of the financial world. Chapter 9 provides an account of the international financial system as a 'communicative commotion' (Shotter 1989) which needs international financial centres like London, New York and Tokyo both to produce and to stabilise this commotion through numerous acts of story telling. Electronic telecommunications have enhanced the communicative resources available to those who work the international financial system but, at the same time, have produced the problem of a larger and larger interpretative load which, paradoxically, forces more and more face-to-face interaction. Thus, the future of places like the City of London, which is examined at length, is assured as, quite literally, a 'talking shop'. Finally, Chapter 10 continues to examine the impact of electronic telecommunications on the international financial system by addressing the idea that its electronic networks form a prototypical 'cyberspace'. The chapter shows that this characterisation is a false one, made possible only by the kind of hyperbole which, in a Gadarene rush to judgement, ignores the sins of technological determinism. What has been produced by the growth of electronic telecommunications is something much more fragmentary and hetero-geneous which requires new, less pompous characterisations of people and electronic technology which resist the temptation to see the world as an epic, and its authors as seers. Using the example of the City of London again, this chapter attempts such a characterisation.

CHAPTER 6

THE RESTRUCTURING OF THE UK FINANCIAL SERVICES INDUSTRY IN THE 1990s

A reversal of fortune?

INTRODUCTION

The late 1980s marked an important watershed in the history of the financial services industry in Britain. Following a decade of unprecedented expansion and growth, the early 1990s saw financial services firms begin a process of retrenchment in response to a downturn in financial markets and growing problems of financial indebtedness. This retrenchment of financial services firms, which is more accurately described as a process of 'restructuring for profit', is wreaking great changes within the industry. On the one hand, financial services labour markets are being remade. They are both shrinking in size, as firms have engaged in unprecedented rounds of voluntary and compulsory redundancies, and taking on new forms, as firms have used the growing mismatch between supply and demand in the labour market to introduce more 'flexible' labour market practices. On the other hand, the process of restructuring for profit is likely to have important long-term implications for urban and regional development, as financial services firms both reorganise their operations over space to reduce costs, and redraw the boundaries of financial markets in order to maximise profits and reduce risks. Whereas in the 1980s the financial services industry acted as an important engine of employment growth within the British economy, the restructuring of financial service labour markets will ensure that very little employment growth will take place in the financial services industry in the 1990s. At the same time, a process of 'financial infrastructure withdrawal', produced by the restructuring of operations and the reconfiguration of markets over space, is likely to have important implications for local economic development within those localities from which financial services firms withdraw their operations. Research in the United States, where this process is much more advanced, has revealed a clear link between financial infrastructure withdrawal and a lack of economic growth (Dymski and Veitch 1992).

The processes of restructuring which are currently transforming the financial services sector are not entirely unfamiliar. Indeed, in many ways, we have been here before. In the early 1980s, the financial services industry went through a similar process of restructuring, which saw important changes in the organisational logic of the financial system accompanied by extensive financial infrastructure withdrawal. However, in the early to mid-1980s this process took place at an international level, as financial institutions withdrew credit and closed operations in less developing countries. As the less developed country debt crisis broke, manifested in unprecedented levels of personal and corporate indebtedness, there occurred a 'flight to quality', as banks abandoned borrowers in less developed countries to concentrate on lending to borrowers within core capitalist economies. On the emergence of a developed countries' debt crisis in the late 1980s, a similar 'flight to quality' occurred, although this time the process of financial infrastructure withdrawal unfolded within the confines of economies such as the United Kingdom and the United States.

The remainder of this chapter seeks to investigate this current round of restructuring within the financial services industry, and does so in three stages. In the first section we seek to uncover the international and national antecedents of the current crisis in the industry, paying particular attention to the changing forms of financial organisation and of financial regulation, and to the changing geographies of the financial system. The second section looks at the process of restructuring within financial services firms, and illustrates the ways in which firms are both remaking their internal labour markets and reorganising themselves over space. The conclusions to the chapter are presented in the third and final section.

A REVERSAL OF FORTUNE

It is possible to interpret the reversal in the fortunes of the financial services industry in Britain as merely the consequence of a cyclical downturn in the economy. The problems of the financial services industry, according to this interpretation, stem from an unfortunate combination of contingent misfortunes. An economic recession, corporate and consumer indebtedness and a housing market slump have combined to lower demand for corporate and personal financial services. Now, while it is true that certain parts of the financial services industry, such as insurance, endure regular cyclical variations in rates of profitability, the description of the crisis as a cyclical downturn *writ large* is not entirely convincing. The crisis facing the financial services sector industry in the early 1990s was systemic in nature. Each of the contingent misfortunes listed above were manifested in problems of indebtedness and declining asset prices, and were constituent of the processes of financial services restructuring which unfolded during the 1980s (Davis 1992).

In the remainder of this section we wish to investigate these earlier rounds of restructuring. We do so at two levels of spatial aggregation: first, at the level of the global financial system, and second, at the level of the UK financial system. We recognise that financial dynamics are of course much more complicated than this, and do not conform to such neat and tidy spatial aggregations. Indeed, the blurring of global and national processes is one of the most important consequences of systemic change within the financial services industry. Nevertheless, there remain sufficient differences between global and national processes to warrant such an approach.

The restructuring of the global financial services industry

The 1980s saw a sea-change in the nature of the international financial system as flows of money and finance conformed to new spatial and organisational logics. During the 1970s it was possible to describe the geography of the international financial system as 'inclusive', dominated as it was by the 'recycling' of large volumes of money from the industrialised and oil-rich nations to developing countries in Latin America, Africa and Asia. Meanwhile, the organisational logic of the financial system during this period was that of intermediated lending; that is, the classic form of financial intermediation, whereby banks make loans to borrowers from pooled deposits, making money from different rates of interest offered to borrowers and depositors. During the 1980s these spatial and organisational logics were overturned. The geography of the international financial system became more 'exclusive' while 'disintermediated' forms of financial organisation became increasingly important within the international financial system.

The catalyst for this sea-change was the breaking of the developing countries' debt crisis in the early 1980s. The history of this crisis is now well known (see Corbridge 1992a). For the developing countries, the crisis was little short of disastrous, and ushered in a decade or so of effective 'de-development'. For the financial system, the crisis was certainly serious, but in the end served mainly to trigger a remarkable process of transformation which overturned the prevailing spatial and organisational logics. A new international financial system came into being as banks, borrowers and investors reorganised in the wake of the crisis (Thrift and Leyshon 1988).

The financial system was remade through the reactions of international banks to the debt crisis. Banks embargoed developing countries, a process of financial withdrawal which excluded much of the developing world from the international financial system. Therefore, although the 1980s witnessed the dawn of a global financial system, it is important to recognise that this system was only global in the sense that money and finance now began to flow more intensively between the three regional blocs of the industrialised world (North America, Europe and South East Asia) (O'Brien 1991; Hirst and Thompson 1992). In consequence, large sections of the world were denied access to this global financial system, the organisation of which became concentrated within just three 'centres of financial co-ordination' or 'financial command posts': London, New York and Tokyo (Leyshon *et al.* 1987; Sassen 1991; Amin and Thrift 1992).

Banks were also instrumental in remaking the organisational logic of the international financial system. During the debt crisis a number of banks seemed close to collapse under the weight of unsecured debt. This fact prompted financial regulators, who are charged with the task of seeking to contain systemic risk within the financial system but without overly restricting competition between agents in financial markets, to take action. Since the less developed countries' debt crisis was evidently of a systemic nature, the regulatory response was to impose tighter restrictions on bank lending. The setting of capital adequacy ratios by the Bank of International Settlements (BIS) is the best example of this process, and required banks to set aside $8 in non-interest-bearing reserves for every $100 advanced to borrowers.[1] However, in their efforts to reduce systemic risk, all that the financial regulators really achieved was to move the centre of the financial system away from the international syndicated loan market and into a new financial arena. During the 1980s disintermediated financial instruments, such as bonds, equity and commercial paper, became increasingly important. One reason for this was that banks earned fee income for the organisation of securitised debt. This activity is 'off balance sheet', and unaffected by capital adequacy requirements. Of more importance, though, was the reactive behaviour of the major groups of international borrowers and investors. Following the embargo imposed upon less developed countries, transnational corporations and developed countries became the major borrowers in international financial markets. The debt crisis damaged the balance sheets of many international banks so badly that they earned credit ratings that were lower than the corporations and governments they sought to lend money to. In other words, transnational corporations and developed sovereign borrowers could obtain money from the wholesale financial markets more cheaply than many international banks. This money was obtained through the issue of paper securities, such as bonds and shares. These financial instruments were bought in increasing volumes by international investment institutions, who in effect began to lend directly to borrowers via disintermediated financial instruments.

The rise of disintermediation broadened the scope of international financial practice as securitised forms of finance took their place alongside more traditional intermediated forms. This development was to have three very important implications for the global financial system. First, it led to increased competition in financial markets. International commercial banks,[2] which had dominated international financial markets during the 1960s and 1970s, increasingly found themselves challenged by other financial institutions such as investment banks, securities houses, other types of financial institutions and even non-financial organisations. Under a logic of intermediation, competition in international financial markets revolved largely around the ability to match assets with liabilities and around the interest rates offered to borrowers and depositors. The skills needed to compete in disintermediated financial markets were very different. Financial institutions needed to be able to assess and price risk much more, to be able to handle the issue and distribution of paper securities on behalf of clients, and to be able to trade in the secondary markets for such securities on their own account. Indeed, this shift in the organisational logic of international financial markets led *The Economist* (1990) to question whether there was still a need for the commercial bank as a unique breed of financial institution.

Second, securitisation and disintermediation sparked a wave of financial innovation and a growth in credit and debt. The financial system has given birth to an extraordinary number of new financial instruments since the late 1970s (Figure 6.1). In effect, money has been mutating into new forms which exist outside existing structures of regulation. Indeed, this is precisely why many of them are developed, although the majority of instruments have been introduced with the overt aim of helping to manage risk in increasingly volatile financial markets (*The Economist* 1993c).

Third, while risk management within disintermediated financial markets became ever more sophisticated, within intermediated markets commercial banks began to turn to more risky types of borrowing. As their best clients began to raise money through the issue of securities, many commercial banks began a search for new borrowers. An important part of

1972	Foreign currency futures
1973	Equity futures
1974	
1975	Morgage-backed bonds futures, T-bill futures
1976	
1977	T-bond futures
1978	
1979	Over-the-counter currency options
1980	Currency swaps, Interest-rate swaps
1981	Bank CD future options, T-bond future options, Equity-index futures, Eurodollar futures, T-note futures
1982	
1983	Equity-index future options, Currency future options, T-note future options, Interest-rate caps & floors
1984	
1985	US dollar & municipal-bond indicies futures, Eurodollar options, Swaptions
1986	
1987	Bond futures & options, Compound options, Average options, Commodity swaps
1988	
1989	Three month Euro-DM futures, Captions, Interest-rate swaps futures, Ecu interest-rate futures
1990	Equity index swaps
1991	Portfolio swaps
1992	Differential swaps

Figure 6.1 Financial innovation 1972–92: the rise of risk management techniques
Source: The Economist (1993c: 9)

this process, especially for banks in the UK and the United States, was to seek to uncover a hitherto untapped demand for credit within their domestic markets. This shift in focus, which saw banks move ever more strongly into the personal finance market, the leveraged buyout end of the corporate finance market and, in particular, into property and real estate lending, was to have particularly disastrous consequences for the banks. By 1992 it was estimated that 35 per cent of all commercial lending to UK residents was property related, either in the form of loans to property companies, to the construction industry, to building societies or to individuals in the form of residential mortgages. However, a significant proportion of this lending was less than secure, given the precipitous decline in the value of property since the late 1980s.[3]

The turn towards disintermediation and securitisation within the international financial system was in fact just one of four wider processes of restructuring within the global financial system. The second was the growing coherence and integration of the world's money and capital markets on a global scale. Modern information and communication technologies (ICTs) now allow regional markets to share data instantaneously and they are leading to the gradual elimination of cash and cheques as primary monetary instruments. It now only takes eleven seconds to post a bank transaction from one part of the globe to another (Crawford and Sihler 1991). And whilst it may be premature to proclaim *The End of Geography*, as some have done (O'Brien 1991), time and space within the global financial system have clearly been compressed in new and remarkable ways (Harvey 1989b). By tying markets together in this way, ICTs have facilitated the pooling of global money and capital to create financial markets which have come to dwarf those for traded goods. For example.

> In 1988 the total volume of [traded goods] flows within [North America, Western Europe and South East Asia] amounted to $600 billion *annually*. By contrast, the *daily* volume in foreign exchange . . . trading amounted to $600 billion.
>
> (Ohmae 1990: 196, *original emphasis*)

By 1992 it was estimated that global turnover in foreign exchange markets had risen to at least $900 billion dollars per day (*The Economist* 1992).

The third process revolved around capital centralisation among international financial institutions. In certain 1980s' scenarios, the global financial system was going to become the province of a few global institutions which would carry out all conceivable financial transactions, and on a world scale to boot. Certainly, in the 1980s there was a large degree of concentration and centralisation amongst financial corporations, leading to fewer, larger, more global firms. Patently, there is room for further concentration. For example, some forecasts predict that the number of commercial banks in the European Community will halve between now and the year 2000. But a recent survey suggested that only sixty-eight truly 'global banks' could be said to exist, and of these only six could claim that at least 50 per cent of their business was conducted outside their home economies (*The Banker* 1991).[4] Most other banks had put aside global ambitions, and were concentrating on particular market niches in specific world regions. However, one of the reasons the largest and most internationalised banks continue to make great store of their 'global reach' is because of the considerable fee income that can be earned from offering fund management services to the world's institutional investors (pension funds, insurance companies, investment funds, and so on).[5] This form of 'money manager capitalism' (Minsky 1989) exerted a growing influence over financial assets in core capitalist countries during the 1980s, as institutional investment institutions both increased in size and number (Davis 1991a, b).

The fourth and final process of restructuring in global financial markets was related to the remaking of international financial regulation. Much has been made in the literature of a bout of so-called 'deregulation'. However, this is not an accurate description of what actually took place (Hancher and Moran 1989; Cerny 1989, 1991; Underhill 1991; Christopherson 1993). In fact, partly in response to American pressure, partly in response to internally generated government ambitions, and partly in response to various financial scandals, the world financial system came increasingly under the spell of American-style procedures, regulations and institutions, which have led to *more* rather than less state control and to a massively increased administrative load for most financial services firms associated with compliance with the new procedures and regulations. Formerly, financial institutions were subjected to a system of 'structural regulation', whereby different types of firms were limited to prescribed areas of the financial system, although the degree to which their activities were supervised within these areas was often minimal. Now, financial institutions have greater freedom to compete across a wider range of markets, but they are subject to a higher level of surveillance (Gardener and Molyneux 1990; Leyshon and Thrift 1992; Marshall *et al.* 1992). In Britain, the Securities and Investment Board (SIB) and the various Self-Regulatory Organisations (SROs), each with their own complex and overlapping rules, are an outgrowth of this move to a new system of regulation. As Michael Moran (1991) puts it:

> the story of the financial services revolution is the story of the rapid creation of new institutions, struggling for regulatory jurisdiction, the development of increasingly complex and unclear rules and the creation of growing numbers of regulations inside and outside firms, all quarrelling over the meaning of an expanding, contradictory and unclear body of jurisprudence.

In summary, these four processes of financial restructuring – financial disintermediation, financial market integration, financial capital centralisation and financial reregulation – meant that the operation of the new international financial system was distinguished by four motifs: an intensified level of *competition* between financial agents; increasingly sophisticated means of issuing and using *debt*; financial innovation linked to the management and exploitation of *risk*; and the importance of *volatility* as a means of amplifying both profits and losses. To this extent, the global financial services industry can perhaps be seen as an example of an industry in which a *modus operandi* based upon notions of 'allocative efficiency' was replaced with one based more upon 'market efficiency', thereby conforming closely to the prescriptive advice of New Right theorists and politicians which enjoyed a similar ascendancy during the 1980s (Thompson 1990a: Cloke 1992; Corbridge 1992b).

However, from the late 1980s onwards, this new international financial system began to run aground. On closer inspection, it became clear that the increasingly dysfunctional nature of the global financial system was a direct consequence of this shift from allocative to market 'efficiency'. Two particularly important problems confronted the global financial services industry in the early 1990s. By far the most important problem was the emergence of a *developed countries' debt crisis*, founded in non-performing personal, corporate property loans. A rapid growth in bank lending during the 1980s (Table 6.1) led to a sharp increase in indebtedness within core capitalist countries. By the late 1980s levels of household indebtedness were more than 90 per cent of disposable income in both the United States and Japan, and more than 100 per cent of disposable income in the UK (Table 6.2).

Problems of indebtedness were exacerbated by the emergence of *new types of risk* within the global financial system. Although financial innovation had in large part been driven by a search for new ways to manage risk in an intermediated financial system, it proved impossible to banish risk from the system altogether. Indeed, while the development of derivative financial instruments has largely succeeded in reducing the level of market risk associated with interest rate and exchange rate volatility,[6] the process of disintermediation has made the international financial system a more risky environment in which to operate. In addition to market risk, international financial institutions now have to deal with seven other types

Table 6.1 Bank lending by destination, 1983–91: percentage growth at annual rate

Destination	Years	USA	Japan	UK	Germany	France	Italy
Business	1983–90	6.5	7.7	18.0	6.3	10.0	15.0
	1991	−4.0	2.4	6.3	14.4	6.2	14.4
Housing	1983–90	14.3	19.0	14.9	5.0	9.1	−
	1991	3.3	4.4	4.3	6.1	5.5	−
Individual	1983–90	8.6	14.6	16.4	7.3	22.5	20.4
	1991	−4.1	6.1	3.6	13.3	−2.6	34.4

Source: Bank for International Settlement (BIS) (1992) *62nd Annual Report*, p. 117, Basle: BIS.

Table 6.2 Household indebtedness in selected countries, 1975–89

	Debt as a percentage of disposable income			
Country	1975	1980	1985	1989
Japan	45	58	68	92
USA	67	77	83	96
Germany	62	76	88	87
UK	47	48	76	105
Canada	77	85	73	87

Source: Bank for International Settlements (BIS) (1991) *61st Annual Report*. p. 107, Basle; BIS.

of risk (Bank for International Settlements, 1992: 14–19). First, the growing importance of off-balance-sheet activities has increased credit risk, inasmuch as it is increasingly difficult to discern the creditworthiness of counterparties in financial markets. A second type of risk – clearing and settlement risk – is related to the first inasmuch as the risk of counterparty default casts a continual shadow over the process of clearing and settling transactions. But this particular risk is further amplified by the increased scale and scope of financial markets, which means that financial institutions are exposed to a larger number and wider range of counterparties than previously. A third type of risk – market liquidity risk – is partly a product of capital centralisation and concentration within financial markets, and partly a product of the growing tendency to use 'expert systems' to spot arbitrage opportunities in securitised financial markets. Large financial institutions are increasingly 'moving the market', with the result that it can be difficult to obtain both buy *and* sell prices in financial markets at any one time. In turn, market illiquidity introduces a fourth type of risk – cash liquidity risk – where institutions may find it difficult to gain access to sufficient capital to fund their activities. A fifth type of risk – legal risk – highlights the fact that while the financial system does indeed operate on a global scale, it has proved impossible to 'disembed' processes of financial exchange from their local economic and social contexts (Giddens 1990). By definition, every financial transaction takes place within at least one geographical–political jurisdiction, and even though the way in which financial institutions are regulated within different countries has become increasingly similar in recent years (Moran 1991), marked differences in what is permitted persist, particularly between what are seen to be 'international' and 'domestic' financial markets, and in the treatment of new financial products. A sixth type of risk, which may be termed innovation risk, stems from the uncertainty which surrounds the introduction of a new financial product, which 'may involve a learning period during which many participants do not fully understand the product's risk properties' (Bank for International Settlements 1992: 18). A seventh and final type of risk is the danger of systemic risk (Davis 1992), which may be seen as an encapsulation of the wide range of risks endemic within a securitised and disintermediated financial system. The rise of a transaction-driven financial system has not only ensured that financial institutions are now more dependent upon, and more highly exposed to, one another in the event of a financial crisis, but the possibility of such a crisis occurring has significantly increased due to time–space compression:

> global information systems disseminated news about problems at a speed that left market participants and central banks very little time to react in the event of a crisis. . . . These systems also spread rumours and misunderstandings widely before they could be countered by denials, clarifications or explanations.
>
> (Bank for International Settlements 1992: 19)

A growing awareness of the inherent riskiness of a disintermediated financial system has seen the management of risk become a competitive strategy in its own right (*The Economist* 1993b). Graham Thompson once argued that financial or banking capital is 'the most "cautious" form of capital, requiring firm collateral before any credit can be given' (Thompson 1977: 270). The behaviour of the financial system in the 1980s seemed to give the lie to such an interpretation, as financial capital operated more in the manner of commercial capital (Thrift 1987c), being chiefly 'concerned with the "turnover" of [financial] commodities, their repeated buying and selling as quickly as possible so as to "realize" its capital in the form of money, with which it can repurchase commodities once again' (Thompson 1977: 270). However, in light of the emergence of a developed countries' debt crisis, there is evidence that the financial sector is rediscovering the merits of caution. Credit lines are being withdrawn or reduced, and much greater attention is being paid to risk management and risk reduction (Bank for International Settlements 1992). As we shall see below, this growing aversion to risk among financial institutions has important implications for the geography of investment and development.

The restructuring of the United Kingdom financial system

A greater concern with the creditworthiness of counterparties in financial transactions has prompted an interesting response on the part of financial institutions. To operate in markets where agents are particularly risk averse, some financial institutions have created separately capitalised operations, organised in such a way that the credit standing of these operations is not affected by the credit standing of the larger financial institution of which they are a part (Bank for International Settlements 1992). This institutional 'balkanisation' is particularly noteworthy because it bears a striking resemblance to the system of structural regulation which governed most national financial systems until the 1980s (Gardener and Molyneux 1990). Structural regulation of the financial system served to maintain a system of discrete financial markets and institutions, the purpose of which was to prevent a contagion of systemic crisis through the financial system. Such regulation was motivated by the belief that by keeping markets and institutions separate from one another, any financial crisis would be contained within the part of the financial system in which it developed (Leyshon and Thrift 1992). What appears to be happening, in some international financial markets at least, is that this form of 'public interest regulation' (Flynn *et al.* 1993), which governed financial markets for so long, is providing the inspiration for a form of institutional regulation within the private sector, by which financial institutions seek to insulate the different parts of their operations from one another.[7]

However, public interest structural regulation in the financial sector was firmly in retreat during the 1980s as barriers between financial markets and institutions were dismantled. In the first instance, the reregulation of the British financial services sector was motivated by an attempt to integrate British financial institutions better with international financial markets, with regulation being shaped to accommodate the imperatives of a global, disintermediated financial system. For example, exchange controls (which since the Second World War had limited the export of capital in the form of foreign portfolio investment) were scrapped only weeks after the Conservatives secured victory at the 1979 General Election. The reform of the rules regulating the Stock Exchange – 'Big Bang' – can also be seen to be part of a wider strategy to integrate British financial capital better with international markets (Leyshon *et al.* 1987; Jessop and Stones 1992). The introduction of a new system for regulating the City of London, codified in the *Financial Services Act* (1986), saw the City's financial markets thrown open to a wide range of financial institutions, which collectively enjoyed a freedom to engage in a wider range of financial markets in exchange for a far higher level of surveillance over their activities (Moran 1991).

Although these examples of reregulation were internationally orientated, they had unforeseen implications for the structural regulation of domestic financial markets in Britain. For example, the removal of exchange controls undermined the efficacy of the 'corset', the regulatory mechanism by which the Bank of England controlled bank lending since 1973. The corset controlled lending by requiring banks to place non-interest-bearing deposits with the Bank of England if lending exceeded certain limits. However, with the abolition of exchange controls in 1979 the corset became redundant as banks began to 'by-pass the corset controls by lending to British customers from overseas subsidiaries' (Smith 1987: 94). The corset was officially abandoned in 1980. Banks took immediate advantage of this new freedom to expand their domestic balance sheets, which became increasingly important to the banks after 1982 as they withdrew from lending to developed countries and refocused activities on domestic banking markets. However, the aggressive expansion of the banks into a range of retail financial markets disturbed the former stability of the domestic financial system. The building society industry was particularly aggrieved, given that building societies . . . could only lend on mortgages secured on freehold or leasehold property and were restricted to raising funds in the retail market. Banks, on the other hand, could lend money in a variety of ways (in the form of overdrafts, personal loans, mortgages, etc.).

(Court and McDowell 1993: 10)

The *Building Societies Act* (1986) sought to redress this imbalance, allowing building societies to enter the retail banking and insurance markets.

This incremental process of regulatory reform, in conjunction with the increased access to a wider range of funds (especially from the wholesale markets) and a period of historically low interest rates, served to promote greater competition between financial institutions and enabled households to borrow more. This competition helped to fuel the now infamous credit boom of the mid- to late 1980s, which stoked up extensive asset price inflation especially, but not only, within the residential property market.

The credit boom of the 1980s was a period of rapid growth for the financial services industry in Britain. Between 1981 and 1989 employment in the financial services industry increased by over 57 per cent, compared with a rate of only 4.3 per cent for employment in the economy as a whole. The growth of financial services employment during the 1980s displayed marked regional variations, and was very much a phenomenon of Britain's 'southern economy'. For example, employment in the financial services industry increased by 88 per cent in both the South East and East Anglia, and by 76 per cent in the South West. Indeed, with the exception of the East Midlands, in every other region the rate of financial services employment growth fell below that within the country as a whole (Table 6.3). One of the key reasons for this was that the credit boom itself was very much a phenomenon of the 'southern economy', being the site for the most

Table 6.3 Regional change in financial services employment, 1981–9 (%)

Region	Male	Female	Total
South East	86.9	89.6	88.4
East Anglia	77.5	96.6	88.2
South West	65.1	84.2	75.9
'Southern economy'	80.1	88.9	85.1
London	42.3	55.5	48.5
West Midlands	46.5	55.0	51.3
East Midlands	58.5	71.2	66.0
Yorkshire and Humberside	38.2	53.8	46.9
North West	36.8	43.0	40.2
Northern	29.9	40.1	36.0
Wales	35.8	54.0	46.2
Scotland	37.7	40.4	39.2
Total	50.7	62.1	56.8

Source: Department of Employment/NOMIS

extreme instances of asset price inflation. In addition, by the late 1980s over 42 per cent of the population of the United Kingdom lived in the South East, the South West and East Anglia, and average earnings in these regions were all above the national average (*Regional Trends* 1991). The 'geo-demographic profile' (Clarke and Wagstaff 1987) of the southern economy proved highly seductive to the financial services industry, which ensured that southern Britain was served by more branches per population than northern regions (Gentle *et al.* 1991).

However, as Peck and Tickell argue, 'in the midst of this boom . . . the seeds of the impending crisis were being sown' (1992: 357). The concentration of credit-based growth within the southern economy was to have severe consequences for the economy in general, and for the financial services industry in particular:

> the recession of 1990–1992, which, though experienced by the entire country, was initially triggered by the chronic overheating of the South's economy. . . . The consumption boom of the mid-1980s occurred primarily in the South following equity gains in southern housing markets and an associated growth in the credit economy. . . . With enormous trade deficits and – in the South – unsustainable growth, the social, economic and geographical base of Thatcherism was undermined. The Government was forced to burst the credit bubble and stabilise wage inflation. The vestigial ideological commitment to 'deregulation' meant that the only option was to increase interest rates, precipitating the downswing which led Britain into its second recession within a decade . . . [although] this recession was based first and foremost in the South. . . . In this way, a crisis . . . within the core region has effectively triggered a national accumulation crisis.
>
> (Peck and Tickell 1992: 359)

The fact that so much of the economic growth of the 1980s had been based on credit meant that the UK financial services industry was badly damaged as recession began to take hold, and was forced to restructure in the face of a second major debt crisis in under a decade. It is to the enforced restructuring of the financial services industry in the face of the developed country debt crisis of the early 1990s that we now turn.

THE RESTRUCTURING OF FINANCIAL SERVICES FIRMS IN THE 1990S

A number of dilemmas are facing financial services firms in Britain in the early 1990s, of which three are of particular importance. First, financial services firms are having to cope with the progressive fusion of international and domestic markets. Drawing a sharp boundary around the British domestic financial system is an increasingly difficult task. The case of housing finance is instructive in this regard. A number of foreign financial institutions were active in the British mortgage market at the peak of the boom. More importantly, money for housing finance was increasingly being raised in the global markets. As a result, the British residential mortgage market became more and more competitive and less and less sheltered from the forces that drive interest rates and dividend yields across global markets. In commercial property markets too, foreign influences were felt. Not only did more and more finance come in from abroad but it is now clear that the flow of funds from foreign (and especially Japanese) investors also kept the London office property market from falling back sooner than it did. The openness of the British domestic financial system can be seen in other ways. In particular, there is the relative ease with which foreign firms can both enter and then influence the system's direction, which contrasts strongly with very many other countries.

The 'merger' of the Midland Bank with the Hong Kong and Shanghai Bank is a good case in point. The battle for control of Midland between the Hong Kong and Shanghai Bank and Lloyds Bank during 1992 helps to illustrate the way in which British financial institutions are now having to turn their attention to international and domestic issues at one and the same time. On the one hand, British institutions are courting, and being courted by, large foreign financial institutions as part of strategies to construct transnational financial services organisations of sufficient scale and geographic reach to be able to respond rapidly to spatial shifts in the global financial market. This can probably be best achieved by entering into an alliance with a foreign financial institution with which some form of geographical and organisational 'synergy' can be achieved. This was certainly the rationale underlying the merger between Midland and the Hong Kong and Shanghai Bank, since the British bank's operations are concentrated in Europe, while the operations of the Hong Kong and Shanghai Bank are more numerous in South East Asia and in North America thereby ensuring the creation not only of the world's largest bank but also one that would be powerful in all the main regional markets of the global financial economy.[8] On the other hand, the increased level of competition at home has encouraged some financial institutions to pursue a more defensive strategy through merger with a domestic rival, seeking to benefit from the consolidation of market share, which could then be exploited through an extensive round of rationalisation. This was the rationale behind the Lloyds Bank bid for Midland. However, apart from the extensive restructurings that a merger between two long-term domestic market rivals would involve, necessitating the eradication of duplicated divisions, offices and branches, and the integration of different operating and technological systems, such mergers are increasingly difficult to get past the anti-competition regulations of the EC, as Lloyds Bank found to its cost.

A second problem facing financial services firms in Britain in the 1990s is that their room for manoeuvre is severely constrained by the problems of debt overhang. The issue here is quite simple, but none the less intractable for that. How can financial services firms expand or create new markets for debt when individuals and firms are rather more concerned with the reduction of outstanding debt? Although Britain's exit from the European Exchange Rate Mechanism in September 1992 certainly helped in this regard, by permitting rates to sink well below the European average, the high levels of indebtedness in Britain ensure that demand for debt-related financial services has indeed been 'satiated' (Gentle and Marshall 1993), at least for the time being.[9]

Given this, the third and final problem facing financial institutions in the 1990s is the need to reduce costs and make more productive use of resources. When markets were expanding, financial institutions were content merely to hold costs steady. But as markets stopped growing and began to contract, financial services firms began to cast around for ways to reduce costs in order to defend their margins. That costs have not been an issue of pressing concern for certain parts of the financial services industry is illustrated by the fact that during the 1980s the operating expenses of British banks accounted for around 65 per cent of gross income (OECD 1992). While this figure was about average for the international banking industry, it was extraordinarily high in comparison with other industrial sectors. These high operating costs persist despite a long history of labour process reorganisation in the financial services sector (Appelbaum and Albin 1989; Crompton 1989).

The high operating costs are explained partly by the extensive and expensive distribution networks that most financial services firms have used to attract customers. For example, it was estimated that the branch networks and the staff that work in them accounted for more than three-quarters of the total operating costs of the British banking sector in 1992 (Gapper 1993a). In the context of the traditional working practices of financial services firms, their branch networks are highly underutilised assets. According to Lloyd,

> If 365 days a year are taken as 100%, the utilisation of an office property is immediately reduced to 260 days (71%) by allowing for a 5-day working week. Annual (25 days) and bank holidays (7 days) bring the figure down further to 228 days (63%).
>
> (quoted in Harris 1992: 13)

According to Lloyd, if one further assumes that a branch office is only being used during a standard working day (eight hours), then an office is only in use for 76 days per annum, or to only 21 per cent of its capacity (ibid.).

The persistence of high operating costs may be seen as a legacy of the industry's history of structural regulation and its tendency towards oligopoly. Such conditions tended to encourage firms to tolerate forms of organisation that were less than fully efficient or to cross-subsidise services that were not strictly profitable in their own right. But in the light of the increased competition of the 1980s, and the contracting financial markets of the 1990s, financial services firms have begun systematically to reduce costs and introduce strategies which seek to make better use of their human and fixed capital resources. Thus, efforts to use resources more productively have dovetailed with a growing tendency for financial services firms to compete upon quality of services (Cressey and Scott 1992), which has often involved extending the opening hours of financial services branches.[10]

In the remainder of this section, we investigate some of the ways in which financial services firms have sought to reduce costs and make more productive use of their resources. We will do this in two stages, turning our attention first to processes of labour market restructuring before going on to consider processes of corporate reorganisation.

Labour market restructuring

The need to cut operating costs has had important implications for the labour market dynamics of the financial services sector in the 1990s, for two reasons in particular. First, in sharp contrast to the 1980s, the 1990s will be a period of considerable labour market retrenchment as the consequences of higher levels of domestic and international competition force firms to realign labour costs with incomes and profits. Within the banking sector, this process began in the late 1980s, as the domestic recession caused banks first to slow and then to halt the process of recruitment. In the 1990s the reduction of labour through 'natural wastage' has been supplemented by voluntary and, increasingly, compulsory redundancies. According to the Banking Insurance and Finance Union (BIFU), the four main British commercial banks – Barclays, National Westminster, Lloyds and Midland – shed around 20,000 jobs in 1991 alone.[11] Cressey and Scott (1992) have estimated that the figure was nearer 23,000. Between 1990 and the end of 1992 BIFU estimate that 75,000 jobs were lost in the banking sector, and that at least 25,000 were under immediate threat. In plans revealed to the union for the period up until the mid- to late 1990s, all four banks indicated that they were looking to push through considerable labour cost savings. One bank indicated that it wished to cut its labour force by one-third, while two of the others wished to cut employment by between 15,000 and 18,000 jobs. Other financial institutions also began to shed labour in the early 1990s, again in response to a downturn in financial and other markets and a drive to produce efficiency savings by making more productive use of the labour they employ. For example, since 1990 employment has been falling sharply within the insurance and building society sectors.

Second, the 1990s will see a continuation and deepening of certain labour market trends initiated during the 1980s. Traditionally, a job in the financial services industry, particularly within the retail side of the business, was viewed as being something of a sinecure, offering significant prospects for advancement within the internal labour market of the firm. New recruits would for the most part join straight from school, with the more able staff being encouraged to sit the examinations of the various professional bodies of the financial industries, thus enabling employees to pursue traditional 'organisational careers' (Savage 1988). In other words, a career in finance fulfilled the criterion of being 'a safe job, with prospects', even if such jobs had the reputation for being a little dull, perhaps a bit regimented, and likely to favour male rather than female employees (Crompton 1989; Crompton and Sanderson 1990). This world was undermined during the 1980s (Cressey and Scott 1992). On the one hand, the rather staid image of finance was replaced by one of considerable allure, as the restructuring of the City of London before and after 'Big Bang' transformed the public perception of the financial services industry. On the other hand, the 1980s also saw an important breach in traditional financial labour market practices. The wage bills of financial institutions increased, but financial markets and earnings became ever more volatile and unpredictable. In response, firms were forced to jettison their traditionally paternalistic labour market practices in favour of models which took greater account of individual and corporate performance. It is worth remembering that at the end of the 1980s, the most important human resources issue for financial services firms was predicted to be a shortage of new recruits, forcing firms to rethink their established recruitment and training procedures. Greater opportunities would have to be offered to those sections of the workforce which hitherto had found it difficult to make significant inroads into the labour market (e.g. women, members of ethnic minorities, older people, etc.), otherwise businesses would be forced out of existence by the sheer shortage of available workers (Rajan and Fryatt 1988). In the early 1990s, these concerns seem curiously dated. The main labour market issue facing financial services firms in the 1990s is bringing labour costs more into line with revenues and with the rate of return on capital. This is being achieved both through the introduction of flexible labour market models (Atkinson 1984; Allen 1988) and through processes of 'capital deepening', the realisation of cost savings through a more extensive use of information technology.

More polarised internal labour markets began to emerge in the financial services sector during the 1980s (Rajan 1987). The old bureaucratic structures, which necessitated entry at the 'bottom' and progression through the ranks of the firm for the most able, have increasingly been replaced with a much more clearly structured and selective recruitment process. In consequence, two distinctive career structures are developing within most firms in the industry. On the one hand, there is the development of a *core* labour force which consists mainly of managerial and professional staff. New recruits tend to be graduates and/or possess some other form of technical qualification. These workers nearly all enjoy full-time conditions of service, with labour market progress tied to the attainment of appraisal targets set by their immediate superiors. In previous, more paternalistic times, promotion procedures were less rigorous, with promotion often being given to those who had served sufficient time in post. Now, the drive to extract greater efficiencies from managerial and professional staff has been given further emphasis by the move away from pay schemes based on general increases and fixed increments and towards reward schemes linked more to individual and corporate performance (Watkins and Bryce 1992). These schemes not only encourage greater efficiencies and productivity but also enable less effective workers to be more accurately identified and sanctioned through the reward system.

On the other hand, there is the development of a more *peripheral* labour force, consisting predominantly of clerical and other support staff, many of whom will be part-time. Clearly ceilings to progress have been placed upon these jobs; it will become increasingly rare for individuals to make the transition from the bottom to the top of financial services firms in the future. In some firms the increased use of part-time labour is seen as a solution to the growing volatility of financial services markets and as an integral part of an attempt to link labour costs more directly to the process of income generation. For example, one large bank has relabelled its part-time staff *key-time staff*, signifying the process by which workers are drawn upon for key periods of the working day. Thus, in the case of counter staff in branches, key-time staff would be needed during the peak hours of demand, typically in the hours between 11.00 and 15.00 hours, when the demand for counter services is highest. Other institutions have devised other solutions to the same problem. One large financial processing institution runs an *hour bank* scheme, where workers are contracted to do a certain number of hours within fixed time periods. The increasingly volatile nature of the business means that at certain times the workload will be very heavy, causing workers to build up 'surpluses' at the hour bank; during less busy times workers draw upon the surpluses of hours they have previously built up. The advantage of this scheme is that it offers workers security of employment in an increasingly volatile business; the drawback of the scheme is the irregularity of the work hours, which can interfere with domestic or social arrangements because employees are expected to be available for work at very short notice.

The search for efficiency savings has other implications for financial service labour markets. Firms are extending the range of duties and responsibilities of their managerial staff. This widening of responsibilities has been associated not just with the shift to incentive- and performance-related reward systems, but also with a marked change in the nature of managerial structures within the financial services sector. Firms are stripping out highly tiered and hierarchical management structures in favour of 'flatter', more responsible and responsive structures, better suited to the new competitive imperatives of the financial services market (Gentle *et al.* 1991; Marshall *et al.* 1992).[12] Such developments are aided by the proliferation of communications and information technology systems within such institutions, which serve to centralise both information processing and handling and, at the same time, facilitate the wide distribution of information to different profit centres in the organisation via management information systems (Watkins and Bryce 1992).

Information technology is also being used to serve another purpose in financial services firms: a reduction in the number of clerical and support staff through the elimination and centralisation of many routine tasks. This is not a new development. Financial services firms have been at the forefront of the introduction of computers and information technology into business practices. However, the long-run expansion of employment within the industry in the past has compensated for the job-displacing effects of information technology. For example, automated teller machines (ATMs) were first introduced into commercial banks in the 1970s, and by 1991, the seven largest UK banks had installed 12,661 ATMs.[13] By 1990, 62 per cent of personal cash withdrawals were made through an ATM (*Social Trends* 1992). The increased use of ATMs during the 1980s helped banks cope with the growing demand for bank services, by freeing counter staff to work in other areas of the business, such as dealing with customer enquiries, processing applications for loans and other services, and other general administrative duties. However, as the banking market has slowed in the early 1990s, so the demand for staff in these areas has declined.

Corporate restructuring

Falling demand for labour in the financial services sector has been accelerated by a wider process of corporate restructuring, and in particular by the tendency towards *spatial specialisation*. We shall illustrate the dimensions of this process with respect to the banking industry. It has three main components. First, a shift towards a profit-centre mode of operation in the banking sector has proceeded in tandem with the construction of new regional templates, with responsibility being centralised in regional headquarters. Efforts to reorganise the structures of control within banking gathered pace during the 1980s, largely in response to the growing competitiveness of the market. Thus, as early as the mid-1980s, Rajan identified an emerging three-tier system of control and responsibility within the retail banking sector (see Figure 6.2):

> The top tier consists of large area corporate offices who perform two functions: provide a comprehensive range of financial services to corporate bodies and private customers; and oversee the 'satellites' in the second tier. Sub-branches providing the primary banking services to small firms and private customers fall in the second tier; and 'full service' branches in rural areas in the third tier.
>
> (Rajan 1985: 76)

Second, the process of spatial specialisation extends to the settlement function, which increasingly is being removed from branches and centralised in regional processing centres. The rationale behind such developments is quite straightforward. The settlement function of matching cheques and balancing accounts has traditionally been undertaken within each bank branch. The large amount of resources that this requires,

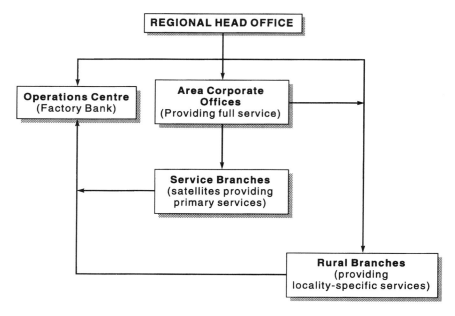

Figure 6.2 Evolving bank branch network systems

both in terms of labour and machinery, has necessitated that the majority of floorspace at each branch is given over to the administrative duties of the bank, rather than to the promotion and sale of services to its customers. Information and communications technology makes it possible for banks to transfer the settlement function out of branches by shipping the cheques and other vouchers to central processing centres, where banks can reap considerable scale economies in the processing function as well as freeing much of the space and staff previously needed at branches to perform such tasks. The network of regional processing centres established by one of the four large clearing banks is illustrated in Figure 6.3. Such centres represent an important departure in the organisation of the commercial banks. They introduce an industrial division into the banking sector. The processing division is integrated with, but necessarily apart from, the main operations of the bank. The industrial character of these operations is reflected not only in the nature of the work, which is highly automated, routinised and large scale, but also in the operation of shift systems and in their suburban locations in industrial or office parks. In addition, processing centres add to the pressure to employ part-time staff. Moreover, the fact that the part-time staff also tend to be women in this development consolidates the feminisation of the banking labour force (Halford and Savage 1993). However, unlike the situation in the 1980s, this process is now taking place against a background of overall employment decline.

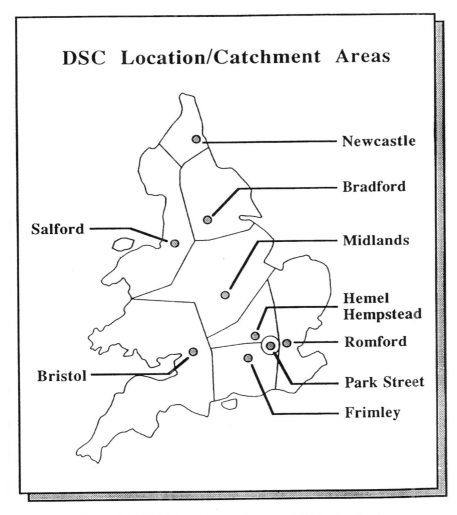

Figure 6.3 District service centres of a UK clearing bank

Third and finally, banks and other financial institutions are paying much closer attention to the geography of their distribution networks. Even during the 1980s, when markets were expanding, banks and building societies continued to close branches, as the processes of corporate reorganization described earlier began to take effect (Table 6.4). But since the late 1980s the rate of closure has accelerated. For example, the four large clearing banks closed almost as many branches between 1989 and 1991 as they had done in the previous eight years. And although much of it is anecdotal, there is evidence to suggest that this reduction in the distribution networks of banks and building societies has proceeded unevenly over space. This reflects the fact that banks and building societies

Table 6.4 Bank and building society branch networks, 1981–91

	1981	1986	1991
Banks	14,738	14,013	12,885
Abbey National[a]	–	–	683
Bank of Scotland	575	550	502
Barclays	2,986	2,842	2,496
Cooperative Bank	71	84	107
Clydesdale Bank	379	360	346
Lloyds	2,292	2,152	1,929
Midland	2,454	2,211	1,824
National Westminster	3,216	3,133	2,683
The Royal Bank of Scotland	903	842	805
Standard Chartered	–	26	4
TSB Group	1,657	1,576	1,399
Yorkshire Bank	205	237	107
Building societies	6,162	6,954	6,051
Girobank[b]	22,475	21,305	20,638
Total	43,375	42,272	39,574

[a] Abbey National became a bank in 1988. It was previously a Building Society
[b] Number of Post Offices

Source: British Bankers Association (BBA) (1992), *Annual Abstract of Banking Statistics* vol. 9, London: BBA.

have embarked upon a more critical appraisal of each unit within their branch networks. This appraisal takes place in a context when financial institutions are concerned above all else with issues of profitability, of risk avoidance and of developing new financial markets in a period of high indebtedness. These concerns have crystallised in a branch restructuring programme which is sensitive to geographical variations in profitability, risk and debt. Thus, at a regional scale, Gentle and Marshall (1993) suggest that the process of bank rationalisation has been concentrated in the south of Britain. The fact that the recession was deeper in the south than the north, they argue, meant that 'banks such as Barclays have been considerably more profitable in the North of England than the South, and as a consequence the former has largely missed the recent branch rationalisation'. At the same time, a concern for a more productive use of resources has led to the closure of branches located in more remote areas, particularly in rural areas, which are seen to be 'overbanked', that is too many branches per head of population. Conversely, this has also led to a renewed focus upon branches in key sites in large metropolitan centres, which are guaranteed a higher 'throughput' of business.

However, at the subregional scale, this concern with profitability, risk and with debt has produced spatial outcomes influenced in part by an underlying geography of income and class. Competition in retail markets during the 1980s saw the cost of financial services fall sharply (a good example was the introduction of free banking for customers in credit), while aggressive marketing strategies widened financial markets by drawing more people into the financial system, many for the first time. However, a large proportion of these new customers were at the lower end of the income scale, and they tended to run very low credit balances. In a post-ERM Britain of historically low interest rates, banks have increasingly been counting the cost of these competitive policies of inclusivity:

> Banks now estimates that they need an average balance of between £1000 and £1500 in each account to generate enough interest income to pay for the annual cost of £60–90 of running each account. . . . One bank estimates that it now loses money on 80% of its current accounts.
>
> (Gapper 1993b: 21)

Banks have responded to this problem in a number of ways. The short-term solution has been to introduce punitive charges for those customers with overdrafts. The medium-term solution is the reintroduction of bank charges to those customers who fail to retain sufficiently high credit balances, representing a shift to true-cost banking. But the long-term solution seems likely to involve a 'flight to quality'. Banks are actively seeking to move their customer base 'up-market', and are making strenuous efforts to attract a client base of 'high net worth individuals'. Three of the four major clearing banks – Barclays, Midland and National Westminster – have introduced their own 'premier' or 'prime' banking services which are offered exclusively to those customers with average incomes well in excess of the national average.[14] These services are attractive to banks in that they deliver a client base with higher than average levels of capital and a much greater propensity to buy investment services, on which the banks earn fee income. The other large clearing bank – Lloyds – has gone further, building a branch network of private banking offices, the geography of which is revealing (Figure 6.4) since it appears to be based on a geography of wealth and class, and upon a logic of exclusion and closure. The following comments, made upon National Westminster's move into these services via its 'up-market' subsidiary Coutts Banks, are instructive in this regard:

> Coutts, where the Queen banks, is part of the NatWest group, and sometimes NatWest customers will be directed to their services. 'We operate at the top end of the market,' said Michael Maslinksi, head of business development. 'Our charges are a little higher as our banking services are aimed at those with above average income and assets.' Customers pay £30 a quarter unless their average balance over the period is more than £3000, in which case the charge is waived.
>
> Customers are expected to have at least £150,000 in investments and income of at least £50,000. The bank has a branch in Eton, which is handy for the boys at the school, who do not meet these criteria, but it is providing a service for the whole family. It opened a new branch in Leeds last October and is considering a modest expansion outside London. '*You will not find us on every high street,*' Mr Malinski added.
>
> (Goldsmith 1993, *our emphasis*)

Figure 6.4 Branch network of Lloyds private banking offices

The corollary of this move up-market, of course, has been to place less emphasis upon those services aimed at a less affluent and less profitable clientele, with particularly important implications for branches in inner-city areas.[15] A similar flight to quality can be observed in the insurance industry, which in the wake of unprecedented losses has begun to engage in far more careful risk pricing. Thus, there have been large increases in insurance premiums charged to small businesses and house and car owners, which have been concentrated in inner-city areas, corresponding closely to a geography of past claims and of anticipated future risks.

These developments within the British banking system have important implications for urban and regional development. They echo the process of spatial specialisation which began in the US financial system during the 1970s and gathered speed during the 1980s. These developments have resulted in a greater spatial concentration of administration, processing and even distribution networks within the US financial system. These processes of spatial specialisation have not only seen financial institutions retreat to more suburban locations, which offer guaranteed supplies of part-time female labour, but have also led to the closure of branches in poorer inner-city and rural areas due to their higher operating costs and lower profitability. A study of bank branch networks in the New York metropolitan area between 1985 and 1989 revealed that there was a net loss of twenty-one full-service branches. In inner-city minority neighbourhoods there was a net decline of fifteen branches. In more affluent suburban areas, there was a net increase of thirty branches over the same period, indicating a marked shift in the geographical organisation of the financial industry within a relatively short period of time (Christopherson 1992). Some banks in the United States have adopted a strategy of concentration, shrinking their client base by 60 per cent to focus only on the more affluent segment of the population (Christopherson 1993), which are the ones more likely to generate fees, buy investment services and retain healthy surpluses in their accounts with the bank. This process of financial infra-structure withdrawal also extends to the insurance industry, which is also closing offices in these areas, but in the case of inner-city areas also risk pricing premiums to such an extent that it has become increasingly difficult for individuals and business to afford insurance.

Clearly, a similar targeting of geographical labour markets and retail financial markets is now taking place within the financial system within the United Kingdom, with reports of disproportionate closures in poorer localities. These trends have important implications for those inner-city and rural locations which fall victim to financial infrastructure withdrawal. Research in the United States has pointed to a correlation between an absence of financial infrastructure and an absence of economic growth (Grown and Bates 1992; Haas 1992; Obermiller 1988). Communities without appropriate financial infrastructure encounter difficulties in gaining access to credit, not least because they increasingly have to depend on what are formulaic out-of-area assessments of financial standing and perceived credit risk. In other words, as financial institutions retreat from certain communities, so their first-hand knowledge of those communities, previously gathered through the employees who worked and perhaps even lived there, declines. This absence of local information encourages conservatism in lending behaviour, particularly when lending to individuals and businesses in poorer or remote communities. The absence of a formal financial infrastructure forces these communities to rely upon more informal credit mechanisms, which tend to be more expensive.

CONCLUSIONS

The issue of financial structure withdrawal in Britain demands urgent attention. Very little work has ever been attempted on access to financial services in Britain. Yet there is good reason to suggest that the problems already documented in the United States are already being manifested in certain inner-city and rural areas in Britain. However, we should not be surprised that this process is taking place. It is the logical response of a private sector financial services industry to problems of indebtedness and a fear of risk. Moreover, as we suggested at the beginning of the chapter, we have been here before, albeit at a different spatial scale. In the wake of the less developed countries' debt crisis, a process of financial infra-structure withdrawal took place on an international scale, as credit and offices were withdrawn from the developing countries, with disastrous economic and social consequences (United Nations Centre on Trans-national Corporations 1988). In the wake of the developed countries' debt crisis of the early 1980s, this process of withdrawal and exclusion is repeating itself, but this time within the space economies of the developed nations. And just as the financial services industry demonstrated a remark-able capacity to adapt and survive in the face of the debt crisis of the early 1980s, so the debt crisis of the early 1990s has been the catalyst for a new round of structural transformation within the industry, from which many firms are emerging strongly and newly invigorated. But the shift from public interest structural regulation towards a form of regulation which forces private sector financial corporations to operate at new levels of competitiveness has profound socio-spatial implications (Flynn *et al.* 1993). The former protection afforded to financial institutions by structural regulation acted as a form of subsidy and encouraged institutions to under-take social functions of critical importance to the economy as a whole (such as cash transmission services, for example), while at the same time permitting them to adhere to a notion of comprehensive service provision. Increased competition between financial institutions and a new concern with profitability and real rates of return mean that neither of these things can now be taken for granted. Indeed, the Chairman of Midland Bank has gone as far as to suggest that risk avoidance and low rates of return will ensure that new bank lending to small businesses will remain limited without some form of government subsidy to the banks (Batchelor and Gapper 1993). Thus, the process of restructuring for profit is forging a new operational logic within the financial services industry, one which is based upon a logic of exclusion and closure and is likely to have important economic, social and geographical consequences during the 1990s.

CHAPTER 7

GEOGRAPHIES OF FINANCIAL EXCLUSION

Financial abandonment in Britain and the United States

INTRODUCTION

Financial crises have profound economic and social consequences. They tend to induce what the financial services industry describes as a 'flight to quality'; that is, a search for 'safer' markets, a process which tends to discriminate in favour of more affluent and powerful social groups and against poor and disadvantaged groups. This much is well known and widely acknowledged. What is less widely acknowledged is that this process of discrimination also has important geographical outcomes, of which two are particularly important. The first is that new patterns of credit creation emerge as money and credit are redirected away from poorer to richer (and therefore 'safer') groups. The second is that new patterns of financial infrastructure develop as financial institutions restructure their operations over space to bring them into line with these new flows of credit and debt.

In recent years there have been two striking examples of the way in which financial crises trigger geographical redistributions of financial flows and financial infrastructure. The first was the less developed countries' (LDCs) debt crisis of the early 1980s. The crisis caused net capital transfers to take place between LDCs and North America, Europe and Japan, thereby contradicting the normative expectation in international economics that funds flow only from developed to less developed countries (Corbridge 1988a, 1992b, 1993; Corbridge and Agnew 1991). This unusual state of affairs arose when, in response to the crisis, international banks refused to lend to LDCs. The reorientation of credit flows was followed by the closure of the offices of international banks in developing countries. Between 1980 and 1985 the world's 100 largest banks closed 24 per cent of their offices in LDCs (United Nations Centre on Transnational Corporations 1988).

The second example followed in the aftermath of the developed countries' debt crisis of the early 1990s (Leyshon *et al.* 1993; see chapter 6) which was engendered by the process of restructuring following the LDC debt crisis of the early 1980s. Having abandoned the LDCs, the international banks began to seek out new customers in the developed countries: from the early 1980s onwards large amounts of credit were provided for the construction and purchase of property (Warf 1994), to facilitate what were often aggressive and predatory rounds of corporate restructuring (Clark 1989a) and to support the consumption of goods and services by individuals through personal loans and other credit facilities.[1]

It was in this way that a new exclusionary pattern of financial recycling emerged. Whereas, in the 1970s, the financial system had recycled funds from developed to less developed countries, in the 1980s money tended to remain within the orbit of the developed economies, circulating at ever faster rates within the tripolar world economy of North America, Europe and South East Asia (Thrift and Leyshon 1988). At the same time, the principal means by which credit was created was transformed, as inter-mediated credit was superseded by disintermediated credit (see Leyshon and Thrift 1992; Thrift and Leyshon 1988).

In the wake of the debt crisis of the early 1990s in the developed countries, the financial services industry has made a typical response. First, there has been a redirection of credit, away from poorer social groups and towards richer groups as part of a strategy of risk avoidance. Second, there has been a process of financial infrastructure withdrawal, this time *within developed countries*. In other words, financial capital is retreating to a middle-class heartland, a process which echoes the earlier retreat of financial capital to the developed countries from the LDCs in the early and mid-1980s.

The withdrawal of financial capital from the LDCs resulted in what Corbridge (1993) describes as a lost decade of development, during which real per capita incomes fell precipitously, development projects were cancelled and infant mortality rates remained at alarmingly high levels. It is important to be reminded of the tragedy of the development crisis of the LDCs in order to place the process of financial infrastructure withdrawal in developed countries in its proper context. Nevertheless, it is becoming increasingly difficult for many citizens of developed countries to gain access to the financial system. Without access, the conduct of everyday life within a contemporary capitalist society can become extremely problematic. One reason for this has been the growth of non-cash financial transmissions which now account for a third of all financial transactions, both in Britain and in the United States (Warley 1994). Employees may find it more difficult to get paid unless they have a bank account, as employers prefer to pay wages and salaries via direct credit transfer for reasons of efficiency and security. For similar reasons governments also attempt to use non-cash financial transmission wherever possible. An increasing number of pensions and benefits are paid by credit transfer or crossed cheque in Britain, despite the fact that as many as 35 per cent of people who receive benefits are not in possession of either a bank or a building society account (National Association of Citizen Advice Bureaux 1993). It is also far more difficult to pay bills without the intermediation of a financial institution, while it is all but impossible to obtain credit from a bank or building society without evidence of a history of personal banking. For all these reasons, access to retail financial services is a social necessity within a contemporary capitalist economy.

In Britain, the United States and other core capitalist countries, the financial services industry's 'flight to quality' promises to have severe social and economic consequences for those groups and localities which are at the wrong end of the process of financial exclusion. These developments signal an insidious and relatively unremarked-upon assault by financial capital upon poorer and disadvantaged groups. It contrasts with the more spectacular assaults launched by financial capital against such groups during the 1980s, which displaced and disrupted many communities living in the shadow of high-profile land and property developments as documented in cities such as London, New York, Los Angeles, Baltimore and many others.[2]

The emergence of the developed countries' debt crisis, founded partly in the debts accumulated by the failure of large-scale property developments to attract sufficient tenants, means that such highly visible assaults will be thin on the ground over the next decade or so. It will be the problems that stem from an inability to access the financial system, and the associated process of financial infrastructure withdrawal, which will become increasingly widespread. Holes are beginning to appear in the geography of retail financial services provision within developed countries such as Britain and the United States. The emergence of these spaces of financial exclusion has important implications for uneven development in these countries for such spaces are associated with economic decline and attendant social problems such as poverty and deprivation.

This chapter has two main objectives. The first is simply to document these exclusionary processes, drawing upon evidence from the United States and Britain. The second is to begin to formulate an alternative agenda that will foster resistance and help to construct institutional alternatives which will deliver basic banking and low-cost loans to low-income households. The remainder of the chapter is, therefore, organised into four main parts. In the following section we make an attempt to come to a theoretical understanding of the processes of financial exclusion and their relation to uneven development. In doing so, we draw upon the work of Gary Dymski and John Veitch (1992) to argue that the tendency towards exclusion is endemic within financial capital but that this tendency waxes and wanes at various historical conjunctures. Next we look at one such conjuncture – the crisis of the British financial services industry in the late 1980s and early 1990s – and at the ways in which this crisis has served to encourage the industry to adopt a rubric of exclusion. Finally, we look at the possibilities for both resisting the process of financial infrastructure withdrawal and countering the effects of financial exclusion by building an alternative financial infrastructure, first in the United States and then in Britain. The conclusions suggest the need to frame the argument made in the rest of the chapter in terms of an idea of 'financial citizenship'.

FINANCIAL EXCLUSION AND UNEVEN DEVELOPMENT

We use the term 'financial exclusion' to refer to those processes that serve to prevent certain social groups and individuals from gaining access to the financial system. Although the criteria for exclusion may vary over time, the financial system has an inherent tendency to discriminate against poor and disadvantaged groups. In other words, the poorer and more disadvantaged an individual, the more likely it is that they will be excluded from the financial system. The reason for this is that the financial services industry operates in a way that favours the socially powerful. Consider how the cost of money is calculated within the financial system. The cost of money is determined by the level of risk which a financial institution believes it incurs in lending money to a borrower. The perceived level of risk is inversely related to the likelihood of the borrower repaying. The higher the perceived level of risk, the more a financial institution will ask a borrower to pay; or, conversely, the more likely it is that the borrower will repay the loan, the less they will have to pay for it.

There are three factors which are taken into account when calculating the risk incurred when lending money. First, risk is determined by the length of time that the money will be out on loan. The longer the borrower requires the loan, the more risky it is considered to be for the lender because the circumstances of the borrower may change over time, making it less likely that the money will be repaid. This means that the more quickly the loan can be repaid, the less it will cost. This state of affairs tends to favour those with greater financial resources, since they will be able to pay back the money more quickly and, therefore, at less expense.

Risk is also determined by the purpose of the loan. Money borrowed to purchase specified, tangible assets (such as property) will usually be cheaper than other sorts of loans (such as personal loans which are for non-specific purposes) because the property rights to the assets bought with the loan can be held in security by the lender until the full payment of the loan is made, as in the case of mortgages on property. Since the ownership of the assets resides with the lender until the full repayment of the loan, the lender can always attempt to sell the asset to recoup the money borrowed against it should the borrower default. This means that lenders are better disposed to lend money for the purchase of assets which are perceived to hold their value over time. In the case of property, all other things being equal, lenders are keener to lend money for investment in more valuable property markets. Finally, risk is determined in large part by the perceived 'credit-worthiness' of the borrower, an assessment which is based not only on some indication of the extant wealth of the borrower but also on an estimate of their future income which gives a further indication of how likely it is that the loan will be repaid.

For all these reasons there tends to be a strong relationship between the economic power of a borrower and the ease with which they gain access to the financial system. In addition, the economic power of a borrower may also determine how much they have to pay for the privilege of such access. The reason why rich and powerful economic agents find it easier to gain access to credit is because they are more 'visible' to the financial system. The most powerful economic actors, such as transnational corporations and governments, can borrow money at very low rates of interest in wholesale financial markets. They can do this by borrowing money in 'spot' credit markets. Here large amounts of credit are available at very short notice, since information about the creditworthiness of borrowers is known a priori owing to the existence of publicly available information about them.[3] Assessing the credit-worthiness of borrowers in wholesale financial markets consumes a great deal of time and energy. This task is undertaken not only by the legions of analysts employed by all the large financial services firms but also by a cohort of independent credit-rating agencies, such as Standard & Poor or Moodys (Sinclair 1994). In such markets, the balance of power tends to lie with the top-rated *borrowers*, since they are able to choose between a wide range of potential lenders, all of which would like to extend money to what are perceived to be extremely good credit risks.

But only a privileged few have access to the cheap credit circulating in the wholesale financial markets. The majority of borrowers have to obtain credit from what Dymski and Veitch (1992: 12) describe as 'contract' credit markets. The reason for this is that information on the borrower, from which the financial institutions could calculate credit risk, is not immediately available. In such markets the balance of power shifts firmly in favour of *lenders*. The borrower has to approach the lender who, in turn, will require the borrower to submit to an assessment of their credit-worthiness before any credit will be granted. 'Contract' credit is more expensive than 'spot' market credit, not only because there is a large absolute difference in the power and wealth of borrowers participating in these markets but also because it is far more expensive to determine the credit-worthiness of borrowers in them as the information needed to calculate any credit risk incurred has to be uncovered and disclosed.[4] Unlike spot or wholesale markets, the cost of money in contract credit markets does not tend to vary too much between borrowers.[5] However, the implications for those who do not qualify as 'good' risks are severe: they are forced to look outside the 'formal' financial system for credit.

If gaining access to credit from the financial system is determined largely by income and wealth, then the geography of income and wealth shapes the geography of access to the financial system. But, as Dymski and Veitch (1992) argue, the relationship is an interdependent and circular one; the geography of income and wealth is determined in part by the geography of access to the financial system. Through a process which they describe as 'financial dynamics', geographical variations in access to the financial system deepen and accentuate prevailing levels of uneven development. In other words, rich areas tend to get richer and poor areas poorer because of the way in which the financial system discriminates between people and communities on the basis of risk.

Thus, Dymski and Veitch (1992) argue that an urban system requires two types of development. In the first instance,

> extensive development involves the conversion of previously agricultural or undeveloped land to residential, commercial, and industrial use.
>
> (ibid: 5)

This type of development is highly capital intensive and is undertaken at great expense by large land and property developers. However, the 'development' of an urban system does not end there:

> Once a community's infrastructure is in place, continued growth and prosperity requires financing, albeit of a different character. Residents and businesses within the community have an ongoing need for financial services. Further residential development itself does not disappear, but changes qualitatively: it becomes *intensive* rather than extensive. . . . Credit is necessary for rehabilitation and property improvements; mortgage credit allows property turnover. Businesses require working capital, and then expansion financing as they mature. These credit flows, along with readily available banking services, facilitate continued economic growth in a maturing community.
>
> (ibid: 7, emphasis added)

It is in this secondary phase of 'intensive development' that the financial system deepens uneven development within an urban system. In normal circumstances the financial system will not only be more disposed to lend to those areas with higher-than-average incomes, since borrowers in such areas are, on the whole, seen to be better credit risks, but financial services firms will also tend to lend greater volumes of money to such areas per capita, since the amount of credit available to a borrower is usually a multiple of income.

The cumulative nature of such a selective process of credit provision becomes particularly noteworthy when the money is advanced for the purchase of geographically fixed assets such as residential property. When money is advanced for the purchase of such assets, the rights are retained by the lender until the loan is fully repaid and the 'immovability' of such assets means that the 'character of the area surrounding these assets enters into the determination of the value of the assets themselves' (ibid: 9). This means that the decision to advance money for the purchase of geographically specific assets 'necessarily involves an assessment of the long-term prospects of that place' (ibid: 10). Such assessments have obvious implications, for the corollary of favouring more affluent areas is the relative neglect of poorer areas. This can lead to a

> downward spiral of decline . . . as residents [of such areas] find it hard to sell or buy property [while] businesses are unable to obtain credit.
>
> (ibid: 34)

THE CRISIS OF THE BRITISH FINANCIAL SERVICES INDUSTRY AND THE RISE OF FINANCIAL INFRASTRUCTURE WITHDRAWAL AND FINANCIAL EXCLUSION

Although the structural predilection of the financial system to favour the rich and powerful over the poor and powerless has important implications for uneven development, it may be ameliorated or intensified at particular historical conjunctures. In Britain during the 1980s, the reregulation of the financial system encouraged a greater level of competition between financial services firms. More people than ever before were drawn into the financial system as it became far easier to obtain credit. The level of outstanding personal debt increased from £9.8 billion in 1980 to £52.5 billion in 1993 (or from £23.1 billion to £50.7 billion at constant 1990 prices). At the same time, the financial system began to move into new parts of the housing market. Indeed, it seemed at times that nowhere was off limits for the financial system in this regard. Mortgages were advanced for the purchase of properties in run-down inner-city areas and even for houses bought in decaying public sector housing estates under the government's 'Right to Buy' legislation. As home ownership rose to unprecedented levels (67 per cent of all housing was owner-occupied in 1989), the financial system began to reach into nooks and crannies of the British social fabric which it had previously shunned, producing commitments to the financial system which would prove to be regressive in the years to come.

In the 1990s, the pendulum began to swing the other way. To recompense for the overextension of credit during the 1980s, the financial system not only rediscovered the merits of caution but is now making it a competitive strategy in its own right as it supports a wider process of restructuring (Leyshon and Thrift 1993). The retreat of the financial system to its traditional middle-class heartland makes perfect economic sense to the financial services industry, given the nature of the crisis that it faced. But, as Susan Christopherson (1993: 285) pointedly reminds us,

> what is useful and rational for individual firms within the context of a particular set of market rules may not be in the interests of the economy as a whole.

Opting for exclusion: the crisis of the British financial services industry in the 1990s

The crisis facing the financial services industry in Britain during the early 1990s was manifested in three main ways. First, intense competition within financial markets began to eat into the revenues of financial services firms. During the 1980s, there was a marked increase in the number of firms participating in financial markets, mainly as a result of neo-liberal reregulation lowering those barriers to entry which had previously restricted the number of firms allowed to compete in any particular financial market

(Gentle 1993). So long as the volume of business in financial markets continued to expand, as it did through much of the 1980s, the growth in the number of market participants had relatively little effect upon overall profit levels in the financial services industry. But when the financial markets began to contract from 1989 onwards, financial services firms began to suffer the effects of a more crowded marketplace and a phase of destructive competition was ushered in.

Second, most financial services firms are saddled with operational costs which are extremely high in comparison with those borne by firms within other industrial sectors. It has been estimated that during the 1980s the operating costs of British banks accounted for as much as 65 per cent of their gross income (OECD 1992a). Such costs were a legacy of the 'structural regulation' which the reforms of the 1980s swept away but which had served to insulate financial markets and institutions from one another. In essence, highly oligopolistic conditions were encouraged in financial markets for fear that too much competition within the financial sector would serve only to destabilise wider processes of capital accumulation (see chapter 3). As a more competitive marketplace made it more difficult to turn a profit, financial services firms began to investigate ways of reducing the burden of their heavy operating costs.

The third manifestation of the crisis facing the financial services industry was an overhang of debt, much of it bad debt. During the early 1990s, levels of debt in developed countries approached or, as in the case of the United Kingdom, surpassed 100 per cent of net income. This meant that the demand for debt-related financial products fell sharply, since many people were unable or unwilling to continue funding purchases with credit. At the same time, a significant proportion of the credit advanced during the 1980s has subsequently been destroyed in the rash of corporate insolvencies, personal bankruptcies and mortgage defaults which reached epidemic proportions during the early 1990s. In addition, banks have been forced to be more circumspect in their lending behaviour because of the imposition of new international regulatory standards which required that all banks in the reporting area of the Bank for International Settlements maintain capital–asset ratios of at least 8 per cent (i.e. for every £100 they lend they must place £8 in a reserve fund in case of default).

For these reasons the financial services industry has begun to turn its attention towards investment-related financial products which offer the greatest prospects for growth during the 1990s. The industry is helped in this regard by the progressive dismantling of what remains of the Keynesian welfare state (Jessop 1993), which is effectively forcing individuals to make their own provisions, be it through the purchase of health insurance, investment in a personal pension or merely building up savings for the future (Hutton 1993). In this sense we are arguably witnessing the 'Japanisation' of the welfare–savings relation. Japan is the industrialised state with both the highest propensity to save *and* the lowest level of state welfare provision (Leyshon 1994).

In order to tackle the problems of competitiveness and high operational costs, the British financial services industry has undergone an extensive process of labour market restructuring involving several rounds of redundancy and the introduction of more flexible systems of working for those who remain.[6] For similar reasons financial services firms have been remaking their corporate structures and cultures. This has involved streamlining managerial levels and reorganising operations over space. Firms have introduced new spatial templates of responsibility and control which have facilitated a more critical appraisal of the value of each level within their corporate structures.

The branch networks of financial services firms have figured prominently in these appraisals for, while branches are the distribution points from which the bulk of retail financial services are sold, they are also responsible for generating most of the costs incurred by such firms.[7] But branch networks have also figured strongly in the efforts of the financial services industry to tackle the problems posed by general indebtedness and the need to develop investment-orientated markets. Branch-restructuring programmes have, therefore, been informed by a sensitivity to spatial variations in costs and profitability, and in levels of debt and perceived risk. In Britain, according to Gentle and Marshall (1993), this has meant a faster rate of branch closure in rural areas than in urban areas, since it is more expensive per capita to serve customers in rural than in urban areas. In addition, there has been a faster rate of branch closure in the south than in the north because indebtedness is higher in the south than in the north (Gentle and Marshall 1993).

But concerns about branch-restructuring programmes have been voiced most often in urban areas. Here, or so it is claimed, the geography of branch restructuring reflects an existing pattern of income and class (Leyshon and Thrift 1994). For example, a recent survey in Birmingham by the Bank of England revealed that a selective pattern of branch closure meant that by the early 1990s five of the city's thirty-nine electoral wards had already lost *all* their bank and building society branches, whilst a further six wards contained only a single branch (Conaty 1993). The wards so affected contained 28 per cent of Birmingham's population, among them some of the city's poorest inhabitants.

Certainly, there are good reasons to suppose that there is a relationship between an underlying geography of income and class, and the pattern of financial service branch closure (Christopherson 1993). Not only are financial services firms less willing to lend money to customers with low incomes and meagre financial resources than they were in the 1980s but such customers can also be expensive to service. Indeed, those of them who succeed in managing their accounts by maintaining low credit balances actually represent a drain on the banks' resources. 'Free' banking, which banks introduced in the 1980s to attract new business, means that prudent low-income customers incur no charges. But their accounts are not large enough for the banks to earn sufficient investment income to cover the fixed costs of servicing their accounts.[8] The losses caused by such customers have been partly offset by increasing the charges levied against those running up overdrafts but banks are considering re-introducing charges for those who fail to run balances high enough to generate enough interest income to cover the costs of running their accounts.

Those who do maintain adequate balances will, of course, continue to enjoy 'free' banking services.[9] This is not just because their deposits enable the banks to make enough money from them to cover the costs of servicing their accounts but also because these are the customers to whom the banks wish to sell investment-related financial products. The shift of emphasis away from debt-related products to the selling of investment services is a clear 'flight to quality' as banks and other financial services firms seek to move their customer base 'up-market' and to refocus upon higher-income and wealthier social groups.

This move has been most clearly marked by the rise of the 'prime' or 'premier' banking service, whereby banks provide preferential services – in the shape of higher rates of interest on deposits and an attentive regime of 'customer care' – to those who can afford it. These services are highly exclusionary. National Westminister's premier service is open to anyone with an annual income of at least £25,000 per annum, while to take advantage of Barclays Bank's premier service an income of at least £30,000 is required. An income of at least £50,000 is required to open a 'premier' account with Midland Bank. For the truly aspirational or the 'high net worth individual', Lloyds Bank can offer the services provided by its Private Banking division (Figure 7.1), while National Westminister has started to build a branch network on behalf of Coutts Bank, its private banking subsidiary, which carries the added cachet that it is the bank reputed to be used by various members of the British royal family.

The corollary of this move 'up-market' has been to place less emphasis upon those services for the rest of the population.[10] Similar moves are afoot in other financial sectors, such as insurance, where firms discriminate against those whom they perceive to be bad insurance risks by sharply raising premiums or even refusing to offer insurance altogether.[11] This development is representative of a more explicit form of socio-spatial risk pricing within the financial services industry[12] and of a greater commodification of the relationship between financial services firms and their customers.

There are now numerous examples of firms introducing practices which exclude and/or discriminate against certain individuals. A particularly revealing source in this regard is the 1993 submission of the National Association of Citizens Advice Bureaux (NACAB) to the Code of Banking Practice Review Committee. Based on evidence compiled from Citizens Advice Bureau across the country, the submission contains some shocking examples of the often brutal way in which banks and building societies are policing the boundaries of the financial system (Figure 7.2). What is clear

Figure 7.1 Moving up-market: advertisement for Lloyds Private Bank in Bristol

is that many of those brought 'inside' the financial system during the 1980s are finding themselves on the 'outside' in the 1990s, as they are expelled through the simple device of banks closing their accounts, or as they leave 'voluntarily' by closing their accounts to avoid the punishing charges incurred when overdraft limits are exceeded.

At the same time, many financial services firms are combining this social distancing with a physical distancing as they concentrate their branch-reduction programme in lower-income communities. This process of financial infrastructure withdrawal has worrying implications for the future development of such communities:

First, the presence of a financial infrastructure improves the viability of any community as a development site. A local financial infrastructure . . . [lowers the cost of] . . . financial transactions. This enhances the amenities of the community, and hence the value of geographically-specific assets located therein. Second, a lending institution located in a given community has a potential cost advantage in gathering information and hence in lending therein. Financial institutions gather information on small borrowers – income levels, account balances – as a byproduct of the financial services they provide. And their proximity to borrowers reduces their costs of assessing any given investment project in the area . . . . Third, the physical distance between lender and borrowers affects the kind of information that is used to assess borrowing projects within a community. When a lending institution is

The commodification of bank-customer relationships

A CAB Citizens Advice Bureau in North London reported the case of a client in multiple debt who has been repaying his debt to the bank for the past three years. He has now been seriously ill for six months. The CAB discussed his situation with the Debt Recovery Office of the bank and explained that if he was pressured he might have a stroke and die. The Debt Recovery Office said that at least then they would get their money through probate. (p. 17)

A CAB in South Wales reported the case of a client with multiple debt including a bank overdraft. When he visited the bank manager on a previous occasion to discuss his financial situation he was charged £75. He cannot afford to go and see the bank again. (p. 17)

A CAB in Cornwall reported an unemployed client who has a £20 overdraft which was increased to £40 because of charges. It was cleared immediately and the account closed. The building society wrote to the client stating that 85 pence was still outstanding and threatening court action and loss of credit worthiness. (p. 22)

A CAB in South Wales reported a client whose building society stopped payments of her five direct debits. She was sent five separate letters at a charge of £20 each. (p. 20)

A CAB in Hertfordshire reported a client with a £300 overdraft limit. When the account was overdrawn by £295 the bank wrote to him to remind him of the limit. He was charged £15 for the letter. (p. 20)

Financial exclusion

A CAB in South Wales reported an unemployed client who went to open a bank account having understood the bank would accept him as a customer. He was refused an account and refused an explanation. (p. 4)

A CAB in Lancashire reported the case of a client with a bank loan. He was made redundant and claimed unsuccessfully on his credit protection insurance. The bank closed his current account and the client only found out when direct debits were not made. (p. 7)

A CAB in Hampshire reported a client living on income support who owed the bank £1,500. The bank transferred the debt to a debt collection agency and the client has been repaying it at £5 a week with no default. The client has now been offered a job and the employer wishes to pay his wages into a bank account. He was refused an account by three banks one of which commented 'we are only interested in quality clients and unofficially I suggest you contact the building societies'. (p. 32)

A CAB in Hertfordshire reported a young disabled client who uses his account to have his salary paid into which he then withdraws for living expenses. The bank are closing his account because of its limited use. (p. 32)

Figure 7.2 The commodification of bank–customer relationships and financial exclusion: evidence from the submission to the Code of Banking Practice Review Committee by the National Association of Citizens Advice Bureaux
Source: National Association of Citizens Advice Bureaux (1993)

located within a community, its officers have knowledge about the potential of local businesses and residential areas. It is more costly for a lender located outside of the community to develop this information. In an assessment of credit worthiness, that lender will substitute generic, and even impressionistic knowledge about overall community characteristics for more project- and borrower-specific information.

(Dymski and Veitch 1992: 15–16)

Although still in its early stages in Britain, the process of financial exclusion has the potential to inflict serious economic and social damage upon communities abandoned by the process of financial infrastructure withdrawal. In the short term, it means that individuals and households in such communities have to look outside the formal 'market-regulated' financial system to satisfy their financial-services needs (Figure 7.3). In the absence of suitable alternatives, such as the non-market-regulated services provided by credit unions and community development banks (see below), or unregulated, non-market financial services, such as family or friendship networks, then communities may become a breeding ground for exploitative and predatory unregulated-market financial services (Haas 1992) where annual interest rates of over 1000 per cent are not unusual (Table 7.1)[13] In the long term, communities abandoned by the financial system are in danger of entering a slow and painful period of decline due to an inability to gain access to funds necessary for the continuous intensive phase of urban development which supports the maintenance of the built environment and provides the possibilities for further economic growth.[14]

	Regulated	Unregulated
Market	**A.** **Regulated market services** e.g. banks, insurance companies, building societies, etc.	**B.** **Unregulated market services** e.g. moneylenders, pawnbrokers, loan sharking, etc.
Non-market	**C.** **Regulated non-market services** e.g. social funds, credit unions, community development banks	**D.** **Unregulated non-market services** e.g. family/friendship networks

Figure 7.3 Typology of retail financial services

Although the process of financial infrastructure withdrawal has obvious implications for class divisions in society, it also has the potential to reinforce other types of oppressions, such as those predicated upon gender and race. Women are likely to be disproportionately affected by the process of financial exclusion because of the occupational segregation which means that they are more likely to be in poorly paid employment, as well the wider incidence of poverty amongst women than men

Table 7.1 Cost of credit to low-income groups, United Kingdom, late 1980s

Source of credit	Annual percentage rate	Availability to low-income groups
Credit unions	12.68	Yes
Banks		
personal loans	19.00	No
Building societies		
mortgages	12.25	No
personal loans	19.50	
Credit cards		
Access, Visa	23.10	No
store cards	29.80	No
Finance companies		
personal loans		
hire purchase	Variable	No
Catalogue companies	n.a.	Yes
Check trading	Expensive	Yes
Licensed moneylenders	300	Yes
Unlicensed moneylenders	1000+	Yes

Source: Adapted from Ford (1991: Table 8)

(McDowell 1991, 1992). Moreover, the requirement for women applying for credit to provide the name of a male guarantor has only relatively recently been rescinded (Mitchell 1992). The exclusionary turn is likely to revive gender-specific discrimination, although in this case the financial system will discriminate between certain types of women rather than against women in general. The process of financial exclusion is also likely to have important racial implications which reflect the higher incidence of poverty within certain ethnic minority groups and the possibilities for racism within an industry which employs a lower than average number of ethnic minority workers (Leyshon *et al.* 1993).

RESISTING FINANCIAL INFRASTRUCTURE WITHDRAWAL AND COUNTERING FINANCIAL EXCLUSION

The United States

Much of what we know about the implications of financial infrastructure withdrawal and the problems associated with financial exclusion comes from the United States. As in Britain, the neo-liberal reregulation of retail financial markets in the United States had the effect of introducing more competition between financial services firms (Dymski *et al.* 1993). But, whereas in Britain it took several years to usher in a wave of more destructive competition, the shock of competition was far more immediate in the United States. One reason for this is that the United States has a far greater number of financial institutions per capita than Britain. Financial regulation inspired by the anti-financial capital sentiments of the New Deal served to confine retail financial services industries to single states (Cerny 1993; Florida 1986). The prohibition of interstate activity protected smaller firms against takeover and acquisition which meant that the institutional fabric of the US financial services industry became highly polarised. On the one hand, it was made up of a core of some very large firms, many of which had grown to such a size as to be able to compete successfully in international financial markets, despite the barriers on interstate activity. But, on the other hand, it was made up of a much larger tail of small and medium-sized financial services firms, many of which operated in what were often highly localised markets (Florida 1986; Holly 1987).

The reregulation of financial markets in the United States contained not only a structural element, allowing firms from different parts of the financial system to compete with one another, but also a spatial element as the restrictions on interstate activity were gradually rolled back (MacDonald 1992). For these reasons the cycle of reregulation from boom (as firms competed with one another to grow their assets) to bust (as the overextension of credit led to indebtedness and default) occurred in a more compressed period of time than was the case in Britain. The response of the US financial services industry to the crisis serves as a warning for economies such as Britain where the industry is only now working its way out of its domestic financial crisis.

The financial services industry in the United States has already retreated to a largely middle-class heartland, refocusing upon predominantly white, suburban communities in the search for fee-income and investment accounts (Mitchell 1990; Christopherson 1993). At the same time, the industry has begun to withdraw from poorer communities, abandoning predominantly African–American and Latino inner-city areas.[15] Haas (1992: 26) has provided a graphic illustration of this process in Los Angeles:

> In 1988, when Bank of America closed the last bank branch in the Vernon-Central neighborhood of South Central, they left a community with no banking service for a three-mile radius . . . The same year . . . Bank America opened a 'Private Banking Center' in Beverley Hills for customers with a net worth of four million dollars and a deposit of one million. Access to the center was by invitation only and these privileged customers were provided with a complete range of full banking, investment, real estate, trust and other services.

Meanwhile, customers in abandoned areas have been disproportionately disadvantaged by the way in which financial services firms have increasingly priced their services to reflect the true costs of providing services in a more competitive marketplace. Whereas low-income customers had previously

> benefited from various forms of non-price competition, such as free or low-fee checking and low or non-existent minimum balance requirements

they now

> have to pay for banking services they use, or tie-up their savings in – for them
> – high minimum balances.
>
> (ibid., 10–11)

In consequence, whereas

> more affluent customers may have benefited from the higher interest rates
> on deposits and balances, reinforced by their knowledge of how to get the
> best value for money, the less well-off are left with feelings of resentment at
> the changes that have been put in place.
>
> (Mitchell 1990: 11)

The restructuring of the financial services industry over space, the shift to 'true cost' finance and the operation of financial dynamics have all played their part in bringing about what Mike Davis (1993: 14) has described as the 'spatial apartheid' of the US urban system. The flight of financial capital has followed the earlier flight of the white middle class to ensure that the suburban fringes of US cities are predominantly white, in work and comparatively wealthy, while inner cities are predominantly African–American or Latino, economically blighted and financially broke.

There have been two main political responses to the advance of the process of financial infrastructure withdrawal and the problems of financial exclusion in the United States. The first response has consisted of efforts to halt the process by which communities are denuded of formal financial infrastructure. The second response has been to counter financial exclusion through the creation of 'alternative' financial infrastructure.

Resisting financial infrastructure withdrawal

That it is possible to resist the process of financial infrastructure withdrawal in the United States at all is due largely to the 1977 Community Reinvestment Act (CRA). This particular piece of federal regulation was passed after a protracted debate over social justice and the future of America's inner cities during the early 1970s, as race riots were followed by divestment and economic decay.[16] The CRA was an explicit recognition by the US Congress that financial abandonment damages local communities. Its purpose was

> to encourage [federally] regulated financial institutions to fulfil their
> continuing and affirmative obligation to meet the credit needs of their com-
> munities, including low- and moderate-income neighborhoods, consistent
> with safe and sound operation of such institutions.
>
> (*Federal Register* 1978: 47 144)

In some states, the CRA is supplemented by state-level community-reinvestment legislation which covers those smaller financial institutions that are state- and not federally chartered (Mitchell 1990).

The CRA significantly empowers local communities in their fight to retain their formal financial infrastructure. The performance of the CRA is regularly monitored and can be taken into account should a bank propose closing branches in particular areas or seek a merger with an out-of-state bank. This has forced many banks to enter into a form of 'negotiated restructuring' to ensure that their plans do not adversely affect 'their communities'. The CRA has ensured that many local communities have clung on to a level of financial service provision that they would otherwise have lost (see Bond (1991) and Mitchell (1990) for examples). It has been estimated that the use of the CRA to resist financial infrastructure withdrawal and financial exclusion succeeded in winning more than $5 billion in lending concessions for low-income areas during the 1980s (Bond 1991). But, given the advance of financial exclusion in the United States during this period the CRA is clearly anything but a watertight barrier against a growing tide of financial abandonment (Fishbein 1989). There would appear to be three main problems with the CRA in this regard.

First, the CRA focuses only upon credit-granting institutions (i.e. banks, and savings and loans institutions) and not upon other financial institutions, such as insurance companies (Hoyt and Choca 1989). This has meant that, while many communities retain a link to credit-granting institutions thanks to the CRA, they may be denied access to insurance by an industry which 'since the mid-1960s . . . [has] concluded that urban communities are uninsurable' (Squires and Velez 1988: 64). Thus, over a long period of time, insurance companies have withdrawn their offices from the poorer parts of US cities (Squires *et al.* 1991). An inability to obtain insurance will, in all probability, affect the chance of an individual obtaining credit even from an institution bound by the CRA since it does not require that banks and thrifts act counter to 'safe and sound' prudential standards. Although it is illegal for insurance companies explicitly to define 'red-line' areas within which they will not write policies, they are now adept at pricing policies in ways that subtly exclude the areas in which the poor and minority groups live, with clear implications for economic development in such areas.[17]

A second problem is that, like any other form of legislation, there are any number of possible readings of the CRA, so that the precise remit of the Act is open to interpretation (cf. Clark 1989b). The main interpretive battleground has been over the definition of 'credit needs' and 'community'. The latter term has been particularly contentious and has provided the legal representatives of financial institutions with the opportunity to engage in protracted legal argument over the meaning of community in each particular case.[18]

A third and final problem is that, while the CRA is certainly a boon to community groups seeking to arrest the process of financial infrastructure withdrawal, all the Act really requires is that banks and thrifts disclose information on their lending activity. As Mitchell (1992: 12) observes, the CRA does not put any formal requirements on banks to make certain kinds of loans, or to extend credit to particular groups . . . [but] . . . by bringing the details of banks' credit decisions into the public domain, so that they are subject to public scrutiny as well as to monitoring by regulators, it provides a powerful incentive to banks to take account of the needs of sections of the community which otherwise might be neglected.

However, there is evidence that the 'monitoring by regulators' referred to above is not as attentive to detail as perhaps it should be. As Haas (1992) points out, banks in Los Angeles which have come under suspicion on the basis of an examination of their pattern of lending behaviour have, nevertheless, been able to achieve 'outstanding' community-reinvestment ratings.

In recent years the provisions of the CRA have been strengthened in the 1989 Financial Institutions Reform, Recovery and Enforcement Act (FIRRE). FIRRE was enacted in the crisis caused by the near collapse of the savings and loan industry under a mountain of debt following deregulation in the early 1980s (MacDonald 1992). The scale of the losses run up by the savings and loans industry, and the manner in which they were incurred, often involving acts of corruption and fraud, caused widespread public outrage in the United States. The extra provisions for the CRA in the FIRRE Act – which widened the scope of institutions covered and required the disclosure of more detailed lending information – may be seen as making the financial services industry do penance for the excesses of the 1980s. However, as MacDonald has noted, the downturn of the US economy in the early 1990s began to shift attention away from the interests of local communities towards the demands of capital as the financial services industry began to lobby for the relaxation of the reform of the CRA.

Nevertheless, the CRA remains a critically important weapon in the armoury of those who seek to defend local communities against the economic and social ravages of financial infrastructure withdrawal.

It is complemented by a second, more proactive strategy which seeks to counter the problems caused by the process of financial exclusion and which involves building an 'alternative' financial infrastructure.

Countering financial exclusion – building an alternative financial infrastructure

In an otherwise pessimistic review of more than a decade of urban policies informed by the neo-liberalism of the Reagan and Bush administrations, Deborah Auger (1993) alights upon Community Development Corporations (CDCs) as offering perhaps the only glimmer of hope for those inner-city communities close to collapse under the weight of capital flight, grinding poverty, spiralling levels of crime and an atmosphere of violence and danger. Auger (ibid.: 812) gives CDCs a glowing testimony for operating in 'the most severely distressed urban neighborhoods, felt to have been largely "abandoned" by government and business alike', and for mobilising funds from a range of public and private sources to attend to 'physical and economic development needs'.

CDCs and similar bodies are informed by the 'localism' which increasingly characterises urban governance on both sides of the Atlantic (Lovering 1994; Peck and Tickell 1993a). In essence, this neo-liberal 'new urban politics' (NUP) (Cox 1993) revolves around the premise that, while capital is potentially globally mobile, 'communities' are by their very nature rooted in particular places. For adherents of NUP this means that urban governance must be about making urban arenas fit places for capital to do business and about competing with other urban arenas to attract and retain hypermobile flows of capital.

However, there are strong grounds for arguing that such genuflection in the face of capital is driven as much by ideology as it is by there being 'no alternative'. Cox (1993) argues that recent changes in the nature of industrial production, revolving around the fragmentation of vertically integrated production and the development of geographically concentrated production *filieres*, mean that capital is becoming more rather than less locationally embedded (see e.g. Amin and Thrift 1992; Storper 1992). On the other hand, to argue that regimes of urban governance have to be bent to suit the demands of mobile capital ignores the fact that within every urban system there are financial resources which can be drawn upon and utilised if the right sort of local institutions are in place to tap and realise them (see e.g. Gaston and Kennedy 1987).

These local institutions can also provide an alternative to the neo-liberal prescriptions of the NUP. As such, they constitute what Christopher and Hazel Gunn (1991) have described as alternative institutions of accumulation (AIA), which can contribute to local economic development in a number of ways. For example, AIA can

- attract resources to the community and recycle them there;
- respond to the community because their governing bodies incorporate a majority of local citizens and make use of democratic decision-making processes;
- aggregate and use social surplus in ways that encourage local development.

(ibid., 60)

What distinguishes AIA from the land and property development agencies favoured by adherents of the NUP is that they operate on behalf of local communities rather than on behalf of capital. Whereas large-scale property development frequently operates around a rubric of displacement, with the implicit aim of bringing in a more affluent residential base via gentrification, AIA focus upon improving the circumstances of the existing residents (Taub 1988). In this sense AIA may be seen as *institutions of resistance* rather than of compliance:

Alternative institutions can . . . be defined in terms of their objectives with respect to social change. Many are organized simply to provide services that are lacking in a community; their goal is to survive from year to year in order to do their work. Others are intended to be, or they become, *oppositional* in character. They shape themselves on the premise that they must be more than ameliorative institutions; they work to change the balance of power and distribution of the fruits of life in their communities.

(Gunn and Gunn 1991: 60–1, emphasis added)

Credit unions and community development banks are the two most important examples of AIA that have emerged in the United States to serve the financial needs of those urban communities most adversely effected by financial infrastructure withdrawals and financial exclusion. These institutions mobilise local pools of savings, sometimes topping them up with private, public and philantrophic funds, and thereby provide a source of credit that would not otherwise be available.

Credit unions are co-operative societies which offer members loans out of a pool of saving accumulated by the members themselves and are the most widespread form of AIA. By the late 1980s, there were estimated to be more than 16,000 credit unions in the United States with a combined membership of 54 million (Berthoud and Hinton 1989).

Community development banks are typically non-profit institutions created to fill the investment gap in communities perceived to be poorly served by the formal financial system (Gunn and Gunn 1991).[19] One of the most successful and certainly the most documented of the community development banks has been the Shorebank Corporation (Barnekov and Jabbar-Bey 1993; Taub 1988). This bank holding company is a private sector organisation but is able to combine profit and non-profit activities in a way not open to more conventional financial institutions, since it enjoys an unusually patient and communitarian shareholder base. The main stakeholders in the bank are foundations, 'concerned individuals' and religious groups, many of them based in the South Shore area of Chicago where the bank operates. The unusual ownership structure of the bank results from an effort to counter an early example of attempted financial infrastructure withdrawal when, in 1972, the bank sought to relocate from South Shore to a more prestigious location in the centre of Chicago. The reasons for this relocation were related to the demographic, economic and racial transformations which the area had undergone during the 1960s and early 1970s. The proportion of African–Americans in the area increased sharply so that by the mid-1970s over 85 per cent of the population was black. This, in turn, was accompanied by a sharp decline in average incomes in the area. According to Taub (1988: 41), the owners of the bank were

certain that it could not survive the period of racial change [and] petitioned to move the license to a downtown location on the grounds that South Shore's new residents would be unable to support a bank.

However, the bank's attempted 'flight to quality' was successfully resisted and community activists took over the bank in 1973 to counter more effectively the problems facing a community subjected to more subtle examples of financial exclusion.

Despite the reservations of the former owners of the bank, the Shorebank Corporation has proved that it is possible to run a successful financial institution in areas abandoned by more formal financial infrastructure. Now consisting of several subsidiary companies, which are engaged in activities ranging from property rehabilitation to the initiation and management of social and economic development projects, the Shorebank Corporation has played a leading role in

> stabilising the economy of the South Shore neighborhood, dramatically improving the quality of housing, fostering new business activity, and instilling a more positive view of the neighborhood by both residents and outsiders.
>
> (Barnekov and Jabbar-Bey 1993: 5)

But, in addition, the bank was also making record profits, earning a pretax income of over $2 million in 1992 from an asset base of almost $250 million (Cowe 1993).

The success of the Shorebank Corporation and similar organisations[20] lies behind the Clinton administration's 1993 Community Development and Financial Institutions Act which proposes to make more than $380 million available between 1994 and 1997 to support a wide range of community development financial institutions (CDFIs). The CDFIs include not only community credit unions and community development banks but also community development loan funds, micro-enterprise funds and minority-owned credit institutions (Barnekov and Jabbar-Bey 1993). The success of this particular piece of legislation would lead to a significant increase in the number of CDFIs, doing much to offset the problems caused by financial infrastructure withdrawal and financial exclusion in many inner-city areas in the United States.[21]

Britain

The situation in Britain is different to that in the United States in a number of respects. Most importantly, the processes of financial infrastructure withdrawal and financial exclusion are much less advanced. However, as we saw earlier, there is strong evidence to suggest that both processes are gathering momentum. Between 1982 and 1992, 17 per cent of bank branches in Britain were closed (*Annual Abstract of Banking Statistics* 1993). In the late 1990s, after a period in which building society branch networks were expanded, building society branches also began to be closed in considerable numbers. The effects of these closures have clearly had differential spatial effects. For example, one study (Skuse 1993) of Midland Bank and Barclays Bank branch closures between 1988 and 1993 found that full branch closures were concentrated in major urban areas (and especially in London, Brighton and Manchester), whilst sub-branch closures were more evenly spread and included many closures in rural areas (see Figures 7.4 and 7.5). To compensate for these closures there were also a small number of branch openings which were nearly all in new office and shopping developments (Figure 7.6). The exact locational effects of these closures await further study. Preliminary research in Hull and Bristol suggests that there is no easy correlation between, for example, poorer areas and branch bank closures but research in larger cities has found such evidence. For example, the finding of a survey in Aston in 1991 was that

> The Trustees Savings Bank . . . is now leaving the ward completely. The TSB (Witton Lane) closed on 10 December and TSB (Newtown Shopping Centre) will close in April 1991. There are only four small building society branches left in Aston and all of these are on Witton Lane in the far north end of the ward. In November 1988, there were 13 major clearing bank branches in the ward. From August 1991, when the Midland closes its Witton branch, there will be only five left and four of these are in the Jewellery Quarter area close to the city centre – well away from the shopping precincts and residential areas of the ward.
>
> (cited in Kempson (1994: 8))

Since 1991, the situation in Aston has deteriorated. There is only one building society branch left in the neighbourhood, one of the branches in the Jewellery Quarter has closed and a second is threatened with closure (ibid.).

The evidence of financial exclusion is more pronounced. We already know that a significant proportion of the British population exist outside the financial system. One survey (Euromonitor 1992) estimated that 81 per cent of adults in the UK had a bank account in 1991. However, these accounts did not automatically come with a cheque book or a cheque-guarantee card. Thus, whereas 70 per cent of adults had a cheque book, only 60 per cent had a cash card and 58 per cent a cheque-guarantee card. Again, while 64 per cent of adults had a building society account, only 13 per cent had an account with a cheque book. Other surveys (e.g. Ford 1991) show that the distribution of account ownership is heavily skewed towards particular socio-economic groups and is more likely to exclude women and certain ethnic groups (Table 7.2). Household surveys, which may be more accurate reflections of financial exclusion, since in many households only one account is held jointly, show that 19 per cent of households in the UK did not have a current account in 1991. Households without current accounts tended to be pensioners, or non-pensioners with an income of less than £150 per week (Table 7.3).

These figures suggest that financial exclusion does not stem so much from the lack of a current account which, according to Kempson (1994), few individuals or households are refused, than from the availability of additional facilities like a cheque-guarantee card or a Switch card which are provided only to those approved by bank or building society credit-scoring systems:

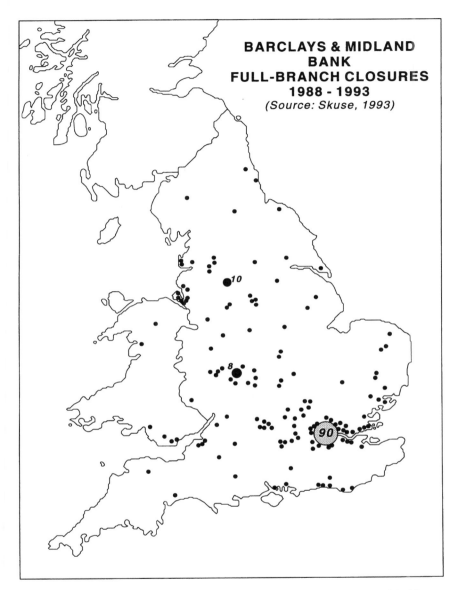

**BARCLAYS & MIDLAND
BANK
FULL-BRANCH CLOSURES
1988 - 1993**
(Source: Skuse, 1993)

Figure 7.4 Barclays and Midland Bank: full-branch closures, 1988–93
Source: Skuse (1993)

A very simple current account, with a cash card and standing order or direct debit facilities is potentially available unless [an applicant] cannot be identified on the voter's register or the applicant's credit reference contains adverse information such as a county court judgement or other credit default. Screening for a cheque book would be only slightly more stringent. But the credit scoring for a cheque guarantee card or a Switch card is likely to be nearly as tough as it is for an overdraft or loan, since both facilities provide an opportunity to overdraw. People who do not have a job, rent their homes from a local authority or housing association, or have any indication of instability in their lives (job loss, relationship breakdown, recent houses moves) would all have a reduced likelihood of getting either a cheque guarantee card or a Switch card.

(Kempson 1994: 9)

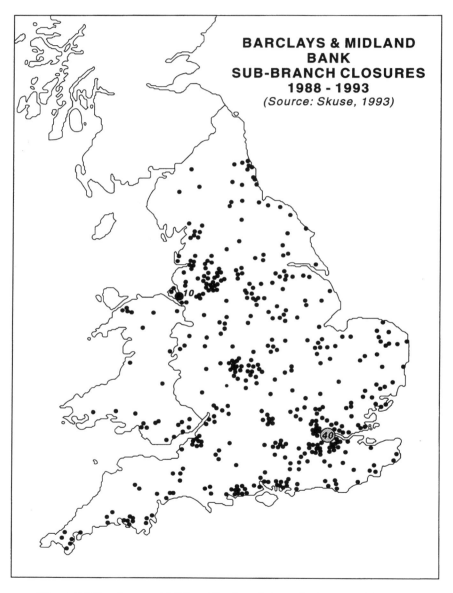

BARCLAYS & MIDLAND BANK SUB-BRANCH CLOSURES 1988 - 1993
(Source: Skuse, 1993)

Figure 7.5 Barclays and Midland Bank: sub-branch closures, 1988–93
Source: Skuse (1993)

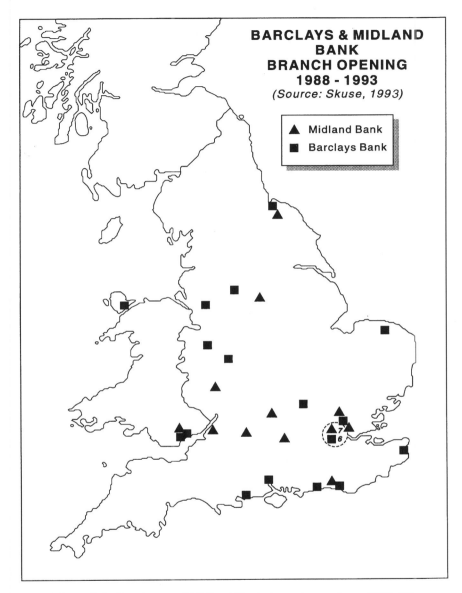

Figure 7.6 Barclays and Midland Bank: branch openings, 1988–93
Source: Skuse (1993)

Taken together, the body of work referred to above would suggest that there is a clear link between income, social class, gender, ethnicity and financial exclusion in Britain which is currently becoming more pronounced.

Given the potential of these processes of financial infrastruture withdrawal and financial exclusion financially to disenfranchise a relatively

Table 7.2 The financially excluded: (1) adults without a current (cheque book) account, United Kingdom, mid-1980s

	Percentage of adults without a current account
Adults	31.2
Adult females	34.6
Adult males	27.4
By social class	
E	58.7
D	43.7
C2	30.8
C1	18.2
AB	11.8
By income (£ per annum)	
Not stated	59.0
2,999 or less	51.3
3,000 to 4,999	34.8
5,000 to 6,999	25.1
7,000 to 8,999	18.5
9,000 to 10,999	14.8
11,000 to 14,999	11.0
15,000 and over	11.3

Source: Adapted from Ford (1991: Table 9)

large proportion of the British population, what likelihood is there of these processes being resisted and counteracted during the 1990s?

Resisting financial infrastructure withdrawal in Britain

There is no legislation approaching the CRA in Britain, nor, in truth, does there seem much chance of any, at least in the foreseeable future. There is no dispute between the British state and the financial services industry that the primary duty of the industry is to please its shareholders first and its clients second. Indeed, as Hunter (1993) has observed,

> [t]he banks are unapologetic for closing branches. A spokesman for the Banking Information Service said: 'Banks are businesses not charities. We do not provide social services.'

But this denial of a wider social responsibility by the banking industry has been challenged on at least two counts. The first challenge has been posed by those who argue that banks should be socially responsible precisely because they are not like other businesses. According to Mitchell (1992), banks in Britain are seen as too big and too important to fail. The collapse of a *major* bank would so destabilise the British economy that it would not be allowed to happen[22] – or at least not without public intervention. This

Table 7.3 The financially excluded: (2) social groups with the lowest penetration of current accounts, United Kingdom, 1991

	Percentage of households without a current account
Age and family circumstances	
Aged over 70	30
Lone parent	52
Separated or divorced in last three years	30
Work and employment status	
Full-time housewife and mother	63
Unemployed	52
Disabled	40
Retired	28
Part-time work	26
Unskilled work	37
Income	
Non-pensioner with income below £100 a week	49
Weekly budget	28
No savings	38
Claims housing benefit	60
Claims income support	58
Claims unemployment benefit	54
Claims retirement pension	28
Housing and neighbourhood	
Council tenant (UK)	47
NIHE tenant	73
Housing association tenant	27
Private tenant	29
Lives in run-down area	39
Lives in very run-down area	55
Pensioners in rural areas	33
Scotland	29
Northern Ireland	31

Source: Kempson (1994: 6)

is different to the experience of all other forms of capitalist enterprise which *are* allowed to fail. Mitchell takes his inspiration from the CRA to argue that in future banks should be forced to provide services to anyone in the 'whole community' who requires them. A concern for community development should be seen as an obligation which is conferred upon banks by the special immunity from failure that they enjoy by being granted a banking licence.

This line of argument begs a number of important questions. It is not entirely clear what Mitchell is referring to when he uses the term 'community'. As we saw earlier, this is a highly contentious concept open to a wide range of interpretations and meanings. Presumably, in this context Mitchell is referring to a national community, since UK banking licences confer nationwide rights, whereas in the United States licences are much more localised, making it easier to identify a community to which the bank should be responsible. Mitchell seems to be suggesting that in return for operating in the British financial system, banks should not be allowed to refuse services to anyone within that national regulatory space. But to determine whether or not a bank was responding to the credit needs of the 'whole community' in this case would require banks to agree to a level of information disclosure which would be unprecedented in Britain. Given the innate opposition of the financial services industry to any legislation that would require such disclosure and the apparent disinterest of the current (and in all likelihood any future) government in calling for disclosure, it would seem that financial exclusion will have to get a lot worse before regulatory change can improve it. Financial regulation is usually only enacted in response to crisis (Leyshon 1992; Moran 1991); we must expect the crisis of financial exclusion to get much worse before any effort is made to tackle the problem via regulatory change along the lines of the CRA.

Clearly, one of the main problems with arguments such as Mitchell's is the fact that the British financial services industry is dominated by a relatively small number of large and powerful institutions who have little or no incentive to pay attention to arguments about community responsibility. A second challenge to the financial services industry's disavowal of responsibility for the social problems caused by financial exclusion may, therefore, be to campaign for the dismantling of the industry on competition grounds. A break-up of an oligopolistic industry into smaller, more competitive groups, perhaps organised on a regional basis, would certainly weaken the power of the industry and, to the extent that it would force firms to embed themselves in local and regional economies, might well counter some of the worst excesses of financial abandonment and exclusion.

An argument along these lines coming from the left would not raise too many eyebrows. However, just this argument has been made by a critic placed firmly on the right of the political divide. In a recent monograph, Alan Duncan (1993: 40) – elected as the Conservative Member of Parliament for the Rutland and Melton constituency in 1992 – makes a strong case for regulation which would, as he puts it, 'unbundle the banks'. Duncan's motivation for launching a broadside against the banks in this way is not hard to fathom. He places much of the blame for the boom and bust of Britain's economy during the 1980s and 1990s at the door of the large clearing banks, which is perhaps disingenuous given his political affiliation. Moreover, his attack upon the banks is inspired in large part by a neo-liberalism which believes that large economic institutions distort what would otherwise be a self-stabilising and equilibrating system of economic competition. But these caveats aside, Duncan's contribution is an interesting addition to those voices who would argue for a reformed, more responsible, more locally orientated financial system.

Duncan's argument runs as follows. The British clearing banks 'are simply too large and diversified . . . to discriminate between sound and unsound banking propositions' (ibid.: 35); they are outdated economic institutions, legacies of an earlier age of capitalism that was national in its orientation but which have been wrong-footed by the globalisation of economic activity, particularly within the financial sphere:

> the entire raison d'être of the old-style clearing bank has disappeared. They were formed in the late nineteenth and early twentieth centuries because it was believed that banks needed to be big enough to service the large industrial corporations which were then being formed through a series of mergers. Today, those corporations borrow not from the banks but from the international capital markets. It was for that reason that the modern clearers were diverted into lending to commercial property developers and into various types of dubious financing used to mount leveraged takeover bids for their former clients.
>
> (ibid.: 36–7; cf. Lash and Urry 1987; Leyshon and Thrift 1993)

Duncan's worry is that in the 1990s banks will 'restrict credit in the same indiscriminate manner that they dispensed it' (ibid.: 37). His prescription is for the banks to return to their roots in the local banking markets from which they emerged in the nineteenth century. He argues that when the banking industry was made up of a constellation of independent banking partnerships they were 'close' to their clients,

> often encountering them socially as well as in business, and knew those whom they could trust and those whom they could not.
>
> (ibid.: 36)

Duncan's primary concern is with small and medium-sized enterprises which, he argues, have suffered over a long period of time because the bank have been more concerned with the credit needs of large and more nationally orientated businesses. It is this which motivates Duncan to call for the 'unbundling' of the highly concentrated and centralised banking industry because if

> the modern clearing banks were broken up into regional, or even local, suppliers of credit akin to the small partnership banks from which most of them were formed, they would get a better understanding of their borrowers.
>
> (ibid.: 36)

This interpretation runs along similar lines to those arguments which insist that a more locally embedded financial system would add to the institutional richness of regional economies, which could ensure their continued viability and competitiveness on a global scale (Murray 1991; cf. Amin and Thrift 1992). But it may well be that a process of unbundling would also help to resist the process of financial infrastructure withdrawal, as banks would be forced to lower their sights, refocus upon more local markets and cultivate areas they could otherwise afford to overlook as nationally orientated organisations.

Duncan even suggests that it is 'conceivable' that the Office of Fair Trading could prepare a legal case against the banks on competition grounds which could force the de-concentration of the industry. There is, he argues, 'strong *prima facie* evidence of an informal [banking] cartel' (Duncan 1993: 36), manifested in the way that all the banks were able to increase charges and widen margins during the deep recession of the early 1990s and by the fact that the market for credit is controlled by just a handful of suppliers.

This is an interesting argument. However, it needs to be treated with due caution. The argument advanced by Duncan may be seen as a variant of the well-rehearsed New Right economic discourse which characterises large, bureaucratic industries as 'inefficient' and 'bad', and small and medium-sized business as 'lean', 'efficient' and, therefore, 'good'. Having seen this discourse used to justify first running down and then selling off the nationalised industries, Duncan could be accused of merely looking for a new set of 'enemies within' in the shape of what perhaps could be described as the nearest thing to a nationalised industry that exists in the private sector.

Moreover, there are a number of problems with Duncan's argument in certain places. First, as the example of the United States makes abundantly clear, a more fragmented, locally integrated banking sector does not automatically ensure that credit will be more accessible than it is in a more centralised banking system. Second, Duncan's call for the break-up of the banking system at a national level ignores the fact that at a transnational level the banking sector is becoming ever more centralised and concentrated, tendencies which within Europe have been considerably hastened by the creation of a Single European Market for many financial products (Begg 1992). Third, and finally, the creation of a set of smaller financial institutions must be set in the context of wider international concerns for the systemic fragility of the financial sector (M. Davis 1992; Underhill 1991), concerns which, for the most part, associate size with financial stability. (It is doubly ironic, therefore, that the independent banking partnerships which Duncan laments actually began to disappear from the early nineteenth century onwards, when in 1826 the Bank of England allowed joint stock banks to form outside the sixty-five-mile 'exclusion zone' surrounding the City of London as part of an effort to strengthen and stabilise a provincial financial system made volatile by the regular collapse of poorly capitalised independent banking partnerships (Black 1989).)

These are powerful countertendencies which make the break-up of the British banking industry, along the lines that Duncan suggests, extremely problematic. It would appear that, while there are certainly possibilities for resisting the withdrawal of formal financial infrastructure in Britain, the chances of success, at least for the foreseeable future, are likely to be slim. With this in mind, let us consider the possibilities of a second strand of resistance: countering financial exclusion through an alternative financial infrastructure.

Countering financial exclusion in Britain

Compared with the situation in the United States, Britain is poorly served by alternative financial infrastructure. This despite the fact that Britain was the birthplace of the co-operative movement which did much to inspire the later development of several forms of co-operative financial institution (Tucker 1967). Although the Co-operative Bank owes its origins to the efforts of the Rochdale Pioneers of 1844, and the Trustees Savings Bank (TSB) is a prominent survivor of the numerous savings banks which grew up in nineteenth-century Britain to mobilise local and regional pools of savings, both institutions are now firmly part of the formal financial infrastructure of Britain, competing with other financial institutions for national and international funds. At the same time, Britain's sole state-owned bank was recently transferred into private hands, when in 1990 the Alliance & Leicester Building Society bought the Girobank, previously a division of the Post Office (Leyshon and Thrift 1994a).

The paucity of alternative institutions of accumulation is not helped by the fact that credit unions, the most numerous form of AIA in the world, have for the most part failed to gain a foothold in Britain. In 1986, only 35,000 people, or 0.1 per cent of the British population, were members of a credit union (Figure 7.7). This compares with a figure of around one in five people in the United States and around one in four in Canada (Berthoud and Hinton 1989). The main advantages of credit union membership are that they can provide credit to people who would not normally be considered credit-worthy by more formal financial institutions and can provide credit at a cost that is well below the market rate. For example, compound rates of interest on credit union loans are usually in the region of 12 per cent per annum, whereas the comparable rates for personal loans, credit cards and charge cards are anything from 20 to 35 per cent per annum or more. This means that credit unions are particularly valuable sources of credit to those individuals and families on low incomes for whom the need to replace an everyday item such as a washing machine can lead to a severe household financial crisis. A credit union loan of a few hundred pounds ensures that a credit union member is able to purchase the goods required with cash and at far less cost than would be the case when using other forms of credit, whereas an application for credit from the retailer or a bank might well have been denied.

In recent years, several local authorities in Britain have sought to promote credit unions for this very reason as well as to counter the problems associated with the use of non-regulated marketed financial services, the growth of which is blighting many public sector housing estates in Britain. Encouragingly, there is evidence to suggest that the use of credit unions will increase if they are actively promoted by concerned bodies. For example, 29 per cent of the Catholic population of Northern Ireland and 30 per cent of the population of the Republic of Ireland are members of credit unions. Indeed, in 1986 there were 3.5

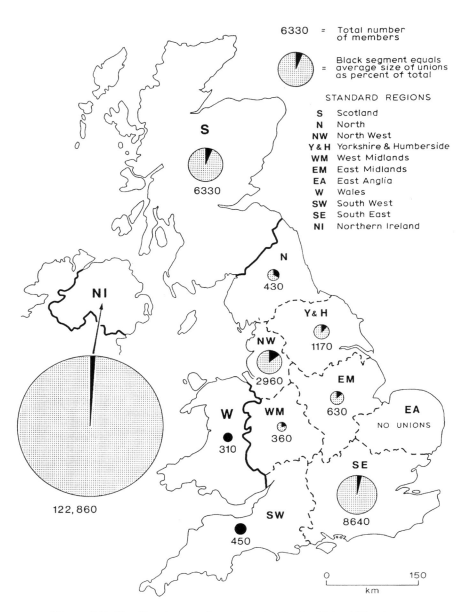

6330 = Total number of members

= Black segment equals average size of unions as percent of total

STANDARD REGIONS

S Scotland
N North
NW North West
Y & H Yorkshire & Humberside
WM West Midlands
EM East Midlands
EA East Anglia
W Wales
SW South West
SE South East
NI Northern Ireland

S
6330

N
430

Y & H
1170

NW
2960

EM
630

EA
NO UNIONS

W
310

WM
360

NI
122,860

SE
8640

SW
450

0   150
km

Figure 7.7 Credit unions and membership in the United Kingdom, by region, 1986
Source: Berthoud and Hinton (1989: Table 1.6)

times more credit union members in Northern Ireland than there were in the whole of Britain. The relatively high number of Catholics who are members of a credit union owes much to their promotion by the Catholic Church, which has a very long history of opposition to financial 'usury' (Parry 1989).

Although credit unions are clearly incapable of solving all the problems caused by financial exclusion, they are certainly a means by which savings can be pooled and then distributed in line with local needs and may even help to stem the process of financial dynamics which would otherwise recycle funds from poorer to richer areas. But it follows that the amount of money that credit unions have available to lend is related to the incomes of their members, since the amount people save is a function of their incomes. It also follows, therefore, that less credit is available in poorer areas than in richer areas. Nor is it certain that credit unions will necessarily stem the rise of unregulated market financial services in poorer areas, since there is evidence that moneylenders are a major cause of indebtedness in certain parts of the Irish Republic, despite the preponderance of credit unions there (Berthoud and Hinton 1989). Indeed, Berthoud and Hinton (ibid.: 93) provide a salutary warning that 'there is little sign that in Britain a credit union is a substitute for other types of credit' but they provide 'a useful extension of the range of credit sources available to middle-income families'.

Moreover, Berthoud and Hinton go on to suggest that credit unions may even be responsible for substituting one type of financial exploitation for another. Figure 7.8 illustrates the relationship between savings and borrowings within a credit union and within the financial system more generally. In the latter case, those on low incomes tend to have borrowings in excess of savings, while those on high incomes tend to have savings in excess of borrowings. This means that the savings of those on high incomes are being recycled in the form of loans to those on low income who pay

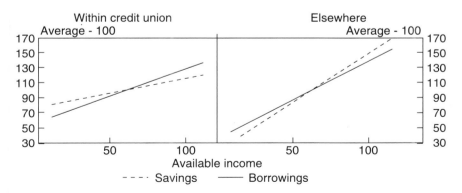

Figure 7.8 Savings and borrowings in credit unions and in the formal finance services market
Source: Berthoud and Hinton (1989: Chart 7.2)

for this money at market rates of interest. However, within a credit union this relationship is inverted. Those on lower incomes tend to have savings in excess of borrowings while those on higher incomes have borrowings in excess of savings. Thus, in the case of a credit union, the savings of those on lower incomes are being recycled into loans for use by those with higher incomes. But, crucially, those on higher incomes are charged at levels of interest which are well below the market rate (ibid.).

However, while credit unions may create their own unique form of financial exploitation, it is nevertheless difficult to disagree with Berthoud and Hinton (ibid.: 122) that while credit unions 'may not have created economic equality . . . they appear to be much less unequal than the outside world'. Being inside a credit union is clearly more favourable than being outside the formal financial system altogether and

> membership of a credit union is more useful to those with low incomes than to those with higher incomes who would have no difficulty in saving or borrowing with financial institutions.
>
> (ibid.: 122)

The problem in Britain really resides in the fact that not only are credit unions thin on the ground but that they are not complemented by other forms of AIA. There are no community development banks to speak of, which would not only serve to mobilise local savings but also act as conduits for flows of external capital into areas that the financial system would otherwise avoid. One hopeful initiative has been the Local Investment Fund (LIF), modelled on US community-investment funds, launched by Business in the Community. The aims of the LIF are laudable, being to provide funds to those inner-city areas increasingly excluded from the financial system and to provide the flows of credit needed to fund economic development. Indeed, the plan is to attempt to repeat the success of community development banks in the United States, such as the Shorebank Corporation. However, in the words of Cowe (1993), the LIF venture

> will not solve Britain's various inner-city crises, even in 20 years . . . For a start, many such areas are much closer to decay than decline, and [LIF's] commercial approach requires a significant residue of capital in the community [to begin with]. Second, the LIF will have all of £3 million once it has finished its current fund-raising exercise – a pitiful effort even by the standards of the $40 million with which Shorebank began 20 years ago.

CONCLUSIONS

Financial infrastructure withdrawal and financial exclusion have the potential significantly to deepen levels of uneven development in economies such as those of Britain and the United States. But there are ways in which these processes can be resisted and countered, some of which we have documented. Although the possibilities of resistance currently seem more hopeful in the United States than Britain, it is important to emphasise that it is still easier to live outside the financial system in Britain than in the United States, largely because of the way in which recipients of benefits and pensions are able to exchange their cheques for cash at the Post Office in a way that is impossible in the United States (Mitchell 1990). Of course, the introduction of automated cash transfer (ACT) to the benefits system in Britain may change this situation.[23]

What the discussion in this chapter suggests is that currently the British case requires two main developments. The first of these is more in the way of resistance. We suggest that one way to achieve this is by focusing on the idea of 'financial citizenship'. Traditional states are, amongst other things, about boundaries. States define spatial and other boundaries of inclusion and exclusion and, on the basis of these boundaries, confer citizenship and rights to those on the inside. States have an 'inside' and an 'outside', a 'here' and a 'there'; they have citizens (on the inside) and non-citizens (on the outside) (Walker 1993). Contemporary financial systems also have these characteristics. They draw borders which are difficult to transgress and which are currently being rolled up. What we need is a concept like financial citizenship which can relate the two, both as a means of putting pressure on states to reform their financial systems so that they include rather than exclude and of putting pressure on financial systems to realise that they have some state-like responsibilities which reach beyond consumer sovereignty into basic human rights. In some other countries there is a more general acceptance of such arguments; for example, in France state law gives everyone the right to a bank account (Kempson 1994). In Britain, the idea that people should be able to be 'dual citizens' of both the state and the financial system clearly still has some way to go.[24]

The second development is to produce imaginative proposals for more in the way of alternative financial infrastructure which can, in particular, supply the basic banking facilities and low-cost loans to low-income households, to replace the infrastructure which is now being lost or which has never existed. The most obvious move would be to allow Post Office Counters, with its network of 20,000 outlets, to provide such services. Because of privatisation proposals this may prove to be a difficult proposition. In such a case, a range of other options suggest themselves, some of which we have mentioned, like community development banks, community development funds and credit unions; others should include non-financial retail outlets providing a range of financial services.[25] What seems certain is that, in present circumstances, processes of financial abandonment within many areas of Britain may well lead to the outbreak of 'financial starvation'. Such a bleak future requires imaginative policy responses and the political will which can be generated only through imaginative campaigning.

CHAPTER 8

MONEY ORDER?

The discursive construction of Bretton Woods and the making and breaking of regulatory space

INTRODUCTION

> We have moved from the metaphysical realm to the metaphorical: that is to say, we have moved away from the idea that economic 'truth' is discovered and towards the idea that it is made.
>
> (Daly 1991: 93)

> Scientific progress is very much about improving the metaphors we use so that our interventions in the world are more successful.
>
> (Sayer 1993: 340)

The way in which we think of 'the economy' in economic geography has undergone a marked shift over recent years. Although the lessons of feminism, poststructuralism, and postmodernism have still to permeate the bedrock of economic geography in the way that they have elsewhere in the academy, there are clear signs that this particular corner of academic endeavour – which many regard to be the last bastion of the 'totalising discourse' – is now too undergoing a period of critical self-reflection. Discourses of the economic, too often assumed to be universal and transcendent, are increasingly recognised as contingent and contextual. Certain economic discourses become dominant at particular times and in particular places, which in turn requires that such discourses, and the theories and ideas associated with them, be subject to critical historical analysis in order to uncover the particular ensembles of power/knowledge upon which they, like all discourses, are founded. To reiterate the argument of Glyn Daly (1991), it is no longer sufficient to seek an immanent, stable economic truth – for as realists have consistently stressed – such a search will be in vain. Rather, what is required is that economic discourses be historicised, in order to reveal the ways in which particular interpretations of 'the economic' have been presented as *the truth* at particular times in particular places in order to serve certain interests and to achieve certain objectives. As Fred Block puts it, it is necessary 'to recognise that social science concepts are not simply analytical abstractions, but are themselves cultural tools that play an important role in creating a semblance of order out of the potential chaos of social life' (1990: 8). Our understanding of the social world, then, is patchy and partial and the concepts we use to describe concrete phenomena help to shape our understandings of these phenomena (Sayer 1993). Moreover, concepts are cultural tools that can have important material effects, inasmuch as prevailing economic discourses can be used to justify the creation or the destruction of economic institutions for the purpose of bringing 'order' to economy and society.

In this chapter we look at one particularly important material intervention within the 'chaos of social life': the Bretton Woods system. This represents perhaps the most ambitious attempt to develop economic order yet attempted within the history of capitalism. The system serves as a particularly good example of the way in which economic discourses can have significant material effects, for the regulatory order which the system sought to impose upon capitalism was profoundly influenced by a shift in the prevailing intellectual climate, associated with the rise of a new practical economic discourse which revolved around the ideas of the 'New Deal' and of Keynesian economic theory. This particular way of conceptualising the economy emerged during an extremely troubling period in the history of capitalism when the major industrialised economies all but collapsed. The economic crisis precipitated an intellectual crisis, as doubt was cast upon prevailing economic orthodoxies, and as the regulatory systems that these orthodoxies had called into existence to order capitalist economies were subject to critical reevaluation (Leyshon 1992).

The remainder of the chapter is organised as follows. In the next two sections we emphasise the need for economic geographers to take economic discourse seriously. The way in which we conceptualise 'the economic' is not completely innocent for, as we hope to illustrate, our theories of the economy can have important material outcomes. To this end in the fourth section we look at two dominant economic discourses that have in the past underpinned economic geography – neoclassicism and Marxism. We then go on to consider two *post-Marxist* economic theories which have particular significance for enquiry within economic geography – regulation theory and neo-Gramscian political economy. In the fifth section we attempt to account for the rise and fall of the regulatory experiment of Bretton Woods. We do this in two parts, drawing upon, first, regulation theory and, second, neo-Gramscian political economy. The conclusions to the chapter are presented in the last section.

TIME, SPACE, AND ECONOMIC DISCOURSE IN ECONOMIC GEOGRAPHY

We wish to make it clear from the outset that to claim that economic geography is entering a period of critical self-reflection is not to suggest that such periods have not occurred before. They have, and have produced significant changes in the scope and content of enquiry within economic geography. Indeed, for a long period of time economic geography has enjoyed a privileged position at, or at least very near to, the heart of human geography, which has meant that critiques emanating from within economic geography have served to bring about ontological and epistemological shifts within the discipline as a whole. This tendency was evident in the 1960s as the 'quantitative revolution' in human geography was ushered in largely on the back of what were, in essence, economic models. Such models were used to explain geographies of settlement (such as in Walter Christaller's central place theory) and of agricultural and industrial production (following the 'rediscovery' of the work of Johann Heinrich von Thünen and Alfred Weber, respectively) among other things. The ascendancy of this form of analysis brought about an important moment of critical self-reflection within human geography, as location models were subject to a radical critique which in the end fatally undermined the hegemony of the quantitative project in human geography (e.g. see the classic contribution from Doreen Massey (1974)).

Many of the criticisms made of the quantitative revolution were voiced from a broadly Marxist perspective, and sought to expose the neoclassical assumptions which underpinned the apparent neutrality of the models being used across the terrain of human geography at the time.[1] Amidst the search for 'optimum locations' and 'efficient solutions', Marxist critics insisted that these concepts were hardly politically neutral. The uncritical use of such concepts in location modelling meant that geographers were advocating solutions that were optimal and efficient for some but not others. That is, the solutions were favourable to 'capital', in that a 'low-cost' location was seen as a positive externality, but not to 'labour', because a higher-than-average wage location was seen as negative externality. The Marxist critique was so persuasive in economic geography that it served to bring about a truly radical reorientation of the nature of enquiry within the subdiscipline. Indeed, some indication of the degree to which Marxist geographers have succeeded in setting the research agenda in economic geography is alluded to by Neil Smith (1994) in his observation that Marxist geographers have, over a long period of time, appeared at or near the top of lists of citation counts in human geography.

The defection of so many economic geographers from neoclassicism to Marxism might appear to be something of a historical curiosity in the history of the discipline, given that the two approaches appear to stand in such stark opposition to one another. However, the leap of faith required to move from neoclassicism to Marxism is, in one sense at least, not as far as one might think. The Marxist critique of location theory certainly provoked a debate about the ethical and moral implications of research, and successfully drew attention to the negative social and political implications of economic processes. But the Marxist critique in geography rarely questioned the way in which neoclassicism placed 'the economic' at the centre of explanation. This was particularly surprising given that a major component of Marx's project was to denaturalise Liberal conceptions of the economy, to emphasise the importance of ideology, the state, and so on. It seemed that, in common with neoclassicalists, Marxist geographers saw the economy as the principal 'engine' of social change, one that conforms to clearly defined 'rational' principles. This line of thinking has obvious appeal within social theory, for it offers the possibility of gaining an analytical purchase over a whole gamut of social processes via economic knowledge alone. The economy, then, is used in such approaches as a 'master concept' (Block 1990: 11), an analytical key which can be used to unlock understanding of society as a whole.

Clearly, Marxists and neoclassicists have very different conceptions of *how* an economy works, but these competing interpretative frameworks each privilege the economic in the final instance which, in turn, requires that other interpretations be afforded secondary analytical status (although, as we shall argue, Marxism's analytical emphasis on the 'social' renders it more amenable to understanding capitalism's specificities and contingent historical forms). Such similarities exist because, although neo-classicalism and Marxism are clearly oppositional interpretations of the economic, they share a number of important systemic similarities (Barnes 1987, 1989, 1992). This is because, in common with all theoretical systems, both neoclassicalism and Marxism have been brought into existence by a process which Trevor Barnes, borrowing from Mary Hesse, describes as 'metaphorical redescription': that is, the process by which scientific explanation is advanced by 'transferring words normally associated with one system . . . to redescribe the explanandum of another system' (1992: 122).[2] Neoclassical economics and its principal creation, *Homo economicus* (economic man), relied heavily upon just such a process of metaphorical redescription. In this case, Barnes argues, nineteenth-century physics was the recruiting ground, with the principle of 'least effort' or energy conservation, derived from the observed behaviour of particles, being conscripted to do service as a metaphor for the economic behaviour of individuals (see Barnes 1987, 1992). The process of metaphorical redescription within Marxism, meanwhile, involves employing a metaphor of reproduction drawn from the field of biology (Barnes 1992). Evidence of the centrality of this metaphor in Marxism may be observed in the central notion of the *circulation* of capital and of the *reproduction* of the capitalist system, as in the circulation of energy necessary for the reproduction of biota.

Although the use of these metaphors served to create two very different economic models, in each case the process of metaphorical redescription introduces an assumption of inherent and immutable rationality into economic processes. In neoclassical economics rationality is assumed at the level of the individual. As each individual seeks to maximise utility, the economy is regulated by a system of rational economic choices. The market ensures that the economy is always moving towards a situation of equilibrium, as imbalances in the supply of and demand for scarce resources are evened out by rational economic actors. Meanwhile, in Marxism, rationality is assumed at the level of the economy as a whole: that is, 'the economy is rational provided there is crisis-free accumulation'

(Barnes 1992: 128). In response to crisis, therefore, the system as a whole must adapt or 'restructure' in order to ensure that the reproductive cycle continues. The use of the word *crisis* to denote a dangerous or unstable economic period is particularly significant here, given its common pathological meaning to signify a crucial stage in the development of a disease or illness within a living organism.

Being aware of these processes of metaphorical redescription, by which notions of physical and biological rationality were imported into explanandums of economic processes, helps explain why members of the neoclassical and Marxist interpretative communities believe so strongly in the certainty of their positions. Moreover, it also reveals why those of a more deconstructionist turn are moved to argue that the 'claims to know' made by both neoclassicism and Marxism should be treated with due caution and scepticism (Block 1990). On the one hand, the assumption of economic utility within neoclassicism excludes any non-rational behaviour at the level of the individual, and denies any role for culture in the unfolding of economic processes, culture being usefully defined in this context as that which one does not *have* to do. On the other hand, the assumption of rationality at the level of the economy as a whole found in some Marxist accounts means that economic activity tends to be explained in functionalist terms; that is, economic activity exists ultimately only because of its role in maintaining systemic equilibrium. In this way, 'appropriate' and 'inappropriate' economic behaviour may be identified in terms of its utility for the survival of the economic system as a whole, an idea which is clearly Darwinian in tone.[3] As Emmanuel Terray puts it, 'reproduction [of the capitalist system] is conceived as a final *cause* from which the ensemble of structures and analyzed institutions proceeds . . . [but] . . . it is necessary to recall first of all that reproduction can only be a *goal*' (Terray, quoted in Lipietz (1993: 128), emphasis added). As Barnes (1992: 132) points out, the use of a metaphor of reproduction in social theory diminishes the importance attached to *reflexivity*, that is the ability of human subjects to 'modify action in the light of its consequences'.

These observations have important implications for theories of all sorts, including those which seek to explain the unfolding of economic processes. It suggests that not only are all theories place specific – that is, they are 'views from somewhere' – but they are also views which are time–space specific (Gregory 1994). In addition, because the world is shrinking, the places from which theoretical observations are made are constantly in motion relative to one another, which means that the confidence we place in social theories of all kinds has been thrown into doubt. In other words, the ground upon which social processes are played out is in motion, making it even more difficult to explicate the ways in which social processes unfold (Leyshon 1994a). But particular doubt has been cast over those forms of social theory which fail to recognise the necessity of contingency and the specificities of time–space. As Andrew Sayer (1993: 335) puts it, the 'supposedly grand totalising visions of liberalism and Marxism have been exposed as partial, particular, situated views of the world masquerading as general, universal views'. This is not to argue that theories have no purchase upon the material world, but that we need to recognise that our understandings are partial and created in a discursive dialogue with material processes.

DISCOURSES *ON* AND *OF* THE ECONOMY

Over the last twenty years or so economic discourses have emerged which take seriously the need for claims to know to be contingent and cognisant of the specificities of time and space. One way of conceptualising this shift in the intellectual climate is to think of the distinction made by Daly (1991) between *discourses of the economy* on the one hand, and *discourses on the economy* on the other. The term 'discourses of the economy' is used to 'refer to the historical construction of all those identities which attempt to establish themselves within the "economic" in a given conjuncture' (Daly 1991: 94). 'Discourses on the economy', meanwhile, include 'all those discursive attempts . . . to conceptually oversee, or domesticate, those identities'. Neoclassicalism and Marxism fall into the category of discourses on the economy, for they attempt to explain the unfolding of economic processes from a privileged vantage point. However, as Peter Dicken and Nigel Thrift (1992) argue, the view from such a position is likely to be restricted and partial, which produces only an impoverished understanding of the ways in which economic processes unfold. Because of this, they argue, it is preferable that capitalism 'be viewed from a number of vantage points', so that the insights gleaned from each position be used to inform the others (Dicken and Thrift 1992: 283; see also Thrift 1994b).

Since the early 1970s discourses on the economy have increasingly been challenged by a set of alternative interpretations which have added substance to the argument that there are a number of perspectives from which 'the economic' (which we would emphasise can be understood as a real social phenomenon) can be viewed. However, the reactions to these challenges to the interpretive frameworks of neoclassicalism and Marxism have been very different. Neoclassicalism has been more or less resistant to this movement. Indeed, Geoffrey Hodgson (1994) maintains that un-diluted neoclassicalism has become hegemonic within the economics profession, dominating the world's leading economic departments and economic journals. Moreover, neoclassical economists are again making claims to other areas of the academy, the most noteworthy of which has been the work of Gary Becker and others who have sought to explain a wide range of social processes by using the analytical tools of neoclassical economics, a claim which has been described as 'economic imperialism' (Block 1990). Significantly in the context of this chapter, part of the reason for the relentless onwards march of neoclassical economics during the 1980s and 1990s has been the way in which this particular economic discourse inspired and legitimated programmes of economic and social reregulation introduced by neo-liberal governments in North America and Europe in order to conform to the perceived 'jungle law' of global economic competition (Peck and Tickell 1994; Zukin and DiMaggio 1990). [4]

In contradistinction, the Marxist interpretive community has in the main been altogether more sympathetic to the call for greater attention to be given to contingency and to the contextualisation of economic theory. This should not be surprising given that Marxism rests upon historical materialism, within which the importance of historical contingency is self-evident. For example, in Volume 1 of *Capital* (1954) Marx takes great care to chart out the evolution of the capitalist labour process over time, and it was Marx who famously observed that individuals,

> make their own history, but they do not make it just as they please; they do not make it under circumstances chosen by themselves, but under circumstances directly encountered, given and transmitted from the past. The tradition of all the dead generations weighs like a nightmare on the brain of the living.
>
> (1968: 96)

A fairly clear indication, if one were needed, of the importance Marx attached to historical contingency. Indeed, Block (1990: 29) goes so far as to argue that Marx

> remains one of the principal sources for the argument that economic arrangements are historically contingent. Marx continually criticised the classical economists for their tendency to assume that the economic patterns that they had identified would exist for all time. His analysis of the fetishism of commodities was a direct attack on a naturalised view of economic arrangements. He recognised that within capitalism social relations among human beings take the ghostly form of relations among things, as when abstract market forces are perceived as determining prices. He stressed that this tendency made it harder to change existing arrangements because people forget that economic institutions are *social creations* that could be recreated in different ways.
>
> (emphasis added)

Yet the Marxism which has tended to prevail within the academy has at times seemed intent more on evacuating an attention to history and contingency than with taking it seriously, replacing it instead with a brand of teleological scientism. Part of the reason for this, argues Block, resides within the inherent contradiction of Marxism, in that in his attempt to identify the 'laws of motion' of capitalism Marx 'ended up naturalizing what he sought to criticize' (1990: 30):

> As a result, subsequent generations of Marxists have struggled with the intractable problem of reconciling the obvious changes in the institutional structures of capitalist societies, such as the increased role of the state and the rise of unions, with Marx's claims about the essential dynamics of a capitalist economy. The problem lies in the notion that there is a transhistorical

essence to capitalism that will continue to exist regardless of changes in the specific institutional arrangements of the economy.

The belief in the existence of a 'transhistorical essence' within capitalism strengthened from the 1960s onwards following the interventions of Louis Althusser and his development of a distinctive brand of Marxism, one which was often read as calling for the removal of both human subjectivity and historical contingency from Marxist economic theory (see Lipietz (1993) and the other contributions in Kaplan and Sprinker (1993)).

Over the last two decades or so a growing sense of dissatisfaction with the limitations of Marxist economic discourse has been the catalyst for many on the Left to disavow economic determinism in favour of making space for a sense of contingency and history within theories of 'the economic'. There has been a proliferation of *post-Marxist* economic discourses. According to Stuart Corbridge (1989: 225), these discourses are distinguished by their 'disavowal of epistemological argument and economism, and [their] sensitivity to the contingencies of capital accumulation in time and space'. Such discourses do not abandon Marxian insights entirely, but take issue with the tendency within Marxism towards overt rationalism and with its advocacy of 'an untenable and mechanistic stages-model of global history which provides communism as the crowning glory of human endeavour' (p. 236). The number of economic discourses which could be grouped under the post-Marxist banner continue to proliferate. They range from what we can describe as weak forms, that is those which remain close to the main tenets of Marxism (including regulation theory and neo-Gramscian political economy which are considered in the next section), and strong forms (such as economic sociology, feminist economics, and critical geopolitics (see Granovetter and Swedberg 1992; Ó Tuathail 1992b, 1993a, b; Popke 1994; Waring 1989; Zukin and DiMaggio 1990)).

POST-MARXIST ECONOMIC DISCOURSES

Regulation theory

One particularly important variant of post-Marxist economic discourse to emerge in recent years is regulation theory. Although regulation theory is in essence a Marxist-inspired growth model, according to Alain Lipietz (1987) regulation theorists seek to reinstate a sensitivity to contingency and historical accident missing within conventional Marxist economic theory. For Lipietz, the limitations of economic Marxism became self-evident during the 1960s and 1970s as the predictive models developed in accordance with the 'laws of motion' of the capitalist system proved incapable of explaining the trajectory of capitalist development in the second half of the twentieth century. As Lipietz (1987: 10) admits:

In the sixties, we argued that the immutable laws of imperialism would inevitably widen the gulf between nations and that they would always lead to a polarity between wealth and poverty. And then we deduced an inevitable sequence of stages of development and underdevelopment. We forecast the impossibility of industrial development in the dominated countries. Yet what did we have to say when, in the seventies, Britain's decline accelerated, the USA slowed down, and the 'Newly Industrializing Countries' started to take off in imperialism's 'backyard'?

Drawing strength from such observations, regulation theory seeks to make a virtue from the point that history is made and cannot be predicted. Hence regulation theorists seek to provide a more nuanced and sensitive account of the unfolding of capitalist economies than is found in conventional Marxist texts (for reviews of the regulation approach see Boyer 1990; Brenner and Glick 1991; Dunford 1990; Jessop 1990; Robles 1994; Tickell and Peck 1992). Regulation theory emphasises contingency by expanding upon Marx's twofold distinction between an economic base and a superstructure. For Marx, the economic base, made up of a variety of labour processes which serve to extract surplus value through the exploitation of labour in the circuit of production, was accommodated by a superstructure. The economic base is the 'engine', as the forces of production drive the economy onwards. The superstructure provides 'a political armature and an ideological justification' to protect the social relations that are produced by capitalist production (Lipietz 1993: 107).[5]

Regulation theory replaces the distinction between an economic base and a superstructure with one between an *accumulation system* on the one hand, and a *mode of social regulation* (MSR) on the other, within the context of a wider regime of accumulation. The relationship between an accumulation system and an MSR is 'the linchpin of the regulationist research project' (Tickell and Peck 1992: 193). The accumulation system

> is a production–consumption relationship which ensures that the individual decisions of capitalists to invest are met by demand for 'their' products, the value of which is realized in the market. [This] is a technical possibility which may or may not be realized. In order for it to become reality, procedures need to be developed which guarantee its reproduction. These procedures consist of habits, customs, social norms and enforceable laws which create 'regulatory systems'. These in turn ensure that individual behaviours are integrated within the overall schema of capitalist reproduction, thus mitigating the conflict inherent in capitalist social relations. It is this ensemble of regulatory mechanisms which is captured by the notion of an MSR.
>
> (p. 192)

An MSR, in other words, allows the capitalist accumulation system to unfold in a relatively crisis-free manner over a fairly long period of time.

One of the reasons that regulation theory represents an important theoretical advance over more conventional Marxist accounts of economic change is because of the way in which the concept of the MSR schematically pays attention to the way in which essentially non-economic phenomena – habits, customs, social norms, and so on – are irrevocably implicated in processes of capitalist accumulation (Barbrook 1990), even if regulationists have more often failed to explore the MSR in reality (Peck and Tickell 1995). Nor is there any doubt that regulation theory has made an important contribution to the ways in which we conceptualise 'the economic', and has succeeded in gathering together a growing interpretive community drawn from a wide range of cognate academic disciplines, including economics, sociology, politics, urban and regional studies, and geography. Moreover, the rise of regulation theory has also served to reawaken Marx's call for history to be taken seriously, by drawing attention to the ways in which current economic developments and their attendant crises often have roots and causes that can be traced back to much earlier phases of capitalist development.

The original regulation theorists were heavily influenced by their readings of Althusser in their understanding of the relationship between the MSR and the mode of growth. Lipietz, for example, has recently maintained that the regime of accumulation

> appears as the macro-economic result of the operation of the mode of regulation on the basis of a model of industrialisation . . . these notions have some connections with the classical Marxist concept of degree of development of productive forces, schemes of reproduction and superstructures.
> (1992b: 311; see also Lipietz 1993)

More recent variants of regulation theory (e.g. Altvater 1992; Hay 1994a; Peck and Tickell 1994) afford the mode of growth and the MSR equal analytical priority, in contrast to the relationship between the base and the superstructure in classical Marxism.

But regulation theory is clearly a 'weak' form of post-Marxist economic discourse. For one thing, it too rests upon the metaphor of reproduction redescribed from biology. Although the concept of regulation might seem to deflect the charge of functionalism directed at mainstream Marxist analyses, we would do well to remember that the 'regulative idea' is a central concept in biological models of production and reproduction (Barnes 1992: 131). Lipietz is candid about regulation theory's link to Marxism through the reproductive metaphor, and the implications this has for the functionalism of regulation theory:

> Let us admit: the introduction of the term 'regulation' does not at all suffice to dissipate the functionalist ambiguities connoted by the term 'reproduction'. In some of our formulations, 'regulation' is designated simply 'what is needed for reproduction to occur'.
> (Lipietz 1993: 129; although compare with Lipietz 1988)

In a sense, therefore, regulation theory seems to rest upon a form of Darwinian logic, where the 'fittest' (i.e. best-fit) MSR 'couples' with an accumulation system. The corollary of this is that all other possible MSRs fade and die because of their unsuitability to the prevailing accumulation system.

Regulation theory clearly represents an advance upon those forms of theoretical Marxism which deny any role for subjectivity, in that the evolution of an 'appropriate' MSR, for any given accumulation system is seen to be an outcome of chance events and the purposive acts of reflexive human subjects. But, regulation theory – in its original Parisian versions at least – remains wedded to a form of 'kapital-logic' in the last instance, because it is the dynamic nature of the accumulation system which forces a change in the accompanying MSR. It is change within the productive forces and capitalist relations of production which serves as the catalyst for a new round of experimentation to find a new MSR to 'fit' with an accumulation system. More recent work, labelled 'third generation' by Bob Jessop (1991), has attempted to bring discourse theory to bear upon regulation theory, stressing that regulationist research should involve analysis of historically developed sets of practices and meanings. The crisis of a regime of accumulation in this conceptualisation is not simply a disjuncture between material processes of accumulation and regulation, it is also discursively created and needs to be discursively resolved (Jenson 1989, 1990; see also Hay 1994a, b). Nevertheless, we would maintain that regulation theory remains a weak form of post-Marxism. This of course explains much of the appeal of regulation theory, as it seems to offer the prospect of a comprehensive understanding of economic processes via the mastery of its theoretical apparatus. Yet, despite its theoretical emphasis on the MSR, little regulationist work emphasises intersubjective power relations or cultural processes. This lacuna is met by other, stronger, forms of post-Marxist economic discourse which provide alternative ways of thinking about 'the economic' and economic change. One such example is neo-Gramscian political economy.

Neo-Gramscian political economy

Two main approaches have traditionally dominated international political economy: Marxism and neorealism. In common with the other theoretical approaches we have looked at in this chapter, both Marxist international political economy and neorealist political theory rely upon processes of metaphorical redescription to bring them into being. However, whereas the earlier examples involved just one such process of redescription, both Marxist and neorealist political economy rely upon a dual process of metaphorical redescription. First, both approaches rely upon a metaphor of spatial enclosure, which serves to delimit the appropriate scale of analysis, although the basis upon which space is so delimited is very different in each case. Within Marxist international political economy lines are drawn around *structural spaces*, whereby space is categorised according to its position within the global capitalist economy (Agnew 1994). To take the example of world systems theory, territory is classified along a centre–periphery hierarchy, based upon the presence or absence of particular capitalist social relations (Taylor 1993; Wallerstein 1979, 1984). Within neorealist international political theory, meanwhile, lines are drawn around a narrower conception of *territorial space* (Agnew 1994). The space of the world is divided up into constellation of sovereign states, because the main object of analysis in neorealist political theory is external relations between states (Walker 1993).

Second, both approaches rely upon a metaphor of equilibrium which is used to explain the 'stability' of the international political economy over time, which is also different in each case. Within Marxist international political theory, the notion of equilibrium is, again, drawn from biology, with the 'centre' of the capitalist world economy existing in a parasitic relationship with the 'periphery'. While this exploitative relationship deepens the level of uneven development within the world economy, it serves to ensure the survival of the centre of the capitalist economy, as the capitalist system is saved from collapse under the weight of its own internal contradictions through the transfer of wealth and resources from the periphery. Within neorealist approaches, meanwhile, the notion of equilibrium is drawn from physics, which means that there are important parallels with neoclassical economics. The state system is seen to be constantly moving towards a position of relative equilibrium in terms of the relative power of states. Any increase in the power of one state will tend to be checked by the response of others. It is this which serves as the basis for the concept of the 'balance of power' (Agnew 1994; Waltz 1979).

These processes of metaphorical redescription ensure that both approaches share a tendency towards transcendence, which in turn leads to a reification of particular political and economic structures which then take on an 'ontological autonomy' (Gill 1991: 52). Over the course of the 1980s and 1990s dissatisfaction with the transcendent nature both of Marxist and of neorealist approaches gave rise to alternative theoretical perspectives within the field of international political economy. An important critique emanating from within the Marxist tradition saw the development of a *neo-Gramscian political economy*, which seeks to provide a more contextual and historically contingent materialist reading of international political economy than hitherto. Where Marxists stressed transcendence, neo-Gramscians stressed transience; where Marxists emphasised the laws of motion of the capitalist economy, neo-Gramscians drew attention to the possibility of reflexive intervention by human subjects within economic, social and political processes (Cox 1992). In doing so, neo-Gramscians seek to move 'towards a more historicist, reflexive and dynamic form of political economy' (Gill 1993b: 21).

Although Gramscian theory has its roots in Marxism, Gramsci refused to reify his writings as a 'timeless set of categories and concepts' (Cox 1993a: 50), so – in common with regulation theory – Gramscian political economy goes beyond the single dualism of economic base and superstructure. Gramsci argued that in addition to an economic structure there are two superstructural levels; political society and civil society. Political society is seen to consist of formal and informal political institutions that enable political life to unfold. Civil society, meanwhile, is conceived as a largely ideological realm, within which identities are forged, intellectual struggles waged, and the intersubjective distribution of social power negotiated (Augelli and Murphy 1993: 129). Through the concept of civil society Gramsci sought to draw attention to the role of reflexive intersubjectivity which, he argued, serves to join economic base and superstructure together. This 'organic' link introduces the possibility of indeterminacy and contingency missing in 'vulgar' orthodox Marxist readings of political economy. It was through his concept of an historic bloc that Gramsci sought to emphasise the fragility and impermanence of social relations over time:

> [An historic bloc] encompasses political, cultural, and economic aspects of a particular social formation, uniting these in historically specific ways to form a complex, politically contestable and dynamic ensemble of social relations. *An historic bloc articulates a world view*, grounded in historically specific socio-political conditions and production relations, which lends substance and ideological coherence to its social power.
>
> (Rupert 1993: 81, emphasis added)

More specifically, an historic bloc was seen to consist of a contingent set of *ideas*, *institutions*, and *material capacities*. Ideas encompass a particular set of theories, ideologies, social myths and intersubjective meanings. Institutions range over particular types of state, market and international organisations. Meanwhile, the notion of material capacities covers distinctive types of productive power and military power (Cox 1987; Gill 1992). These components of the historic bloc are seen to be reflexively and discursively constructed by subjects whom Gramsci described as 'organic intellectuals'; that is, 'the entire social structure which exercises an organisation function in the wider sense – whether in the field of culture or production or political administration' (Gramsci, quoted in Gill (1986: 211)):

> Gramsci developed the unique concept of the 'organic intellectual' to show how the processes of intellectual production were themselves in dialectical relation to the processes of historical change. Intellectual work directed towards social explanation was often directly or indirectly linked to political strategies, themselves developed from different perspectives. *Such perspectives exist in political time and space.* Thus, by linking the theory of knowledge production to a theory of identity and interest, Gramsci was able to show how, at least in this sense, *theory is always for someone and for some purpose.*
>
> (Gill 1991: 56, emphasis added)

Usually, such purposive intellectual work makes justificatory claims for the 'ordering' of economic, social and political life in particular ways that favour powerful social groups. If such claims succeed in gaining recognition as being what André Drainville (1994: 109) describes as 'coherent formulations of the general interest', then they are likely to become 'hegemonic', and begin to exert a commanding influence over the ways in which economic, social, and political processes unfold. Such hegemonic ideas establish a set of universal principles for the ordering of social and, in particular, economic life. Although they favour more powerful social groups, they are nevertheless adhered to by less powerful social groups because they have been successfully cast as being in the general interest of society as a whole. In this sense, the advantage that powerful social groups enjoy from the establishment of such guiding principles is 'ethical', for social power is exercised with the 'critical, reflective consent' of more subordinate groups (Augelli and Murphy 1993: 127). The ability of dominant social groups to develop plausible theories of the ways in which social and economic life unfolds, replete with blueprints for the construction of institutions for the regulation of such processes is, therefore, of critical importance, and accounts for the significance afforded to the role of intellectual work by Gramsci. In building the alliances and links of an historic bloc, intellectuals effectively write the scripts and discourses of hegemonic order. According to Gramsci, 'The intellectuals of the hegemonic class must produce a philosophy, political theory, and economics which together constitute a coherent world-view, the principles of which can be translated from one discipline to another' (quoted in Augelli and Murphy (1993: 131). As such organic intellectuals are participants in an ideological and power struggle between different social groups, and through intellectual work seek either to confirm or to refute the world-view of the current hegemonic order.

There are clear parallels between the Gramscian notion of political economy and regulation theory, not least because the survival of historic blocs over time serves to deliver a degree of stability to social, economic and political life (parallels which Jessop (1991) makes explicit, nor should it be forgotten that the term 'Fordism', which figures so prominently within regulation theory, was first coined by Gramsci in his *Prison Notebooks* (Hoare and Nowell Smith 1971)). However, on balance Gramscian political economy is probably closer to economic sociology than it is to regulation theory. Thus, the existence of an historic bloc with a distinctive concept of control is seen to cause the ideas, institutions and material capabilities to become *embedded* within social, economic and political structures over time (Cox 1992; compare Polanyi 1944; Granovetter 1985; Granovetter and Swedberg 1992). Moreover, inasmuch as historic blocs are likely to be undermined through on-going processes of economic and political struggle, there occur periodic processes of *disembedding* when ideas are challenged and institutions and material capabilities are restructured. In addition, much greater priority is given to the role of reflexive human subjects in both the making and the breaking of such periods of relative stability. In particular, Gramscian political economy focuses upon the role of elites as 'interpreters' and 'constructors' of the dominant structures which serve as the basis for ordering political economy. Elites are seen as 'structurally literate' reflexive subjects who play an important role in generating plausible discoveries for the ordering of political and economic life. As Drainville (1994: 109) puts it, 'elites not only share a particularly meaningful position in the structures of accumulation, they are also structurally literate. They read structures of dynamics, constraints and imperatives, and invent fitting political projects'. This 'reflexive authoring' of political and economic discourses plays an important role in constructing the 'comprehensive concepts of control' referred to earlier.

However, orthodox Gramscian political economy has its limitations. Of particular significance in this context is the Gramscian conception of space. Gramsci conceived historic blocs as explicitly national phenomena (Augelli and Murphy 1993; Gill 1991, 1993a), which only cohered because they brought disparate social, political and economic interests together within the 'imagined community' of the nation state (Anderson 1983). It is precisely this spatial delimiting of the extent and influence of historic blocs within orthodox Gramscian political economy that neo-Gramscian approaches seek to overcome. Indeed, a central plank of such approaches is that the explanatory importance attached to national historic blocs is misplaced. Neo-Gramscians argue that over a long period of time the internationalisation and globalisation of social and economic processes have brought into being a transnational civil society, so that it is possible to speak of *transnational historic blocs* that have served to order the world economy (Cox 1981, 1987, 1993a, b; Drainville 1994; Fennema and Van der Pijl 1987; Gill 1986, 1990, 1991, 1992, 1993b, c; Gill and Law 1989; Overbeek 1990; Van der Pijl 1984, 1989a; b). Neo-Gramscian political economists argue that an historical analysis of the capitalist world economy reveals periods during which universal principles for the governance of economic life become hegemonic. The transnational hegemony of a set of ideas, institutions and material capacities serves to deliver extended periods of relative stability to the international economy. Periods of hegemonic stability are usually brought to an end under the weight of economic crises, which undermine the authority of hegemonic social groups and associated systems of governance, for economic crises cast doubt on the efficacy of regulatory mechanisms (Augelli and Murphy 1993). This means that periods of hegemony are interspersed with non-hegemonic phases during which fierce intellectual and political struggles are fought within civil society as elites and organic intellectuals search for a new set of universal principles for the governance of economic life.

Neo-Gramscians identify two main periods of transnational hegemony in the history of capitalism. The first of these periods covered the second half of the nineteenth century, and the second began around about 1945 and ended some twenty or thirty years later. The two periods are each associated with the rise to power of individual national economies – Britain and the United States – that acted as bases from which hegemonic ideas were disseminated through the international economy. However, it is important to note that the concept of hegemony used here does not mean that these particular national economies dominated the world economy by virtue of their economic and military power alone, calling a tune to which all other nations were forced to dance. Rather, powerful groups within these states used the position of dominance that their national economy enjoyed to establish hegemony in the Gramscian sense, that is to formulate universal principles for the governance of economic life which gained the support of less powerful social groups across a large number of different national economies. In this sense, the hegemony established in each period was 'ethical' in the Gramscian sense, because the system of governance was seen to serve more than just the narrow interests of elite groups within the dominant state of the global economy. Indeed, the hegemonic order was widely interpreted as being in the general interest.

The first period of hegemony revolved around a transnational historic bloc inspired by the ideas and theories of the classical economics of Adam Smith and David Ricardo, which placed faith in the ability of an unfettered market economy to deliver the best of all possible worlds. The main regulatory institutions of this period of hegemony were the international gold standard (IGS) and the system of liberal free trade. By inversely linking the flow of internationally traded goods to that of specie, the IGS was erroneously believed to impose a self-regulating monetary order upon the international economy (Walter 1991). In this sense, the international economy was accepted as having moved 'beyond politics', because – for the first time since the Treaty of Westphalia in 1648 and the birth of the modern state system – economic life within individual territorial states was governed by an authority which existed 'above' and 'beyond' the control of the political authorities of the nation state (Arrighi 1993; Ashley 1987; Walker 1993).

However, the system was in no way politically neutral, for it disproportionately favoured the interests of capitalist and political elites within Britain. This was for two main reasons. First, although free trade opened up the British market to foreign competition, the relatively advanced state of capitalist organisation in Britain meant that this price was well worth paying to gain access to foreign markets. Second, the international regulatory system was effectively policed by financial elites in the City of London, for it was in the City that the overwhelming majority of the world's foreign currency and bullion trading was transacted (Cain and Hopkins 1993a; Michie 1992). But, although the benefits of the system were skewed in favour of powerful social groups in Britain, these ideas and institutions became widely accepted elsewhere because of the powerful claim that the regulatory order would also serve to enhance the 'wealth of nations' by virtue of the allocative efficiency of the workings of the market at an international level (Arrighi 1993; Polanyi 1944), while the anti-inflationary disciplinary logic of the IGS served to protect the invested wealth of powerful social groups in the major capitalist economies.

However, in time this apparently 'self-regulating' international order was undermined by capitalist and political elites in North America and Europe who began to count the costs as well as the benefits of the IGS and the system of free trade. Of particular concern was the manner in which deficit economies were disciplined by the international financial markets, which was particularly harsh and extremely disruptive of long-term processes of capital accumulation. In response, the virtues of a transnational financial and economic liberalism began to be called into question and there began a movement whereby national governments sought to reclaim control over the governance of economic life. The transnational historic bloc of the late nineteenth century collapsed as economic space increasingly became territorial once more. The borders of states were again taken to be the natural delimiters of economic activity, and barriers were drawn around such spaces in the form of import tariffs and quotas in order to protect 'internal' capitalist accumulation from 'outside' competition.

The turn towards autocentric forms of capitalist accumulation characterised the period from the turn of the century and the outbreak of the Second World War. The IGS collapsed on the outbreak of the First World War and, abortive attempts to restore the link between sterling and gold notwithstanding (Brown 1987; Ingham 1984), the interwar period saw the emergence of ever more distinctive national models of capitalist accumulation (Cox 1987). Neo-Gramscians follow Karl Polanyi (1944) in arguing that the fragmentation of an international and interdependent world economy into a series of largely self-enclosed, autocentric, national economies sowed the seeds of the conflict of the Second World War. They also argue that the closing years of the war sowed the seeds of the creation of a new period of hegemony, as the world economy was rebuilt in line with new sets of economic ideas and theories, and regulated by a distinctive set of economic institutions. As we shall see below, the Bretton Woods system was a significant material expression of this new era.

BRETTON WOODS AND THE GOLDEN AGE

In 1944 US and British elites set about to plan the postwar international monetary system. International monetary policy would have to resolve the contradiction between national economic autonomy and national monies on the one hand and the provision of a stable international means of exchange and the plurality of international currencies on the other (Aglietta 1985; Ingham 1994). The conditions under which economic expansion could occur were to be consistent with the social advances of both the New Deal in the United States and putative social democracy in the United Kingdom (see Gardner 1980). International monetary policy would, therefore, aim to prevent the kinds of external balance-of-payments imbalances that contributed to deflation in the prewar period. The particular compromise reached at Bretton Woods represented one possible solution to the generic problem of international money (Altvater 1993) and reflected the constellation of power at the conference, where it was agreed to set up a system of fixed exchange rates, an international development bank (the International Bank for Reconstruction and Development or 'World Bank') and the International Monetary Fund (IMF), charged with managing the global monetary system (Walter 1991). Although the system of fixed exchange rates was swept away during the early 1950s, the period between the end of the Second World War and the late 1960s, when the US dollar acted as an international reserve currency, was largely set up at Bretton Woods. Rather than outline the economic and regulatory dynamics of the Bretton Woods system (excellent reviews exist elsewhere; see Block 1977; Bordo and Eichengreen 1993; Gardner 1980; Parboni 1981; Strange 1986; Van Dormael 1978; Walter 1991), below we explore the ways in which regulation theory and neo-Gramscian political economy understand the role of the Bretton Woods system in the postwar economic order. In regulation theory, we argue, the inadequate characterisation of the postwar international monetary order has been a significant lacuna.

National monetary order? Regulation theory and the golden age

With its explicit emphasis on the necessity of complementarity between the mode of social regulation and the mode of growth, regulation theory aims to unpack capitalism as a persistently enduring structure. However, the theory has most successfully been used in accounts of the 'golden age of Fordism', from the end of the Second World War to the 1980s when the capitalist world experienced unprecedented economic growth coupled with narrowing social and economic divisions. According to regulation theorists, technical progress in the consumer goods industries after the First World War was not matched by sufficient consumer spending power to create an effective demand for increased production. This produced a structural crisis during the 1930s. The core of the problem was that the prewar MSR was unable to form a social framework in which wages could increase in line with productivity growth (Aglietta 1979). In order for the crisis of the 1930s to be resolved it was essential that a new coupling between the accumulation system and the MSR be established. For regulation theorists, the Fordist golden age emerged out of a social compromise anchored in the Keynesian welfare state, under which collective bargaining and monopoly pricing were institutionalised; policy instruments were deployed to maintain and manage aggregate demand; and norms of mass consumption were generalised (see Jessop 1992; Lipietz 1987, 1992b). These processes of social regulation were rooted, first and foremost, in and around the *nation* state, with nation state authorities conceptualised as holding the levers of macroeconomic policy. In his analysis of US Fordism, for example, Aglietta (1979: 365) maintains that

> The process of inflation is the form taken by the financial crisis under the regime of predominantly intensive accumulation established after the New Deal, when the monetary constraint is expressed as the formation of a national money with an enforced currency.

(see also de Vroey 1984)

The regulationist emphasis on the nation state as the key site of institutional compromise arises from perceived functionalism and ahistoricism of both Althusserian Marxism and dependency theory. Accordingly, 'we do not . . . have an international regime of accumulation in the true sense of the term', but a set of national Fordisms within a particular international configuration whose 'coherence is simply of the interaction between . . . various national regimes of accumulation' (Lipietz 1987: 40, 25).

In this analysis, then, the nature of the Fordist compromise and its subsequent breakdown largely emerged within national specificities, albeit within certain parameters allowed by the nature of Fordism. Lipietz argues that the crisis of Fordism was primarily a crisis in the labour process. During the late 1960s, the productivity gains engendered by the Taylorist division of labour began to slow down as full employment, education, 'and a widespread desire for work satisfaction and dignity led to an increasingly open revolt against the denial of personality by the starkest forms of separation between those who designed and those who performed tasks' (Lipietz 1992b; 315). Firms subsequently responded to falling profitability by increasing the cost of their products, thus contributing to growing inflationary pressures and a slowdown in demand, and, subsequently, recession. For Lipietz, then, this illustrates that

> for purely internal reasons . . . the Fordist compromise became economically unsustainable . . . [and] the crisis of the Fordist development model should be seen primarily as a supply-side crisis – a crisis of the labour process which, because it dehumanizes the worker, ends up by not being efficient, even from the employer's point of view.
>
> (1992b: 317)

Although this account captures much of the reality of the Fordist golden age, it remains partial because it understates the role of international processes – particularly those set up at Bretton Woods – in creating and underscoring national money and the ways in which their breakdown contributed to the growing crisis of Fordism after the late 1960s (see also Davis 1978). Yet, whereas some regulation theorists may initially have viewed Fordism as being national in character, more recently there has been a recognition that it is important to conceptualise the role played by the *global* regime within which these national systems existed (see, particularly, Aglietta, 1985; Altvater 1992, 1993; Boyer 1990: xv; Mistral 1986; Robles 1994).

One of the fundamental tensions of the Fordist regime lay in the conflict between *national-*level regulation and the *globalising* dynamic of accumulation, and regulationists emphasise that the Bretton Woods agreement set the framework within which countries were able to pursue national growth strategies within the context of substantial interdependence (Aglietta 1985). The Fordist system may have been rooted in the Taylorist labour process, and its regulatory 'logic' may have been in the nationally constituted Keynesian welfare state, but these were predicated on a specifically configured international order. Essential to the viability of national state systems in core Fordist countries was the institutionalisation of international economic and political relations under the Bretton Woods system, itself a reflection of US hegemony.

In this more recent regulation theoretical account, attention turns from the labour process to the global status of both the money form and the financial markets. In an important contribution to regulation theory, Elmar Altvater (1993) stresses that the Bretton Woods system was designed to regulate money as a circulatory function, rather than solely as a means of payment, and thus to facilitate the expansion of world trade. This required that a single currency operate as a world money in order to limit the extent to which nations engage in competitive devaluations (an action not without risks to the devaluing currency) and to reduce risks on currency markets. In turn, this condition requires either an artificial world money (which the Bretton Woods conference considered but failed to set up) or a hegemonic power which makes its own currency operate simultaneously as national money. The establishment of the United States as global hegemon – which was backed up by the country's military, economic and political might and institutionalised under Bretton Woods – thus allowed other nation states to operate their own macroeconomic policies (Altvater 1992; Corbridge 1988b; Walter 1991). We can therefore conceive of global Fordism, inasmuch as global market mechanisms were regulated at a global level which allowed national Fordisms to thrive, in just the same way as the Keynesian welfare state underwrote the Taylorist labour process.

However, regulationist theorists insist that any regulation can only temporarily overcome inherent contradictions within capitalism, and the Bretton Woods system was no exception. During the 1950s and 1960s, the US dollar found itself on the horns of the 'Triffin dilemma', which states that a world currency is subject to contradictory forces. Because of the value of the US dollar ultimately depended on its gold value, the United States attempted to maintain this gold value by keeping the dollar in short supply. Yet the consequence of this policy was a shortage of international liquidity, which could have led to a contraction in world trade. Accordingly, central banks began to prefer to denominate their reserves in gold rather than the dollar which both eroded the US gold stock and the gold convertability of the dollar (Altvater 1993; Walter 1991). While the United States attempted to solve the problem by reducing its external deficit and for the whole of the 1960s maintaining the convertability of the dollar, the global monetary order moved from the equilibrium of the 1950s into disequilibrium during the 1960s. Yet rather than maintaining the value of the dollar, US overseas debt increased threefold between 1960 and 1973 (Walter 1991), further increasing the growing instability in the system.

Having engendered a state of dynamic interdependency between the US economy and the global economy, the hegemonic position of the United States consequently posed the constant threat of crisis tendencies being transmitted from the domestic US economy to the world economy and vice versa (see Cooper 1987; Corbridge 1994). At the same time, the hegemonic advantage of the United States turned into a 'seignorage disadvantage' (Altvater 1993: 116) as competitor nations were able to take advantage of stability without having to meet any of the costs. As Eurocurrency markets allowed financial institutions to evade US dollar regulations and as both money capital and productive capital internationalised, a global credit system emerged which was not simply based on trade. The structures set up at Bretton Woods proved incapable of coping with the newly emergent global financial system (Swyngedouw 1992; Walter 1991). As Altvater argues,

> the international monetary system was ... eclipsed by the functional requirements of the international credit system, and the IMF changed from an institution regulating money as a means of circulation to one guaranteeing money as a means of payment and defending precarious international credit relations. In this way, the institutional regulation of financial instabilities was quite feasible for a certain period. But institutions are designed for the carrying out of certain functions. The [Bretton Woods institutions were] best suited to reckon institutionally with the circulatory function of money: and ... can no longer do this when the function of money as a means of payment predominates within the expanding credit system.
>
> (1993: 121)

Yet it was not solely in terms of macroeconomic policy that the Bretton Woods system proved contradictory. Global Fordism stimulated an internationalisation of both trade and production which undermined those national economies which provided the system with its strength. Along with the IMF and the World Bank, the General Agreement on Tariffs and Trade (GATT) constituted one of the central pillars of the Fordist world economy. The GATT was set up in 1947 in order to facilitate trade, initially between developed countries, through the multilateral removal of tariff and nontariff barriers (Dicken 1992a). Like the two Bretton Woods institutions, the GATT was maintained by the strong support provided by the United States in its role as Fordist hegemon. As the GATT expanded during the 1960s, however, it began to undermine accumulation in some sectors in the Fordist countries, as cheaper or technologically more sophisticated imports successfully competed with indigenous industries which were reaching the limits of the Taylorist division of labour. Tensions within the United States between nationally oriented and internationally oriented capital contributed to a retreat from multilateralism in the 1970s and concomitant growth in bilateralism and protectionism (Dicken 1992a, b; Friedmann 1993).

In contrast, then, to the earlier regulation–theoretical position which stressed the integrity of national social formations, Altvater and, in his more recent work, Michel Aglietta, place the nation state within the context of the global credit system. As private capital began increasingly to circuit globally on a deregulated basis, Keynesian nation states progressively lost control of one of the most important macroeconomic levers – the setting of interest rates. The loss of interest rate sovereignty was a significant contributor to the breakdown of the fragile international order established under Fordism (Glyn *et al.* 1991). 'Unregulated global credit was [consequently] a factor of erosion of the (political institutional) regulation of the whole Fordist system' (Altvater 1992: 37).

A transnational historic bloc? Neo-Gramscian political economy and the golden age

The neo-Gramscian version of the rise and fall of the Bretton Woods system bears a number of similarities to that of regulation theory. One reason for these similarities is that neo-Gramscian political economists and regulation theorists alike are concerned with an important problematic; that is, the attempt to come to understand theoretically the increasingly erratic trajectory of the international capitalist system since the late 1960s and early 1970s. For neo-Gramscians, the recent turbulence of the international economy is caused by the ending of the second period of hegemonic stability of historical capitalism. The golden age of postwar capitalism was made possible by a hegemonic congruence of a dominant set of ideas, institutions and material capabilities, much of which the Bretton Woods system embodied, providing a system for the transnational governance of capitalist accumulation. But, as the contradictions of the system became ever more difficult to reconcile, and economic crises became evermore frequent, so the ideas, institutions, and even the material capabilities of the Bretton Woods system have been undermined, ushering in a period of *posthegemony*, where confusion and uncertainty reign. For neo-Gramscians, we are all caught up in an era of reflexive anxiety, engaged in a protracted ideological and political struggle in search of a new set of universal principles by which international capitalism should be governed.

The hegemonic stability of the golden age was delivered out of just such an exercise which took place among a set of international political and intellectual elites who met at the US holiday resort of Bretton Woods. Their brief was to agree upon the plans drawn up by US and British elites for the rebuilding of the world economy after the Second World War. This international economic summit indicated how different the postwar international economic order would be from the one which preceded it, for it signalled the willingness of national governments to co-operate in order to manage the international economy (Ikenberry 1992: 298). In particular, there was a concerted effort on the part of particularly influential academic and political participants to neutralise the power of international financial capital, to limit its influence within the system of international economic governance. The reason for this was largely because the 1930s represented the nadir of the credibility and influence of those ideas and institutions which had once held hegemonic sway over the international economy during the nineteenth century. Confidence in international finance all but evaporated from the end of the 1920s as a worldwide financial crisis was followed by a widespread destruction of credit and debt, and wild unpredictable movements of capital on an international scale (Brown 1987). In weakening the social power and influence of the elites responsible for the propagation of existing economic orthodoxy, the crisis created a space within which an alternative vision of economic order could develop. According to Eric Helleiner (1993: 122):

> The [1929–]1931 international financial crisis was important not just in bringing the collapse of international capital markets and of the international gold standard . . . it [also] marked the beginning of a kind of *ideological* *'structural' break in financial affairs.* As one German financier noted at the end of the crisis: 'What I have experienced means the end of a way of life, certainly for Germany and perhaps other countries as well. . . . The common vision of the future has been destroyed.' Largely discredited by the crisis, the private and central bankers who had dominated financial politics before the 1930s were increasingly replaced at the levers of financial power by *professional economists, industrialists and labour groups* working through their respective finance ministries or treasuries. Where the bankers had advocated a laissez-faire approach to domestic financial issues and the following of automatic 'rules of the game' in the international financial sphere, these new groups favoured a more interventionist approach that would make domestic and international finance serve broader political and economic goals.
>
> (emphasis added)

As the power and influence of the financial capitalist class declined, so did the adherence to economic orthodoxy. In its place there emerged a greater concern for issues of economic democracy and welfarism. Indeed, the discussions at the Bretton Woods conference seem to have been preoccupied with neutralising the power of international financial capital in order to consolidate the welfare gains made during the turn to more autocentric and 'productivist' models of capitalist accumulation during the 1930s. Thus, the spatial configuration of the postwar international order was one of more or less coherent national economies, which were seen as somehow the 'natural' spaces within which accumulation strategies should be pursued (Radice 1984; Sunley 1992). This conception of economic space owed much to the world view of John Maynard Keynes, who led the British delegation to the Bretton Woods conference, and argued strongly against an international economy made of homogeneous financial space, across which financial capital could travel freely:

> Freedom of capital movements is an essential part of the old laissez faire system and assumes that it is right and desirable to have an equalisation of interest rates in all parts of the world . . . In my view the whole management of the domestic economy depends upon being free to have the appropriate rate of interest without reference to the rates prevailing elsewhere in the world. Capital control is a corollary of this.
>
> (Keynes, quoted in Helleiner (1993: 27))

Keynes's thinking on this issue was in line with that of Harry Dexter White, leader of the US delegation. White was a convert to Keynesianism and an enthusiastic supporter both of the New Deal and of the comprehensive reregulation of the US financial system which the latter encompassed, which imposed strict controls on the geographical movement of financial capital within the US economy (Cerny 1993). Keynes and White agreed that the control of financial capital would not only serve to preserve the welfare gains enjoyed in many national economies during the 1930s but would also further the prospect of the growth of a liberal international trading order. Trade flows between national economic spaces were further encouraged by a system of fixed-but-flexible currency exchange rates, which would prevent volatile oscillations in currency that might otherwise deter international trade. Processes of financial adjustment between deficit and surplus trading nations would be managed by the newly constructed international institutions of the IMF and the World Bank, with private financial capital relegated to the sidelines (Block 1977).

However, as Helleiner (1993) points out, the original plans for the construction of a new international regulatory order did not go unchallenged. Indeed, despite their weakened position, the financial elites of the New York banking community retained sufficient power to mobilise a rearguard action against the plans for the political sterilisation of international financial flows through the imposition of capital controls. Their ability to do this bore testament to the embeddedness of the old financial orthodoxy within key institutions of the US state, particularly in the Federal Reserve and the State Department, 'which housed prominent liberal academic thinkers . . . and many figures from Wall Street' (Helleiner 1993: 33). These vestiges of the old hegemonic order served to weaken one of the key cornerstones of the Keynesian and New Deal-inspired attempt to bring about the 'euthanasia of the rentier' through the Bretton Woods settlement. The final Bretton Woods Agreement called not for compulsory but only voluntary controls on capital moving into and out of national economies.

The victory of this rearguard action on the part of the financial elites was revealed, according to Helleiner (1993: 36), at the final press conference of the Bretton Woods meetings:

> Just as Keynes . . . finished announcing that the agreement 'provides that capital movements must be controlled, and indeed that it is an essential condition', White interrupted to state that countries who wish to use capital controls were permitted to do so but that 'the United States does not wish to have them'. Moreover, just to be certain, the US delegation also succeeded . . . in changing a clause which had allowed the IMF as late as the 1944 Joint Statement to 'require' the imposition of capital controls if its resources were being drained by a member for the purpose of financing a deficit stemming from speculative capital movements. Keynes and White had granted the IMF this power to ensure that its resources would be used only for the purpose of financing deficits on the current account or those stemming from productive capital movements. Under US pressure, the IMF's power was reduced to the extent that it could only now 'request' controls to prevent

such use, with refusal to cooperate penalised by the member being declared ineligible to use the resources of the Fund. . . . In the words of the US technical group at the conference, this change was made because 'the US does not want to be forced to control an export of capital'.

This important change to the original Bretton Woods blueprint illustrates that the building of the postwar order was a great deal more than merely an exercise in the practical application of economic theory writ large. The birth of the Bretton Woods system was a manifestation of an attempt by what Kees Van der Pijl (1984) has described as an 'Atlantic ruling class', the most powerful members of which were based in the United States, to mould the international economic order in their interest. For purposes of public consumption, the Bretton Woods settlement was scripted as a system of international economic order which served the interests of the wider world economy. However, the new regulatory order served to facilitate the dissemination on a global scale of the 'key institutions and practices of the American corporate–liberal democratic order' (Agnew 1993: 211). The ideas, institutions and material capacities of this hegemonic offensive were successfully implanted within the major industrialised countries during the immediate postwar years, 'either through processes of "external inducement" and coercion, as in the British and French cases, or through direct intervention and reconstruction, as in the German and Japanese cases' (Agnew 1993: 211).

This ideological construction of economic order, which was skewed in favour of US capitalist and political elites, succeeded in becoming hegemonic as successful alliances were made with elites in other countries and the United States embarked upon a series of geopolitical manoeuvres which succeeded in winning the 'hearts and minds' of subordinate groups in Western Europe and elsewhere. The key ideological offensive in Europe was the Marshall Plan which served to pump large volumes of US capital into Western European countries for the purposes of postwar reconstruction. As John Agnew (1993: 221) observes, this manoeuvre 'provided an image of a giving America in the service of an open world-economy that even the most cynical Europeans found difficult to challenge'. However, the funds were provided in large part to 'save' Western European capitalism from collapse in the face of the Soviet 'threat', and were only available to Western European governments if they played by the 'rules of the game' dictated by US political elites, which for the most part involved agreements to free up their economies to international (i.e. US) goods and services. In other words, the Marshall Fund helped make Europe a fit place for US firms to do business.

Meanwhile, Japan was also given considerable assistance in its road to capitalist renewal, mainly by an extremely favourable dollar–yen exchange rate which remained unchanged for twenty-two years (Leyshon 1994b). This neglect of the dollar–yen exchange rate, which over time caused the yen to be substantially undervalued in the foreign exchange markets, ensured that Japanese producers gained a considerable competitive advantage in international markets for traded goods. The favourable treatment meted out to Japan also stemmed from US geopolitical anxiety over the Soviet threat, Japan being seen as a capitalist stronghold in a region of the world where the influence of both the USSR and the People's Republic of China loomed large.[6] But, despite these underlying geopolitical and geo-economic motivations, through the support given to local capitalist interests and to those political elites who conformed to the 'rules of the game', and through the material and social gains derived from an unprecedented period of economic expansion coupled with the growth of the 'Keynesian welfare state', US elites managed successfully to build a transnational historic bloc which encompassed the majority of the industrial world.

According to Robert Cox (1993a), this period of hegemonic stability came to an end in the mid-1960s. The main reason for the collapse of the transnational historic bloc which had grown up around the Bretton Woods system was the way in which US political elites began to make economic policy decisions that were widely perceived as not only self-serving but actively detrimental to other industrialised countries. In other words, US leadership of the system of international governance before the mid-1960s could be classified as 'ethical' in the Gramscian sense; from the late 1960s onwards, the turn towards narrow self-interest within US policy compromised the transnational alliances that held the international regulatory order together. The immediate cause of this Gramscian 'crisis of authority' (Augelli and Murphy 1993) was caused by a looming financial and monetary crisis in the United States, the roots of which could be traced back to the subversion of the original White–Keynes plans for the Bretton Woods order by financial and political elites in the United States. The problems revolved around the role of the US dollar in the postwar financial system. Keynes had originally called for the creation of a synthetic 'xenocurrency' to act as the numeraire of the international financial system, partly in fear of tying the fate of the international monetary order to 'the vagaries of American politics' (Block 1977: 48). However, on US insistence, the dollar was implanted as the international numeraire, for reasons of geo-economic advantage. This, coupled with the failure to impose compulsory controls on the movement of capital between national economies, meant that when the United States expanded its domestic financial system it also tended to increase the stock of world money, as dollars readily flowed into the rest of the international financial system, and tended not to return, accumulating instead in the 'offshore' euro-dollar markets which developed from the late 1950s. The rise of the euromarkets signalled the end of the Bretton-Woods-inspired period of hegemonic stability (see Agnew and Corbridge 1989; Block 1977; Clarke 1988; Corbridge 1988b; Corbridge and Agnew 1991; Daly and Logan 1989; Walter 1991).

The consequences of the collapse of Bretton Woods for the international financial system has been told many times, and there is insufficient space to rehearse it here. However, four features are worth foregrounding. First, the 'threat' the euromarkets posed to US gold reserves was sufficient to encourage the United States to begin to unwind the international monetary order by ending the right of dollar holders to exchange their dollars for gold, a decision which in turn led to the collapse of the fixed exchange rate system. By acting unilaterally in this way, US political elites signalled their unwillingness for the US economy to bear any longer the costs of managing the key currency of the international monetary order in 'the general interest' (Ingham 1994), so that the 'ethical' basis of US hegemony evaporated.

Second, the rise of the euromarkets led to a significant increase in the structural power of financial capital (Gill and Law 1989). The euromarkets were 'beyond' political control which meant that money could be diverted to them to escape the control of national financial regulations. By providing a bolt-hole from regulations often designed to limit the power of financial capital in the interests of the national accumulation strategies of the Keynesian welfare state, the euromarkets heralded the dawn of an era of regulatory arbitrage (Cerny 1993; see chapter 2), whereby geo-graphical–political spaces competed to create regulatory environments conducive to financial capital (Roberts 1994).

Third, these developments combined to usher in a protracted period of economic crisis founded in monetary disorder and a generalised inflation. US political elites were the authors of both. By removing the threat to gold supplies, the United States was free to expand the domestic money supply without compunction, a process which also served the dual purpose of pushing down the value of the dollar in the foreign exchange markets which made US-produced goods more competitive in international markets. However, the main effect of this geo-economic offensive was to usher in a period of protracted economic uncertainty, as financial volatility and an accelerating inflation rate served to disrupt the accumulation strategies of capitalist organisations by making the process of economic calculation far more difficult than it was in the earlier period of hegemonic stability (Corbridge 1994; Swyngedouw 1992).

Fourth, these crises fuelled an intellectual debate around issues of economic governance which undermined the dominance of Keynesian ideas. In a world economy where cross-border flows of capital counted for so much, Keynes's national–centric and abstract sense of time came in for a great deal of criticism. However, although an attempt to build upon and modify Keynesian ideas in light of changed material circumstances led to the development of post-Keynesian economics within the academy (Sunley 1992), this particular strand of economic discourse was overshadowed by the rise of monetarism, an economic credo which not only stood in opposition to the Keynesian orthodoxy but which seemed to speak directly to those financial, industrial and political elites disturbed by what they saw as the corrosive effects of inflation upon processes of economic calculation and capitalist accumulation:

The creeping inflation of the late 1960s and early 1970s gave encouragement to a growing group of monetarist economists whose voices had been all but ignored in the 1950s and 1960s. These economists pointed out that Keynesian macroeconomics lacked a substantial microeconomic foundation, and that Keynesianism – unlike monetarism – was unable to predict the post-1960s phenomenon of stagflation.

(Corbridge 1994: 70)

In turn, the work of Milton Friedman and other monetarist economists helped to provide the theoretical and empirical armature to justify an over-haul of the institutional structure of the postwar economic order in a move to reassert the primacy of market forces because monetarists concluded that inflations were created by governments, which for reasons of political advantage maintained 'artificially' high levels of employment through the simple recourse of printing money. For example, Friedman gave intellectual comfort to those who were concerned about the collapse of the Bretton Woods system of fixed exchange rates by arguing that in severing the link to the US economy through the fixed dollar exchange rate, a 'system of floating exchange rates would in theory open up a window for national economic policy making, specifically with regard to anti-inflationary measures through monetary policies' (Corbridge 1994: 74). This compared with the situation under the system of fixed exchange rates where 'the creation of high-powered money to excess in the USA was more or less bound to fuel inflation in the economies of the USA's main trading partners' (1994: 73).

In practice, the decoupling of the currencies of the major industrialised countries from the dollar did encourage a shift towards a rubric of anti-inflationism, but this was as much to do with exogenous pressure from the 'invested interests' of a more powerful and more geographically mobile financial capital than anything else. From the early 1970s onwards foreign exchange crises became more frequent as the markets sanctioned the currencies of those national economies which seemed to offer an insufficient return on capital invested. According to the currency dealers, investment managers, chief economists and the like who make up the interpretive community of the world's leading centres (Thrift 1994b; see chapter 9), high-inflation economies were 'goods' and low-inflationary communities were 'bads', for the real value of invested wealth was eroded faster over time in inflationary economies. This form of calculative rationality encouraged those political elites who were not already disposed towards anti-inflationary monetary policies to give them serious considera-tion, if only to avoid the periodic outbreak of currency crises.

In summary, then, the neo-Gramscian argument is that the internation-alisation of economic activity 'beyond' and across the space of individual states, a process in which financial capital has taken a vanguard role, has served to undermine the coherence of the old hegemonic order. In response, alternative formulations for the ordering of political economy began to gain ground during the 1960s and 1970s. In particular, it was

New Right economic discourse which garnered sufficient intellectual currency to influence the reform and overthrow of the institutions and regulations associated with the old transnational historic bloc. In this way, neo-Gramscians argue, a 'Keynesian capitalism' organised on a national scale based upon social democratic principles, linked on an international scale via public interest international organisations, gave way to a transnational 'disciplinary neo-liberalism' and to an undemocratic 'new constitutionalism', which has involved concentrated effort to 'insulate economic institutions and agents from popular scrutiny or political accountability' (Gill 1992: 279). In other words, the international economy is increasingly subject to *governance without government* (Rosenau 1992a, b; Sinclair 1994). And the most important force within this non-governmental form of economic governance is the community of financial elites. As Scott Lash and John Urry have pointedly remarked, it is now not so much that money makes the world go round, but that 'money *is* the world going around, faster and faster' (1994: 292). For many financial elites, wedded to the enduring metaphors of liberal economics, this is only as the economic world should be. The purview within the financial community would seem to be that the Bretton Woods system was a misguided aberration, a product of society's fear of finance, an international social experiment in which the competitive, allocative efficiency of raw financial forces was tamed in the interests of managerialism and welfarism. But now, 'natural' order has been restored to the universe of which the financial community are the masters, a self-regulating order of market forces, of allocative efficiency, a universe of winners and losers.

CONCLUSIONS

The Bretton Woods system evolved from an attempt on the part of Anglo-American political elites to 'rewrite' the economic world in an audacious bid to call an alternative economic and social order into being. However, the 'failure' of the system has seen its replacement with an economic order within which a far greater importance is given to a 'naturalised' conception of the operation of economic and social forces. Rather than provide a straightforward narrative account of this important episode in the history of capitalism, we have sought to interpret Bretton Woods through the analytical lens of two very important strands of post-Marxist economic discourse – regulation theory and neo-Gramscian political economy. Of these it was the neo-Gramscian account which had more to say about the Bretton Woods system, mainly because neo-Gramscian theorists have traditionally been far more concerned with the way in which 'economic order' was constituted at an international level.

Although both economic discourses share much in common, there are important differences in their analyses of the rise and fall of the Bretton Woods system. Regulation theory, with its emphasis on how national Fordisms operated, has tended to examine the structural factors which constituted the emergent international order. Neo-Gramscian theory, with its emphasis on the intellectual and political genesis of the system, has accentuated the role of transnational agents. This dissimilarity of approach is also reflected in the explanations given for the subsequent breakdown of the system. Again, regulation theorists have tended to argue that the crisis was caused by the transmission of the crisis in the US economy together with the undermining of Fordist regulation by the growth of internationalisation of production and finance. This crisis was, crucially, transmitted via the international monetary system, in the form of rising interest rates and crises of liquidity. Neo-Gramscians have interpreted the crisis as being rooted in the retreat of US elite actors from their hegemonic role in order to use US power for their own (narrowly interpreted) self-interest. The crisis, for neo-Gramscians, therefore was transmitted because there was a crisis of authority and a decomposition of the 'Atlantic ruling class'.

The greater attention to issues of money and finance and the greater importance afforded to issues of discursivity are developments that are constituent of one another in both accounts. For one thing, the more one analyses the realm of money and finance, the more one realises that an attention to discursivity is required to come to an understanding of it. As we argue in the following chapter, the world of money is a world of interpretative power struggles, where competing sets of scripts and discourses conjure up alternative plausible 'orderings' of the economic world for purposes of financial advantage: in other words, the social power of financial wealth increasingly attaches itself to those able to offer the most convincing interpretations. It is also a world which can act on these constructions with an unusual efficacy. For another, the speed at which this discursive world of money and finance transforms itself has accelerated greatly in recent years, which has meant that time–space horizons of this world are now at odds with much conventional academic and political thinking. In consequence, the possibilities of political interventions within a world in which the social power of financial elites has increased will remain limited so long as political ontologies remain 'caught within discursive horizons that express the spatiotemporal configurations of another era' (Walker 1993: x). This ontological disjuncture is well illustrated by Stephen Gill's analysis of the intergovernmental meetings of the Group of Seven, which now stands as the most important forum for international policy co-ordination within the contemporary world economy (Gill 1993c). As Gill points out, despite the fact that

> we now appear to be in a post-hegemonic, hierarchical, market-determined system, dominated by the scale and power and swift reflexes of internationally-mobile capital . . . international diplomacy between the leaders of the world's largest capitalist nations appears to be caught in a conceptual and institutional time-warp.

(1993c: 86)

In other words, whereas the horizons of the world of money and finance are global and deterritorialised, the political imagination seems wedded to territorialism and the borders of the nation state.

Such an ontological disjuncture signifies an important imbalance between the social power of powerful financial elites and those who would wish to bring about a reordering of the economic world in the general interest of other less powerful social groups. Until this disjuncture can be overcome, a Bretton Woods Mark 2, which might redress the current geopolitical and geo-economic imbalance in social power in the global economy, will be a long time in coming.

CHAPTER 9

A PHANTOM STATE?

The de-traditionalisation of money, the international financial system and international financial centres

My concern with the limits of the modern political imagination is informed both by a sense of the need for alternative forms of political practice under contemporary conditions and a sense that fairly profound transformations are currently in progress. But it is also informed by a sense that our understanding of these transformations, and of the contours of alternative political practices, remains caught within discursive horizons that express the spatiotemporal configurations of another era.

(Walker 1993: ix–x)

On television news . . . almost any striking event . . . now fetches to the screen a row of cream-faced young men called 'analysts', who are asked for their opinions. These people are really stockbrokers' clerks, but drawn these days from the public schools instead of the plebs. They know a bit about money, in the sense of short-term speculation prospects. But their views on politics, so readily offered, are amateurish. Any of us, given a couple of whiskies and a read of that morning's *Independent*, could do as well. But they come from the City of London, and the City knows about money, and money is what politics is really about.

(Ascherson 1992: 25)

INTRODUCTION

This chapter arises out of a previous paper (Thrift 1994a) in which an attempt was made to answer a more and more frequently heard charge – that international financial centres will become redundant in a world where electronic flows of information predominate. As *The Economist* (1993a: 15) puts it: 'the very idea that financial markets need a geographic centre is being gradually refuted by electronics'. The argument of that paper was couched in terms of a set of factors, apart from the obvious ones of external economies and the sheer amount of capital sunk into international financial centres, which meant that such centres were still needed in the decentralised realm of electronic space. Chief amongst these were a set of social and cultural factors that, so it was argued, would force the continuance of face-to-face interaction in recognised international financial centres. This chapter attempts to extend that argument in two ways.

The first of these is through a consideration of the characteristics of modern money. To read some accounts, money has become a free-floating signifier, endlessly circulating in an electronic space of flows. In these accounts, money is an increasingly abstract, increasingly fluid, increasingly frantic affair, watched over and tended by greedy young men and women who are shades of the usurers of old. Denzin (1991: 91) provides a particularly good example of this kind of account in a passage from *Images of Postmodern Society*:

> Numbers flashing across screens, numbers which can be erased with the touch of a finger, or a loud voice. Numbers which point to imaginary properties or imaginary things. Companies with made-up names, whose productivity is measured by imaginary numbers concerning losses and gains. Money going in and out of hidden accounts. Money attached to nothing but imaginary numbers attached to made-up accounts, built on the transactions and imagined doings of imaginary companies. Careers built on who can best manipulate this imaginary political economy of signs. This is what 'Wall Street' is. A site where a political economy of signs circulates across an imaginary computerised space where nothing is any longer real.

Our purpose in the first part of this chapter is to challenge this kind of conception of money as the new sublime, beyond representation (Eagleton 1993). We want to suggest, through a brief examination of the international financial system, that money has become both more universal and more particular. This is hardly a revolutionary observation, of course. It is exactly the point made by Marx, Simmel and many others (Dodd 1993). But what seems to have been forgotten in many recent accounts is precisely the dialectical nature of the development of money.

The second way in which we want to extend the argument of the first paper is by suggesting that, in contradistinction to the idea of an abstracted electronic system of monetary creation and circulation, the international financial system has actually become *more* social, *more* reflexive and *more* interpretative since the breakdown of Bretton Woods. In many ways, what we see is the return to a system with many of the characteristics of the international financial system before the era of state control. It is a system that is now, without doubt, dependent upon electronic telecommunications but, ironically perhaps, the increasingly intricate patterns of connection that are able to be produced as a result may in turn trigger off demands for more rather than less face-to-face interaction (Walker 1993). The second part of the chapter attempts to answer the question of how we might now describe this system via actor–network theory.

In other words, we want to suggest that money, the international financial system, and international financial centres have all 'de-traditionalised' over the last thirty years or so, because of the continuing dialectic between the universal and the particular and because of the breakdown of state authority and its replacement by more diffuse sources of governance. In turn, this de-traditionalisation has produced an enormous discursive task of 'understanding'. The international financial system is now disordered, contingent and mobile and so are the interpretations of it – the links are reciprocal.

In the third and fourth parts of the chapter, we want to illustrate these two extensions to our argument by considering the case of one major international financial centre – the City of London – before and after the decline of Bretton Woods. Finally, some brief, speculative conclusions are made to round the chapter out.

POSTMODERN MONEY

Money is conventionally described as consisting of four functions: a medium of exchange, a unit of account, a means of payment and a standard for deferred payment. As history has proceeded, so the last function, in which money increasingly becomes distributed over time and space as part of a burgeoning system of credit, has become the most important: credit money has displaced commodity money (Altvater 1993). In one sense, there is now only international credit money, ceaselessly 'circulating' bits of information, ceaselessly regenerating obligations as old obligations shrivel and die: 'modern money is everywhere debt' (Peebles 1991: 131).

This system of international credit money depends on the pupillage of time, space and risk. First of all, credit money 'brackets' time since a period of the future is reserved or 'colonised' as a stream of obligations (Giddens 1991). The time structure of credit money is clearly important and it has become increasingly complex (Shackle 1972; Cencini 1988). Further, the time horizon over which enterprises and other agents must calculate,

> turns out to be an endogenous aspect of these credit relations: when expectations concerning future system-wide developments are stable and widely shared, then a wide spectrum of private liabilities will be regarded as liquid and will find a place in the portfolios of those units whose current operations generate a surplus of revenues over expenditures.
>
> (Grahl 1991: 172–3)

Second, credit money 'brackets' space since 'standardised value allows transactions between a multiplicity of individuals who never physically meet one another' (Giddens 1991: 18). More importantly, in the process of bracketing, it is increasingly able to erode the territorial controls of the state. In the seventeenth century the bill of exchange was hailed in part because it enabled merchants to move their money out of the hands of absolutist states. In the same way, one of the purposes of many modern monetary instruments is to elude state controls – over interest rates, currencies and the regulation of money.

Of course, no clear distinction can be made between the configuration of money, time and space. From the use of the share as a means of financing long-distance exploration by extending monetary obligations over the period of time needed to complete a voyage to the use of the swap as a means of providing the best probable interest rate structure on a loan in the best possible currencies, money has been about the complex articulation of time and space.

Finally, credit money 'brackets' risk. What constitutes risk is, of course, a constantly changing notion. Since its invention in the thirteenth century, 'risk' has been a shifting ensemble of meanings about the timing and spacing of credit and debt which depict whether a credit/debt relation is viable. Early notions of risk were akin to wagers, encapsulated in devices like tontines and lotteries. Although banks began to understand and articulate risk early on – even as early as the seventeenth century the Bank of Amsterdam understood the difference between liquidity and credit risk – it was not until the late eighteenth century that calculation of risk became possible and not until the late nineteenth century that risk became an integral part of the monetary system as speculation came to be seen as a wholly legitimate activity: 'as risk became an integral part of the . . . economic system, certain forms of risk taking and speculation assumed new respectability. Rational speculation that dealt with already existent risks was differentiated from pure gambling which created artificial risk' (Zelizer 1979: 86). However, risk in modern monetary systems has presented something of a paradox, especially since the death of the Bretton Woods system of fixed exchange rates and capital controls and extensive national systems of regulation has produced new and higher levels of volatility in the money and capital markets. More is now known about risk, and that knowledge is often formalised in the credit ratings of firms like Moodys or Standard and Poor as well as in expert systems dependent upon mathematics and computing power (OECD 1992b). But this knowledge can, in turn, be used to produce new forms of money (which have often started out as instruments to control risk) whose exact risk profile is unknown (Table 9.1) and may even lead to systemic risk. The case of derivatives (financial instruments like options, futures and swaps) shows this paradox only too clearly. Originally instruments for hedging, derivations have often become simply tools of speculation. As a result they may as often have increased volatility as they have damped it down (Bank for International Settlements 1992). In other words, the systematic assessment of risk allows new forms of risk to be generated (Table 9.2) and promotes volatility in time and space, which is now both necessary in order to make money, and itself creates more risks. No clearer illustration can be found of Giddens's (1991: 118) assertion that the international monetary system is an institutionally structured risk environment which is constituted through risk, rather than risk being an incidental factor.

Table 9.1 Different forms of monetary risk

Balance sheet risks: mismatches between the interest rate, maturity and currency structure of assets and the liabilities funding these assets results in:
1 interest rate mismatch risk
2 liquidity risk
3 foreign exchange risk

Transaction risk: risks resulting from transactions, including:
1 credit risks (risks due to default or determination)
2 price risks (risks due to change in value of assets and liabilities)
3 operating and liquidity risks (risks due to technical failures, settlement systems, etc.)

Source: The Economist (1993a: 4).

Table 9.2 Risks arising from the use of derivatives

- counterparty credit risk (arising from counterparty default)
- market risk (arising from price risks of the derivative market and the market or markets underlying the derivative)
- settlement risk (arising from delays in settlement)
- operating risk (arising from operating systems without adequate controls)
- liquidity risk (arising from the drying up of markets)
- legal risk (arising from uncertainty about the legality of some derivative contracts)
- aggregation or interconnection risk (arising from the sheer complexity of exposure to many markets)

Source: The Economist (1993a: 35)

An important part of the study of international credit money is usually considered to be its increasingly chimerical character (a contention usually illustrated by reference to the stomach-churning world of foreign exchange). Money, so the saying goes, has become disembedded. Through the medium of electronic communications and expert systems post-modern money can flow efficiently without barriers. It has become simply a set of accounts; credits and debits constantly notching up like the tally sticks of old, a single quality-less and rationalising market money. Now, in a sense, this is precisely what has happened, or is happening. But, at the same time, precisely in order to achieve this kind of universalism, inter-national monetary instruments have become *more* complex and specific. In order to attain exactly the right articulation of time, space and risk, new international monetary instruments have been invented at a breakneck pace. Nowhere is this clearer than in the sphere of derivatives, complex financial instruments whose values derive from other assets and indices of these asset values, and whose function, at least to begin with, was simply to transfer price risks associated with fluctuations in these assets' values.

Further, the apparently quality-less and rationalising universalism of credit money is also mediated by culture. As Simmel put it, 'money is influenced by the broad cultural trends and is, at the same time, an independent cause of these trends' (Simmel cited in Frisby (1992: 93)). Money has a broad range of meanings associated with it which influence how it is used. Yet we still know relatively little about the range of these meanings, hindered as we still are by the idea that money is 'not socio-logical enough' (Collins 1979: 190). Yet research has constantly shown that social and cultural structures set important limits on what is regarded as money and thereby on the practices of money. There are multiple monies, with qualitatively different characteristics generated by their situations and meanings (Zelizer 1989) which are, in turn, influenced by much larger and longer-term shifts in the meaning of money which work to open up cultural spaces in which new meanings and practices of money can flourish. These longer-term shifts in the meaning of money have been well documented. For example, there is the gradual redefinition of usury documented by Le Goff (1988), Kerridge (1988) and others involving in particular the invention of new ideas of risk, and a general concept of purgatory, which opened up a cultural space for new practices of money in the thirteenth century: 'The hope of escaping Hell, thanks to purgatory, permitted the usurer to propel the economy and society of the thirteenth century ahead toward capitalism' (Le Goff, 1988: 93). Again, there is the social and intellectual history of 'the money question' in the later nineteenth century and especially the spread of bimetallism, with its potent arguments about what constituted the 'intrinsic value' of money in an increasingly international monetary system (e.g. Unger 1964; Nugent 1967). At much the same time Zelizer (1979) shows that there was a general revaluation of notions of risk and what counted as rational specu-lation which can be seen as part of a more general reassessment of time and human life which opened up a cultural space for life assurance and thereby solved 'the cultural and structural dilemma of putting death on the market' (p. 26). Finally, we can note the struggle in the twentieth century between socialist notions of a 'passive' money, serving the interests of the state and often taken to be simply an expression of labour, and modern western economic rhetorics with their ideas of money as an exces-sive force (Goux 1990a). (Indeed, not the least interesting of observations is the way in which many 'postmodern' accounts of money as a free-floating signifier often simply simulate these rhetorics (Goux 1990b).)

To summarise, credit money has a number of properties which mean that although it is often thought of as abstracted, it can never become an entirely abstract system, because it must remain a complex articulation of time, space, risk and more general cultural trends which, to some extent, define how time, space and risk are conceived. In other words, at root credit money must depend upon conventions – relatively stable intersubjective represen-tations – of what economic life is all about. These conventions will be forced by one final property of credit money which is that its value is critically dependent upon credibility, upon *trust* that money assets will not lose their value. The material and symbolic costs incurred in building trust in credit money have become much greater since the decline of Bretton Woods (de Grauwe 1989).

THE INTERNATIONAL FINANCIAL SYSTEM: GOVERNING WITHOUT GOVERNMENT?

From the middle of the nineteenth century until the decline of Bretton Woods, the international financial system was, in effect, run by nation states, latterly under US hegemony. National banks, government departments and civil servants held power over much of the business of international finance Money capitalists were a critical and vibrant part of this international financial system, often operating with a considerable degree of independence, but they were held in check by state regulation of credit and state power to define what counted as money.

With the decline of Bretton Woods, much of the power over the international financial system, and especially power over how credit is created, bought and sold, has transferred back to money capitalists who are increasingly able to 'define money through their collective acts', that is to legislate on 'what is used as money and how money is used' (Baker 1987: 110). With the growth of electronic telecommunications, these money capitalists are able to operate on a global scale and with a speed of reaction which states find very difficult to emulate. In this new international financial system, 'the balance has shifted from a financial structure which was predominantly state-based with some transnational links, to a predominantly global system in which some residual local differences in markets, institutions and regulation persist' (Stopford and Strange 1991: 41).

However, the exact status of this new international financial system is unclear. There are clearly structures of *governance* but whether the interaction between these structures constitutes an independently functioning system of *government* is less clear.

Perhaps the best way to conceive of the status of this untidy but decidedly influential system is by drawing on actor–network theory (Callon 1986, 1991; Latour 1986, 1993; Law 1994). Actor–network theory suits our purposes well because it echoes a number of themes which are integral to this chapter:

> It is symbolic interaction with an added dash of Machiavellian political theory, a portion of (suitably diluted) discourse analysis, and a commitment to the project of understanding the material character of the networks of the social.
>
> (Law 1994: 100)

Actor–networks are networks which are defined by actors who are constantly acting through intermediaries – texts, humans, non-humans and money – which are put into circulation in attempts to construct and maintain power relations. In these networks, actors can never be completely stable entities, they must constantly redefine one another in interaction via intermediaries which themselves cannot be considered as passive; in other words, an actor is 'any entity able to associate texts, humans, non-humans and money' (Callon 1991: 140) and thus put intermediaries into circulation. Most particularly, actor–network theory is concerned to study the recursive processes of ordering and elaboration which are generated within and by actor–networks. Further, it does not take the stability of these networks for granted. They are considered open to shifts in their boundaries which may mean that they can be redefined. But, to the extent that these networks are maintained, this will depend upon the degree to which actor–networks are able to 'translate' situations, that is 'assemble the bits and pieces needed to assemble a coherent actor' (Law 1994: 161). In turn, this process of translation demands the utilisation of materials of association which are able to act at a distance, thus constructing time and space *within* these networks. These materials, whether dependent upon voice, or body or text, are socio-technical innovations like 'writing, paper, money, a postal system, cartography, navigation, ocean-going vessels, cannons, gunpowder [and] telephony' (Law 1994: 103) which can generate required effects that will last over varying periods of time and cover varying distances. Thus, in actor–network theory, agency, power and size are always uncertain capillary effects which have to be constantly worked on by an actor–network. They are achieved, they are not a right.

In the current international financial system it is possible to note four overlapping but relatively stable actor–networks. These networks have been able to assemble the agency, power and size needed to develop, produce and distribute money. We might see these actor–networks as the chief structures of governance in the international financial system, which together constitute the fragmenting 'post-politics' of international money.

The first of these is the nation state. It would be foolish to contend that the nation state has lost all its powers to order the international financial system. State financial regulation still imposes important limits (and creates its own problems of interpretation, as the large number of compliance officers in many financial services firms only too readily attest to). States can still, to some extent, rein in parts of the financial services industry through concerted action, as the impact of the Bank for International Settlements' capital adequacy ratios on banks shows only too clearly. State monetary policy still makes a difference, as the effects of German monetary policy on other European countries makes clear. Further, nation states continually struggle to extend their powers over the international financial system, both through new modes of regulation (e.g. international contract law, international accounting standards or the struggle by states to extend control to derivatives) and through new international organisations of nation states (e.g. G7 or the EU; see Held 1991). But state networks are not as extensive or as concentrated as they once were. To a large extent, the international financial system has been privatised and this privatisation has involved not just the circulation of money but increasingly also its production, as new forms of money like derivatives are constantly invented which are outside state control (see Baker 1987). The result is a more complex, sprawling, volatile and reflexive international financial system, with many different networks of players dealing in many different types of financial market, with associated risks which are very difficult to calculate. Further, it is a system which is now, in effect, designed continually to outrun prevailing state norms and rules.

The second actor–network is the media. The press and television have become powerful ordering forces in the modern international financial system. The inception of a modern financial press in the nineteenth century has been followed by the increasing ability of the media to influence events for four main reasons. First, there has been the extension of the media into new arenas concerned with the supply of electronic information – from market quotation systems to CD-ROM databases. By one estimate, the market for such electronic information grew at 35 per cent a year in the 1980s (Parsons 1989). Second, there has been an increase in specialised financial publishing tied to particular segments of the market. Some commentators have even talked of the disagreggation of economic news and commentary. Third, there has been the growth of global media outlets, newspapers like the *Financial Times* (Kynaston 1989), and television stations like CNN. Fourth, there has been the demise of grand interpretative schemes like Keynesianism or monetarism, and the growth of a multiplicity of different explanations of financial events, leading some commentators to talk of 'the relativism of the electronic age' (Smith 1983: 325). In other words:

> the powerful macro-frameworks of the past are no longer adequate as contexts of reporting modern transnational capitalism. The continued privatisation of economic discourse has not helped to provide any new popular paradigm. But another reason for this splintering process is the sheer expansion in the availability of greater qualities of information itself.
>
> (Parsons 1989: 218)

Thus, it is debatable whether the media now gain their influence from the interpretative schemes they diffuse through, for example, economic and market commentaries, or through the sheer weight of information they provide, or both.

The third actor–network, and the one to which we want to devote considerable attention, consists of the organisations of the money capitalists themselves, which go to make up the modern global financial services industry. It is debatable whether this group of money capitalists actually cohere as a class. Some argue that they do (see Van der Pijl 1989c), others that they do not. Whatever the actual case it is clear that there are certain processes in common that do bind these actors together and allow them to exert a degree of control over the international financial system, over and above their ability to own or manipulate large sums of money. Four of these processes seem particularly important, each of them closely interrelated with the others.

The first of these is the need for trust and reciprocity. Enough has been written of the need for trust and reciprocity in monetary systems to forestall further expansion here. Suffice it to say that building and maintaining co-operative relationships of trust and reciprocity in the monetary system has always been a high priority because of the need to retain the credibility of the value of money and monetary instruments. Ironically, it is now probably greater than ever, because of the overwhelming importance of credit money, because the international monetary system has become a system of institutionalised risk, and because the overall level of trust has declined. This decline can be traced, in particular, to the decline in one-to-one relationships between firms and clients as price competition has become more important; clients have become more and more likely to want to do business on a competitive, 'transactional' deal-by-deal basis. Two strategies have been initiated to cope with this decline in trust. One is simply the institution of more formal controls on employees (down to and including video-taping and tape-recording of deals made in dealing rooms). The other is 'relationship management': money capitalists have to try harder to get to know more people and to get to know them better (Eccles and Crane 1988). In turn, the interactional frenzy that has resulted from relationship management has made work on presenting the self a central project of the international financial system (Thrift 1994b). Work on the self is of crucial importance since it is only through such work that money capitalists can now build up trust and reciprocity. In many of the situations of negotiation, especially those involving a high degree of uncertainty, it is presentation of knowledge and self (the two being related) that is the main resource brought to the situation by participants. Self-identity can therefore become a crucial determinant of economic success.

The second process is the increasing requirement for interpretation. The international financial system today generates a massive load of information and the power goes, to an extent, to those able to offer the most convincing interpretations (Soros 1988). The problem is no longer necessarily a shortage of information but how to make sense of the masses of information that exist. As a *Wall Street Journal* journalist explains in a Robert Erdman novel, 'Well I'm plugged in and, true, I've got information coming out of my ears. But what that information *means* I haven't got a clue about' (cited in Parsons (1989: 227)). Thus the generation of interpretative schemes is now crucial.

This uncertainty is perhaps most clear in the stock markets where 'the one obvious problem is that you're only as good as your last bargain. Each day starts a new, complete sheet' (stockbroker, cited in Lazar (1990: 58)). Smith (1983) suggests that the reaction to uncertainty in these markets has been the generation of four main discursive schemes or 'orientations'. The first of these is the fundamentalist/economic orientation which can be summarised in the phrase 'market values reflect economic values' (p. 33), such as a firm's profits, interest rates and so on. The second orientation is an 'insider/influence' one which conceives market events strictly in inter-personal terms with the result that powerful institutions and individuals are considered important. The third 'cyclist/charist' orientation involves the belief that 'the market has a life of its own' (p. 48) and therefore cannot be explained by reference to 'outside' factors. Finally, the fourth 'trader/market action' view stresses understanding of the market as involv-ing 'feel' for the mood of the market and market psychology (see Heath *et al.* 1993) and Jirotka *et al.* (1993) on the way in which share traders come to a collaborative view of the market in the City of London).

A third process is the growth of formalised 'knowledge structures' or 'expert systems' which modify and constantly revise knowledge about the international financial system (Strange 1988; Giddens 1991). International finance has gone from being something approaching a craft industry, learnt on the job, to an industry in which workshops, seminars, videos and round tables teach an endless round of not only vital textual knowledge (such as the importance of credit rating agencies) but also interpersonal skills.

The fourth and most important process has been the growth of the 'immutable mobile' (Law 1994) of information technology and, most especially, the advent of 'intelligent networks' that integrate information and communication services (Mansell 1993; Mansell and Jenkins 1993).

The growth of this technology has proved to be a particularly complex process because of the multiplicity of effects such technology has had. Four of these have marked the development of money capitalist organisations. First, information technology has, as Zuboff (1988) puts it, 'informated' these organisations. That is, information technology generates informa-tion that was previously unavailable which both provides the possibility of more control but also provides a more complex and uncertain information environment of 'electronic texts'.

Second, this new information is used to generate new products, thus adding further to complexity and uncertainty. Third, information tech-nology allows less hierarchical, more open, 'networked' organisations to develop. But, again, this is a two-edged sword. Such organisations allow 'positional' control strategies to be developed which can more easily accommodate complexity and uncertainty but such organisations (which, in any case, have a long tradition in the financial service industry (Eccles and Crane 1988)) also tend to have their own problems. Thus, the spread of these communication and control systems 'is as much a response to increasing uncertainty as a clear strategy to enhance control [and] the proliferation of industry response systems creating more interconnections and more transactions tends to undermine predictability rather than enhance it' (Mulgan 1991: 242). Fourth, the importance of interpretation has become even more pressing. The turn to information technology solves few interpretative problems. Indeed it may even increase them. To begin with, information technology produces output which still has to be read, and read *in action*. As Wynne (1991: 37) puts it: 'Of one thing . . . I am sure, even if there were no longer any printed texts to read, only screens . . . there will still be the question of reading and the limits and effects of reading that-which-is-read upon its readable meaning.' Thus, increasingly, money capitalists are becoming:

> a group of people gathered around a central core that is the electronic text. Individuals take up their relationship toward that text according to their responsibilities and their information needs. In such a scenario, work is, in large measure, the creation of meaning, and the methods of work involve the application of intellective skill to data.
>
> (Zuboff 1988: 394)

Then again, the rhetorics and narrative possibilities of the software involved in electronic texts are very complex and demand new communicable forms which involve innovative and constantly developing combinations of actors, messages and stories (Dunlop and Kling 1991; Sproull and Kiesler 1991; Lea 1992). As if this were not enough, it also has to be remembered that the total load of interpretation has become more rather than less pressing because all organisations tend to be acting in the light of improved information, with the effect that knowledge and certainty may actually be reduced, not enhanced.

The mention of information technology points to a fourth actor—network. This is the network that is the most shadowy and the least understood. It is, quite simply, machine 'intelligence'. Until recently, intelligent machines could be subsumed under the general rubric of information technology as intermediary 'immutable mobiles' without much harm. They had not been able to construct agency or power. That may now be changing, both practically and also theoretically as the networks of the social are seen to come in a variety of material forms of which people are only one (Haraway 1991; Latour 1993; Law 1994; Thrift 1994a). Increasingly, the international financial system provides examples of networks of machine intelligence, usually in the form of artificial intelligence systems, usually deploying neural network techniques. These networks, which first came to general awareness because of the furore over the role of programme trading in the October 1987 stock market crash, have become more and more sophisticated.

> Last year Citibank, which handles at least 15 per cent of the currency dealings in London, gave a neural network system $10 million to play with for a few months. It made an 18 per cent annual return compared with the 12 per cent typically achieved by traders using more conventional forecasting methods. A large pension fund in the United States is believed to be using the technique with larger sums of money.
>
> (Holderness 1993: 23)

These four actor–networks clearly interact with each other in myriad ways. In particular, Moran (1991) has pointed to the importance in the new international financial system of transient but still potent 'issue coalitions', made up of groupings of states, media, money capitalists, machines and other interested parties. Such coalitions focus on only one particular issue (usually a crisis or a financial scandal) and come together only around that issue to force through change.

It is clearly possible to describe these four actor–networks as overlapping sources of governance of a new, privatised international financial system. But is it possible to describe this system as in any sense governed? The international financial system may have structures of governance, made up of the diverse and overlapping actor–networks of nation states, the media, private money capitalists and machines. Do they add up to anything like a government? Is there, in other words, a hand at the tiller?

There are a number of different theoretical schemata that we can draw on to answer this question. We will concentrate on just three. The first of these is regulation theory (Boyer 1990; Jessop 1990). One of the most notable aspects of recent intellectual history has been the degree to which the original attempts by Aglietta and others to integrate monetary phenomena into the general framework of a regime of accumulation have been lost in subsequent discussions (Aglietta 1979; Aglietta and Orlean 1982; Lipietz 1987). Yet, the regulationist scheme of things, with its synthesis of Marxian and Keynesian monetary concepts, allows the greater importance of credit in the modern world to be recognised, as well as the constantly shifting balance of power between creditors and debtors (Grahl 1991). Under optimal conditions, stability of the regime of accumulation can be achieved because of a general match between supply and demand and the confidence of economic agents that this match will continue. However:

> When ... the coherence of the regime is disturbed, and when this disturbance is seen as undermining commercial asset values, the monetary authorities are forced to make critical strategic choices. On the one hand, the widespread refinance of illiquid deficit units can be encouraged in order to prevent the fragmentation of the networks of exchange relations, but this will provoke inflation to the extent that restructuring by debtors does not succeed in eliminating imbalances between cost and demand. This is a centralising strategy which carries the risk that initial imbalances may persist and even widen. On the other hand, a decentralising deflationary strategy – refusing or strictly curtailing refinance – although it will compel rapid adjustment of deficit positions, may prove too difficult for industrial agents, and then the elimination of loss-making units will threaten a cumulative breakdown of existing relations.
>
> (Grahl 1991: 173)

But creditors and debtors will want to have their say. Thus,

> given the successful reproduction of an established regime of accumulation, creditors and debtors will be bound together by a solidarity that rests on an agreed valuation of financial investments. But when the regime can no longer orient investment activity towards a commercially accepted future for the system, this solidarity is disturbed. Nevertheless a collapse is not inevitable – debtors will pressure banks and monetary authorities to shield them

from creditors; but the latter, although now anxious for rapid repayment or transfers of ownership, may hold back from foreclosure through the fear of failures that will devalorise their assets. The structures of intermediation, which determine the possibility of aggregating debtor or creditor interests, clearly play a key role in the development of these relations. Essentially the central bank now has to choose between antagonistic and incompatible restructuring projects, formulated by groups of agents who no longer share a common vision of the broad trends in the system as a whole, nor agree to the time horizon appropriate for individual investments and reconstructions.

(Grahl 1991: 173–4)

Accounts like these, and similar ones offered by the North American economic governance school (see Christopherson 1993), have clear advantages in describing certain situations. However, they also have very real disadvantages as accounts of the international financial system post-Bretton Woods. Most particularly, there are three disadvantages. The first is that such accounts are state centred. They therefore only poorly account for situations, such as the current one, in which states are weaker sources of governance, having lost some of their power to order the financial system because of the growth in the power of private money capitalists and the media, because of their inability to react as rapidly to events as private money capitalists and the media, and because of the difficulty that states have faced engaging in monetary cooperation, as a result of a general lack of political and institutional integration (de Grauwe 1989). In other words, such accounts find it difficult to conceive of the international financial system as autocentric. The second disadvantage is that the international financial system is reduced to an effect of capitalism or is allowed only the most limited differentiation from it, usually as part of a mode of social regulation. In other words, accounts like that proffered by regulation theory deny the performative capacity of the international financial system. The third disadvantage is that these accounts have real difficulties in describing the fluid nature of the international financial system, especially its speed of reaction, adaptability and speculative spirals. They find it difficult to take into their accounts the fact that 'time and space in the bankers' world [are] pliable, moveable, profitable constructions which might or might not correspond with the mundane geography of national territories' (Daly and Logan 1989: 103).

Are there any theoretical approaches which might be more forthcoming? We will briefly note two. The first of these is Luhmann's (1982, 1989) theory of autopoietic systems. Such a theory might envisage the current international financial system as having been built up from the interaction of varying social forces until it has reached the point where it has achieved a good deal of autonomy, and has become something close to an independently functioning system:

autopoiesis . . . is a property of a certain type of system and can be defined, in a nutshell, as a condition of radical autonomy. It emerges when the system in question defines its own boundaries relative to its environment, developing its own unifying operational code, implements its own programmes, reproduces its own elements in a closed system, obeys its own laws of motion. When a system achieves what we might call 'autopoietic take-off', its operations can no longer be controlled from outside. Autopoieticist social theorists agree that modern societies have seen many such systems develop along functional lines and have therefore become so highly differentiated and polycentric that no centre could coordinate all diverse interactions, organisations and institutions. Nor is there a single functionally dominant system which could, *pace* Marxists, determine societal development 'in the last instance'.

(Jessop 1990: 320)

In other words, to translate Luhmann's insights into realist parlance, the new international financial system is demonstrating 'emergent powers'.

The second approach might be to call on poststructuralism. In this approach, the international financial system might be seen as an open and constantly moving field of increasingly electronic discourses with the power to define and force the pace of events. The field is a massive structure of communication in which the subject's relation to the world has been reconfigured and in which time and space have been retooled so that the absent is as important as the present (Poster 1990; Deleuze 1991). Following Poster (1990), we might see a new and unrecognisable mode of community coming into being in which electronically mediated communication both supplements and substitutes for existing forms of communication. To put it another way, we might conceive of the international financial system as an electronically networked, constantly circulating, nomadic 'state', operating twenty-four hours a day around the world.

These three theoretical schemata therefore provide different answers to the question of whether the international financial system constitutes a government. In regulation theory, the international financial system remains, in its essentials, an adjunct of capitalism. In contrast, in autopoietic and poststructuralist theory, the international financial system has taken on a life of its own, has become something like a self-governing (although not sovereign) entity. Certainly the switch in theoretical emphasis from regulation theory to autopoietic or poststructuralist theory makes it somewhat easier to envisage what international financial centres are becoming as *electronic* flows of information begin to predominate. They are both waveform and point.

Thus, on the one hand, the international financial system has become increasingly 'disembedded'. It now consists of multiple discourse networks (Kittler 1990), networks of evaluation which are possible because of the new information technology. In turn, these networks generate new forms of discourse that would not be possible without them (Lea 1992) and which involve new forms of 'actant' (Haraway 1991) subjects based on new combinations of the body, self and machines producing new financial products (Poster 1990). In other words, a new space of communicative materiality has been constituted over time (Beninger 1991).

On the other hand, although this '"virtual" world of information hubs, data bases and networks' (Mulgan 1991: 3) may appear as a kind of universal, its very universalism forces a new set of particulars. The pressures of the interpretative load of multiple networks of electronic texts and the 'fictive sociality' (Gergen 1991) that it produces are so great that they force embodied, interpersonal, face-to-face interaction as the only way to come to fully finished mutual understandings. Helped by the fact that so many new financial instruments are more, rather than less, specific, this means that people have to make physical contact to argue their position: there is still a compulsion of proximity (Boden and Molotch 1993) – but in very specific locations. In other words greater universalism forces new kinds of particularism.

Thus the space of this new 'informated' international financial system bends both ways. There is an invisible and a visible hand. There is a dis-embedded electronic space. But there is also a re-embedded set of meeting places (from restaurants to trading floors) where many of the *practices* of this first space still have to be negotiated because 'there are now teeming images from which to draw, often fleeting in duration, and the options for action are enormous. The audience for such actions is also complex; what plays with ease in one context may seem superficial in another' (Gergen 1991: 223). In other words the second, re-embedded space is increasingly an outcome of the first; it is an integral part of disembedded electronic space rather than a relict feature (see Heath *et al.* 1993; Jirotka *et al.* 1993; Kahn and Cooper 1993).

In turn, this electronic world, with its emphasis on meaning and increased social connectedness (Gergen 1991), forces an even greater reflexivity into the conduct of many meeting places. This increase in reflexivity is partly a result of the need to negotiate a wider spectrum of relationships as a result of an increase in the cosmopolitanism of the international financial system, partly the result of the need to cement relationships formed in the fragile and symbolic communities of electronic space, and, no doubt, partly a result of the general increase in reflexivity in societies as a whole (Giddens 1991; Beck 1992; Lash 1993; Lash and Urry 1994). Thus these meeting places become soups of reflexivity, where people work hard to present themselves.

Further, the relationship between this new electronic world and meeting places is not all one way. There is a dynamic and reciprocal relationship between telecommunication and context (Lea 1992). Thus, social activity in these meeting places can resonate back through the electronic world.

Conventionally, the meeting places of the international financial system have been international financial centres. What seems to have happened post-Bretton Woods is that the number of these international financial centres that count – as meeting places, as generators of news and new meanings and, in general, as significant nodes of reflexivity in electronic discourse networks – has decreased but, in turn, those places that are left in contention have become more important. In other words, the inter-dependent connectedness of disembedded electronic networks promotes dependence on just a few places like London, New York and Tokyo where representations can be mutually constructed, negotiated, accepted and acted upon (Amin and Thrift 1992). In effect, these are the places that make the non-place electronic realm conceivable. They are what Law (1994: 104) calls 'ordering centres', the centres of translation of actor–networks 'constituted by gathering, simplifying, representing, making calculations about, and acting upon the flow of immutable mobiles'.

In the next section, we want to turn to one of these ordering centres – the City of London – to exemplify some of the points made in this and the first part of the chapter. In describing the City of London, it is important to note that the City is not a static object of study. In particular, the character of the City has varied over the course of its history in four significant ways. First, it has consisted of a differing mix of industries over time, which, to an extent, have had different social and cultural structures. For example, Michie (1992) distinguishes over time between a commercial or trading City, a credit or banking City, a capital market City, and a client or financial services City, each of which has shown some degree of dominance over the course of the City's history. Second, the size of firms in the City has varied over time. Until quite recently, the size distribution of firms in the City was overwhelmingly biased towards small firms, although this has now changed. Third, it has varied over space. Until after the Second World War, the financial City of banking, capital markets and financial services occupied only a small part of the 'square mile' and it is only in comparatively recent times that the City has outgrown this boundary. Fourth, the numbers working in the City have fluctuated from 170,000 in 1866, to a peak of 500,000 in 1935 to about 300,000 in 1992 (even these numbers are difficult to rely on, since they depend upon what industries are counted as City industries).

All these comments made, it is still possible, and indeed conventional, to study the City as a relatively coherent whole and, in turn, to make a break between the 'traditional' City which existed before the death of Bretton Woods and the 'de-traditionalising' City which existed thereafter. The break therefore takes in the point at which the City casts off the gloom of a moribund wartime and postwar trough and becomes a dynamic international financial centre again, partly because of the progressive collapse of the Bretton Woods system which the City, as the major centre of the growing eurodollar market, had a hand in. The break also captures the point at which many social and cultural aspects of the City changed quite decisively in ways which are intimately linked to its transformation into an outpost of an electronic phantom state in which distinctions between 'inside' and 'outside' become increasingly difficult to make (Walker 1993).

THE 'TRADITIONAL' CITY: THE CITY OF LONDON
PRE-BRETTON WOODS

Before the death of the Bretton Woods system, the City's power to reproduce itself rested on four main foundation stones (Thrift 1994b). The first
of these was the City's relationship with the British state. Often the City was
described as a 'state within a state'. This is an exaggerated description since
at various times the British state intervened very effectively in the City in
ways which were undoubtedly to its detriment (Michie 1992). It is more
accurate to describe the City's relationship with the British state as 'meso-
corporatist' (Cawson 1986), one in which 'representation and regulation
were fused' (Moran 1991: 61). In other words, the City was able to maintain
a relatively self-contained system of collective governance, with the Bank of
England acting as a buffer against pluralist regulatory systems (Hennessy
1992; Sayers 1976).

The second foundation stone of the City's power to reproduce itself
consisted of a 'traditional' social structure, a 'gentlemanly order' (Cain and
Hopkins 1993a) based on highly visible class, gender and ethnic divisions
which in turn generated strong senses of self-identity. The divisions
provided the means with which it was possible to recognise the insider
and the outsider, the trustworthy and the non-trustworthy. Transgression of
these divisions was therefore a potentially serious social and/or cultural
offence.

In essence, until the 1960s, the City was composed of three relatively
distinct *class* strata. At the top of the pile were the directors and partners
of the numerous city firms (see e.g. Cassis 1987). In the past, these
directors and partners have often been seen as being drawn into the
landed gentry over the course of the nineteenth century, their collective
identity becoming increasingly bound up in aristocratic mores and
practices. Such a depiction of a kind of mimetic aristocracy is now
regarded with increasing suspicion. Current opinion on the class status of
the directors and partners of the City is probably best summarised by
Harris and Thane (1984: 83) who describe them as

> a distinct stratum, combining elements of bourgeois and aristocratic cultures
> but reducible to neither. It was a culture that (despite the trappings of
> landownership) was urban rather than rural, functionally progressive rather
> than reactionary, and combined grand dynastic aspiration with an un-
> pretentious devotion to the ethic of work.

This description became, if anything, increasingly accurate after the
professionalisation of British society in the late nineteenth century (Perkin
1989) with its systems of public schools and universities, which offered the
potential for City partners and directors to construct their own common
background. Thus, through the nineteenth and into the twentieth century
the proportion of partners and directors going through the mill of public
schools and Oxbridge gradually increased.

Of course, the directors and partners were not the only class stratum in the City. Increasingly, over time, they were joined by a professional and managerial middle class as a result of four linked processes. The first of these was the expanding system of professional institutions described above, and the credentials that resulted from them. The second process was the increasing demand for managers as firms increased in size. There were managers in the City in the 1830s but the chief influx was after the middle of the nineteenth century, as the retail banks and insurance companies increased markedly in size. The third process was an increasing demand for professionals, especially from the late nineteenth century. Indeed, some parts of the City suffered skill shortages because of lack of appropriate professionals (e.g. actuaries). The fourth process was simply the expanding division of labour which, by the end of the nineteenth century, led to the presence of 'hordes of specialists each making their own particular contribution to an increasingly complex process' of monetary creation and circulation (Michie 1988: 196).

There was one final class stratum which also needs to be noted. This was the clerical labour force. By 1866, commercial clerks in the City numbered 17,225 (20 per cent of all commercial clerks in Britain). At first, clerks tended to come from relatively elevated backgrounds but after the 1860s working-class clerks became more common. Even so, clerical wages were relatively high compared with the rest of the country, but reduced over time, probably reaching their lowest point in the 1950s. Clerks worked in diverse conditions. In the private banks, conditions were often paternalist. By contrast, in the developing stock banks and insurance companies, they tended to be more regimented.

The social atmosphere of the City was not just based on class, of course. It was characterised by other divides as well. Of these, the most important was *gender*. The City was a classically 'homosocial' (Kanter 1976) environment, based on the interaction of class and a severe form of masculinity that produced what, in retrospect, seem like stifling forms of masculine identity based on quaint uniforms, exact dress codes, various boyish market rituals and japes, heavy drinking, etc. Of course, to a degree such forms of identity were only exaggerations of upper- and upper middle-class British society at large, but it is difficult not to come to the conclusion that their weight was sufficient to have produced a distinctive City patina. Certainly, in the early 1960s, Sampson (1965: 26) still found the atmosphere stuffy and uninspiring:

> Nearly everyone wears a dark suit and carries an umbrella, and discount brokers and gilt-edged stockbrokers still wear top hats. The restaurants are crowded with rows of pale faced, blackcoated men.

The closed effect of this environment was considerably reinforced by a network of men-only social institutions that functioned inside and outside work and which were both mechanisms of social regulation and ways of extending contact networks and, by implication, trust. These social institutions were diverse. They included institutions with formal membership requirements like the City Corporation, the Livery Companies, the London Clubs, Freemasons' Lodges, and so on. They also included more general social arenas, of which the pubs and chophouses were perhaps the most important. All these institutions helped to dim the distinction between work and leisure: indeed, in a sense, for many a 'City man', work and leisure both involved mixing with the same round of people.

The effect of this homosocial environment was to exclude women from the City's labour force. Women first made an appearance as City workers in this forbidding environment only in 1872, as clerks at the Prudential Insurance Company (only daughters of 'professional men' were allowed to apply). By 1890, there were 200 female clerks at the Prudential. Then, in 1894, the Bank of England hired twenty-five female clerks, but, again, the conditions were strict: the women had to be nominated by directors of the Bank and they had to pass entrance examinations (in other words they had to be 'gentlewomen' of good family) (Sayers 1976).

The First and Second World Wars both saw large but temporary increases in female clerical labour in the City – for example, the Bank of England employed 400–500 women in the First World War, whilst in the Second World War women were allowed to become settling room clerks in that male bastion, the Stock Exchange (a 'privilege' promptly withdrawn in 1946) – but it was not until sometime after the Second World War that women appeared in the City in large numbers. By 1961, the proportion of women office workers was actually greater than the average for England and Wales and even for Central London (Pryke 1991), chiefly as a result of three labour force factors: the advent of the typewriter and shorthand, which produced both a system of credentials and an occupational niche for women, the fact that women could be paid less than men, and the possibility of excluding women from any real career structure.

Another important social schism in the City was based on *ethnicity*. Various social groups were seen as 'foreign' to the City's collective body. But this sense of foreignness was ambivalent, since the history of the City's success was in part based on a constant infusion of foreign immigrants, often as a result of persecution elsewhere in Europe (e.g. the Huguenots). There were three main 'foreign' presences in the City, often inter-connected. The first of these was the Anglo-Jewish group that had built up in the City. This group was seen as insiders (e.g. the Rothschilds and other Anglo-Jewish gentry) but also as outsiders. Indeed many of the group actively resisted assimilation into the City. Second, there was a constant stream of foreign immigrants, often German–Jewish, who set up in the City throughout the period and who were often very successful. Finally, note most be taken of the foreigners connected with the growth of foreign bank branches – which date from a surprisingly early point in the City's history. From the 1860s onwards, foreign banks had been established in the City. By 1910 there were twenty-eight such banks in the City, by 1913 there were thirty, including German, Japanese and Russian branches. These figures ignore the large number of colonial bank branches of the time. By 1938 there were eighty-five foreign bank branches in the City 'which was more than ever before despite the disappearance of German banks during the First World War and American banks in the wake of the 1929 crash' (Michie 1992: 82).

The ambiguous relationship with foreigners only rarely seems to have given way to outright hostility, usually as a result of warfare. For example, both world wars led to discrimination against particular groups, especially the Germans, who were excluded from membership of such bodies as the Baltic Exchange (Michie 1992: 44). But a more generalised scepticism about foreigners does seem to have been general. In particular, foreign firms were often looked down upon by City partners and directors, who routinely worked only from 10.00 a.m. to 4.00 p.m., for starting work early and finishing work late (which, it is now generally acknowledged, gave these firms a major competitive edge).

The third foundation stone of the City's power to reproduce itself was its knowledge base, consisting of an expanding archive of knowledge, particular kinds of expertise, and extensive networks of interconnected contacts. This network was vital to the City's reproduction as is evidenced by the example of the two world wars. Thus Michie (1992: 45) argues that

> the Second World War represented a disaster for the City's trading interests, not so much from the physical damage but from the loss of contacts and expertise. During the war, valuable contacts were lost, while key staff left with many not returning.

The crucial elements of this knowledge base were the discourses that structured it which in turn produced particular judgements about the worth of people and practices. The most obvious of these was the narrative of the 'gentleman' (sic), a widespread discourse based on values of honour, integrity and courtesy, and manifested in ideas of how to act, ways of talk, suitable clothing and so on. This gentlemanly discourse, in part imported from the aristocracy and in part from the new professionalisation, was sustained by the City's high level of face-to-face contacts, and the consequent need to be able to value people/business. In the famous words of Lord 'the first thing is character', by which was meant character of a gentlemanly type. Most especially, such a discourse enabled people to scent when contacts did not 'fit', when something was 'wrong'. In other words, the discourse enabled them to judge when, and when not, to extend trust and reciprocity. However, this discourse was hardly the only one circulating through the City. Many others did too, increasingly through the expanding medium of texts. In particular, through the nineteenth century the power of the financial press became much greater, as did the press's ability to distribute information, monitor actions, and so on. In other words, texts increasingly constituted 'the City'. They 'kept the City informed about itself' (Michie 1992: 184). Starting with *Lloyds List* in 1734 the financial press became increasingly important (Parsons 1989). Thus in 1825 *The Times* started a regular City Feature. In 1843 *The Economist* began to publish. In 1888 the *Financial Times* started up (from a merger with the *Financial News*). In 1983 the *Investors Chronicle* began life. Finally, the knowledge base of the City was also becoming increasingly specialised. This process was enshrined in a set of epistemic communities, each with their own particular vocabularies.

The fourth foundation stone of the City's power to reproduce itself came from spatial concentration. The City's activities were concentrated into a very small area with numerous recognisably monumental buildings that declared that the City was a centre of financial power. Further, this concentration was strongly policed. From the micro-space of the partners' rooms in the merchant banks to the larger spaces of streets and squares the City was spatially regulated. In particular, a multitude of rules and rounds kept the City in the City. There were, first of all, the rules about spatial location. For example, all Stock Exchange members had to maintain an office within 700 yards of the Exchange to meet settlement deadlines. There was an (unwritten) Accepting Houses rule that all members had to locate within the City. The Bank of England insisted that all foreign bank offices were in close proximity to it. Second, there were rules that were the result of the need to intermesh time and space in various settlement systems. There were the daily discount house rounds. There were the 'walks' of the banks, trodden each hour to pick up cheques and other paper to pay into the Bank of England. There were the various clearing systems. Most especially there was the cheque clearing system, used by the banks routinely but then extended to cover the Stock Exchange, insurance companies, and so on. 'General' clearing took place from 8.00 a.m. to 11.15 a.m. A later 'town' clearing took place at 3.50 p.m. Institutions had to be within a half mile radius of the Clearing House to be included in this system. Third, there were the numerous prohibited spaces that could only be gained entry to by insiders, from market floors to clubs.

The City was not just reproduced by these intricate intermeshings of time and space, important though they were in producing a coherent City space and confirming the identity of place and person. The spatial concentration of the workforce that resulted from these rules and rounds was mirrored by residential concentration. Until the early nineteenth century, this was the result of the isomorphism between City workplaces and residences. Then, over time, as commuting into the City grew and residence in the City declined, so specific City residential areas sprang up. For example, by the end of the nineteenth century, a specific 'stockbroker belt' had formed in the Home Counties which persisted into the 1950s (Cassis 1984, 1987).

However, this emphasis on spatial concentration can be misleading. Even in the nineteenth century there was no walled City. The world economy impinged in numerous ways. The thriving Port of London brought in a constant stream of visitors (and information) from overseas. There was a vast flow of bills and documents into and out of the City. Most importantly, the electronic space of flows so beloved of modern commentators had actually been a part of the City's operation over many years, the result of the invention and early application of the telegraph and telephone. The telegraph was first used in the City by Reuter in 1851 to transmit Stock Exchange prices between Paris and London. In 1866, the first telegraph connection was made between London and New York, with immediate effect on the rapidity of market adjustment between the two cities. The telegraph made it possible

> for the first time to trade systematically, and with a fair degree of confidence, in future delivery, rather than taking a gamble on a very risky speculation since it was possible to anticipate expected supply and demand with reasonable certainty . . . The telegraph, and later the telephone, and their use by intermediaries meant a qualitative change in the degree of risk . . .
>
> (Michie 1992: 55–63)

Again, the City had the first telephone exchange in Britain, in 1879, and had large numbers of telephone users early on – by 1910 the number of telephone subscribers had reached more than 10,000. In 1937 a telephone link between London and New York was installed. By 1939 there were three City telephone exchanges, serving some 46,000 subscribers. By 1940 it was already possible for one commentator to describe a foreign exchange dealing room of the 1930s in terms redolent of those used today:

> To describe exactly what goes on in the foreign exchange room of any of the big banks or foreign exchange brokers who compose the London Foreign Exchange market is beyond me. It is the nearest thing to Bedlam that I know – half a dozen men in a little room, shouting in incomprehensible jargon into Telephones, pushing switches up and down all the time in response to the flashing indicator lights.
>
> (Hobson 1940: 71)

The innovations of the telegraph and telephone certainly reduced the need for physical proximity in certain cases but this was not as strong a phenomenon as might have been expected. Rather, what seems to have happened is that to existing levels of contact was added the supplement of the electronic realm and the new markets it made possible. Thus, at certain times before the 1950s, the City, through this realm, was able to become the centre of both a *global* foreign exchange market and an integrated *global* securities market. Thus Michie (1992: 55–63) points out that, even before the First World War:

> with international communications transformed with the coming of the telegraph, and later the telephone, and the need to mobilise funds on a world scale for the finance of infrastructure developments, there appeared the possibility of creating global trading in securities. Information and orders could be quickly transmitted between exchanges and there existed a substantial pool of commonly-held securities, ownership of which could easily be changed between the nationals of different countries, especially in the absence of exchange controls. By 1913, securities with a paid-up value of $2 bn were common to both the London and New York Stock Exchanges, and it took less than a minute to communicate between the two.

THE DE-TRADITIONALISED CITY: THE CITY
OF LONDON POST-BRETTON WOODS

Since the decline of Bretton Woods in the 1960s the City of London has changed its nature. To a degree, this shift has been prompted by a number of related changes in the nature and extent of international financial systems which have boosted the City's competitive position. These have included: the rise of a privatised credit system on a global scale (and especially the euromarkets); the dramatic increase in the number, size, speed of response, volatility and interaction of markets, with a consequent increase in the general indeterminacy of the markets; an increase in risk and the need for risk management; the increase in rates of product/market innovations; the rise of large oligopolistic financial service firms; the rise of large institutional investors (pension funds, insurance companies) and block trades; large amounts of technological change, especially in the field of telecommunications, leading to greater computing power, the decline of fixed open outcry markets, and the rise of paperless settlement systems and the spread of American-style regulatory systems.

Changes like these may have contributed to the success of the post-Bretton Woods City but they have also included actual or potential threats to the City's ability to reproduce itself, which the City has had to contend with in a number of ways. Two chief threats are usually perceived. The first of these is technological change which, in principle at least, allows financial markets to operate from anywhere, bypassing accepted geographic centres. However, this threat may be exaggerated. To begin with, there are still some formidable technological obstacles to this decentred vision. For example, paperless settlement and clearing systems have proved extremely difficult to implement and, even now, the financial system's appetite for paper and paper transactions is voracious. But, more to the point, this may be to misrecognise the problem. Not only is the City the hub of many electronic networks but its frenzy of face-to-face interaction may be seen, as has been argued above, as increasingly the result of the vast penumbra of electronic networks that surround the City and the associated pressures of interpretation they exert. The second threat to the City is usually seen as arising from its changed relationship with the British state. The old meso-corporatist structure has faced unrelenting pressures – from technological change, from scandals and crises, and from the changing character of the British state (and, in particular, a new fair trading ideology and a greater inclination by those in government to intervene in City affairs). In turn, these pressures have led to the death of the monopoly powers of many of its institutions, typified by the desertion of one of the bastions of old-style regulation, the Stock Exchange, by the Bank of England in 1983 (Moran 1991). Thus, the old meso-corporatist structure has been replaced by new North-American-style regulatory structures. However, to an extent, one might again argue that the perception of this threat is overdone. The British state's ability to intervene in the City is limited by its ability to target the City inasmuch as much of what the City is has moved on to electronic networks which are outside formal state (or even parastatal) jurisdiction. In other words there is less 'there' to regulate.

But, given that the City's power to reproduce is under threat, how has it managed to stay at least relatively successful? There are three possible answers: its de-traditionalising social structure, its knowledge structure and spatial policing. We will address each of these in turn.

The traditional social structures on which the City's collective self-definition in large part relied have quite clearly weakened and, in some cases, even faded away. Certainly, transgression of the identities forged by these social structures is a much less serious offence than before. Thus, so far as class is concerned, it is still possible to find a core of old-style white, upper middle-class, homosocial merchant banks in which the directors and partners are recruited from only certain public schools and Oxbridge, as one 1986 survey found (Bowen 1986). Such results are echoed by one of Pahl's (1989) respondents in the late 1980s who noted that 'During most of these two years [in such a merchant bank], I was the only non-Etonian in the room and felt quite a social outcast.' But even these firms are nowhere near as closed as they were, especially if generational shifts are taken into account. Nor are they as influential: many of them are now relatively small firms in a larger complex of multinational financial services firms. Thus, *pace* Cain and Hopkins (1993b), we do not believe that the old gentlemanly order has survived into the present.

Increasingly, expertise and influence in the City reside in a reflexive group of managers and professionals. These managers and professionals have a more heterogeneous social background, partly because in the 1970s and 1980s the City was forced to recruit from a wider pool of people to satisfy its demand for more and more skilled labour and partly because, even though many managers and professionals are still recruited from independent schools and from Oxford, Cambridge and a 'milk run' of other universities like Bristol, Durham and Exeter, the social class constitution of these institutions has become more heterogeneous (see chapter 5).

The influx of managers and professionals in such large numbers is relatively new.

> As late as 1965, few university careers advisers would mention finance as a possible choice for a first class honours student; it would be regarded as having rather low social status, and was seen to be unsuccessful and out of political fashion.
>
> (Fay, 1970: 23)

In 1961, for example, the proportion of managers in the City was lower than in the rest of Central London, and England and Wales. By the 1980s it was much higher. The influx was the result of a number of processes, including a more complex division of labour, an increasing foreign (especially North American) presence which encouraged more meritocratic selection procedures, an increase in the requirements for credentials, greater financial rewards and earlier career responsibility.

The primacy of professionals and managers was underlined by a considerable decline in the number of clerical workers, especially as a result of the general decentralisation of low-skilled jobs out of London. Many of these clerical jobs were held by women and this brings us conveniently on to the question of gender.

The homosocial environment of the City has also weakened as the gender composition of the City has changed. After the Second World War, there was a rapid increase in the number of women working in the City, but nearly all these women were clerical workers who were socially and spatially segregated from the City's homogeneity by prevailing codes of sexuality, by the gendered nature of the labour process, and by these women's class position – many were working-class women from the East End. Even in the early 1970s, Sampson (1972: 67) could still write of these female clerical workers as almost a separate race which was

> automatically segregated in sandwich bars or canteens. The austere masculinity frightens away the more sophisticated secretaries who prefer the brightness and shops of the West End. The City remains the stronghold of male domination, whether social or financial, and women are kept out of nearly all the centres of its power.

But since the 1970s, the social composition of women in the City has changed. Thus, even as clerical jobs have been declining, women have been able to keep and, in some cases, increase their proportional presence in the City because of the influx of professional and managerial women, especially into jobs which require skills and credentials, because they have increasingly been able to take up jobs which require high-level social interaction.

The result is that women have to be admitted into what were once segregated male-only spaces. In turn, this change has required a renegotiation of modes of identification by both men and women. As one woman put it: 'I was not sure what my universe of men expected from me, but often neither were they' (Davies 1993: 33). Most research has been into the problems faced by women in the City (e.g. McDowell 1993). For example, professional and managerial women have had to take care in how they are identified in matters like dress: 'If you dressed casually it would be quite difficult for people to distinguish between you and a secretary' (cited in Dix 1990: 171).

Ethnic divisions within the City have also been declining as a result of the increasing cosmopolitanism of the City (Hannerz 1992). There are now a large number of foreign workers in the City. There are more British workers, working for the large number of foreign financial service firms. More British workers also have considerable overseas experience, especially as a result of secondments. Indeed, for many professionals and managers overseas experience is a vital part of their career (Beaverstock 1991). In turn, the new cosmopolitanism has had other effects. For example, US banks and securities houses are more likely to hire women, and more likely to promote them to positions of responsibility. (However, it is worth noting that lower down the hierarchy, the City's record in hiring British people who belong to ethnic minorities has not been outstanding – see Rajan (1990) and Rajan and Fryatt (1988).)

The weakening of the social structures on which the old City's integrity was based has gone hand in hand with a heightening of the City's reflexivity. In the past, the City's business was chiefly based on face-to-face contacts which were made in order to stabilise relations of trust and reciprocity. However, much of the content of these transactions was fore-ordained, since they involved reading 'badges of office' which were readily recognisable signs of class, gender and ethnicity. This was what was meant by the famous phrase 'the first thing is character'. But, in current circumstances, the need for reflexivity has been much enhanced: because of the pressures for interpretation and negotiation arising out of electronic texts; because of the need to be able to gather information in a hurry so as to make appropriate market responses (which requires carefully tutored social networks); because of the general tendency in society towards greater reflexivity, leading to a greater emphasis on presentation of self, face-work, negotiating skills, and so on; because of the increasing requirement to be able to read people because the signs of their social positions are no longer necessarily foreordained; and because of the increasingly uncertain 'transactional' nature of business relationships between firms and clients. Thus trust now has to be *constituted* through *work on relationships*, not *read off* from *signs of trustworthiness*. The formal gavottes of the Old City have therefore become much more complicated dances: 'the first thing is presentation of self'.

This increased emphasis on reflexivity in the City has another consequence. The City's thick network of social institutions not only still exists but is actually thriving. In the past, such institutions were the continuation of the social structures of work by other means: places where the extant social structures of the City were confirmed and reinforced. Now they have become places in which to do face-work much more actively: to make contacts, to check people out, to tap into and to transmit discourses. There is certainly an enormous web of such social institutions including the City Corporation (with 18,000 on the electoral roll in 1990), the Livery Companies (there are eighty-three guilds in the City with new ones still coming into existence, such as the Company of Information Technologists), the London Clubs which were very successful in the 1980s, and the Freemasons' Lodges (of which there are hundreds, including special Lodges for the Bank of England, Lloyds, and so on).

Of course, none of the foregoing is meant to suggest that social divisions no longer exist in the City. They clearly do. For example, women are still excluded from many City social networks because so many of the City's social institutions are still men only (although it is also the case that women have set up their own networks such as Women in Banking and the City Women's Network). However, we would suggest that these social divisions have weakened (Beck 1992) and that, as a consequence, the need for reflexivity has become greater. In this, the City has now become much closer to the rest of British society (e.g. the managerial and professional women in the City that McDowell (1993) describes have the same problems of identification in every other sector of British industry). If the City's social structure is still able to claim any uniqueness, then, it is probably on the basis of its very high degree of reflexivity: the City is, even more than in the past, a 'communicative commotion' (Shotter 1989) that enables money capitalists – from corporate financiers to stock market traders – to interpret and construct their world.

To summarise, collective self-definition has widened and weakened in the City. People come from more diverse social backgrounds. As a result, the networks that run the City are increasingly constructed out of the demands of reflexivity and not just social structure. Personal relationships are still vital in the City but they have to be worked at, rather than through, constructed for their own sakes rather than for the sake of maintaining social structures. Indeed, this tireless working on relationships – whether face to face or at a distance – is now, more than ever, the primary focus of the City. The City no longer looks for the signs of trust; it constructs them.

Such an emphasis on the City as a reflexivity machine also begins to account for why the second foundation stone of the City's power to reproduce itself has become more important. That is, quite simply, the City's role as a knowledge structure at the heart of numerous discourse networks. Clearly the City has seen an explosion of information on the financial services industry, and expertise in interpreting and disseminating that information, which has manifested itself in four very closely related ways. First, and as already pointed out, the City is a nexus of *face-to-face* communication through which information is interpreted – and gathered. Second, the City is a centre for *electronic* information gathering and transmission. For example, by 1989 Reuters 'maintained 184 300 screens worldwide, providing groups of customers not only with instant access to information, but also allowing groups of them to communicate with each other, and so provide an international electronic market-place' (Michie 1992: 185). Third, the City is a centre of *textual* interpretation, whether the texts are printed or read from screens. The text can be a quotation system, a credit rating, a research analyst's report or even a humble tipsheet. But, most particularly, the City is now a centre of the *global financial media* – including *Euromoney, The Banker, The Economist,* and the *Financial Times.* The *Financial Times* started a continental European edition in 1979, with a New York edition following in 1985. By 1993, 40 per cent of the paper's circulation was abroad (Kynaston 1989; *Financial Times* 1993). The newspaper has now extended into television programmes, as well as numerous reports and conferences. Fourth and finally, the City is increasingly home to many different global 'epistemic communities', occupational communities each with their own specialised vocabularies, rhetorics, knowledges, practices and texts. From economists to foreign exchange dealers to eurobond traders, each of these communities tends to live in an increasingly specialised narrative world.

This emphasis on discursivity extends in other ways. Increasingly, the City markets itself as a centre of 'cultural authority' for global financial services. It is a place where people meet from around the world because of its associations with finance (and the knowledge, expertise and contracts concentrated there). In turn, the City has consciously begun to play to this role. The old gentlemanly discourse may have dissolved but the 'trappings of trust' still remain: quiet, wood-panelled dining rooms, crested china, discount round top hats, City police uniforms, etc., are all used to 'brand' the City, to boost its image of solidity and trustworthiness. 'The rediscovery of tradition is the key to City trendsetting' (Pugh 1989: xx). Indeed, so prominent has this heritage style become that it might be argued that it has spilled over even into City 'fashion' for men. In the 1960s, the City seemed to begin to reflect broader trends in British society. There were distinct signs of a loosening of the sartorial ties: one author of the time noted the presence of 'bright ties', 'soft collars', 'bright blue silky suits with a transatlantic feel', even 'ties with horizontal stripes in the continental fashion' (Fay 1970). But by the 1980s a strict dress code had reasserted itself to an even greater extent than in Britain as a whole, one based on the dark suit: 'if you're not in a suit, you're invisible'; 'if you're not in a suit you must be a bike boy delivering sandwiches' (Pugh 1989: 126). The dress code varied with age, with younger people tending to dress more sharply in bright shirts and ties and partners and directors clothed in tailored suits but there are few signs of life outside the suit. Even the much vaunted (and rather rare) working-class 'barrow boy' traders conformed (Kahn and Cooper 1993). Only the bright trading floor jackets of the London International Financial Futures Exchange (LIFFE) showed any measure of sartorial difference.

One might assume from all this that the last foundation stone of the City's power to reproduce itself, its tight spatial orbit, would melt away. Certainly there are at least three indicators of dissolution. First, the controls on the bounds of the City are much less strong than before. For example, in 1985 the Bank of England decided to take a less directive role in where foreign bank offices could locate (Pryke 1991). Further, many of the walks and rounds which acted as a kind of socio-spatial glue are also dying out as electronic settlement systems come on line. Second, and as this example shows, the City's space is itself increasingly electronic. 'The City' is no longer fixed in the same way. Its space includes a massive shadow world of electronic networks. Third, the City's workers are now increasingly mobile. Many of them have lived abroad. Many of them spend much of their time travelling.

Yet, the City shows surprisingly few signs of deconstructing in the face of these tendencies. Since the 1960s it has become larger in extent, gradually extending its boundaries north and across the river. A few foreign bank offices have moved to the West End. Back-office operations tend to be dotted around London. Yet few foreign bank offices have moved very far away. London Docklands never really took off as an extension of the City. The spatial matrix of the City has enlarged only a little. Why? There are three main reasons, reasons which go to the heart of this chapter.

First, the need for face-to-face contact has not diminished. Indeed it has been argued above that it has, if anything, become greater as the need for reflexivity has increased. Second, there is little evidence to suggest that the growth of electronic space necessarily threatens the spatial integrity of the City. As has also been argued above, it may even help it to cohere. Further, it is worth pointing out again that the history of the City has been tied into this space of flows for over 100 years now. For example, in 1956, the Foreign Exchange market reopened as an all-telephone market and has operated in such a mode ever since. Even in 1967, 3 million telephone calls into and out of the City were being made daily (excluding inter office calls) (Dunning and Morgan 1971). This figure has clearly increased since then as a result of expanding business, satellite communications, computing demands, faxes, and so on. In other words, electronic communication seems to have fuelled the connectedness of the City by acting as a supplement to face-to-face communication, rather than an alternative, increasing the overall amount of communication between the City and the rest of the world (and this is to ignore the corresponding increase in paper communication, indexed by the rise in postal items delivered in, into and out of the City and by the rise of the motorbike messenger). Third, the increase in mobility actually seems to have helped the City to continue to cohere. The City is now an important transient space for international financiers, a place to do business. It has become a global node for circulating stories, sizing up people and doing deals. Thus, at any one time, much of the City's population will consist of visitors, but they are not incidental. They are part of why the City continues to exist. They are part of the communicative commotion that places the City in the electronic spaces of global finance.

CONCLUSIONS: A PHANTOM STATE?

We want to conclude this chapter by drawing on a distinction that Habermas (1992) makes between money power, administrative power and communicative power to add a certain nuance to the preceding parts of this chapter. In these preceding sections, we have very tentatively outlined the rise of a new 'phantom state', both constituting and representing money power, that is based on the communicative power of electronic networks and a few, selected (g)localities. It consists of actor–networks which increasingly rely on money power and communicative power without having to call on the degree of bureaucratic administrative power usually associated with the state form.

One reason for the success of this new kind of state has been the continuing evolution of a 'public sphere' for money capitalists. As Habermas (1992) points out, an extended public sphere was originally able to develop, at least in part, because of the ability of early merchants (many of whom were the precursors of money capitalists), combined with the discovery of new communicative techniques associated with print, to extend market economies beyond local arenas, leading to long-distance trafficking in commodities, financial instruments, news and opinion: 'the flow of international news attendant on the growth of trading networks generated a new category of public knowledge and information' (Eley 1992: 291). This archetypal public sphere was the prototype of a more general bourgeois public sphere that grew up in the eighteenth and nineteenth centuries between the state and the market.

But now, we might speculate, two changes have come about. First, the public sphere has split into a number of interlocking but increasingly self-contained 'public' spheres. One of these spheres belongs to money capitalists. In this sphere they are able to use money power to operate at very high levels of discursivity. Thus money power, especially through the construction of electronic networks and localities, drives communicative power. But the presence of this particular public sphere also shows how communicative power increasingly drives money power. In this sense, the discourses of money have become money. Second, none of this could have happened to the same degree if it were not for the decline in the administrative power deployed by the nation state. To an extent at least, the old nation state form has been outfoxed by a combination of money power and communicative power. In one sense, the power of the new 'phantom state' is still based in institutions, but in another sense it is based in the flow of communication itself. To this extent, Habermas (1992: 452) may be wrong to write that:

> The responsibility for practically consequential decisions must be based in an institution. Discourses do not govern. They generate a communicative power that cannot take the place of administration but can only influence it. This influence is linked to the procurement and withdrawal of legitimation. Communicative power cannot supply a substitute for the systematic inner logic of public bureaucracies.

More and more, we might argue that, in the modern world, money power and communicative power have been able to replace state authority based on administrative power with a discursive authority which is based in electronic networks and particular 'world cities'. This discursive authority is the stuff of a phantom state whose resonances are increasingly felt by all.

CHAPTER 10

NEW URBAN ERAS AND OLD TECHNOLOGICAL FEARS

Reconfiguring the goodwill of electronic things

INTRODUCTION

My approach will be marked by mechanical confidence or creative uncertainty, according to whether I consider everything to be worked out in advance or everything to be there for the taking . . .

(Guattari 1995: 134)

Introduction 1

What is 'new'? It is only recently that the question of novelty has been explicitly addressed by writers in the social sciences. Yet the idea of novelty is at the root of these writers' *raison d'être* since the delegation of what is (and what is not) 'new' is a critical part of these practices. Most particularly, this delegation is bound up with conceptions like 'modernity' whose very existence depends upon the identification of a different time in which novelty is continually and remorselessly generated (Osborne 1995). Nowhere is the question of novelty brought into starker relief than in recent work on electronic communication technologies. For many writers these technologies are the living proof of a powered-up modernity, and one of the lemmas of this proof is that these technologies are self-evidently 'new' (Henning 1995). To expound any other point of view is to be open to the criticism of a 'retro-orientation' which denies the existence of a whole new world of 'warp-speed accelerations', 'telecommercial hyper-manic cultures', 'hungrily expanding spatialities', and 'virtual human obsolescence' (Land 1995).

But, in principle at least, this view of the role of the new electronic telecommunications cultures is not one that automatically has to be drawn upon. We want to suggest that the elements of an alternative account, an account which ranges itself against the bluster and hyperbole of the epic and epochal accounts which are now almost automatically associated with writing on the new electronic telecommunications technologies, are starting to be put in place.

This account will be made up from the following elements: an attention to the cultural practices of electronic communications technology, of the kind found in the literature on computer-mediated control of work (Star 1995); an attempt to refigure the relationship between people and machines that leaves neither term inside or outside of the other one but brings both terms together in specific actor–networks; and a turning away from the sterile notion of modernity towards notions of historical change which are slow moving, complex and interconnected, and in pieces (Latour 1993).

At one level, this stance simply allows the history of electronic telecommunication technologies to be seen as long and sinuous, as evolutionary rather than revelatory: 'what we have is not so much a digital culture in the sense of new media overtaking and displacing old ones, as the increasing digitalisation of older media' (Henning 1995: 231). For example, Winston (1995: 230–1), in reply to one of Bukatman's (1993a) more extreme paragraphs describing the advent of a new information age, writes:

> Telephones worked by 1880, television by the early 1930s. Digitalisation, the key to the current phase of development was demonstrated as a technique in 1938. A computer ran a factoring programme in 1948. And the convergence of these technologies, via telephony, has gone on as each has come on-stream.
>
> If one adds gestation periods, one can note that the essential architecture of the computer was first articulated in 1837, the physics of the solid-state electronic device were outlined in 1879, the idea of television was patented in 1884, and the basic mathematics of digitalisation theorised in 1928. Indeed if one were to conceptualise these developments as starting with the physical exploration of electromagnetic phenomenon one could say that they had been coming on-stream for the better part of two centuries – or even four.
>
> So what has been proliferating recently? Certainly not television screens and telephone wires which have been diffused for decades. The cable television system has been building since the late 1940s. As for digital devices in the home, they are not yet as ubiquitous as analog television and telephones, despite being introduced in 1974 (Atari Video Game), 1976 (Apple II Computer) and 1978 (CDs). It is therefore two decades since this 'new' three-pronged domestic 'proliferation' of the digital began.

But at another level, this stance is part of a more general attempt to refigure historical change as a complex set of different times which: conjures up a 'present' which no longer has to be considered as contemporary; produces a past which is no longer out of date; and constructs a future which is no longer the race for first place. As Serres (in Serres and Latour 1995: 45) puts it:

> In order to say 'contemporary', we must already be thinking of a certain time and thinking of it in a certain way . . . . So let's put the question differently: What things are contemporary? Consider a late-model car. It is a disparate aggregate of scientific and technical solutions dating from different periods. One can date it component by component: this part was invented at the turn of the century, another, ten years ago, and Carnot's cycle is almost two

hundred years old. Not to mention that the wheel dates back to neolithic times. The ensemble is only contemporary by assemblage, by its design, its finish, sometimes only by the slickness of the advertising surrounding it.

This chapter is a first attempt to sort out some of these issues as they impinge upon how we attend to electronic communication technologies. Our intention is to produce narratives of these technologies which do not attempt to impose a particular additive and singular politics of time by hijacking history in the name of the new.

Introduction 2

There is a mode of writing about electronic telecommunications technologies which is now becoming ubiquitous. According to this body of literature what we are seeing is nothing less than a new dimension coming into existence. This new space (and, interestingly, it is nearly always a space) goes under many names – Graham (1996) lists the 'space of flows' (Castells 1989); 'postmodern hyperspace' (Jameson 1984); the 'netscape' (Hemrick 1992); the 'network' (Harasim 1993); 'data spaces' (Murdoch 1993); 'telegeography' (Staple 1992) and 'cyberspace' (Gibson 1986; Benedikt 1991) to name just a few – but they all signify the same thing:

> The space of information. This proliferating multidimensional space is virtual, densely webbed, and infinitely complex, a vast and sublime realm accessed through the mediation of our imaginative and technical representations. How powerfully we engage this information space depends on how powerfully we both manipulate and inhabit these representations, these phantoms ghosting the interface.
>
> (Davis 1993: 86)

Cue moody or even menacing music, soaring corporate towers that are lit up like Christmas trees, slowly moving rivers of headlights, and all the other sub-*Blade Runner* clichés we now see almost nightly on television documentaries about the growth of cyberspace.

What is interesting is how often the space of information is represented in these urban terms: as a parallel urban landscape with its own key nodes of command and control; as a means of visualising information space with databases transformed into corporate towers and computer networks into information highways; and, more generally, as a means of generating all manner of new metaphors and metonyms. At the same time, the modern city is itself transformed by its information space 'shadow'. Thus Graham (1996) can also list the contemporary city redescribed as the 'non-place urban realm' (Webber 1968), as 'the invisible city' (Batty 1990); 'the informational city' (Castells 1989); 'the wired city' (Dutton *et al.* 1987); 'the telecity' (Fathy 1991); 'the intelligent city' (Laterasse 1992); 'the virtual city' or 'the virtual community' (Rheingold 1994); 'the electronic community' (Poster 1990), 'the overexposed city' (Virilio 1987); and even 'teletopia' (Piorinski 1991).

In this chapter, we want to lay down a challenge to the kinds of 'new era' accounts of information spaces which we usually associate with those kinds of urban clichés. Three of these new era accounts seem to hold a particular power at present. The first consists of *fin-de-siècle* celebrations of the end of life as we know it, which usually involve a good helping of the kind of 'reverse humanism' (Poster 1995) favoured by Baudrillard, De Landa (1991), Kroker and Weinstein (1994), and Land (1994, 1995). The second account is made up of doom-laden pronouncements about our acquiescence to the means–end values embedded in high technology which duly threaten our ability to encounter experience meaningfully. Dating especially from a revival of interest in Heidegger's discussion of technology and Habermas's later ruminations on instrumental reason, recent examples of these pronouncements can be found in Feenberg (1991) and Simpson (1995). Finally, there are solipsistic ramblings of the 'me and my computer' variety which paint the technological experiences of the author as somehow symptomatic of a postmodern culture (e.g. Wiley 1995; Spender 1995).

We want to argue that each of these very different accounts of information spaces tends to sink very quickly into remarkably similar forms of 'highway hype', 'techno-babble', or 'digital dreaming', inflated claims about the power of electronic communications technologies which commit one or more of a series of besetting sins.[1] In particular, these accounts seem to us to be: motivated by a passion for absolute certainty and order, masquerading as its opposite; transfixed by a series of elite representational discourses caught up in their own denial; and driven by a desire to fix on metaphors of modern life like speed, circulation and travel, which were already tired before they were recycled last time around. Ironically, the real message of each of these accounts of informational spaces seems to be '*inevitability* – not what the future *might* hold, but the inevitable hold of the present over the future – what the future could not fail to see' (Landon 1989: 143). Most depressing of all, too often these accounts seem to lack any *social* dimension, the sense that living, breathing, corporeal human beings arrayed in various creatively improvised networks of relation and affinity still exist as something more than machine fodder, and that human concerns like 'sex, death, race, and gender strongly infiltrate (each) little corner of cybernetic paradise, just as they inhabit the visionary musings of any-one concerned with how the cultural tensions of today will unfold in the unpredictable worlds of tomorrow' (Springer 1994: 732).

Why should this be? Why should these accounts so quickly slough off the uncertain and the human? We want to argue that, whether these accounts of new informational spaces claim to predict the future (as some of the more 'economic' accounts actually seem to want to do) or are operating in a 'symptomatic mode', providing a prognosis about the place of technology in current western societies, or recognise themselves as 'not primarily about understanding new technologies but rather how to take active pleasure in them' (Springer 1993), they have all retained deeply engrained habits of reading technology which 'date from exigencies of the industrial and resolutely patriarchal nineteenth century' (Springer 1993), habits which even now can still be encapsulated in the phrase 'technological determinism'.

This chapter is about how we can begin to expunge these habits so that we can, at last, begin to see our technological landscapes in a non-deterministic way. In turn that means that we have to modify our claims to knowledge, and no longer attempt to conjure up images of the world as a purified order, comprised of epics and tragedies, but rather see it as a commotion of situated knowledges which we can only ever chip away at (Thrift 1996).

This chapter is therefore in three parts. In the first part, we want to outline some of the nineteenth-century habits of technological determinist thinking that still reveal themselves in 'new era' writing on new informational dimensions and city forms. We want to argue that these habits of thinking cannot hold and we want to sketch some alternatives which can 'move us away from what has turned equally sour – cultural nostalgia and technological euphoria' (Pfeiffer 1993: 12). In the second part of the chapter we want to fix on what is currently one of the most concentrated examples of an 'informational space', the City of London. Here we want to show that this space, replete with instantaneous communications, real-time corporate databases, artificial intelligences, and the like, is also the most social of places, partly *because* it now exists in 'cyberspace'. Finally, by way of a double conclusion to the chapter we want to point to what *does* seem to be novel about the present technological conjuncture by attempting to listen to the groans and whispers of previous historical experiences.

NEW ERAS, OLD ERRORS

From the postal system and the electric telegraph to the telephone and the computer, every major innovation in the transmission and processing of information has been hailed by contemporary observers as a harbinger of a new order of the ages.

(John 1994: 101)

It is always dangerous to generalise, but we might say that new era accounts of informational spaces and their accompanying telematic cities have been characterised by the following identifiers:

- they are produced by the rise of electronic networks and databases;
- they invoke new modes of time (Lash and Urry 1994; Urry 1994) including an instantaneous world time which results in 'a type of *general arrival* in which everything arrives so quickly that departure becomes unnecessary' (Virilio 1993: 8; Pinney 1992), and a new 'depthless' historical time (Jameson 1991);
- they signal new spatial logics which respect none of the apparently Newtonian constructs of space which characterise our physical lives in cities;

- they are connected to the rise of images and signs as the means by which our society makes sense of itself;
- they deal in metaphors of flow, movement and circulation;
- they speculate about new means of control, based on telecommunications (Deleuze 1991);
- they provide new options for commodification;
- they provide a challenge to current forms of subjectivity or, *in extremis*, they challenge the notion of subjectivity itself, thereby generating new subject positions which Bukatman (1993a: 26), for example, calls 'terminal identities': 'an unmistakably doubled articulation in which we find the end of the subject and a new subjectivity constructed at the computer station or television screen';
- they question corporeality, even suggesting it may have had its day.

Now, what we do not want to do here is to describe the exact status of these changes – whether they are happening, the pace at which they are happening, and so on. We are, it is true, suspicious of some (but not all) of the claims and even more suspicious of their extent (Thrift 1995), and other authors share these views. For example, Woudhuysen (1994) has documented at some length the history of exaggeration associated with new era writing, and the reasons why new informational spaces and telematic cities will never reach the ascendancy that is often claimed for them. But what we are more concerned with here is how new era accounts are made over discursively into techno-epics heralding techno-epochs and how we can forge alternatives to this strategy which recognise the importance of new technologies without either jettisoning the human or assuming that it is under mortal threat (Poster 1995).

Why do we find that new era accounts so often end up producing masculine fantasies of omnipotent machine power or of human beings set free by machines? There are two reasons. One is quite straightforward and is hardly either surprising or unique in the social sciences. These accounts have 'an a priori agenda which overdetermines their readings of their materials, without any care for their historical placement or their generic properties' (Barker 1995: 189). The other reason is more subtle but, ultimately, more important. These accounts have bumped up against the limits of nineteenth-century thinking on electronic telecommunications technology, limits which, with the benefit of several rounds of techno-logical hindsight – from the telegraph on – are now much clearer to see than was perhaps once the case.

Let us expand on this latter point. We want to call on the thinking from the period when these 'old technologies were new', to use Carolyn Marvin's (1988) felicitous phrase, and especially thinking about the telegraph and the telephone which produced the prototypical electronic informational spaces, to illuminate the problems that we still face in thinking about technologies now (Marvin 1988; Czitrom 1982; John 1994). As we find now with their contemporary descendants, these 'new electronic media were sources of endless fascination and fear, and provided constant fodder for social experimentation' (Marvin 1988: 9).

When we look back at this thinking, we can see that the commentators of the time ran up against eight main imaginative borders, borders which still seem to persist and which, taken together, describe the kind of thinking that we want to label technological determinism. First of all, commentators tended to fix on and argue from *extremes*. Thus, the usage of a new electronic telecommunications technology in one particular way was too often extended to how it would be used overall and everywhere. For example, the early commentators on the telephone were convinced it would mainly be a tool of business. Domestic appliances were rarely considered (Fischer 1992).

Second, these technologies were assumed to replace technologies that had gone before. Thus, attention was focused on the new technologies to the exclusion of the old with the result that the combination of 'modern' technologies with 'anachronistic' technologies was rarely if ever considered, whilst the real alternatives that existed at particular points in time were written out (Gershuny 1992).

Third, new electronic telecommunications technologies were nearly always presented as *de novo*, prompted by the enthusiastic writings of the scientists and engineers for whom these technologies were important investments. They were described as smooth, crystalline systems, which rarely broke down and needed repair. In particular, these systems seemed to need no work to keep going. The mistakes and imaginative improvisations which are normal elements of technological systems were almost never mentioned, thereby writing out much of these technologies' human component.[2]

Fourth, the new electronic communications technologies were nearly always presented as a coherent, consistent and cumulative whole. Yet, recent historical analysis suggests they often had divergent effects, and operated in different ways for different people, at different periods in history as particular technologies and their accepted uses evolved.

Fifth, new electronic communications technologies were often assumed to be likely to spread everywhere rapidly, and to have the same effects everywhere and rapidly, a kind of 'techno-orientalism' that, in part, has been linked to nineteenth-century fantasies of empire, and especially to the fantasy of the empire as a total archive of information gathered up through the new technologies (Richards 1993; Barker 1995). Thus, it is worth remembering that, even now, between a third and a half of the world's population still lives more than two hours from the nearest telephone (Sabbagh 1994).[3] Equally, it seems unlikely 'that participation in the emerging information, imaging and communications technologies will ever (in the meaningful future) expand beyond a minority of people on the planet' (Crary 1994: 20).

Sixth, new technologies were rarely seen as part of a linked repertoire of practices. But no technology is ever found working in splendid isolation as though it is the central node of the social universe. It is linked – by the social purposes to which it is put – to humans and other technologies of different kinds. It is linked to a chain of other activities involving other technologies. And, it is heavily contextualised. Thus the telephone, say, at someone's place of work had (and has) different meanings than the telephone in, say, their bedroom, and is often used in quite different ways.

Seventh, the metaphorical structure that was used to understand the onset of new electronic telecommunications technologies nearly always configured them as part of a second, usually distanced, nature. The primary reference point was usually the orders (and disorders) of the human body (Armstrong 1992; Marvin 1988; Nye 1990; Selzer 1992). The metaphors of change were waves, shocks, currents and various natural disasters, and the stories were of how this second nature would bite back. For example, one common concern was that people's subjectivity would come under threat. As one commentator described the new electrical age:

> It seems to us that we are getting perilously near the ideal of the modern utopia when life is to consist of sitting in armchairs, and pressing a button. It is not a desirable prospect; we shall have no work, no money, no motivation, no youth, no vices, no individuality.
>
> (*The Electrician*, cited in Marvin (1988: 124))

Another concern was that people's bodies would be transformed, made over into electronic machines. Thus:

> Nineteenth century observers were especially interested in how men might change their biological constitutions or their ways of waging war in response to machine imperatives, and both experts and laymen wondered how man measured up to electricity conceived as a supernatural or supercultural form. Perhaps electrical machines were cultural artifacts superior to man himself. Perhaps they were debased cultural forms, or perhaps they were a highly advanced form of nature, destined to drive man from his fragile position in the cosmos, rather than to help him establish its security.
>
> (Marvin 1988: 141)

Eighth, and finally, new technologies were *re-presented* through texts and in images. These re-presentations, which tend to accord primacy to textuality and imageability, inevitably filtered out the performative 'presentations', the 'showings' and the 'manifestations', that characterise technology actually *in use* (Thrift 1996). In turn, these re-presentations washed away other important aspects of new technologies. In particular, they tended to underplay the sensuous nature of their presence in lived experience, what Prendergast (1992) has called 'epidermal sensibility'. But, of course, new technologies always register in a whole series of sensory modes – the ocular, but also the tactile, kinesthetic and auditory. For example, reading involves not just the art of seeing but also the feel of the paper, the smell of the book, and so on. That the sensuous nature of new technologies was lost was also, at least, in part, the result of the way in which intellectual commentators tended to use people to 'represent the most creative energies and functions of critical reading. In the end they are not simply the cultural student's object of study, his native informants. The people are also the textually delegated, allegorical emblem of the critic's own activity' (Morris 1988: 17).

Nowadays, these bounds to thinking about new technology are often encapsulated as four different but related traps that we fall into when writing about technology and society. First, writing about new technologies has nearly always involved the idea of a purified system which moves indomitably on its way through a society, an unstoppable glacier, changing all before it and stamping out everything behind it. But, as Latour (1993: 138) has pointed out, the idea that such purified systems exist is the enemy of good social science:

> Where does the threat come from? From those who seek to reduce (the *anthropos*) to an essence and who – by scanning things, objects, machines and the social, by cutting off all delegations and senders – make humanism a fragile and precious thing at risk of being overwhelmed by nature, society and God.

Or, one might add, technology. In other words, we need to return to more modest and less formidable ideas of technology as implicated in actor–networks which take work to build up and maintain:

> Take some small business-owner hesitatingly going after a few market shares, some conqueror trembling with fever, some poor scientist tinkering in his lab, a lowly engineer piecing together a few more or less favourable relationships of force, some stuttering and fearful politicians; turn the critics loose on them, and what do you get? Capitalism, imperialism, science, technology, domination – all equally absolute, systematic, totalising. In the first scenario, the actors were trembling; in the second they were not. The actors in the first scenario could be defeated; in the second they no longer can. In the first scenario, the actors were still quite close to the modest work of fragile and modifiable mediations, now they are purified and they are all equally formidable.
>
> (Latour 1993: 126)

Second, the idea of technologies as purified systems can take hold because societies are depicted as smoothly functioning wholes through which technologies can pass unproblematically, rather than as only partly connected networks through which technologies pass not *unevenly*, *but differently*, providing complex outcomes which are mediated in numerous ways. (The importance of difference is only accentuated in the case of electronic technologies which demand an active relationship with their users (Strathern 1992).)

Third, and following on, too often these purified technological systems are, to use Bernstein's (1994) phrase, 'foreshadowed'. That is, they provide an apocalyptic history of inevitable moments leading inevitably towards a predefined goal or fate which historians already know, a goal or fate in which everything becomes faster, and more compressed in space and time, more commodified, and so on. This logic of historical inevitability depends upon the dubious idea that history has a coherence other than what we impress upon it. It is rather like someone running through the town after the Pruitt-Igoe Flats were dynamited in 1972 shouting 'postmodern capitalism has begun'. (In its most pernicious variant, foreshadowing leads to what Bernstein (1994: 16) calls 'backshadowing' in which 'the shared knowledge of the outcome of a series of events by narrator and listener is used to judge the participants in those events, as though they too should have known what was to come'. Found most commonly in retroactive accounts of the Shoah, this practice is also common in accounts of the onset of new technologies.)

Fourth, too many accounts of purified and purifying technology systems suppose that they form part of a general erosion of the social and that we are moving inevitably towards a more abstract, decontextualised, de-humanised, and generally disenchanted world, one in which the lifeworld is taken over by the system, 'authentic' spaces by programmed consumer spaces, tactics by strategies, humans by machines, and so on. But this argument is more often assumed than demonstrated and many authors are now beginning to believe that our world may not be so very different from the worlds that have gone before it and that such a view rests on a series of false and unproductive oppositions: nature and culture, technology and society, and primitive and modern, for example (Knorr-Cetina 1994; Latour 1993; Ingold 1995; Moore 1995; Stafford 1995). Perhaps the assumption of disenchantment arises, then, from sticking with descriptions of something which are increasingly what Douglas (1966) has called 'out of category'. This means that we cannot recognise (or have not recognised until recently) the depth and complexity of the 'sociations' that surround us which have become, now, the source of so much comment (see Giddens 1991; Beck *et al.* 1994). Thus, to take just one example, that of the apparent increase in secularisation in some western countries, the fact that some regions of the world have apparently experienced secularisation may just mean that new forms of religion are out of category with what we have conventionally regarded as religion (as the blossoming study of new age religion, implicit religion, and so on seems to imply). In other words,

> The thesis of the disenchantment of the world fails in several ways. First, it rests on the equation of the content of particular belief systems or modes of operation – which have changed – with 'substance', 'meaning', 'the life-world', etc in general. If the proposition of the 'loss of meaning' in modern and postmodern life is stripped of this equation it amounts to a historically plausible but trivial assertion about the changing nature of meaning structures. Second, the assumption of the increase in formal, technical and abstract systems ignores the phenomenon that these systems are never abstract when enacted. Presumably, the meaning of abstract elements lies not in their formal definition but in their use. Third, the thesis fails in that it has

not been systematically documented empirically. In fact, assessments like that of a trend towards the elimination of the life-world are ironic in the face of the . . . microsociological studies in the last thirty years which demonstrate the procedures and forms of organisation of the life-world.

(Knorr-Cetina 1994: 6)

Certainly, much of the current literature on new electronic technologies suffers from the same difficulties of explicit or implicit technological determinism as was found in the writings of the nineteenth century. Two forms are the most prominent (Fischer 1992). The first is a 'symptomatic' form in which new electronic technologies are metaphorical expressions of a current culture or geist. In this form of determinism, the new technological order provides the narrative mill. The new machines become both the model for society and its most conspicuous sign. The second form of technological determinism is less sweeping, but is still highly directed. Here, the new electronic technologies alter history by a process of cultural and psychological transfer of their essential properties to their users. For example, Kern (1983) takes on board a wide – and long-held – view (see Porter 1993) which infers that space-transcending technologies like the telegraph and telephone, and the bicycle and automobile, were able to communicate their essential properties of instantaneity and speed to their users, who became more tense, alert and time-conscious as a result. Leaving aside the difficulties of evidence, such a relationship is by no means self-evident. For example,

In the use of the automobile, one could reason that the replacement of the horse and train by the automobile would have sped up users' experiences. This may sometimes be so, but not always or perhaps even mostly. Traveling by car rather than train probably led, according to a historian of touring, to a more leisurely pace. People could pull over and enjoy the countryside, 'smell the roses'. Similarly, farmers who replaced their horses with motor vehicles could travel faster to market, but many apparently used the time to sleep in longer on market day.

(Fischer 1992: 11)

Similarly, Meyrowitz (1985: 115) argues that electronic media 'lead to a near total dissociation of physical place and social "place". When we communicate through telephone, radio, television, or computer where we are physically no longer determines where and who we are socially.' Thus all places become like others, cultural distances between places are erased and privacy is reduced as areas of life previously sheltered from public view are recorded. Like Kern, 'Meyrowitz reasons from the properties of the technologies to the consequences. Electronic media are "place-less", so people lose their sense of place' (Fischer 1992: 11). Yet, like Kern's account, the reasoning is defective. For example,

Meyrowitz argues that, unlike letter writers, telephone callers can pierce other people's facades by hearing sounds in the background of the other party. Thus the telephone breaks down privacy. But why not instead compare the telephone call to the personal visit or the front-step conversation? If telephone calls have replaced more face-to-face talks than letters, then the telephone has increased privacy.

(Fischer 1992: 12)

In other words, what is still not well understood is that each new technology must take on complex cultural meanings which are by no means self-evident and which allow certain machines, for example the piano, to be seen as 'natural' and others, like the computer, to be seen as unnatural. Why? Because, we live in a culture

that has over time slowly grown a language and models for close relationships with certain machines. The harpsichord, like the visual artist's pencils, brushes, and paints, is a tool, and yet we understand the artist's relationship with these can (and indeed, will most probably) be close, sensuous and relational.

(Turkle and Papert 1990: 153)

This process of social acquaintance is still taking place with the new electronic communications technologies. And, even in their comparatively short life span, these technologies have changed their meaning. At the most general level, cultural anxieties expressed in metaphors of information excess, overload, bombardment or glut are now being replaced by more positive orientations expressed in metaphors of highway, dance and surfing (Collins 1995). More specifically, the process of social acquaintance has produced many new forms of 'techno-textuality' which rest on markedly different interpretations of the cultural legacy of electronic telecommunications, which do not cohere, and which do not have to cohere. Thus Collins (1995: 6) can write of the impact of information technology on music in these terms:

These radically new forms of textual production are obviously constative elements of the Age of Information, but in order to understand the complex interaction of cultural expression and information technology, we need to examine how excess of information and its accessibility have affected all those other 'anachronistic' low-tech areas of cultural activity as well. This is not just a matter of recognising the sophisticated forms of resistance to the semiotic excess that have developed alongside radically new technologies . . . It also involves recognising the ways in which both deconstructive and neoclassical architecture, both industrial rock and 'neo-traditionalist' country music are reactions to the same semiotic excess, and their realisations depend on their ability to access and refashion the 'already said', which is now decidedly the still being said due to the technologies of information storage and retrieval. In other words, the Age of Information is defined not by the ongoing struggle between the futuristic and the anachronistic (which is in and of itself not sufficiently appreciated by techno theory), but even more importantly, by the ways in which that very opposition is being reconceptualised in cultures defined by the simultaneous presence of phenomena like cyberpunk fiction and neoclassical architecture, but also 'cutting-edge' Early Music ensembles.

(Collins 1995: 6–7)

Let us summarise the argument so far. What is missing from techno-logically determinist accounts, and what must be re-embedded if we are to understand modern informational spaces and telematic cities, is any concerted sense of new electronic communications technologies as part of a long history of rich and often wayward social *practices* (including the interpretations of these practices) through which we have become *socially acquainted* with these technologies. As Marvin (1988: 4–5) has argued, that means that what she calls the 'instrument-centred' perspective, in which the instrument determines the effect, is much too narrow[4] because the history of electronic technologies

is less the revolution of technical efficiencies in communication than a series of arenas for negotiating issues crucial to the conduct of social life: among them, who is inside and outside, who may speak, who may not, and who has authority and may be believed. Changes in the speed, capacity, and perfor-mance of communications devices tell us little about these questions. At best, they provide a cover of functional meanings beneath which social meanings can elaborate themselves undisturbed.

If artifactual approaches foster the belief that social processes connected to media logically and historically begin with the instrument, then new media are presumed to fashion new social groups called audiences from voiceless collectives and to inspire new uses bred on novel technological properties. When audiences become organised around these bases, the history of a new media begins. The model used here is different. Here the focus is shifted from the instrument to the drama in which existing groups perpetually negotiate power, authority, representation and knowledge with whatever resources are available. New media intrude on these negotiations by providing new platforms on which old groups confront one another. Old habits of transacting between groups are projected onto new technologies that alter, or seem to alter, critical social distances. New media may change the perceived effectiveness of one group's surveillance of another, the per-missible familiarity of exchange, the frequency and intensity of contact, and the efficiency of customary tests for truth and deception. Old practices are then painfully revised, and group habits are refined. New practices do not so much flow directly from the technology that inspire them as they are improvised out of old practices that no longer work in new settings. Efforts are made to restore social equilibrium, and these efforts have significant social risks. In the end, it is less in new media practices, which come later and point toward a resolution of these conflicts (or, more likely, a temporary truce), than in the uncertainty of emerging and contested practices of communication that the struggle of groups to define and locate themselves is most easily observed.

We want to illustrate some of these points in the next section of this chapter by considering one particular set of communities of practice which are often regarded as at the heart of the modern informational space.[5] This is the set of communities who are involved in international finance. It has become one of the fixed clichés of modern life that massive amounts of money now circulate the globe at the press of a button (or, more accurately, the touch on a screen) and this virtual monetary space is often regarded as the avatar of postmodernity (e.g. Denzin 1991; Jameson 1991; Castells 1989; Harvey 1989b; Wark 1994). Yet, we will argue, when we move away from the instrument-centred perspective we find something very different. The rise of electronic telecommunications networks may well have produced more, not less, sociation, much of it face to face. In other words, we do not find an electronic world swept of people, we find hybrid 'actor–networks' of people and electronic things (Haraway 1991; Latour 1993; Law 1994), 'communities of practice' (Lave and Wenger 1991; Star 1995) which have long and involved histories and traditions. New forms of electronic detachment have therefore produced new forms of social involvement. It is not a case of either/or, but of both/and. In other words, the example of international finance yet again shows the sterility of a 'cybercultural history that believes only in the newness of all phenomena, as though the world itself had been entirely reborn in the electronic era' (Bukatman 1993b: 628). Historical depth is not, therefore, an incidental moment in the task of explanation, but a necessity.

THE FIRST TELEMATIC CITY? THE CITY OF LONDON

We want to fill out these thoughts by reference to the example of an archetypal telematic city: the City of London. Over the last 140 years this small space has been one of the key centres of a globally extensive web of telecommunications; what was once the telegraphic heart of the Empire of British commercial capital is now one of the electronic hearts of an international imperium of commercial capital. More than most spaces, it can therefore be figured as a way station in an extraordinary world of speed and immediacy, dematerialised like the money it serves, the haunt of the ineffaceable real, a moment in the constitution of the monetary sublime. Indeed this is a favourite interpretation of contemporary intellectuals (Harvey 1989b; Wark 1994). But in a series of papers (Thrift 1990b, 1994a, b, 1995; chapter 9), we have tried to show that such a depiction is flawed, blinded by its own technological hyperbole which prevents its authors from seeing that this world is still, even given the growth in quasi-mediated interaction (Thompson 1995), a world of ordinary human practices which have a complex historical genealogy.

Seen in this light, electronic communications technologies are no longer an economic, social and cultural earthquake but rather a part of a continuing performative history of 'technological' practices, a complex archive of stances, emotions, tacit and cognitive knowledges, and presentations and representations, which seek out and construct these technologies in certain ways rather than others (sometimes before they even exist) and which therefore ascribe what is new about them (Pickering 1995).

In this section we want to illustrate some of these propositions by reference to the history of the three key instruments of electronic communication

– the telegraph, the telephone and computerised telecommunications – in the City. We want to show, first of all, the impossibility of separating out the instrument from the practices of which it is always only a mutable and mobile part. Then, second, we want to argue that, as in the past, so in the present, there is no sense that the latest developments in electronic communications have produced an abstract and inhuman world, strung out on the wire, by reference to developments in City practices which both contain the germ of older technological practices and are being constantly adjusted to the performative possibilities provided by getting acquainted with new electronic communication instruments.

The growth of the City's informational space began with the installation of *the telegraph* which gradually integrated British financial spaces (e.g. the London and Glasgow Stock Exchange were linked in 1847), allowing prices to converge and small time period arbitrage to become a possibility (Thrift 1990b). The process of integration was slow at first – the first telegraph systems were vulnerable to the weather and suffered from considerable problems of capacity. But these problems were overcome so that by 1905

> it was estimated by the Post Office that the average time of transmission on [the London–Glasgow] route was a mere 2½ minutes; 70 per cent of all telegrams were sent within 5 minutes of report and 97 per cent under 10 minutes. Though delays could, and did, continue to take place 'due either to falling wires or sudden pressure', it was normal to send a message, have the deal done and receive confirmation well within the half-hour, and this had been the case since at least the 1870s.
>
> (Michie 1987: 9)

In any case, many of the problems of the system were able to be overcome by those City firms who installed private wires. For example, between 1870 and 1895 about sixty of these wires were installed between London and Glasgow.

Until the invention of the telegraph, the City's global reach had relied on the mails and, fastest of all, the carrier pigeon.[6] But, in 1851 the first element in the City's global informational space was put into place, with the laying of a submarine cable between London and Paris.[7] The two cities were then able to be linked by telegraph, allowing news (including stock prices) to be transmitted back and forth within business hours. Other European cities followed suit and by 1860 the Barings' banker John Bates could note 'Received a telegram that the contract had been signed and despatched per mail, so that we shall have it in 5 days. The Telegraph is beginning to be much used and very useful' (cited in Kynaston (1994: 168)). In July 1866, the first submarine cable connection was made between London and New York, with immediate effect on the rapidity of market adjustment between the two cities (Kynaston 1994). In 1871 some 42,000 telegrams were already being sent between the two cities and by 1877 *The Economist* was able to remark that, so embedded had the use of telegraph become in the business of international finance, that telegraphic transfers, together with international coupons, were superseding the bill as a means of remittance (King 1972). The telegraph and its attendant 'cable boys' made it possible

> for the first time to trade systematically, and with a fair degree of confidence, in future delivery, rather than taking a gamble on a very risky speculation since it was possible to anticipate expected supply and demand with reasonable certainty. . . . The telegrams, and later the telephone, and their use by intermediaries meant a qualitative change in the degree of risk.
>
> (Michie 1992: 55–6)

This is not to say that the new business practices attendant on the telegraph were never contested. For example, even as late as the 1880s and 1890s there was still concern at the way in which the telegraph made forward commodity trading a possibility. In a debate which still has echoes today, concerns were expressed over the propriety of future rather than actual delivery on the American model. Was it an incitement to speculation, or a harmless way of hedging bets in a fluctuating market? Thus, as Kynaston (1995: 20) notes:

> in 1894 some of the qualms surfaced in a reprobatory article in the *Contemporary Review* on 'Market Gambling'. The author . . . noted the vastly increased amount of futures dealing in corn that had taken place in recent years in both the USA and Liverpool, and went on
>
> > It is satisfactory to state that the great majority of merchants in Mark Lane set themselves resolutely against the abominable system, and regard any firm taking part in it with suspicion. On the Baltic, the importer's market in London, option dealing takes place, and the men who deal in options have their Produce Exchange [i.e. the London Commercial Sale Rooms in Mincing Lane] and Clearing-house. It is considered on Mark Lane, however, somewhat 'shoddy' to belong to the comparatively small clique in London who have adopted the American fashion of dealing in grain.
>
> It was clear, however, which way the trend was going, and especially clear that by providing facilities for forward dealing, the City was safeguarding its international position. Perhaps significantly, the markets that dealt in futures preferred not to use that term, an American one, but instead preferred to call themselves 'terminal' markets deriving from the French word for time.

Whatever the particular reservations associated with particular financial instruments, by the 1880s the telegraph was an integral part of the City business day, etched into the practices of the City as though electronic stock dealing had always existed, as this account by *The Statist* of the situation in 1886 as the New York market opened at 3 o'clock makes clear:

> visitors to the City who are not familiar with its ways must observe a good many scenes which puzzle them. If they chance to be loitering about Bartholomew-lane or Throgmorton-street between three and four o'clock in the afternoon they may see telegraph boys racing along at a breakneck pace. . . . They dash across streets, shoot round corners like greased lightning, dodge past hansoms, and rush up stairs into demure looking offices in the most unceremonious fashion. As soon as they reach the door

they shout 'cable!'. . . . But these fleet footed youngsters may make as much noise as they please, and nobody objects . . .

The afternoon cable race is one of the recent developments of Stock Exchange enterprise. It is carried on in the interest of the 'arbitrageurs', who buy and sell on the small margins of difference there may happen to be between London and New York markets. Arbitrage is also practised between London and the chief Continental Bourses, but on a smaller scale and with less scientific methods. On the Continent it is done largely between one Bourse and another; in fact, it is of foreign origin, and foreigners take the lead in it even here. The market which offers the finest scope for it is American railways, the daily fluctuations in these stocks being active, and the deviations from parity between the New York and London prices being often considerable . . .

Translating dollar prices into sterling prices at the exchange of the day – a rate which is seldom two days alike – involves intricate calculation. Tables have been framed to facilitate the process, but an expert 'arbitrageur' carries in his head about all that he needs for his purpose . . .

From a quarter past 3 o'clock onwards the cables come pouring in. They have to be sent out from the cable offices to the offices of the arbitrage houses. There they have to be turned into sterling prices, and these compared with the London prices at the moment. Like a flash of lightning the 'arbitrageur' has to decide what he will buy and what he will sell. He rushes to the House and has his business done for him. . . . Then he cables back to New York to 'cover' his transactions, that is, to buy against what he had sold or to sell against what he has bought. It may be also that his partner or agent in New York has entered into transactions which he must cover here if he can. The game is played simultaneously from both ends, and like duplex telegraphy there are generally two accounts of speculation crossing each other. Scores of buyings and sellings may be going on together, each of which carries a certain degree of risk, but the arbitrageur's hope is to come out right on the general balance. He makes his risks, so to speak, insure each other, and so long as the differences are comparatively small he stands a fair chance to come out well. The arbitrageurs themselves say that it is the small profits they make most by. A wide fluctuation in a stock, while a transaction in it is being covered, is pretty sure to end badly. If it is against the arbitrageurs, great judgement has to be exercised in deciding whether the loss should be cut at once, or the transaction kept open on the chance of its righting itself . . .

Having the first cable from Wall Street of an afternoon is better that having a 'moral certainty' for the Derby. The second cable is worth a good deal less, as the jobbers are quick enough to see how the wind blows from the west. If the arbitrageurs are buying they put up prices, and if they are selling they put them down. It is only the early bird that catches the arbitrage worm, and the late birds are more likely to be caught themselves. That is the moral of the headlong racing among the cable boys, of the lightning calculations, and the rushes of excited clerks into the House about half-past 3 o'clock. Capel Court and Wall Street are like two arms of a delicately poised balance. They are always deviating from the level, but the slightest touch brings them back to it. By forestalling that slight touch the arbitrageur makes his living.

(cited in Kynaston (1994: 348–9))

The high point of telegraph usage in the City was the turn of the century. For example, in 1903 an average of 2.4 telegrams per minute were being transmitted into and out of the Baltic Exchange (Kynaston 1995). But the ascendancy of this instrument was now threatened by the practice of the telephone. Thus, by 1904, *the telephone* had also impinged on the operation of arbitrage between the London and New York markets.

> By rapid degrees the American fluctuations became generally circulated; one market seems to be full of the little pink slips that came flying in at the hands of boys and clerks stationed in a line that stretches from the offices of the cable companies outside the House to the very heart of the Yankee Market in the Stock Exchange. Again, the telephone and telegraph come into requisition, and the House usually finishes up, unless there is really nothing doing, in a state of more or less mild excitement.
>
> (Duguid, cited in Kynaston (1995: 301))

The telephone added to the array of electronic telecommunications that the City wielded in significant ways and it is no surprise that the City had the first two telephone exchanges in Britain (in 1879)[8] and had many telephone users from an early point in time, including worthies like the Baltic Exchange, which installed lines as early as 1881 (Barty-King 1977). In 1902, the Bank of England finally installed telephones, symbolically assuring their importance for the City, and by 1910 the number of telephone subscribers had already reached 10,000.

Some of these subscribers were putting their telephones to heavy use. For example, in October 1908, 81,883 outwards and 23,916 inward calls were made or received at the Stock Exchange telephones linked to brokers offices. 'In approximate terms, this meant that a telephone call was made every 6 seconds and one received every 21 seconds during the whole day, and this excluded all subsequent office calls' (Michie 1987: 13).

At first, the telephone had been used purely for local calls within the City but, as in the case of the telegraph, telephone wires gradually linked Britain's financial spaces together. Indeed, by 1889 a programme was in hand to link the London Stock Exchange with the provincial stock exchanges by means of direct cables, thereby avoiding delays created by routing via local telephone exchanges. But, around 1900, again just like the telegraph, private dedicated telephone wires began to be used by a few City firms, each line costing about £20,000 per annum to rent. The example of the Stock Exchange is again instructive. By 1904, ten London Stock Exchange firms had rented direct lines to the provinces and

> by keeping [the line between the offices of Stock Exchange markets and provincial brokers] open throughout the day, and allied to each broker's different telephonic links from his office to his own exchange, a continuous and immediate two-way contact was established between trading in London and activity elsewhere. This facility was superior to that of the public wires, which were soon relegated to handling the less important business.
>
> (Michie 1987: 14)

The existence of the direct lines led to the increasing importance of certain financial practices like the 'shunting' of securities and also, ironically, to the strengthening of the dual-capacity system of brokers and jobbers, precisely in order to give the Stock Exchange the means to fend off such practices.

As this example makes clear there was still significant resistance to the new telecommunications technologies in some parts of the City. For example,

> a residual mistrust (of telephones) was felt even at a progressive firm like Schröders, where Baron Bruno allowed one only on condition that the firm's number was omitted from the telephone directory, on the ground that incoming calls would be a distraction from business.
>
> (Kynaston 1995: 252)[9]

Bastions of conservatism held out even longer against the new technology and the most conservative of all was the Stock Exchange which consistently refused to make full use of the new telegraphic, and then telephonic, communications, encouraged by the Stock Exchange's lack of control over the building it used (which was provided by a company which derived its income from the fees paid by the members). Thus in 1868, a request to install an exchange telegraph was turned down by the management and much pressure had to be exerted by the members to make the management give way. The telephone was also perceived as a threat.

> The first application to introduce a telephone service between the London Stock Exchange and the outside subscribers was made in November 1879. It was rejected. It was not until the Exchange was enlarged in 1882–3 that a telephone room was provided and even then the facilities remained inadequate, inconvenient and of limited use. Faced with the continued refusal to provide proper facilities for telephones, in July 1888 the members threatened to find an alternative to the facilities provided by the Stock Exchange unless the managers gave way. The management backed down, putting only normal obstruction in the way of further expansion; the year 1888 marked the end of any serious resistance by the management to the changes created by the communications revolution.
>
> (Michie 1987: 20)

Yet, even as late as 1905, one frustrated member of the Exchange was able to write to the *Financial News*:

> Our members have every right to expect facilities such as do exist on other Exchanges. Every frequenter of the Exchange is aware of the quantity of outside institutions which have sprung up, and which, by the aid of private telephone boxes outside the Exchange, are doing a large and increasing business, securing their customers in the provinces, on the Continent, or in America, either as outside brokers or arbitrage dealers, on terms more advantageous than the 'House' man can offer. Look around Shorter's Court, under the new building . . . and you will see innumerable busy telephone manipulators. You have in this Court two cable companies, who, unable to

gain access to a corner of the 'House', again swell the messenger boy's brigade.

Why should the members of the 'House' not be able to install their direct telephonic connections inside the building? Why again, should the cable companies not be permitted to have their room within the building, thus gaining our paying members a slight start in receiving, and sending their messages?

At Lloyd's, the Baltic, and elsewhere, the exchanges provide a most exhaustive supply of telephonic communications, which are posted up as soon as received. Barring a very scanty supply of news over the Exchange (tape) machine, we are left to our own resources.

(cited in Kynaston (1995: 403))

Even by the second decade of the twentieth century, the Stock Exchange still doggedly held to its own telegraphic way of proceeding; and even this was generally slow and inefficient relative to competitors.

The Stock Exchange's record in the international sphere was only slightly more inspiring. The Exchange proved itself reluctant to increase opening hours after the opening of the Anglo-American telegraph in 1866.[10] Even as late as 1904

the ten firms doing large-scale arbitrage business in the American market had vainly asked the managers for pneumatic tubes to be provided from the offices of the Anglo-American Telegraph and Commercial Cable Companies into the Stock Exchange: in 1907 the managers gave their usual niggardly response when the Exchange Telegraph Company sought improved facilities in order to speed up the process of transferring price changes to the tape, which, the company stated, compared unfavourably with the swiftness of the 'ticker' service on the New York Stock Exchange: over the next two years the managers agreed with only the greatest reluctance to erect more telephone boxes; and in 1911 a number made a vain complaint . . . about the poor telegraphic facilities between the Stock Exchange and the Continental bourse.

(Kynaston 1995: 403)

It is no surprise that an American visitor to the Stock Exchange in 1913 could so easily contrast the difference in attitude to the new communications technology between the London and New York Exchange:

Here in New York there is a slapdash come and go system that is greatly facilitated by the use of the telephone and the private telegraph lines. A single commission house has 10,000 miles of licensed lines. In London, where telephone and private lines are but sparingly used, both by brokers and clients, a broker often finds on his desk in the morning, three or four hundred letters and telegrams; the care and attention required to handle an enormous lot of orders given in this deliberate manner are something with which the New York stock brokers are quite unfamiliar.

(cited in Morgan and Thomas (1962: 164))

Still, for all the frustrations, the number of telephone subscribers continued to increase. Thus by 1939 there were three City telephone exchanges, serving 46,000 subscribers in all, and the City had become one of the hubs of global telephonic space. In 1937, a telephone link between London and New York was initiated. By 1940, it was already possible for one commentator to describe a foreign exchange dealing room of the 1930s in terms redolent of those used today.

> To describe exactly what goes in the foreign exchange room of many of the big banks or foreign exchange brokers who comprise the London Foreign Exchange market is beyond me. It is the nearest thing to the Bedlam that I know – half a dozen men in a little room, shouting in incomprehensible jargon into Telephones, pushing switches up and down all the time in response to the flashing indicator lights.
>
> All the telephone talk, moreover, is not confined to the London network of lines. Every now and again a bank in Paris or Amsterdam or Zurich will come through on the touch line, and in the afternoon when the American market has opened, there may be a stream of telegrams coming in from New York. The fact reminds us that the foreign exchange market of London . . . is not an isolated market, but is part of a single active market in world currencies.
>
> (Hobson 1940: 61)

In 1956, the Foreign Exchange market reopened after the war as an all-telephone market and it has operated as such ever since.

By the 1920s, the telegraph and the telephone had been integrated with other forms of electronic telecommunications like wireless telegraphy (introduced in the 1920s) to produce a City of London that was becoming recognisably modern in its attitudes to the use of technology. Along the way, the telegraph and telephone had also stimulated many other *hybrid technologies*. There was, for example, the pneumatic tube, used to communicate the short distances between terminals (e.g. linking the floor of the Stock Exchange with the Telegraph office pre-telephone). Then there was the tickertape, a teleprinter with an operator and a staff of reporters collecting prices from the Stock Exchange floor which provided a record of prices – at six words a minute. Invented in 1867, it was used on Wall Street for some time before being imported to London by the Exchange Telegraph Company in 1872, as a service to Stock Exchange members, but also some merchant banks and outside brokers. But, the service was not as popular as in the United States, perhaps because it transmitted a list of prices only four or five times a day compared with the continuous American services. For example, one American writer of 1913 noted that the machines were 'limited in number, almost nobody looks at them, and many enterprising houses do not install them at all' (cited in Morgan and Thomas 1962: 163)). However, in 1928, a continuous service was installed by Reuters, providing commodity and currency as well as stock prices (Read 1992).

From an early point in time, the City had been interested in the potential of *computers* for payment and settlement purposes to replace the high-speed mechanical sorting and tabulating equipment that had been the norm. For example, in the late 1950s the London-based Association of Clearing Banks had an Electronics Sub-Committee, with a major assignment to automate bank payment processes (and indeed in 1971 this did indeed happen when the Bankers Automated Clearing Services Ltd (BACS) began trading in London (Kirkman 1987)). But computers made their major appearance in the City in the 1960s. In 1966, for example, even the normally reticent Stock Exchange installed one. Even so, adoption of computers was a relatively slow business (in 1971, *The Banker* revealed that 'the computerisation plans of some of the British banks are seriously behind schedule'), most particularly because it took time for their uses to be explored.

Even so, that process of exploration meant that in the 1960s the telephone and telex were already being merged with the new computers to produce recognisably modern forms of *telecommunications*. There were four main imperatives behind this amalgamation. The first was that the extant telephone systems were becoming simply overburdened.[11] Second, information was needed more and more quickly because of the reciprocal increase in generally available information and connectivity, and the speed-up in response times resulting from new technological–organisational arrangements. Third, this information then had to be analysed, sieved and sorted. Fourth, it became correspondingly more important to be able to locate people quickly[12] to put them in touch with information and analysis.

To begin with at least, commercial news and information was able to be transmitted directly to customers, and did not have to go through intermediate offices and agents to be redirected on via a combination of teleprinter, telex, telephone, mail and messenger. Then, in 1964, the first computerised price quotation service was offered. By 1968, over 10,000 commodity prices were available at push button demand, at first in fifteen seconds, later in two seconds. In 1970, this system was put onto screen display:

> there is an entirely new Market Price Display Service. More than 1200 television receivers have been installed in some 250 offices around the City, and each of them can display information on 22 channels. The System is linked to a Ferranti computer.
>
> (Jenkins 1973: 102)

In 1973, spurred on by the break-up of Bretton Woods, and the consequent expansion in foreign exchange dealing, a real-time interactive quotation service was established which, for the first time, allowed customers to input data. This was necessary because dependency on telephones and telex was proving unsatisfactory. 'Since by the time an answer to a request for (say) a bank's dollar/sterling price had been given and transmitted, that price might well have changed. Seconds were important' (Read 1992: 30). Finally, in 1981, came computerised dealing. Advertisements for this new product emphasised speed – how the new product offered the opportunity to conclude deals in two to four seconds, compared with up to ten seconds with the then current methods.

> Only through Reuters could dealers communicate with each other at high speed to buy, sell, or lend money through the same screen, taking hard copies of transactions from an associated teleprinter. They still had to work out their own deals, since this was not yet 'matching' but the new scheme was a great advance . . . By the second anniversary in February 1983 the Dealing Service had 400 subscribers in 24 countries; 37 of the world's top 50 banks were participating; calls through the system were averaging 10,000 per day. A year later calls had doubled again, with peaks of 40,000 in active markets.
>
> (Read 1992: 311)

In the 1990s, the City is still one of the world's major telecommunications hubs providing high-volume, low-cost services (Ireland 1994; City Research Project 1995) via a wide variety of different modes of connection.[13] These modes of connection now include direct small-disk satellite delivery (first made available in 1982), microwave, and fibre optic rings (the first of which began construction in 1983; there are currently five operating in the City controlled by BT, Mercury, Energis, Colt and MFS) as well as older modes. These new modes of connection, along with increasing computational power, have produced the following results: electronic networks which operate in all stages of the process of trading and settlement (Mansell and Jenkins 1993); so-called intelligent networks (which, for example, allow 0800 numbers to be transferred from city to city around the world according to time zone, offer specific services to different customer segments, provide private networks, and can offer billing on floppy disk); and certain primitive forms of artificial intelligence (e.g. neural network systems involved in currency dealing). The City, in other words, is one of the major hubs of a global 'informational space' which is probably one of the closest approximations to information space and the telematic city that currently exist.

Yet, there is no sense that these developments have produced an abstract and inhuman world, strung out on the wire. And there are good reasons why this is so. Three of these stand out. First, the new informational space has produced as much confusion as certainty. The problem is no longer lack of information. Instead, it is too much. As one of the vice-presidents of the New York Stock Exchange put it, 'we're drowning in data' (cited in *The Economist* 25 August 1995: 75). The information explosion in part comes from the simple process of being able to use information technology to make much more information available to many more people (Khan and Ireland 1993). But there is more to the process than this. Information technology can also be used to generate information that was previously unavailable (Zuboff 1988). This information which can be used to generate new products, as in the case of the exotic financial products produced by 'rocket scientists', adds to the uncertainty. Further, information technology is not a neutral medium. It produces new forms of communication, new forms of rhetoric and narrative possibilities, new norms and conventions, which complicate how and what 'information' is delivered (Ferrara *et al.* 1991).

In turn, this means that the major task in the information spaces of telematic cities like the City of London becomes interpretation, and, moreover, interpretation *in action* under the pressures of real-time events. Since the international financial system generates such a massive load of information, power goes to those who are able to offer the most convincing interpretations of the moment. The problem is no longer necessarily a shortage of information but how to make sense of the masses of information that exist. Thus the generation of convincing interpretive schemes becomes both crucial and, at the same time, a more and more difficult achievement in the face of growing numbers of possible interpretations of each and every event.

Part of the hunger for interpretation has been answered by the media. Increasingly global in character, the media provide a bewildering variety of interpretations from newspapers, to specialised financial publishing, to tipsheets, increasingly in electronic form (Parsons 1989). But it is possible to argue that the media are 'as much a part of the problem of interpretation in that they often provide multiple and confusing explanations of financial events, leading some commentators to talk of the relativism of the electronic age' (Smith 1983: 325).

Another part of the hunger for interpretation has been answered by the new forms of representation that the more recent electronic telecommunications technologies themselves made possible: from graphical interfaces to computer graphics and animation. But these can only help to a limited degree.

Thus the many workers in the City who depend on 'correct' interpretations for their living tend to fall back on other means. These practices are most obvious in the largest and most volatile markets where, as one stock dealer put it, 'the one obvious problem is that you're only as good as your last bargain. Each day starts a new complete sheet' (Lazar 1990: 58). In these circumstances, dealers tend to fall back on specific social cliques (Baker 1984) which cleave to particular interpretive schemes. Four of these schemes seem most common. We might call these schemes, fundamentalist, evangelical, charismatic and spiritualist (Cosgrove 1996). There are first of all, then, those who believe in economic fundamentals. They constitute the blunt end of the financial markets:

> They are looking at economies and the fundamental values which lie behind currencies and the demand there. When fundamentalists analyse shares they dissect individual companies' accounts, assessing the true worth of the share. In commodity markets, they study crop reports, mining returns, and the changing patterns of demand in consumer countries. In all cases, there will, of course, be as many different schools of thought about the relative importance of various factors as Christianity has sects.
>
> (G. Roberts 1995: 116)

The Bank of England's view is typical of a relatively fundamentalist stance. For the Bank, market movements are

a reflection of a host of factors and underlying forces, some driven by fundamental economic developments, some responding to movements in relative interest rates and asset prices, some moved by technical or seasonal conditions, and some reflecting long-term trends. Understanding these factors can give us useful information about how economic goals are responding to the monetary stance we are pursuing and hence how far we are succeeding in pursuing our monetary objective of price stability. But the information is inevitably jumbled and laced with a great deal of extraneous 'noise'. It needs to be decoded.

(Associate Director, Bank of England, cited in G. Roberts (1995: 114))

The second 'evangelical' interpretative scheme is concerned with price, regardless of value. It involves the belief that 'the market has a life of its own' (Smith 1983: 48), and is best studied technically via charts of various kinds. One study of the City (Taylor and Allen 1989) found that for short-term time horizons, 90 per cent of dealing institutions used some charting and for two-thirds charts were at least as important as economic fundamentals. So-called Chartists have formulated their own well-formed vocabulary and methods of analysis over time: 'You work very hard at your charts. You look at them twice a day on a consistent basis across a variety of currencies. And you try and work out what's going on' (trader, cited in G. Roberts (1995: 120)).

The third 'charismatic' interpretative scheme is one which conceives market events in strictly interpersonal terms with the result that key individuals ('who really know what's going on') and powerful institutions who can move markets are taken as benchmarks. The fourth and final 'spiritualist' interpretative scheme is one which is based on market psychology, on a 'feel' for the market.

I think that it really comes down to is psychology. The markets are all about psychology. It's not about how intelligent you are. It's about how lucky you are and how well you can read what the next guy's trying to do.

(trader, cited in G. Roberts (1995: 120))

Certainly, the fact that 'irrational' indicators like round numbers (de Grauwe and Decupere 1992), low trading levels on Mondays, as well as the existence of bubbles and fads, have been shown to be important in market behaviour over and over again, suggests that this last schema has as much to recommend it as any other.

Of course, these four schemes are often merged in practice. Thus one trader (cited in G. Roberts (1995: 176)) uses most of the schemes:

There are people who trade off fundamentals and others who trade off the feeling they have for the movement and the flows. There's not one particular approach that a dealer should use. The dealers have access to all types of information which is necessary for them to take. And they pick and choose what is important to them for the way they trade and their particular style of trading.

I like to look at charts as a confirmation of something that I'm feeling anyway. If I feel strongly about something I look at the chart and say 'Is the chart agreeing with me, is it telling me that my timing's wrong or that I'm totally wrong?'. . . . Another thing that I really find valuable is contacts in the market. I know a good few people in the market, talking to these people during the day. They'll say different things to us which will help you form a view.

The uncertainty of the markets breeds other interpretative schemes as well. Astrology has become an increasingly popular means of interpretation. And superstitions are rife:

unpredictability breeds superstition, too. We had one very good dealer and we had a building site just outside with a crane. . . . And he'd say 'The crane's moving to the left, that's sterling going down, going to the right, it's going up'. People have their little ideas like that, as well.

(G. Roberts 1995: 180)

The second reason why it is impossible to see information space as an abstract and inhuman space, strung out on the wire, stems from the way that City people interact knowledgeably with the available electronic communications technology. Here it is important to remember, first of all, that City people are practised in this kind of technology, socialised into its use over more than a century. We can therefore expect that they are relatively unimpressed by the newer electronic communications technologies coming on-line and soon become acquainted with and incorporate them (Fischer 1992). Outbreaks of 'techno-fear' seem to have been comparatively rare in the City. For example, Read (1992) mentions some resistance to screen-based trading when it was first bought in the early 1980s but this seems to have soon broken down. Second, City people stress the use of a repertoire of electronic technologies, working side by side, in new combinations: the old coextensive with the new. For example, a trader will still use the telephone and messengers along with touch screens, e-mail and fax. Third, electronic communications do not take place in one step in a smooth and integrated cyberspace (Mansell and Jenkins 1993). Rather, they take place through a series of overlapping channels which usually work on a step-by-step basis. Fourth, new electronic communications technology is not, in any case, used equally everywhere in the City. As we have seen from the history of the use of such technology in the City, certain firms and institutions heartily embrace new technologies. But others drag their heels. 'In spite of predictions that technology would eliminate distinctions between financial institutions, they have remained separate in culture, management style and business strategy' (*Financial Times* 16 September 1992: 1). The City's information space cannot therefore be all of a piece since even the fact of connection (which cannot be guaranteed) does not automatically signify use. Fifth and finally, electronic communications technology is rarely used in the City in isolation. For example, in the case of traders it is a part of an 'actor–network' built up to produce profit. The trader acts as one node in this collective along with other traders and, integrally, the technology they use. Most important for the trader in this situation is the 'image' he or she conveys to colleagues, an image made up of particular forms of masculinity (or femininity), bodily stance (including speech), favoured interpretative schemes, *and style of use of the available technology* (intense, carefree, indifferent, and so on).

> It's very important – especially when you're working in a big team like we have here – that whatever you're feeling inside it shouldn't always be shown. ... There is also the simple reality that emotional displays give away information to rivals with whom you are dealing. It's all about how you display your image as well.
>
> (G. Roberts 1995: 179)

In other words, telecommunications are not just used universally, but also *differently* by different groups of people.

The third reason why it is impossible to see the burgeoning information space as an abstract and inhuman space, strung out on the wire, is that its complexity and uncertainty, coupled with other factors like increasing competition, increasing cosmopolitanism and an increasingly female work-force, have driven the denizens of the City towards having to construct a more and more structured space of face-to-face interaction/interpretation. This 'dialogical City' of recent years, drawing on the close social traditions of the older City but extending them and also changing them, has produced a whole series of new or adjusted face-to-face social practices through which the 'informational frenzy' can be stabilised. These practices take many forms. There is the growth of the business card. Exchanging business cards is now a part of the ritual of meetings in the City in a way it never was before. There is the growth of the business lunch. There was always a lunching culture in the City – dating from the chophouses of the nineteenth century (see Kynaston 1994) – but this has now been 'civilised' – becoming less masculine and less based on consumption of meat and drink – and much more widely practised.

> Laughing in the face of doomsters who forecasted the arrival of the desk sandwich lunch and the demise of the traditional City lunch, many restaurants claim they have never been busier. Evidence of restaurants bulging at the rafters at lunch periods provides ample testimony of the continued potency of lunch as an important part of the business tool (*sic*).
>
> The most active criticism of City food in the late eighties revolved around the lack of good choice and the poor value . . . both these criticisms have to a large extent been removed. While the central London restaurant community still has the edge, the City is no longer the gastronomic desert that perhaps it was.
>
> (Square Meal 1994: 10)

Then there is the growth of the conference and the convention. As McRae (1994: 16) puts it:

> The world economy is developing in such a way that people need to communicate far more widely in order to do their jobs well. Professional jobs

are becoming very complex and anyone doing them needs to find ways of meeting other people in a similar field to improve performance . . . their peers in other corporations or countries. A conference is often the only way people can meet.

Finally, there is the growth of the corporate hospitality industry. First formalised in the 1970s, corporate hospitality is now one of the mainstays of city sociability. Covering the full range of sporting and artistic events, as well as more mundane corporate golf and other sporting days ('few will disagree that as a way of building a relationship golf has few equals'), corporate hospitality is now estimated to be a £1 billion industry by itself.

These comparatively new practices of face-to-face interaction have been backed up by increasing formalisation of the social encounter itself. This formalisation has been of three kinds. First, there has been the growth of formal 'relationship management'. Relationship management is the attempt by City firms to bring order and coherence to the pursuit of personal relations so that they are more likely to bear business fruit and 'insider' information and interpretation. Second, much greater attention has been paid to work on the self, so as to produce more acute social skills. Workshops, round tables, videos, are all used to achieve a more personable workforce, again so as to produce more business. Finally, to complete the circle, electronic technology is used as a technological supplement to face-to-face contacts, as well as in its own right. The telephone, fax and e-mail are all used as means of ordering face-to-face interaction. (Indeed, a number of workers now use computer programs to schedule people to call and have lunch with on a regular basis in the pursuit of 'insider' information and interpretation.)

To summarise, what we see in the City of London looks less like an outbreak of a new and alien information space, inhabited by the plugged in and the zoned out, and more like a more complex, historically constructed set of 'technological' practices, peopled by the active and aware, built up out of negotiations and struggles amongst inventors, investors, competitors, organised customers, agencies of government, the media and others which gradually result in accepted definitions/uses of new electronic communications technologies, in a sense in their 'reinvention' (Fischer, 1992). To put it in another vocabulary, the actors in these actor–networks redefine each other *in action* in ways which mean that there are no simple one-to-one relationships from technology to people but rather a constantly on-going, constantly inventive and constantly reciprocal process of social acquaintance and reacquaintance.

At the same time, the example of the City of London casts some doubt on the idea of the telematic city as a new kind of city at the nexus between a single, unified, relativistic space of flows and a more prosaic Euclidean urban space. It is more accurate to say that contemporary telematic cities are the hybrid outcome of multiple processes of social figuration (Elias 1982), processes which are specific to particular differentially extensive actor–networks (made up of people and things holding each other together) and generate their own spaces and times, which will sometimes, and sometimes not, be coincident. There is, in other words, no big picture of the modern City to be had but only a set of constantly evolving sketches.

The example of the City of London also suggests that new era theorists' ways of understanding modern cities are rather less different from ways of understanding earlier cities than they might want to admit. In particular, it suggests the images and the rhetoric that new era theorists employ are the outcome of a complex genealogy of fantasies about technology. For example, there is the imperial fantasy of the City's role at the 'heart of empire' which seems to be intimately linked with fantasies about the control of information spaces (Cain and Hopkins 1993a, b). Thus Richards (1993) has traced the beginnings of the idea of an all-conquering information space to nineteenth-century fantasies of a total Imperial archive. That such fantasies of unity persist, but now, as Richards points out, transferred to the medium of technology, suggests that the processes of decolonisation of thinking which postcolonial theorists have instigated may have farther to go than some of these theorists have imagined. 'Understanding the fantasy of knowledge elevated to global power takes us a long way towards understanding the lure, and finally the persistence, of the much larger fantasy of empire itself' (Richards 1993: 9).

CONCLUSIONS

The historian's musings proposed in the present work thus lead to a question essential in our own present time – not the overworked question of the supposed disappearance of writing, which is more resistant than has been thought, but the question of a possible revolution in the forms of its dissemination and appropriation.

(Chartier 1994: p. 91)

Conclusion 1: The Order of the Screen

We do not want this chapter to be perceived as simply an exercise in the debunking of new era writings, although they certainly need debunking. There also has to be, indeed there must be, something 'new' about the present conjuncture: 'there is no question that something new is at work while we all slip into a state of terminal identity' (Bukatman 1993b: 629).

That 'something new' seems to us to be the move from spatialising the largely invisible processes of information in one way – via writing – to spatialising them in another – via visual images.[14] For, as Barbara Maria Stafford (1991, 1994, 1995), one of the chief proponents of the view that we are now in transit to a new form of *oral–visual* culture, has argued:

No one who has watched the computer graphic and interactive techniques revolution can doubt that we are returning to an oral–visual culture.

Animation, virtual reality, fiber-optic video, laser disks, computer modelling, even e-mail, are part of a new vision and visionary art-science.

(Stafford 1994: xxx)

But, as Stafford goes on to argue, our ability to recognise, yet alone understand, this new oral–visual culture has been shrouded by two different sets of actors. One of these is the manufacturers of the new digital devices whose sales pitch is bound up with techno-hyperbole. The other set of actors are certain media critics who have inherited the suspicion of non-textualisable phenomena dating from the Enlightenment. They have 'reproduced, without realising it, the Enlightenment critique of merely beautiful appearances. Like the early moderns, they too deride the charlatanism of a bewitching optical technology and a cunning manual skill without compelling content performed to trick the masses' (Stafford 1994: xxvii). But, says Stafford, there is a third way. That is, to welcome, though not uncritically, the new oral–visual culture rather than to see it as a new form of papist idolatry and to do so for two main reasons. The first of these is its emphasis on recuperating physical objects (including images) as important means of patterning existence, as 'semiophores, or couriers of meaning (bearing witness) to a positive and instrumental materialism (and not just as) the passive drugs feeding our habit of consumption, but as cherished possessions' (Stafford 1994: 3). In other words, physical objects can again take their place as major sources of knowledge.

The second reason is because, while reading gradually became a silent and, to an extent, isolated and isolating activity, the return of oral–visual culture also bears the possibility of again promoting a more open and interactive universe crisscrossed by 'extra-linguistic messages, interactive speech acts, gestured conversations, and vivid pantomime' (Stafford 1994: 3) in which the exchange of information is both creative *and* playful. Most particularly, it is to recognise the possibility of entrenching 'a culture of high-level visual education to accompany the advances in visualisation', and to dispel the idea of a dichotomy between higher cognitive functions, represented by serious textual methods, and the physical manufacture of 'pretty pictures', which are merely hedonistic entertainment. In other words, Stafford is working towards the idea of reinstating the mobile thought of colloquial discussion in new ways as an oral–visual drama in which concepts are variably generated and played with as tangible objects. In turn, argues Stafford, this kind of pleasurable 'learning' will require a new 'culture of politeness' (of the kind already found on e-mail) which can cope with this kind of discussion. To summarise, Stafford (1994: 286) argues that:

we are returning to the oral–visual culture of early modernism. To be sure, our world is more heterogeneous, fragmented, indeterminate and speeded up, because of computers and robotic systems. Indeed, it is difficult to imagine students in the manipulative and 'movieola' period of video or of electronic texts returning to scribal techniques. It is all the more important, then, to understand the role of visual analysis for abstract concepts such as human development, cognition, memory, intelligence. No longer preliterate, we are postliterate. Yet, ironically, even within 'postcolonial critical discourses' emphasising the global importance of 'hybridity' and the value of 'alterity' the temporal linearity of texts serves as a model for a transnational countermodernity. Might the patterns and shape of cultures, their transformation, and shifting relations, not be explored more effectively through randomisation, animation, computer modelling and morphing?

Such a view is echoed by Sherry Turkle who argues that the iconic style of modern computerised telecommunications can support a move towards a much greater emphasis on 'concrete' thinking based on the rise of computational 'objects', and towards greater 'epistemological pluralism' which is more inclusive.

> The development of a new computer culture would require more than environments where there is permission to work with highly personal approaches. It would require a new social construction of the computer, with a new set of intellectual and emotional values more like those applied to harpsichord than hammer. Since, increasingly, computers are the tools people use to write, to design, to play with ideas and shapes and images, they should be addressed with a language that reflects the full range of human experiences and abilities. Changes in this direction would necessitate the reconstruction of our cultural assumptions about formal logic as the 'law of thought'.
>
> (Turkle and Papert 1990: 153)

Stafford and Turkle may exaggerate (much of the new information space will remain resolutely based on text as the example of e-mail makes clear (Pound 1993)), but they also seem to us to have produced an original point of view on the rise of informational space.

Conclusion 2: Back to the Future?

This brings us to a final point. If we had to choose a space and a time to which the current City seems closest, it would be an eighteenth-century city. This might seem a bizarre choice. Yet one might argue, on the basis of current historical research which has, to an extent, pushed back the historical frontier of 'modernity', that many of the current indexes of our present were already in place in the eighteenth-century city – from blossoming consumer cultures, through to many and variegated senses of time, from insecure nation states through to large and powerful financial markets (which, for example, already used futures), from greater freedom for certain kinds of women through to the heterogeneity of social groupings, from various new forms of public sphere (like the press and pamphlets) through to the play of many different forms of cultural apprehension (such as astrology and various forms of science). Most especially, the eighteenth-century city was the site of a blooming oral–visual culture (Stafford 1991) to which we would argue that we are currently 'returning', one in which the boundaries between art and science were less clear (see Serres 1982), and one which was, partly through the sheer force of noise and smell, more entirely aware of the *vécu*, more open to what Prendergast (1992) calls an 'epidermal sensibility'. We would argue that what followed the eighteenth-century city – the controlled spaces of the nineteenth-century specular order, based upon the hegemony of print – are now being either cleared away or highly modified. We are moving, in other words, towards a city which generates, attends and reflects an oral–visual culture, a city in which pixels are replacing movable type, a city which offers new 'affordances', that is new cultural resources, new vocabularies, new senses of how to do things, some of which are good, some of which are bad, and each of which offers new ocular, kinesthetic, tactile and auditory skills (Thrift 1996; Stallabrass 1995).

This new 'city of bits' (Mitchell 1995) displays many of the same elements as the eighteenth-century city, from its emphasis on consumption to its many and variegated senses of time, from the insecurity of the nation state through to large and powerful financial markets, from greater freedom for certain women (in certain senses) through to the diversity of social groups, from various new forms of the public sphere (like e-mail and the Internet), through to the play of many different forms of cultural apprehension (from new-age religions, through many implicit religions, to the fact that we probably live at the high point of astrology), from a belief in all manner of monsters and mythologies (lurking in the sewers, or coming out of the television and computer screens), through to a renewed appreciation of the ordinary marvels of everyday (and night) life (Thrift 1994a). Most particularly, it seems to me that, in opposition to Jameson's ideas of vaulting and dysfunctional postmodern cities or Sennett's (1994) and others' laments for community lost, what we see is a city – a more dispersed city it is true – which still exists on a human (but not humanistic) scale and is still caught up in identifiably human concerns. We therefore find it oddly reassuring that the largest number of Internet bulletin boards are concerned with *Star Trek*, and that much of the discussion on Internet is concerned with sex (Sabbagh 1994; Moore 1995; Stone 1995; Wiley 1995). It also suggests that we should be about as worried about the 'return' of electronic oral–visual cultures as non-electronic oral–visual cultures were worried by the rise of literate cultures. These new cultures will certainly change our apprehension of the urban world and in quite severe ways, but we will still have many customs in common with the past. The new era will still contain many echoes of the old. In other words, business will go on, but never as usual – because it never has.[15]

NOTES

1 INTRODUCTION

1 This was the dilemma faced by Athens in 407 BC when Sparta blocked its supply of silver, forcing the Athenian authorities to resort to minting coins in gold realised from the melting down of statues and other treasures in the city (Davies 1994: 76). However, as the blockade continued the Athenian authorities sought recourse in the phenomenon that bedevils all forms of commodity money system: debasement. This occurs when the precious metal content of coins is lowered and replaced by a less-valued base metal. However, as happened in this case, debasement serves to introduce uncertainty into the process of monetary exchange, particularly when the debased coinage is introduced to supplement coins of higher intrinsic value already circulating in the currency system. In this particular instance the Athenian authorities issued bronze coins with a thin coating of silver, 'with the result that the good coins tended to disappear, which made the short-age even worse' (ibid.). As Davies notes, 'This infamous situation was made the occasion of what was probably the world's first statement of Gresham's Law, that bad money drives out good' (ibid.).

2 For example, by the beginning of the eleventh century there were a sufficient number of mints scattered the length and breadth of the country that no-one need travel more than twenty miles to exchange old coins for new (Davies 1994: 131).

3 Nevertheless, commodity money remained vulnerable to abuse from all its users owing to its embodiment of value. The precious metal that made them up could be extracted through devices such as clipping, filing or 'sweating', the latter being where coins are ground together to generate filaments of precious metal. These problems of incremental debasement were not really circumvented until coins became mere token money, made of base metal (e.g. see Galbraith 1975).

4 For example,

> Money has a younger sister, a very useful and officious servant in Trade, but if she be ever so little disappointed she grows sullen, sick and ill-natur'd and will be gone for a great while together: Her name in our Language is call'd Credit, in some countries Honour, and in others, I know not what.
>
> (Defoe, cited in Nicholson (1994: 48))

5 And, not the least, Defoe, of course, who was declared bankrupt twice, in 1692 and 1706.

6 Locke emphasises market relations between individuals as the natural order of things.

7 This act of default was hitherto known as the 'Stop of the Exchequer'.

8 The one nineteenth-century effort to produce a state-sponsored insurance scheme in Britain failed and the market was left to private insurance companies and friendly societies.

9 This is a discourse that is hardly dead, of course!

10 It is, of course, possible that in the future electronic cash will become a possibility, whether it takes the form of the Mondex Card now on trial in Swindon, or payment via the Internet.

11 There were, of course, markedly different technological regimes in Britain and North America. The Americans relied much more on electronic technology, on a large network of private lines, and so on.

12 One of the predecessors of the credit card, the travellers' cheque, itself has a fascinating historical geography, laid out in Booker (1994). The first of these 'circular notes' were offered by Robert Harris in 1769 and could be cashed in numerous agencies around Europe by British tourists taking the Grand Tour. In turn, their precursors were letters of credit used in Britain by travellers which in turn were preceded by bills of exchange. Thus the same kind of intra-regional, inter-regional and international compression of space and time was taking place in the retail financial arena.

13 Some of Marx's contempt for money may have come from Hegel for whom money was 'a monstrous system' that requires 'continual dominance and taming like a beast' (Hegel, cited in Shell (1982: 154)).

14 Keynes' fear of speculation needs to be qualified. His major fear was of monetary instability and the dangers this posed to capitalist economies, and he saw speculation as an important cause of such instability. However, on an individual basis, Keynes was deeply involved in the day-to-day workings of financial markets, and was responsible for perhaps more than his fair share of speculative financial practices. Keynes made and lost fortunes gambling on the movement of currencies during the early 1920s, while in 1921 he was made Chairman of the National Mutual Life Assurance Company and introduced an investment policy 'which combined investing in real assets . . . with constant switching of investments' (Skidelsky 1992: 25).

PART I HIGH SUMMER: INTRODUCTION

1 The term 'financial capital' is used in preference to 'banking capital' because institutions other than banks are increasingly advancing capital in return for interest paid out of surplus value. Therefore, to make it clear that we are talking about a particular function within the process of capital accumulation and not just one sector of the economy, the term financial capital is used.

2 The functions performed by financial, productive and commercial capital may not necessarily be located in different economic units. Some organisations may perform at different times all three of the functions of financial, productive and commercial capital.

3 In the long term, discipline will be reasserted, for the provision of credit does not solve the problems caused by extending production beyond the limits of the market. The extension of credit merely postpones the resolution of the problem. In other words, 'the use of credit tends to make matters worse in the long run because it can only deal with problems that arise in exchange and never with those in production' (Harvey 1982: 286).

4 Some indication of the relative dominance that financial capital has over productive capital is revealed by the fact that in return for the technical functions performed by money-dealing capitalists to facilitate the circulation of money and which impose financial orthodoxy upon productive capitalists, money-dealing capitalists extract a charge from the productive capitalists themselves through the appropriation of a part of surplus value. The failure to realise 'fictitious value' is extremely perilous to productive capitalists who are in debt. Lenders are legally entitled to bring into question the solvency of borrowers who fail to pay the 'price' of their debt. Therefore, indebted productive capitalists can be made insolvent by creditors who are not given their agreed share of future surplus value (i.e. their repayments of money capital advanced) which can lead to the liquidation of their assets, so creditors can obtain at least part of the value contained within the fixed capital of borrowers. However, it is far from certain that the value contained within the fixed capital will compensate for the value equivalent contained within the money capital advanced, which in addition may need to be shared out among a host of competing creditors.

5 Other important tendencies within capitalism facilitated by the credit system include the equalisation of the profit rate and the centralisation of capital.

2 THE REGULATION OF GLOBAL MONEY

1 Boyer (1990) insists that the two definitions of regulation described above should be differentiated from a third interpretation which arises in the corpus of work known as Regulation Theory. Here regulation is defined as 'the conjunction of the mechanisms working together for social reproduction, with attention to the prevalent economic structures and social forms' (Boyer 1990: 20). Nevertheless, despite Boyer's claims of

fundamental theoretical schism, there would seem to be some justification in exploring the common ground between conventional interpretations of *regulation* and *Regulation Theory*, not least since there would seem to be parallels between the ways in which regulation as a form of systemic equilibrium can be linked to regulation as a legal and administrative framework on the one hand, and the fusion of regimes of accumulation and modes of social regulation as used in Regulation Theory on the other.

2 This is not to suggest that the state is no longer an important actor upon the stage of the global political economy, as MacEwan and Tabb (1989) and Pooley (1991), among others, have stressed. Indeed, given the advent of an intensified geo-economic competition within the global economy, the role of the nation state assumes a new significance.

3 These were the 1810 Select Committee on the High Price of Gold Bullion and the 1811 parliamentary debate on the nature of money and its management. The purpose of these investigations and debates was to answer the question 'does money influence the economy or does money respond to the economy?' (Galbraith 1975: 46).

3 LIBERALISATION AND CONSOLIDATION

1 But note that the Cecchini Report has rightly been criticised for a tendency towards hyperbole in its evaluation of the economic benefits generated by the integration process (Cutler *et al.*, 1990; London Business School, 1989). However, even if the *absolute* level of economic gains penetrated by the 1992 programme fails to reach the inflated predictions of the Cecchini Report, the *relative* importance of the financial sector within the programme has not, as far as we are aware, been brought into question.

2 The implications of such liberalisation measures often seem not to be taken into account when first introduced, because they are usually designed to have dynamic effects upon the non-financial sector of the economy. For example, the introduction of legislation to liberalise the advancement of credit in the United Kingdom in the early 1970s (Competition and Credit Control) was intended to accelerate the provision of credit to UK productive capital (compare Fay 1988). Meanwhile, in the late 1970s the Japanese government introduced competition into its capital markets to lower the costs of its budget deficit financing (Hayes and Hubbard 1990). In both cases, liberalisation had long-run and for the most part unintended implications upon the competitive and institutional structures of the financial sectors of both countries, accelerating inherent tendencies towards capital centralisation and concentration.

3 Accounts can be found in Daly and Logan (1989), Evans (1988), Lipietz (1985, 1987), Strange (1986, 1988), and Thrift and Leyshon (1988).

4 The state often played an important role in facilitating the rise of international investment institutions to positions of importance within the circuit of financial capital. For example, in Europe where the state intervention in the accumulation process was highly developed, the level of employment supported by the nationalised industries meant that the pension funds organised by these industries were responsible for handling very large volumes of capital. Moreover, the international Keynesian–Fordist settlement, where rising levels of industrial productivity were balanced by a greater distribution of surpluses to the personal sector to support consumption, was responsible for producing higher level of disposable income, which often found its way into the circuit of financial capital via the purchase of insurance policies.

5 Until 1971 the United States was ultimately constrained in the extent to which it could push domestic accumulation by cheapening credit because of the link between the dollar and gold established at Bretton Woods. Cheap credit had the effect of increasing the volume of dollars in circulation, making the promise made by the United States to convert dollars into gold ever harder to keep. To prevent the growing number of dollar holders from cleaning out the US gold reserve, the gold window was unilaterally revoked by the United States in 1971. This decision had the additional short-term benefit to the United States of allowing it to accelerate the process of credit provision within the domestic economy, thereby encouraging accumulation. At the same time the severing of the link between the dollar and gold destroyed the fixed currency exchange rate system which was one of the cornerstones of the Bretton Woods system, and enabled the United States to push down the value of the dollar in relation to other currencies simply by encouraging an increase in the supply of dollars, thereby improving the competitiveness of US productive capital in world markets.

6 The collapse of the German Herstatt Bank in 1974 is generally recognised as the catalyst which spurred national financial regulators to move towards the creation of more unified, multinational standards of financial regulation (Dale 1989).

7 This included the purchase of real estate, which through the 1980s increasingly came to take on all the hallmarks of a securitised financial investment (Haila 1988, 1990).

8 There are two important points to note here. First, uncompetitive credit markets were manifested as national problems, and weighed heavily only on those borrowers who were unable to gain access to credit in the euromarkets. Therefore, national companies with international operations or those which were large enough to generate credit in such markets were not hindered by the cost of nationally derived credit, for credit could be obtained much more cheaply by entering into the global circuit of financial capital. The costs were borne by smaller borrowers, typically smaller companies and the personal sector (Dale, 1990). Second, the existence of long-term banking links in several European countries saw many borrowers gain access to funds at levels cheaper than the price posted in the open market.

9 This was later countered by waves of reactive reregulation in other key European centres. For an outline of reregulatory processes in European financial centres see Davis and Latter (1989: table J, p. 522).

10 A consideration of variations in the cost of motor insurance, notwithstanding the fact that the liberalisation of this market is in fact precluded from the proposed reforms, immediately highlights one of the main weaknesses of a plan for institutional restructuring rooted entirely in orthodox economic thinking. The cost of motor insurance, as reflected in the insurance premium, is a product not merely of the 'efficiency' and 'cost-effectiveness' of insurance companies, but is also a product of the local conditions in which insurance policies are offered: that is, the spatial variation in the incidence of car accidents can be expected to influence the relative costs of premiums. Therefore, the relatively high cost of motor insurance in Italy compared with the United Kingdom may indeed be a product of the differences in the 'efficiency' of Italian and UK insurers. But one cannot dismiss the possibility that the variations in the cost of premiums are a product of national variations in motor vehicle safety (Cutler et al., 1990; Evans and Smales 1989).

11 Of course, adherents of this view overlook the fact that many nation states retain very little control over the process of credit creation. The irony here is that the banks which states wish to retain as national monetary assets were largely responsible for liberating the credit system from the control of the state.

12 As was discovered by US banks such as Citicorp and Chase Manhattan in the 1980s, whose policies of branch expansion in Europe were subsequently reversed.

13 However, the ability of City-based institutions to continue to prosper within the European corporate finance market will inevitably decline as the focus shifts away from the purchase of UK companies. Not only does the European corporate finance market throw up more barriers to non-domestic financial institutions, because of the bank-orientated financial systems prevalent within many core EC economies, but the regulatory structure of the capital markets in many such countries means that rounds of capital centralisation operate at a much lower amplitude than in more transparent capital markets such as the United Kingdom (and the United States) (Franks and Mayer 1990).

14 The centralisation of political and economic power within a unified European state has been identified by many as a process which will allow for the introduction of more interventionist economic policies than is presently possible in individual European nation states given the sanctioning. These sentiments are particularly prevalent on the European left. For example, Jean-Pierre Cot, leader of the Socialist Group in the European Parliament, has argued that 'the only answer [to the erosion of national interventionist mechanisms] is to try and get some kind of control on public intervention at an international or at least a European level' (quoted in Lloyd (1991: 1)).

15 It should be noted that the German commitment to anti-inflationism has a longer history than that of the other European states. Outside Germany, the fear of inflation grew in direct proportion to the rising power of international financial capital, as experienced through the pressure exerted on national currencies in the foreign exchange markets. The inherent fear of German policy makers of inflationary conditions is rooted in the experiences of the 1930s when hyperinflation contributed to the destruction of the economic and the political bases of that society. The German economy has less to fear from rising inflation than other European states, thanks both to the strength of its industrial base, which makes the DM a safer bet than most other currencies, even in

conditions of rising inflations, and to the fact that the partial development of its capital markets means that it is less exposed to the highly volatile flows of mobile money that forces states to bend monetary policies to the imperatives of financial capital.

4 'SEXY GREEDY'

1 All such quotations in this chapter are from Churchill (1987: 92, 29, 22, 25, 25).

2 There are three probable reasons for the decline in relationship banking. First, the effective distribution of bonds to investors is primarily a sales task and banks need to be closely attuned to the market. The selling of securities to investors in a disintermediatory environment is much more performance driven and open to evaluation than is the matching of anonymous borrowers and lenders through the provision of loans. Therefore, borrowers will be attracted to banks who they perceive as possessing efficient distribution systems. Second, the initial advantage of disintermediation to many borrowers is the cost benefits inherent in obtaining securitised debt. Therefore, it is likely that price will be an important factor in the choice of a bank for an issue. Moreover, the competition between banks has risen sharply, placing downward pressure on costs as, on the one hand, international banks experienced in cross-border debt have endeavoured to become involved in securitisation, while on the other, investment banks and securities houses have moved further into the provision of cross-border debt. The increased competition between banks is linked to the third factor, namely financial diversification. A plethora of debt instruments has been developed by banks in the past few years in an attempt to increase market share. The innovations rage from note issuance facilities, through revolving underwriting facilities to swaps that make debt cheaper and/or more flexible for the borrower. These three developments have served to make borrowers more service driven and to loosen their ties with long-term financial advisers.

3 The initial attack on the working practices in the City came from the then Prices and Consumer Protection Minister, Roy Hattersley, who extended the powers of the Office of Fair Trading to include service industries as well as the manufacturing sector. The OFT duly commenced an action against the Stock Exchange intending to challenge its rule-book in the Restrictive Practices court. The case was eventually dropped in 1983 when the then Secretary of State for Trade and Industry, Cecil Parkinson, secured a commitment from the Chairman of the Stock Exchange to dismantle the fixed commission and other restrictive practices in the exchange before the end of 1986.

4 As an indication of London's position as Europe's premier financial centre Deutsche Bank moved its capital market headquarters from Frankfurt to the City during 1986.

5 It is important to note that the major part of these effects are concentrated in the south east of England, strengthening the argument of this chapter, if anything.

6 Findlay found that short-term professional and managerial migrants from Britain were more likely to be from the South East.

7 Every sign is that there will be a rationalisation of employment numbers in the City, beginning in 1988.

8 In fact, the situation is in many ways similar to that found in the 1970s when exchange rates floated and there was a shortage of foreign exchange traders, driving up wages.

9 In 1987, Morgan Stanley offered one Cambridge undergraduate a starting salary of £26,000 (plus perquisites, bonuses, etc.) (*Business,* June 1987: 18).

10 According to Inland Revenue figures, before tax, there were 704,000 incomes of £20,000 to £50,000 in 1983–4, 44,000 of £50,000 to £100,000 and 8,000 of over £100,000. Our estimates proceed from these figures but without updating them to 1986 and by taking the lowest possible figure. Therefore our estimates are very conservative indeed.

11 Remember that earnings, income and wealth are not the same. Thus some people in the City might have relatively low earnings but still be millionaires. Thus the figures on earnings, wealth and income should not be expected to tally automatically, although some correlation is clearly likely in certain cases.

12 According to Rentoul (1987) and *New Society* (1986) 43,500 people had assets of more than £740,000 in 1986. Thus a figure for the City of 13,000 such people seems entirely likely and probably conservative.

13 One might legitimately question the spatial extent of the 'South East' now, of course. In

many ways, as the London commuter shed has grown, so the South East has grown with it until it is now stretching along the M4 corridor at the least (see Thrift 1987a).

14 The number of USM-created millionaires was at least 500 between 1980 and 1986 (see Thrift 1987b).

15 The City, of course, produces only some of the South East's wealth. There are other sources as well.

16 The figures were derived by multiplying the average yearly full-time woman's salary by the number of women workers and the average full-time man's salary by the number of male workers. The figure is ex-bonuses. Tax is assumed to be charged at 40 per cent, probably an overestimate.

17 As Ascherson (1986a,b,c) points out, domestic service is returning.

18 We ignore here corporate spending on private health schemes.

19 As Rubinstein (1977) points out, the South Eastern middle class has always been nearer to upper-class mores and values than the middle class in the north.

20 One might well question current depictions of capital as 'depersonalised' (e.g. Abercrombie and Urry 1983). Perhaps they have moved further away from production.

PART II FALL: INTRODUCTION

1 A similar history could be constructed for many other centres. For example, in the United States, it could again start with the Bible but then move on through Theodore Dreiser's *Sister Carrie*, ending up in Tom Wolfe's *Bonfire of the Vanities*.

2 Eliot moved to the Colonial and Foreign Department of Lloyds in 1917, aged 29:

> He was to remain here for the next nine years, arguably the most important years in his creative life. The man who wrote *The Waste Land* was a man behind his desk, a bank official indistinguishable from other such officials except perhaps for the absolute decorum of his dress, arriving at 9.30 and leaving at 5.30, working one Saturday in four, taking his lunch at Baker's Chop House with its curved front windows, visiting the wine shop in Cowper's Court with its dusty shelves and corners, a little cog in the machine of Britain's commercial empire.
>
> (Ackroyd, 1984: 78–9)

3 Mottram, the author of more than sixty books, died in 1971 aged 87. He once wrote 'I am an escaped bank clerk. I don't even look like a writer' (*Daily Telegraph* 1971).

4 A term which, as Chapman (1992) notes, has its antecedents in the work of Bagehot on *Lombard Street*, and in the work of Chapman and Cassis on the so-called 'aristocratic bourgeoisie'.

5 We are grateful to Lesley Budd for this reference. We shall do no more than note here that if gentlemanly capitalism was so gentlemanly, how was it that the City's history is filled with examples of fraud and general financial wrong-doing (Daunton 1995)?

6 The assumptions of this work spilt over into work on interlocking directorships carried out by Whitley, Giddens and Stanworth, and others in the 1960s in a remarkably unexamined way.

7 This discursive approach has been developed in Thrift (1983, 1985a, 1986b) and in particular in Thrift (1991, 1992, 1993, 1995b). We take it that the study of culture formation is the study of the production and distribution of meaning, and that production and distribution of meaning takes place through the medium of accounts, the ways in which practices are justified in dialogical interaction, continually constituting consciousness and mastery of self, and identity. However, it is important to make clear that we have to understand accounts in a rather broader sense than is found in some of the literature. Whilst we would want to endorse the social constructivist project which sees people as cultural artefacts created in the course of collective action by accounts, we do not want, as many social constructivists seem to do, to assert that practices/accounts are produced only or even chiefly by speech/talk. In one sense this is because we want to broaden out the meaning of language. Thus we would agree with Derrida that speech has been colonised by reading and writing over time, and, as a result, the immediacy of speech has been joined to the 'absence' of writing in much (but not all) of what we do: speech cannot be privileged.

But in another sense, we see no reason to restrict ourselves to the frame of language. For, as Levine (1987: 29) puts it:

The fact is that we don't even know if we know all the ways of thinking and perceiving and we certainly don't know much about the ones we have so far attempted to classify. Language is muddled up with everything else the body does and there is no general reason – even a pragmatist one – to isolate it and declare this is what we're all about, the rest is conceptually insignificant.

Thus, we would also want to include the non-verbal within the substance of accounts. That means visual images certainly, a common enough departure since Barthes (Fyfe and Law 1988). But it means more than this. We would also want to include bodies in their many manifestations and all manner of objects, especially commodities. We take these to be a fundamental part of communication, the image schemata through which we create the world, and a fundamental part of the cultural sphere.

To summarise, accounts are best conceived of as 'social thoughts' constantly being refurbished through interaction, using whatever resources are to hand (speech, texts, images, music, bodies, commodity objects and no doubt other ways of communication that we have yet to discover).

These social thoughts have four chief characteristics (Lakoff 1987). First they are embodied. They grow out of bodily experience and make sense in terms of it. Second, they are imaginative, they employ all manner of aesthetics, metaphors, metonymies, and mental images to go beyond simple representation. Third, they are always and everywhere collective. Even when others are not present, this presence is assumed. Fourth, they are contextual. They depend on position in, and the setting of, time and space.

The fuel for the process of accounting is provided by stocks of knowledge, which are constantly being built up and torn down. Knowledge can be obtained directly (as in the case of emotional and social knowledge). But increasingly, as technology has progressed, so stocks of knowledge have become indirect and institutionalised, existing at a distance from interaction (although their trace may be present in the interaction), with rules governing access to them.

The process of social thought is always geographical. Accounts of practices and the selves and the identities they engender are acutely contextual. They are co-ordinations of time and space that constantly refer to co-ordinations of time and space. For example, 'research has shown that there are distinct personas adjusted to each socially distinct kind of situation in which a person acts. Personality is not a simple and constant property of each human being; but rather a presentational style that varies from one situation to another' (Harré et al. 1985: 89). Stocks of knowledge are acutely contextual as well. They do not exist everywhere, only in certain places, and so they can only be used as resources to constitute self and identify in those places where they are available (Thrift 1985a). Finally, both accounts and stocks of knowledge assume particular orderings of time and space, what Bakhtin called chronotopes.

What dynamises this whole system? We would want to suggest that it is a combination of material circumstance and discourses; the dominant modes of conceiving social life. Whereas accounts can be thought of as drops of rain, and stocks of knowledge as pools, discourses are more like rivers. They are hegemonic ways of ordering, of categorising experience. They are shared social categorisations with their own stocks of knowledge (special kinds of speech, text, image and other kinds of cultural capital), their own criteria for membership of the discourse, their own norms of representation, like specific kinds of metaphor and rhetorics, their own contents, even their own personas, which are routinely drawn on in accounts to justify actions:

> dominant discourse is not a thing but a complex shifting formation. It is as diffuse as a way of feeling, of experiencing the body, of perceiving sensorially, of living work and leisure, of assimilating information, of communicating with others within the social world, of comprehending the organisation of conflict, of experiencing the inevitable hierarchicalisations of social existence.
>
> (Terdiman 1985: 57)

6 THE RESTRUCTURING OF THE UK FINANCIAL SERVICES INDUSTRY IN THE 1990s

1 For more on the relative efficacy of this form of regulation, see Underhill (1991) and OECD (1992a).

2 That is, the equivalent of clearing banks in the UK or money-center banks in the United States.

3 At least part of the blame for the emergence of the less developed countries' debt crisis has been laid at the door of the elites of these countries who used the money they borrowed to fund 'Pharaonic projects', which were spectacular but ultimately unproductive uses of borrowed money (Corbridge 1992: 291). Large property developments in large financial centres, such as the Canary Wharf project in London's Docklands will in time surely be seen as the 'Pharaonic projects' of the developed countries' debt crisis, since they were equally spectacular but equally unproductive uses of borrowed money (e.g. see Hallsworth and Bobe 1993: Daniels and Bobe 1993).

4 The six 'global' banks were the two large Hong Kong banks – Hong Kong and Shanghai Bank and Standard Chartered Bank; the three largest Swiss banks, Union Bank of Switzerland, Swiss Bank Corporation and Credit Suisse; and the US bank Bankers Trust.

5 The international pretensions of such services are revealed by their industry description: global custody services (e.g. see *The Financial Times* 1992).

6 The European Monetary System (EMS) and the regular meetings of the Group of Five (G5) and Group of Seven (G7) industrial nations, which have sought to counteract the worst excess of international macroeconomic instability, however, have also been highly significant in this regard (Thompson 1990b; Leyshon and Thrift 1994b).

7 The difference between this form of private sector institutional regulation and the public sector form of structural regulation is that the former is taking place to insulate activities in newer, more profitable financial markets from the damage inflicted in more established markets where crises have already broken out. In other words, it is more a *reactive* than a *proactive* form of regulation. It aims to sustain competitive market power in an increasingly volatile system.

8 However, it must also be acknowledged that the Hong Kong and Shanghai Bank's interest in Midland was part driven by its search for a refuge for its assets ahead of Hong Kong's absorption into the People's Republic of China in 1997.

9 Investment-related financial products, on the other hand, are likely to become more important. With lower rates of interest more money has to be invested to make the same rate of return on investment realised under earlier regimes of more expensive money. Although during the 1980s lower interest rates actually saw the propensity to save go into sharp decline, there are a number of reasons to suggest that indebtedness on this scale will not reappear, at least for the foreseeable future. One reason is simply the bitter experience of 1980s' indebtedness, and the highly publicised consequences of what can be described as 'debt over-reach' (e.g. house repossession due to mortgage default, personal bankruptcy, etc.). Perhaps of more importance is the progressive dismantling of the state system of welfare provision. This will require people to save more from their own income for formerly socialised items such as health care and retirement provision. It is no coincidence that Japan is the industrialised state with both the lowest level of state welfare provision *and* the highest propensity to save.

10 Calculations such as these help to explain the attractions of the centralised telephone-based financial services pioneered by Midland Bank, through its First Direct banking service, and by the Royal Bank of Scotland, through its Direct Line insurance service. Both services have been highly profitable.

11 Interview with Senior BIFU Official, London, January 1992.

12 In consequence, by the early 1990s large numbers of middle-ranking managerial staff in the financial services industry had been made redundant.

13 The banks include Bank of Scotland, Barclays, Lloyds, Midland, National Westminster, The Royal Bank of Scotland and TSB (British Banking Association 1992).

14 For example, Barclays premier banking service requires an income of at least £30,000 per annum, that of Midland £50,000. National Westminster run a rather less exclusive service, which requires a mere £25,000 per annum salary (Goldsmith 1993).

15 An example of such 'risk pricing' might be the Bristol & West Building Society's proposed policy to introduce mortgages with tiered interest rates linked to family status. Married couples with children would receive preferential treatment, following a calculation by the

building society that 'unmarried couples were 50% more likely to fall into arrears than married couples. Childless couples were more likely to default after they had children because their bills had increased' (Gapper 1992).

7 GEOGRAPHIES OF FINANCIAL EXCLUSION

1 See Berthoud and Kempson (1992), Ford (1988, 1991), Kempson (1994).
2 For London, see Bird (1993), Brownhill (1990) and Keith and Pile (1993); for New York, see Fainstein (1994) and Smith (1993); for Los Angeles, see Davis (1990); for Baltimore, see Merrifield (1993).
3 This is why lending money to such powerful economic agents is sometimes described as 'investing'; that is, when money is exchanged with a public company in return for some of its share capital, or to a government in return for a government bond.
4 But note that in Britain, at least, financial institutions have dramatically reduced the costs of calculating the credit-worthiness of borrowers in contract credit markets by automating the process. Potential borrowers are required to complete application forms which are then assessed by credit-scoring computer systems. This is far more cost effective than the relatively expensive face-to-face interview with a bank manager which was once the predominant way in which access to the financial system was policed. However, tellingly, while the *costs* have been lowered, financial institutions have done little to pass on these savings in the *price* charged for such credit.
5 Although in Britain this is changing with the introduction of 'premier' banking accounts for more affluent customers. Certain credit cards (e.g. American Express Optima) also charge differential interest rates based on indicators of customer probity.
6 See Cressey and Scott (1991, 1992), Halford and Savage (1993, 1995), Leyshon *et al.* (1993), O'Reilly (1992a, b).
7 However, it should be noted that a study by the Boston Consulting Group (1992) has argued that, while a typical bank branch has an annual cost of £300,000, in a well-run bank few branches would fail to cover their costs. Further, branch closures make it more difficult to retain and recruit customers. In summary, Boston Consulting Group calculated that a closure of 20 per cent of branches would lead to only a 2 per cent saving in total costs and therefore suggested that branch remodelling (making a branch more like a retail outlet) was more effective than closure in most cases. Moreover, banks have various options other than closure which could reduce their costs and exposure to risk in low-income areas (Alex Ball, Banking Consultant, personal communication, 1994). First, banks could cut overhead costs by sharing facilities in multiple-occupancy 'banking halls'. Second, banks could externalise costs and risks through franchising services and/or by encouraging management buyouts of branches. In this way, branches would retain a formal link to the bank but would take a greater responsibility for their economic fortunes. Third, banks could create low-cost subdivisions which would exist specifically to provide basic financial services to low-income communities.
8 Which in 1992 was estimated to be between £60 and £90 per account per annum (Gapper 1992).
9 In 1992, it was estimated that an account would have to run average balances of at least £1,000 before it generated sufficient income to cover the cost of running the account. With interest rates at lower levels, this figure would need to be revised upwards.
10 Although the rise of telephone banking has the potential to compensate for some of the worst excesses of financial infrastructure withdrawal and financial exclusion, it must be pointed out that these services are designed specifically to attract more affluent middle-class customers. First Direct, Midland Bank's highly successful telephone banking subsidiary, is a good case in point. According to Richardson (1993: 17)

> its customer profile differs from that of the high street bank with most customers falling into the A, B, and C1 socio-economic bands, with 66 per cent in the 25–44 age group. The bank describes its customers as 'upscale, confident and articulate' and it would appear that Midland has, so far, been successful in carving out an up-market client base through telebanking.

11 As the Consumers Association (1994: 4) found out when it conducted an impromptu survey in response to complaints that some of its members were being denied insurance cover in certain areas:

As well as putting up prices, often by ridiculous amounts, and paying out on less claims . . . some insurers are trying to cut their losses by refusing cover to those people they consider to be high risk. Our survey suggests that a couple of claims may be enough to put you in the 'high-risk' category . . . we contacted 16 insurers anonymously, asking for quotes on a three-bedroomed house in London with two theft claims (£900 and £1,400) in the last year. Only one insurer would quote.

12 For example, in 1994 *The Sunday Times* reported that Provincial Insurance had set up a telephone-based motor insurance subdivision to exploit the commercial advantages of socio-spatial risk pricing by focusing exclusively upon low-risk customers. The company utilises a geographical information system package called 'Premium Watch' which, it is claimed 'identifies the best risks by analysing the applicant's claims record, lifestyle and residential area' (Gardner 1994: 5.1). The philosophy of the company is made clear by a comment made by the Managing Director:

Motor insurers have tended to lump people together in large groups in a way that does not fully reward careful people. We can assess their risk ratings by looking at exactly where they live – using all the letters of the postcode – therefore basing premiums on locations as precise as groups of just 15 houses. Our data show that these 'micro-localities' very well define their lifestyles and characteristics'.

(ibid.: 5.1)

13 Indeed, Conaty (1993) reports that an investigation into such services in Birmingham revealed some lenders were charging interest rates approaching 5,000 per cent per annum.

14 However, it might be argued that the proliferation of automated teller machines (ATMs) counteracts the effect of bank branch closure in poorer communities. But this misses an important difference between bank branches and ATMs. While the growing number of ATMs in Britain means that *cash* transmission is still possible in areas subjected to financial infrastructure withdrawal, they do not provide *credit* which is more important for long-term local economic development.

15 See Caskey (1994), Cloud and Galster (1993), Hoyt and Choca (1989), Leven and Sykuta (1994), Robinson (1991).

16 See, for example, Erickson (1971), Harvey (1973), Harvey and Chaterjee (1974), Stone (1975), Werner *et al.* (1976), Yaspan (1970).

17 See Badain (1980), Heimer (1982), Hoyt and Choca (1989), Squires *et al.* (1979), Squires and Velez (1987, 1988).

18 The problem of coming to a hard and fast definition of 'community' is revealed by the fact that the CRA makes a distinction between two types of community and suggests two ways of delineating them. On the one hand, banks serve an 'entire' community which is seen to be made up of one or more 'local' communities. On the other hand, local communities may be taken to reside within existing geographical areas, such as counties, or within what the CRA describes as 'the effective lending area territory'. Adding fuel to the problems of interpretation, the CRA adds that, 'Both types of territory are subject to certain adjustments' (*Federal Register* 1978).

19 However, it would be mistaken to assume that all credit unions are communitarian in orientation. To work at all, the members of the credit union must be united by a common bond. This may well be the fact that they live in the same local community. But many more credit unions are based on non-residential communities, such as workplaces, where the members may live in very different types of residential community. Indeed, the vast majority of credit unions in the United States are based on workplaces (77 per cent) (Berthoud and Hinton 1989: 7–8).

20 For example, The Founders National Bank, based in the south central district of Los Angeles and owned by a consortium of community-minded investors, managed to earn $1.3 million in 1992 on an asset base of $74 million, mainly through the provision of mortgage finance in another area largely abandoned by more formal financial infrastructure (*The Economist* 1993b).

21 However, an important note of caution about such developments has been sounded by that astute chronicler of the US urban landscape, Mike Davis. He warns that 'community developers . . . are being promoted not as auxiliaries, but as surrogates for federal government spending' (M. Davis 1993: 51). He argues that it is impossible for such organisations, no matter how laudable their aims, to compensate for the severe cutbacks in government funding of inner-city development.

22 The exceptions that prove the rule here, of course, are the way in which the Bank of England allowed BCCI to collapse in 1991 and the failure of the Bank to construct a rescue package for Barings in February 1995. BCCI played only a minor role within the British economy as a whole. The collapse of the bank did immense economic damage to the many Asian communities where the bank did most of its business in Britain, as well as forcing up local taxes in the Highlands and Islands where the local authority was lending money to the bank at relatively high levels of interest at the time of the collapse. However, the Bank of England clearly calculated that these localised losses were a price well worth paying to close down a bank engaged in extensive Ponzi financing operations, which in time could have ensnared larger and, for the British economy as a whole, more important banks. The collapse of Barings was widely attributed to a failure of internal control mechanisms to control 'rogue' dealing. Certainly, this was the view of Kenneth Clarke, the UK Chancellor of the Exchequer, in his statement to the House of Commons on 27 February 1995.

23 The Employment Service introduced ACT on a rolling programme between May 1993 and autumn 1994. The Benefits Agency introduced ACT for Income Support from October 1993 and for incapacity benefits from the end of January 1994. Currently, clients can choose whether to receive benefit by order book and girocheque or to opt for ACT (Kempson 1994).

24 One avenue that is currently being explored by members of the New Economics Foundation and the UK Social Investment Forum to bring pressure to bear for an EU Banking Directive which emphasises the social responsibilities of banks.

25 A number of retailers already offer 'cash-back' facilities.

8 MONEY ORDER?

1 Although the radical critique of the quantitative revolution was important, it was not the only one. The quantitative project was also undermined by critics writing from a 'behavioural' and 'humanistic' perspective. See Cloke *et al.* (1991) for a summary of radical and humanistic critiques of the 'quantitative turn' in human geography which emerged from the early 1970s onwards.

2 As, for example, in the description of 'sound waves'. As we cannot see sound we can have no visual picture of the movement of sound, but through a process of metaphorical redescription we can imagine sound moving in patterns similar to ocean waves (see Barnes 1992: 122).

3 Indeed, Marx was much impressed with Darwin's theory of evolution. After reading *Origin of Species* in 1860 Marx wrote to Engels to argue that, 'although it is developed in the crude English style, this is the book which contains the basis in natural history for our view' (quoted in Young (1985: 52)). Darwin's evolutionary metaphor, meanwhile, owed a considerable debt both to Malthus's understanding of population dynamics and, more importantly, to Adam Smith's understanding of the invisible hand. Russian evolutionists, such as Kropotkin, meanwhile developed theories which stressed co-operation and mutual aid (Gould 1991; Todes 1988). These debts were embarrassing to Marx and Engels, given their earlier criticisms of Malthus and Smith (Young 1985).

4 Interestingly, the dominance of neoclassical economics within the financial community – the guerrilla wing of the economics profession – is increasingly under pressure from another metaphorical transformation derived from the physical and biological sciences. Chaos theory and fuzzy logic are both being used in attempts to outperform the securities markets. Similarly, neural networks, which attempt to mimic the pattern of acitvity in the human brain, are being used to 'evolve' solutions to problems (Davidson 1994: 7). Illustrative of their influence is that half of the theoretical physics PhD graduates from Harvard in recent years now work on Wall Street.

5 As with so much of Marx's work, there are a number of competing ways in which the relationship between the economic base and the legal and political superstructure can be read. Although Marx at times was technologically determinist (most notably in his claim that 'the hand mill will give you a society with the feudal lord, the steam mill a society with the industrial capitalist' (Marx 1977: 202; see also Cohen (1978)), we would dispute a reading which generalises this statement. In *The Poverty of Philosophy*, for example, Marx placed the working class firmly in the economic base, referring to them as 'the greatest productive power of all the instruments of production' (cited in McLellan (1980: 137)).

6 The favourable treatment of Japan came to an abrupt end in the 1980s as geo-economic anxieties came to rival geopolitical concerns (Luttwak 1990). Powerful social groups in the United States began to seek the 'liberalisation' of the Japanese economy in much the way that an earlier generation had succeeded in 'liberalising' the economies of Western Europe during the 1940s and 1950s (e.g. see Grant 1993; Leyshon 1994b; Ó Tuathail 1992b, 1993a, b).

10 NEW URBAN ERAS AND OLD TECHNOLOGICAL FEARS

1 Even the accounts of that most subtle of the writers in this area, Donna Haraway, are not immune from this kind of hyperbole (Barker 1995).
2 One thinks of the enormous number of repair functions in any *Yellow Pages* (see also Sayer and Walker 1992).
3 And this is not all. Until recently, for example, the Amish 'shunned' telephones. Even now, they only use jointly accessed community telephones (Umble 1992).
4 Spurred on, of course, by the way in which many new electronic communications technologies have reversed the idea of a 'broadcast' model of few producers and many consumers (Poster 1995).
5 There are, of course, many communities of practice using electronic communications technologies in more or less techno-literate ways to particular ends. What we need are studies which attend to the range and depth of this cultural variation.
6 Several Stock Exchange syndicates maintained pigeon lofts in the 1830s and 1840s.
7 The cable was linked to the Stock Exchange in 1853.
8 These exchanges, both run by private companies, were located at 6 Lombard Street (Edison Company) and 36 Coleman Street (Telephone Company), both in the heart of the City.
9 Similarly, 'one well-known firm had (the telephone) installed in the lavatory, apparently believing that if it were in any more accessible place, it would encourage the clerks to waste time on private calls' (Morgan and Thomas 1962: 163).
10 Even though much business was forced to go on outside the Exchange.
11 In part, the new Stock Exchange building, opened in 1972, was built in order to accommodate increasing telecommunications demands.
12 Which lead to the use of pagers. Thus Jenkins (1973: 103) could write of the Stock Exchange in 1972:

> The new paging system, specifically designed by Modern Telephones Ltd, is one of the fastest in the world and can handle 1200 calls per minute. There are 1,500 receivers, remotely controlled from 280 points, and the system could be expanded to 4,000 receivers if necessary. This is perhaps the greatest change noticed by older Members. From 1801 until 1970, the normal method of calling a Member on the Floor was the stentorian voice of 'a waiter' (so-called from coffee-house days) or a flashing number above a Member's stand. Now Members carry pocket 'bleepers' – small microwave radios by which they can be reached anywhere on the Floor or . . . in neighbouring pubs and cafes.

The mobile phone has changed all this again. Yet, throughout the history of the City private messenger and courier services have continued to operate, nowadays especially to guarantee secure delivery of documents. Thus, it is important to note that international document delivery, by United Parcel Services in the City still, in part at least, relies on eleven walking couriers (*The Independent* 15 June 1994: 23). Again, the rise of the bicycle courier in the City in the 1980s cannot be ignored.

13 On one reckoning, 60 per cent of all British telecommunications expenditure originates or ends in London. Firms in the City spend £200 million a month on international direct dialling, which does not take into account their expenditure on private calls (City Research Project 1995).
14 This tendency is now as far advanced in the world of international finance as elsewhere. Firms like Visible Decisions specialise in three-dimensional graphics for international finance, as an aid to traders and investors in seeing what they are doing, as a risk-management tool, and as a way of making speedier decisions (*The Economist* 25 August

1995: 75). But, the greatest use of visualisation may well be in allowing managers to understand what is going on, a problem the Barings débâcle suggests is still widespread, even in an age of 'rocket science' (Motluk 1995).

15 In any case, as other new technologies proceed, we believe that the current obsession with electronic spaces may well diminish. See for example, Stephenson's (1995) remarkable move into nanotechnology.

REFERENCES

Abercrombie, N. and Urry, J. (1983) *Capital, Labour and the Middle Classes*, London: Allen & Unwin.

Accountancy Personnel (1986) *Summary of Salaries in Accountancy*, London: Accountancy Personnel.

Ackroyd, P. (1984) *T.S. Eliot*, London: Hamish Hamilton.

Aglietta, M. (1979) *A Theory of Capitalist Regulation: The US Experience*, London: Verso.

—— (1985) 'The emergence of international liquidity', in *The Political Economy of International Money*, ed. L. Tsoukalis, pp. 171–202, London: Sage.

Aglietta, M. and Orlean, A. (1982) *La Violence de la Monnaie*, Paris: Plon.

Agnew, J.A. (1991) 'Timeless space and state-centricism: the geographical assumptions of international relations theory', Department of Geography, Syracuse University, New York (mimeo).

—— (1993) 'The United States and American hegemony', in *Political Geography of the Twentieth Century: A Global Analysis*, ed. P.J. Taylor, pp. 209–38, London: Belhaven Press.

—— (1994) 'The territorial trap: the geographical assumptions of international relations theory', *Review of International Political Economy* 1: 53–80.'

Agnew, J.A. and Corbridge, S. (1989) 'The new geopolitics: the dynamics of geopolitical disorder', in *A World in Crisis?*, ed. R.J. Johnston and P.J. Taylor, 2nd edition, pp. 266–88, Oxford: Basil Blackwell.

Aitchison, N.B. (1988) 'Roman wealth, native ritual: coin hoards within and beyond Roman Britain, *World Archaeology* 20(2): 270–84.

Allen, J. (1988), 'Towards a post-industrial economy?', in *The Economy in Question*, ed. J. Allen and D. Massey, pp. 92–135, London: Sage.

Althusser, L. and Balibar, E. (1970) *Reading Capital*, London: New Left Books.

Altvater, E. (1992) 'Fordist and post-Fordist international division of labor and monetary regimes', in *Pathways to Industrialisation and Regional Development*, ed. M. Storper and A.J. Scott, pp. 21–45, London: Routledge.

—— (1993) *The Future of the Market. An Essay on the Regulation of Money and Nature after the Collapse of Actually Existing Socialism*, London: Verso.

Amin, A. and Thrift, N. (1992) 'Neo-Marshallian nodes in global networks', *International Journal of Urban and Regional Research* 16: 571–87.

Anderson, B. (1983) *Imagined Communities*, London: Verso.

Anderson, P. (1987) 'The figures of descent', *New Left Review* 161: 20–77.

Andreff, W. (1984) 'The international centralization of capital and the re-ordering of world capitalism', *Capital and Class* 22: 58–80.

Angell, N. (1930) *The Story of Money*, London: Cassell.

Annual Abstract of Banking Statistics (1993) Vol. 10, London: Statistical Unit, British Bankers Association.

Appelbaum, D. (1991) 'Money and the City', *Parable: The Magazine of Myth and Tradition* 16: 40–5.

Applebaum, E. and Albin, P. (1989) 'Computer rationalization and the transformation of work: lessons from the insurance industry', in *The Transformation of Work? Skill, Flexibility and the Labour Process*, ed. S. Wood, pp. 247–65, London; Unwin Hyman.

Ardener, S. and Burman, S. (eds) (1995) *Money-Go-Rounds: The Importance of Rotating Savings and Credit Associates for Women*, Oxford: Berg.

Armstrong, T. (1992) 'The electrification of the body', *Textual Practice* 8: 16–32.
Arrighi, G. (1993) 'The three hegemonies of historical capitalism', in *Gramsci, Historical Materialism and International Relations*, ed. S. Gill, pp. 148–85, Cambridge: Cambridge University Press.
Ascherson, N. (1986a) 'London's new class: the great cash-in', *The Observer* 25 May.
—— (1986b) 'The new rich spend, the old rich sulk', *The Observer* 13 July.
—— (1986c) 'Stoke Newington: settlers and natives', *The Observer* 3 August.
—— (1992) 'Will the mice run from the Budget box to ballot box?', *The Independent on Sunday* 15 March: 25.
Ashley, R.K. (1987) 'The geopolitics of geopolitical space: toward a critical social theory of international politics', *Alternatives* 12: 403–34.
Atkinson, J. (1984) 'Manpower strategies for flexible organizations', *Personnel Management* August: 28–31.
Augelli, E. and Murphy, C.N. (1993) 'Gramsci and international relations: a general perspective and an example from recent US policy towards the third world', in *Gramsci, Historical Materialism and International Relations*, ed. S. Gill, pp. 127–47, Cambridge: Cambridge University Press.
Auger, D.A. (1993) 'Urban realities, US national policy and the Clinton administration', *Regional Studies* 27: 807–15.
Ayling, D.E. (1986) *The Internationalisation of Stockmarkets*, Aldershot: Gower.
Badain, D.I. (1980) 'Insurance redlining and the future of the urban core', *Colombia Journal of Law and Social Problems* 16: 1–83.
Baker, W.E (1984) 'Fear, trading and crowd dynamics', *The Social Dynamics of Financial Markets*, ed. P. Adler, Greenwich, CT: JAI Press.
—— (1987) 'What is money? A social structural interpretation', in *Intercorporate Relations. The Structural Analysis of Business*, ed. M. Mizruchi and M. Schwartz, pp. 109–44, Cambridge: Cambridge University Press.
Bank for International Settlements (1992) *Recent Developments in International Interbank Relations*, Basle: Bank for International Settlements.
Bank of England (1989) 'The single European market: survey of the UK financial services industry', *Bank of England Quarterly Bulletin* 29: 407–12.
Barbrook, R. (1990) 'Mistranslations: Lipietz in London and Paris', *Science as Culture* 8: 80–117.
Barker, M. (1995) 'Drawing attention to the image: computers and comics', in *The Photographic Image in Digital Culture*, ed. M. Lister, London: Routledge, 188–213.
Barnekov, T. and Jabber-Bey, R. (1993) 'Letter from America: credit and development financing for low-income and minority communities', *Regions: The Newsletter of the Regional Studies Association* No. 188, December: 4–8.
Barnes, T. (1987) 'Homo economicus, physical metaphors, and universal models in economic geography', *Canadian Geographer* 31: 299–308.
—— (1989) 'Place, space, and theories of economic value: contextualism and essentialism in economic geography', *Transactions of the Institute of British Geographers* New Series 14: 299–316.
—— (1992) 'Reading the texts of theoretical economic geography: the role of physical and biological methaphors', in *Writing Worlds: Discourse, Text and Metaphor in the Representation of Landscape*, ed. T.J. Barnes and J.S. Duncan, pp. 118–35, London: Routledge.
Barrett, M. (1987) 'The coming crunch for banks', *Euromoney* April: 99–103.
Barty-King, H. (1977) *The Baltic Exchange*, London: Hutchinson.
—— (1991) *Worst Poverty: A History of Debt and Debtors*, London: Alan Sutton.
Batchelor, C. and Gapper, J. (1993) 'Midland calls for subsidised bank loans', *Financial Times* 28 February:
Batty, M. (1990) 'Invisible cities', *Environment and Planning B* 17: 127–30.
Beaverstock, J. (1991) 'Skilled international migration: an analysis of the geography of international secondments within large accountancy firms', *Environment and Planning A* 23: 1133–46.
Beaverstock, J., Leyshon, A., Thrift, N. and Williams, P. (1990) *The estate agency sector in transition*, Working Papers in Producer Services 17, University of Bristol, Bristol, and Portsmouth Polytechnic, Portsmouth.
Beck, U. (1992) *Risk Society: Towards a New Modernity*, London: Sage.
Beck, U., Lash, S. and Giddens, A. (1994) *Reflexive Modernisation*, Cambridge: Polity Press.
Begg, I. (1992) 'The spatial impact of the EC internal market for financial services', *Regional Studies* 26: 333–47.

Benedikt, M. (ed.) (1991) *Cyberspace: First Steps*, Cambridge, MA: MIT Press.
Beninger, J.R. (1991) *The Control Revolution*, Cambridge, MA: Harvard University Press.
Bernstein, J. (1994) *Foregone Conclusions*, Berkeley, CA: University of California Press.
Berthoud, R. and Hinton, T. (1989) *Credit Unions in the United Kingdom*, London: Policy Studies Institute.
Berthoud, R. and Kempson, E. (1992) *Credit and Debt: The PSI Report*, London: Policy Studies Institute.
Best, M. (1990) *The New Competition*, Cambridge: Polity Press.
Bhabha, H. (1994) *The Location of Culture*, New York: Routledge.
Bhaskar, R. (1980) 'Scientific explanation and human emancipation', *Radical Philosophy* 26: 16–28.
Bird, J. (1993) 'Dystopia on the Thames', in *Mapping the Futures: Local Cultures, Global Change*, ed. J. Bird *et al.*, pp. 120–35, London: Routledge.
Birmingham, P. (1989) 'Local theory', in *The Question of the Other*, ed. A. Dalley and C.E. Scott, pp. 205–12, Albany, NY: SUNY Press.
Black, I. (1989) 'Geography, political economy and the circulation of finance capital in early industrial England', *Journal of Historical Geography* 15: 366–84.
Block, F. (1977) *The Origins of International Economic Disorder: A Study of United States International Monetary Policy from World War II to the Present*, Berkeley, CA: University of California Press.
—— (1990) *Postindustrial Possibilities: A Critique of Economic Discourse*, Berkeley, CA: University of California Press.
Board of Inland Revenue (1987) *Survey of Personal Income, 1983/84*, London: HMSO.
Boden, D. and Molotch, H. (1993) 'The compulsion of proximity', in *Now/Here. Time, Space and Modernity*, ed. R. Friedland and D. Boden, Berkeley, CA: University of California Press.
Bond, P. (1990) 'The new US class struggle: financial industry power vs. grass-roots populism', *Capital and Class* 40: 150–81.
—— (1991) 'Alternative politics in the inner city: the financial explosion and the campaign for community control of capital in Baltimore', in *Hollow Promises: Rhetoric and Reality in the Inner City*, ed. M. Keith and A. Rogers, pp. 141–68, London: Mansell.
Booker, J. (1994) *Traveller's Money*, Stroud: Alan Sutton.
Bordo, M.D. and Eichengreen, B. (eds) (1993) *A Retrospective on the Bretton Woods System: Lessons for International Monetary Reform*, Chicago: Chicago University Press.
Born, K.E. (1983) *International Banking in the Nineteenth and Twentieth Century*, Leamington Spa: Berg.
Bose, M. (1988) *The Crash*, London: Bloomsbury.
Boss, H. (1990) *Theories of Transfer and Surplus: Parasites and Producers in Economic Thought*, London: Unwin Hyman.
Boston Consulting Group (1992) *Retail Banking: Will Pruning Branches Kill the Tree?*, London: Boston Consulting Group.
Bourdieu, P. (1979) 'Les trois états du capital culturel', *Actes de la Recherché en Sciences Sociales* 24: 2–22.
—— (1980) 'Le capital social', *Actes de la Recherche en Sciences Sociales* 31: 2–3.
—— (1984) *Distinction. A Social Critique of the Judgement of Taste*, London: Routledge and Kegan Paul.
—— (1987) 'What makes a social class? On the theoretical and practical existence of groups', *Berkeley Journal of Sociology* 3: 1–17.
—— (1988) *Homo Academicus*, Cambridge: Polity Press.
Bowen, D. (1986) 'The class of 86', *Business* November: 34–41.
Boyer, R. (1990) *The Regulation School. A Critical Introduction*, New York: Columbia University Press.
Brennan, J. (1989) 'Agents caught short', *Financial Times* 7 October, Property Supplement.
Brenner, R. and Glick, M. (1991) 'The regulation approach: theory and history', *New Left Review* 188: 45–120.
Brett, E.A. (1985) *The World Economy Since the War: The Politics of Uneven Development*, London: Macmillan.
Brewer, A. (1990) *Marxist Theories of Imperialism: A Critical Survey*, 2nd Edition, London: Routledge.
British Bankers Association (BBA) (1992) *Annual Abstract of Banking Statistics*, Vol. 9, London: BBA.
Brown, B. (1987) *The Flight of International Capital: A Contemporary History*, London: Routledge.

Brownhill, S. (1990) *Developing London's Docklands: Another Great Planning Disaster?*, London: Paul Chapman.'

Browning, P.J. (1986) 'Changes in the international capital market', in *Corporate Finance in Multinational Companies*, ed. D.B. Zenoff, London: Euromoney.

Bukatman, S. (1993a) *Terminal Identity*, Durham, NC: Duke University Press.

—— (1993b) 'Gibson's typewriter', *South Atlantic Quarterly* 92: 627–46.

Burke, P. (1978) *Popular Culture in Early Modern Europe*, London: Temple Smith.

Burkett, P. (1989) 'Financial innovation, crises, and the contradictions of central bank policy under capitalism: the case of investment fund money', *Capital and Class* No. 38: 37–62.

Byrne, J.A. (1987) *The Headhunters*, London: Kogan Page.

Cain, P.J. and Hopkins, A.G. (1986) 'Gentlemanly capitalism and British expansion overseas', *Economic History Review* 2nd Series, 39: 501–25.

—— (1993a) *British Imperialism. Innovation and Expansion, 1688–1914*, London: Longman.

—— (1993b) *British Imperialism. Crisis and Deconstruction, 1914–1990*, London: Longman.

Callon, M. (1986) 'Some elements of a sociology of translation', in *Power, Action and Belief. A New Sociology of Knowledge*, ed. J. Law, pp. 196–232, London: Routledge and Kegan Paul.

—— (1991) 'Techno-economic networks and irreversibility', in *A Sociology of Monsters?*, ed. J. Law, pp. 132–61, London: Routledge.

Carchedi, G. (1983) *Problems in Class Analysis: Production, Knowledge and the Function of Capital*, London: Routledge and Kegan Paul.

Carrier, J.G. (ed.) (1995) *Occidentalism*, Oxford: Oxford University Press.

Caskey, J.P. (1994) 'Bank representation in low-income and minority urban communities', *Urban Affairs Quarterly* 29: 617–38.

Cassis, Y. (1984) *Les Banquiers de la City à L'Epoque Edouardienne 1890–1914*, Geneva: Droz.

—— (1987) *La City de Londres, 1870–1914*, Paris: Belin.

Castells, M. (1989) *The Informational City: Information Technology, Economic Restructuring and the Urban-Regional Process*, Oxford: Blackwell.

Cawson, A. (ed.) (1986) *Organised Interests and the State*, London: Sage.

Cecchini, P. (1988) *The European Challenge 1992: The Benefits of a Single Market*, Aldershot, Hants: Wildwood House.

Cencini, A. (1988) *Money, Income and Time. A Quantum-Theoretical Approach*, London: Frances Pinter.

Census of Population 1981 Workplace and Transport to Work Tables (1984) London: OPCS.

Centre for Medieval and Renaissance Studies (1979) *Banking in Europe*, Cambridge, MA: Harvard University Press.

Cerny, P.G. (1989) 'The "little Big Bang" in Paris: financial deregulation in a *dirigiste* system', *European Journal of Political Research* 17: 169–92.

—— (1990) *The Changing Architecture of Politics: Structure, Agency and the Future of the State*, London: Sage.

—— (1991) 'The limits of deregulation: transnational interpenetration and policy change', *European Journal of Political Research* 19: 173–96.

—— (1993) 'Money and power: the American financial system from free banking to global competition', *PAIS Working Paper* No. 116, Department of Politics and International Studies, University of Warwick.

Chapman, S. (1984) *The Rise of Merchant Banking*, London: Routledge.

—— (1992) *Merchant Enterprise in Britain. From the Industrial Revolution to World War 1*, Cambridge: Cambridge University Press.

Chartier, R. (1994) *The Order of Books*, Cambridge: Polity Press.

Christopherson, S. (1992) 'How the state and the market are remaking the landscape of inequality', Department of City and Regional Planning, Cornell University (mimeo).

—— (1993) 'Market rules and territorial outcomes: the case of the United States', *International Journal of Urban and Regional Research* 17: 274–88.

Churchill, C. (1987) *Serious Money. A City Comedy*, London: Methuen.

City of London Research Project (1992) *Intermediate Report*, London: City Corporation.

City Research Project (1995) *The Competitive Position of London's Financial Services: Final Report*, London: Corporation of London.

Clark, G.L. (1989a) 'Remaking the map of corporate capitalism: the arbitrage economy of the 1980s', *Environment and Planning A* 21: 997–1000.

—— (1989b) 'Law and the interpretive turn in the social sciences', *Urban Geography*, 10: 209–28.

Clarke, M. and Wagstaff, S. (1987) 'Spatial analysis and geodemographics of financial services', School of Geography, University of Leeds (mimeo, copy available from authors).

Clarke, S. (1988) *Keynesianism, Monetarism and the Crisis of the State*, Aldershot, Hants: Edward Elgar.

Clarke, W.M. (1965) *The City in the World Economy*, London: Institute for Economic Affairs.

—— (1986a) *How the City Works*, London: Waterloo.

—— (1986b) *Inside the City*, London: Waterloo.

Cleaver, H. (1989) 'Close the IMF, abolish debt and end development: a class analysis of the international debt crisis', *Capital and Class* 39: 17–50.

Cloke, P. (ed.) (1992) *Policy and Change in Thatcher's Britain*, Oxford: Pergamon.

Cloke, P., Philo, C. and Sadler, D. (1991) *Approaching Human Geography*, London: Paul Chapman.

Cloud, C. and Galster, G. (1993) 'What do we know about racial discrimination in mortgage markets?', *The Review of Black Political Economy* 22: 101–20.

Coakley, J. and Harris, L. (1983) *The City of Capital: London's Role as a Financial Centre*, Oxford: Blackwell.

Cobbett, D. (1986) *Tales of the Old Stock Exchange. Before the Big Bang*, Portsmouth: Milestone Publications.

Cobham, D. (ed.) (1992) *Markets and Dealers. The Economics of the London Financial Markets*, London: Longman.

Cockburn, P. (1989) 'Taking a cautious view of the single market', *Financial Times* 6 November.

Cohen, G. (1978) *Karl Marx's Theory of History*, Oxford: Oxford University Press.

Collins, R. (1979) 'Review of *The Bankers* by Martin Meyer', *American Journal of Sociology* 85: 190.

Collins, J. (1995) *Architectures of Excess. Cultural Life in the Information Age*, New York: Routledge.

Collins, M. (1988) *Money and Banking in the UK: A History*, London: Croom Helm.

Commission of the European Communities (1992) *Perspectives on Advanced Communications in Europe*, Volume I, Summary.

Conaty, P. (1993) 'Communities', in *Bank Watch*, ed. E. Mayo, pp. 18–20, London: The New Economics Foundation.

Conley, V.A. (ed.) (1993) *Rethinking Technologies*, Minneapolis: University of Minnesota Press.

Consumers Association (1994) *Which* January: 4.

Cooke, P. (1985) 'Class practices as regional markers: a contribution to labour geography', in *Social Relations and Spatial Structures*, pp. 213–41, ed. D. Gregory and J. Urry, London: Macmillan.

Cooper, R. (1987) *The International Monetary System*, Cambridge, MA: MIT Press.

Copeland, T. (1995) *Women Writing About Money: Women's Fiction in England, 1750–1820*, Cambridge: Cambridge University Press.

Corbridge, S. (1986) *Capitalist World Development: A Critique of Radical Development Geography*, London: Macmillan.

—— (1988a) 'The debt crisis and the crisis of global regulation', *Geoforum* 19: 109–30.

—— (1988b) 'The asymmetry of interdependence: the United States and the geopolitics of international financial relations', *Studies in Comparative International Development* 23: 3–29.

—— (1989) 'Marxism, post-Marxism, and the geography of development', in *New Models in Geography, Volume 1*, ed. R. Peet and N. Thrift, pp. 224–54, London: Unwin Hyman.

—— (1992a) *Debt and Development*, Oxford: Blackwell.

—— (1992b) 'Discipline and punish: the new right and the policing of the inter-national debt crisis', *Geoforum* 23: 285–301.

—— (1993) *Debt and Development*, Oxford: Blackwell.

—— (1994) 'Plausible worlds: Friedman, Keynes and the geography of inflation', in *Power and Space*, ed. S. Corbridge *et al.*, pp. 63–90, Oxford: Blackwell.

Corbridge, S. and Agnew, J. (1991) 'The US trade and budget deficits in global perspective: an essay in geopolitical-economy', *Environment and Planning D: Society and Space* 9: 71–90.

Cosgrove, D. (1996) 'Discussants' comments', *Urban Studies* 33: forthcoming.

Country Life (1989) 'Getting the edge', in *Buying a Country House. A County Guide to Value*, *Country Life*/Knight, Frank and Rutley, pp. 19–22, London: *Country Life*.

Country Life/Knight, Frank and Rutley (1987) *Buying a Country House*, London: *Country Life*.

—— (1988) *Buying a Country House. A County Guide to Value*, London: *Country Life*.

—— (1989) *Buying a Country House. A County Guide to Value*, London: *Country Life*.

Court, G. and McDowell, L. (1993) 'Serious trouble? Financial services and structural change', South East Programme Occasional Paper No. 4, Faculty of Social Sciences, Open University, Milton Keynes.

Cowe, R. (1993) 'Slumming it in the city', *The Guardian* 31 July.

Cox, A. (ed.) (1986) *States, Industry and Finance*, Brighton, Sussex: Harvester Press.

Cox, K.R. (1993) 'The local and the global in the new urban politics: a critical view', *Environment and Planning D: Society and Space* 11: 433–48.

Cox, R. (1981) 'Social forces, states and world orders: beyond international relations theory', *Millennium: Journal of International Studies* 10: 126–55.

—— (1987) *Production, Power and World Order: Social Forces in the Making of History*, New York: Colombia University Press.

—— (1992) 'Towards a post-hegemonic conceptualization of world order: reflections on the relevancy of Ibn Khaldun', in *Governance Without Government: Order and Change in World Politics*, ed. J.N. Rosenau and E. Czempiel, pp. 132–59, Cambridge: Cambridge University Press.

—— (1993a) 'Gramsci, hegemony and international relations: an essay in method', in *Gramsci, Historical Materialism and International Relations*, ed. S. Gill, pp. 49–66, Cambridge: Cambridge University Press.

—— (1993b) 'Structural issues of global governance: implications for Europe', in *Gramsci, Historical Materialism and International Relations*, ed. S. Gill, pp. 259–89, Cambridge: Cambridge University Press.

Coyle, S. (1995) 'Cash, cash, cash', *The Independent* 15 July: 18.

Crary, J. (1994) 'Critical reflections' *Artforum* February.

Crawford, R.D. and Sihler, W.W. (1991) *The Troubled Money Business*, New York: Harper & Collins.

Creigh, S. and Rees, A. (1989) 'Graduates and the labour market in the 1980s', *Employment Gazette* January: 17–28.

Cressey, P. and Scott, P. (1991) 'Industrial relations and innovation in services', Report for the Ministry of Labour, Employment Vocational Training, Republic of France and IRIS-Travail et Société, University of Paris-Dauphine.

—— (1992) 'Employment, technology and industrial relations in the UK clearing banks: is the honeymoon over?', *New Technology, Work and Employment* 3: 83–96.

Crompton, R. (1989) 'Women in banking: continuity and change since the Second World War', *Work, Employment and Society* 3: 141–56.

Crompton, R. and Sanderson, K. (1990) *Gendered Jobs and Social Change*, London: Unwin Hyman.

CSO (1984) *Social Trends, 1983*, London: HMSO.

Cutler, T., Haslam, C., Williams, J. and Williams, K. (1990) *1992 – The Struggle For Europe*, Leamington Spa: Berg.

Czitrom, D.J. (1982) *Media and the American Mind from Morse to McLuhan*, Chapel Hill, NC: University of North Carolina Press.

Daily Telegraph (1971) 'Obituary. R.H. Mottram, author of 60 books', 17 April.

Dale, R. (1989) 'International financial regulation', in *The Age of Regulatory Reform*, ed. K. Button and D. Swann, pp. 217–35, Oxford: Clarendon Press.

—— (1990) '1992–2002: the future evolution of financial markets in Europe', *Royal Bank of Scotland Review* No. 152: 13–14.

Dalton, G. (1965) 'Primitive money', *American Anthropologist* 67(1): 44–65.

Daly, G. (1991) 'The discursive construction of economic space: logics of organization and disorganization', *Economy and Space* 20: 79–102.

Daly, M.T. and Logan, M. (1989) *The Brittle Rim. Finance, Business and the Pacific Region*, Harmondsworth: Penguin.

Daniels, P.W. and Bobe, J.M. (1993) 'Extending the boundary of the City of London? The development of Canary Wharf', *Environment and Planning A* 25: 539–52.

Daniels, P.W., Leyshon, A. and Thrift, N.J. (1988a) 'Trends in the growth and location of professional producer services: UK property consultants', *Tijdschrift voor Economische en Sociale Geografie* 79: 162–74.

—— (1988b) 'Large accountancy firms in the UK: operational adaptation and spatial development', *The Service Industries Journal* 8: 317–46.

Daniels, P.W., Thrift, N. and Leyshon, A. (1989) 'Internationalisation of professional producers' services: accountancy conglomerates', in *Multinational Service Firms*, ed. P. Enderwick, p. 106, London: Routledge.

Daunton, M.J. (1989) '"Gentlemanly capitalism" and British industry, 1820–1914', *Past and Present* No. 122: 119–58.

—— (1995) 'Rascals and regulations', *The Times Literary Supplement* 18 August: 9–10.

Davidson, C. (1994) 'Head for figures', *The Guardian*, Online Section, 9 June: 7.

Davies, G. (1994) *A History of Money: From Ancient Times to the Present Day*, Cardiff: University of Wales Press.

Davies, L. (1993) 'A raw deal', *The Sunday Times Magazine* 4 July: 30–7.

Davis, E. (1993) 'Techgnosis, magic, memory and the angels of information', *South Atlantic Quarterly* 92: 585–617.

Davis, E. and Latter, A.R. (1989) 'London as an international financial centre', *Bank of England Quarterly Bulletin* 29: 516–28.

Davis, E. and Smales, C. (1989) 'The integration of European financial services', in *1992: Myths and Realities*, ed. E. Davis *et al.*, pp. 91–117, London: London Business School.

Davis, E.P. (1991a) 'The development of pension funds – an international comparison', *Bank of England Quarterly Bulletin* 31: 380–90.

—— (1991b) 'International diversification of institutional investors', *Bank of England Discussion Papers Technical Series* No. 44.

—— (1992) *Debt, Financial Fragility, and Systemic Risk*, Oxford: Clarendon.

Davis, M. (1978) '"Fordism" in crisis: a review of Michel Aglietta's Régulation et Crises: L'Expérience des États-Unis', *Review* 2: 207–69.

—— (1990) *City of Quartz: Excavating the Future in Los Angeles*, London: Verso.

—— (1992) 'Who killed LA? A political autopsy', *New Left Review* No. 197: 3–28.

—— (1993) 'Who killed Los Angeles? Part two: The verdict is given', *New Left Review* No. 198: 29–54.

de Cecco, M. (1987) *Changing Money: Financial Innovation in Developing Countries*, Oxford: Blackwell.

de Grauwe, P. (1989) *International Money. Post-war Trends and Theories*, Oxford: Oxford University Press.

de Grauwe, P. and Decupere, D. (1992) 'Psychological barriers in the foreign exchange market', *Centre for Economic Policy Research Working Paper*.

de Jonquieres, G. (1990) 'UK favoured for foreign takeovers', *Financial Times* 5 February.

De Landa, M. (1991) *War in the Age of Intelligent Machines*, Cambridge, MA: MIT Press.

Deleuze, G. (1991) 'Postscript on the societies of control', *October* 59: 3–7.

Denzin, N. (1991) *Images of Postmodern Society*, London: Sage.

Department of Employment (1986) *New Earnings Survey*, London: Department of Employment.

Desai, M. (1988) 'Foreword' to Cencini, A. (1988a) *Money, Income, Time*, Oxford: Blackwell.

de Vroey, M. (1984) 'Inflation: a non-monetarist monetary interpretation', *Cambridge Journal of Economics* 8: 381–400.

Diacon, S. (1990) 'Strategies for the Single European Market: the options for insurers', *The Service Industries Journal* 10: 197–211.

Dicken, P. (1992a) 'International production in a volatile regulatory environment: the influence of national regulatory policies on the spatial strategies of transnational corporations', *Geoforum* 23: 303–16.

—— (1992b) *Global Shift: The Internationalization of Economic Activity*, 2nd edition, London: Paul Chapman.

Dicken, P. and Thrift, N. (1992) 'The organisation of production and the production of organisation: why business enterprises matter in the study of geographical organisation', *Transactions of the Institute of British Geographers, New Series* 17: 279–91.

Dix, C. (1990) *A Chance for the Top*, London: Bantam Press.

Dodd, N. (1994) *The Sociology of Money: Economics, Reason and Contemporary Society*, Cambridge: Polity Press.

—— (1995) 'The sociology of money: questions of trust and risk', Conference Paper, Sociology and the Limits of Economics, Liverpool, England, 20–22 April.

Douglas, M. (1966) *Purity and Danger*, London: Routledge and Kegan Paul.

Drainville, A.C. (1994) 'International political economy in the age of open Marxism', *Review of International Political Economy* 1: 105–32.

Duncan, A. (1993) *An End to Illusions*, Demos Pamphlet No. 2, London: Demos.

Dunford, M. (1990) 'Theories of regulation', *Environment and Planning D: Society and Space* 8: 297–321.

Dunford, M. and Perrons, D. (1983) *The Arena of Capital*, London: Macmillan.

Dunkling, A. and Room, L. (1990) *The Guinness Book of Money*, London: Guinness Publications.

Dunlop, C. and Kling, R. (eds) (1991) *Computerisation and Controversy: Value Conflicts and Social Choice*, New York: Academic Press.

Dunning, J.H. and Morgan, E.V. (1971) *An Economic Study of the City of London*, London: Allen & Unwin.

Dutton, W., Blumler, J. and Kraemer, K. (eds) (1987) *Wired Cities: Shaping the Future of Communications*, Communications Library, Washington, DC.

Dymski, G., Epstein, G. and Pollin, R. (eds) (1993) *Transforming the U.S. Financial System: Equity and Efficiency in the 21st Century*, Armonk, NY: M.E. Sharp.

Dymski, G. and Veitch, J. (1992) 'Race and the financial dynamics of urban growth: L.A. as Fay Wray', Working Paper 92–21, Department of Economics, University of California, Riverside, CA.

Eagleton, T. (1989) *Marxism and Literary Criticism*, London: Routledge.

—— (1993) 'The new sublime', *London Review of Books*.

Eccles, R.G. and Crane, D.B. (1988) *Doing Deals. Investment Banks at Work*, Boston, MA: Harvard Business School Press.

Eichengreen, B. (1990) 'One money for Europe? Lessons from the US currency union', *Economic Policy* 10: 117–87.

Einzig, P. (1966) *Primitive Money*, 2nd Edition, Oxford: Pergamon.

Eley, G. (1992) 'Nations, publics and political cultures: placing Habermas in the nineteenth century', in *Habermas and the Public Sphere*, ed. C. Calhoun, Cambridge, MA: MIT Press.

Elias, N. (1975) *The Civilising Process. Volume 1*, Oxford: Blackwell.

—— (1982) *State Formation and Civilization*, Oxford: Blackwell.

—— (1995) 'Technicization and civilization: introductory remarks', *Theory, Culture and Society* 12: 7–42.

Employment Gazette (1987) (January), London: Department of Employment.

Enzensberger, H.M. (1990) 'Blind-Man's-Buff economics', in *Political Crumbs*, pp. 85–96, London: Verso.

Erickson, R. (ed.) (1971) *Antipode* 3(1), Special issue on access to essential public services.

Euromoney (1986a) 'The power league', February: 83–95.

—— (1986b) 'Latin America isn't rich yet', September: 154–84.

—— (1987a) 'The most powerful men in Japan', March: 118–23.

—— (1987b) 'The Power League', February: 85–95.

—— (1987c) 'Swaps: new moves', Supplement, July.

—— (1987d) 'Japan: the land where money grows', Supplement, April.

Euromonitor (1992) *Consumer Banking and Personal Finance in Europe*, London: Euromonitor.

Evans, A.W. and Crampton, G. (1989) 'Myth, reality and employment in London', *Journal of Transport Economics and Policy* January.

Evans, T. (1988) 'Money makes the world go around', in *New Perspectives on the Financial System*, ed. L. Harris *et al.*, pp. 41–68, Andover, Hants: Croom Helm.

Fainstein, S.S. (1994) 'Government programs for commercial redevelopment in poor neighbourhoods: the cases of Spitalfields in East London and downtown Brooklyn, NY', *Environment and Planning A* 26: 215–34.

Family Expenditure Survey (1985) London: HMSO.

Farmborough, H. (1987) 'Atomic reaction', *Financial Weekly* 18 June: 28–34.

Fathy, T. (1991) *Telecity: Information Technology and its Impact on City Form*, London: Praeger.

Fay, B. (1970) *A Banker's World*, London: Heinemann.

Fay, S. (1988) *Portrait of an Old Lady*, Harmondsworth: Penguin.

Federal Register (1978) 'The regulation: Community Reinvestment Act of 1977; implementation', Vol. 43, No. 198.

Feenberg, A. (1991) *Critical Theory of Technology*, New York: Oxford University Press.

Fennema, M. and Van der Pijl, K. (1987) 'International bank capital and the new liberalism', in *Intercorporate Relations: The Structural Analysis of Business*, ed. M.S. Mizruchi and M. Schwartz, pp. 298–319, Cambridge: Cambridge University Press.

Ferrara, K., Brunner, H. and Whittemore, G. (1991) 'Interactive written discourse as an emergent register', *Written Communication* 8: 8–34.

Financial Times (1993) '100 years in the pink', *Financial Times* 4 January: i–x.

Findlay, A. (1987) 'From settlers to skilled transients. The changing nature of British international migration'. Paper presented to the Workshop of the Skilled International Migration Working Party, University of Liverpool, 6–7 July.

Fischer, C.S. (1992) *Calling America. The Social History of the Telephone*, Berkeley, CA: University of California Press.

Fishbein, A.J. (1989) 'Banks giving credit with a conscience', *Business and Society* 68: 33–7.

Florida, R.L. (1986) 'The political economy of financial deregulation and the reorganization of housing finance in the United States', *International Journal of Urban and Regional Research* 10: 207–31.

Flynn, A., Marsden, T. and Ward, N. (1993) 'Retailing, the food system and the regulatory state', in *Regulating Agriculture*, ed. P. Lowe, T. Marsden and S. Whatmore, London: Fulton.

Foley, D. (1989) 'Money in economic activity', in *The New Palgrave*, ed. J. Eatwell *et al.*, pp. 248–62, London: Macmillan.

Ford, J. (1988) *The Indebted Society: Credit and Default in the 1980s*, London: Routledge.

—— (1991) *Consuming Credit: Debt and Poverty in the UK*, London: Child Poverty Action Group.

Frankel, S.H. (1977) *Money: Two Philosophies: The Conflict of Trust and Authority*, Oxford: Blackwell.

Franklin, D. (1991) 'Economic and monetary union', in *The City and the Single European Market*, ed. W. Kay, Cambridge: Woodhead-Faulkner, pp. 15–33.

Franks, J. and Mayer, C. (1990) 'Capital markets and corporate control: a study of France, Germany and the UK', *Economic Policy* 10: 189–231.

French, M. (1987) 'Swapping debt – just hot air?', *Euromoney* May: 115–22.

Frieden, J.A. (1987) *Banking on the World: The Politics of American International Finance*, New York: Harper & Row.

Friedman, A. (1989) 'Marriage Italian style', *Financial Times*, 23 March.

Friedman, J. (1987) 'Beyond otherness on the spectacularization of anthropology', *Telos* 71: 16–23.

—— (1995) 'Global system, globalisation and the parameters of modernity', in *Global Modernisations*, ed. M. Featherstone *et al.*, pp. 69–90, London: Sage.

Friedmann, H. (1993) 'The political economy of food: a global crisis?', *New Left Review* 197: 29–57.

Frisby, D. (1992) *Simmel and Since. Essays on Georg Simmel's Social Theory*, London: Routledge.

Fyfe, G. and Law, J. (eds) (1988) *Picturing Power*, London: Routledge.

Galbraith, J.K. (1975) *Money: Whence it Came, Where it Went*, London: Penguin.

Ganßmann, H. (1988) 'Money – a symbolically generalised medium of communication? On the concept of money in recent sociology', *Economy and Society* 17: 285–316.

Gapper, J. (1992) 'Bristol & West to price mortgages by family status', *Financial Times*, 3 December.

—— (1993a) 'Banks launch root and branch reform', *Financial Times* 18 January: 11.

—— (1993b) 'A charge that's set to shock', *Financial Times* 10 February, 21.

Gardner, E.P.M. and Molyneux, P. (1990) *Changes in Western European Banking*, London: Unwin Hyman.

Gardner, N. (1994) 'Insurer targets "careful" drivers', *The Sunday Times* 10 July: 5.1.

Gardner, R.N. (1980) *Sterling-Dollar Diplomacy in Current Perspective*, New York: Columbia University Press.

Gaston, M. and Kennedy, M. (1987) 'Capital investment or community development? The struggle for land control by Boston's black and latino community', *Antipode* 19: 178–209.

Gentle, C. (1993) *The Financial Services Industry: The Impact of Corporate Reorganisation on Regional Economic Development*, Aldershot: Avebury.

Gentle, C. and Marshall, N. (1993) 'Corporate restructuring in the financial services industry: converging markets and divergent organisational structures', mimeo.

Gentle, C.J.S., Marshall, J.N. and Coombes, M. (1991) 'Business reorganization and regional development: the case of the British building societies movement', *Environment and Planning A* 23: 1759–77.

Gergen, K.J. (1991) *The Saturated Self. Dilemmas of Identity in Contemporary Life*, New York: Basic Books.

Gershuny, J. (1992) 'Postscript: revolutionary technologies and technological revolutions', in *Consuming Technologies*, ed. R. Silverstone and E. Hirch, pp. 227–33, London: Routledge.

Gershuny, J. and Miles, I. (1983) *The New Services Economy*, London: Frances Pinter.

Gewertz, D.B. and Errington, F.K. (1995) 'Dwelling currencies in East New Britain: the construction of shell money as national cultural property', in *Occidentalism, Images of the West*, ed. J.G. Carrier, pp. 161–91, Oxford: Clarendon Press.

Gibson, W. (1986) *Neuromancer*, London: Collins.

Giddens, A. (1985) *The Nation-State and Violence: Volume Two of a Contemporary Critique of Historical Materialism*, Cambridge: Polity Press.

—— (1990) *Consequences of Modernity*, Cambridge: Polity Press.

—— (1991) *Modernity and Self-Identity*, Cambridge: Polity Press.

Gill, S. (1986) 'Hegemony, consensus and Trilateralism', *Review of International Studies* 12: 205–21.

—— (1990) *American Hegemony and the Trilateral Commission*, Cambridge: Cambridge University Press.

—— (1991) 'Historical materialism, Gramsci and international political economy', in *The New International Political Economy*, ed. C. Murphy and R. Tooze, pp. 51–75, Boulder, CO: Lynne Reiner.

—— (1992) 'Economic globalization and the internationalization of authority: limits and contradictions', *Geoforum* 23: 269–83.

—— (1993a) 'Gramsci and global politics: towards a post-hegemonic research agenda', in *Gramsci, Historical Materialism and International Relations*, ed. S. Gill, pp. 1–18, Cambridge: Cambridge University Press.

—— (1993b) 'Epistemology, ontology and the "Italian School"', in *Gramsci, Historical Materialism and International Relations*, ed. S. Gill, pp. 21–48, Cambridge: Cambridge University Press.

—— (1993c) 'Global finance, monetary policy and cooperation among the Group of Seven, 1944–92', in *Finance and World Politics: Markets, Regimes and States in the Post-hegemonic Era*, ed. P.G. Cerny, pp. 86–113, Aldershot: Edward Elgar.

Gill, S. and Law, D. (1989) 'Global hegemony and the structural power of capital', *International Studies Quarterly* 36: 475–99.

Gilroy, P. (1993) *The Black Atlantic: Modernity and Double Consciousness*, London: Verso.

Glancy, J. (1988) 'Togging up for the country', in *Buying a Country House. A Country Guide to Value*, Knight, Frank and Rutley/*Country Life*, pp. xxiii–xxiv, London: *Country Life*.

Glyn, A. (1989) 'The macro-anatomy of the Thatcher years', in *The Restructuring of the UK Economy*, ed. F. Green, pp. 65–79, Hemel Hempstead: Harvester Wheatsheaf.

Glyn, A., Hughes, A., Lipietz, A. and Singh, A. (1991) 'The rise and fall of the Golden Age', in *The Golden Age of Capitalism*, ed. S. Marglin and J.B. Schor, pp. 39–125, Oxford: Clarendon Press.

Goddard, J. (1968a) 'Changing office location patterns in Central London', *Urban Studies* 4: 276–85.

—— (1968b) 'Multivariate analysis of office location patterns in the City Centre: a London example', *Regional Studies* 2.

Goldsmith, R.W. (1983) *The Financial Development of Japan, 1868–1977*, New Haven, CT, and London: Yale University Press.

Goldsmith, V. (1993) 'Flying first class to the bank', *The Independent* 27 February.

Goodhart, C. (1987) 'The economics of Big Bang', *Midland Bank Review* Summer: 6–15.

—— (1989) *Money, Information and Uncertainty*, London: Macmillan.

Gould, S.J. (1991) *Bully for Brontosaurus*, London: Hutchinson.

Goux, J.J. (1990a) *Symbolic Economies. After Marx and Freud*, Ithaca, NY: Cornell University Press.

—— (1990b) 'General economics and postmodern capitalism', *Yale French Studies* No. 78: 206–24.

Graham, S. (1996) 'Cities in the real-time age: the paradigm challenge of telecommunications to the conception and planning of urban space', *Environment and Planning A* 27.

Grahl, J. (1991) 'Economies out of control', *New Left Review* 185: 170–83.

Granovetter, M. (1985) 'Economic action and social structure: the problem of embeddedness', *American Journal of Sociology* 91: 481–510.

Granovetter, M.S. and Swedberg, R. (eds) (1992) *The Sociology of Economic Life*, Boulder, CO: Westview Press.

Grant, R. (1993) 'Trading blocs or trading blows? The macroeconomic geography of US and Japanese trade policies', *Environment and Planning A* 25: 273–91.

Greenshields, A. (ed.) (1989) *Who's Who in the City*, London: Stock Exchange Press.

Gregory, D. (1978) *Ideology, Science and Human Geography*, London: Hutchinson.

—— (1994) *Geographical Imaginations*, Oxford: Blackwell.

Grenier, J.Y. *et al.* (1993) *A Propos de 'Philosophie de L'Argent' de Georg Simmel*, Paris: L'Harmattan.

Grilli, V. (1989) 'Europe 1992: issues and prospects for the financial markets', *Economic Policy* 4: 387–421.

Grown, T. and Bates, T. (1992) 'Commercial bank lending practices and the development of Black-owned construction companies', *Journal of Urban Affairs* 14: 25–41.

Guattari, F. (1995) *Chaosmosis. An Ethico-Asthetic Paradigm*, Sydney: Power Publications.

Gunn, S. (1988) 'The "failure" of the Victorian middle class: a critique', in *The Culture of Capital: Art, Power and the Nineteenth-century Middle Class*, ed. J. Wolff and J. Seed, pp. 17–43, Manchester: Manchester University Press.

Gunn, C. and Gunn, H.D. (1991) *Reclaiming Capital: Democratic Initiatives and Community Development*, Ithaca, NY: Cornell University Press.

Haas, G. (1992) Testimony before the Subcommittee on Housing and Community Development and the Subcommittee on Consumer Affairs and Coinage of the U.S. House of Representatives Committee on Banking, Finance, and Urban Affairs, May 7.

Habermas, J. (1992) 'Further reflections on the public sphere', in *Habermas and the Public Sphere*, ed. C. Calhoun, Cambridge, MA: MIT Press.

Haila, A. (1988) 'Land as a financial asset: the theory of urban land rent as a mirror of economic transformation', *Antipode* 20: 79–101.

—— (1990) 'The theory of land rent at the crossroads', *Environment and Planning D: Society and Space* 8 249–374.

Halford, S. and Savage, M. (1993) 'Changing the culture of the organization: gender and cultural restructuring in banking and local government', Paper presented to the 9th Urban Change and Conflict Conference, University of Sheffield, 14–16 September.

—— (1994) 'Changing masculinities, management and careers', mimeo.

—— (1995) 'Restructuring organizations, changing people: gender and restructuring in banking and local government', *Work, Employment and Society* 9: 97–122.

Hall, M. (1990) 'The Bank for International Settlements capital adequacy rules: implications for banks operating in the UK', *The Service Industries Journal* 10: 145–71.

Hallsworth, A.G. and Bobe, J.M. (1993) 'How the interest rate cat ate the Docklands canary', *Area* 25: 64–9.

Hamilton, A. (1986) *The Financial Revolution. The Big Bang Worldwide*, Harmondsworth: Penguin.

Hamilton, J.D. (1986) *Stockbroking Tomorrow*, London: Macmillan.

Hammond, G.S. (1987) 'Recent developments in the swap market', *Bank of England Quarterly Bulletin* February: 66–74.

Hancher, L. and Moran, M. (1989) 'Introduction: regulation and deregulation', *European Journal of Political Research* 17: 129–36.

Hannah, L. (1986) *Inventing Retirement: The Development of Occupational Pensions in Britain*, Cambridge: Cambridge University Press.

Hannerz, U. (1992) *Cultural Complexity*, New York: Columbia University Press.

Harasim, L. (1993) 'Global networks: an introduction', in *Global Networks: Computers and International Communication*, ed. L. Harasim, pp. 3–14, London and Cambridge, MA: MIT Press.

Haraway, D. (1991) *Simians, Cyborgs and Women. The Reinvention of Nature*, London: Free Association Books.

Harré, R., Clarke, D. and de Carlo, N. (1985) *Machines and Mechanisms. An Introduction to the Psychology of Action*, London: Methuen.

Harris, D. (1988a) 'British MBOs still thriving', *Euromoney Supplement* April: 25–6.

—— (1988b) 'The adventurous British', *Euromoney Supplement* April: 27.

Harris, J. and Thane, P. (1984) 'British and European bankers, 1880–1914: an aristocratic bourgeoisie?', in *The Power of the Past*, ed. P. Thane *et al.*, London: Methuen.

Harris, L. (1988) 'Alternative perspectives on the financial system', in *New Perspectives on the Financial System*, ed. L. Harris *et al.*, pp. 7–35, Andover, Hants: Croom Helm.

Harris, R. (1992) 'The property development industry: a blueprint for change', Stanhope Properties plc, London (mimeo).

Hart, K. (1986) 'Heads or tails? Two sides of the coin', *Man* 21: 641–2.

Harvey, D. (1973) *Social Justice and the City*, London: Edward Arnold.

—— (1982) *The Limits to Capital*, Oxford: Blackwell.

—— (1985) 'The geopolitics of capitalism', in *Social Relations and Spatial Structures*, ed. D. Gregory and J. Urry, pp. 128–63, London: Macmillan.

—— (1989a) *The Urban Experience*, Oxford: Blackwell.

—— (1989b) *The Condition of Postmodernity: An Enquiry into the Origins of Cultural Change*, Oxford: Blackwell.

Harvey, D. and Chaterjee, L. (1974) 'Absolute rent and the structuring of space by governmental and financial institutions', *Antipode* 6: 22–36.

Hay, C. (1994a) 'Crisis, what crisis? Re-stating the problem of regulation', Lancaster Working Paper in Political Economy 47, Department of Sociology, University of Lancaster.

—— (1994b) 'The structural and ideological contradictions of Britain's post-war reconstruction', *Capital and Class* 54: 25–59.

Hayes, S.L. and Hubbard, D.M. (1990) *Investment Banking: A Tale of Three Cities*, Boston, MA: Harvard Business School Press.

Heath, C., Jirotka, M., Luff, P. and Hindmarsh, J. (1993) 'Unpacking collaboration: the interactional organisation of trading in a City dealing room', *Proceedings of the European Conference on Computer Supported Cooperative Work (CSCW) '93, Milan*.

Heimer, C.A. (1982) 'The racial and organizational origins of insurance redlining', *Journal of Intergroup Relations* 10: 42–60.

Held, D. (1991) 'Democracy, the nation-state and the global system', *Economy and Society* 20: 138–72.

Helleiner, E. (1993) 'When finance was the servant: international capital movements in the Bretton Woods order', in *Finance and World Politics: Markets, Regimes and States in the Post-hegemonic Era*, ed. P.G. Cerny, pp. 20–48, Aldershot: Edward Elgar.

—— (1994) *The Resurgence of Global Finance*, Ithaca, NY: Cornell University Press.

—— (1995) 'Explaining the globalization of financial markets: bringing states back in', *Review of International Political Economy* 2(2): 315–41.

Hemrick, C. (1992) 'Building today's global computer internetworks', *IEEE Communications Magazine* October: 44–9.

Hennessy, M. (1992) *A Domestic History of the Bank of England, 1930–1960*, Cambridge: Cambridge University Press.

Henning, M. (1995) 'Digital encounters: mythical pasts and electronic presence', in *The Photographic Image in Digital Culture*, ed. M. Lister, pp. 217–35, London: Routledge.

Hewison, R. (1987) *The Heritage Industry*, London: Methuen.

Hewlett, N. and Toporowski, J. (1985) 'All change in the city: a report on recent changes and future prospects in London's financial markets', *Economist* Intelligence Unit, Special Report 222.

Hirsch, F. (1977) *The Social Limits to Growth*, London: Routledge and Kegan Paul.

Hirschman, A.O. (1977) *The Passion and the Interests*, Princeton, NJ: Princeton University Press.

Hirst, J., Taylor, M. and Thrift, N. (1982) 'The geographical pattern of the Australian trading banks' overseas representation', in *The Geography of Multinationals*, ed. M.J. Taylor and N.J. Thrift, pp. 117–38, London: Croom Helm.

Hirst, P. and Thompson, G. (1992) 'The problem of "globalization": international economic relations, national economic management and the formation of trading blocs', *Economy and Society* 21: 357–96.

Hoare, Q. and Nowell Smith, G. (eds) (1971) *Selections from the Prison Notebooks of Antonio Gramsci*, London: Lawrence & Wishart.

Hobsbawm, E. (1975) *The Age of Capital*, London: Weidenfeld & Nicolson.

Hobson, J.A. (1902) 'The last chance for a liberal party', *The New Age* 9 January.

Hobson, O.R. (1940) *How the City Works*, London: The Dickens Press.

Hodgson, G.M. (1994) 'Some remarks on "economic imperialism" and international political economy', *Review of International Political Economy* 1: 21–8.

Holberton, S. (1987) 'Tokyo on the Thames', *Financial Times* 25 July.

—— (1989) 'Charting a course for European union', *Financial Times* 18 April: 3.

Holderness, M. (1993) 'It all adds up to money', *The Independent* 13 December: 23.

Holly, B. (1987) 'Regulation, competition and technology: the restructuring of the US commercial banking system', *Environment and Planning A* 19: 633–52.

Hopwood, A.G. and Miller, P. (eds) (1994) *Accounting as Social and Institutional Practice*, Cambridge: Cambridge University Press.

Howkins, A. (1986) 'The discovery of rural England', in *Englishness: Politics and Culture 1880–1920*, ed. R. Colls and P. Dodd, pp. 62–88, London: Croom Helm.

Hoyt, J. and Choca, M. (1989) *The Silent Partner: The Insurance Industry Potential For Community Reinvestment*, Chicago: Woodstock Institute.

Hübner, K. (1991) 'Flexibilization and autonomization of world money markets: obstacles for a new long expansion', *Politics and Flexibility: Restructuring States and Industry in Britain, Germany and Scandinavia*, ed. B. Jessop *et al.*, pp. 50–66, Aldershot: Edward Elgar.

Hunter, T. (1993) 'Banks shutting their doors to the poor', *The Guardian* 18 September: 33.

Hutton, W. (1993) 'State has betrayed pensions promise', *The Guardian* 13 December.
—— (1995) *The State We're In*, London: Jonathan Cape.
Ikenberry, G.J. (1992) 'A world economy restored: expert consensus and the Anglo–American postwar settlement', *International Organization* 46: 289–321.
Independent Schools Information Service (1987) *Annual Census 1987*, Independent School Information Service, London.
Ingham, G. (1984) *Capitalism Divided? The City and Industry in British Social Development*, London: Macmillan.
—— (1994) 'States and markets in the production of world money: sterling and the dollar', in *Money, Power and Space*, ed. S. Corbridge *et al.*, pp. 29–48, Oxford: Basil Blackwell.
—— (1995) 'British capitalism: empire, merchants and decline', *Social History* (forthcoming).
Ingold, T. (1995) 'Building, dwelling, living: how animals and people make themselves at home in the world', in *Shifting Contexts*, ed. M. Strathern, pp. 57–80, London: Routledge.
Ingram, D.H.A. (1987) 'Changes in the Stock Exchange and regulation in the City', *Bank of England Quarterly Bulletin* February: 54–65.
International Stock Exchange (1990) *Quality of Markets Quarterly Review* Spring issue.
Ireland, J. (1994) 'The importance of telecommunications to London as an international financial centre', *City Research Project Subject Report 6*.
Jackson, K. (ed.) (1995) *The Oxford Book of Money*, Oxford: Oxford University Press.
Jameson, F. (1984) 'Postmodernism, or the cultural logic of late capitalism', *New Left Review* 146: 53–92.
—— (1991) *Postmodernism, or The Cultural Logic of Late Capitalism*, London: Verso.
Jenkins, A. (1973) *The Stockbridge Story*, London: Heinemann.
Jenson, J. (1989) '"Different" but not "exceptional": Canada's permeable Fordism', *Canadian Review of Sociology and Anthropology* 26: 69–94.
—— (1990) 'Representation in crisis: the roots of Canada's permeable Fordism', *Canadian Journal of Political Science* 24: 653–83.
Jessop, B. (1990) *State Theory: Putting Capitalist States in Their Place*, Oxford: Blackwell.
—— (1991) 'Regulation und Politik: integrale Ökonomie und integraler Staat', in *Regulation, Staat und Hegemonie*, ed. A. Demirovic *et al.*, pp. 65–87, Münster: Westfälisches Dampfboot.
—— (1992) 'Fordism and post-Fordism: a critical reformulation', in *Pathways to Industrialization and Regional Development*, ed. M. Storper and A.J. Scott, pp. 47–69, London: Routledge.
—— (1993) 'Towards a Schumpeterian workfare state? Preliminary remarks on post-Fordist political economy', *Studies in Political Economy* 40: 7–39.
Jessop, B., Bonnett, K. and Bromley, S. (1990) 'Farewell to Thatcherism? Neo-liberalism and "new times"', *New Left Review* No. 179: 81–102.
Jessop, B. and Stones, R. (1992) 'Old City and New Times: economic and political aspects of deregulation', in *Global Finance and Urban Living: A Study of Metropolitan Change*, ed. L. Budd, and S. Whimster, pp. 177–92, London: Routledge.
Jirotka, M., Luff, P. and Heath, C. (1993) 'Requirements engineering and interactions in the workplace: a case study in City dealing rooms', *Proceedings of the Workshop on Social Science, Technical Systems and Cooperative Work*, Paris.
John, R.R. (1994) 'American historians and the concept of the communications revolution', in *Information Acumen. The Understanding and Use of Knowledge in Modern Business*, ed. L. Bud-Frierman, pp. 98–112, London: Business Press.
Jones, S. (1989) *The Headhunting Business: A Practical Users' Guide*, London: Van Nostrand Reinhold.
Kahn, H. and Cooper, C.L. (1993) *Stress in the Dealing Room. High Performers under Pressure*, London: Routledge.
Kanter, R.M. (1976) *Men and Women of the Corporation*, New York: Basic Books.
Kaplan, E.A. and Sprinker, M. (eds) (1993) *The Althusserian Legacy*, London: Verso.
Kaufman, H. (1986) *Interest Rates, the Markets and the New Financial World*, London: I.B. Tauris.
Kay, J. (1993) *Foundations of Corporate Success*, Oxford: Oxford University Press.
—— (1995) 'The foundations of national competitive advantage', *ESRC Fifth Annual Lecture*, London: ESRC.
Kay, W. (1991) *The City and the Single European Market*, Cambridge: Woodhead-Faulkner.
Keith, M. and Pile, S. (1993) 'Introduction Part 1: The politics of place ...', in *Place and the Politics of Identity*, ed. M. Keith and S. Pile, pp. 1–21, London: Routledge.
Kempson, E. (1994) *Outside the Banking System: A Review of Households Without a Current Account*, Social Security Advisory Committee, Research Paper 6, London: HMSO.

Kennedy, E. (1991) *The Bundesbank: Germany's Central Bank in the International Monetary System*, London: RIIA/Pinter.

Kern, S. (1983) *The Culture of Time and Space, 1880–1918*, Cambridge, MA: Harvard University Press.   :

Kerridge, E. (1988) *Trade and Banking in Early Modern England*, Manchester: Manchester University Press.

Kettell, B. and Magnus, G. (1986) *The International Debt Game*, London: Graham & Trotman.

Key, J.S.T. (1981) 'Services in the UK economy', *Bank of England Quarterly Bulletin* 25: 404–14.

Keynes, J.M. (1930) *A Treatise on Money, Volume 1: The Pure Theory of Money*, London: Macmillan.

—— (1936) *The General Theory of Employment, Interest and Money*, London: Macmillan.

Khan, B. and Ireland, J. (1993) 'The use of technology for competitive advantage. A study of screen vs floor trading', *City Research Project Subject Report 4*.

Kindleberger, C.P. (1984) *Financial History of Western Europe*, Oxford: Oxford University Press.

—— (1986) *The World in Depression, 1929–1939*, Revised Edition, London: Pelican.

King, A.D. (1990) *Global Cities. Post-Imperialism and the Internationalisation of London*, London: Routledge.

—— (1995) 'The times and spaces of modernity (or who needs postmodernism?)', in *Global Modernities*, ed. M. Featherstone *et al.*, pp. 108–23, London: Sage.

King, W. (1972) *History of the London Discount Market*, London: Cass.

Kirkman, F. (1987) *Electronic Funds Transfer*, Oxford: Oxford University Press.

Kittler, F.A. (1990) *Discourse Networks 1800/1900*, Stanford, CA: Stanford University Press.

Knight, Frank and Rutley (1989) 'The family housing cycle', *Knight, Frank and Rutley Residential Reports 2*, London: Knight, Frank and Rutley.

Knights, D. and Vurdubakis, T. (1993) 'Calculations of risk. Towards an understanding of insurances of moral and political technology', *Accounting, Organization and Society* 18: 729–64.

Knorr-Cetina, K. (1994) 'Primitive classification and post modernity: towards a notion of fiction', *Theory, Culture and Society* 11: 1–22.

Kroker, A. and Weinstein, M.A. (1994) *Data Trash. The Theory of the Virtual Class*, Montreal: New World Perspectives.

Kynaston, D. (1989) *The Financial Times. A Centenary History*, London: Viking.

—— (1994) *The City of London. Volume One. A World of its Own 1815–1890*, London: Chatto & Windus.

—— (1995) *The City of London. Volume Two. Golden Years: 1890–1914*, London: Chatto & Windus.

Labour Research (1986) 'Divided city', November: 11–14.

Laclau, E. and Mouffe, C. (1985) *Hegemony and Socialist Strategies*, London: Verso.

Lakoff, C. (1987) *Women, Fire and Dangerous Things*, Cambridge, MA: MIT Press.

Lakoff, C. and Johnson, M. (1980) *Metaphors We Live By*, Chicago: University of Chicago Press.

Lamont, M. (1992) *Money, Morals and Manners. The Culture of the French and the American Upper Middle Class*, Chicago: University of Chicago Press.

Land, N. (1994) 'Machinic desire', *Textual Practice* 11: 471–82.

—— (1995) 'Machines and technological complexity', *Theory, Culture and Society* 12: 131–40.

Landon, B. (1989) 'Bet on it: cyber video punk performance', *Mondo 2000* 1: 145–95.

Langdale, J. (1985) 'Electronics funds transfer and the internationalisation of the banking and finance industry', *Geoforum* 16: 1–13.

—— (1987) 'Telecommunications and electronic information services in Australia', in *The Spatial Impact of Technological Change*, pp. 89–103, ed. J.F. Brotchie *et al.*, Beckenham: Croom Helm.

Lascelles, D. *et al.* (1991) *Behind Closed Doors*, London: Financial Times.

Lash, S. (1993) 'Reflexive modernisation: the aesthetic dimension', *Theory, Culture and Society* 10: 1–23.

Lash, S. and Urry, J. (1987) *The End of Organised Capitalism*, Cambridge: Polity Press.

—— (1994) *Economies of Signs and Space*, London: Sage.

Laterasse, J. (1992) 'The intelligent city: Utopia or tomorrow's reality?', in *Telecom, Companies, Territories*, ed. F. Rowe and P. Veltz, Presses De L'ENPC.

Latour, B. (1986) 'The powers of association', in *Power, Action and Belief. A New Sociology of Knowledge?*, ed. J. Law, pp. 264–80, London: Routledge and Kegan Paul.

—— (1993) *We Have Never Been Modern*, Hemel Hempstead: Harvester Wheatsheaf.

Lave, J. and Wenger, M. (1991) *Situated Learning: Legitimate Peripheral Participation*, Cambridge: Cambridge University Press.

Law, J. (1994) *Organising Modernity*, Oxford: Blackwell.

Lawless, J. (1987) 'Back from the brink', *Business* May: 84–6.

Lazar, D. (1990) *Markets and Ideology in the City of London*, London: Macmillan.

Lea, M. (ed.) (1992) *Contexts of Computer-Mediated Communication*, Brighton: Harvester Wheatsheaf.

Leborgne, D. and Lipietz, A. (1990) 'Avoiding a two-tier Europe', *Labour and Society* 15: 177–99.

Lee, C.H. (1984) 'The service sector, regional specialisation and economic growth in the Victorian economy', *Journal of Historical Geography* 10(2): 139–55.

—— (1986) *The British Economy Since 1700: A Macroeconomic Perspective*, Cambridge: Cambridge University Press.

Lee, R. (1995) 'Moral money? Making local economic geographies: LETS in Kent, south east England', Paper presented at the 91st Annual Meeting of the Association of American Geographers, Chicago, March.

Le Goff, J. (1988) *Your Money or Your Life, Economy and Religion in the Middle Ages*, New York: Zone Books.

Leven, C.L. and Sykuta, M.E. (1994) 'The importance of race in home mortgage loan approvals', *Urban Affairs Quarterly* 29: 479–89.

Levine, C. (1987) 'Review of *Self and Society: Narcissism, Collectivism and the Development of Morals*', *Canadian Journal of Sociology* 12: 168–70.

Lewis, J. and Marsh, C.C. (1990) 'Too many hungry mouths to feed', *Euromoney* December: 33–9.

Lewis, M. (1989) *Liar's Poker*, London: Coronet.

Leys, C. (1988) 'The formation of British capital', *New Left Review*.

Leyshon, A. (1990) 'Review essay on *The United States in the World Economy*', *Environment and Planning A* 22: 1267–74.

—— (1992) 'The transformation of regulatory order: regulating the global economy and environment', *Geoforum* 23: 249–67.

—— (1994) 'Under pressure: finance, geoeconomic competition and the rise and fall of Japan's post-war growth economy', in *Money, Power, Space*, ed. S. Corbridge *et al.*, Oxford: Blackwell.

—— (1995a) 'Annihilating space: The speed-up of communications', in *A Shrinking World?*, ed. J. Allen and C. Hammet, pp. 11–54, Oxford: Oxford University Press.

—— (1995b) 'Geographies of money and finance 1', *Progress in Human Geography* 19(4): 531–43.

—— (1996a) 'Dissolving distance? Money, disembedding and the creation of "global financial space"', in *The Global Economy in Transition*, ed. P. Daniels and W. Lever, pp. 62–80, London: Longman.

—— (1996b) 'Geographies of money and finance 2', *Progress in Human Geography* 20 (forthcoming).

Leyshon, A., Boddy, M. and Thrift, N. (1989) 'Socio-economic restructuring and changing patterns of long-distance commuting', Department of Geography/School of Advanced Urban Studies, University of Bristol, mimeo.

Leyshon, A. and Thrift, N. (1994a) 'Access to financial services and financial infrastructure withdrawal: problems and policies', *Area* 26: 268–75.

—— (1994b) 'European financial integration: the search for an "island of monetary stability" in the seas of global financial turbulence', in *An Enlarged Europe: Regions in Competition?*, ed. L. Albrechts *et al.*, pp. 109–44, London: Jessica Kingsley.

Leyshon, A., Thrift, N. and Daniels, P. (1987) 'The urban and regional consequences of the restructuring of world financial markets: the case of the City of London', *Working Papers on Producer Services*, No. 4, University of Bristol and University of Liverpool.

Leyshon, A., Thrift, N. and Daniels, P. (1990) 'The operational development and spatial expansion of large commercial property firms', in *Land and Property Development Processes in a Changing Context*, ed. P. Healey and R. Nabbarro, pp. 60–97, Aldershot: Gower.

Leyshon, A., Thrift, N. and Justice, M. (1993) *A Reversal of Fortune? Financial Services and South East of England*, Stevenage: South East Economic Development Strategy.

Leyshon, A., Thrift, N. and Tommey, C. (1989) 'The rise of the British provincial financial centre', *Progress in Planning* 31: 151–229.

Liefferink, J.D. and Moi, A.P.J. (1991) 'Environmental policy making in the European Community: an evaluation of theoretical perspectives', Paper presented at the European integration and environmental policy seminar, Woudschofen, 29–30 November.

Lilwall, C. and Allcock, K. (1988) 'Value at a glance', in *Buying a Country House. A County Guide to Value, Country Life/*Knight, Frank and Rutley, London: *Country Life*.

Lim, Q.P. (1986) 'The *Euromoney* risk ratings', *Euromoney* September: 364–9.

Lipietz, A. (1985) *The Enchanted World*, London: Verso.

—— (1987) *Mirages and Miracles: The Crises of Global Fordism*, London: Verso.

—— (1988) 'Reflections on a tale: the Marxist formulation of the concepts of regulation and accumulation', *Studies in Political Economy* 26: 7–36.

—— (1989) 'The debt problem, European integration and the new phase of world crisis', *New Left Review* 178: 37–50.

—— (1992a) *Towards A New Economic Order: Postfordism, Ecology and Democracy*, Cambridge: Polity Press.

—— (1992b) 'The regulation approach and capitalist crisis: an alternative compromise for the 1990's', in *Cities and Regions in the New Europe: The Global–Local Interplay and Spatial Development Strategies*, ed. M. Dunford and G. Kafkalas, pp. 309–34, London: Belhaven Press.

—— (1993) 'From Althusserianism to "regulation theory"', in *The Althusserian Legacy*, ed. E.A. Kaplan and M. Sprinker, pp. 99–138, London: Verso.

Llewelyn, D.T. (1989) 'The changing structure of regulation in the British financial system', in *The Age of Regulatory Reform*, ed. K. Button and D. Swann, pp. 189–215, Oxford: Clarendon Press.

Lloyd, J. (1988a) 'The crumbling of the establishment', *Financial Times* 16 July: 6.

—— (1988b) 'Preaching in the market place', *Financial Times* 18 July: 15.

—— (1988c) 'Serving Thatcher's children', *Financial Times* 20 July: 20.

—— (1988d) 'Death of the honourable Englishman', *GQ* December: 152–5.

—— (1991) 'For Queen and community?', *Financial Times* 2 February: 1.

London Business School (1989) *1992: Myths and Realities*, London: London Business School.

Lovering, J. (1994) 'Creating discourses rather than jobs: the crisis in the cities and the transition fantasies of intellectuals and policy makers', School of Geography and Earth Resources, University of Hull, mimeo.

Luhmann, N. (1982) *The Differentiation of Society*, New York: Columbia University Press.

—— (1989) *Ecological Communication*, Cambridge: Polity Press.

Luke, T. (1993) 'Space-time compression and de-traditionalisation: identity, meaning and globalisation', Paper presented to the conference on De-traditionalisation, Lancaster University, 8–10 July.

Luttwak, E.N. (1990) 'From geopolitics to geo-economics: logic of conflict, grammar of commerce', *The National Interest* 20: 17–24.

McCulloch, T. (1988) 'International competition in services', in *The United States in the World Economy*, ed. M. Feldstein, pp. 367–406, Chicago: NBER.

MacDonald, H.I. (1992) 'Special interest politics and the crisis of financial institutions in the USA', *Environment and Planning C: Government and Policy* 10: 123–46.

McDowell, L. (1991) 'Life without father and Ford: the new gender order of post-Fordism', *Transactions of the Institute of British Geographers* 16: 400–19.

—— (1992) 'Social divisions, income inequality and gender relations in the 1980s', in *Policy and Change in Thatcher's Britain*, ed. P. Cloke, pp. 355–78, Oxford: Pergamon.

—— (1993) 'The missing subject in economic geography', mimeo.

McDowell, L. and Court, G. (1994) 'Performing work: bodily representations in merchant banks', *Environment and Planning D: Society and Space* 12: 727–50.

MacEwan, A. and Tabb, W. (1989) 'The economy in crisis: national power and international instability', *Socialist Review* 19: 67–91.

McLellan, D. (1980) *The Thought of Karl Marx*, London: Macmillan.

McMichael, P. and Myhre, D. (1991) 'Global regulation vs. the nation-state: agro-food systems and the new politics of capital', *Capital and Class* 43: 83–105.

McRae, H. (1994) *The Independent*.

Magdoff, H. and Sweezy, P. (1987) *Stagnation and the Financial Explosion*, New York: Monthly Review Press.

Mandel, E. (1984) 'Gold, money and the transformation problem', in *Riccardo, Marx, Sraffa: The Langston Memorial Volume*, ed. E. Mandel and A. Freeway, pp. 141–62, London: Verso.

Mann, M. (1984) 'The autonomous power of the state: its origins, mechanisms and results', *Arch. Eur. Soc.* 15: 185–213.

Mansell, R. (1993) *The New Telecommunications. A Political Economy of Network Evolution*, London: Sage.

Mansell, R. and Jenkins, M. (1993) 'Electronic-trading networks, the emergence of new productive networks', *Commission of the European Communities. FAST Dossier. Continental Europe. Science, Technology and Community Cohesion*, Vols 23–4, Annex 5: 127–72.

Mantel, H. (1989) *Fludd*, London: Viking.

Marceau, J. (1989) *A Family Business? The Making of an International Business Class*, Cambridge: Cambridge University Press.

Marden, P. (1992) '"Real" regulation reconsidered', *Environment and Planning A* 24: 751–67.

Mars, G. (1982) *Cheats at Work*, London: Heinemann.

Marsh, F. (1986) *Japan's Next Export Success: The Financial Services Industry*, Special Report No. 1066, *Economist* Intelligence Unit, London.

Marshall, J.N., Gentle, C.J.S., Raybould, S. and Coombes, M. (1992) 'Regulatory change, corporate restructuring and the spatial development of the British financial sector', *Regional Studies* 26: 453–67.

Marvin, C. (1988) *When Old Technologies Were New*, New York: Oxford University Press.

Marx, K. (1885) *Kapital*, Volume 1.

Marx, K. (1954) *Capital: A Critique of Political Economy*, Vol. I, London: Lawrence & Wishart.

—— (1959) *Capital: A Critique of Political Economy*, Vol. III, London: Lawrence & Wishart.

—— (1963a) *Capital*, Volume 1, Moscow: Progress Publishers.

—— (1963b) *Theories of Surplus Value*, Volume 1, Moscow: Progress Publishers.

—— (1968) 'The 18th Brumaire of Louis Bonaparte', in *Selected Works in One Volume*, ed. K. Marx and F. Engels, pp. 96–179, London: Lawrence & Wishart.

—— (1973) *Grundrisse*, Harmondsworth: Penguin.

—— (1977) *Selected Writings*, ed. D. McLellan, Oxford: Oxford University Press.

Massey, D. (1974) 'Towards a critique of industrial location theory', London: RP5, Centre for Environmental Studies.

May, M. (1987) 'City reward that equals £111,000', *The Times* 21 July: 25.

Merrifield, A. (1993) 'The struggle over place: redeveloping American Can in southeast Baltimore', *Transactions of the Institute of British Geographers* NS 18: 102–21.

Meyrowitz, J. (1985) *No Sense of Place: The Impact of Electronic Media on Social Behaviour*, New York: Oxford University Press.

Michie, R.L. (1987) *The London and New York Stock Exchange, 1850–1914*, London: Macmillan.

—— (1988) 'Dunn, Fisher and Co. in the City of London', *Business History* 30: 195–218.

—— (1992) *The City of London. Continuity and Change, 1850–1990*, London: Macmillan.

Minsky, H.P. (1982) *Can 'It' Happen Again?*, Armonk, NY: M.E. Sharpe.

—— (1989) 'Financial crises and the evolution of capitalism: the crash of '87 – what does it mean?', in *Capitalist Development and Crisis Theory: Accumulation, Regulation and Spatial Restructuring*, ed. M. Gottdiener and N. Koninos, pp. 391–403, New York: St Martins Press.

Mistral, J. (1986) 'Régime international et trajectoires nationales', in *Capitalismes: Fin de Siècle*, ed. R. Boyer, pp. 167–202, Paris: Presses Universitaires de France.

Mitchell, J. (1990) *Access to Basic Banking Services: The Problems of Low-income American Consumers*, Providence, RI: Rhode Island Consumers Council.

—— (1992) 'Obligations to society: banks and their obligations', Paper presented to Institute of Bankers, Cambridge Seminar.

Mitchell, W.T.J. (1995) *City of Bits*, Cambridge, MA: MIT Press.

Molyneux, P. (1989) '1991 and its impact on local and regional banking markets', *Regional Studies* 23: 523–33.

Moore, L. (1995) 'Teledildonics: Virtual lesbians in the fiction of Jeanette Winterson', in *Sexy Bodies*, ed. E. Grosz and E. Probyn, pp. 104–27, London: Routledge.

Moran, M. (1991) *The Politics of the Financial Services Revolution*, London: Macmillan.

Morgan, E.V. and Thomas, W.A. (1962) *The Stock Exchange*, London: Elek.

Morris, M. (1988) 'Banality in cultural studies', *Discourse X* 2: 3–29.

Motluk, A. (1995) 'The City's latest takeover bid', *New Scientist* 19 August: 12–13.

Mottram, R.H. (1924) *Spanish Farm Trilogy*, London: Chatto & Windus.

—— (1929) *A History of Financial Speculation*, London: Chatto & Windus.

Mulford, D. (1989) 'Needed: bolder steps towards freer access', *Financial Times* 29 November.

Mulgan, G.J. (1991) *Communication and Control: Networks and the New Economics of Communication*, London: Routledge.

Murdoch, G. (1993) 'Communications and the constitution of modernity', *Media, Culture and Society* 15: 521–39.

Murray, R. (1991) *Local Space: Europe and the New Regionalism*, Manchester/Stevenage: CLES/SEEDS.

National Association of Citizen's Advice Bureaux (1993) 'Don't bank on it', Submission to the Code of Banking Practice Review Committee, July.

National Association of Pension Funds (1990) 'Creative tension?', National Association of Pension Funds Ltd, 12 Grosvenor Gardens, London SW1W 0PS. ·

Naylor, R.T. (1987) *Hot Money and the Politics of Debt*, London: Unwin.

Neal, L. (1990) *The Rise of Financial Capitalism: International Capital Markets in the Age of Reason*, Cambridge: Cambridge University Press.

New Earnings Survey (1977) London: Department of Employment.

—— (1981) London: Department of Employment.

—— (1984) London: Department of Employment.

New Society (1986) 'The rich in Britain', 22 August: Special Supplement.

Nicholson, C. (1994) *Writing and the Rise of Financial Capital Satires of the Early Eighteenth Century*, Cambridge: Cambridge University Press.

Nomura Research Institute (1986) *The World Economy and Financial Markets in 1995*, Tokyo: Nomura Research Institute.

Nugent, W.T.K. (1967) *The Money Question During Reconstruction*, New Haven, CT: Yale University Press.

Nye, D. (1990) *Electrifying America*, Cambridge, MA: MIT Press.

Obermiller, P.J. (1988) 'Banking at the brink: the effects of banking deregulation on low-income neighbourhoods', *Business and Society* 27: 7–13.

O'Brien, R. (1991) *Global Financial Integration. The End of Geography*, London: Pinter.

OECD (1986) *Financial Market Trends*, November, Paris: OECD.

—— (1992a) *Banks Under Stress*, Paris; OECD.

—— (1992b) *Risk Management in Financial Services*, Paris: OECD.

Ohmae, K. (1990) *The Borderless World: Power and Strategy in the Interlinked Economy*, London: Collins.

O'Leary, J. (1986) 'The powerhouse beckons with a pot of gold', *Times Higher Education Supplement* 20 June: 12.

O'Reilly, J. (1992a) 'Subcontracting in banking: some evidence from Britain and France', *New Technology, Work and Employment* 3: 107–15.

—— (1992b) 'Where do you draw the line? Functional flexibility, training and skill in Britain and France', *Work, Employment and Society* 6: 369–96.

Osborne, P. (1995) *The Politics of Time. Modernity and Avant-Garde*, London: Verso.

Ó Tuathail, G. (1992a) 'Japan and the Bush Administration's "New World Order"', Paper presented in the session 'Towards New World Order? The International System after Stalinism', British Political Studies Conference, Queen's University, Belfast, 7–9 April.

—— (1992b) '"Pearl Harbour without bombs": a critical geopolitics of the US-Japan "FSX" debate', *Environment and Planning A* 24: 975–94.

—— (1993a) 'Japan as threat: geo-economic discourses on the USA-Japan relationship in US civil society, 1987–91', in *The Political Geography of the New World Order*, ed. C.H. Williams, pp. 181–209, London: Belhaven Press.

—— (1993b) 'The new East-West conflict? Japan and the Bush administration's "New World Order"', *Area* 25: 127–35.

Overbeek, H. (1990) *Global Capitalism and National Decline: The Thatcher Decade in Perspective*, London: Unwin Hyman.

Pagano, M. (1986) 'Graduates bank on the Big Bang bucks', *Guardian* 12 August: 22.

Pagano, M. and Roell, A. (1990) 'Trading systems in European stock exchanges: current performance and policy options', *Economic Policy* 10: 63–115.

Pahl, R.E. (1989) 'St. Matthews and the golden handcuffs', mimeo.

Paice, C. (1989) 'Modern country houses. Winners or white elephants?', *Savills Magazine* No. 23: 55–7.

Parboni, R. (1981) *The Dollar and Its Rivals: Recession, Inflation and International Finance*, London: Verso.

Parry, J. (1989) 'On the moral perils of exchange', in *Money and the Morality of Exchange*, ed. J. Parry and M. Bloch, pp. 64–93, Cambridge: Cambridge University Press.

Parry, J. and Bloch, M. (eds) (1989) *Money and the Morality of Exchange*, Cambridge: Cambridge University Press.

Parsons, W. (1989) *The Power of the Financial Press*, London: Edward Elgar.

Peck, J.A. and Tickell, A. (1992) 'Local modes of social regulation? Regulation theory, Thatcherism and uneven development', *Geoforum* 23: 347–63.

—— (1993a) 'Business goes local: dissecting the "business agenda" in post-democratic Manchester', Paper presented at the 9th Urban Change and Conflict Conference, University of Sheffield, 14–16 September.

—— (1993b) 'Social regulation *after*-Fordism: regulation-theory, neo-liberalism and the global-local nexus', Manchester: WP6, Manchester International Centre for Labour Studies, University of Manchester.

—— (1994) 'Searching for a new institutional fix: the after-Fordist crisis and global-local disorder', in *Post-Fordism: A Reader*, ed. A. Amin, pp. 280–313, Oxford: Blackwell.

—— (1995) 'The social regulation of uneven development: "regulatory deficit", England's South East, and the collapse of Thatcherism', *Environment and Planning A* 27: 15–40.

Peebles, G. (1991) *A Short History of Socialist Money*, London: Allen & Unwin.

Pensions Management (1987) 'The survey: fund managers' performance – surviving the squall?', *Pensions Management* December: 51–79.

Perkin, H. (1989). *The Rise of Professional Society. Britain Since 1880*, London: Routledge.

Pfeiffer, K.L. (1993) 'The materiality of communication', in *Materialities of Communication*, ed. H.L. Gumbrecht and K.L. Pfeiffer, pp. 1–12, Stanford, CA: Stanford University Press.

Pfeil, F. (1990) *Another Tale to Tell. Politics and Narrative in Postmodern Culture*, London: Verso.

Picciotto, S. (1991) 'The internationalisation of the state', *Capital and Class* 43: 43–63.

Pickering, A. (1995) *The Mangle of Practice. Time, Agency and Science*, Chicago: University of Chicago Press.

Pinney, C. (1992) 'Future travel. Anthropology and cultural distance in an age of virtual reality, or, a past seen from a possible future', *Visual Anthropology Review* 8.

Piorinski, R. (1991) 'Télétopia: nouvelles technologies et aménagement de territoire', *Futures* November: 47–65.

Plender, J. (1987) 'Under the skin of an image problem', *Financial Times* 15 June.

—— (1990a) 'Malaise in need of long-term remedy', *Financial Times* 20 July.

—— (1990b) 'Throw sand in the take-over machine', *Financial Times* 24 July.

Plender, J. and Wallace, P. (1985) *The Square Mile*, London: Century.

Poggi, G. (1993) *Georg Simmel's Philosophy of Money*, Berkeley, CA: University of California Press.

Polanyi, K. (1944) *The Great Transformation*, New York: Farrar & Rinehart.

—— (1957) *The Great Transformation: Origins of Our Time*, Boston: Beacon Press.

—— (1968) 'The semantics of money-uses', in *Primitive, Archaic and Modern Economics: Essays of Karl Polanyi*, ed. G. Dalton, pp. 175–203, Boston: Beacon Press.

Pooley, S. (1991) 'The state rules, OK? The continuing political economy of nation-states', *Capital and Class* 43: 65–82.

Popke, E.J. (1994) 'Recasting geopolitics: the discursive scripting of the International Monetary Fund', *Political Geography* 13: 255–69.

Porter, M. (1990) *The Competitive Advantage of Nations*, London: Macmillan.

Porter, R. (1993) 'Baudrillard, hysteria and consumption', in *Forget Baudrillard*, ed. C. Rojek and B. Turner, London: Routledge.

Poster, M. (1990) *The Mode of Information: Poststructuralism and Social Context*, Cambridge: Polity Press.

—— (1995) *The Second Media Age*, Cambridge: Polity Press.

Pound, C. (1993) 'Imagining in-formation: the complex disconnections of computer networks', in *Technoscientific Imaginaries*, ed. G.E. Marcus, pp. 527–48, Chicago: Chicago University Press.

Power, M. (1993) 'The politics of financial auditing', *Political Quarterly* 64: 272–84.

Prendergast, C. (1992) *Paris and the Nineteenth Century*, Oxford: Blackwell.

Presnell, L.S. (1956) *Country Banking in the Industrial Revolution*, Oxford: Oxford University Press.

Price, K.A. (1986) *The Global Financial Village*, London: Banking World.

Probyn, E. (1991) *Sexing the Subject*, London: Routledge.

Pryke, M. (1991) 'An international city going global', *Environment and Planning: Society and Space* 9: 197–222.

Pugh, J. (1989) *The Penguin Guide to the City*, Harmondsworth: Penguin.

Quinn, S. (1995) 'Balances and goldsmith-bankers: the co-ordination and control of inter-banker debt clearing in seventeenth-century London', in *Goldsmiths, Silversmiths and Bankers: Innovation and the Transfer of Skill, 1550–1750*, ed. D. Mitchell, Centre for Metropolitan History Working Paper Series, No. 2 (Alan Sutton Publishing Limited and Centre for Metropolitan History, London).

Radice, H. (1984) 'The national economy: a Keynesian myth?', *Capital and Class* 22: 111–40.

Rajan, A. (1985) *New Technology and Employment in Insurance, Banking and Building Societies: Recent Experience and Future Impact*, Aldershot: Gower.

—— (1987) 'New technology and career progression on financial institutions', *The Service Industries Journal* 7: 33–40.

—— (1990) *Capital People*, London: Industrial Society.

Rajan, A. and Fryatt, J. (1988) *Create or Abdicate: The City's Human Resource Choice for the 1990s*, London: Witherby.

Read, D. (1992) *The Power of News. The History of Reuters*, Oxford: Oxford University Press.

Reading, B. (1989a) 'A return to stop-go', *Sunday Times* 15 October: D9.

—— (1989b) 'Letter to the editor', *Financial Times* 19 October: 25.

Reddy, W. (1987) *Money and Liberty in Modern Europe*, Cambridge: Cambridge University Press.

Regional Trends (1983) London: HMSO.

—— (1986) London: HMSO.

—— (1987) London: HMSO.

—— (1991) London: HMSO.

Reid, M. (1988) *All Change in the City. The Revolution in Britain's Financial Sector*, London: Macmillan.

Reifner, U. and Ford, J. (eds) (1992) *Banking for People*, Berlin: Walter de Gruyter.

Remuneration Economics (1987) *Guide to Current Salaries in Banking*, March, London: Jonathan Wren Recruitment Consultants.

Rentoul, J. (1987) *The Rich Get Richer. The Growth of Inequality in Britain in the 1980's*, London: Unwin Hyman.

Rheingold, H. (1994) *The Virtual Community*, London: Secker & Warburg.

Richards, T. (1993) *The Imperial Archive. Knowledge and the Fantasy of Empire*, London: Verso.

Richardson, R. (1993) 'The geography of new telemediated services: opportunity or threat for the UK's provincial cities?', Centre for Urban and Regional Development Studies, University of Newcastle-upon-Tyne (mimeo).

Ritzer, G. (1995) *Expressing America: A Critique of the Global Credit Card Society*, Thousand Oaks, CA: Pine Forge.

Roberts, G. (1995) *$1000 Billion A Day. Inside the Foreign Exchange Markets*, London: Harper-Collins.

Roberts, M. (1995) 'Beyond revisionism: New Labour, socialist basics and the dynamic economy', *Radical Philosophy* 73: 13–21.

Roberts, R. and Kynaston, D. (1995) *Bank of England: Money, Power and Influence, 1694–1994*, Oxford: Oxford University Press.

Roberts, S. (1994) 'Fictitious capital, fictitious spaces: the geography of offshore financial flows', in *Money, Power and Space*, ed. S. Corbridge *et al.*, pp. 91–115, Oxford: Blackwell.

Robinson, C.J. (1991) 'Racial disparity in the Atlanta housing market', *Review of Black Political Economy* 19: 87–109.

Robinson, J.M. (1984) *The Latest Country Houses*, London: Bodley Head.

Robles, A.C. (1994) *French Theories of Regulation and Conceptions of the International Division of Labour*, London: Macmillan.

Rogers, B. (1988) *Men Only. An Investigation into Men's Organisations*, London: Pandora Press.

Rosenau, J.N. (1992a) 'Governance, order and change in world politics', in *Governance Without Government: Order and Change in World Politics*, ed. J.N. Rosenau and E.O. Czempiel, pp. 1–29, Cambridge: Cambridge University Press.

—— (1992b) 'Citizenship in a changing global order', in *Governance Without Government: Order and Change in World Politics*, ed. J.N. Rosenau and E.O. Czempiel, pp. 272–94, Cambridge: Cambridge University Press.

—— (ed.) (1993) *Global Voices. Dialogues in International Relations*, Boulder, CO: Westview Press.

Rosenau, J.N. and Czempiel, E. (eds) (1992) *Governance Without Government. Order and Change in World Politics*, Cambridge: Cambridge University Press.

Rubinstein, W.D. (1977) 'The Victorian middle classes: wealth, occupation and geography', *Economic History Review* 30.

—— (1980) *Men of Property*, London: Croom Helm.

—— (1986) *Wealth and Inequality in Britain*, London: Faber & Faber.

—— (1987) *Elites and the Wealthy in Modern British History*, Brighton: Harvester.
Rupert, M. (1993) 'Alienation, capitalism and the inter-state system: towards a Marxian/Gramscian critique', in *Gramsci, Historical Materialism and International Relations*, ed. S. Gill, pp. 67–92, Cambridge: Cambridge University Press.
Sabbagh, T. (1994) *Demos Quarterly* 3: 6–8.
Sampson, A. (1965) *The Anatomy of Britain*, London: Hodder & Stoughton.
—— (1972) *The Anatomy of Britain*, 2nd Edition, London: Hodder & Stoughton.
Samuel, R. (1989) 'Introduction: exciting to be English', in *Patriotism: The Making and Unmaking of British National Identity, Volume 1. History and Politics*, ed. R. Samuel, London: Routledge.
Sandelson, V. (1959) 'The confidence trick', in *The Establishment*, ed. H. Thomas, pp. 127–68, London: Anthony Blond.
Sassen, S. (1991) *The Global City: New York, London, Tokyo*. Princeton, NJ: Princeton University Press.
Savage, M. (1988) 'The missing link? The relationship between spatial mobility and social mobility', *British Journal of Sociology* 39: 554–77.
Savills (1987a) *Savills Magazine* 16, Spring.
—— (1987b) 'In search of perfection', *Savills Magazine* 17: 5–8.
—— (1988) *Placing Prospectus*, London: Savills/Kleinwort Benson.
Sayer, A. (1993) 'Postmodernist thought in geography: a realist view', *Antipode* 25: 320–44.
Sayer, A. and Walker, R. (1992) *The New Social Economy*, Oxford: Blackwell.
Sayer, D. (1979) *Marx's Method. Ideology, Science and Critique in 'Capital'*, Hassocks: Harvester Press.
Sayer, S. (1992) 'The City, power and economic policy in the U.K.', *International Review of Applied Economics* 6: 125–51.
Sayers, R.S. (1976) *The Bank of England 1891–1944*, (3 vols), Cambridge: Cambridge University Press.
Scott, J. (1986) *Capitalist Property and Financial Power: A Comparative Study of Britain, the United States and Japan*, London: Wheatsheaf.
Selzer, M. (1992) *Bodies and Machines*, New York: Routledge.
Sennett, R. (1994) *Flesh and Stone*, London: Allen Lane.
Serres, M. (1982) *Hermes. Literature, Science, Philosophy*, Baltimore, MD: Johns Hopkins University Press.
—— (1995) *Angels: A Modern Myth*, Paris: Flammarion.
Serres, M. and Latour, B. (1995) *Conversations on Science, Culture and Time*, Ann Arbor, MI: University of Michigan Press.
Servais, D. (1988) *The Single Financial Market*, Brussels: Commission of the European Communities.
Shackle, G.L.S. (1972) *Epistemics and Economics. A Critique and Economic Doctories*, Cambridge: Cambridge University Press.
Shell, M. (1982) *Money, Language and Thought*, Berkeley, CA: University of California Press.
Shotter, J. (1989) '"Duality of Structure" and "Intentionality" in an ecological psychology: towards a science of individuality', *Journal for the Theory of Social Behaviour* 12: 19–43.
Simmel, G. (1978) *The Philosophy of Money*, London: Routledge.
—— (1990) *The Philosophy of Money*, 2nd Edition, London: Routledge.
Simpson, L.C. (1995) *Technology, Time and the Conversations of Modernity*, London: Routledge.
Sinclair, T.J. (1994) 'Passing judgement: credit rating processes as regulatory mechanisms of governance in the emerging world order', *Review of International Political Economy* 1: 133–60.
Skidelsky, R. (1992) *John Maynard Keynes: The Economist As Saviour 1920–1937*, London: Macmillan.
Skuse, B. (1993) *The Incidence of Retail Bank Branch Closure in the United Kingdom, 1988–1993: A Case Study in the Bristol Region*, BA Dissertation, University of Bristol.
Smelser, N.J. and Swedberg, R. (eds) (1994) *The Handbook of Economic Sociology*, Princeton, NJ: Princeton University Press.
Smiles, S. (1859) *Self-Help and the Acquisition of Character and Perseverance*, London: Murray.
Smith, A. (1968) *The Wealth of Nations*, Harmondsworth: Penguin.
Smith, C.W. (1983) *The Mind of the Market*, New York: Harper Colophon.
Smith, D. (1987) *The Rise and Fall of Monetarism: The Theory and Politics of an Economic Experiment*, London: Pelican.

Smith, N. (1993) 'Homeless/global: scaling places', in *Mapping the Futures: Local Cultures, Global Change*, ed. J. Bird *et al.*, pp. 87–119, London: Routledge.

—— (1994) 'Marxist geography', in *Dictionary of Human Geography*, 3rd Edition, ed. R.H. Johnston *et al.*, pp. 365–73, Oxford: Blackwell.

Social Trends (1992) London: HMSO.

Soper, K. (1990) *Troubled Pleasures*, London: Verso.

Soros, G. (1988) *The Alchemy of Finance*, London: John Wiley.

Spender, D. (1995) *Nattering on the Net: Women, Power and Cyberspace*, Melbourne: Spinifex Press.

Springer, C. (1993) 'Sex, memory and angry women', *South Atlantic Quarterly* 92: 713–35.

—— (1994) 'The pleasures of the interface', *Screen* 32: 303–23.

Sproull, L. and Kiesler, S. (1991) *Connections: New Ways of Working in the Networked Organisation*, Cambridge, MA: MIT Press.

Spufford, P. (1988) *Money and its Use in Medieval Europe*, Cambridge: Cambridge University Press.

Square Meal (1994) *Square Meal*, London: Monomax.

Squires, G.D. (1992) 'Community reinvestment: an emerging social movement', in *From Redlining to Reinvestment: Community Responses to Urban Disinvestment*, ed. G.D. Squires, pp. 1–37, Philadelphia: Temple University Press.

Squires, G.D., Dewolfe, R. and Dewolfe, A.S. (1979) 'Urban decline or disinvestment: uneven development, redlining and the role of the insurance industry', *Social Problems* 27: 79–95.

Squires, G.D. and Velez, W. (1987) 'Insurance redlining and the transformation of an urban metropolis', *Urban Affairs Quarterly* 23: 63–83.

—— (1988) 'Insurance redlining and the process of discrimination', *The Review of Black Political Economy* 16: 63–75.

Squires, G.D., Velez, W. and Tauber, K.E. (1991) 'Insurance redlining, agency location and the process of urban disinvestment', *Urban Affairs Quarterly* 26: 567–88.

Stafford, B.M. (1991) *Body Criticism*, Cambridge, MA: MIT Press.

—— (1994) *Artful Science*, Cambridge, MA: MIT Press.

—— (1995) 'Desperately seeking connections: four scenes from eighteenth century laboratory life', *Ecumene* 2: 378–98.

Stallabrass, J. (1995) 'Empowering technology: the exploration of cyberspace', *New Left Review* No. 211: 3–32.

Staple, G. (1992) *Telegeography: Global Telecommunications, Traffic Statistics and Commentary*, International Institute For Communications.

Star, S.L. (ed.) (1995) *Cultures of Computing*, Oxford: Blackwell.

Stark, T. (1989) 'The changing distribution of income under Mrs Thatcher', in *The Restructuring of the UK Economy*, ed. F. Green, Hemel Hempstead: Wheatsheaf.

Stephenson, N. (1995) *The Diamond Age*, London: Viking.

Stewart, I. (1988) '1988: the year of the country house', *Savills Magazine* No. 21: 9–11.

—— (1989) 'A layman's guide to country house costs', *Savills Magazine* No. 25: 55–7.

Stone, A.R. (1995) 'Sex and death among the disembodied; VR, cyberspace and the natural academic discourse', in *The Cultures of Computing*, ed. S.L. Star, pp. 243–55, Oxford: Blackwell.

Stone, M.E. (1975) 'The housing crisis, mortgage lending and class struggle', *Antipode* 7: 22–37.

Stopford, J. and Strange, S. (1991) *Rival States, Rival Firms: Competition for World Market Shares*, Cambridge: Cambridge University Press.

Storper, M. (1992) 'The limits to globalization: technology districts and international trade', *Economic Geography* 68: 60–93.

Strange, S. (1986) *Casino Capitalism*, Oxford: Blackwell.

—— (1988) *States and Markets*, London: Frances Pinter.

Strathern, M. (1992) 'Foreword: the mirror of technology', in *Consuming Technologies*, ed. R. Silverstone and E. Hirsch, pp. vii-xiii, London: Routledge.

Streeck, W. and Schmitter, P.C. (1991) 'From national corporatism to transnational pluralism: organized interests in the Single European Market', *Politics and Society* 19: 133–64.

Sunley, P. (1992) 'An uncertain future: a critique of Post-Keynesian economic geographies', *Progress in Human Geography* 16: 58–70.

Swyngedouw, E.A. (1992) 'The Mammon quest; "glocalisation", interspatial competition and the monetary order: the construction of new spatial scales', in *Cities and Regions in the New*

Europe: The Global-Local Interplay and Spatial Development Strategies, ed. M. Dunford and G. Kafkalas, pp. 39–67, London: Belhaven Press.

Taub, R. (1988) *Community Capitalism*, Boston: Harvard Business School.

Taylor, A. (1987) 'Salaries low, office costs high in London', *Financial Times* 13 May.

Taylor, M. and Allen, H. (1989) 'Chart analysis and the foreign exchange market', *Bank of England Quarterly* November.

Taylor, M. and Thrift, N. (1982) *The Geography of Multinationals*, London: Croom Helm.

Taylor, P.J. (1989) *Political Geography: World-economy, Nation-state and Locality*, Harlow: Longman.

—— (1993) 'Geopolitical world orders', in *Political Geography of the Twentieth Century: A Global Analysis*, ed. P.J. Taylor, pp. 31–61, London: Belhaven Press.

Taylor, R. (1990) 'High interest from financial liberation', *Financial Times* 22 January.

Terdiman, R. (1985) *Discourse/Counter-Discourse: Theory and Practice of Symbolic Resistance in Nineteenth Century France*, Ithaca, NY: Cornell University Press.

The Banker (1968) 118: 915–23.

—— (1977) 127: 129–77.

—— (1986) 136: 69–132.

—— (1991) 'Global gamble', 8–17 February.

The Economist (1986) 'The consumer is sovereign: a survey of international banking', 28 March: 1–68.

—— (1987a) 'Till debt us do part', 28 February: 89–90.

—— (1987b) 'Over-weight, over-rich and over here', 4 April: 73–4.

—— (1987c) 'Crying for Argentina', 25 April: 91–2.

—— (1987d) 'Why America needs Japan as much as Japan needs America', 22 May, Supplement.

—— (1987e) 'End of binge: a survey of euromarkets', 22 May, Supplement.

—— (1987f) 'Yanks slither on the City slick', 30 May: 77.

—— (1987g) 'Nice market, shame about the backlog', 29 August: 71.

—— (1987h) 'Big or boutique?', 29 August: 16–17.

—— (1988) 'A survey of Japanese finance', 10 December.

—— (1989) 'Top and bottom of the art market', 29 October: 125.

—— (1990) 'A question of definition: a survey', 7 April: 84–96.

—— (1991) 'Europe's reluctant superbanks', 5 January: 69–70.

—— (1992) 'Fear of finance: a survey of the world economy', 19 September.

—— (1993a) 'Putting the City together again', 1 May: 15.

—— (1993b) 'Phoenix in south-central', 14 August.

—— (1993c) 'Survey of international banking', 10 April.

—— (1994a) 'Recalled to life: A survey of international banking', 30 April: 1–46.

—— (1994b) 'Mind over matter', 23 April: 105–6.

Thomas, H. (ed.) (1959) *The Establishment*, London.

Thompson, E.P. (1961) 'The Long Revolution', *New Left Review* 9: 24–33 and 10: 34–9.

Thompson, F.M.L. (1963) *English Landed Society in the Nineteenth Century*, London: Routledge and Kegan Paul.

Thompson, G. (1977) 'The relationship between the financial and industrial sector in the United Kingdom economy', *Economy and Society* 6: 235–83.

—— (1990a) *The Political Economy of the New Right*, London: Pinter.

—— (1990b) 'Monetary policy and international finance', in *Reactions to the Right*, ed. B. Hindess, pp. 50–77, London; Routledge.

Thompson, J.B. (1995) *The Media and Modernity. A Social Theory of the Media*, Cambridge: Polity Press.

Thrift, N. (1979) 'Unemployment in the inner city: urban problems or structural imperative? A review of the British experience', in *Geography and the Urban Environment Vol. 2*, ed. D.T. Herbert and R.J. Johnston, pp. 125–6, Chichester: John Wiley.

—— (1983) 'On the determination of social action in space and time', *Environment and Planning D: Society and Space* 1: 23–57.

—— (1985a) 'Flies and germs: a geography of knowledge', in *Social Relations and Spatial Structures*, ed. D. Gregory and J. Urry, pp. 330–73, London: Macmillan.

—— (1985b) 'Taking the rest of the world seriously? British urban and regional research in a time of economic crisis', *Government and Planning A* 17: 7–24.

—— (1986a) 'The internationalisation of producer services and the integration of the Pacific Basin property market', in *Multinationals and the Restructuring of the World Economy*, ed. M.J. Taylor and N.J. Thrift, Beckenham, Kent: Croom Helm.

—— (1986b) 'The geography of international economic disorder', in *A World in Crisis*, ed. R.J. Johnston and P.J. Taylor, pp. 12–67, Oxford: Blackwell.

—— (1987a) 'Manufacturing rural geography?', *Journal of Rural Studies* 3: 77–81.

—— (1987b) 'Serious money. Capitalism, class, consumption and culture in late twentieth century Britain', Paper presented to the IBG Conference on 'New Directions in Cultural Geography', London, 1–3 September.

—— (1987c) 'The fixers: the urban geography of international commercial capital' in *Global Restructuring and Territorial Development*, ed. J. Henderson and M. Castells, pp. 219–97, Beverly Hills, CA: Sage.

—— (1987d) 'A new world? Global finance in an investor's market: comment on Corbridge's paper', *Studies in Comparative International Development*

—— (1989a) 'New times and spaces? The perils of transition models', *Environment and Planning D: Society and Space* 7: 127–30.

—— (1989b) 'The geography of international economic disorder', in *A World in Crisis?, Geographical Perspectives*, 2nd Edition, ed. R. Johnston and P. Taylor, pp. 16–78, Oxford: Blackwell.

—— (1989c) 'Images of social change', in *The Changing Social Structure*, ed. C. Hamnett, L. McDowell and P. Sarre, pp. 12–42, London: Sage.

—— (1990a) 'The perils of the international financial system', *Environment and Planning A* 22: 1135–6.

—— (1990b) 'Transport and communication 1730–1914', in *An Historical Geography of England and Wales*, 2nd Edition, ed. R.A. Dodgshon and R.A. Butlin, pp. 453–86, London: Academic Press.

—— (1991) 'Muddling through: world order and globalisation', *Professional Geographer* 14: 272–9.

—— (1992) 'Light out of darkness? Social theory in Britain in the 1980s', in *Policy and Change in Thatcher's Britain*, ed. P.J. Cloke, pp. 1–32, Oxford: Pergamon.

—— (1993) 'For a new regional geography 3', *Progress in Human Geography* 17: 92–100.

—— (1994a) 'Inhuman geographies', in *Reading the Rural*, ed. P.J. Cloke *et al.*, London: Paul Chapman.

—— (1994b) 'On the social and cultural determinants of international financial centres', in *Money, Space and Power*, ed. S. Corbridge *et al.*, pp. 327–55, London: Blackwell.

—— (1995) 'A hyperactive world', in *Geographies of Global Change: Remapping the World in the Late Twentieth Century*, ed. R.J. Johnston *et al.*, pp. 2–35, Oxford: Blackwell.

—— (1996) *Spatial Formations*, London: Sage.

Thrift, N. and Leyshon, A. (1988) '"The gambling propensity": banks, developing country debt exposures and the new international financial system', *Geoforum* 19: 55–69.

Tickell, A. and Peck, J.A. (1992) 'Accumulation, regulation and the geographies of post-Fordism: missing links in regulationist research', *Progress in Human Geography* 16: 190–218.

Todes, D.P. (1988) 'Darwin's Malthussian metaphor and Russian evolutionary thought', *Isis* 78: 537–51.

Townsend, P. (1987) *Poverty and Labour in London*, London: Low Pay Unit.

Tucker, D.S. (1967) [1922] *The Evolution of People's Banks*, New York: AMS Press.

Turkle, S. and Papert, S. (1990) 'Epistemological pluralism: styles and voices within the computer culture', *Signs* 16: 125–57.

Tussie, D. (1991) 'Trading in fear? U.S. hegemony and the open world economy in perspective', in *The New International Political Economy*, ed. C.N. Murphy and R. Toose, pp. 79–95, Boulder, CO: Lynne Reiner.

Turner, J.T. (1987) *Rediscovering the Social Group. A Self-Categorisation Theory*, Oxford: Blackwell.

Umble, D.Z. (1992) 'The Amish and the telephone: resistance and reconstruction', in *Consuming Technologies*, ed. R. Silverstone and E. Hirsch, pp. 183–94, London: Routledge.

Underhill, G.R.D. (1991) 'Markets beyond politics? The state and the internationalisation of financial markets', *European Journal of Political Research* 19: 197–225.

Unger, I. (1964) *The Greenback Era*, Princeton, NJ: Princeton University Press.

United Nations Centre on Transnational Corporations (1988) *Transnational Corporations in World Development*, New York: UNCTC.

—— (1990) 'Regional economic integration and transnational corporations in the 1990s: Europe 1992, North America and developing countries', UNCTC Current Studies 15, New York: United Nations.

Urry, J. (1990) 'Globalisation, localisation and the nation-state', *Lancaster Regionalism Group Working Paper*, 40, University of Lancaster.

—— (1994) 'Time, leisure and social identity', *Time and Society* 3: 131–50.

Van Cutsem, G. (1988) 'On the move: update', *Savills Magazine* No. 20: 9.

Van der Pijl, K. (1984) *The Making of the Atlantic Ruling Class*, London: Verso.

—— (1989a) 'Ruling classes, hegemony, and the state system', *International Journal of Political Economy* 19: 7–35.

—— (1989b) 'Restructuring the Atlantic ruling class in the 1970's and 1980's', in *Atlantic Relations Beyond the Reagan Era*, ed. S. Gill, pp. 62–87, New York; St Martin's Press.

—— (1989c) 'Is there an Atlantic class?', *Capital and Class* 25: 1–18.

Van Dormael, A. (1978) *Bretton Woods: Birth of a Monetary System*, London: Macmillan.

Virilio, P. (1987) 'The overexposed city', *Zone* 1(2).

—— (1993) 'The third interval: a critical transition', in *Rethinking Technologies*, ed. V.A. Conley, pp. 3–12, Minneapolis: University of Minnesota Press.

Walker, R.B.J. (1993) *Inside/Outside: International Relations as Political Theory*, Cambridge; Cambridge University Press.

Waller, D. (1990) 'Alive and well and buying in Europe', *Financial Times* 13 December.

Wallerstein, I. (1979) *The Capitalist World-economy*, Cambridge: Cambridge University Press.

—— (1984) *The Politics of the World-economy*, Cambridge: Cambridge University Press.

Walter, A. (1991) *World Power and World Money: The Role of International Monetary Order*, Hemel Hempstead: Harvester Wheatsheaf.

Waltz, K.E. (1979) *Theory of International Politics*, New York: Random House.

Warf, B. (1994) 'Vicious circle: financial markets and commercial real estate in the United States', in *Money, Power, and Space*, ed. S. Corbridge *et al.*, pp. 309–26, Oxford: Blackwell.

Waring, M. (1989) *As If Women Counted: A New Feminist Economics*, London: Macmillan.

Wark, M. (1994) *Virtual Geography*, Bloomington, IN: Indiana University Press.

Warley, P. (1994) 'Take a long view', *The Banker* February: 32–3.

Watkins, J. and Bryce, V. (1992) *Horatio: A Survey of Human Resource Ratios in the Retail Financial Services Sector*, Bristol: University of Bristol/KPMG Management Consulting.

Webber, M. (1968) 'The post-City age', *Daedalus* Fall.

Werner, F.E., Frej, W.M. and Madway, D.M. (1976) 'Redlining and disinvestment: causes, consequences, and proposed remedies', *Clearing House Review* October: 501–42.

Wiener, M. (1981) *English Culture and the Decline of the Industrial Spirit, 1850–1980*, Cambridge: Cambridge University Press.

Wiley, J. (1995) 'Nobody is doing it: cybersexuality as a postmodern narrative', *Body and Society* 1: 145–62.

Williams, C.C. (1995) 'Informal networks as a means of local economic development: the case of Local Exchange Trading Systems (LETS)', Paper presented to the Institute of British Geographers Annual Conference, 3–6 January, University of Northumbria at Newcastle.

Williams, R. (1970) 'Introduction', in *Dombey and Son*, C. Dickens, pp. 11–34, Harmondsworth: Penguin.

—— (1973) *The Country and the City*, New York: Oxford University Press.

—— (1985) *Loyalties*, London: Chatto & Windus.

Winston, B. (1995) 'Tyrell's Owl: the limits of the technological immigration in an epoch of hyperbolic discourse', in *Theorising Culture*, ed. B. Adam and S. Allan, pp. 225–35, London: UCL Press.

Wolf, M. (1990) 'One continent – one currency', *Financial Times Survey: 1992: Redrawing the Map of Europe* 2 July.

Wolff, K.H. (1964) *The Sociology of Georg Simmel*, New York: Free Press.

Woudhuysen, A. (1994) *Demos Quarterly* 3: 12–15.

Wright, P. (1985) *On Living in an Old Country*, London: Verso.

—— (1988) 'Brideshead and the tower blocks', *London Review of Books*, 10(11): p. 3–7.

Wynne, A. (1991) 'Electric writing. Things, texts, people: agency and action', mimeo.

Yaspan, R. (1970) 'Property insurance and the American ghetto: a study in social responsibility', *Southern California Law Review* 44: 218–74.

Young, R.M. (1985) *Darwin's Metaphor: Nature's Place in Victorian Culture*, Cambridge: Cambridge University Press.

Zelizer, V. (1979) *Morals and Markets. The Development of Life Insurance in the United States*, New York: Columbia University Press.

—— (1989) 'The social meaning of money: special monies', *American Journal of Sociology* 95: 342–77.

—— (1994) *The Social Meaning of Money*, New York: Basic Books.

Zuboff, S. (1988) *In the Age of the Smart Machine. The Future of Work and Power*, London: Heinemann.

Zukin, S. and DiMaggio, P. (eds) (1990) *Structures of Capital: The Social Organization of the Economy*, Cambridge: Cambridge University Press.

Zysman, J. (1983) *Governments, Markets and Growth: Financial Systems and the Politics of Industrial Change*, Oxford: Martin Roberts.

INDEX